WEBSTER'S
NEW WORLD®

Pocket French Dictionary

Houghton Mifflin Harcourt
Boston • New York

ISBN: 978-1-118-35660-9

Manufactured in the United States of America

DP 10 9 8 7 6 5 4 3

Contents

Free Audio Content

Go to www.wiley.com/go/wnwpocketfrench to access free audio downloads featuring pronunciation of twenty-five key French verbs. You will hear three regular verbs given in their full conjugations in all tenses and the remaining twenty-two in their full conjugations in the most common tenses.

Preface

This revised *Pocket French Dictionary* offers wide coverage of both French and English, in a portable format with a clear, user-friendly design. With more than 25,000 words and expressions and a focus on American English, it is an accurate, reliable tool for learners of French.

This new edition provides a wide-ranging selection of the most useful and up-to-date vocabulary, including colloquial language and terms from the ever-expanding fields of information technology and telecommunications. All English headwords have been syllabified to further assist the user.

The dictionary has been designed for easy navigation through the entries. Different senses of the headword are shown by source-language indicating material in brackets, as in **chance** *(luck)* hasard *m*; *(opportunity)* chances *fpl*. Further contextualization is provided by target-language indicators which are given after the translation in cases where its sense is ambiguous, eg **scrapbook** album *m (pour collages etc)*. Finally, source-language labels such as *Grammar, Sports, Cartes* and so on are provided for items belonging to specific fields of vocabulary.

The different grammatical divisions of an entry (such as noun, verb or adjective) are easily identified by bold numbers **1, 2, 3** and so on. Similarly, sense divisions within longer entries are clearly indicated by a ▪ symbol.

For added clarity, English phrasal verbs (such as **go ahead**), many French pronominal verbs (such as **se laver**) and the most common English compound nouns (such as **heat wave**) are all presented as separate entries.

Various space-saving devices help to maximize the content of this pocket-sized book. A headword is represented by its first letter when it appears as an example within the entry, for example **on the h.** in the entry **horizon**. In addition, a slash (/) within an entry is used both to separate non-interchangeable parts of a phrase matched exactly in English and in French, such as **qui/quoi encore?** who/what else? and to show productive expressions such as **how many apples/etc?** combien de pommes/etc?.

Finally, the book contains helpful supplementary material to aid communication. In the centre, the user will find information on French verbs as well as names of countries, regions and nationalities. And in an exciting new feature, ten conversation panels have been added throughout the text, with useful phrases for situations like meeting people, expressing opinions and using the telephone.

French grammar notes

In French, the feminine of an adjective is formed, when regular, by adding **e** to the masculine form (eg grand, grande; carré, carrée; fin, fine). If the masculine already ends in **e**, the feminine is the same as the masculine (eg utile). Both regular and irregular feminine forms of adjectives (eg généreux, généreuse; léger, légère; doux, douce) are given on the French-English side of the dictionary. On the English-French side, French adjectives are shown in the masculine, but highly irregular feminine forms (eg frais, fraîche; faux, fausse) have also been included to help the user.

To form the plural of a French noun or adjective **s** is usually added to the singular (eg arbre, arbres; taxi, taxis; petit, petits). The plural form of a noun ending in **s**, **x** or **z** (eg pois, croix, nez) is the same as that of the singular. Plurals of nouns and adjectives which do not follow these general rules (eg where **x** or **aux** is added in the plural, or where there is a highly irregular plural such as œil, yeux) are listed in the French section. Also included are the plurals of French compounds where the formation of the plural involves a change other than the addition of final **s** (eg chou-fleur, choux-fleurs; arc-en-ciel, arcs-en-ciel). The irregular plurals of French nouns (and irregular masculine plurals of French adjectives) ending in **al, eau, eu, au, ail** and **ou** are listed on the French-English side (eg cerveau, -x; général, -aux). Included on the English-French side, to help the user, are the plurals of French nouns (and adjectives) ending in **al, eu** and **au** where **s**, and not the usual **x**, forms the plural (eg pneu, pneus; naval, navals) and of those nouns in **ail** and **ou** where the plural is formed with **x**, and not the usual **s** (eg travail, travaux; chou, choux).

Pronunciation of French

Table of phonetic symbols

Vowels

[i] vite, cygne, sortie
[e] été, donner, légal
[ε] elle, mais, père, prêt
[a] chat, fameux, toit [twa]
[ɑ] pas, âge, tâche
[ɔ] donne, fort, album
[o] dos, chaud, peau, dôme
[u] tout, cour, roue, goût

[y] cru, sûr, rue
[ø] feu, meule, nœud
[ï] œuf, jeune, cueillir [kœjir]
[ə] le, refaire, entre
[ɛ̃] vin, plein, faim, saint
[ɑ̃] enfant, temps, paon
[ɔ̃] mon, nombre, honte
[œ̃] lundi, humble, un

Consonants

[p] pain, absolu, taper, frapper
[b] beau, abbé, robe
[t] table, nette, vite
[d] donner, sud, raide
[k] camp, képi, qui, taxe [taks], accès [aksɛ]
[g] garde, guerre, second, exister [ɛgziste]
[f] feu, siffler, phase
[v] voir, trouver, wagon

[s] son, cire, ça, chasse, nation
[z] cousin, zéro, rose
[ʃ] chose, hache, schéma
[ʒ] gilet, jeter, âge
[l] lait, facile, elle
[r] rare, rhume, sortir, barreau
[m] mon, flamme, aimer
[n] né, canne, animal
[ɲ] campagne, agneau
[ŋ] jogging

Semi-consonants

[j] piano, voyage, fille, yeux
[w] ouest, noir [nwar], tramway
[ɥ] muet, lui, huile

Abbreviations

abbreviation	*abbr, abrév*	abréviation
adjective	*adj*	adjectif
adverb	*adv*	adverbe
article	*art*	article
auxiliary	*aux*	auxiliaire
Canadian	*Can*	canadien
conjunction	*conj*	conjonction
definite	*def, déf*	défini
demonstrative	*dem, dém*	démonstratif
et cetera	*etc*	et cetera
feminine	*f*	féminin
familiar	*Fam*	familier
feminine plural	*fpl*	féminin pluriel
French	*Fr*	français
indefinite	*indef, indéf*	indéfini
interjection	*int*	interjection
invariable	*inv*	invariable
masculine	*m*	masculin
masculine and feminine	*mf*	masculin et féminin
masculine plural	*mpl*	masculin pluriel
noun	*n*	nom
plural	*pl*	pluriel
possessive	*poss*	possessif
past participle	*pp*	participe passé
preposition	*prep, prép*	préposition
present participle	*pres p*	participe présent
pronoun	*pron*	pronom
	qch	quelque chose
	qn	quelqu'un
registered trademark	®	marque déposée
relative	*rel*	relatif
somebody	*sb*	
singular	*sing*	singulier
something	*sth*	
United States	*US*	États-Unis
auxiliary verb	*v aux*	verbe auxiliare
intransitive verb	*vi*	verbe intransitif
pronominal verb	*vpr*	verbe pronominal
transitive verb	*vt*	verbe transitif
transitive and intransitive verb	*vti*	verbe transitif et intransitif

English – French
Anglais – Français

A

a (*before vowel or mute h* **an**) *indef art* un, une; **a man** un homme; **an apple** une pomme; **two dollars a pound** deux dollars la livre; **30 miles an hour** 50 km à l'heure; **he's a doctor** il est médecin; **twice a month** deux fois par mois.

a·ban·don *vt* abandonner.

ab·bey abbaye *f*.

ab·bre·vi·a·tion abréviation *f*.

a·bil·i·ty capacité *f* (**to do** pour faire); **to the best of my a.** de mon mieux.

a·ble *adj* capable; **to be a. to do** être capable de faire, pouvoir faire; **to be a. to swim/drive** savoir nager/conduire.

a·ble-bod·ied *adj* robuste.

ab·nor·mal *adj* anormal.

a·board 1 *adv* (*on ship*) à bord; **all a.** (*on train*) en voiture. **2** *prep* **a. the ship** à bord du navire; **a. the train** dans le train.

a·bol·ish *vt* supprimer.

a·bor·tion avortement *m*; **to have an a.** se faire avorter.

a·bout 1 *adv* (*approximately*) à peu près, environ; **(at) a. two o'clock** vers deux heures; **out and a.** (*after illness*) sur pied; **up and a.** (*out of bed*) levé, debout. **2** *prep* (*concerning*) au sujet de; **to talk a.** parler de; **a book a.** un livre sur; **what's it (all) a.?** de quoi s'agit-il?; **what** *or* **how a. me?** et moi?; **what** *or* **how a. a drink?** que dirais-tu de prendre un verre? ■ (+ *infinitive*) **a. to do** sur le point de faire.

a·bove 1 *adv* au-dessus; **from a.** d'en haut; **floor a.** étage *m* supérieur. **2** *prep* au-dessus de; **a. all** par-dessus tout; **he's a. me** (*in rank*) c'est mon supérieur.

a·bove-men·tioned *adj* susmentionné.

a·breast *adv* **four a.** par rangs de quatre; **to keep a. of** se tenir au courant de.

a·broad *adv* à l'étranger; **from a.** de l'étranger.

a·brupt *adj* (*sudden, rude*) brusque.

ab·scess abcès *m*.

ab·sence absence *f*.

ab·sent *adj* absent (**from** de).

ab·sent-mind·ed *adj* distrait.

ab·so·lute *adj* absolu; (*coward etc*) parfait.

ab·so·lute·ly *adv* absolument.

ab·sorb *vt* (*liquid*) absorber; **absorbed in one's work** absorbé dans *or* par son travail.

ab·surd *adj* absurde.

a·buse 1 *n* abus *m* (**of** de); (*of child etc*) mauvais traitements *mpl*; (*insults*) injures *fpl*. **2** *vt* (*use badly or wrongly*) abuser de; (*ill-treat*) maltraiter; (*insult*) injurier.

a·bu·sive *adj* grossier.

ac·a·dem·ic 1 *adj* (*year, diploma etc*) universitaire; (*teacher*) universitaire *mf*.

ac·cel·er·ate *vi* (*in vehicle*) accélérer.

ac·cel·er·a·tor accélérateur *m*.

ac·cent accent *m*.

ac·cept *vt* accepter.

ac·cept·a·ble *adj* acceptable.

ac·cess accès *m* (**to sth** à qch; **to sb** auprès de qn).

ac·ces·si·ble *adj* accessible.

ac·ces·so·ries *npl* (*objects*) accessoires *mpl*.

ac·ci·dent accident *m*; **by a.** (*without meaning to*) accidentellement; (*by chance*) par hasard.

ac·ci·den·tal *adj* accidentel.

ac·ci·den·tal·ly *adv* accidentellement.

ac·com·mo·date *vt* (*of house*) loger; (*oblige*) rendre service à.

ac·com·mo·da·tion(s) logement *m*

ac·com·pa·ny vt accompagner.

ac·com·plish vt accomplir; (aim) réaliser.

ac·cord of my own a. volontairement.

ac·cor·dance in a. with conformément à.

ac·cord·ing·ly adv en conséquence.

ac·cord·ing to prep selon.

ac·cor·di·on accordéon m.

ac·count (with bank or firm) compte m; (report) compte rendu m; **accounts** (of firm) comptabilité f; **to take into a.** tenir compte de; **on a. of** à cause de.

ac·count·ant comptable mf.

▶ **account for** vt (explain) expliquer; (represent) représenter.

ac·count·ing comptabilité f.

ac·cu·mu·late 1 vt accumuler. **2** vi s'accumuler.

ac·cu·rate adj exact, précis.

ac·cu·rate·ly adv avec précision.

ac·cu·sa·tion accusation f.

ac·cuse vt accuser (**of** de).

ac·cused the a. l'accusé, -ée mf.

ac·cus·tomed adj habitué (**to sth** à qch; **to doing** à faire); **to get a. to** s'habituer.

ace (card, person) as m.

ache 1 n douleur f; **to have an a. in one's arm** avoir mal au bras. **2** vi faire mal; **my head aches** ma tête me fait mal; **I'm aching all over** j'ai mal partout.

a·chieve vt réaliser; (success, result) obtenir; (victory) remporter.

a·chieve·ment (success) réussite f.

ach·ing adj douloureux.

ac·id adj & n acide (m).

ac·knowl·edge vt reconnaître (**as** pour); **to a.** (**receipt of**) accuser réception de.

ac·ne acné f.

a·corn gland m.

ac·quaint vt **to be acquainted with sb** connaître qn; **we are acquainted** on se connaît.

ac·quain·tance connaissance f.

ac·quire vt acquérir.

a·cre acre f (= 0,4 hectare).

ac·ro·bat acrobate mf.

ac·ro·bat·ic adj acrobatique.

a·cross adv & prep (from side to side (of)) d'un côté à l'autre (de); (on the other side (of)) de l'autre côté (de); (so as to cross, diagonally) en travers (de); **to be half a mile a.** (wide) avoir un kilomètre de large; **to walk** or **go a.** (street) traverser.

a·cryl·ic acrylique m; **a. sweater etc** pull m/etc en acrylique.

act 1 n (deed, part of play) acte m; (in circus) numéro m; **caught in the a.** pris sur le fait. **2** vt (role in play or film) jouer. **3** vi (do sth, behave) agir; **to a. as** (secretary etc) faire office de; (of object) servir de.

▶ **act for** vt représenter.

ac·tion action f; (military) combat m; **to take a.** prendre des mesures; **to put into a.** (plan) exécuter; **out of a.** hors d'usage; (person) hors (de) combat.

ac·tive 1 adj actif; (interest, dislike) vif. **2** n Grammar actif m.

ac·tiv·i·ty activité f; (in street) animation f.

▶ **act (up)on** vt (affect) agir sur; (advice) suivre.

ac·tor acteur m.

ac·tress actrice f.

ac·tu·al adj réel; **the a. book** le livre même.

ac·tu·al·ly adv (truly) réellement; (in fact) en réalité.

a·cute adj aigu (f -uë); (emotion) vif; (shortage) grave.

AD abbr (anno Domini) après Jésus-Christ.

ad Fam pub f; (private, in newspaper) annonce f; **want ad** petite annonce.

a·dapt vt adapter (**to** à); **to a.** (**oneself**) s'adapter.

a·dapt·a·ble adj (person) souple.

a·dap·ter, **a·dap·tor** *(plug)* prise *f* multiple.

add *vt* ajouter (**to** à; **that** que); *(total)* additionner.

ad·dict TV a. fana *mf* de la télé; **drug a.** drogué, -ée *mf*.

ad·dict·ed *adj* **to be a. to** *(TV)* se passionner pour; **a. to alcohol** alcoolique; **to be a. to cocaine** avoir une dépendance à la cocaïne, être cocaïnomane.

ad·dic·tion drug a. toxicomanie *f*.

▸ **add in** *vt (include)* inclure.

ad·di·tion addition *f*; **in a.** de plus; **in a. to** en plus de.

ad·di·tion·al *adj* supplémentaire.

ad·di·tive additif *m*.

ad·dress 1 *n (on letter etc)* adresse *f*; *(speech)* allocution *f*. **2** *vt (person)* s'adresser à; *(audience)* parler devant; *(letter)* mettre l'adresse sur.

▸ **add to** *vt (increase)* augmenter.

▸ **add together** *vt (numbers)* additionner.

▸ **add up 1** *vt (numbers)* additionner. **2** *vi* **to a. up to** *(total)* s'élever à; *(mean)* signifier; *(represent)* constituer.

ad·e·noids *npl* végétations *fpl* (adénoïdes).

ad·e·quate *adj (quantity etc)* suffisant; *(acceptable)* convenable; *(person)* compétent.

ad·e·quate·ly *adv* suffisamment; convenablement.

▸ **ad·here to** *vt* adhérer à; *(decision, rule)* s'en tenir à.

ad·he·sive *adj & n* adhésif *(m)*.

ad·ja·cent *adj (building, angle)* adjacent (**to** à).

ad·jec·tive adjectif *m*.

ad·just *vt (machine)* régler; *(salaries)* ajuster; **to a. (oneself) to** s'adapter à.

ad·just·a·ble *adj (seat)* réglable.

ad·just·ment réglage *m*; *(of person)* adaptation *f*.

ad lib *vi* improviser.

ad·min·is·ter *vt* administrer.

ad·min·is·tra·tion administration *f*; *(government)* gouvernement *m*.

ad·min·is·tra·tive *adj* administratif.

ad·min·is·tra·tor directeur, -trice *mf*, administrateur, -trice *mf*.

ad·mi·ral amiral *m*.

ad·mi·ra·tion admiration *f*.

ad·mire *vt* admirer (**for** pour; **for doing** de faire).

ad·mis·sion *(to movies etc)* entrée *f*; **a. charge** prix *m* d'entrée.

ad·mit *vt (let in)* laisser entrer, admettre; *(acknowledge)* reconnaître, admettre (**that** que).

ad·mit·tance entrée *f*; **'no a.'** 'entrée interdite'.

▸ **admit to** *vt (confess)* avouer.

ad·o·les·cent adolescent, -ente *mf*.

a·dopt *vt (child, attitude)* adopter.

a·dopt·ed *adj (child)* adoptif.

a·dop·tion adoption *f*.

a·dor·a·ble *adj* adorable.

a·dore *vt* adorer (**doing** faire).

a·dult 1 *n* adulte *mf*. **2** *adj (animal etc)* adulte; **a. class/film/etc** classe *f*/film *m*/*etc* pour adultes.

ad·vance 1 *n (movement, money)* avance *f*; **advances** *(sexual)* avances *fpl*; **in a.** à l'avance, d'avance. **2** *adj (payment)* anticipé; **a. reservation** réservation *f*. **3** *vt (put forward, lend)* avancer. **4** *vi (go forward, progress)* avancer.

ad·vanced *adj* avancé; *(studies, level)* supérieur; *(course)* de niveau supérieur.

ad·van·tage avantage *m* (**over** sur); **to take a. of** profiter de; *(person)* exploiter.

ad·ven·ture aventure *f*.

ad·ven·tur·ous *adj* aventureux.

ad·verb adverbe *m*.

ad·ver·tise 1 *vt (commercially)* faire de la publicité pour; *(pri-*

vately) passer une annonce pour vendre; *(make known)* annoncer. **2** *vi* faire de la publicité; *(privately)* passer une annonce **(for** pour trouver).

ad·ver·tise·ment publicité *f;* *(private, in newspaper)* annonce *f;* *(poster)* affiche *f;* **classified a.** petite annonce.

ad·vice conseil(s) *m(pl);* **a piece of a.** un conseil.

ad·vis·a·ble *adj (wise)* prudent **(to do** de faire).

ad·vise *vt* conseiller; *(recommend)* recommander; **to a. sb to do** conseiller à qn de faire.

▸**advise against** *vt* déconseiller.

ad·vis·er conseiller, -ère *mf.*

ad·vo·cate 1 *n (supporter)* défenseur *m.* **2** *vt* préconiser.

aer·i·al antenne *f.*

aer·o·bics *npl* aérobic *m.*

aer·o·sol aérosol *m.*

aes·thet·ic *adj* esthétique.

af·fair affaire *f;* **(love) a.** liaison *f.*

af·fect *vt (concern, move)* toucher, affecter; *(harm)* nuire à.

af·fec·tion affection *f* (**for** pour).

af·fec·tion·ate *adj* affectueux.

af·flu·ent *adj* riche.

af·ford *vt (be able to pay for)* avoir les moyens d'acheter; *(time)* pouvoir trouver.

af·ford·a·ble *adj (price etc)* abordable.

a·float *adv (ship, swimmer, business)* à flot.

a·fraid *adj* **to be a.** avoir peur **(of,** to de); **he's a. (that) she may be sick** il a peur qu'elle (ne) soit malade; **I'm a. he's out** *(I regret to say)* je regrette, il est sorti.

Af·ri·can 1 *n* Africain, -aine *mf.* **2** *adj* africain.

af·ter 1 *adv* après; **the month a.** le mois suivant. **2** *prep* après; **a. all** après tout; **a. eating** après avoir mangé; **a. you!** je vous en prie!; **ten a. four** quatre heures dix; **to**

be a. sth/sb *(seek)* chercher qch/ qn. **3** *conj* après que.

af·ter·ef·fects *npl* suites *fpl.*

af·ter·noon après-midi *m or f inv;* **in the a.** l'après-midi; **good a.!** *(hello)* bonjour!

af·ter·noons *adv* l'après-midi.

af·ter·shave après-rasage *m.*

af·ter·ward(s) *adv* après, plus tard.

a·gain *adv* de nouveau, encore une fois; **never a.** plus jamais; **a. and a., time and (time) a.** bien des fois, maintes fois.

a·gainst *prep* contre; **a. the law** illégal.

age 1 *n* âge *m;* **(old) a.** vieillesse *f;* **the Middle Ages** le Moyen Âge; **five years of a.** âgé de cinq ans; **under a.** trop jeune. **2** *vti* vieillir.

aged *adj* **a. ten** âgé de dix ans.

a·gen·cy *(office)* agence *f.*

a·gen·da ordre *m* du jour.

a·gent agent *m;* *(dealer)* concessionnaire *mf.*

ag·gra·vate *vt (make worse)* aggraver; *(annoy) Fam* exaspérer.

ag·gra·va·tion *(annoyance)* ennui(s) *m(pl).*

ag·gres·sion agression *f.*

ag·gres·sive *adj* agressif.

ag·ile *adj* agile.

ag·i·tat·ed *adj* agité.

a·go *adv* **a year a.** il y a un an; **how long a.?** il y a combien de temps (de cela)?

ag·o·ny **to be in a.** souffrir horriblement.

a·gree 1 *vi (come to an agreement)* se mettre d'accord; *(be in agreement)* être d'accord **(with** avec); *(of facts, dates)* concorder; *Grammar* s'accorder; **to a. to sth/to doing** consentir à qch/à faire; **it doesn't a. with me** *(food, climate)* ça ne me réussit pas. **2** *vt* **to a. to do** accepter de faire; **to a. that** admettre que.

a·gree·a·ble *adj (pleasant)* agréable.

a·greed adj (time, place) convenu;
we are a. nous sommes d'accord;
a.! entendu!

a·gree·ment accord m; **in a. with**
d'accord avec; **to reach an a.** tomber d'accord.

▸**agree (up)on** vt convenir de.

ag·ri·cul·tur·al adj agricole.

ag·ri·cul·ture agriculture f.

a·head adv (in space) en avant;
(leading) en tête; (in the future)
dans l'avenir; **a. (of time)** en
avance (sur l'horaire); **to be one
hour a.** avoir une heure d'avance
(of sur); **a. of** (space) devant; (time)
en avance sur; **straight a.** (to walk)
tout droit; (to look) droit devant soi.

aid aide f, (device) accessoire m,
support m; **with the a. of** (a stick
etc) à l'aide de; **in a. of** (charity) au
profit de.

AIDS abrev (acquired immune defi-
ciency syndrome) SIDA m.

aim 1 n but m; **with the a. of** dans le
but de. **2** vt (gun) braquer (at sur);
aimed at children/etc (product)
destiné aux enfants/etc. **3** vi viser;
to a. at sb viser qn; **to a. to do** or
at doing avoir l'intention de faire.

air 1 n air m; **in the open a.** en plein
air; **by a.** (to travel, send) par avion;
(up) in(to) the a. en l'air. **2** adj
(raid, base) aérien. **3** vt (room)
aérer.

air-con·di·tioned adj climatisé.

air con·di·tion·ing climatisation f.

air·craft inv avion(s) m(pl).

air·craft car·ri·er porte-avions
m inv

air·fare prix du billet d'avion.

air force armée f de l'air.

air·line ligne f aérienne.

air·line tick·et billet m d'avion.

air·mail poste f aérienne; **by a.** par
avion.

air·plane avion m.

air·port aéroport m.

air·sick·ness mal m de l'air.

air ter·mi·nal aérogare f.

air·tight adj hermétique.

air traf·fic con·trol·ler aiguilleur m du ciel.

aisle (walkway in plane, theater) allée f, (in church) nef f latérale; (row
of seats) rangée f, (section of supermarket) rayon m.

a·jar adj (door) entrouvert.

a·larm 1 n (warning, device in
house or car) alarme f, (mechanism) sonnerie f (d'alarme); **a. (clock)**
réveil m. **2** vt alarmer.

al·bum (book, record) album m.

al·co·hol alcool m.

al·co·hol·ic 1 adj (drink) alcoolisé. **2** n (person) alcoolique mf.

a·lert adj (watching carefully) vigi-
lant.

al·ge·bra algèbre f.

a·li·as 1 n (pl aliases) nom m d'emprunt. **2** adv alias.

al·i·bi alibi m.

a·li·en étranger, -ère mf.

a·light adj (fire) allumé; **to set a.**
mettre le feu à.

a·like 1 adj (people, things) sem-
blables; **to look** or **be a.** se ressembler. **2** adv de la même
manière.

a·live adj vivant, en vie.

all 1 adj tout, toute, pl tous, toutes;
a. day toute la journée; **a. (the)
men** tous les hommes. **2** pron tous
mpl, toutes fpl; (everything) tout;
my sisters are a. here toutes mes
sœurs sont ici; **he ate it a., he ate
a. of it** il a tout mangé; **a. (that) he
has** tout ce qu'il a; **a. of us** nous
tous; **in a., a. told** en tout; **a. but** (almost) presque; **if there's any wind
at a.** s'il y a le moindre vent; **not at
a.** pas du tout; (after 'thank you')
pas de quoi. **3** adv tout; **a. alone** tout
seul; **six a.** Sport six buts partout.

al·le·giance fidélité f (to à).

al·ler·gic adj allergique (to à).

al·ley ruelle f, (in park) allée f.

al·li·ance alliance f.

al·lied *adj (country)* allié; *(matters)* lié.

al·li·ga·tor alligator *m.*

al·lo·cate *vt* allouer (**to** à); *(distribute)* répartir.

al·lot·ment *(land)* lopin *m* de terre *(loué pour la culture).*

all-out *adj (effort)* énergique.

al·low *vt* permettre; *(give)* accorder; *(as discount)* déduire; **to a. sb to do** permettre à qn de faire; **you're not allowed to go** on vous interdit de partir.

al·low·ance allocation *f, (for travel, housing, food)* indemnité *f, (for duty-free goods)* tolérance *f, (for children)* argent *m* de poche; **to make allowances for sb** être indulgent envers qn.

▸ **allow for** *vt* tenir compte de.

all-pur·pose *adj (tool)* universel.

all-right 1 *adj (satisfactory)* bien *inv, (unharmed)* sain et sauf; *(undamaged)* intact; *(without worries)* tranquille; **it's a.** ça va; **I'm a.** *(healthy)* je vais bien. **2** *adv (well)* bien; **a.!** *(agreement)* d'accord!; **I got your letter a.** *(emphatic)* j'ai bien reçu votre lettre.

all-round *adj* complet.

al·ly allié, -ée *mf.*

al·mond amande *f.*

al·most *adv* presque; **he a. fell**/*etc* il a failli tomber/*etc.*

a·lone *adj & adv* seul; **to leave a.** *(person)* laisser tranquille; *(thing)* ne pas toucher à.

a·long 1 *prep (all)* **a.** (tout) le long de; **to go** *or* **walk a.** *(street)* passer par; **a. with** avec. **2** *adv* **all a.** *(time)* dès le début.

a·long·side *prep & adv* à côté (de).

a·loud *adv* à haute voix.

al·pha·bet alphabet *m.*

al·pha·bet·i·cal *adj* alphabétique.

Alps *npl* the **A.** les Alpes *fpl.*

al·read·y *adv* déjà.

al·right *adv Fam* = **all-right**.

al·so *adv* aussi.

al·tar autel *m.*

al·ter *vt* changer; *(clothing)* retoucher. **2** *vi* changer.

al·ter·a·tion changement *m; (of clothing)* retouche *f.*

al·ter·nate 1 *adj* alterné; **on a. days** tous les deux jours. **2** *vi* alterner (**with** avec).

al·ter·na·tive 1 *adj (other)* autre. **2** *n* alternative *f.*

al·ter·na·tive·ly *adv* comme alternative.

al·though *adv* bien que (+ *subjunctive*).

al·to·geth·er *adv (completely)* tout à fait; *(on the whole)* somme toute; **how much a.?** combien en tout?

a·lu·mi·num aluminium *m.*

al·ways *adv* toujours.

am *see* be.

a.m. *adv* du matin.

am·a·teur 1 *n* amateur *m.* **2** *adj* **a.** painter/*etc* peintre/*etc* amateur.

a·maze *vt* étonner.

a·mazed *adj* stupéfait (**at sth** de qch; **at seeing** de voir); *(filled with wonder)* émerveillé.

a·maz·ing *adj* stupéfiant; *(incredible)* extraordinaire.

am·bas·sa·dor ambassadeur *m; (woman)* ambassadrice *f.*

am·ber **a. (light)** *(of traffic signal)* (feu *m*) orange *m.*

am·big·u·ous *adj* ambigu (f-uë).

am·bi·tion ambition *f.*

am·bi·tious *adj* ambitieux.

am·bu·lance ambulance *f.*

am·bu·lance driv·er ambulancier, -ière *mf.*

a·mend *vt (text)* modifier; *(law)* amender.

A·mer·i·can 1 *n* Américain, -aine *mf.* **2** *adj* américain.

a·mid(st) *prep* au milieu de, parmi.

am·mu·ni·tion munitions *fpl.*

a·mong(st) *prep* parmi, entre; **a. the crowd/books** parmi la foule/les livres; **a. themselves/friends** entre eux/amis.

a·mount quantité *f*; *(sum of money)* somme *f*; *(total of bill etc)* montant *m*.

▸ **amount to** *vt* s'élever à; *(mean)* signifier; *(represent)* représenter.

am·ple *adj (enough)* largement assez de; **you have a. time** tu as largement le temps.

am·pli·fi·er amplificateur *m*.

am·pu·tate *vt* amputer.

a·muse *vt* amuser.

a·muse·ment amusement *m*.

a·mus·ing *adj* amusant.

an *see* a.

an·a·ly·sis, *pl* **-ses** analyse *f*.

an·a·lyst analyste *mf*; *(psychoanalyst)* (psych)analyste *mf*.

an·a·lyze *vt* analyser.

an·ar·chy anarchie *f*.

a·nat·o·my anatomie *f*.

an·ces·tor ancêtre *m*.

an·chor ancre *f*.

an·chored *adj* ancré.

an·cho·vy anchois *m*.

an·cient *adj* ancien; *(pre-medieval)* antique.

and *conj* et; **two hundred a. two** deux cent deux; **better a. better** de mieux en mieux; **go a. see** va voir.

an·es·thet·ic anesthésie *f*; *(substance)* anesthésique *m*; **general a.** anesthésie générale.

an·gel ange *m*.

an·ger colère *f*.

an·gle angle *m*; **at an a.** en biais.

an·gler pêcheur, -euse *mf* à la ligne.

an·gri·ly *adv (to speak etc)* avec colère.

an·gry *adj* fâché; *(letter)* indigné; **to get a.** se fâcher (**with** contre).

an·i·mal *n & adj* animal *(m)*.

an·kle cheville *f*.

an·kle sock socquette *f*.

an·nex *(building)* annexe *f*.

an·ni·ver·sa·ry *(of event)* anniversaire *m*.

an·nounce *vt* annoncer; *(birth, marriage)* faire part de.

an·nounce·ment *(statement)* annonce *f*; *(notice)* avis *m*.

an·nounc·er *(on TV)* speaker *m*, speakerine *f*.

an·noy *vt (inconvenience)* ennuyer; *(irritate)* agacer.

an·noyed *adj* fâché; **to get a.** se fâcher (**with** contre).

an·noy·ing *adj* ennuyeux.

an·nu·al 1 *adj* annuel. **2** *n (book)* annuaire *m*.

an·nu·al·ly *adv* annuellement.

a·non·y·mous *adj* anonyme.

an·oth·er *adj & pron* un(e) autre; **a. man** un autre homme; **a. month** *(additional)* encore un mois; **a. ten** encore dix; **one a.** l'un(e) l'autre, *pl* les un(e)s les autres; **they love one a.** ils s'aiment (l'un l'autre).

an·swer 1 *n* réponse *f*, *(to problem)* solution *f* (**to** à). **2** *vt (person, question, phone)* répondre à; *(prayer, wish)* exaucer; **to a. the door** ouvrir la porte. **3** *vi* répondre.

▸ **answer back** *vt* répondre à.

▸ **answer for** *vt* répondre de.

an·swer·ing ma·chine répondeur *m*.

ant fourmi *f*.

an·te·lope antilope *f*.

an·ten·na antenne *f*.

an·them national a. hymne *m* national.

an·thol·o·gy recueil *m*.

an·ti- *prefix* anti-.

an·ti·bi·ot·ic antibiotique *m*.

an·ti·bod·y anticorps *m*.

an·tic·i·pate *vt (foresee)* prévoir; *(expect)* s'attendre à.

an·tic·i·pa·tion in a. of en prévision de.

an·tics *npl* singeries *fpl*.

an·ti·freeze antigel *m*.

an·ti·his·ta·mine antihistaminique *m*.

an·tique 1 *adj (furniture etc)* ancien. **2** *n* antiquité *f.*

an·tique deal·er antiquaire *mf.*

an·tique shop magasin *m* d'antiquités.

an·ti·sep·tic *adj & n* antiseptique *(m).*

anx·i·e·ty *(worry)* inquiétude *f;* *(fear)* anxiété *f.*

anx·ious *adj (worried)* inquiet *(about* de, pour); *(afraid)* anxieux; *(eager)* impatient *(to do* faire).

anx·ious·ly *adv (to wait)* impatiemment.

an·y 1 *adj (with question)* du, de la, des; **do you have a. milk/tickets?** avez-vous du lait/des billets? ▪ *(negative)* de; **he hasn't got a. milk/tickets** il n'a pas de lait/de billets. ▪ *(no matter which)* n'importe quel. ▪ *(every)* tout; **in a. case, at a. rate** de toute façon. **2** *pron (no matter which one)* n'importe lequel; *(somebody)* quelqu'un; **if a. of you** si l'un d'entre vous. ▪ *(quantity)* en; **do you have a.?** en as-tu? **3** *adv* **(not) a. happier/etc** (pas) plus heureux/*etc*; **I don't see him a. more** je ne le vois plus; **a. more tea?** encore du thé?; **a. better?** c'est mieux?

an·y·bod·y *pron (somebody)* quelqu'un; **do you see a.?** vois-tu quelqu'un? ▪ *(negative)* personne; **he doesn't know a.** il ne connaît personne. ▪ *(no matter who)* n'importe qui.

an·y·how *adv (at any rate)* de toute façon; *(badly)* n'importe comment.

an·y·one *pron* = **anybody.**

an·y·place *adv* = **anywhere.**

an·y·thing *pron (something)* quelque chose. ▪ *(negative)* rien; **he doesn't do a.** il ne fait rien. ▪ *(everything)* tout; **a. you like** *(tout)* ce que tu veux. ▪ *(no matter what)* **a. (at all)** n'importe quoi.

an·y·way *adv (at any rate)* de toute façon.

an·y·where *adv (no matter where)* n'importe où. ▪ *(everywhere)* partout; **a. you go** partout où vous allez; **a. you like** là où tu veux. ▪ *(negative)* nulle part; **he doesn't go a.** il ne va nulle part.

a·part *adv* **we kept them a.** *(separate)* on les tenait séparés; **with legs a.** les jambes écartées; **they are three feet a.** ils se trouvent à un mètre l'un de l'autre; **a. from** *(except for)* à part.

a·part·ment appartement *m;* **a. house** *or* **building** immeuble *m* (d'habitation).

ape singe *m.*

a·pé·ri·tif apéritif *m.*

a·pol·o·get·ic *adj* **to be a.** s'excuser *(about* de).

a·pol·o·gize *vi* s'excuser *(for* de); **to a. to sb** faire ses excuses à qn *(for* pour).

a·pol·o·gy excuses *fpl.*

a·pos·tro·phe apostrophe *f.*

ap·pall *vt* consterner.

ap·pall·ing *adj* épouvantable.

ap·pa·ra·tus appareil *m;* *(in gym)* agrès *mpl.*

ap·par·el vêtements *mpl.*

ap·par·ent *adj* apparent; **it's a. that** il est évident que.

ap·par·ent·ly *adv* apparemment.

ap·peal¹ *(charm)* attrait *m;* *(interest)* intérêt *m.*

ap·peal² **1** *n (in court)* appel *m.* **2** *vi* faire appel.

▸ **appeal to** *vt (attract)* plaire à; *(interest)* intéresser.

ap·pear *vi (become visible)* apparaître; *(present oneself)* se présenter; *(seem, be published)* paraître; *(in court)* comparaître; **it appears that** il semble que *(+ subjunctive or indicative).*

ap·pear·ance *(act)* apparition *f;* *(look)* apparence *f.*

ap·pen·di·ci·tis appendicite *f.*

ap·pen·dix, *pl* **-ixes** *or* **-ices** *(in book, body)* appendice *m.*

ap·pe·tite appétit *m.*

ap·pe·tiz·ing *adj* appétissant.

ap·plaud *vti (clap)* applaudir.

ap·plause applaudissements *mpl.*

ap·ple pomme *f;* **cooking a.** pomme *f* à cuire; **a. pie** tarte *f* aux pommes.

ap·pli·ance appareil *m.*

ap·pli·ca·ble *adj* applicable (**to** à).

ap·pli·cant candidat, -ate *mf* (**for** à).

ap·pli·ca·tion *(for job)* candidature *f, (for membership)* demande *f* d'adhésion; **a. (form)** *(for job)* formulaire *m* de candidature.

ap·ply 1 *vt* appliquer; *(brake)* appuyer sur; **to a. oneself to** s'appliquer à. **2** *vi (be relevant)* s'appliquer (**to** à).

▶ **apply for** *vt (job)* poser sa candidature à.

ap·point *vt (person)* nommer (**to sth** à qch; **to do** pour faire).

ap·point·ment nomination *f, (meeting)* rendez-vous *m inv.*

ap·point·ment book agenda *m.*

ap·prais·al évaluation *f.*

ap·praise *vt* évaluer.

ap·pre·ci·ate *vt (enjoy, value)* apprécier; *(understand)* comprendre; *(be grateful for)* être reconnaissant de.

ap·pre·ci·a·tion *(gratitude)* reconnaissance *f.*

ap·pren·tice apprenti, -ie *mf.*

ap·pren·tice·ship apprentissage *m.*

ap·proach 1 *vt (person, door etc)* s'approcher de; *(age, result, town)* approcher de; *(subject)* aborder. **2** *vi (of person, vehicle)* s'approcher; *(of date)* approcher. **3** *n (method)* façon *f* de s'y prendre.

ap·pro·pri·ate *adj* convenable.

ap·prov·al approbation *f,* **on a.** *(goods)* à l'essai.

▶ **ap·prove of** *vt (conduct etc)* approuver; **I don't a. of him** il ne me

plaît pas; **I a. of his going** je trouve bon qu'il y aille.

ap·prox·i·mate *adj* approximatif.

ap·prox·i·mate·ly *adv* à peu près.

a·pri·cot abricot *m.*

A·pril avril *m.*

a·pron tablier *m.*

apt *adj (remark, reply)* juste, convenable; **to be a. to** avoir tendance à.

ap·ti·tude aptitude *f* (**for** à, pour).

a·quar·i·um aquarium *m.*

Ar·ab *adj & n* arabe *(mf).*

Ar·a·bic *adj & n (language)* arabe *(m);* **A. numerals** chiffres *mpl* arabes.

arc *(of circle)* arc *m.*

arch *(of bridge)* arche *f, (of building)* voûte *f.*

arch·er archer *m.*

arch·e·ry tir *m* à l'arc.

ar·chi·tect architecte *mf.*

ar·chi·tec·ture architecture *f.*

Arc·tic the A. l'Arctique *f.*

are *see* **be**.

ar·e·a *(in geometry)* superficie *f, (of country)* région *f, (of town)* quartier *m;* **parking a.** aire *f* de stationnement.

ar·e·a code *(phone number)* indicatif *m.*

a·re·na arène *f.*

ar·gue 1 *vi (quarrel)* se disputer (**with** avec; **about** au sujet de); *(reason)* raisonner (**with** avec, **about** sur). **2** *vt* **to a. that** *(maintain)* soutenir que.

ar·gu·ment *(quarrel)* dispute *f, (reasoning)* argument *m;* **to have an a.** se disputer.

a·rise* *vi (of problem, opportunity)* se présenter; *(result)* résulter *(from* de).

a·rith·me·tic arithmétique *f.*

arm 1 *n* bras *m; (weapon)* arme *f.* **2** *vt* armer (**with** de).

arm·band brassard *m.*

arm·chair fauteuil *m.*

ar·mor *(of knight)* armure *f; (of tank etc)* blindage *m.*

arm·ored *adj (car etc)* blindé.

arm·pit aisselle *f.*

ar·my 1 *n* armée *f.* **2** *adj* militaire.

a·round 1 *prep* autour de; *(approximately)* environ. **2** *adv* autour; **a. here** par ici; **he's still a.** il est encore là; **there's a lot of flu a.** il y a pas mal de grippes dans l'air; **there's a rumor going a.** il y a un bruit qui court; **up and a.** *(after illness)* sur pied.

a·rouse *vt* éveiller.

ar·range *vt* arranger; *(time, meeting)* fixer; **to a. to do** s'arranger pour faire.

ar·range·ment *(layout, agreement)* arrangement *m;* **arrangements** préparatifs *mpl; (plans)* projets *mpl.*

ar·rears *npl* **in a.** en retard dans ses paiements.

ar·rest 1 *vt* arrêter. **2** *n* arrestation *f;* **under a.** en état d'arrestation.

ar·ri·val arrivée *f.*

ar·rive *vi* arriver.

ar·row flèche *f.*

art *m;* **work of a.** œuvre *f* d'art.

ar·te·ry artère *f.*

ar·thri·tis arthrite *f.*

ar·ti·cle *(object, in newspaper, in grammar)* article *m.*

ar·tic·u·late[1] *adj (speech)* clair; *(person)* qui s'exprime clairement.

ar·tic·u·late[2] *vti* articuler.

ar·ti·fi·cial *adj* artificiel.

ar·tist *(actor, painter etc)* artiste *mf.*

ar·tis·tic *adj* artistique; *(person)* artiste.

as *adv & conj (manner etc)* comme; **as you like** comme tu veux; **as much** *or* **as hard as I can** (au)tant que je peux; **as (it) is** *(to leave sth)* comme ça, tel quel; **as if, as though** comme si. ▪ *(comparison)* **as tall as you** aussi grand que vous; **as white as a sheet** blanc comme un linge; **as much** *or* **as hard as you** autant que vous; **twice as big as** deux fois plus grand que. ▪ *(though)* **(as) smart as he is** si intelligent qu'il soit. ▪ *(capacity)* **as a teacher** comme professeur; **to act as a father** agir en père. ▪ *(reason)* puisque; **as it's late** puisqu'il est tard. ▪ *(time)* **as I was leaving** comme je partais; **as he slept** pendant qu'il dormait; **as from, as of** *(time)* à partir de. ▪ *(concerning)* **as for that** quant à cela. ▪ *(+ infinitive)* **so as to** de manière à; **so stupid as to** assez bête pour.

asap *abbr (as soon as possible)* le plut tôt possible.

as·cer·tain *vt* établir, déterminer.

ash cendre *f.*

a·shamed *adj* **to be a.** avoir honte *(* of de*)*.

a·shore *adv* **to go a.** débarquer.

ash·tray cendrier *m.*

A·sian 1 *n* Asiatique *mf.* **2** *adj* asiatique.

a·side *adv* de côté; **a. from** en dehors de.

ask 1 *vt* demander; *(a question)* poser; *(invite)* inviter; **to a. sb (for) sth** demander qch à qn; **to a. sb to do** demander à qn de faire. **2** *vi* demander; **to a. for sth/sb** demander qch/qn; **to a. about sth** se renseigner sur qch; **to a. about sb** demander des nouvelles de qn; **to a. sb about** interroger qn sur.

a·sleep *adj* **to be a.** dormir; **to fall a.** s'endormir.

as·par·a·gus asperges *fpl.*

as·pect aspect *m.*

as·pi·rin aspirine *f.*

as·sault 1 *n (crime)* agression *f.* **2** *vt (attack)* agresser.

as·sem·ble 1 *vt* assembler; *(people)* rassembler; *(machine)* monter. **2** *vi* se rassembler.

as·sem·bly *(meeting)* assemblée *f, (in school)* rassemblement *m.*

as·sert *vt* affirmer; **to a. oneself**

s'affirmer; **to a. one's rights** faire valoir ses droits.

as·sess *vt* (*estimate*) évaluer; (*decide amount of*) fixer le montant de.

as·set (*advantage*) atout *m*; **assets** (*of business*) actif *m*.

as·sign *vt* (*give*) attribuer (**to** à).

as·sign·ment (*task*) mission *f*.

as·sist *vti* aider (**in doing, to do** à faire).

as·sis·tance aide *f*; **to be of a. to sb** aider qn.

as·sis·tant **1** *n* assistant, -ante *mf*; (*in shop*) vendeur, -euse *mf*. **2** *adj* adjoint.

as·so·ci·ate 1 *vt* associer; **associated with sth/sb** associé à qch/avec qn. **2** *n & adj* associé, -ée (*mf*).

as·so·ci·a·tion association *f*.

as·sort·ed *adj* variés; (*foods*) assortis.

as·sort·ment assortiment *m*.

as·sume *vt* (*suppose*) présumer (**that** que); (*take on*) prendre; (*responsibility, role*) assumer.

as·sur·ance assurance *f*.

as·sure *vt* assurer (**sb that** à qn que; **sb of** qn de).

as·ter·isk astérisque *m*.

asth·ma asthme *m*.

asth·mat·ic *adj & n* asthmatique (*mf*).

a·ston·ish *vt* étonner; **to be astonished** s'étonner (**at sth** de qch).

a·ston·ish·ing *adj* étonnant.

a·stray *adv* **to go a.** s'égarer.

as·trol·o·gy astrologie *f*.

as·tro·naut astronaute *mf*.

as·tron·o·my astronomie *f*.

a·sy·lum asile *m*; **to seek a.** chercher asile; (**mental**) **a.** asile *m* (d'aliénés).

at *prep* à; **at work** au travail; **at six** (o'clock) à six heures; **at sign** (*in e-mail address*) arrobas *m*, arobase *f*. ▪ chez; **at the doctor's** chez le médecin. ▪ en; **at sea** en mer. ▪ contre; **angry at** fâché contre. ▪ sur; **to shoot at** tirer sur. ▪ de; **to**

laugh at rire de. ▪ (au)près de; **at the window** (au)près de la fenêtre. ▪ par; **six at a time** six par six.

ath·lete athlète *mf*.

ath·let·ic *adj* athlétique.

ath·let·ics *npl* athlétisme *m*.

At·lan·tic 1 *adj* atlantique. **2** *n* **the A.** l'Atlantique *m*.

at·las atlas *m*.

ATM *abbr* (*automatic teller machine*) DAB *m f*.

at·mos·phere atmosphère *f*.

at·om atome *m*.

a·tom·ic *adj* (*bomb etc*) atomique.

at·tach *vt* attacher (**to** à); (*document*) joindre (**to** à); **attached to** (*fond of*) attaché à.

at·ta·ché case attaché-case *m*, mallette *f*.

at·tach·ment (*tool*) accessoire *m*; (*to e-mail*) fichier *m* joint.

at·tack 1 *n* attaque *f*. **2** *vti* attaquer.

at·tack·er agresseur *m*.

at·tain *vt* (*aim*) atteindre; (*goal, ambition*) réaliser; (*rank*) parvenir à.

at·tempt 1 *n* tentative *f*; **to make an a.** tenter de. **2** *vt* tenter; (*task*) entreprendre; **to a. to do** tenter de faire.

at·tend 1 *vt* (*meeting etc*) assister à; (*course*) suivre; (*school, church*) aller à. **2** *vi* assister.

at·ten·dance présence *f* (**at** à); (**school**) a. scolarité *f*.

at·ten·dant employé, -ée *mf*; (*in gas station*) pompiste *mf*; (*in museum*) gardien, -ienne *mf*.

▶**attend to** *vt* (*customer, task*) s'occuper de.

at·ten·tion attention *f*; **to pay a.** faire attention (**to** à).

at·ten·tive *adj* attentif (**to** à).

at·tic grenier *m*.

at·ti·tude attitude *f*.

at·tor·ney avocat, -e *mf*.

at·tract *vt* attirer.

at·trac·tion (*charm*) attrait *m*.

at·trac·tive *adj* (*price, offer etc*) intéressant; (*person*) attirant, séduisant.

at·trib·ute 1 *n (quality)* attribut *m.*
2 *vt* attribuer (**to**) à.
auc·tion (off) *vt* vendre (aux
enchères).
auc·tion·eer commissaire-pri-
seur *m.*
au·di·ble *adj* perceptible.
au·di·ence *(of speaker, musician)*
auditoire *m; (in theater)* spectateurs *mpl; (of radio broadcast)* auditeurs *mpl;* TV *a.* téléspectateurs *mpl.*
au·di·o *adj* audio *inv.*
au·di·o·vi·su·al *adj* audiovisuel.
au·dit 1 *n* audit *m.* **2** *vt* vérifier.
Au·gust août *m.*
aunt tante *f.*
aunt·ie, aunt·y *Fam* tata *f.*
au pair 1 *adv* au pair. **2** *n* **au p.**
(girl) jeune fille *f* au pair.
Aus·tra·li·an 1 *n* Australien,
-ienne *mf.* **2** *adj* australien.
Aus·tri·an 1 *n* Autrichien, -ienne
mf. **2** *adj* autrichien.
au·then·tic *adj* authentique.
au·thor auteur *m.*
au·thor·i·ty autorité *f; (permission)* autorisation *f* (**to do** à faire).
au·thor·i·za·tion autorisation *f*
(**to do** à faire).
au·to·bi·og·ra·phy autobiogra-
phie *f.*
au·to·graph 1 *n* autographe *m.* **2**
vt dédicacer (**for** à).
au·to·mat·ic *adj* automatique.
au·to·mat·i·cal·ly *adv* automatiquement.
au·to·mo·bile auto(mobile) *f.*
au·ton·o·mous *adj* autonome.
au·tumn automne *m.*
aux·il·ia·ry *adj & n* **a. (verb)**
(verbe *m*) auxiliaire *m.*
a·vail·a·bil·i·ty disponibilité *f.*
a·vail·a·ble *adj* disponible; **a. to**
all accessible à tous.
av·a·lanche avalanche *f.*
av·e·nue avenue *f.*
av·er·age 1 *n* moyenne *f;* **on a.** en
moyenne. **2** *adj* moyen.
a·vi·a·tion aviation *f.*

av·o·ca·do, *pl* -os avocat *m.*
a·void *vt* éviter; **to a. doing** éviter
de faire.
a·void·a·ble *adj* évitable.
a·wake 1 *vi** se réveiller. **2** *adj*
éveillé; **to keep sb a.** empêcher qn
de dormir; **he's (still) a.** il ne dort
pas (encore).
a·ward 1 *vt (money, prize)* attribuer. **2** *n (prize)* prix *m; (scholarship)* bourse *f;* **awards ceremony**
distribution *f* des prix.
a·ware *adj* **a. of** *(conscious)* conscient de; *(informed)* au courant
de; **to become a. of** prendre conscience de.
a·way *adv (distant)* loin; **far a.** au
loin; **3 miles a.** à 5km (de distance);
to play a. *(of team)* jouer à l'extérieur. ▪ *(in time)* **ten days a.** dans
dix jours. ▪ *(absent)* parti. ▪ *(con-
tinuously)* **to work/talk/etc a.** tra-
vailler/parler/*etc* sans relâche.
aw·ful *adj* affreux; *(terrifying)*
épouvantable; **an a. lot of** *Fam* un
nombre incroyable de.
aw·ful·ly *adv (very) Fam* affreusement.
awk·ward *adj (clumsy)* maladroit;
(difficult) difficile; *(tool)* peu commode; *(time)* inopportun.
awn·ing *(over shop)* store *m.*
ax 1 *n* hache *f.* **2** *vt (job etc)* supprimer.
ax·is, *pl* -es axe *m.*
ax·le essieu *m.*

B

ba·by bébé *m;* **b. boy** petit garçon
m; **b. girl** petite fille *f.*
ba·by car·riage landau *m (pl* -aus).
ba·by clothes vêtements *mpl* de
bébé.

ba·by·sit vi garder les enfants.

ba·by·sit·ter baby-sitter mf.

bach·e·lor célibataire m; **B. of Arts/of Science** licencié, -ée mf ès lettres/ès sciences.

back[1] **1** n dos m; (of chair) dossier m; (of hand) revers m; (of house) derrière m, arrière m; (of room) fond m; (of vehicle) arrière m; (of page) verso m; **at the b. of the book** à la fin du livre; **b. to front** devant derrière; **in b. of** derrière. **2** adj arrière inv; de derrière; **b. door** porte f de derrière; **b. tooth** molaire f. **3** adv (behind) en arrière; **to come b.** revenir; **he's b.** il est de retour, il est revenu.

back[2] vt (support) appuyer; (with money) financer; (horse etc) parier sur.

back·ache mal m de dos; **to have a b.** avoir mal au dos.

back·fire vi (of vehicle) pétarader.

back·ground fond m; (events) antécédents mpl; (education) formation f; (environment) milieu m; **b. music** musique f de fond.

back·ing (aid) soutien m; (material) support m.

back·log (of work) arriéré m.

▸ **back out** vi (withdraw) se retirer.

back·pack sac m à dos.

back·side (buttocks) Fam derrière m.

back·stage adv dans les coulisses.

▸ **back up** vt (support) appuyer qn.

back·ward adj (retarded) arriéré; (glance) en arrière.

back·wards adv en arrière; (to walk) à reculons; (to put on garment) à l'envers.

back·yard jardin m.

ba·con bacon m.

bac·te·ri·a npl bactéries fpl.

bad adj mauvais; (wicked) méchant; (accident, wound) grave; (arm, leg) malade; (pain) violent; **to feel b.** (ill) se sentir mal; **things**

are b. ça va mal; **not b.!** pas mal!

badge (plastic) badge m; (metal) pin's m; (of policeman etc) plaque f.

badg·er blaireau m.

bad·ly adv mal; (hurt) grièvement; **b. affected** très touché; **to want b.** avoir grande envie de.

bad-man·nered adj mal élevé.

bad·min·ton badminton m.

bad-tem·pered adj grincheux.

baf·fle vt déconcerter.

bag sac m; **bags** (baggage) valises fpl; (under eyes) poches fpl.

bag·gage bagages mpl.

bag·gage check consigne f.

bag·gy adj (out of shape) déformé; (by design) large.

bag·pipes npl cornemuse f.

bail (in court) caution f; **on b.** en liberté provisoire.

bait amorce f, appât m.

bake 1 vt (faire) cuire (au four). **2** vi (of cook) (make cakes) faire de la pâtisserie; (make bread) faire du pain; (of cake etc) cuire (au four).

baked beans npl haricots mpl blancs (à la tomate).

bak·er boulanger, -ère mf.

bak·e·ry boulangerie f.

bal·ance 1 n équilibre m; (of account) solde m; (remainder) reste m; **to lose one's b.** perdre l'équilibre. **2** vt tenir en équilibre (on sur); (account) équilibrer. **3** vi (of person) se tenir en équilibre; (of accounts) être en équilibre.

bal·ance sheet bilan m.

bald adj chauve.

bald-head·ed adj chauve.

bald·ness calvitie f.

ball[1] (round object) balle f; (inflated) (for sports) ballon m; (of string, wool) pelote f; (any round shape) boule f; (of meat or fish) boulette f; **on the b.** Fam (alert) éveillé; (efficient) au point.

ball[2] (dance) bal m (pl bals).

bal·le·ri·na ballerine f.

bal·let ballet m.

bal·loon ballon *m*.

bal·lot *(voting)* scrutin *m*.

ball·park stade *m* de base-ball; **a b. figure** une estimation.

ball·point stylo *m* à bille, bic® *m*.

ball·room salle *f* de danse.

ban 1 *n* interdiction *f*. 2 *vt* interdire (**sb from doing** à qn de faire); *(exclude)* exclure (**from** de).

ba·na·na banane *f*.

band *(strip)* bande *f*; *(musicians)* (petit) orchestre *m*; *(pop group)* groupe *m*; **rubber b.** élastique *m*.

band·age bande *f*.

▸ **bandage up** *vt (arm, wound)* bander.

Band-Aid® pansement *m* adhésif.

bang 1 *n* coup *m* (violent); *(of door)* claquement *m*. 2 *vt* cogner; *(door)* (faire) claquer. 3 *vi* cogner; *(of door)* claquer.

▸ **bang down** *vt (lid)* rabattre (violemment).

▸ **bang into** *vt* heurter.

ban·gle bracelet *m* (rigide).

bangs *npl (of hair)* frange *f*.

ban·is·ter(s) *n(pl)* rampe *f* (d'escalier).

bank *(of river)* bord *m*; *(for money)* banque *f*.

bank ac·count compte *m* en banque.

bank·er banquier *m*.

bank·ing *(activity)* la banque.

▸ **bank on** *vt* compter sur.

bank·rupt *adj* **to go b.** faire faillite.

bank·rupt·cy faillite *f*.

ban·ner *(at rallies, on two poles)* banderole *f*.

bar 1 *n* barre *f*; *(of gold)* lingot *m*; *(of chocolate)* tablette *f*; *(on window)* barreau *m*; *(pub, counter)* bar *m*. 2 *vt (way)* bloquer; *(prohibit)* interdire (**sb from doing** à qn de faire); *(exclude)* exclure (**from** de).

bar·be·cue barbecue *m*.

barbed *adj* **b. wire** fil *m* de fer barbelé.

bar·ber coiffeur *m*.

bare *adj* nu; *(tree)* dénudé; **with his b. hands** mains nues.

bare·foot *adv* nu-pieds.

bare·ly *adv (scarcely)* à peine.

bar·gain 1 *n (deal)* marché *m*; **a b.** *(cheap buy)* une affaire; **b. price** prix *m* exceptionnel. 2 *vi* négocier.

▸ **bargain for** *vt (expect)* s'attendre à.

barge chaland *m*.

▸ **barge in** *vi (enter a room)* faire irruption; *(interrupt sb)* interrompre.

bark 1 *n (of tree)* écorce *f*. 2 *vi (of dog)* aboyer.

bark·ing aboiements *mpl*.

bar·ley orge *f*.

bar·maid serveuse *f* de bar.

bar·man barman *m*.

barn *(for crops)* grange *f*.

ba·rom·e·ter baromètre *m*.

bar·racks *npl* caserne *f*.

bar·rage *(barrier)* barrage *m*.

bar·rel *(cask)* tonneau *m*; *(of oil)* baril *m*; *(of gun)* canon *m*.

bar·ren *adj* stérile.

bar·rette barrette *f*.

bar·ri·cade 1 *n* barricade *f*. 2 *vt* barricader.

bar·ri·er barrière *f*.

bar·tend·er barman *m*.

base 1 *n* base *f*; *(of tree, lamp)* pied *m*. 2 *vt* baser.

base·ball base-ball *m*.

base·board plinthe *f*.

base·ment sous-sol *m*.

bash 1 *n (bang)* coup *m*. 2 *vt (hit)* cogner.

▸ **bash up** *vt* **to b. sb up** tabasser qn.

ba·sic 1 *adj* essentiel, de base; *(elementary)* élémentaire; *(pay)* de base. 2 *n* **the basics** l'essentiel *m*.

ba·si·cal·ly *adv* au fond.

ba·sin bassin *m*; *(sink)* lavabo *m*.

ba·sis *(of agreement etc)* bases *fpl*; **on the b. of** d'après; **on that b.** dans ces conditions; **on a weekly b.** chaque semaine.

bask *vi* se chauffer.

bas·ket panier *m*; *(for bread, laundry, litter)* corbeille *f*.

bass 1 *n (singer)* basse *f*; *(notes)* graves *mpl*. **b. drum** grosse caisse *f*, **b. (guitar)** *(guitare f)* basse *f*. 2 *adj* grave, bas *(f* basse).

bat 1 *n (animal)* chauve-souris *f*; *Sports* batte *f*. 2 *vt* **she didn't b. an eyelid** elle n'a pas sourcillé.

batch *(of people)* groupe *m*; *(of letters)* paquet *m*; *(of papers)* liasse *f*.

bath 1 *n* bain *m*; *(tub)* baignoire *f*; **to take a b.** prendre un bain. 2 *vt* baigner.

bathe 1 *vt* baigner. 2 *vi (swim)* se baigner; *(take a bath)* prendre un bain. 3 *n* bain *m* (de mer).

bath·ing suit maillot *m* de bain.

bath·robe robe *f* de chambre.

bath·room salle *f* de bain(s); *(toilet)* toilettes *fpl*.

bath·tub baignoire *f*.

bat·ter 1 *n* pâte *f* à frire. 2 *vt (child)* martyriser.

▶**batter down** *vt (door)* défoncer.

bat·tered *adj (car)* cabossé.

bat·te·ry batterie *f*; *(in radio, appliance)* pile *f*.

bat·tle 1 *n* bataille *f*; *(struggle)* lutte *f*. 2 *vi* se battre.

bat·tle·ship cuirassé *m*.

bawl (out) *vti* beugler; **to b. sb out** *Fam* engueuler qn.

bay *(part of coastline)* baie *f*; *(for loading)* aire *f*.

BC *abbr (before Christ)* avant Jésus-Christ.

be* *vi* être; **she's a doctor** elle est médecin; **it's 3 o'clock** il est trois heures. ■ avoir; **to be hot/right/ lucky** avoir chaud/raison/de la chance; **he's 20** il a 20 ans; **to be 7 feet high** avoir 2 mètres de haut. ■ *(health)* aller; **how are you?** comment vas-tu? ■ *(go, come)* **I've been to see her** je suis allé *or* j'ai été la voir; **he's (already) been here** il est (déjà) venu. ■ *(weather, cal-*

culations) faire; **it's sunny** il fait beau; **2 and 2 are 4** 2 et 2 font 4. ■ *(cost)* faire; **how much is it?** ça fait combien? ■ *(auxiliary)* **I am/was doing** je fais/faisais; **he was killed** il a été tué; **I've been waiting (for) two hours** j'attends depuis deux heures; **isn't it?/aren't you?/etc** n'est-ce pas?, non? ■ *(+ infinitive)* **he is to come** *(must)* il doit venir. ■ **there is** *or* **are** il y a; *(pointing)* voilà!; **here is** *or* **are** voici.

beach plage *f*.

bea·con balise *f*.

bead perle *f*; *(of sweat)* goutte *f*; **(string of) beads** collier *m*.

beak bec *m*.

beak·er *(for drinking)* gobelet *m*; *(in laboratory)* vase *m* à bec.

beam *(of wood)* poutre *f*; *(of light)* rayon *m*; *(of headlight)* faisceau *m*.

beam·ing *adj (radiant)* radieux.

bean haricot *m*; *(of coffee)* grain *m*; **(broad) b.** fève *f*.

bean·sprouts *npl* germes *mpl* de soja.

bear¹ *(animal)* ours *m*.

bear²* 1 *vt (carry, show)* porter; *(endure)* supporter; *(responsibility)* assumer; **to b. in mind** tenir compte de. 2 *vi* **to b. left/right** tourner à gauche/droite.

bear·a·ble *adj* supportable.

beard barbe *f*.

beard·ed *adj* barbu.

bear·ing *(relevance)* relation *f* (**on** avec); **to get one's bearings** s'orienter.

▶**bear out** *vt* corroborer.

beast bête *f*; *(person)* brute *f*.

beast·ly *adj (bad) Fam* vilain.

beat 1 *n (of heart, drum)* battement *m*; *(of policeman)* ronde *f*. 2 *vt** battre.

beat down 1 *vt (door)* défoncer. 2 *vi (of rain)* tomber à verse; *(of sun)* taper.

beat·ing *(blows, defeat)* raclée *f*.

▶**beat off** *vt* repousser.

▶**beat up** vt tabasser.

beau·ti·ful adj (très) beau (f belle).

beau·ty (quality, woman) beauté f.

beau·ty mark (on skin) grain m de beauté.

beau·ty par·lor institut m de beauté.

beau·ty spot (on skin) grain m de beauté.

bea·ver castor m.

be·cause conj parce que; **b. of** à cause de.

be·come* vi devenir; **to b. a painter** devenir peintre; **what has b. of her?** qu'est-elle devenue?

bed lit m; **to go to b.** (aller) se coucher; **in b.** couché; **to get out of b.** se lever; **b. and breakfast** chambre f avec petit déjeuner.

bed·clothes npl couvertures fpl et draps mpl.

bed·room chambre f à coucher.

bed·side chevet m; **b. lamp/book** lampe f/livre m de chevet.

bed·time heure f de coucher.

bee abeille f.

beech (tree, wood) hêtre m.

beef bœuf m.

bee·hive ruche f.

been pp de **be**.

beep 1 n bip m; (on answering machine) bip m sonore. **2** vt biper.

bee·per récepteur m d'appels, bip m.

beer bière f; **b. glass** chope f.

beet betterave f (potagère).

bee·tle scarabée m.

be·fore 1 adv avant; (already) déjà; (in front) devant; **the day b.** la veille. **2** prep (time) avant; (place) devant; **the year b. last** il y a deux ans. **3** conj avant que (+ ne + subjunctive), avant de (+ infinitive); **b. he goes** avant qu'il (ne) parte; **b. going** avant de partir.

be·friend vt prendre en amitié, se prendre d'amitié pour.

beg 1 vt **to b. (for)** solliciter;

(bread, money) mendier; **to b. sb to do** supplier qn de faire. **2** vi mendier.

beg·gar mendiant, -ante mf.

be·gin* 1 vt commencer; (campaign) lancer; **to b. doing** or **to do** commencer or se mettre à faire. **2** vi commencer (**with** par; **by doing** par faire); **to b. with** (first) d'abord.

be·gin·ner débutant, -ante mf.

be·gin·ning commencement m, début m.

be·grudge vt (envy) envier (**sb sth** qch à qn); **to b. doing sth** faire qch à contrecœur.

be·half on b. of (to act) pour le compte de; (to call, write) de la part de.

be·have vi se conduire; (of machine) fonctionner; **to b. (oneself)** se tenir bien; (of child) être sage.

be·hav·ior conduite f.

be·hind 1 prep derrière; (in making progress) en retard sur. **2** adv derrière; (late) en retard. **3** n (buttocks) Fam derrière m.

beige adj & n beige (m).

belch 1 vi faire un renvoi. **2** n renvoi m.

Bel·gian 1 n Belge mf. **2** adj belge.

be·lief croyance f (in en); (trust) confiance f, foi f; (opinion) opinion f.

be·liev·a·ble adj croyable.

be·lieve vti croire (**in sth** à qch; **in God** en Dieu); **I b. so** je crois que oui; **to b. in doing** croire qu'il faut faire.

be·liev·er (religious) croyant, -ante mf.

be·lit·tle vt dénigrer.

bell cloche f; (small) clochette f; (in phone) sonnerie f; (on door, bicycle) sonnette f.

bell·boy groom m.

bel·ly ventre m; **b. button** Fam nombril m.

bel·ly·ache mal m au ventre.

be·long vi appartenir (**to** à); **to b.**

to (*club*) être membre de.
be·long·ings *npl* affaires *fpl*.
be·low 1 *prep* au-dessous de. **2** *adv* en dessous.
belt ceinture *f*; (*in machine*) courroie *f*.
belt·way périphérique *m*.
bench (*seat*) banc *m*; (*work table*) établi *m*.
bend 1 *n* courbe *f*; (*in river*) coude *m*; (*in road*) virage *m*; (*of arm, knee*) pli *m*. **2** *vt** courber; (*leg, arm*) plier. **3** *vi* (*of road*) tourner.
bend (down) *vi* se baisser.
bend (over) *vi* se pencher.
be·neath 1 *prep* au-dessous de. **2** *adv* (au-)dessous.
ben·e·fi·cial *adj* bénéfique.
ben·e·fit 1 *n* avantage *m*; (*money*) allocation *f*; **child b.** allocations familiales; **for your (own) b.** pour vous. **2** *vt* faire du bien à; (*be useful to*) profiter à. **3** *vi* you'll **b. from it** ça vous fera du bien.
bent *adj* (*nail*) tordu; **b. on doing** résolu à faire.
be·reave·ment deuil *m*.
ber·ry baie *f*.
ber·serk *adj* **to go b.** devenir fou.
berth (*in ship, train*) couchette *f*.
be·side *prep* à côté de; **that's b. the point** ça n'a rien à voir.
be·sides 1 *prep* en plus de; (*except*) excepté. **2** *adv* de plus; (*moreover*) d'ailleurs.
best 1 *adj* meilleur; (*in de*); **the b. part of** (*most*) la plus grande partie de. **2** *n* **the b.** le meilleur, la meilleure; **at b.** au mieux; **to do one's b.** faire de son mieux; **to make the b. of** s'accommoder de. **3** *adv* (**the**) **b.** (*to play, sing etc*) le mieux; **the b. loved** le plus aimé.
best man (*at wedding*) garçon *m* d'honneur.
best-sell·er best-seller *m*.
bet 1 *n* pari *m*. **2** *vti** parier (**on** sur; **that** que).
be·tray *vt* trahir.

be·tray·al trahison *f*.
bet·ter 1 *adj* meilleur (**than** que); **she's (much) b.** (*in health*) elle va (beaucoup) mieux; **that's b.** c'est mieux; **to get b.** (*recover*) se remettre; (*improve*) s'améliorer; **it's b. to go** il vaut mieux partir. **2** *adv* mieux; **I had b. go** il vaut mieux que je parte. **3** *vt* **to b.** oneself améliorer sa condition.
betting pari(s) *m*(*pl*).
be·tween 1 *prep* entre; **in b. sth and sth/two things** entre qch et qch/deux choses. **2** *adv* **in b.** au milieu; (*time*) dans l'intervalle.
bev·er·age boisson *f*.
be·ware *vi* **to b. of** se méfier de; **b.!** méfiez-vous!
be·wil·der *vt* dérouter.
be·yond 1 *prep* au-delà de; (*reach, doubt*) hors de; **b. my means** au dessus de mes moyens; **it's b. me** ça me dépasse. **2** *adv* au-delà.
bi·as penchant *m* (**towards** pour); (*prejudice*) préjugé *m*.
bi·as(s)ed *adj* partial; **to be b. against** avoir des préjugés contre.
bib (*baby's*) bavoir *m*.
Bi·ble bible *f*; **the B.** la Bible.
bi·cy·cle bicyclette *f*.
bid* **1** *vt* (*money*) offrir. **2** *vi* faire une offre (**for** pour). **3** *n* (*at auction*) offre *f*; (*for job*) tentative *f*.
big *adj* grand, gros (*f* grosse); (*in age, generous*) grand; (*in bulk, amount*) gros; **b. deal!** Fam (bon) et alors!
big·head Fam (*conceited*) prétentieux, -euse *mf*; (*boasting*) vantard, -arde *mf*.
big-shot Fam gros bonnet *m*.
bike Fam vélo *m*.
bike path Fam piste *f* cyclable.
bi·ki·ni deux-pièces *m inv*; **b. briefs** mini-slip *m*.
bile bile *f*.
bi·lin·gual *adj* bilingue.
bill 1 *n* (*invoice*) facture *f*, note *f*; (*in restaurant*) addition *f*; (*in hotel*)

note f; *(money)* billet m; *(proposed law)* projet m de loi. **2** vt **to b. sb** envoyer la facture à qn.
bill·board panneau m d'affichage.
bill·fold portefeuille m.
bil·liards npl (jeu m de) billiard m.
bil·lion milliard m.
bin boîte f; *(for trash)* poubelle f.
bind vt* lier; *(book)* relier.
bind·er *(for papers)* classeur m.
bind·ing *(of book)* reliure f.
bin·go loto m.
bin·oc·u·lars npl jumelles fpl.
bi·o·log·i·cal adj biologique.
bi·ol·o·gy biologie f.
bi·o·tech·nol·o·gy biotechnologie f.
birch (silver) b. *(tree)* bouleau m.
bird oiseau m; *(fowl)* volaille f; **b.'s-eye view** vue f d'ensemble.
birth naissance f; **to give b.** to donner naissance à.
birth cer·tif·i·cate acte m de naissance.
birth·day anniversaire m; **happy b.!** bon anniversaire!
birth·mark tache f de naissance.
bis·cuit petit pain m.
bish·op évêque m.
bit morceau m; **a b.** *(a little)* un peu; **quite a b.** *(very)* très; *(a lot)* beaucoup; **not a b.** pas du tout; **b. by b.** petit à petit.
bitch **1** n *(dog)* chienne f; *(spiteful woman)* Fam garce f. **2** vi **to b.** (about) Fam *(criticize)* déblatérer (contre).
bite **1** n *(wound)* morsure f; *(from insect)* piqûre f; **a b. to eat** quelque chose à manger. **2** vti* mordre; **to b. one's nails** se ronger les ongles.
bit·ter adj amer; *(cold, wind)* glacial; *(conflict)* violent.
bit·ter·ness amertume f, *(of conflict)* violence f.
bi·zarre adj bizarre.
black **1** adj noir; **b. eye** œil m poché; **to give sb a b. eye** pocher

l'œil à qn; **b. and blue** *(bruised)* couvert de bleus. **2** n *(color)* noir m; *(person)* Noir, -e mf.
black·ber·ry mûre f.
black·bird merle m.
black·board tableau m (noir); **on the b.** au tableau.
black·cur·rant cassis m.
black·list **1** n liste f noire. **2** vt mettre sur la liste noire.
black·mail **1** n chantage m. **2** vt faire chanter.
black·mail·er maître-chanteur m.
black·out panne f d'électricité; *(fainting fit)* syncope f.
▶**black out** vi *(faint)* s'évanouir.
blad·der vessie f.
blade lame f, *(of grass)* brin m.
blame **1** vt accuser; **to b. sb for sth** reprocher qch à qn; **you're to b.** c'est ta faute. **2** n faute f.
blame·less adj irréprochable.
bland adj *(food)* fade.
blank **1** adj *(paper, page)* blanc *(f* blanche); *(check)* en blanc. **2** adj & n **b.** (space) blanc m.
blan·ket couverture f.
blare (out) vi *(of radio)* beugler; *(of music)* retentir.
blast **1** n explosion f; *(air from explosion)* souffle m. **2** int Fam zut!
blast·ed adj Fam fichu.
blast-off *(of spacecraft)* mise f à feu.
blaze **1** n *(fire)* flamme f, *(large)* incendie m. **2** vi *(of fire)* flamber; *(of sun)* flamboyer.
blaz·er blazer m.
blaz·ing adj en feu; *(sun)* brûlant.
bleach *(household)* eau f de Javel.
bleak adj morne.
bleed* vti saigner.
blem·ish *(fault)* défaut m; *(mark)* tache f.
blend **1** n mélange m. **2** vt mélanger. **3** vi se mélanger.
blend·er *(for food)* mixer m.
bless vt bénir; **b. you!** *(after sneeze)* à tes souhaits!

bles·sing bénédiction f; (benefit) bienfait m.

blew pt de **blow¹**.

blind 1 adj aveugle; **b. person** aveugle mf. **2** n (on window) store m; **the b.** les aveugles mpl.

blind·fold 1 n bandeau m. **2** vt bander les yeux à.

blind·ly adv aveuglément.

blind·ness cécité f.

blink 1 vi (of person) cligner des yeux; (of eyes) cligner. **2** n clignement m.

bliss félicité f.

blis·ter (on skin) ampoule f.

bliz·zard tempête f de neige.

bloat vt gonfler.

blob goutte f; (of ink) tache f.

block 1 n (of stone) bloc m; (of buildings) pâté m (de maisons); (child's toy) cube m. **2** vt (obstruct) bloquer.

block·age obstruction f.

▸**block off** vt (road) barrer.

▸**block up** vt (pipe, hole) bloquer.

blog blog m.

blog·ger blogueur, -euse mf.

blond adj & n blond (m).

blonde adj & n blonde (f).

blood sang m; **b. donor** donneur, -euse mf de sang; **b. group** groupe m sanguin; **b. pressure** tension f (artérielle); **to have high b. pressure** avoir de la tension.

blood·shed effusion f de sang.

blood·shot adj (eye) injecté de sang.

blood·y adj sanglant.

bloom 1 n fleur f; **in b.** en fleur(s). **2** vi fleurir.

blos·som 1 n fleur(s) f(pl). **2** vi fleurir.

blot tache f.

blotch·y adj couvert de taches.

blot·ting pa·per buvard m.

blouse chemisier m.

blow¹* 1 vt (of wind) pousser (un navire), chasser (la pluie); (of person) (smoke) souffler; (bubbles) faire; (trumpet) souffler dans; **to b. one's nose** se moucher; **to b. a whistle** siffler. **2** vi (of wind, person) souffler.

blow² (with fist, tool etc) coup m.

▸**blow away 1** vt (of wind) emporter. **2** vi (of hat, newspaper etc) s'envoler.

▸**blow down, blow over 1** vt (chimney etc) faire tomber. **2** vi tomber.

blow-dry Brushing® m.

blow-dry·er sèche-cheveux m.

▸**blow off 1** vt (hat etc) emporter. **2** vi s'envoler.

▸**blow out** (candle) souffler.

blow-torch chalumeau m.

▸**blow up 1** vt (building) faire sauter; (tire, balloon) gonfler. **2** vi exploser.

blue 1 adj bleu (mpl bleus). **2** n bleu m (pl bleus).

blue·ber·ry myrtille f.

blue·print bleu m; (plan) plan m, projet m.

bluff 1 vti bluffer. **2** n bluff m.

blun·der 1 n (mistake) bévue f. **2** vi faire une bévue.

blunt adj (edge) émoussé; (person, speech) franc, brusque.

blur 1 n tache f floue. **2** vt rendre flou.

blurred adj flou.

blush vi rougir (with de).

blus·te·ry adj (weather) de grand vent.

board¹ 1 n (piece of wood) planche f; (for notices) tableau m; (cardboard) carton m; **b. (of directors)** conseil m d'administration; **on b.** (ship, aircraft) à bord (de). **2** vt monter à bord de; (bus, train) monter dans.

board² (food) pension f; **room and b.** pension f (complète).

board·er pensionnaire mf.

board·ing (of passengers) embarquement m.

board·ing house pension f (de famille).

board·ing school pensionnat m.

board·walk promenade f (de planches).

boast vi se vanter (**about, of** de).

boat bateau m; (small) barque f, canot m; (liner) paquebot m.

bob·by pin pince f à cheveux.

bob·by socks, bob·by sox npl socquettes fpl (de fille).

bod·i·ly adj (need) physique.

bod·y corps m; (institution) organisme m.

bod·y·guard garde m du corps.

bod·y·work carrosserie f.

bogged down adj to get b. s'enliser.

bo·gus adj faux (f fausse).

boil[1] (pimple) furoncle m.

boil[2] 1 n to come to the b. bouillir. 2 vt faire bouillir. 3 vi bouillir.

boiled adj bouilli; (potato) à l'eau; **b. egg** œuf m à la coque; **hard-b. egg** œuf m dur.

boil·er chaudière f.

boil·ing adj b. (hot) bouillant; it's b. (hot) (weather) il fait une chaleur infernale.

▶ **boil over** vi (of milk) déborder.

▶ **boil up** vt faire bouillir.

bold adj hardi.

bold·ness hardiesse f.

bolt 1 n (on door) verrou m; (for nut) boulon m. 2 vt (door) fermer au verrou. 3 vi (dash) se précipiter.

bomb 1 n bombe f. 2 vt bombarder.

bomb·er (aircraft) bombardier m.

bomb·ing bombardement m.

bond (link) lien m; (investment certificate) bon m.

bone os m; (of fish) arête f.

bon·fire (celebration) feu m de joie; (for dead leaves) feu m (de jardin).

bon·net (hat) bonnet m; (of car) capot m.

bo·nus prime f.

bon·y adj (thin) osseux; (fish) plein d'arêtes.

boo 1 vti siffler. 2 n boos sifflets mpl.

boo·by-trap vt piéger.

book 1 n livre m; (of tickets) carnet m; (exercise) b. cahier m (de brouillon); **books** (accounts) comptes mpl. 2 vt (room etc) réserver.

book·case bibliothèque f.

booked up adj (hotel) complet.

book·ing réservation f.

book·keep·er comptable mf.

book·keep·ing comptabilité f.

book·let (pamphlet) brochure f.

book·mak·er bookmaker m.

book·sell·er libraire mf.

book·shelf rayon m.

book·store librairie f.

boom (economic) expansion f.

boost vt (increase) augmenter; (product) faire de la réclame pour; (economy) stimuler.

boot (footwear) botte f; (ankle) b. bottillon m; **to get the b.** Fam être mis à la porte; (Denver) b. (on car) sabot m (de Denver).

booth (for phone) cabine f.

▶ **boot out** vt mettre à la porte.

booze Fam 1 n alcool m. 2 vi picoler.

bor·der (of country) frontière f; (edge) bord m.

bor·der (on) vt (country) toucher à.

bor·der·line case cas m limite.

bore 1 vt ennuyer; **to be bored** s'ennuyer. 2 n (person) raseur, -euse mf; (thing) ennui m.

bore·dom ennui m.

bor·ing adj ennuyeux.

born adj né; **to be b.** naître; **he was b.** il est né.

bor·ough municipalité f.

bor·row vt emprunter (**from** à).

boss patron, -onne mf, chef m.

▶ **boss around** vt donner des ordres à.

boss·y adj Fam autoritaire.

botch (up) vt (ruin) bâcler.

both 1 adj les deux. 2 pron tous/toutes (les) deux; **b. of us** nous deux. 3 adv (at the same time) à la fois; **b. you and I** vous et moi.

both·er 1 vt (annoy, worry) ennuyer; (disturb) déranger; (pester) importuner; **to b. doing** or **to do** se donner la peine de faire; **I can't be bothered** je n'en ai pas envie. **2** n (trouble) ennui m; (effort) peine f; (inconvenience) dérangement m.

▶**bother about** vt (worry about) se préoccuper de.

bot·tle bouteille f; (small) flacon m; (for baby) biberon m; **hot-water b.** bouillotte f.

bot·tle o·pen·er ouvre-bouteilles m inv.

bot·tom 1 n (of sea, box) fond m; (of page, hill) bas m; (buttocks) Fam derrière m; **to be at the b. of the class** être le dernier de la classe. **2** adj (part, shelf) inférieur, du bas; **b. floor** rez-de-chaussée m.

boul·der rocher m.

bounce 1 vi (of ball) rebondir; (of check) Fam être sans provision. **2** vt faire rebondir. **3** n (re)bond m.

bound adj **b. to do** (obliged) obligé de faire; (certain) sûr de faire; **it's b. to happen/snow/etc** ça arrivera/il neigera/etc sûrement; **b. for** en route pour.

bound·a·ry limite f.

bounds npl **out of b.** (place) interdit.

bou·quet (of flowers) bouquet m.

bou·tique boutique f (de mode).

bow¹ (weapon) arc m; (knot) nœud m.

bow² **1** n révérence f; (nod) salut m. **2** vi s'incliner (**to** devant); (nod) incliner la tête (**to** devant).

bow·els npl intestins mpl.

bowl (for food) bol m; (for sugar) sucrier m; (for salad) saladier m; (for fruit) coupe f.

bowl·ing (tenpin) **b.** bowling m.

bowl·ing al·ley bowling m.

bow tie nœud m papillon.

box 1 n boîte f; (large) caisse f. **2** vi (of boxer) boxer.

box·er boxeur m.

box·er shorts caleçon m.

▶**box in** vt (enclose) enfermer.

box·ing boxe f; **b. ring** ring m.

box of·fice guichet m (pour spectacles).

boy garçon m; **American b.** jeune Américain m; **oh b.!** mon Dieu!

boy·cott 1 vt boycotter. **2** n boycottage m.

boy·friend petit ami m.

bra soutien-gorge m.

brace·let bracelet m.

brack·et (in typography) crochet m; (for shelf etc) équerre f.

brag vi se vanter (**about, of** de).

brag·ging vantardise f.

braid 1 n (of hair) tresse f. **2** vt tresser.

brain cerveau m; **to have brains** avoir de l'intelligence.

brain·storm (brilliant idea) idée f géniale.

brain·wash vt faire un lavage de cerveau à.

brain·y adj Fam intelligent.

brake 1 n frein m. **2** vi freiner.

brake light (signal m de) stop m.

branch branche f; (of road) embranchement m; (of store, office) succursale f.

▶**branch off** vi (of road) bifurquer.

▶**branch out** vi (of firm, person) étendre ses activités (**into** à).

brand (trademark) marque f.

brand-new adj tout neuf (f toute neuve).

bran·dy cognac m.

brass cuivre m.

brave adj courageux, brave.

brav·e·ry courage m.

brawl bagarre f.

brawn·y adj musclé.

bread inv pain m; **loaf of b.** pain m; **(slice** or **piece of) b. and butter** tartine f.

bread·box coffre m à pain.

bread·crumb miette f (de pain); **breadcrumbs** (in cooking) chapelure f.

breadth largeur *f*.

bread·win·ner soutien *m* de famille.

break 1 *vt** casser; *(into pieces)* briser; *(silence, spell)* rompre; *(strike, heart, ice)* briser; *(sports record)* battre; *(law)* violer; *(one's word, promise)* manquer à; *(journey)* interrompre; *(news)* révéler (**to** à). **2** *vi* (se) casser; *(into pieces)* se briser; se rompre; *(of news)* éclater; *(stop work)* faire la pause. **3** *n* cassure *f*, *(in bone)* fracture *f*, *(with person, group)* rupture *f*, *(in journey)* interruption *f*, *(rest)* repos *m*; *(in activity, for tea etc)* pause *f*, *(in school)* récréation *f*, **a lucky b.** une chance.

break·a·ble *adj* fragile.

▸ **break away** *vi* se détacher.

break·down *(of vehicle, machine)* panne *f*, *(in talks)* rupture *f*, *(nervous)* dépression *f*.

▸ **break down 1** *vt* *(door)* enfoncer. **2** *vi* *(of vehicle, machine)* tomber en panne; *(of talks)* échouer; *(collapse) (of person)* s'effondrer.

break·fast petit déjeuner *m*.

▸ **break in 1** *vi* *(of burglar)* entrer par effraction. **2** *vt* *(door)* enfoncer; *(vehicle)* roder.

break-in cambriolage *m*.

▸ **break into** *vt* *(house)* cambrioler; *(safe)* forcer.

▸ **break loose** *vi* s'échapper.

▸ **break off 1** *vt* détacher; *(relations)* rompre. **2** *vi* se détacher; *(stop)* s'arrêter; **to b. off with sb** rompre avec qn.

▸ **break out** *vi* *(of war, fire)* éclater; *(escape)* s'échapper.

break·through percée *f*, découverte *f*.

break·up *(of marriage)* rupture *f*.

▸ **break up 1** *vt* mettre en morceaux; *(fight)* mettre fin à. **2** *vi* *(of group)* se disperser; *(of marriage)* se briser.

breast sein *m*; *(of chicken)* blanc *m*.

breast·feed *vt* allaiter.

breast·stroke brasse *f*.

breath haleine *f*, souffle *m*; **out of b.** (tout) essoufflé.

Breath·a·lyz·er® alcootest® *m*.

breathe *vti* respirer; **to b. in** aspirer; **to b. out** expirer.

breath·ing respiration *f*, **b. space** moment *m* de repos.

breath·tak·ing *adj* époustouflant.

breed 1 *vt** *(animals)* élever. **2** *vi* *(of animals)* se reproduire. **3** *n* race *f*.

breed·er éleveur, -euse *mf*.

breed·ing *(of animals)* élevage *m*; *(good manners)* éducation *f*, **b. ground** foyer *m*, terrain *m* propice.

breeze brise *f*.

breez·y *adj* *(weather)* frais.

brew *vi* *(storm)* se préparer; *(of tea)* infuser; **something is brewing** il se prépare quelque chose.

brew·e·ry brasserie *f*.

bribe 1 *n* pot-de-vin *m*. **2** *vt* *(person)* acheter.

brick brique *f*.

brick·lay·er maçon *m*.

bride mariée *f*, **the b. and groom** les mariés *mpl*.

bride·groom marié *m*.

brides·maid demoiselle *f* d'honneur.

bridge pont *m*.

brief 1 *adj* bref (*f* brève). **2** *vt* *(inform)* mettre au courant (**on** de). **3** *n* briefs *(underpants)* slip *m*.

brief·case serviette *f*.

brief·ing instructions *fpl*.

brief·ly *adv* *(quickly)* en vitesse.

bright 1 *adj* brillant; *(weather, room)* clair; *(clever)* intelligent; *(idea)* génial. **2** *adv* **b. and early** de bonne heure.

bright·en (up) 1 *vt* *(room)* égayer. **2** *vi* *(of weather)* s'éclaircir.

bright·ly *adv* avec éclat.

bright·ness éclat *m*.

bril·liance éclat *m*; *(of person)* grande intelligence *f*.

bril·liant *adj (light)* éclatant; *(clever)* brillant.

bring* *vt (person, vehicle)* amener; *(thing)* apporter; *(to cause)* amener; **to b. to an end** mettre fin à; **to b. to mind** rappeler.

▸ **bring about** *vt* provoquer.

▸ **bring along** *vt (object)* emporter; *(person)* emmener.

▸ **bring around** *vt* ranimer.

▸ **bring back** *vt (person)* ramener; *(object)* rapporter; *(memories)* rappeler.

▸ **bring down** *vt (object)* descendre; *(overthrow)* faire tomber; *(reduce)* réduire.

▸ **bring in** *vt (object)* rentrer; *(person)* faire entrer; *(introduce)* introduire.

▸ **bring out** *vt (object)* sortir; *(person)* faire sortir; *(meaning)* faire ressortir; *(book)* publier; *(product)* lancer.

▸ **bring to** *vt* ranimer.

▸ **bring together** *vt (reconcile)* réconcilier.

▸ **bring up** *vt (object)* monter; *(child)* élever; *(subject)* mentionner.

brink bord *m.*

brisk *adj* vif.

brisk·ly *adv (to walk)* vite.

bris·tle poil *m.*

Brit·ish 1 *adj* britannique. 2 *n* the B. les Britanniques *mpl.*

Brit·ish Isles îles *fpl* Britanniques.

Brit·on Britannique *mf.*

brit·tle *adj* fragile.

broad *adj (wide)* large; *(outline)* général; **in b. daylight** en plein jour.

broad·band ADSL *m.*

broad·cast 1 *vt** diffuser, retransmettre. 2 *n* émission *f.*

broad·en *vt* élargir.

broc·co·li *inv* brocolis *mpl.*

bro·chure brochure *f.*

broke 1 *pt de* break. 2 *adj (penniless)* fauché.

bro·ken *pp de* break.

bro·ken-down *adj (machine)* délingué.

bron·chi·tis bronchite *f.*

bronze bronze *m.*

brooch broche *f.*

brood 1 *n* couvée *f.* 2 *vi* méditer tristement (**over** sur).

brook ruisseau *m.*

broom balai *m.*

broom·stick manche *m* à balai.

broth·er frère *m.*

broth·er-in-law, *pl* brothers-in-law beau-frère *m.*

brought *pt & pp de* bring.

brow *(forehead)* front *m;* *(eyebrow)* sourcil *m;* *(of hill)* sommet *m.*

brown 1 *adj* marron; *(hair)* châtain; *(tanned)* bronzé. 2 *n* marron *m.*

brown·ie brownie *m.*

browse *vi (in bookstore)* feuilleter des livres; *(in store)* regarder.

bruise 1 *vt* **to b. one's knee/etc** se faire un bleu au genou/etc. 2 *n* bleu *m (pl* bleus), contusion *f.*

bruised *adj* couvert de bleus.

brunch brunch *m.*

bru·nette brunette *f.*

brush 1 *n* brosse *f;* *(for painting)* pinceau *m.* 2 *vt (teeth, hair)* (se) brosser.

▸ **brush aside** *vt* écarter.

▸ **brush away, brush off** *vt* enlever.

▸ **brush up (on)** *vt (language)* se remettre à.

bru·tal *adj* brutal.

bru·tal·i·ty brutalité *f.*

brute brute *f.*

BS, BSc *abbr* = **Bachelor of Science.**

bub·ble 1 *n* bulle *f.* 2 *vi* bouillonner.

▸ **bubble over** *vi* déborder.

buck *Fam* dollar *m.*

buck·et seau *m.*

buck·le 1 *n* boucle *f.* 2 *vt* boucler. 3 *vti (warp)* voiler.

▸ **buck up** 1 *vt (person)* remonter le moral à. 2 *vi (become livelier)* reprendre du poil de la bête.

bud 1 n (of tree) bourgeon m; (of flower) bouton m. **2** vi (of tree) bourgeonner; (of flower) pousser des boutons.

Bud·hist adj & n bouddhiste (mf).

bud·dy Fam copain, -ine mf.

budge vi bouger.

budg·et budget m.

▸ **budget for** vt inscrire au budget.

buf·fa·lo, pl -oes or -os buffle m; (American) b. bison m.

buff·er (device) tampon m; (in computer) tampon, mémoire f intermédiaire.

buf·fet (table, meal) buffet m.

bug¹ punaise f; (any insect) bestiole f; (germ) microbe m, virus m; (in machine) défaut m; (in computer program) erreur f; (listening device) micro m clandestin.

bug² vt (annoy) Fam embêter.

bu·gle clairon m.

build 1 n (of person) carrure f. **2** vt* construire; (house) construire, bâtir.

build·er maçon m; (contractor) entrepreneur m.

build·ing bâtiment m; (of apartments, offices) immeuble m.

▸ **build up 1** vt (increase) augmenter; (collection) constituer; (business) monter; (speed) prendre. **2** vt (of tension, pressure) augmenter.

built-in adj (closet) encastré; (part of machine) incorporé.

built-up a·re·a agglomération f.

bulb (of plant) oignon m; (of lamp) ampoule f.

bulge renflement m.

bulge (out) vi se renfler.

bulg·ing adj renflé.

bulk inv grosseur f; **the b. of** (most) la majeure partie de.

bulk·y adj gros (f grosse).

bull taureau m.

bull·dog bouledogue m.

bull·doz·er bulldozer m.

bul·let boule f (de révolver etc).

bul·le·tin bulletin m.

bul·le·tin board tableau m d'affichage.

bul·let·proof adj (vest) pare-balles inv; (car) blindé.

bull·fight corrida f.

bul·ly 1 n (grosse) brute f. **2** vt brutaliser.

bum Fam (tramp) clochard, -arde mf; (good-for-nothing) propre mf à rien.

bum·ble·bee bourdon m.

bump 1 vt (of car) heurter; **to b. one's head/knee** se cogner la tête/le genou. **2** n (impact) choc m; (jerk) cahot m; (on road, body) bosse f.

bump·er pare-chocs m inv.

▸ **bump into** vt se cogner contre; (of car) rentrer dans; (meet) tomber sur.

bump·y adj (road, ride) cahoteux.

bun (roll) petit pain m au lait.

bunch (of flowers) bouquet m; (of keys) trousseau m; (of people) bande f; **b. of grapes** grappe f de raisin.

bun·dle 1 n paquet m; (of papers) liasse f. **2** vt (put) fourrer; (push) pousser (**into** dans).

▸ **bundle up** vi (dress warmly) se couvrir.

bun·ga·low bungalow m.

bunk couchette f; **b. beds** lits mpl superposés.

bun·ny Fam Jeannot m lapin.

buoy bouée f.

bur·den 1 n fardeau m; (of tax) poids m. **2** vt accabler (**with** de).

bu·reau, pl bureaux (office) service m, office m; (chest of drawers) commode f.

bu·reau·cra·cy bureaucratie f.

bu·reau·crat bureaucrate mf.

burg·er hamburger m.

bur·glar cambrioleur, -euse mf.

bur·glar a·larm alarme f antivol.

bur·glar·ize vt cambrioler.

bur·gla·ry cambriolage m.

bur·gle vt cambrioler.

bur·i·al enterrement m.

burn 1 n brûlure f. **2** vti* brûler; **burnt alive** brûlé vif.

▸ **burn down 1** vt détruire par le feu. **2** vi être détruit par le feu.

burn·er (of stove) brûleur m.

burn·ing adj en feu; (fire, light) allumé.

burp 1 n rot m. **2** vi roter.

burst 1 n (of laughter) éclat m; (of thunder) coup m. **2** vi* (with force) éclater; (of bubble, balloon, boil, tire) crever.

burst·ing adj (full) plein à craquer.

▸ **burst into** vt (room) faire irruption dans; **to b. into tears** fondre en larmes.

▸ **burst out** vi **to b. out laughing** éclater de rire.

bur·y vt enterrer; (hide) enfouir; (plunge, absorb) plonger.

bus (auto) bus m; (long-distance) (auto) car m.

bush buisson m.

bush·y adj broussailleux.

busi·ness 1 n affaires fpl, commerce m; (shop) commerce m; (task, concern, matter) affaire f; **on b.** pour affaires; **it's your b. to...** c'est à vous de...; **that's none of your b.!, mind your own b.!** ça ne vous regarde pas! **2** adj commercial; (meeting, trip) d'affaires; **b. hours** heures fpl de bureau; **b. card** carte f de visite.

busi·ness·man, pl -men homme m d'affaires.

busi·ness·wom·an, pl -women femme f d'affaires.

bus shel·ter abribus m.

bus sta·tion gare f routière.

bus stop arrêt m d'autobus.

bust 1 n (sculpture) buste m; (woman's breasts) poitrine f. **2** adj **to go b.** Fam (bankrupt) faire faillite.

bus·tle 1 vi s'affairer. **2** n activité f.

bus·tling adj (street, town) bruyant.

bus·y adj occupé (**doing** à faire); (active) actif; (day) chargé; (street) animé; (phone) occupé; **to be b. doing** (in the process of) être en train de faire; **b. signal** sonnerie f occupé.

bus·y·bod·y Fam fouineur, -euse mf.

but 1 conj mais. **2** prep (except) sauf; **b. for that/him** sans cela/lui. **3** adv (only) seulement.

butch·er boucher, -ère mf; **b.'s shop** boucherie f.

but·ler maître m d'hôtel.

butt (of cigarette) mégot m; (buttocks) Fam cul m.

but·ter 1 n beurre m. **2** vt beurrer.

but·ter·cup bouton-d'or m.

but·ter·fly papillon m.

▸ **butt in** vi interrompre.

but·tock fesse f.

but·ton bouton m; (of phone etc) touche f, (bearing slogan) pin's m.

button (up) vt (garment) boutonner.

but·ton·hole boutonnière f.

buy 1 vt* acheter (**from sb** à qn; **for sb** à or pour qn). **2** n **a good b.** une bonne affaire.

buy·er acheteur, -euse mf.

buzz 1 vi bourdonner. **2** n bourdonnement m.

▸ **buzz off** vi Fam décamper.

by 1 prep (agent, manner) par; hit/ etc by frappé/etc par; surrounded/ etc by entouré/etc de; **by doing** en faisant; **by sea** par mer; **by car** en voiture; **by bicycle** à bicyclette; **by day** de jour; **by oneself** tout seul. ▪ (next to) à côté de; (near) près de; **by the lake** au bord du lac. ▪ (before in time) avant; **by Monday** avant lundi; **by now** à cette heure-ci. ▪ (amount) à; **by weight** au poids; **paid by the hour** payé à l'heure. **2** *adv* **close by** tout près; **to go by, pass by** passer; **by and large** en gros.

bye(-bye)! *int Fam* salut!

by·pass 1 *n* (*of highway*) bretelle *f* (de contournement); (*heart surgery*) pontage *m*. **2** *vt* contourner.

by·stand·er spectateur, -trice *mf*.

C

cab taxi *m*.

cab·bage chou *m* (*pl* choux).

cab·in (*on ship*) cabine *f*; (*hut*) cabane *f*.

cab·i·net¹ armoire *f*; (*for display*) vitrine *f*; (**filing**) **c.** classeur *m* (de bureau).

cab·i·net² (*in politics*) gouvernement *m*; **c. meeting** conseil *m* des ministres.

ca·ble câble *m*; **c. television** la télévision par câble.

ca·ble car téléphérique *m*; (*on tracks*) funiculaire *m*.

cac·tus, *pl* -ti *or* -tuses cactus *m*.

caf·e·te·ri·a cafétéria *f*.

caf·feine caféine *f*.

cage cage *f*.

cake gâteau *m*.

cal·cu·late *vti* calculer.

cal·cu·la·tion calcul *m*.

cal·cu·la·tor calculatrice *f*.

cal·en·dar calendrier *m*.

calf, *pl* **calves** (*animal*) veau *m*; (*part of leg*) mollet *m*.

call 1 *n* appel *m*; (*shout*) cri *m*; (*visit*) visite *f*; (**telephone**) **c.** communication *f*; **to make a c.** (*phone*) téléphoner (**to** à). **2** *vt* appeler; (*shout*) crier; (*attention*) attirer (**to** sur); **he's called David** il s'appelle David; **to c. a meeting** convoquer une assemblée; **to c. sb a liar/etc** qualifier

qn de menteur/*etc*. **3** *vi* (*cry out*) crier; (*visit*) passer.

▸ **call back** *vti* rappeler.

   call·er visiteur, -euse *mf*; (*on phone*) correspondant, -ante *mf*.

▸ **call for** *vt* (*require*) demander; (*summon*) appeler; (*collect*) passer prendre.

▸ **call in** *vt* (*into room etc*) faire entrer.

   call·ing card (*for telephone*) télécarte *f*.

▸ **call off** *vt* (*cancel*) annuler.

▸ **call on** *vt* (*visit*) passer voir; **to c. sb to do** inviter qn à faire; (*urge*) presser qn de faire.

▸ **call out 1** *vt* (*shout*) crier; (*doctor*) appeler. **2** *vi* crier; **to c. out for** demander à haute voix.

▸ **call up** *vt* (*phone*) appeler.

calm 1 *adj* calme; **keep c.!** du calme! **2** *n* calme *m*. **3** *vt* calmer.

▸ **calm down 1** *vi* se calmer. **2** *vt* calmer.

calm·ly *adv* calmement.

cal·o·rie calorie *f*.

cam·cord·er caméscope *m*.

came *pt of* **come**.

cam·el chameau *m*.

cam·er·a appareil photo *m*; (**TV** *or film*) **c.** caméra *f*.

camp camp *m*.

camp (out) *vi* camper.

cam·paign campagne *f*.

camp·er (*person*) campeur, -euse *mf*; (*recreational vehicle*) camping-car *m*; (*trailer*) caravane *f*.

camp·fire feu *m* de camp.

camp·ing camping *m*; **c. site** camping *m*.

camp·site camping *m*.

cam·pus campus *m*, complexe *m* universitaire.

can¹ *v aux* (*pt* **could**) pouvoir; (*know how to*) savoir; **he couldn't help me** il ne pouvait pas m'aider; **she c. swim** elle sait nager; **you could be wrong** (*possibility*) tu as peut-être tort; **he can't be old**

(probability) il ne doit pas être vieux; **c. I come in?** puis-je entrer?

can² *(for food)* boîte *f*; *(for drinks)* cannette *f*.

Ca·na·di·an 1 *n* Canadien, -ienne *mf*. **2** *adj* canadien.

ca·nal canal *m*.

ca·nar·y canari *m*.

can·cel *vt (flight, appointment etc)* annuler; *(goods, taxi)* décommander; *(train)* supprimer.

can·cel·la·tion *(of flight, appointment etc)* annulation *f*; *(of train)* suppression *f*.

can·cer cancer *m*.

can·did *adj* franc *(f* franche*)*.

can·di·date candidat, -ate *mf*.

can·dle bougie *f*; *(in church)* cierge *m*.

can·dle·stick bougeoir *m*; *(tall)* chandelier *m*.

can·dy bonbon(s) *m(pl)*.

can·dy·store confiserie *f*.

cane 1 *n (stick)* canne *f*; *(for punishment)* baguette *f*. **2** *vt (punish)* fouetter.

can·na·bis *(drug)* haschisch *m*.

canned *adj* en boîte; **c. food** conserves *fpl*.

can·ni·bal cannibale *mf*.

ca·noe canoë *m*.

ca·noe·ing **to go c.** faire du canoë.

can·o·la colza *m*.

can·o·pen·er ouvre-boîtes *m inv*.

can·o·py *(hood of baby carriage)* capote *f*; *(small roof)* auvent *m*.

can·ta·loup(e) *(melon)* cantaloup *m*.

can·teen *(place)* cantine *f*; *(flask)* gourde *f*.

can·vas toile *f*.

can·yon canyon *m*.

cap *(hat)* casquette *f*; *(for shower)* bonnet *m*; *(of soldier)* képi *m*; *(of bottle, tube)* bouchon *m*; *(of milk or beer bottle)* capsule *f*; *(of pen)* capuchon *m*; *(of child's gun)* amorce *f*.

ca·pa·bil·i·ty capacité *f*.

ca·pa·ble *adj (person)* capable *(of sth de qch; of doing de faire).*

ca·pac·i·ty *(of container)* capacité *f*; *(ability)* aptitude *f*; **in my c. as** en ma qualité de.

cape *(cloak)* cape *f*; *(of cyclist)* pèlerine *f*.

cap·i·tal *(money)* capital *m*; **c. (city)** capitale *f*; **c. (letter)** majuscule *f*.

cap·size *vti* chavirer.

cap·sule capsule *f*.

cap·tain capitaine *m*.

cap·ture *vt (of person, town)* prendre.

car·a·mel caramel *m*.

car·a·van caravane *f*; *(horse-drawn)* roulotte *f*.

car·bon carbone *m*; **c. copy** double *m* (au carbone).

car·bon pa·per *(papier m)* carbone *m*.

car·bu·re·tor carburateur *m*.

card carte *f*; *(cardboard)* carton *m*; **(index) c.** fiche *f*; **to play cards** jouer aux cartes.

card·board carton *m*.

car·di·gan gilet *m*.

car·di·nal *adj (number, point)* cardinal.

card in·dex fichier *m*.

care 1 *vi (like)* aimer; **would you c. to try?** aimeriez-vous essayer?; **I don't c.** ça m'est égal; **who cares?** qu'est-ce que ça fait? **2** *n (attention)* soin(s) *m(pl)*; *(protection)* garde *f*; *(anxiety)* souci *m*; **to take c. not to do** faire attention à ne pas faire; **to take c. to do** veiller à faire; **to take c. of** s'occuper de; *(keep safely)* garder *(for sb* pour qn*)*; *(sick person)* prendre soin de; **to take c. of one-self** *(manage)* se débrouiller; *(keep healthy)* faire bien attention à soi.

▸ **care about** *vt* se soucier de.

ca·reer carrière *f*.

▶ **care for** vt (want) avoir envie de; **to c. for sb** (look after) s'occuper de qn; (sick person) soigner qn; (like) avoir de la sympathie pour qn; **I don't c. for it** je n'aime pas beaucoup ça.

care•free adj insouciant.

care•ful adj (exact, thorough) soigneux (**about** de); (cautious) prudent; **to be c.** of or **with** faire attention à.

care•ful•ly adv avec soin; (cautiously) prudemment.

care•giv•er (professional) aide mf à domicile; (relative) = personne s'occupant d'un parent malade ou âgé.

care•less adj négligent; (absent-minded) étourdi.

care•tak•er gardien, -ienne mf.

car fer•ry ferry-boat m.

car•go, pl -os cargaison f.

car•ing adj (loving) aimant; (understanding) très humain.

car•na•tion œillet m.

car•ni•val carnaval m (pl -als).

car•ol chant m (de Noël).

carp (fish) carpe f.

car•pen•ter charpentier m; (for light woodwork) menuisier m.

car•pen•try charpenterie f; menuiserie f.

car•pet tapis m; (fitted) moquette f.

car•pet•ing (wall-to-wall) c. moquette f.

car•pet sweep•er balai m mécanique.

car•riage (of train, horse-drawn) voiture f.

car•ri•er (company) entreprise f de transport; (of disease) porteur, -euse mf.

car•rot carotte f.

car•ry vt porter; (goods) transporter; (sell) stocker; (in calculation) retenir.

car•ry•all fourre-tout m inv.

▶ **carry away** vt emporter; **to get carried away** (excited) s'emballer.

▶ **carry back** vt rapporter; (person) ramener.

▶ **carry off** vt emporter; (prize) remporter; **to c. it off** réussir.

▶ **carry on 1** vt continuer; (conduct) diriger; (sustain) soutenir. **2** vi continuer (**doing** à faire).

▶ **carry out** vt (plan, order, promise) exécuter; (repair, reform) effectuer; (duty) accomplir; (meal) emporter.

▶ **carry through** vt (plan) mener à bien.

cart (horse-drawn) charrette f; (in supermarket) caddie® m; (serving) c. table f roulante.

cart (a•round) vt Fam trimbal(l)er.

▶ **cart away** vt emporter.

car•ton (box) carton m; (of milk etc) brique f, (of cigarettes) cartouche f; (of cream) pot m.

car•toon dessin m (humoristique); (film) dessin m animé; (strip) c. bande f dessinée.

car•tridge cartouche f.

carve vt tailler (**out of** dans); (initials etc) graver.

carve (up) vt (meat) découper.

car wash (machine) lave-auto m.

case¹ (instance, in hospital) cas m; (in court) affaire f; **in any c.** en tout cas; **in c. it rains** pour le cas où il pleuvrait; **in c. of** en cas de; (just) **in c.** à tout hasard.

case² (bag) valise f, (crate) caisse f, (for pen, glasses, camera, cigarettes) étui m; (for jewels) coffret m.

cash 1 n argent m; **to pay (in) c.** payer en espèces. **2** vt **to c. a check** encaisser un chèque; (of bank) payer un chèque.

cash•box caisse f.

cash•ier caissier, -ière mf.

cash ma•chine distributeur m de billets.

cash price prix m (au) comptant.

cash re•gis•ter caisse f enregistreuse.

ca•si•no, pl -os casino m.

cas·se·role cocotte *f*; *(stew)* ragoût *m* en cocotte.

cas·sette *(audio, video)* cassette *f*; *(film)* cartouche *f*.

cas·sette play·er lecteur *m* de cassettes.

cas·sette re·cord·er magnétophone *m* à cassettes.

cast[1] *(actors)* acteurs *mpl*; *(list of actors)* distribution *f*; *(for broken bone)* plâtre *m*.

cast[2]* *vt* jeter; *(light, shadow)* projeter; *(doubt)* exprimer; **to c. a vote** voter.

cast-i·ron *adj (pan)* en fonte; *(alibi)* inattaquable, en béton.

cas·tle château *m*; *Chess* tour *f*.

cas·tor *(wheel)* roulette *f*.

ca·su·al *adj (remark)* fait en passant; *(stroll)* sans but; *(offhand)* désinvolte; *(worker)* temporaire; *(work)* irrégulier; **c. clothes** vêtements *mpl* sport.

ca·su·al·ty *(dead)* mort *m*, morte *f*; *(wounded)* blessé, -ée *mf*.

cat chat *m*; *(female)* chatte *f*; **c. food** pâtée *f*.

cat·a·log catalogue *m*.

cat·a·pult catapulte *f*.

ca·tas·tro·phe catastrophe *f*.

catch* **1** *vt (ball, thief, illness, train etc)* attraper; *(grab, surprise)* prendre; *(understand)* saisir; *(attention)* attirer; *(on nail etc)* accrocher **(on** à); *(finger etc)* se prendre **(in** dans); **to c. fire** prendre feu; **to c. one's breath** *(rest)* reprendre haleine. **2** *vi* **her skirt (got) caught in the door** sa jupe s'est prise dans la porte; **to c. on fire** prendre feu. **3** *n (trick)* piège *m*; *(on door)* loquet *m*.

catch·ing *adj* contagieux.

▸ **catch on** *vi (become popular)* prendre; *(understand)* saisir.

▸ **catch out** *vt* prendre en défaut.

▸ **catch up 1** *vt* **to c. sb up** rattraper qn. **2** *vi* se rattraper; **to c. up with sb** rattraper qn.

cat·e·go·ry catégorie *f*.

▸ **cater for, cater to** *vt (need, taste)* satisfaire.

cat·er·pil·lar chenille *f*.

ca·the·dral cathédrale *f*.

Cath·o·lic *adj & n* catholique *(mf)*.

cau·li·flow·er chou-fleur *m*.

cause 1 *n* cause *f*. **2** *vt* causer; **to c. sth to move/etc** faire bouger/etc qch.

cau·tion *(care)* prudence *f*; *(warning)* avertissement *m*.

cau·tious *adj* prudent.

cau·tious·ly *adv* prudemment.

cave caverne *f*.

▸ **cave in** *vi (fall in)* s'effondrer.

cav·i·ty cavité *f*.

CCTV *f (closed-circuit television)* télévision *f* en circuit fermé.

CD *abbr (compact disc)* CD *m*; **CD player** lecteur *m* de CD.

cease *vti* cesser **(doing** de faire).

cease-fire cessez-le-feu *m inv*.

ceil·ing plafond *m*.

cel·e·brate 1 *vt* fêter; *(mass)* célébrer. **2** *vi* faire la fête.

ce·leb·ra·tion fête *f*.

ce·leb·ri·ty *(person)* célébrité *f*.

cel·er·y céleri *m*.

cell cellule *f*.

cel·lar cave *f*.

cel·lo·phane® cellophane® *f*.

cell·phone *(téléphone m)* portable *m*.

ce·ment 1 *n* ciment *m*. **2** *vt* cimenter.

ce·ment mix·er bétonnière *f*.

cem·e·ter·y cimetière *f*.

cen·sus recensement *m*.

cent *(coin)* cent *m*.

cen·ter 1 *n* centre *m*. **2** *vt* centrer.

cen·ti·grade *adj* centigrade.

cen·ti·me·ter centimètre *m*.

cen·ti·pede mille-pattes *m inv*.

cen·tral *adj* central.

cen·tral·ize *vt* centraliser.

cen·tu·ry siècle *m*.

ce·ram·ic *adj (tile)* de céramique.

ce·re·al céréale *f*.

cer·e·mo·ny cérémonie *f*.

cer·tain *adj (sure, particular)* certain; **she's c. to come** c'est certain qu'elle viendra; **I'm not c. what to do** je ne sais pas très bien ce qu'il faut faire; **to be c. of sth/that** être certain de qch/que; **to make c. of** *(fact)* s'assurer de; *(seat etc)* s'assurer.

cer·tain·ly *adv* certainement; *(yes)* bien sûr.

cer·tain·ty certitude *f*.

cer·tif·i·cate certificat *m; (from university)* diplôme *m.*

cer·ti·fied *adj* certifié, agréé; **C. Public Accountant** expert-comptable *m.*

cer·ti·fy *vt (document etc)* certifier.

chain *(of rings, mountains)* chaîne *f.*

chain (up) *vt (dog)* mettre à l'attache; *(person)* enchaîner.

chain saw tronçonneuse *f.*

chain store magasin *m* à succursales multiples.

chair chaise *f*, *(armchair)* fauteuil *m.*

chair lift télésiège *m.*

chair·man, *pl* **-men** président, -ente *mf.*

cha·let chalet *m.*

chalk 1 *n* craie *f.* 2 *vti* écrire à la craie.

chal·lenge 1 *n* défi *m; (task)* challenge *m*, gageure *f.* 2 *vt* défier (**sb to do** qn de faire); *(dispute)* contester.

chal·leng·ing *adj (job)* exigeant.

cham·ber c. of commerce chambre *f* de commerce.

cham·ois *(leather)* peau *f* de chamois.

cham·pagne champagne *m.*

cham·pi·on champion, -onne *mf.*

cham·pi·on·ship championnat *m.*

chance 1 *n (luck)* hasard *m; (possibility)* chances *fpl, (opportunity)* occasion *f*, **by c.** par hasard. 2 *vt* **to c. it** risquer le coup.

chan·cel·lor *(head of state, in embassy)* chancelier *m.*

chan·de·lier lustre *m.*

change 1 *n* changement *m; (money)* monnaie *f*, **for a c.** pour changer; **it makes a c. from** ça change de; **a c. of clothes** des vêtements de rechange. 2 *vt* changer; *(exchange)* échanger (**for** contre); *(money)* changer; **to c. trains/one's skirt/etc** changer de train/de jupe/etc; **to c. the subject** changer de sujet. 3 *vi* changer; *(change clothes)* se changer.

change·a·ble *adj* changeant.

▶**change over** *vi* passer (**from** de; **to** à).

change·o·ver passage *m* (**from** de; **to** à).

chang·ing room vestiaire *m.*

chan·nel *(on television)* chaîne *f; (for inquiry etc)* voie *f*, **the English C.** la Manche; **to go through the normal channels** passer par la voie normale.

chant 1 *vt (slogan)* scander. 2 *vi (of demonstrators)* scander des slogans.

cha·os chaos *m.*

cha·ot·ic *adj* sens dessus dessous.

chap·el chapelle *f.*

chapped *adj* gercé.

chap·ter chapitre *m.*

char *vt* carboniser; *(scorch)* brûler légèrement.

char·ac·ter caractère *m; (in book, film)* personnage *m; (strange person)* numéro *m.*

char·ac·ter·is·tic *adj & n* caractéristique (*f*).

charge¹ 1 *n (cost)* prix *m;* **charges** *(expenses)* frais *mpl;* **there's a c.** **(for it)** c'est payant; **free of c.** gratuit. 2 *vt (amount)* demander (**for** pour); *(person)* faire payer.

charge² 1 *n (in court)* accusation *f; (care)* garde *f*, **to take c. of** prendre en charge; **to be in c. of** *(child)* avoir la garde de; *(office)* être responsable de. **2** *vt (battery, soldiers)* charger; *(accuse)* accuser (**with** de). **3** *vi (rush)* se précipiter.

char·ger *(for battery, phone)* chargeur *m*.

char·i·ty *(society)* fondation *f* charitable; **to give to c.** faire la charité.

charm 1 *n* charme *m*; *(trinket)* amulette *f*. **2** *vt* charmer.

charm·ing *adj* charmant.

chart *(map)* carte *f*, *(graph)* graphique *m*; *(pop)* **charts** hit-parade *m*.

char·ter 1 *n (of institution)* statuts *mpl*. **2** *vt (plane, boat)* affréter.

char·ter flight charter *m*.

chase 1 *n* poursuite *f*. **2** *vt* poursuivre.

▶ **chase after** *vt* courir après, poursuivre.

▶ **chase away** *or* **off** *vt* chasser.

chasm abîme *m*, gouffre *m*.

chas·sis *(of vehicle)* châssis *m*.

chat 1 *n* petite conversation *f*; **to have a c.** bavarder. **2** *vi* causer.

chat·ter 1 *vi (of person)* bavarder; **his teeth are chattering** il claque des dents. **2** *n* bavardage *m*.

chat·ter·box bavard, -arde *mf*.

chat·ty *adj* bavard.

chauf·feur chauffeur *m*.

cheap 1 *adj* bon marché *inv*; *(rate)* réduit; *(worthless)* sans valeur; **cheaper** meilleur marché. **2** *adv* *(to buy)* (à) bon marché.

cheap·ly *adv* (à) bon marché.

cheat 1 *vt* tromper; **to c. sb out of sth** escroquer qch à qn. **2** *vi (at games etc)* tricher.

cheat·er tricheur, -euse *mf*.

check 1 *vt (examine)* vérifier; *(inspect)* contrôler; *(stop)* arrêter; *(baggage)* mettre à la consigne. **2** *vi* vérifier. **3** *n* vérification *f*, *(inspection)* contrôle *m*; *Chess* échec *m*; *(mark)* = coche *f*, *(receipt)* reçu *m*; *(bill in restaurant)* addition *f*, *(in banking)* chèque *m*.

check·book carnet *m* de chèques.

checked, check·ered *adj* à carreaux.

check·ers *npl* jeu *m* de dames.

check-in enregistrement *m* (des bagages).

▶ **check in 1** *vt (luggage)* enregistrer. **2** *vi (at hotel)* signer le registre; *(arrive)* arriver; *(at airport)* se présenter (à l'enregistrement).

check·ing ac·count compte *m* courant.

check·mate *Chess* échec et mat *m*.

▶ **check off** *vt (names on list etc)* cocher.

check·out *(in supermarket)* caisse *f*.

▶ **check on** *vt* vérifier.

▶ **check out 1** *vt* confirmer. **2** *vi (at hotel)* régler sa note.

check·up bilan *m* de santé.

▶ **check up** *vi* vérifier.

ched·dar *(cheese)* cheddar *m*.

cheek joue *f*, *(impudence)* culot *m*.

cheek·y *adj* effronté.

cheer 1 *n* **cheers** acclamations *fpl*; **cheers!** *Fam* à votre santé! **2** *vt (applaud)* acclamer. **3** *vi* applaudir.

cheer·ful *adj* gai.

cheer·ing acclamations *fpl*.

▶ **cheer up** *vt* donner du courage à; *(amuse)* égayer. **2** *vi* prendre courage; *(become happier)* s'égayer; **c. up!** (du) courage!

cheese fromage *m*.

cheese·burg·er cheeseburger *m*.

cheese·cake tarte *f* au fromage, cheesecake *m*.

chef *(cook)* chef *m*.

chem·i·cal 1 *adj* chimique. **2** *n* produit *m* chimique.

chem·ist chimiste *mf*.

chem·is·try chimie *f*.

cher·ry cerise *f*.

cher·ry bran·dy cherry *m*.

chess échecs *mpl*.

chess·board échiquier *m*.

chest *(part of body)* poitrine *f*, *(box)* coffre *m*; **c. of drawers** commode *f*.

chest·nut châtaigne f.

chew 1 vt to c. (up) mâcher. **2** vi mastiquer.

chew·ing gum chewing-gum m.

chick poussin m.

chick·en 1 n poulet m. **2** adj (cowardly) Fam froussard.

▸**chicken out** vi Fam se dégonfler.

chick·en·pox varicelle f.

chick·pea pois m chiche.

chic·o·ry (for salad) endive f.

chief 1 n chef m; in c. en chef. **2** adj principal.

chief·ly adv principalement.

chil·blain engelure f.

child, pl **children** enfant mf.

child care (for working parents) crèches fpl et garderies fpl.

child·hood enfance f.

child·ish adj puéril.

chil·i, pl **-ies** piment m (de Cayenne).

chill 1 n froid m; (illness) refroidissement m; to catch a c. prendre froid. **2** vt (wine, melon) faire rafraîchir; (meat) réfrigérer.

chilled adj (wine) frais.

chill·y adj froid; it's c. il fait (un peu) froid.

chime vi (of clock) sonner.

chim·ney cheminée f.

chim·ney·pot tuyau m de cheminée.

chim·pan·zee chimpanzé m.

chin menton m.

chi·na n inv porcelaine f. **2** adj en porcelaine.

Chi·nese 1 n inv Chinois, -oise (mf); (language) chinois m. **2** adj chinois.

chip 1 vt (cup etc) ébrécher; (paint) écailler. **2** n (break) ébréchure f; (microchip) puce f; (counter) jeton m; (potato) chips mpl.

chi·ro·po·dist pédicure mf.

chis·el ciseau m.

chives ciboulette f.

chock·a·block adj Fam archiplein.

choc·o·late 1 n chocolat m; **milk c.** chocolat m au lait; **bittersweet c.** chocolat m à croquer. **2** adj (cake) au chocolat.

choice choix m.

choir chœur m.

choke 1 vt (person) étrangler; (clog) boucher. **2** vi s'étrangler (on avec).

cho·les·ter·ol cholestérol m.

choose* 1 vt choisir; to c. to do (decide) juger bon de faire. **2** vi choisir.

choos·(e)y adj difficile.

chop 1 n (of lamb, pork) côtelette f. **2** vt couper (à la hache); (food) hacher.

▸**chop down** vt (tree) abattre.

▸**chop off** vt (branch, finger etc) couper.

chop·per hachoir m.

chop·sticks npl baguettes fpl.

▸**chop up** vt couper en morceaux.

chord (in music) accord m.

chore travail m (routinier); (unpleasant) corvée f; **chores** travaux mpl ménagers.

cho·rus (of song) refrain m.

chris·ten vt baptiser.

chris·ten·ing baptême m.

Chris·tian adj & n chrétien, -ienne (mf).

Christ·mas 1 n Noël m; **Merry C.** Joyeux Noël; **C. Eve** la veille de Noël. **2** adj de Noël.

chrome chrome m.

chron·ic adj chronique.

chry·san·the·mum chrysanthème m.

chub·by adj potelé.

chuck vt Fam (throw) jeter; (job etc) laisser tomber.

▸**chuck out** vt (old clothes etc) Fam balancer.

chum Fam copain m, copine f.

chunk (gros) morceau m.

church église f.

chute (for refuse) vide-ordures m inv; (in pool) toboggan m.

ci·der cidre *m.*

ci·gar cigare *m.*

cig·a·rette cigarette *f.*

cig·a·rette butt mégot *m.*

cig·a·rette light·er briquet *m.*

cin·e·ma cinéma *m.*

cin·na·mon cannelle *f.*

cir·cle 1 *n* cercle *m*; **circles** *(political etc)* milieux *mpl.* **2** *vt* faire le tour de; *(word)* encadrer. **3** *vi (of aircraft etc)* décrire des cercles.

cir·cuit *(electrical path, in sports etc)* circuit *m.*

cir·cu·lar 1 *adj* circulaire. **2** *n (letter)* circulaire *f*; *(advertisement)* prospectus *m.*

cir·cu·late 1 *vi (of blood etc)* circuler. **2** *vt (pass around)* faire circuler.

cir·cu·la·tion *(of newspaper)* tirage *m.*

cir·cum·fer·ence circonférence *f.*

cir·cum·stance circonstance *f*; **in or under no circumstances** en aucun cas.

cir·cus cirque *m.*

cite *vt (quote)* citer.

cit·i·zen citoyen, -enne *mf*; *(of town)* habitant, -ante *mf.*

cit·y (grande) ville *f.*

cit·y coun·cil conseil *m* municipal.

cit·y hall hôtel *m* de ville.

civ·ic *adj (authority, building)* municipal; *(duty, rights)* civique.

civ·il *adj* civil.

ci·vil·ian *adj & n* civil, -ile *(mf).*

civ·i·li·za·tion civilisation *f.*

civ·il ser·vant fonctionnaire *mf.*

civ·il ser·vice fonction *f* publique.

claim 1 *vt* réclamer; **to c. that** prétendre que. **2** *n (demand)* revendication *f*; *(statement)* affirmation *f*; *(right)* droit *m* (**to** à); **(insurance) c.** demande *f* d'indemnité.

clam *(shellfish)* palourde *f.*

clap *vti* applaudir; **to c. (one's hands)** battre des mains.

clap·ping applaudissements *mpl.*

clar·i·fy *vt* clarifier.

clar·i·net clarinette *f.*

clash 1 *vi (of plates)* s'entrechoquer; *(of interests)* se heurter; *(of colors)* jurer (**with** avec); *(of people)* se bagarrer; *(coincide)* tomber en même temps (**with** que). **2** *n (noise)* choc *m*; *(of interests)* conflit *m.*

clasp 1 *vt* serrer. **2** *n (fastener)* fermoir *m*; *(of belt)* boucle *f.*

class 1 *n* classe *f*, *(lesson)* cours *m.* **2** *vt* classer.

clas·sic 1 *adj* classique. **2** *n (work etc)* classique *m.*

clas·si·cal *adj* classique.

clas·si·fy *vt* classer.

class·mate camarade *mf* de classe.

class·room (salle *f* de) classe *f.*

clause *(in sentence)* proposition *f.*

claw griffe *f*; *(of lobster)* pince *f.*

clay argile *f.*

clean 1 *adj (not dirty)* propre; *(clearcut)* net (*f* nette). **2** *adv (utterly)* complètement; *(to break, cut)* net. **3** *vt* nettoyer; *(wash)* laver; *(wipe)* essuyer. **4** *vi* faire le nettoyage.

clean cop·y copie *f* au propre.

clean·er *(dry)* c. teinturier, -ière *mf.*

clean·ing nettoyage *m*; *(housework)* ménage *m.*

clean·ing la·dy femme *f* de ménage.

clean·ly *adv (to break, cut)* net.

▸**clean out** *vt (room etc)* nettoyer; *(empty)* vider.

cleans·ing cream crème *f* démaquillante.

▸**clean up 1** *vt* nettoyer. **2** *vi* faire le nettoyage.

clear 1 *adj (sky, outline, sound, thought etc)* clair; *(glass)* transparent; *(road)* libre; *(profit)* net; *(obvious)* évident, clair; **to be c. (free of)** être libre de; **to make one-**

self c. se faire comprendre. **2** *adv* **to keep** *or* **steer c. of** se tenir à l'écart de; **to get c. of** s'éloigner de. **3** *vt* *(path, table)* débarrasser; *(fence)* franchir; *(accused person)* disculper; *(check)* faire passer (sur un compte); *(through customs)* dédouaner; **to c. one's throat** s'éclaircir la gorge. **4** *vi* *(of weather)* s'éclaircir; *(of fog)* se dissiper.

clear·ance *(sale)* soldes *mpl*; *(space)* dégagement *m*.

▸ **clear away** *vt (remove)* enlever.

clear-cut *adj* net *(f* nette).

clear·ing *(in wood)* clairière *f*.

clear·ly *adv* clairement; *(obviously)* évidemment.

▸ **clear out 1** *vt* vider; *(clean)* nettoyer; *(remove)* enlever. **2** *vi* *(go)* *Fam* décamper.

▸ **clear up 1** *vt (room)* ranger; *(mystery)* éclaircir. **2** *vi (tidy)* ranger.

cleat *(sports shoe)* crampon *m*.

clem·en·tine clémentine *f*.

clench *vt (fist)* serrer.

cler·gy clergé *m*.

cler·i·cal *adj (job)* d'employé; *(work)* de bureau.

clerk employé, -ée *mf* (de bureau); *(in store)* vendeur, -euse *mf*.

clev·er *adj* intelligent; *(smart)* astucieux; *(skillful)* habile; *(machine, book etc)* ingénieux.

click 1 *n (noise)* petit bruit *m* sec; *(with mouse)* clic *m*. **2** *vi (make noise)* faire un bruit sec; *(with mouse)* cliquer (**on** sur).

cli·ent client, -ente *mf*.

cliff falaise *f*.

cli·mate climat *m*.

cli·max point *m* culminant.

climb (o·ver) *vt (wall)* escalader.

climb (up) 1 *vt (stairs, steps)* monter; *(hill, mountain)* gravir; *(tree, ladder)* monter à. **2** *vi* monter.

▸ **climb down 1** *vt (wall, tree, hill)* descendre. **2** *vi* descendre (**from** de).

climb·er *(mountaineer)* alpiniste *mf*.

cling* *vi* se cramponner; *(stick)* adhérer (**to** à).

clin·ic *(private)* clinique *f*; *(public)* centre *m* médical.

clip 1 *vt* couper; *(hedge)* tailler; *(ticket)* poinçonner; *(attach)* attacher. **2** *n (paper)* trombone *m*; *(of brooch, of cyclist, for hair)* pince *f*.

▸ **clip on** *vt* attacher (**to** à).

clip·pers *npl (for hair)* tondeuse *f*; *(for nails)* coupe-ongles *m inv*.

clip·ping *(newspaper article)* coupure *f*.

cloak *(grande)* cape *f*.

cloak·room vestiaire *m*.

clock horloge *f*; *(small)* pendule *f*; **around the c.** vingt-quatre heures sur vingt-quatre.

clock·wise *adv* dans le sens des aiguilles d'une montre.

clone 1 *n* clone *m*. **2** *vt* cloner.

close¹ 1 *adj (place, relative etc)* proche (**to** de); *(collaboration, connection)* étroit; *(friend)* intime; *(atmosphere)* lourd. **2** *adv* **c. (by)** *(tout)* près; **c. to** près de; **c. behind** juste derrière.

close² 1 *n (end)* fin *f*. **2** *vt (door, shop etc)* fermer; *(road)* barrer; *(deal)* conclure. **3** *vi* se fermer; *(of shop)* fermer.

closed *adj* fermé; **c.-circuit television** télévision *f* en circuit fermé.

▸ **close down** *vti (for good)* fermer (définitivement).

▸ **close in** *vi* approcher.

close·ly *adv (to follow, guard)* de près; *(to listen)* attentivement.

clos·et *(for linens, clothes etc)* placard *m*; *(for clothing only)* penderie *f*.

▸ **close up 1** *vt* fermer. **2** *vi (of shopkeeper)* fermer; *(of line of people)* se rapprocher.

clos·ing time heure *f* de fermeture.

clo·sure fermeture *f*.

clot 1 *n (of blood)* caillot *m*. **2** *vi* se coaguler.

cloth tissu *m*; *(for dusting)* chiffon *m*; *(for dishes)* torchon *m*; *(table-cloth)* nappe *f*.

clothes *npl* vêtements *mpl*; **to put one's c. on** s'habiller.

clothes brush brosse *f* à habits.

clothes·line corde *f* à linge.

clothes·pin pince *f* à linge.

cloth·ing vêtements *mpl*; **an article of c.** un vêtement.

cloth·ing store magasin *m* d'habillement.

cloud nuage *m*.

▸ **cloud over** *vi (of sky)* se couvrir.

cloud·y *adj (weather)* couvert.

clove c. of garlic gousse *f* d'ail.

clown clown *m*.

club *(society, stick for golf)* club *m*; **club(s)** *(at cards)* trèfle *m*.

club so·da eau *f* gazeuse.

clue indice *m*; *(of crossword)* définition *f*; **I don't have a c.** *Fam* je n'en ai pas la moindre idée.

clum·sy *adj* maladroit; *(tool)* peu commode.

clunk·er *(car) Fam* tacot *m*.

clus·ter **1** *n* groupe *m*. **2** *vi* se grouper.

clutch **1** *vt (hold)* serrer; *(grasp)* saisir. **2** *n (in vehicle)* embrayage *m*; *(pedal)* pédale *f* d'embrayage.

▸ **clut·ter up** *vt (room etc)* encombrer *(with* de).

cm *abbr (centimeter)* cm.

Co *abbr (company)* Cie.

coach **1** *n (part of train)* voiture *f*; *(bus)* autocar *m*. **2** *vt (pupil)* donner des leçons (particulières) à.

coal charbon *m*.

coal·mine mine *f* de charbon.

coarse *adj (person, fabric)* grossier.

coast côte *f*.

coat **1** *n* manteau *m*; *(jacket)* veste *f*; *(of animal)* pelage *m*; *(of paint)* couche *f*. **2** *vt* couvrir *(with* de).

coat·hang·er cintre *m*.

coat·ing couche *f*.

cob corn on the c. épi *m* de maïs.

cob·bled *adj* pavé.

cob·web toile *f* d'araignée.

co·caine cocaïne *f*.

cock *(fowl)* coq *m*.

cock·le *(shellfish)* coque *f*.

cock·pit poste *m* de pilotage.

cock·roach *(insect)* cafard *m*.

cock·tail cocktail *m*; **fruit c.** macédoine *f* (de fruits); **shrimp c.** crevettes *fpl* à la mayonnaise.

cock·tail par·ty cocktail *m*.

co·coa cacao *m*.

co·co·nut noix *f* de coco.

cod morue *f*.

code code *m*.

cod·liv·er oil huile *f* de foie de morue.

co·ed·u·ca·tion·al *adj (school etc)* mixte.

cof·fee café *m*; **c. with milk** café *m* au lait; *(in restaurant)* (café *m*) crème *m*.

cof·fee bar café *m*.

cof·fee break pause-café *f*.

cof·fee·pot cafetière *f*.

cof·fee ta·ble table *f* basse.

cof·fin cercueil *m*.

co·gnac cognac *m*.

co·her·ent *adj* cohérent.

coil **1** *n (of wire, rope etc)* rouleau *m*. **2** *vt* enrouler.

coin pièce *f* (de monnaie).

coin bank tirelire *f*.

co·in·cide *vi* coïncider (*with* avec).

co·in·ci·dence coïncidence *f*.

coke *(Coca-Cola®)* coca *m*.

col·an·der passoire *f*.

cold **1** *n* froid *m*; *(illness)* rhume *m*; **to catch c.** prendre froid. **2** *adj* froid; **to be** *or* **feel c.** avoir froid; **my hands are c.** j'ai froid aux mains; **it's c.** *(of weather)* il fait froid; **to get c.** *(of weather)* se refroidir; *(of food)* refroidir.

cold cuts assiette *f* anglaise.

cold·ness froideur *f*.

cole·slaw salade *f* de chou cru.

col·lab·o·rate *vi* collaborer (*on* à).

col·lab·o·ra·tion collaboration f.

col·lapse 1 vi (of person, building) s'effondrer. **2** n effondrement m.

col·lar col m; (of dog) collier m.

col·lar·bone clavicule f.

col·league collègue mf.

col·lect 1 vt (pick up) ramasser; (gather) rassembler; (taxes) percevoir; (rent) encaisser; (stamps etc) collectionner; (fetch) (passer) prendre; **to c. (money)** (in street, church) quêter. **2** vi (of dust) s'accumuler. **3** adv **to call c.** téléphoner en PCV.

col·lec·tion (group of objects) collection f; (of poems etc) recueil m; (of mail) levée f.

col·lec·tor (of stamps etc) collectionneur, -euse mf.

col·lege université f.

col·lide vi entrer en collision (with avec).

col·li·sion collision f.

col·lo·qui·al adj familier.

co·logne eau f de Cologne.

co·lon Grammar deux-points m inv.

colo·nel colonel m.

co·lo·ni·al adj colonial.

col·o·ny colonie f.

col·or 1 n couleur f. **2** adj (photo, TV set) en couleurs. **3** vt colorer.

col·ored adj (pencil) de couleur.

col·or·ful adj coloré; (person) pittoresque.

▸ **col·or in** vt (drawing) colorier.

col·or·ing book album m de coloriages.

col·umn colonne f; (newspaper feature) chronique f.

co·ma coma m; **in a c.** dans le coma.

comb 1 n peigne m. **2** vt **to c. one's hair** se peigner.

com·bi·na·tion combinaison f.

com·bine 1 vt joindre (with à); **our combined efforts achieved a result** en joignant nos efforts nous

avons obtenu un résultat. **2** vi s'unir.

come* vi venir (from de; to à); **to c. first** (in race) arriver premier; (in exam) être le premier; **to c. close to doing** faillir faire.

▸ **come about** vi (happen) se faire, arriver.

▸ **come across** vt (thing, person) tomber sur.

▸ **come along** vi venir (with avec); (progress) avancer; **c. along!** allons!

▸ **come apart** vi (of two objects) se séparer.

▸ **come around** vi (visit) venir; (of date) revenir; (regain consciousness) revenir à soi.

▸ **come away** vi (leave, come off) partir.

come·back to make a c. faire un come-back.

▸ **come back** vi revenir; (return home) rentrer.

▸ **come by** vt obtenir; (find) trouver.

co·me·di·an (acteur m) comique m, actrice f comique.

▸ **come down** vi descendre; (of rain, price) tomber.

▸ **come down with** vt attraper.

com·e·dy comédie f.

▸ **come for** vt venir chercher.

▸ **come forward** vi s'avancer; (volunteer) se présenter; **to c. forward with sth** offrir qch.

▸ **come in** vi entrer; (of tide) monter; (of train) arriver.

▸ **come into** vt (room etc) entrer dans; (money) hériter de.

▸ **come off 1** vi (of button etc) se détacher; (succeed) réussir. **2** vt (fall from) tomber de; (get down from) descendre de.

▸ **come on** vi (progress) avancer; **c. on!** (reproving, encouraging) allons!, allez!

▸ **come out** vi sortir; (of sun, book) paraître; (of stain) partir.

▸ **come over 1** vi (visit) venir. **2** vt (of feeling) saisir.

▸**come through 1** *vi (survive)* s'en tirer. **2** *vt (crisis etc)* se tirer indemne de.

▸**come to 1** *vt (amount to)* revenir à; *(a decision)* parvenir à. **2** *vi (regain consciousness)* revenir à soi.

▸**come under** *vt (heading)* être classé sous; *(sb's influence)* tomber sous.

▸**come up** *vi (rise)* monter; *(of plant)* sortir; *(of question, job)* se présenter.

▸**come up against** *vt (wall, problem)* se heurter à.

▸**come up to** *vt (reach)* arriver jusqu'à.

▸**come up with** *vt (idea, money)* trouver.

com·fort 1 *n* confort *m*; *(consolation)* réconfort *m.* **2** *vt* consoler.

com·fort·a·ble *adj (chair etc)* confortable; *(rich)* aisé; **he's c.** *(in chair etc)* il est à l'aise; **make yourself c.** mets-toi à l'aise.

com·fort·er *(quilt)* édredon *m*, couette *f.*

com·ic 1 *adj* comique. **2** *n (magazine)* bande *f* dessinée.

com·ings *npl* **c. and goings** allées *fpl* et venues.

com·ma virgule *f.*

com·mand 1 *vt (order)* commander (**sb to do** à qn de faire). **2** *n (order)* ordre *m*; *(mastery)* maîtrise *f* (**of** de); **to be in c. (of)** *(army etc)* commander; *(situation)* être maître (de).

com·mand·er commandant *m.*

com·mem·o·rate *vt* commémorer.

com·mence *vti* commencer (**doing** à faire).

com·ment commentaire *m.*

com·men·tar·y commentaire *m*; **(live) c.** reportage *m.*

com·men·ta·tor reporter *m.*

▸**comment on** *vt (event etc)* commenter.

com·merce commerce *m.*

com·mer·cial 1 *adj* commercial.

2 *n* **commercial(s)** *(on television)* publicité *f.*

com·mis·sion *(fee, group)* commission *f.*

com·mit *vt (crime)* commettre; **to c. suicide** se suicider.

com·mit·ment *(promise)* engagement *m.*

com·mit·tee comité *m.*

com·mod·i·ty produit *m.*

com·mon *adj (shared, frequent etc)* commun; **in c.** *(shared)* en commun (**with** avec); **in c. with** *(like)* comme.

com·mon·ly *adv (generally)* en général.

com·mon·place *adj* banal (*mpl* banals).

com·mon room salle *f* commune.

com·mon sense *m* sens *m* commun.

com·mo·tion agitation *f.*

com·mu·nal *adj (bathroom etc)* commun.

com·mu·ni·cate *vti* communiquer.

com·mu·ni·ca·tion communication *f.*

com·mun·ion communion *f.*

com·mu·ni·ty communauté *f.*

com·mu·ni·ty cen·ter centre *m* socio-culturel.

com·mute *vi* faire la navette (**to work** pour se rendre à son travail).

com·mut·er banlieusard, -arde *mf.*

com·mut·ing trajets *mpl* journaliers.

com·pact 1 *adj* compact. **2** *n (for face powder)* poudrier *m.*

com·pact disc *or* **disk** disque *m* compact.

com·pan·ion compagnon *m.*

com·pa·ny *(being with others, firm)* compagnie *f*; *(guests)* invités, -ées *mfpl*; **to keep sb c.** tenir compagnie à qn.

com·pa·ra·ble *adj* comparable (**to, with** à).

com·pa·ra·tive·ly *adv* relativement.

com·pare *vt* comparer (**with, to** à); **compared to** *or* **with** en comparaison de.

com·par·i·son comparaison *f* (**with** avec).

com·part·ment compartiment *m*.

com·pass *(for direction)* boussole *f*; *(on ship)* compas *m*; **(pair of) compasses** *(for drawing etc)* compas *m*.

com·pat·i·ble *adj* compatible.

com·pel *vt* forcer, contraindre (**to do** à faire).

com·pen·sate 1 *vt* **to c. sb** dédommager qn (**for** de). **2** *vi* compenser (**for sth** qch).

com·pen·sa·tion dédommagement *m*.

com·pete *vi (take part)* concourir (**in** à; **for** pour); **to c.** *(with sb)* rivaliser (avec qn); *(in business)* faire concurrence (à qn).

com·pe·tent *adj* compétent (**to do** pour faire).

com·pe·tent·ly *adv* avec compétence.

com·pe·ti·tion *(rivalry)* compétition *f*; **a c.** *(contest)* un concours; *(in sports)* une compétition.

com·pet·i·tive *adj (price etc)* compétitif; *(person)* aimant la compétition.

com·pet·i·tor concurrent, -ente *mf*.

com·pile *vt (dictionary)* rédiger; *(list)* dresser.

com·plain *vi* se plaindre (**of, about** de; **that** que).

com·plaint plainte *f*; *(in shop etc)* réclamation *f*; *(illness)* maladie *f*.

com·ple·ment 1 *n* complément *m*. **2** *vt* compléter.

com·plete 1 *adj (total)* complet; *(finished)* achevé; **a c. idiot** un parfait imbécile. **2** *vt* compléter; *(finish)* achever; *(a form)* remplir.

com·plete·ly *adv* complètement.

com·plex 1 *adj* complexe. **2** *n (feeling, buildings)* complexe *m*.

com·plex·ion *(of face)* teint *m*.

com·pli·cate *vt* compliquer.

com·pli·cat·ed *adj* compliqué.

com·pli·ca·tion complication *f*.

com·pli·ment compliment *m*.

com·pli·men·ta·ry *adj (praising)* flatteur; *(free)* gratuit.

com·ply *vi* obéir (**with** à).

com·pose *vt* composer; **to c. oneself** se calmer.

com·posed *adj* calme.

com·pos·er compositeur, -trice *mf*.

com·po·si·tion *(school essay)* rédaction *f*.

com·pound *(substance, word)* composé *m*.

com·pre·hen·sive *adj* complet; *(insurance)* tous risques.

com·prise *vt* comprendre.

com·pro·mise compromis *m*.

com·pul·sive *adj (smoker etc)* invétéré; **c. liar** mythomane *mf*.

com·pul·so·ry *adj* obligatoire.

com·put·er ordinateur *m*; **c. technician** informaticien, -enne *mf*.

com·put·er·ized *adj* informatisé.

com·put·er sci·ence informatique *f*.

com·put·ing informatique *f*.

con *vt (deceive) Fam* escroquer.

con·ceal *vt* dissimuler (**from sb** à qn); *(plan)* tenir secret.

con·cede *vt* concéder (**to** à).

con·ceit·ed *adj* vaniteux.

con·ceiv·a·ble *adj* concevable.

con·ceive *vti* concevoir.

con·cen·trate 1 *vt* concentrer. **2** *vi* se concentrer (**on** sur); **to c. on doing** s'appliquer à faire.

con·cen·tra·tion concentration *f*.

con·cern 1 *vt* concerner; **to be concerned with/about** s'occuper de/s'inquiéter de. **2** *n (matter)* affaire *f*; *(anxiety)* inquiétude *f*; **his c. for** son souci de; *(business)* **c.** entreprise *f*.

con·cerned adj (anxious) inquiet.

con·cern·ing prep en ce qui concerne.

con·cert concert m.

con·ces·sion concession f.

con·cise adj concis.

con·clude 1 vt conclure; **to c. that** conclure que. **2** vi se terminer (**with** par); (of speaker) conclure.

con·clu·sion conclusion f.

con·crete 1 n béton m. **2** adj en béton; (real) concret.

con·demn vt condamner (**to** à).

con·den·sa·tion (mist) buée f.

con·di·tion condition f; **on c. that one does** à condition de faire, à condition que l'on fasse.

con·di·tion·er (hair) c. après-shampooing m.

con·do, pl -os abbr = **condominium**.

con·dom préservatif m.

con·do·min·i·um (building) copropriété f; (apartment) appartement m dans une copropriété.

con·duct 1 n conduite f. **2** vt conduire; (orchestra) diriger.

con·duct·ed tour excursion f accompagnée.

con·duc·tor (of orchestra) chef m d'orchestre; (on bus) receveur, -euse mf; (on train) chef m de train.

cone cône m; (of ice cream) cornet m.

con·fer 1 vt (title) conférer, accorder (**on** à). **2** vi (discuss) se consulter (**on**, **about** sur).

con·fer·ence conférence f; (scientific, etc) congrès m.

con·fess 1 vt avouer (**that** que). **2** vi **to c.** (**to**) avouer.

con·fes·sion aveu(x) m(pl).

con·fet·ti confettis mpl.

con·fi·dence (trust) confiance f; (self-)c. confiance f en soi; **in c.** en confidence.

con·fi·dent adj sûr; (self-)c. sûr de soi.

con·fi·den·tial adj confidentiel.

con·fi·dent·ly adv avec confiance.

con·fine vt limiter (**to** à); **to c. oneself to doing** se limiter à faire.

con·fined adj (space) réduit; **c. to bed** cloué au lit.

con·firm vt confirmer (**that** que).

con·fir·ma·tion confirmation f.

con·firmed adj (bachelor) endurci.

con·fis·cate vt confisquer (**from sb** à qn).

con·flict 1 n conflit m. **2** vi être en contradiction (**with** avec).

con·flict·ing adj (views etc) contradictoires; (dates) incompatibles.

con·form vi (of person) se conformer (**to** à).

con·front vt (problems, danger) faire face à; **to c. sb** (be face to face with) se trouver en face de qn; (oppose) affronter qn.

con·fron·ta·tion confrontation f.

con·fuse vt (make unsure) embrouiller; **to c. with** (mistake for) confondre avec.

con·fused adj (situation) confus; **to be c.** (of person) s'y perdre; **to get c.** s'embrouiller.

con·fus·ing adj déroutant.

con·fu·sion confusion f.

con·gest·ed adj (street) encombré.

con·ges·tion (traffic) encombrement(s) m(pl).

con·grat·u·late vt féliciter (**sb on sth** qn de qch).

con·grat·u·la·tions félicitations fpl (**on** pour).

con·gre·gate vi se rassembler.

con·gress congrès m; **C.** (political body) le Congrès.

Con·gress·man, pl -men membre m du Congrès.

con·ju·gate vt (verb) conjuguer.

con·ju·ga·tion conjugaison f.

con·junc·tion Grammar conjonction f.

con·jur·er prestidigitateur, -trice *mf*.

con·jur·ing trick tour *m* de prestidigitation.

con man *Fam* escroc *m*.

con·nect 1 *vt* relier (**with, to** à); *(telephone etc)* brancher; **to c. sb with sb** *(by phone)* mettre qn en communication avec qn. **2** *vi* **to c. with** *(of train, bus)* assurer la correspondance avec.

con·nect·ed *adj (facts)* liés; **to be c. with** *(have dealings with, relate to)* être lié à.

con·nec·tion *(link)* rapport *m* (**with** avec); *(train etc)* correspondance *f*; *(phone call)* communication *f*; **connections** *(contacts)* relations *fpl*; **in c. with** à propos de.

con·quer *vt (country)* conquérir; *(enemy, habit)* vaincre.

con·quest conquête *f*.

con·science conscience *f*.

con·sci·en·tious *adj* consciencieux.

con·scious *adj (awake)* conscient; **c. of sth** *(aware)* conscient de qch; **to be c. of doing** avoir conscience de faire.

con·sen·sus consensus *m*.

con·sent 1 *vi* consentir (**to** à). **2** *n* consentement *m*.

con·se·quence *(result)* conséquence *f*.

con·se·quent·ly *adv* par conséquent.

con·ser·va·tion *(of energy)* économies *fpl*, d'énergie; *(of nature)* protection *f* de l'environnement.

con·ser·va·tive *adj & n* conservateur, -trice *(mf)*.

con·ser·va·to·ry *(room)* véranda *f*.

con·serve *vt* **to c. energy** faire des économies d'énergie.

con·sid·er *vt* considérer (**that** que); *(take into account)* tenir compte de; **to c. doing** envisager de faire.

con·sid·er·a·ble *adj (large)* considérable; *(much)* beaucoup de.

con·sid·er·ate *adj* plein d'égards (**to** pour).

con·sid·er·a·tion considération *f*; **to take into c.** prendre en considération.

con·sid·er·ing *prep* compte tenu de.

con·sign·ment *(goods)* arrivage *m*.

con·sis·ten·cy consistance *f*.

con·sis·tent *adj (unchanging)* constant; *(ideas)* logique; **c. with** compatible avec.

con·sis·tent·ly *adv (always)* constamment.

▸ **con·sist in** *vt* consister dans; **to c. in doing** consister à faire.

▸ **con·sist of** *vt* consister en.

con·so·la·tion consolation *f*; **c. prize** lot *m* de consolation.

con·sole¹ *vt* consoler.

con·sole² *(control desk)* console *f*.

con·so·nant consonne *f*.

con·spic·u·ous *adj* visible; *(striking)* remarquable.

con·spir·a·cy conspiration *f*.

con·stant *adj (frequent)* incessant; *(unchanging)* constant.

con·stant·ly *adv* constamment.

con·sti·pat·ed *adj* constipé.

con·sti·tu·tion constitution *f*.

con·straint contrainte *f*.

con·struct *vt* construire.

con·struc·tion construction *f*; **under c.** en construction.

con·struc·tive *adj* constructif.

con·sul consul *m*.

con·su·late consulat *m*.

con·sult 1 *vt* consulter. **2** *vi* **to c. with** discuter avec.

con·sult·ant *(doctor)* spécialiste *mf*; *(financial, legal)* expert-conseil *m*.

con·sul·ta·tion consultation *f*.

con·sult·ing firm cabinet *m* d'experts-conseils.

con·sume *vt (food, supplies)* consommer.

con·sum·er consommateur, -trice *mf.*

con·sump·tion consommation *f* (of de).

con·tact 1 *n* contact *m; (person)* contact *m,* relation *f;* **in c. with** en contact avec. **2** *vt* contacter.

con·tact lens·es lentilles *fpl* or verres *mpl* de contact.

con·ta·gious *adj* contagieux.

con·tain *vt* contenir.

con·tain·er récipient *m; (for goods)* conteneur *m.*

con·tem·po·rar·y *adj & n* contemporain, -aine *(mf).*

con·tempt mépris *m.*

▸**con·tend with** *vt (problem)* faire face à; *(person)* avoir affaire à.

con·tent¹ *adj* satisfait (**with** de).

con·tent² *(of text etc)* contenu *m;* **contents** *(of container)* contenu *m;* **(table of) contents** *(of book)* table *f* des matières.

con·tent·ed *adj* satisfait.

con·test concours *m; (fight)* lutte *f.*

con·tes·tant concurrent, -ente *mf; (in fight)* adversaire *mf.*

con·text contexte *m.*

con·ti·nent continent *m.*

con·ti·nen·tal *adj* continental; **c. breakfast** petit déjeuner *m* à la française.

con·tin·u·al *adj* continuel.

con·tinu·al·ly *adv* continuellement.

con·tin·ue 1 *vt* continuer (**to do** or **doing** à or de faire); **to c. (with)** *(work etc)* poursuivre; *(resume)* reprendre. **2** *vi* continuer; *(resume)* reprendre.

con·tin·u·ous *adj* continu.

con·tin·u·ous·ly *adv* sans interruption.

con·tra·cep·tion contraception *f.*

con·tra·cep·tive *adj & n* contraceptif *(m).*

con·tract contrat *m.*

con·trac·tor entrepreneur *m.*

con·tra·dict *vt* contredire.

con·tra·dic·tion contradiction *f.*

con·tra·ry 1 *adv* **c. to** contrairement à. **2** *n* **on the c.** au contraire.

con·trast contraste *m;* **in c. to** par opposition à.

con·trast·ing *adj (colors, opinions)* opposés.

con·trib·ute 1 *vt* donner (**to** à); *(article)* écrire (**to** pour); **to c. money to** contribuer à. **2** *vi* **to c. to** contribuer à; *(publication)* collaborer à.

con·tri·bu·tion contribution *f; (to fund etc)* cotisation(s) *f(pl).*

con·trive *vt* **to c. to do** trouver moyen de faire.

con·trived *adj* artificiel.

con·trol 1 *vt (organization)* diriger; *(traffic)* régler; *(prices, quality, situation, emotion)* contrôler; **to c. oneself** se contrôler. **2** *n* autorité *f* (**over** sur); *(over prices, quality)* contrôle *m;* **controls** *(of train etc)* commandes *fpl; (of TV set etc)* boutons *mpl;* **everything is under c.** tout est en ordre; **in c. of** maître de; **to lose c. of** perdre le contrôle de.

con·trol tow·er tour *f* de contrôle.

con·va·lesce *vi* être en convalescence.

con·va·les·cence convalescence *f.*

conva·les·cent home maison *f* de convalescence.

con·ven·ience commodité *f;* **c. foods** plats *mpl* tout préparés; **(public) conveniences** toilettes *fpl.*

con·ven·ient *adj* commode; *(well-situated)* bien situé (**to shopping**/*etc* par rapport aux magasins/*etc*); *(moment)* convenable; **to be c. (for)** *(suit)* convenir (à).

con·vent couvent *m.*

con·ver·sa·tion conversation *f.*

con·verse *vi* s'entretenir (**with** avec).

con·ver·sion conversion *f*; *(of building)* aménagement *m*.

con·vert *vt* convertir (**into** en; **to** à); *(building)* aménager (**into** en).

con·vert·i·ble *(car)* (voiture *f*) décapotable *f*.

con·vey *vt* *(goods, people)* transporter; *(sound, message)* transmettre; *(idea)* communiquer.

con·vey·or belt tapis *m* roulant.

con·vict *vt* déclarer coupable.

con·vic·tion *(for crime)* condamnation *f*; *(belief)* conviction *f*.

con·vince *vt* convaincre (**of** de).

con·vinc·ing *adj* convaincant.

con·voy *(cars)* convoi *m*.

cook 1 *vt* *(food)* (faire) cuire. **2** *vi* *(of food)* cuire; *(of person)* faire la cuisine. **3** *n* cuisinier, -ière *mf*.

cook·book livre *m* de cuisine.

cook·ie biscuit *m*.

cook·ing cuisine *f*.

cook·ing ap·ple pomme *f* à cuire.

cool 1 *adj* *(weather, place, drink etc)* frais (*f* fraîche); *(manner)* calme; *(unfriendly)* froid; *(fashionable, good)* cool *inv*; **to keep sth c.** tenir qch au frais. **2** *n* *(of evening)* fraîcheur *f*; **to lose one's c.** perdre son sang-froid.

cool (down) 1 *vi* *(of angry person)* se calmer; *(of hot liquid)* refroidir. **2** *vt* refroidir.

cool·er *(for food)* glacière *f*.

cool·head·ed *adj* calme.

cool·ness fraîcheur *f*; *(unfriendliness)* froideur *f*.

▶**cool off** *vi* *(refresh oneself)* se rafraîchir.

co-op appartement *m* en copropriété.

co·op·er·ate *vi* coopérer (**in** à; **with** avec).

co·op·er·a·tion coopération *f*.

▶**coop up** *vt* *(person)* enfermer.

co·or·di·nate 1 *vt* coordonner. **2**

n **coordinates** *(clothes)* coordonnés *mpl*.

cop *(policeman)* Fam flic *m*.

cope *vi* **to c. with** s'occuper de; *(problem)* faire face à; **(to be able) to c.** *(savoir)* se débrouiller.

cop·per *(metal)* cuivre *m*.

cop·y 1 *n* copie *f*; *(of book, magazine etc)* exemplaire *m*. **2** *vti* copier.

▶**copy out, copy down** *vt* *(address etc)* (re)copier.

cord cordon *m*; *(electrical)* cordon *m* électrique.

cor·dial *(fruit)* **c.** sirop *m*.

▶**cor·don off** *vt* *(of police etc)* interdire l'accès de.

cor·du·roy velours *m* côtelé; **corduroys** pantalon *m* en velours (côtelé).

core *(of apple etc)* trognon *m*.

cork liège *m*; *(for bottle)* bouchon *m*.

cork (up) *vt* *(bottle)* boucher.

cork·screw tire-bouchon *m*.

corn maïs *m*; *(on foot)* cor *m*.

corn·bread pain *m* à la farine de maïs.

corned beef corned-beef *m*.

cor·ner 1 *n* coin *m*; *(bend in road)* virage *m*. **2** *vt* *(person in corridor etc)* coincer; *(market)* monopoliser.

corn·flakes céréales *fpl*.

corn·starch fécule *f* de maïs.

corn·y *adj* *(joke)* rebattu.

cor·o·nar·y infarctus *m*.

cor·po·ral caporal(-chef) *m*.

corps *inv* corps *m*.

corpse cadavre *m*.

cor·rect 1 *adj* exact, correct; *(proper)* correct; **he's c.** *(right)* il a raison. **2** *vt* corriger.

cor·rec·tion correction *f*.

cor·rect·ly *adv* correctement.

cor·re·spond correspondre (**to, with** à); *(by letter)* correspondre (**with** avec).

cor·re·spon·dence correspondance *f*; **c. course** cours *m* par correspondance.

cor·re·spond·ing adj (matching) correspondant.

cor·ri·dor couloir m.

cor·ru·gat·ed adj c. iron tôle f ondulée.

cor·rupt adj corrompu.

cor·rup·tion corruption f.

cos·met·ic produit m de beauté.

cost 1 vti coûter; **how much does it c.?** ça coûte combien? 2 n prix m; **at all costs** à tout prix.

cost·ly adj coûteux.

cos·tume costume m.

cos·tume ball bal m masqué.

cos·tume jew·el·ry bijoux mpl de fantaisie.

cot lit m d'enfant; (camp bed) lit m de camp.

cot·tage petite maison f de campagne; **(thatched) c.** chaumière f.

cot·tage cheese fromage m blanc (maigre).

cot·ton coton m; (yarn) fil m (de coton); **c. wool** coton m hydrophile.

couch canapé m.

cou·chette (on train) couchette f.

cough 1 n toux f; **c. syrup** sirop m contre la toux. 2 vi tousser.

cough up 1 vt (blood) cracher. 2 vti (pay) Fam casquer.

could see **can¹.**

coun·cil conseil m; **(city) c.** conseil m municipal, municipalité f.

coun·cil·man (city) **c.** conseiller m municipal.

coun·sel·ing aide f psychologique.

count¹ 1 vt compter. 2 vi (calculate, be important) compter. 3 n he's lost **c. of the books he has** il ne sait plus combien il a de livres.

count² (title) comte m.

count·down compte m à rebours.

coun·ter (in shop, bar etc) comptoir m; (in bank etc) guichet m; (in games) jeton m.

coun·ter- prefix contre-.

coun·ter·at·tack contre-attaque f.

coun·ter·clock·wise adj & adv dans le sens inverse des aiguilles d'une montre.

coun·ter·part (thing) équivalent m; (person) homologue mf.

▸ **count in** vt inclure.

▸ **count on** vt (rely on) compter sur; **to c. on doing** compter faire.

▸ **count out** vt exclure; (money) compter.

coun·try pays m; (regarded with affection) patrie f; (opposed to town) campagne f; **c. house** maison f de campagne.

coun·try·side campagne f.

coun·ty comté m.

coup coup m d'état.

cou·ple (of people) couple m; **a c. of** deux ou trois; (a few) quelques.

cou·pon (voucher) bon m.

cour·age courage m.

cou·ra·geous adj courageux.

cou·ri·er (messenger) messager m.

course 1 n (duration, movement) cours m; **c. (of action)** ligne f de conduite; (option) parti m; **in the c. of** au cours de. ▪ (lessons) cours m; **c. of lectures** série f de conférences. ▪ **c. (of treatment)** traitement m. ▪ (of meal) plat m; **first c.** entrée f. ▪ **(golf) c.** terrain m de golf. 2 adv **of c.!** bien sûr!; **of c. not!** bien sûr que non!

court (of king etc, for trials) cour f; **(tennis) c.** court m (de tennis); **to take sb to c.** poursuivre qn en justice.

cour·te·ous adj poli.

cour·te·sy politesse f, courtoisie f.

court·room salle f du tribunal.

court·yard cour f.

cous·in cousin, -ine mf.

cov·er 1 n (lid) couvercle m; (of book) couverture f; (for furniture etc) housse f; **the covers** (on bed) les couvertures fpl et les draps mpl; **to take c.** se mettre à l'abri. 2 vt couvrir (**with** de); (insure) assurer.

cov·er·age couverture f.

cov·er·alls bleu m (de travail).

cov·er charge (in restaurant) couvert m.

cov·er·ing (wrapping) enveloppe f; (layer) couche f.

cov·er let·ter lettre f jointe (à un document); (seeking job) lettre f de motivation.

▸ **cover over** vt (floor etc) recouvrir.

▸ **cover up 1** vt recouvrir; (truth, tracks) dissimuler; (scandal) étouffer. **2** vi (wrap up) se couvrir.

▸ **cover up for** vt couvrir.

cow vache f.

cow·ard lâche mf.

cow·ard·ice lâcheté f.

cow·ard·ly adj lâche.

cow·boy cow-boy m.

co·zy adj douillet.

CPA abbr = **Certified Public Accountant**.

crab crabe m.

crack 1 n fente f; (in glass, china, bone) fêlure f; (noise) craquement m; (of whip) claquement m; (joke) Fam plaisanterie f. **2** vt (glass, ice) fêler; (nut) casser; (whip) faire claquer; (joke) lancer. **3** vi se fêler; (of branch, wood) craquer; **to get cracking** (get to work) Fam s'y mettre.

crack·er (biscuit) biscuit m (salé).

crack·pot Fam cinglé, -ée mf.

▸ **crack up** vi (mentally) Fam craquer.

cra·dle berceau m.

craft (skill) art m; (job) métier m (artisanal).

crafts·man, pl -men artisan m.

craft·y adj astucieux.

cram 1 vt **to c. into** (force) fourrer dans; **to c. with** (fill) bourrer de. **2** vi **to c. into** (of people) s'entasser dans; **to c. (for an exam)** banchoter.

cramp (muscle pain) crampe f (in à).

cramped adj à l'étroit.

crane (machine, bird) grue f.

crank¹ (handle) manivelle f.

crank² Fam (person) excentrique mf.

crash 1 n accident m; (of firm) faillite f; (noise) fracas m. **2** int (of fallen object) patatras! **3** vt (car) avoir un accident avec; **to c. one's car into** faire rentrer sa voiture dans. **4** vi (of car, plane) s'écraser; **to c. into** rentrer dans.

crash course cours m intensif.

crash di·et régime m intensif.

▸ **crash down** vi (fall) tomber; (break) se casser.

crash hel·met casque m (antichoc).

crash-land vi atterrir en catastrophe.

crash land·ing atterrissage m en catastrophe.

crate caisse f.

crav·ing désir m (for de).

crawl 1 vi ramper; (of child) marcher à quatre pattes; (of vehicle) avancer au pas; **to be crawling with** grouiller de. **2** n (swimming stroke) crawl m.

cray·on crayon m de couleur (en cire).

craze manie f (for de).

cra·zy adj fou (f folle); **c. about sth** fana de qch; **c. about sb** fou de qn.

creak vi (of hinge) grincer.

cream crème f, **c. cake** gâteau m à la crème.

cream cheese fromage m blanc.

cream·y adj crémeux.

crease 1 vt (wrinkle) froisser. **2** vi se froisser. **3** n (in trousers) pli m.

cre·ate vt créer; (impression, noise) faire.

cre·a·tion création f.

cre·a·tive adj créatif.

crea·ture animal m; (person) créature f.

crèche (nursery) crèche f.

cred·i·bil·i·ty crédibilité f.

cred·i·ble adj croyable; (politician etc) crédible.

cred·it 1 *n (financial)* crédit *m*; *(merit)* mérite *m*; *(from university)* unité *f* de valeur; **to be a c. to** faire honneur à; **on c.** à crédit; **my account shows a c. balance of** mon compte est créditeur de. 2 *vt (of bank)* créditer (**sb with sth** qn de qch).

cred·it card carte *f* de crédit.

cred·it terms facilités *fpl* de paiement.

cred·it·wor·thy *adj* solvable.

creek *(stream)* ruisseau *m*.

creep* *vi* ramper; *(silently)* se glisser; *(slowly)* avancer lentement.

creep·y *adj (causing fear)* Fam terrifiant.

cre·mate *vt* incinérer.

cre·ma·tion crémation *f*.

cre·ma·to·ri·um, cre·ma·to·ry crématorium *m*.

crêpe pa·per papier *m* crépon.

cress cresson *m*.

crest *(of wave etc)* crête *f*, *(of hill)* sommet *m*.

crew *(of ship, plane)* équipage *m*.

crew cut *(coupe f en)* brosse *f*.

crib *(cot)* lit *m* d'enfant; *(list of answers)* pompe *f*, anti-sèche *f*.

crick·et *(insect)* grillon *m*.

crime crime *m*; *(not serious)* délit *m*; *(criminal practice)* criminalité *f*.

crim·i·nal *adj & n* criminel, -elle *(mf)*.

cri·sis, *pl* **-ses** crise *f*.

crisp *adj (cookie)* croustillant; *(apple)* croquant.

cri·te·ri·on, *pl* **criteria** critère *m*.

crit·ic critique *m*.

crit·i·cal *adj* critique.

crit·i·cal·ly *adv (ill)* gravement.

crit·i·cism critique *f*.

crit·i·cize *vti* critiquer.

cro·chet 1 *vt* faire au crochet. 2 *vi* faire du crochet. 3 *n (travail m au)* crochet *m*.

croc·o·dile crocodile *m*.

cro·cus crocus *m*.

crook *(thief)* escroc *m*.

crook·ed *adj (stick)* courbé; *(path)* tortueux; *(hat, picture)* de travers.

crop *(harvest)* récolte *f*, *(produce)* culture *f*.

▶**crop up** *vi* se présenter.

cro·quet croquet *m*.

cross[1] 1 *n* croix *f*; **a c. between** *(animal)* un croisement entre *or* de. 2 *vt (street, room etc)* traverser; *(barrier)* franchir; *(legs)* croiser. 3 *vi (of paths)* se croiser.

cross[2] *adj (angry)* fâché **(with** contre).

cross-coun·try race cross(-country) *m*.

cross-eyed *adj* qui louche.

cross·ing *(by ship)* traversée *f*.

▶**cross off** *or* **out** *vt (word, name etc)* rayer.

▶**cross over** *vti* traverser.

cross-ref·er·ence renvoi *m*.

cross·roads carrefour *m*.

cross-sec·tion coupe *f* transversale; *(sample)* échantillon *n*.

cross·walk passage *m* clouté.

cross·word (puz·zle) mots *mpl* croisés.

crouch (down) *vi* s'accroupir.

crow corbeau *m*.

crow·bar levier *m*, pied *m* de biche.

crowd foule *f*, *(particular group)* bande *f*.

crowd·ed *adj* plein **(with** de).

▶**crowd into** *vt (of people)* s'entasser dans.

▶**crowd round** *vt* se presser autour de.

crown couronne *f*.

cru·cial *adj* crucial.

crude *adj (manners, language)* grossier; *(work)* rudimentaire.

cru·el *adj* cruel.

cru·el·ty cruauté *f*; **an act of c.** une cruauté.

cru·et petit flacon *m*; *(for oil and vinegar)* huilier *m*.

cruise 1 *vi (of ship)* croiser; *(of car)*

rouler; *(of plane)* voler. **2** *n* croisière
f; **to take a c.** faire une croisière.
crumb miette f.
crum·ble 1 *vt (bread)* émietter. **2**
vi (in small pieces) s'effriter; *(of
bread)* s'émietter; *(become ruined)*
tomber en ruine.
crum·bly *adj* friable.
crum·my *adj Fam* moche.
crum·ple *vt* froisser.
crunch *vt (food)* croquer.
crunch·y *adj (apple etc)* croquant;
(bread, cookie) croustillant.
crush 1 *n (crowd)* cohue f; *(rush)*
bousculade f. **2** *vt* écraser; *(clothes)*
froisser; *(cram)* entasser (**into**
dans).
crust croûte f.
crust·y *adj (bread)* croustillant.
crutch *(of invalid)* béquille f.
cry 1 *n (shout)* cri m; **to have a c.**
Fam pleurer. **2** *vi* pleurer; *(shout)*
pousser un cri.
cry·ing *(weeping)* pleurs mpl.
▸ **cry off** *vi* se décommander.
▸ **cry out 1** *vi* pousser un cri; *(exclaim)* s'écrier. **2** *vt* crier.
▸ **cry out for** *vt* demander (à grands
cris); **to be crying out for sth** avoir
grand besoin de qch.
▸ **cry over** *vt* pleurer (sur).
crys·tal cristal m.
cub *(scout)* louveteau m.
cube cube m; *(of meat etc)* dé m.
cu·bic *adj (meter etc)* cube.
cu·bi·cle *(in office building)* box
m.
cuck·oo *(bird)* coucou m.
cu·cum·ber concombre m.
cud·dle 1 *vt (hug)* serrer; *(caress)*
câliner. **2** *vi* se serrer. **3** *n* caresse f.
▸ **cuddle up to** *vt* se serrer contre.
cud·dly *adj* câlin; *(toy)* doux (f
douce).
cue *(in theatre)* réplique f; *(signal)*
signal m.
cuff *(of shirt)* poignet m; *(of trousers)* revers m.
cuff link bouton m de manchette.

cul-de-sac impasse f.
cul·prit coupable mf.
cult culte m; **c. film** film m culte.
cul·ti·vate *vt* cultiver.
cul·ti·vat·ed *adj* cultivé.
cul·tur·al *adj* culturel.
cul·ture culture f.
cul·tured *adj* cultivé.
cum·ber·some *adj* encombrant.
cun·ning 1 *adj* astucieux. **2** *n* astuce f.
cup tasse f; *(prize)* coupe f.
cup·board armoire f, *(built-in)*
placard m.
cup·cake petit gâteau m.
cup·ful tasse f.
cur·a·ble *adj* guérissable.
curb bord m du trottoir.
cure 1 *vt* guérir *(qn)* *(of* de). **2** *n* remède m *(for* contre); **rest c.** cure f
de repos.
cu·ri·os·i·ty curiosité f.
cu·ri·ous *adj (odd)* curieux; *(inquisitive)* curieux *(about* de).
curl 1 *vti (hair)* boucler. **2** *n* boucle f.
curl·er bigoudi m.
▸ **curl up** *vi* se pelotonner.
curl·y *adj (hair)* bouclé.
cur·rant *(dried grape)* raisin m de
Corinthe.
cur·ren·cy monnaie f; *(foreign)*
devises fpl (étrangères).
cur·rent 1 *adj* actuel; *(opinion)*
courant; *(year)* courant. **2** *n (of river, electric)* courant m.
cur·rent af·fairs questions fpl
d'actualité.
cur·rent·ly *adv* actuellement.
cur·ric·u·lum programme m (scolaire).
cur·ry curry m.
curse *vi (swear)* jurer.
cur·sor *(of computer)* curseur m.
cur·tain rideau m.
curt·s(e)y 1 *n* révérence f. **2** *vi*
faire une révérence.
curve 1 *n* courbe f, *(in road)* virage
m. **2** *vi* se courber; *(of road)* faire
une courbe.

cush·ion coussin m.
cus·tard crème f anglaise; (when set) crème f renversée.
cus·to·dy garde f.
cus·tom coutume f, (customers) clientèle f.
cus·tom·ar·y adj habituel.
cus·tom·er client, -ente mf.
cus·tom·er ser·vice service m après-vente.
cus·toms la douane; **c. (duty)** droits mpl de douane; **c. officer** douanier m.
cut 1 n (mark) coupure f, (stroke) coup m; (of clothes, hair) coupe f, (in salary, prices etc) réduction f, (of meat) morceau m. **2** vt* couper; (meat) découper; (glass, tree) tailler; (salary etc) réduire; **to c. open** ouvrir (au couteau etc). **3** vi (of person, scissors) couper; **to c. in line** passer avant son tour.
▸**cut away** vt (remove) enlever.
 cut·back réduction f.
▸**cut back (on)** vti réduire.
▸**cut down** vt (tree) abattre; (reduce) réduire.
▸**cut down on** vt réduire.
 cute adj Fam (pretty) mignon (f mignonne).
▸**cut into** vt (cake) entamer.
 cut·ler·y couverts mpl.
 cut·let côtelette f.
▸**cut off** vt couper; (isolate) isoler.
 cut·out (picture) découpage m.
▸**cut out 1** vi (of engine) caler. **2** vt (article) découper; (remove) enlever; **to c. out drinking** s'arrêter de boire; **c. it out!** Fam ça suffit!; **c. out to be a doctor**/etc fait pour être médecin/etc.
 cut·ting 1 n (from newspaper) coupure m; (plant) bouture f. **2** adj (wind, remark) cinglant.
▸**cut up** vt couper (en morceaux).
 cy·cle 1 n (bicycle) bicyclette f, (series, period) cycle m. **2** vi aller à bicyclette (to à).
 cy·cling cyclisme m.

cy·clist cycliste mf.
cyl·in·der cylindre m.
cym·bal cymbale f.
cyn·i·cal adj cynique.

D

dab vt (wound) tamponner; **to d. sth on sth** appliquer qch sur qch.
Da·cron® tergal® m.
dad·dy Fam papa m.
daf·fo·dil jonquille f.
daft adj Fam idiot, bête.
dai·ly 1 adj quotidien. **2** adv quotidiennement. **3** n **d. (paper)** quotidien m.
dair·y adj (product) laitier.
dai·sy pâquerette f.
dam barrage m.
dam·age 1 n dégâts mpl, (harm) préjudice m. **2** vt (spoil) abîmer; (harm) nuire à.
dam·ag·ing adj préjudiciable.
damn Fam **1** int **d. (it)!** merde!; **d. him!** qu'il aille au diable! **2** adj (awful) fichu. **3** adv (very) vachement.
damp 1 adj humide. **2** n humidité f.
damp·en vt humecter.
damp·ness humidité f.
dance 1 n danse f, (social event) bal m (pl bals). **2** vti danser.
dance hall salle f de danse.
danc·er danseur, -euse mf.
danc·ing danse f.
dan·de·li·on pissenlit m.
dan·druff pellicules fpl.
Dane Danois, -oise mf.
dan·ger danger m (**to** pour); **in d.** en danger; **to be in d. of falling**/etc risquer de tomber/etc.
dan·ger·ous adj dangereux (**to** pour).

Dan·ish 1 adj danois. **2** n (language) danois m.

dare vt oser (**do** faire); **to d. sb to do** défier qn de faire.

dar·ing adj audacieux.

dark 1 adj obscur, noir; (color, eyes) foncé; (skin, hair) brun; **it's d.** il fait nuit or noir; **d. glasses** lunettes fpl noires. **2** n noir m, obscurité f.

dark-haired adj aux cheveux bruns.

dark·ness obscurité f, noir m.

dark-skinned adj brun.

dar·ling (my) d. (mon) chéri, (ma) chérie.

dart fléchette f; **darts** (game) fléchettes fpl.

dart·board cible f.

dash 1 vi se précipiter. **2** n (stroke) trait m.

▸ **dash away, dash off** vi partir en vitesse.

dash·board tableau m de bord.

da·ta npl données fpl.

dat·a bank banque f de données.

dat·a pro·cess·ing informatique f.

date¹ 1 n (time) date f; (meeting) Fam rendez-vous m inv (galant); (person) Fam copain, -ine mf; **up to d.** moderne; (information) à jour; (well-informed) au courant (on de); **out of d.** (old-fashioned) démodé; (expired) périmé. **2** vt (letter etc) dater; (girl, boy) Fam sortir avec.

date² (fruit) datte f.

dat·ed adj démodé.

date stamp (tampon m) dateur m; (mark) cachet m.

daugh·ter fille f.

daugh·ter-in-law, pl daughters-in-law belle-fille f.

daw·dle vi traîner.

dawn aube f.

day jour m; (whole day long) journée f; **all d. (long)** toute la journée; **the following** or **next d.** le lendemain; **the day before** la veille; **the**

d. before yesterday avant-hier; **the d. after tomorrow** après-demain.

day·break point m du jour.

day·care (for ages 3 and below) crèche f, (for older children) garderie f.

day·light (lumière f du) jour m.

day·time journée f, jour m.

dead 1 adj mort; (battery) à plat. **2** adv (completely) absolument; (very) très.

dead-end (street) impasse f.

dead-line date f limite; (time) heure f limite.

dead·ly 1 adj mortel; **d. weapon** arme f meurtrière. **2** adv (very) mortellement.

deaf adj sourd; **d. and dumb** sourd-muet (f sourde-muette).

deaf·ness surdité f.

deal¹ a good or **great d.** (a lot) beaucoup (**of** de).

deal² n (in business) marché m, affaire f; **it's a d.** d'accord. **2** vi* (trade) traiter (**with sb** avec qn); **to d. in** faire le commerce de; **to d. with** s'occuper de; (concern) traiter de. **3** vt (cards) donner.

deal·er marchand, -ande mf (**in** de); (agent) dépositaire mf, (for cars) concessionnaire mf.

deal·ings npl relations fpl (**with** avec); (in business) transactions fpl.

dear 1 adj (loved, expensive) cher; **D. Sir** (in letter) Monsieur; **oh d.!** oh là là! **2** n (my) d. (darling) (mon) chéri, (ma) chérie; (friend) mon cher, ma chère.

death mort f.

death cer·tif·i·cate acte m de décès.

de·bate vti discuter. **2** n débat m, discussion f.

deb·it 1 n débit m; **my account shows a d. balance of** mon compte est débiteur de. **2** vt débiter (**sb with sth** qn de qch).

DATE AND TIME

Days of the week
lundi; mardi; mercredi; jeudi; vendredi; samedi; dimanche

Months of the year
janvier; février; mars; avril; mai; juin; juillet; août; septembre; octobre; novembre; décembre

Days and months are written without a capital letter in French. The first of the month is *le premier*, other dates are expressed in cardinal numbers (**March 3rd** *le trois mars*).

What day is it today?
On est quel jour aujourd'hui ?

It's Friday.
On est vendredi.

What's today's date?
On est le combien aujourd'hui ?

It's April 15th, 2008.
On est le quinze avril deux mille huit.

It's Wednesday April 12th.
On est le mercredi douze avril.

It's Thursday tomorrow.
Demain c'est jeudi.

I was born in 1980.
Je suis né(e) en mille neuf cent quatre-vingt.

I came to Paris a few years ago.
Je suis venu(e) à Paris il y a quelques années.

How long are you staying?
Vous restez jusqu'à quand ?

We leave on Sunday/the 8th.
Nous partons dimanche/le huit.

We got here last weekend.
Nous sommes arrivés le weekend dernier.

I waited all day.
J'ai attendu toute la journée.

See you on Saturday!
À samedi !

See you next week!
À la semaine prochaine !

> Use the masculine words an, jour, matin, soir when talking about time in general. Use the feminine année, journée, matinée, soirée to express duration.

Take it three times a day.
Prenez-le trois fois par jour.

I see them every two weeks.
Je les vois toutes les deux semaines.

> The French commonly use the 24-hour clock and write times with an *h* for *heure(s)*, eg 7.30 a.m. = 7h30 (*sept heures trente*), 7.30 p.m. = 19h30 (*dix-neuf heures trente*).

What's the time?
Quelle heure est-il ?

It's 2 o'clock.
Il est deux heures.

It's nearly midday/midnight.
Il est presque midi/minuit.

It's half four/four-thirty.
Il est quatre heures et demie/quatre heures trente.

It's a quarter to seven.
Il est sept heures moins le quart.

It's twenty after seven.
Il est sept heures vingt.

I'll be there about eight.
Je serai là vers huit heures.

I'll meet you in half an hour.
On se retrouve dans une demi-heure.

My plane was two hours late.
Mon avion a eu deux heures de retard.

I'm early/late/on time.
Je suis en avance/en retard/à l'heure.

I don't have time (to...).
Je n'ai pas le temps (de...).

It's time to go.
C'est l'heure de partir.

debt dette *f*; **to be in d.** avoir des dettes.

debt·or débiteur, -trice *mf*.

de·but début *m*; **to make one's d.** faire ses débuts.

dec·ade décennie *f*.

de·caf·fein·at·ed *adj* décaféiné.

de·cal décalcomanie *f*.

de·cay (*of tooth*) carie(s) *f(pl)*.

de·ceive *vti* tromper.

De·cem·ber décembre *m*.

de·cent *adj* (*respectable*) convenable, décent; (*good*) *Fam* bon; (*kind*) *Fam* gentil.

de·cep·tion tromperie *f*.

de·cide 1 *vt* (*question etc*) décider; **to d. to do** décider de faire; **to d. that** décider que. 2 *vi* (*make decisions*) décider (**on** de); (*make up one's mind*) se décider (**on doing** à faire); (*choose*) se décider (**on** pour).

dec·i·mal 1 *adj* **d. point** virgule *f*. 2 *n* décimale *f*.

de·ci·sion décision *f*.

de·ci·sive *adj* décisif; (*victory*) net (*f* nette).

deck (*of ship*) pont *m*; (*of cards*) jeu *m*; (*of house*) terrasse *f*.

deck-chair transat *m*.

de·clare *vt* déclarer (**that** que); (*verdict, result*) proclamer.

de·cline 1 *vi* (*become less*) (*of popularity etc*) être en baisse. 2 *vt* (*invitation*) refuser.

dec·o·rate *vt* (*cake, house, soldier*) décorer (**with** de); (*hat, skirt etc*) orner (**with** de); (*paint etc*) peindre (et tapisser).

dec·o·ra·tion décoration *f*.

dec·o·ra·tive *adj* décoratif.

dec·o·ra·tor peintre *m* décorateur; (*interior*) **d.** décorateur, -trice *mf*.

de·crease 1 *vti* diminuer. 2 *n* diminution *f* (**in** de).

de·cree 1 *n* (*by court*) jugement *m*. 2 *vt* décréter.

ded·i·cate *vt* consacrer (**to** à); (*book*) dédier (**to** à).

ded·i·cat·ed *adj* (*teacher etc*) consciencieux.

de·duct *vt* déduire (**from** de); (*from wage, account*) prélever (**from** sur).

de·duc·tion déduction *f*.

deed action *f*, acte *m*; (*document*) acte *m* (notarié).

deep *adj* profond; (*voice*) grave; **to be 20 feet/etc d.** avoir six mètres/ *etc* de profondeur; **the d. end** (*in pool*) le grand bain.

deep-freeze 1 *vt* surgeler. 2 *n* congélateur *m*.

deer *inv* cerf *m*.

de·fault **by d.** par défaut; **to win by d.** gagner par forfait.

de·feat 1 *vt* battre. 2 *n* défaite *f*.

de·fect défaut *m*.

de·fec·tive *adj* défectueux.

de·fend *vt* défendre.

de·fen·dant (*accused*) prévenu, -ue *mf*.

de·fense défense *f*.

de·fen·sive 1 *adj* défensif; **to be d.** être sur la défensive. 2 *n* **to be on the d.** être sur la défensive.

de·fi·ant *adj* (*tone, attitude*) de défi; (*person*) rebelle.

de·fi·cien·cy manque *m*; (*of vitamins etc*) carence *f*.

de·fi·cient *adj* insuffisant; **to be d. in** manquer de.

def·i·cit déficit *m*.

de·fine *vt* définir.

def·i·nite *adj* (*date, plan*) précis; (*reply, improvement*) net (*f* nette); (*order, offer*) ferme; (*certain*) certain; **d. article** *Grammar* article *m* défini.

def·i·nite·ly *adv* certainement; (*considerably*) nettement; (*to say*) catégoriquement.

def·i·ni·tion définition *f*.

de·formed *adj* (*body*) difforme.

de·frost *vt* (*fridge*) dégivrer; (*food*) décongeler.

de·fy vt défier (qn); **to d. sb to do** défier qn de faire.

de·gen·er·ate vi dégénérer (**into** en).

de·gree (angle, temperature) degré m; (from university) diplôme m; (Bachelor's) licence f; (Master's) maîtrise f; (PhD) doctorat m; **to such a d.** à tel point (**that** que).

de·ice vt (car window etc) dégivrer.

de·ic·er (substance) dégivreur m.

de·ject·ed adj abattu.

de·lay 1 vt retarder; (payment) différer. **2** vi (be slow) tarder (**doing** à faire); (linger) s'attarder. **3** n retard m; (waiting period) délai m; **without d.** sans tarder.

del·e·gate 1 vt déléguer (**to** à). **2** n délégué, -ée mf.

del·e·ga·tion délégation f.

de·lete vt rayer.

de·lib·er·ate adj (intentional) intentionnel.

de·liber·ate·ly adv (intentionally) exprès.

del·i·ca·cy (food) mets m délicat.

del·i·cate adj délicat.

del·i·ca·tes·sen traiteur m, épicerie f fine.

de·li·cious adj délicieux.

de·light 1 n délice m; **to take d. in sth/in doing** se délecter de qch/à faire. **2** vt réjouir. **3** vi **to d. in doing** se délecter à faire.

de·light·ed adj ravi (**with** sth de qch; **to do** de faire; **that** que).

de·light·ful adj charmant; (meal) délicieux.

de·lin·quent délinquant, -ante mf.

de·liv·er vt (goods etc) livrer; (letters) distribuer; (hand over) remettre (**to** à); (speech) prononcer; (warning) lancer.

de·liv·er·y livraison f; (of letters) distribution f; (handing over) remise f; (birth) accouchement m.

de·lude vt tromper; **to d. oneself** se faire des illusions.

de·lu·sion illusion f.

de·luxe adj de luxe.

de·mand 1 vt exiger (sth from sb qch de qn); (rights, more pay) revendiquer; **to d. that** exiger que. **2** n exigence f; (claim) revendication f; (for goods) demande f; **in great d.** très demandé.

de·mand·ing adj exigeant.

dem·o Fam (demonstration) manif f; **d. tape** cassette f de démonstration.

de·moc·ra·cy démocratie f.

dem·o·crat·ic adj démocratique; (person) démocrate.

de·mol·ish vt démolir.

dem·o·li·tion démolition f.

de·mon démon m.

dem·on·strate 1 vt démontrer; (machine) faire une démonstration de. **2** vi manifester.

dem·on·stra·tion démonstration f; (protest) manifestation f.

de·mon·stra·tive adj & n Grammar démonstratif (m).

dem·on·stra·tor (protester) manifestant, -ante mf.

de·mor·al·ize vt démoraliser.

den tanière f.

de·ni·al (of rumor) démenti m.

den·im (toile f de) coton m.

de·nounce vt (person, injustice etc) dénoncer (**to** à).

dense adj dense; (stupid) Fam lourd, bête.

dent 1 n (in car etc) bosse f. **2** vt cabosser.

den·tal adj dentaire.

den·tist dentiste mf.

den·tures npl dentier m.

de·ny vt nier (**doing** avoir fait; **that** que); (rumor) démentir; **to d. sb sth** refuser qch à qn.

de·o·dor·ant déodorant m.

de·part vi partir; (deviate) s'écarter (**from** de).

de·part·ment département m; (in office) service m; (in shop) rayon m; (of government) = ministère m;

D. of State Ministère des Affaires Etrangères.
de·part·ment store grand magasin *m*.
de·par·ture départ *m*; **a d. from** *(rule)* un écart par rapport à.
de·pend *vi* dépendre (**on, upon** de); **to d. (up)on** *(rely on)* compter sur (**for sth** pour qch).
de·pend·a·ble *adj* sûr.
de·pen·dant personne *f* à charge.
de·pen·dent *adj* dépendant; **to be d. on sth** dépendre de qch.
de·pict *vt (describe)* dépeindre; *(in pictures)* représenter.
de·plor·a·ble *adj* déplorable.
de·plore *adj* déplorer.
de·pos·it **1** *vt* déposer; **to d.** *(check)* verser (**to one's account** sur son compte). **2** *n* dépôt *m*; *(part payment)* acompte *m*, arrhes *fpl*; *(against damage)* caution *f*; *(on bottle)* consigne *f*.
de·pot *(railroad station)* gare *f*; **bus d.** gare *f* routière.
de·press *vt (discourage)* déprimer.
de·pressed *adj* déprimé; **to get d.** se décourager.
de·pres·sion dépression *f*.
de·prive *vt* priver (**of** de).
de·prived *adj (child etc)* déshérité.
depth profondeur *f*.
dep·u·ty *(replacement)* remplaçant, -ante *mf*; *(assistant)* adjoint, -ointe *mf*.
de·rail·ment déraillement *m*.
der·e·lict *adj* abandonné.
de·rive *vt* **to d. from sth** *(pleasure etc)* tirer de qch; **to be derived from** *(of word etc)* dériver de.
de·scend *vi* descendre (**from** de). **2** *vt (stairs)* descendre.
de·scen·dant descendant, -ante *mf*.
► **descend upon** *vt (of tourists)* envahir.
de·scent *(of aircraft etc)* descente *f*.

de·scribe *vt* décrire.
de·scrip·tion description *f*; *(on passport)* signalement *m*; **of every d.** de toutes sortes.
des·ert¹ désert *m*; **d. island** île *f* déserte.
de·sert² *vt* abandonner.
de·sert·ed *adj (place)* désert.
de·serve *vt* mériter (**to do** de faire).
de·sign **1** *vt (car etc)* dessiner; **designed to do/for sb** conçu pour faire/pour qn; **well designed** bien conçu. **2** *n (pattern)* motif *m*; *(sketch)* plan *m*, dessin *m*; *(type of dress or car)* modèle *m*.
des·ig·nate *vt* désigner.
de·sign·er dessinateur, -trice *mf*.
de·sign·er clothes vêtements *mpl* griffés.
de·sir·a·ble *adj* désirable.
de·sire **1** *n* désir *m*; **I have no d. to** je n'ai aucune envie de. **2** *vt* désirer (**to do** faire).
desk *(in school)* pupitre *m*; *(in office)* bureau *m*; *(in shop)* caisse *f*; *(reception)* réception *f*.
desk clerk *(in hotel)* réceptionniste *mf*.
desk·top bureau *m*; **d. publishing** publication *f* assistée par ordinateur.
de·spair **1** *n* désespoir *m*; **to be in d.** être au désespoir. **2** *vi* désespérer (**of sb** de qn; **of doing** de faire).
des·per·ate *adj* désespéré; **to be d. for** avoir désespérément besoin de; *(cigarette, baby)* mourir d'envie d'avoir.
des·pic·a·ble *adj* méprisable.
de·spise *vt* mépriser.
de·spite *prep* malgré.
des·sert dessert *m*.
des·sert·spoon cuillère *f* à dessert.
des·ti·na·tion destination *f*.
des·ti·tute *adj* indigent.
de·stroy *vt* détruire.
de·struc·tion destruction *f*.

de·struc·tive adj destructeur.
de·tach vt détacher (**from** de).
de·tach·a·ble adj (lining) amovible.
de·tached house maison f individuelle.
de·tail détail m; **in d.** en détail.
de·tailed adj détaillé.
de·tain vt retenir; (prisoner) détenir.
de·tect (find) découvrir; (see, hear) distinguer.
de·tec·tive inspecteur m de police; (private) détective m.
de·tec·tor détecteur m.
de·ten·tion (school punishment) retenue f.
de·ter vt **to d. sb** dissuader qn (**from doing** de faire; **from sth** de qch).
de·ter·gent détergent m.
de·te·ri·o·rate vi se détériorer.
de·te·ri·o·ra·tion détérioration f.
de·ter·mi·na·tion (intention) ferme intention f.
de·ter·mine vt déterminer; (price) fixer.
de·ter·mined adj déterminé; **d. to do** or **on doing** décidé à faire.
de·ter·rent **to be a d.** être dissuasif.
de·test vt détester (**doing** faire).
de·tour déviation f.
dev·as·tat·ing adj (news, results) accablant.
de·vel·op 1 vt développer; (area, land) mettre en valeur; (habit, illness) contracter. 2 vi se développer.
▸ **develop into** vt devenir.
de·vel·op·ment développement m; **housing d.** lotissement m; (large) grand ensemble m; **a (new) d.** (in situation) un fait nouveau.
de·vi·ate vi dévier (**from** de).
de·vice dispositif m; **left to one's own devices** livré à soi-même.
dev·il diable m; **what/where/why the d.?** que/où/pourquoi diable?

de·vise vt (a plan) combiner; (invent) inventer.
de·vote vt consacrer (**to** à).
de·vot·ed adj dévoué.
de·vo·tion dévouement m (**to sb** à qn).
dew rosée f.
di·a·be·tes diabète m.
di·a·bet·ic diabétique mf.
di·ag·nose vt diagnostiquer.
di·ag·no·sis, pl **-oses** diagnostic m.
di·ag·o·nal 1 adj diagonal. 2 n **d.** (line) diagonale f.
di·ag·o·nal·ly adv en diagonale.
di·a·gram schéma m.
di·al 1 n cadran m. 2 vt (phone number) faire; (person) appeler.
di·a·lect dialecte m.
di·al tone tonalité f.
di·a·log dialogue m.
di·am·e·ter diamètre m.
di·a·mond diamant m; (shape) losange m; Baseball terrain m; **diamond(s)** Cards carreau m; **d. necklace** collier m de diamants.
di·a·per couche f.
di·ar·rhe·a diarrhée f.
di·a·ry journal m (intime).
dice 1 n inv dé m (à jouer). 2 vt (food) couper en dés.
dic·tate vti dicter (**to** à).
dic·ta·tion dictée f.
dic·tion·ar·y dictionnaire m.
did pt de **do**.
die* vi mourir (**of**, **from** de); **to be dying to do** mourir d'envie de faire; **to be dying for sth** avoir une envie folle de qch.
▸ **die away** vi (of noise) mourir.
▸ **die down** vi (of storm) se calmer.
▸ **die out** vi (of custom) mourir.
die·sel adj & n **d.** (engine) (moteur m) diesel m; **d.** (oil) gazole m.
di·et 1 n (to lose weight) régime m; (usual food) alimentation f; **to go on a d.** faire un régime. 2 vi suivre un régime.
dif·fer vi différer (**from** de); (dis-

agree) ne pas être d'accord (**from** avec).

dif·fer·ence différence *f* (**in** de); **d. (of opinion)** différend *m;* **it makes no d.** ça n'a pas d'importance; **it makes no d. to me** ça m'est égal.

dif·fer·ent *adj* différent (**from, to** de); *(another)* autre; *(various)* divers.

differ·ent·ly *adv* autrement (**from, to** que).

dif·fi·cult *adj* difficile (**to do** à faire); **it's d. for us to** il nous est difficile de.

dif·fi·cul·ty difficulté *f;* **to have d. doing** avoir du mal à faire.

dig* 1 *vt* (*ground*) bêcher; *(hole)* creuser. 2 *vi* creuser.

di·gest *vti* digérer.

di·ges·tion digestion *f.*

dig·ger *(machine)* pelleteuse *f.*

dig·it *(number)* chiffre *m.*

dig·i·tal *adj* numérique.

dig·ni·ty *vt* dignité *f.*

▶ **dig out** *vt* (*from ground*) déterrer; *(accident victim)* dégager; *(find)* dénicher.

▶ **dig up** *vt* (*from ground*) déterrer; *(weed)* arracher; *(earth)* retourner; *(street)* piocher.

di·lap·i·dat·ed *adj* délabré.

di·lem·ma dilemme *f.*

di·lute *vt* diluer.

dim 1 *adj* (*light*) faible; *(room)* sombre; *(memory, outline)* vague; *(person)* stupide. 2 *vt* (*light*) baisser; **to d. one's headlights** se mettre en code.

dime (pièce *f* de) dix cents *mpl;* **d. store** magasin *m* à prix unique.

di·men·sion dimension *f.*

di·min·ish *vti* diminuer.

dimmed head·lights codes *mpl.*

din vacarme *m.*

dine *vi* dîner (**on** de).

▶ **dine out** *vi* dîner en ville.

din·er dîneur, -euse *mf;* (*restaurant*) petit restaurant *m.*

din·ghy petit canot *m;* (**rubber**) d. canot *m* pneumatique.

din·gy *adj* (*room etc*) minable; *(color)* terne.

din·ing car wagon-restaurant *m.*

din·ing room salle *f* à manger.

din·ner dîner *m;* (*lunch*) déjeuner *m;* **to have d.** dîner.

din·ner jack·et smoking *m.*

din·ner par·ty dîner *m* (à la maison).

din·ner ser·vice *or* **set** service *m* de table.

di·no·saur dinosaure *m.*

dip 1 *vt* plonger. 2 *vi* (*of road*) plonger; **to d. into** (*pocket, savings*) puiser dans. 3 *n* (*in road*) petit creux *m;* **to go for a d.** (*swim*) faire trempette.

diph·thong diphtongue *f.*

di·plo·ma diplôme *m.*

dip·lo·mat diplomate *mf.*

dip·lo·mat·ic *adj* Pol diplomatique; *(tactful)* diplomate.

di·rect 1 *adj* direct. 2 *adv* directement. 3 *vt* diriger; *(remark)* adresser (**to** à); **to d. sb to** (*place*) indiquer à qn le chemin de.

di·rec·tion direction *f,* **directions** (**for use**) mode *m* d'emploi; **in the opposite d.** en sens inverse.

di·rect·ly 1 *adv* directement; *(at once)* tout de suite. 2 *conj* aussitôt que (+ *indicative*).

di·rec·tor directeur, -trice *mf;* (*board member in firm*) administrateur, -trice *mf;* (*of film*) metteur *m* en scène.

di·rec·to·ry (**telephone**) d. annuaire *m* (téléphonique).

di·rec·to·ry as·sis·tance renseignements *mpl.*

dirt saleté *f,* (*earth*) terre *f,* **d. cheap** *Fam* très bon marché.

dirt·y 1 *adj* sale; *(job)* salissant; *(word)* grossier; **to get d.** se salir; **to get sth d.** salir qch; **a d. joke** une histoire cochonne. 2 *vt* salir.

dis- *prefix* dé-, dés-.

dis·a·bil·i·ty infirmité f.

dis·a·bled 1 adj handicapé. **2** n the d. les handicapés mpl.

dis·ad·van·tage désavantage m.

dis·a·gree vi ne pas être d'accord (with avec); **to d. with sb** (of food etc) ne pas réussir à qn.

dis·a·gree·a·ble adj désagréable.

dis·a·gree·ment désaccord m; (quarrel) différend m.

dis·ap·pear vi disparaître.

dis·ap·pear·ance disparition f.

dis·ap·point vt décevoir; **I'm disappointed with it** ça m'a déçu.

dis·ap·point·ing adj décevant.

dis·ap·point·ment déception f.

dis·ap·prov·al désapprobation f.

dis·ap·prove vi **to d. of sb/sth** désapprouver qn/qch; **I d.** je suis contre.

dis·arm vt désarmer.

dis·as·ter désastre m.

dis·as·trous adj désastreux.

dis·card vt se débarrasser de.

dis·charge vt (patient, employee) renvoyer; (soldier) libérer.

dis·ci·pline 1 n discipline f. **2** vt discipliner; (punish) punir.

disc jock·ey disc-jockey m.

dis·close vt révéler.

dis·co, pl -os disco f.

dis·com·fort douleur f; **I have d. in my wrist** mon poignet me gêne.

dis·con·nect vt détacher; (unplug) débrancher; (wires) déconnecter; (gas, telephone) couper.

dis·con·tent·ed adj mécontent.

dis·con·tin·ued adj (article) qui ne se fait plus.

dis·co·theque (club) discothèque f.

dis·count (on article) remise f, réduction f; **at a d.** à prix réduit.

dis·count store solderie f.

dis·cour·age vt décourager; **to get discouraged** se décourager.

dis·cov·er vt découvrir (that que).

dis·cov·er·y découverte f.

dis·creet adj discret.

dis·crim·i·nate vi **to d. against** faire de la discrimination contre.

dis·crim·i·na·tion (against sb) discrimination f.

dis·cuss vt discuter de; (plan, question, price) discuter.

dis·cus·sion discussion f.

dis·ease maladie f.

dis·em·bark vti débarquer.

dis·fig·ured adj défiguré.

dis·grace 1 n (shame) honte f (to à). **2** vt déshonorer.

dis·grace·ful adj honteux.

dis·guise 1 vt déguiser (as en). **2** n déguisement m; **in d.** déguisé.

dis·gust 1 n dégoût m (for, at, with de); **in d.** dégoûté. **2** vt dégoûter.

dis·gust·ed adj dégoûté (at, by, with de); **d. with sb** (annoyed) fâché contre qn.

dis·gust·ing adj dégoûtant.

dish (container, food) plat m; **the dishes** la vaisselle; **to do the dishes** faire la vaisselle.

dish·cloth (for washing) lavette f; (for drying) torchon m.

di·shev·eled adj débraillé.

dis·hon·est adj malhonnête.

dis·hon·es·ty malhonnêteté f.

▶ **dish out, dish up** vt (food) servir.

dish tow·el torchon m.

dish·wash·er (machine) lave-vaisselle m inv.

dis·il·lu·sioned adj déçu (with de).

dis·in·cen·tive mesure f dissuasive.

dis·in·fect vt désinfecter.

dis·in·fec·tant désinfectant m.

disk disque m.

dis·like 1 vt ne pas aimer (doing faire). **2** n aversion f (for, of pour); **to take a d. to sb/sth** prendre qn/qch en grippe.

dis·lo·cate vt (limb) démettre.

dis·mal adj morne.

dis·man·tle vt (machine) démonter.

dis·may vt consterner.

dis·miss vt (from job) renvoyer (**from** de).

dis·miss·al renvoi m.

dis·o·be·di·ence désobéissance f.

dis·o·be·di·ent adj désobéissant.

dis·o·bey 1 vt désobéir à. 2 vi désobéir.

dis·or·der (confusion) désordre m; (illness) troubles mpl.

dis·or·gan·ized adj désorganisé.

dis·patch vt expédier; (troops, messenger) envoyer.

dis·pel vt dissiper.

dis·pens·er (device) distributeur m; **cash d.** distributeur m de billets.

dis·perse 1 vt disperser. 2 vi se disperser.

dis·play 1 vt montrer; (notice, electronic data) afficher; (painting, goods) exposer; (courage etc) faire preuve de. 2 n (in shop) étalage m; (of data) affichage m; **on d.** exposé.

dis·pleased adj mécontent (**with** de).

dis·pos·a·ble adj (plate etc) à jeter, jetable.

dis·pos·al **at the d. of** à la disposition de.

dis·pose vi **to d. of** (get rid of) se débarrasser de; (sell) vendre.

dis·pute 1 n (quarrel) dispute f; (industrial) conflit m. 2 vt contester.

dis·qual·i·fy vt rendre inapte (**from** à); (in sport) disqualifier.

dis·re·gard vt ne tenir aucun compte de.

dis·re·spect·ful adj irrespectueux.

dis·rupt vt (traffic, class etc) perturber; (plan etc) déranger.

dis·rup·tion perturbation f; (of plan etc) dérangement m.

dis·rup·tive adj (child) turbulent.

dis·sat·is·fac·tion mécontentement m.

dis·sat·is·fied adj mécontent (**with** de).

dis·sent 1 n désaccord m. 2 vi être en désaccord (**from** avec).

dis·solve 1 vt dissoudre. 2 vi se dissoudre.

dis·suade vt dissuader (**from doing** de faire).

dis·tance distance f; **in the d.** au loin; **from a d.** de loin; **it's within walking d.** on peut y aller à pied; **to keep one's d.** garder ses distances.

dis·tant adj éloigné; (reserved) distant.

dis·taste aversion f (**for** pour).

dis·taste·ful adj désagréable.

dis·tinct adj (voice, light) distinct; (difference, improvement) net (f nette); (different) distinct (**from** de).

dis·tinc·tion distinction f; (at graduation) **with d.** avec mention f.

dis·tinc·tive adj distinctif.

dis·tinct·ly adv distinctement; (definitely) sensiblement.

dis·tin·guish vti distinguer (**from** de; **between** entre).

dis·tin·guished adj distingué.

dis·tort vt déformer.

dis·tract vt distraire (**from** de).

dis·trac·tion distraction f.

dis·tress (pain) douleur f; (anguish) détresse f; **in d.** (ship) en détresse.

dis·tress·ing adj affligeant.

dis·trib·ute vt distribuer; (spread evenly) répartir.

dis·tri·bu·tion distribution f.

dis·trib·u·tor (in car) distributeur m; (of goods) concessionnaire mf.

dis·trict région f; (of town) quartier m; **d. attorney** = procureur m (de la République).

dis·trust vt se méfier de.

dis·turb vt (sleep) troubler; (pa-

pers, belongings) déranger; **to d. sb** *(bother)* déranger qn; *(worry)* troubler qn.

dis·tur·bance *(noise)* tapage *m*; **disturbances** *(riots)* troubles *mpl*.

dis·turb·ing *adj (worrying)* inquiétant.

ditch fossé *m*.

dit·to *adv* idem.

di·van divan *m*.

dive* **1** *vi* plonger; *(rush)* se précipiter. **2** *n (of swimmer, goalkeeper)* plongeon *m*; *(of aircraft)* piqué *m*.

div·er plongeur, -euse *mf*.

di·ver·sion *(on road)* déviation *f*; *(distraction)* diversion *f*.

di·vert *vt (traffic)* dévier; *(aircraft)* dérouter.

di·vide *vt* diviser (**into** en); *(share out)* partager; *(separate)* séparer (**from** de).

▶**divide off** *vt* séparer (**from sth** de qch).

▶**divide up** *vt (share out)* partager.

di·vid·ed high·way route *f* à quatre voies.

div·i·dend dividende *m*.

div·ing plongée *f* sous-marine.

div·ing board plongeoir *m*.

di·vi·sion division *f*.

di·vorce **1** *n* divorce *m*. **2** *vt (husband, wife)* divorcer d'avec.

di·vorced *adj* divorcé (**from** d'avec); **to get d.** divorcer.

DIY *abbr (do-it-yourself)* bricolage *m*.

diz·zi·ness vertige *m*.

diz·zy *adj* **to be** *or* **feel d.** avoir le vertige; **to make sb (feel) d.** donner le vertige à qn.

DJ *abbr* = **disc jockey**.

do* **1** *v aux* **do you know?** savez-vous?, est-ce que vous savez?; **I do not** *or* **don't see** je ne vois pas; **he did say so** *(emphasis)* il l'a bien dit; **do stay** reste donc; **you know him, don't you?** tu le connais, n'est-ce pas?; **neither do I** moi non plus; **so do I** moi aussi. **2** *vt* faire; **what does**

she do? *(in general)*, **what is she doing?** *(now)* qu'est-ce qu'elle fait?; **what have you done (with)...?** qu'as-tu fait (de)...?; **well done** *(congratulations)* bravo!; *(steak)* bien cuit; **to do sb out of sth** escroquer qch à qn; **he's done for** *Fam* il est fichu. **3** *vi (get along)* aller; *(suit)* faire l'affaire; *(be enough)* suffire; *(finish)* finir; **how do you do?** *(introduction)* enchanté; **he did well** *or* **right to leave** il a bien fait de partir; **do as I do** fais comme moi; **to have to do with** *(relate to)* avoir à voir avec; *(concern)* concerner.

▶**do away with** *vt* supprimer.

dock **1** *n (for ship)* dock *m*. **2** *vi (at pier)* se mettre à quai.

dock·er docker *m*.

dock·yard chantier *m* naval.

doc·tor médecin *m*; *(academic)* docteur *m*.

doc·tor·ate doctorat *m*.

doc·trine doctrine *f*.

doc·u·ment document *m*.

doc·u·men·ta·ry *(film)* documentaire *m*.

dodge **1** *vt* esquiver; *(pursuer)* échapper à; *(tax)* éviter de payer. **2** *vi* **to d. through** *(crowd)* se faufiler dans.

does *see* **do**.

dog chien *m*; *(female)* chienne *f*; **d. food** pâtée *f*.

dog·gy bag *(in restaurant)* petit sac *m* pour emporter les restes.

dog·house niche *f*.

dog tags plaque *f* d'identité.

do·ing **that's your d.** c'est toi qui as fait ça.

do-it-your·self **1** *n* bricolage *m*. **2** *adj (store, book)* de bricolage.

doll poupée *f*.

dol·lar dollar *m*.

doll·house maison *f* de poupée.

dol·phin dauphin *m*.

do·main domaine *m*; **d. name** nom *m* de domaine.

dome dôme m.
do·mes·tic adj domestique; (trade, flight) intérieur.
dom·i·nant adj dominant; (person) dominateur.
dom·i·nate vti dominer.
dom·i·no domino m; dominoes (game) dominos mpl.
do·nate 1 vt faire don de; (blood) donner. 2 vi donner.
do·na·tion don m.
don·key âne m.
do·nor (to charity) donateur, -trice mf; (of organ, blood) donneur, -euse mf.
door porte f.
door·bell sonnette f.
door·knob poignée f de porte.
door·knock·er marteau m.
door·man, pl **-men** (of hotel) portier m.
door·mat paillasson m.
door·step seuil m.
door·stop butoir m (de porte).
door·way in the d. dans l'encadrement de la porte.
▸ **do over** vt (redecorate) refaire.
dope (drugs) Fam drogue f.
dor·mi·to·ry dortoir m; (at university) résidence f (universitaire).
dos·age (amount) dose f.
dose dose f.
dot point m.
dot·ted line pointillé m.
dou·ble 1 adj double; **a d. bed** un grand lit; **a d. room** une chambre pour deux personnes. 2 adv (twice) deux fois, le double; (to fold) en deux. 3 n double m. 4 vti doubler.
▸ **double back** vi (of person) revenir en arrière.
dou·ble-breast·ed adj (jacket) croisé.
dou·ble-cross vt trahir, doubler.
dou·ble-deck·er (bus) autobus m à impériale.
dou·ble-glaz·ing double vitrage m.

▸ **double up** vi (with pain, laughter) être plié en deux.
doubt 1 n doute m; **no d.** (probably) sans doute. 2 vt douter de; **to d. whether** or **that** or **if** douter que (+ subjunctive).
doubt·ful adj **to be d.** (about sth) avoir des doutes (sur qch); **it's d. whether** or **that** or **if** ce n'est pas sûr que (+ subjunctive).
doubt·less adj sans doute.
dough pâte f, (money) Fam fric m.
dough·nut beignet m (rond).
▸ **do up** vt (coat, button) boutonner; (zipper) fermer; (house) refaire, décorer; (goods) emballer.
dove colombe f.
▸ **do with** vt **I could do with that** j'aimerais bien ça.
▸ **do without** vt se passer de.
down 1 adv en bas; (to the ground) par terre; (of curtain, temperature) baissé; (in writing) inscrit; (out of bed) descendu; **to come** or **go d.** descendre; **d. there** or **here** en bas; **d. with flu** grippé; **to feel d.** avoir le cafard. 2 prep (at bottom of) en bas de; (from top to bottom of) du haut en bas de; (along) le long de; **to go d.** (hill, street, stairs) descendre.
down-and-out adj **to be d.** être sur le pavé.
down·fall chute f.
down·hill adv **to go d.** descendre; (of sick person, business) aller de plus en plus mal.
down·load 1 n téléchargement m. 2 vt télécharger.
down pay·ment acompte m, arrhes fpl.
down·pour averse f.
down·right 1 adj (rogue etc) véritable; (refusal) catégorique. 2 adv (rude etc) franchement.
down·stairs 1 adj (room, neighbors) d'en bas. 2 adv en bas; **to come** or **go d.** descendre l'escalier.
down-to-earth adj terre-à-terre.
down·town adj au centre-

ville; **d. Chicago** le centre de Chicago.

down·ward(s) *adv* vers le bas.

doze 1 *n* petit somme *m*. **2** *vi* sommeiller.

doz·en douzaine *f*; **a d.** *(books etc)* une douzaine de.

▸ **doze off** *vi* s'assoupir.

Dr *abbr (Doctor)* Docteur.

drab *adj* terne; *(weather)* gris.

draft courant *m* d'air.

draft beer bière *f* pression.

draft·y *adj (room)* plein de courants d'air.

drag *vti* traîner.

▸ **drag along** *vt* (en)traîner.

▸ **drag away** arracher *(from* à).

drag·on dragon *m*.

▸ **drag on, drag out** *vi (last a long time)* se prolonger, s'éterniser.

drain 1 *n (sewer)* égout *m*; *(outside house)* puisard *m*; *(in street)* bouche *f* d'égout. **2** *vt (tank)* vider; *(vegetables)* égoutter.

drain (off) 1 *vt (liquid)* faire écouler. **2** *vi (of liquid)* s'écouler.

drain·board paillasse *f*.

drain·er *(board)* paillasse *f*, *(rack, basket)* égouttoir *m*.

drain·pipe tuyau *m* d'évacuation.

dra·ma *(event)* drame *m*; *(dramatic art)* théâtre *m*.

dra·mat·ic *adj* dramatique; *(very great, striking)* spectaculaire.

dra·mat·i·cal·ly *adv (to change etc)* de façon spectaculaire.

drapes *npl (heavy curtains)* rideaux *mpl*.

dras·tic *adj* radical.

dras·ti·cal·ly *adv* radicalement.

draw¹* **1** *n (in sports, games)* match *m* nul. **2** *vt* (pull) tirer; *(attract)* attirer.

draw²* *vt (picture)* dessiner; *(circle)* tracer. **2** *vi* dessiner.

draw·back inconvénient *m*.

draw·er tiroir *m*.

draw·ing dessin *m*.

draw·ing room salon *m*.

▸ **draw near** *vi* s'approcher; *(of time)* approcher.

▸ **draw near to** *vt* s'approcher de; *(of time)* approcher de.

▸ **draw on** *vt (savings)* puiser dans.

▸ **draw up 1** *vt (list, plan)* dresser. **2** *vi (of vehicle)* s'arrêter.

dread 1 *vt (exam etc)* appréhender; **to d. doing** appréhender de faire. **2** *n* crainte *f*.

dread·ful *adj* épouvantable; *(child)* insupportable; *(ill)* malade.

dread·ful·ly *adv* terriblement; **to be d. sorry** regretter infiniment.

dream 1 *vi* * rêver *(of* de; *of going* de faire). **2** *vt* rêver *(that* que). **3** *n* rêve *m*; **to have a d.** faire un rêve *(about* de); **a d. house**/*etc* une maison/*etc* de rêve.

▸ **dream up** *vt* imaginer.

drea·ry *adj (gloomy)* morne; *(boring)* ennuyeux.

drench *vt* tremper; **to get drenched** se faire tremper.

dress 1 *n (woman's)* robe *f*, *(style of dressing)* tenue *f*. **2** *vt (person)* habiller; *(wound)* panser; **to get dressed** s'habiller. **3** *vi* s'habiller.

dress·er *(furniture)* coiffeuse *f*.

dress·mak·er couturière *f*.

▸ **dress up** *vi (smartly)* bien s'habiller; *(in disguise)* se déguiser *(as* en).

drew *pt de* **draw¹,²**.

drib·ble 1 *vi (of person)* couler lentement. **2** *vti (in sports)* dribbler.

dried *adj (fruit)* sec *(f* sèche); *(flowers)* séché.

drift *vi* être emporté par le vent *or* le courant, dériver.

drill 1 *n (tool)* perceuse *f*, *(bit)* mèche *f*, *(dentist's)* roulette *f*. **2** *vt (hole)* percer.

drink 1 *n* boisson *f*, *(glass of sth)* verre *m*; **to give sb a d.** donner (quelque chose) à boire à qn. **2** *vt* * boire *(out of* dans); **to d. to sb** boire à la santé de qn.

drink·a·ble *adj* potable; *(not unpleasant)* buvable.

▸**drink down** *vt* boire.

drink·ing wa·ter eau *f* potable.

▸**drink up 1** *vt* boire. **2** *vi* finir son verre.

drip 1 *vi* dégouliner; *(of laundry, vegetables)* s'égoutter; *(of faucet)* fuir. **2** *vt (paint etc)* laisser couler. **3** *n* goutte *f*; *(fool) Fam* nouille *f*.

drip-dry *adj (shirt etc)* sans repassage.

drip·ping *adj & adv* **d. (wet)** dégoulinant.

drive 1 *n* promenade *f* en voiture; *(energy)* énergie *f*; *(road to house)* allée *f*; **an hour's d.** une heure de voiture; **four-wheel d. (vehicle)** quatre-quatre *m*. **2** *vt* (vehicle, train, passenger)* conduire; *(machine)* actionner; *(chase away)* chasser; **to d. sb to do** pousser qn à faire; **to d. sb mad or crazy** rendre qn fou. **3** *vi (drive a car)* conduire; *(go by car)* rouler.

▸**drive along** *vi (in car)* rouler.

▸**drive away 1** *vt (chase)* chasser. **2** *vi* partir (en voiture).

▸**drive back 1** *vt (enemy)* repousser; *(passenger)* ramener (en voiture). **2** *vi* revenir (en voiture).

▸**drive in** *vt (nail)* enfoncer.

driv·el idioties *fpl*.

▸**drive off** *vi* partir (en voiture).

▸**drive on** *vi (in car)* continuer.

▸**drive out** *vt (chase away)* chasser.

driv·er conducteur, -trice *mf*; *(train or engine)* **d.** mécanicien *m*; **she's a good d.** elle conduit bien.

driv·er's li·cense permis *m* de conduire.

▸**drive up** *vi* arriver (en voiture).

driv·ing conduite *f*.

driv·ing les·son leçon *f* de conduite.

driv·ing school auto-école *f*.

driv·ing test examen *m* du permis de conduire.

driz·zle 1 *n* bruine *f*. **2** *vi* bruiner.

drool *vi* baver.

droop *vi (of flower)* se faner.

drop 1 *n (of liquid)* goutte *f*; *(fall)* baisse *f* (en **d.** in de). **2** *vt* laisser tomber; *(price, voice)* baisser; *(passenger, goods from vehicle)* déposer; *(put)* mettre; *(leave out)* omettre; **to d. a line** to écrire un mot à. **3** *vi* tomber; *(of price)* baisser.

▸**drop back, drop behind** *vi* rester en arrière.

▸**drop in** *vi (visit)* passer (**to sb's house** chez qn).

▸**drop off 1** *vi (fall asleep)* s'endormir; *(fall off)* tomber; *(of sales)* diminuer. **2** *vt (passenger)* déposer.

▸**drop out** *vi (withdraw)* se retirer.

drought sécheresse *f*.

drown 1 *vi* se noyer. **2** *vt* **to d. oneself, to be drowned** se noyer.

drows·y *adj* **to be** *or* **feel d.** avoir sommeil.

drug 1 *n* médicament *m*; *(narcotic)* stupéfiant *m*; **drugs** *(narcotics in general)* la drogue; **to be on drugs, to take drugs** se droguer. **2** *vt* droguer *(qn)*.

drug ad·dict drogué, -ée *mf*.

drug deal·er trafiquant *m* de drogue.

drug·gist pharmacien, -ienne *mf*.

drug·store drugstore *m*.

drum tambour *m*; *(for oil)* bidon *m*; **the drums** *(in pop or jazz group)* la batterie.

drum·mer *(joueur, -euse* *mf* de) tambour *m*; *(in pop or jazz group)* batteur *m*.

drum·stick baguette *f* (de tambour); *(of chicken)* pilon *m*.

drunk *(pp of drink)* **1** *adj* ivre; **to get d.** s'enivrer; **d. driving** conduite *f* en état d'ivresse. **2** *n* ivrogne *mf*.

drunk·ard ivrogne *mf*.

dry 1 *adj* sec (*f* sèche); *(well, river)* à sec; *(day)* sans pluie; *(book)* aride; **to feel** *or* **be d.** *(thirsty)* avoir soif. **2** *vt* sécher; *(by wiping)* essuyer.

dry-clean *vt* nettoyer à sec.

dry clean·er teinturier, -ière *mf*.

dry clean·ing nettoyage *m* à sec.

dry·er séchoir *m*; *(helmet-style for hair)* casque *m*; *(for laundry)* sèche-linge *m*.

▸ **dry off** *vti* sécher.

▸ **dry up 1** *vt* sécher. **2** *vi* sécher; *(dry the dishes)* essuyer la vaisselle.

du·al *adj* double.

dub *vt (film)* doubler.

du·bi·ous *adj* douteux; **I'm d. about going** je me demande si je dois y aller.

duch·ess duchesse *f*.

duck 1 *n* canard *m*. **2** *vi* se baisser (vivement).

due *adj (money)* dû *(f* due) *(to* à); *(rent, bill)* à payer; **to fall d.** échoir; **he's d. (to arrive)** il doit arriver; **in d. course** en temps utile; *(finally)* à la longue; **d. to** dû à; *(because of)* à cause de.

du·el duel *m*.

duf·fel coat, duf·fle coat duffel-coat *m*.

duke duc *m*.

dull *adj (boring)* ennuyeux; *(color)* terne; *(weather)* maussade; *(sound, ache)* sourd.

dull·ness *(of life, town)* monotonie *f*.

du·ly *adv (properly)* dûment; *(as expected)* commme prévu.

dumb *adj* muet *(f* muette); *(stupid)* idiot.

dum·my *(for clothes)* mannequin *m*; *(person) Fam* idiot *m*.

dump 1 *vt (garbage)* déposer. **2** *n (dull town) Fam* trou *m*; **(garbage) d.** tas *m* d'ordures; *(place)* dépôt *m* d'ordures; *(room)* dépotoir *m*.

dump truck camion *m* à benne basculante.

du·plex *(apartment)* duplex *m*.

du·pli·cate double *m*; **in d.** en deux exemplaires; **a d. copy** une copie en double.

du·ra·ble *adj (material)* résistant.

du·ra·tion durée *f*.

dur·ing *prep* pendant.

dusk crépuscule *m*.

dust 1 *n* poussière *f*. **2** *vt (furniture etc)* essuyer (la poussière de). **3** *vi* faire la poussière.

dust cloth chiffon *m* (à poussière).

dust jack·et *(for book)* jaquette *f*.

dust·y *adj* poussiéreux.

Dutch 1 *adj* hollandais, néerlandais. **2** *n (language)* hollandais *m*, néerlandais *m*; **the D.** les Hollandais *mpl*, les Néerlandais *mpl*.

Dutch·man, *pl* **-men** Hollandais *m*, Néerlandais *m*.

Dutch·wom·an, *pl* **-women** Hollandaise *f*, Néerlandaise *f*.

du·ty devoir *m*; *(tax)* droit *m*; **duties** *(responsibilities)* fonctions *fpl*; **on d.** *(policeman, teacher)* de service; *(doctor)* de garde; **off d.** libre.

du·ty-free *adj (goods, shop)* hors-taxe *inv*.

du·vet couette *f*.

DVD *abbr (digital versatile disk, digital video disk)* DVD *m*; **D. player** lecteur *m* (de) DVD.

dwarf nain *m*, naine *f*.

dye 1 *n* teinture *f*. **2** *vt* teindre; **to d. green** teindre en vert.

dy·nam·ic *adj* dynamique.

dy·na·mite dynamite *f*.

dy·na·mo, *pl* **-os** dynamo *f*.

dys·lex·ic *adj & n* dyslexique *(mf)*.

E

each 1 *adj* chaque. **2** *pron* **e. (one)** chacun, -une; **e. other** l'un(e) l'autre, *pl* les un(e)s les autres; **e. of us** chacun, -une d'entre nous.

ea·ger *adj* impatient **(to do** de faire); *(enthusiastic)* plein d'enthousiasme; **to be e. to do** *(want)* tenir (beaucoup) à faire.

ea·ger·ly adv avec enthousiasme; (to await) avec impatience.

ea·ger·ness impatience f (to do de faire).

ea·gle aigle m.

ear oreille f.

ear·ache mal m d'oreille; **to have an e.** avoir mal à l'oreille.

ear·ly 1 adj (first) premier; (age) jeune; **it's e.** (on clock) il est tôt; (referring to meeting) c'est tôt; **it's too e. to get up** il est trop tôt pour se lever; **to be e.** (ahead of time) être en avance; **to have an e. meal/night** manger/se coucher de bonne heure; **in e. summer** au début de l'été. **2** adv tôt, de bonne heure; (ahead of time) en avance; **as e. as possible** le plus tôt possible; **earlier (on)** plus tôt.

earn vt gagner; (interest) rapporter.

ear·nest 1 adj sérieux, -euse. **2** n **in e.** sérieusement.

earn·ings npl (wages) rémunérations fpl.

ear·phones npl casque m.

ear·plug boule f Quiès®.

ear·ring boucle f d'oreille.

earth (world, ground) terre f; **where/what on e.?** où/que diable?

earth·quake tremblement m de terre.

ease 1 n facilité f; **with e.** facilement; **(ill) at e.** (mal) à l'aise. **2** vt (pain) soulager; (mind) calmer.

ease (off or up) vi (become less) diminuer; (of pain) se calmer; (not work so hard) se relâcher.

ea·sel chevalet m.

▸ **ease off** vti enlever doucement.

eas·i·ly adv facilement; **e. the best**/etc de loin le meilleur/etc.

east 1 n est m; **(to the) e. of** à l'est de. **2** adj (coast) est inv; (wind) d'est. **3** adv à l'est.

east·bound adj en direction de l'est.

Eas·ter Pâques m sing or fpl; **Happy E.!** joyeuses Pâques!

east·ern adj (coast) est inv; **E. Europe** Europe f de l'Est.

east·ward(s) adj & adv vers l'est.

eas·y 1 adj facile; (life) tranquille; **it's e. to do** c'est facile à faire. **2** adv doucement; **go e. on** (sugar etc) vas-y doucement avec; (person) ne sois pas trop dur avec; **take it e.** calme-toi; (rest) repose-toi; (work less) ne te fatigue pas.

eas·y chair fauteuil m.

eas·y·go·ing adj (carefree) insouciant; (easy to get along with) facile à vivre.

eat* 1 vt manger; (meal) prendre. **2** vi manger.

eat·er big e. gros mangeur m, grosse mangeuse f.

▸ **eat out** vi manger dehors.

▸ **eat up** vt (finish) finir.

e-bank·ing banque f électronique.

ec·cen·tric adj & n excentrique (mf).

ech·o, pl -oes **1** n écho m. **2** vi the explosion/etc echoed l'écho de l'explosion/etc se répercuta.

ec·o·nom·ic adj économique; (profitable) rentable.

ec·o·nom·i·cal adj économique.

e·con·o·mize vti économiser (on sur).

e·con·o·my class (on aircraft) classe f touriste.

edge bord m; (of forest) lisière f; (of town) abords mpl; (of page) marge f; (of knife) tranchant m; **on e.** énervé; (nerves) tendu.

▸ **edge forward** vi avancer doucement.

ed·i·ble adj comestible; (not unpleasant) mangeable.

ed·it vt (newspaper) diriger; (article) mettre au point; (film) monter; (text) éditer; (compile) rédiger.

e·di·tion édition f.

ed·i·tor (of newspaper) rédacteur m en chef; (compiler) rédacteur, -trice mf.

ed·i·to·ri·al e. staff rédaction f.

ed·u·cate vt éduquer; (pupil, mind) former.

ed·u·cat·ed adj (well-)e. instruit.

ed·u·ca·tion éducation f, (teaching, training) formation f.

ed·u·ca·tion·al adj (establishment) d'enseignement; (game) éducatif.

eel anguille f.

ef·fect effet m (on sur); to put into e. mettre en application; to come into e., to take e. (of law) entrer en vigueur; to take e. (of drug) agir; to have an e. (of medicine) faire de l'effet.

ef·fec·tive adj (efficient) efficace; (striking) frappant.

ef·fec·tive·ly adv efficacement; (in fact) effectivement.

ef·fi·cien·cy efficacité f, (of machine) performances fpl.

ef·fi·cient adj efficace; (machine) performant.

ef·fi·cient·ly adv efficacement; to work e. (of machine) bien fonctionner.

ef·fort effort m; to make an e. faire un effort (to pour); it isn't worth the e. ça ne or n'en vaut pas la peine.

e.g. abbr par exemple.

egg œuf m.

egg·cup coquetier m.

egg·plant aubergine f.

egg tim·er sablier m.

e·go amour-propre m; to have an enormous e. être imbu de soi-même.

E·gyp·tian 1 n Égyptien, -ienne mf. 2 adj égyptien, -ienne.

ei·der·down édredon m.

eight adj & n huit (m).

eight·een adj & n dix-huit (m).

eighth adj & n huitième (mf).

eight·y adj & n quatre-vingts (m); e.-one quatre-vingt-un.

ei·ther 1 adj & pron (one or other) l'un(e) ou l'autre; (with negative) ni l'un(e) ni l'autre; (each) chaque; on e. side de chaque côté. 2 adv she can't swim e. elle ne sait pas nager non plus; I don't e. (ni) moi non plus. 3 conj e...or ou (bien)...ou (bien); (with negative) ni...ni.

e·lab·o·rate 1 vt (work out) élaborer; (explain) décrire en détail. 2 vi donner des détails; to e. on sth développer qch. 3 adj (meal, system) élaboré; (pattern, design) compliqué; (style, costume) recherché.

e·las·tic adj & n élastique (m).

el·bow 1 n coude m. 2 vt to e. one's way se frayer un chemin (à coups de coude) (through à travers).

eld·er adj & n (of two people) aîné, -ée (mf).

eld·er·ly adj âgé.

eld·est adj & n aîné, -ée (mf); his/her e. brother l'aîné de ses frères.

e·lect vt élire (qn) (to à).

e·lec·tion 1 n élection f. 2 adj (campaign) électoral; (day, results) du scrutin.

e·lec·tor·ate électorat m.

e·lec·tric adj électrique; e. blanket couverture f chauffante; e. chair chaise f électrique; e. shock décharge f électrique.

e·lec·tri·cal adj électrique.

e·lec·tri·cian électricien m.

e·lec·tri·cian's tape chatterton m.

e·lec·tric·i·ty électricité f.

e·lec·tro·cute vt électrocuter.

e·lec·tron·ic adj électronique.

e·lec·tron·ics électronique f.

el·e·gance élégance f.

el·e·gant adj élégant.

el·e·gant·ly adv avec élégance.

el·e·ment élément m; (of heater) résistance f.

el·e·men·ta·ry adj élémentaire; (school) primaire.

el·e·phant éléphant m.

el·e·va·tor ascenseur m.

e·lev·en adj & n onze (m).

e·lev·enth adj & n onzième (mf).

el·i·gi·ble *adj (for post)* admissible (**for** à); **to be e. for** *(entitled to)* avoir droit à.

e·lim·i·nate *vt* supprimer; *(applicant, possibility)* éliminer.

e·lite élite *f.*

else *adv* d'autre; **everybody e.** tous les autres; **somebody/nobody/ nothing e.** quelqu'un/personne/ rien d'autre; **something e.** autre chose; **anything e.?** encore quelque chose? **somewhere e.** ailleurs; **how e.?** de quelle autre façon?; **or e.** ou bien.

else·where *adv* ailleurs.

e·lude *vt (of word, name)* échapper à *(qn).*

e-mail 1 *n* e-mail *m, Can* courriel *m*; **by e.** par e-mail; **to send sb an e.** envoyer un e-mail à qn. **2** *vt (person)* envoyer un e-mail à; *(document)* envoyer par e-mail.

em·bark *vi* (s')embarquer.

▸**embark on** *vt (start)* commencer.

em·bar·rass *vt* embarrasser.

em·bar·rass·ing *adj* embarrassant.

em·bar·rass·ment embarras *m.*

em·bas·sy ambassade *f.*

em·blem emblème *m.*

em·brace 1 *vt (hug)* étreindre. **2** *vi* s'étreindre. **3** *n* étreinte *f.*

em·broi·der *vt (cloth)* broder.

em·broi·der·y broderie *f.*

em·bry·o embryon *m.*

em·er·ald émeraude *f.*

e·merge *vi* apparaître (**from** de); *(from hole)* sortir; *(of truth, from water)* émerger.

e·mer·gen·cy 1 *n* urgence *f*; **in an e.** en cas d'urgence. **2** *adj (measure)* d'urgence; *(exit, brake)* de secours; **e. room** salle *f* des urgences; **e. landing** atterrissage *m* forcé.

em·i·grate *vi* émigrer.

e·mo·tion *(strength of feeling)* émotion *f*; *(joy, love etc)* sentiment *m.*

e·mo·tion·al *adj (person, reaction)* émotif; *(story)* émouvant.

em·per·or empereur *m.*

em·pha·sis *(in word or phrase)* accent *m*; **to lay** *or* **put e. on** mettre l'accent sur.

em·pha·size *vt* souligner (**that** que).

em·pire empire *m.*

em·ploy *vt* employer.

em·ploy·ee employé, -ée *mf.*

em·ploy·er patron, -onne *mf.*

em·ploy·ment emploi *m*; **place of e.** lieu *m* de travail.

em·ploy·ment a·gen·cy bureau *m* de placement.

emp·ty 1 *adj* vide; *(stomach)* creux; *(threat, promise)* vain; **to return e.-handed** revenir les mains vides. **2** *vi (of building, tank etc)* se vider.

emp·ty (out) *vt (box, liquid etc)* vider; *(vehicle)* décharger; *(objects in box etc)* sortir (**from** de).

e·mul·sion émulsion *f.*

en·a·ble *vt* **to e. sb to do** permettre à qn de faire.

e·nam·el 1 *n* émail *m (pl* émaux). **2** *adj* en émail.

en·chant·ing *adj* charmant, enchanteur (*f* -eresse).

en·close *vt (send with letter)* joindre (**in, with** à); *(fence off)* clôturer.

en·closed *adj (space)* clos; *(receipt etc)* ci-joint.

en·clo·sure *(in letter)* pièce *f* jointe; *(place)* enceinte *f.*

en·coun·ter 1 *vt* rencontrer. **2** *n* rencontre *f.*

en·cour·age *vt* encourager (**to do** à faire).

en·cour·age·ment encouragement *m.*

en·cy·clo·pe·di·a encyclopédie *f.*

end 1 *n (of street, box etc)* bout *m*; *(of meeting, month, book etc)* fin *f*; *(purpose)* but *m*; **at an e.** *(discussion etc)* fini; *(patience)* à bout; **in the e.** à la fin; **to come to an e.** prendre fin; **to put an e. to, to bring**

to an e. mettre fin à; **no e. of** *Fam* beaucoup de; **for days on e.** pendant des jours et des jours. **2** *vt* finir (**with** par); (*rumor*) mettre fin à. **3** *vi* finir; **to e. in failure** se solder par un échec.

en·dan·ger *vt* mettre en danger.

end·ing fin *f*; (*of word*) terminaison *f*.

en·dive (*curly*) chicorée *f*, (*smooth*) endive *f*.

end·less *adj* interminable.

en·dorse *vt* (*check*) endosser; (*action*) approuver.

en·dorse·ment (*signature*) aval *m*; (*backing*) appui *m*; (*on check*) endossement *m*.

▶**end up** *vi* to e. up doing finir par faire; **to e. up in** (*place*) se retrouver à; **he ended up in prison/a doctor** il a fini en prison/par devenir médecin.

en·dur·ance endurance *f*.

en·dure *vt* supporter (**doing** de faire).

en·e·my *n & adj* ennemi, -ie (*mf*).

en·er·get·ic *adj* énergique.

en·er·gy **1** *n* énergie *f*. **2** *adj* (*crisis, resources etc*) énergétique.

en·force *vt* (*law*) faire respecter.

en·gaged *adj* e. (**to be married**) fiancé; **to get e.** se fiancer.

en·gage·ment (*to marry*) fiançailles *fpl*; (*meeting*) rendez-vous *m inv*; **e. ring** bague *f* de fiançailles.

en·gine (*of vehicle*) moteur *m*; (*of train*) locomotive *f*, (*of jet*) réacteur *m*.

en·gi·neer ingénieur *m*; (*repairer*) dépanneur, -euse *mf*.

en·gi·neer·ing ingénierie *f*, génie *m*.

Eng·lish 1 *adj* anglais; (*teacher*) d'anglais; **the E. Channel** la Manche. **2** *n* (*language*) anglais *m*; **the E.** les Anglais *mpl*.

Eng·lish·man, *pl* -**men** Anglais *m*.

Eng·lish-speak·ing *adj* anglophone.

Eng·lish·wom·an, *pl* -**women** Anglaise *f*.

en·grave *vt* graver.

en·grav·ing gravure *f*.

en·joy *vt* aimer (**doing** faire); (*meal*) apprécier; **to e. the evening** passer une bonne soirée; **to e. oneself** s'amuser; **to e. being in Paris** se plaire à Paris.

en·joy·a·ble *adj* agréable.

en·joy·ment plaisir *m*.

en·large *vt* agrandir.

en·light·en *vt* éclairer (**sb on** or **about sth** qn sur qch).

en·list 1 *vt* (*recruit*) engager; (*supporter*) recruter; (*support, help*) s'assurer. **2** *vi* (*in the army*) s'engager.

e·nor·mous *adj* énorme.

e·nor·mous·ly *adv* (*very much*) énormément; (*very*) extrêmement.

e·nough 1 *adj & n* assez (de); **e. time/cups/etc** assez de temps/de tasses/*etc*; **to have e. to live on** avoir de quoi vivre; **e. to drink** assez à boire; **to have had e. of** en avoir assez de; **that's e.** ça suffit. **2** *adv* assez; **big/good/etc e.** assez grand/bon/*etc* (**to** pour).

en·quire *vi* = **inquire.**

en·quir·y *n* = **inquiry.**

en·roll *vi* s'inscrire (**in, for** à).

en·roll·ment inscription *f*.

en·sure *vt* assurer; **to e. that** s'assurer que.

en·tail *vt* (*consequence*) entraîner; (*risk*) comporter.

en·ter 1 *vt* (*room, vehicle etc*) entrer dans; (*university*) s'inscrire à; (*race, competition*) s'inscrire pour; (*write down*) inscrire (**in** dans); **to e. sb/sth in** (*competition*) présenter qn/qch à; **it didn't e. my head** or **mind** ça ne m'est pas venu à l'esprit. **2** *vi* entrer.

▶**enter into** *vt* (*conversation*) entrer en; (*career*) entrer dans; (*agreement*) conclure.

en·ter·prise (*undertaking, firm*)

entreprise f; (spirit) initiative f.

en·ter·pris·ing adj plein d'initiative.

en·ter·tain 1 vt amuser; (guest) recevoir. **2** vi (receive guests) recevoir.

en·ter·tain·er artiste mf.

en·ter·tain·ing adj amusant.

en·ter·tain·ment amusement m; (show) spectacle m.

en·thu·si·asm enthousiasme m.

en·thu·si·ast enthousiaste mf; jazz/etc e. passionné, -ée mf de jazz/etc.

en·thu·si·as·tic adj enthousiaste; (golfer etc) passionné; **to be e. about** (hobby) être passionné de; (gift) être emballé par; **to get e.** s'emballer (**about** pour).

en·thu·si·as·ti·cal·ly adv avec enthousiasme.

en·tire adj entier.

en·tire·ly adv tout à fait.

en·ti·tle vt **to e. sb to do** donner à qn le droit de faire; **to e. sb to sth** donner à qn (le) droit à qch.

en·ti·tled adj **to be e. to do** avoir le droit de faire; **to be e. to sth** avoir droit à qch.

en·trance entrée f (**to** de); (to university) admission f (**to** à); **e. exam** examen m d'entrée.

en·trant (in race) concurrent, -ente mf; (for exam) candidat, -ate mf.

en·try (way in, action) entrée f, (bookkeeping item) écriture f; (dictionary term) entrée f; (in competition) objet m (or œuvre f or projet m) soumis au jury; **'no e.'** 'entrée interdite'; (road sign) 'sens interdit'.

en·try form feuille f d'inscription.

en·ve·lope enveloppe f.

en·vi·ous adj envieux (**of sth** de qch); **e. of sb** jaloux de qn.

en·vi·ron·ment milieu m; (natural) environnement m.

en·vi·ron·men·tal adj du milieu; (natural) de l'environnement; (group) écologiste; (issue) écolo-

gique, lié à l'environnement.

en·vis·age, en·vi·sion vt (imagine) envisager; (foresee) prévoir.

en·vy 1 n envie f. **2** vt envier (**sb sth** qch à qn).

ep·i·dem·ic épidémie f.

ep·i·sode épisode m.

e·qual 1 adj égal (**to** à); **to be e. to** (number) égaler; **she's e. to** (task) elle est à la hauteur de. **2** n (person) égal, -ale mf.

e·qual·i·ty égalité f.

e·qual·ize vi (score) égaliser.

e·qual·ly adv également; (to divide) en parts égales.

e·qua·tion équation f.

e·qua·tor équateur m.

e·quip vt équiper (**with** de); (well-) **equipped with** pourvu de; (well-) **equipped to do** compétent pour faire.

e·quip·ment équipement (m).

e·quiv·a·lent adj & n équivalent (m).

e·ra époque f, (historical, geological) ère f.

e·rase vt effacer.

e·ras·er gomme f.

e·rect 1 adj (upright) (bien) droit. **2** vt construire; (statue etc) ériger; (scaffolding, tent) monter.

e·ro·sion érosion f.

er·rand commission f.

er·rat·ic adj (service, machine etc) capricieux; (person) lunatique.

er·ror erreur f; **to do sth in e.** faire qch par erreur.

e·rupt vi (volcano) entrer en éruption; (war, violence) éclater.

e·rup·tion (of volcano) éruption f, (of violence) flambée f.

es·ca·la·tor escalier m roulant.

es·cape 1 vi s'échapper; **to e. from** (person) échapper à; (place) s'échapper de. **2** vt (death) échapper à; (punishment) éviter; **her name escapes me** son nom m'échappe. **3** n (of gas) fuite f, (of person) évasion f.

es·cort 1 n *(soldiers etc)* escorte f.
2 vt escorter.

Es·ki·mo, pl **-os** Esquimau, -aude mf.

es·pe·cial·ly adv (tout) spécialement; **e. as** d'autant plus que.

es·pres·so, pl **-os** (café m) express m inv.

es·say *(at school)* rédaction f.

es·sen·tial adj essentiel.

es·sen·tial·ly adv essentiellement.

es·tab·lish vt établir.

es·tab·lished adj *(company)* solide; *(fact)* reconnu; *(reputation)* établi.

es·tab·lish·ment *(institution, firm)* établissement m.

es·tate *(land)* terre(s) f(pl); *(property after death)* succession f.

es·ti·mate 1 vt estimer (**that** que).
2 n évaluation f; *(price for work to be done)* devis m.

etch·ing eau-forte f.

e·ter·nal adj éternel.

eth·ics *(study)* éthique f; *(principles)* morale f; *(of profession)* déontologie f.

e·tick·et billet m électronique.

et·i·quette bienséances fpl.

Euro- prefix euro-.

Eu·ro·pe·an 1 adj européen, -éenne. **2** n Européen, -éenne.

Eu·ro·pe·an Un·ion Union f européenne.

e·vac·u·ate vt évacuer.

e·vade vt éviter; *(pursuer, tax)* échapper à; *(law, question)* éluder.

e·val·u·ate vt évaluer (**at** à).

e·vap·o·rat·ed milk lait m concentré.

eve on the **e. of** à la veille de.

e·ven 1 adj *(flat)* uni; *(equal)* égal; *(regular)* régulier; *(number)* pair; **to get e. with sb** se venger de qn; **we're e.** nous sommes quittes; *(in score)* nous sommes à égalité; **to break e.** *(financially)* s'y retrouver.
2 adv même; **e. better/more** en-

core mieux/plus; **e. if** or **though** même si; **e. so** quand même.

eve·ning soir m; *(whole evening, event)* soirée f; **in the e.** le soir; **at seven in the e.** à sept heures du soir; **every Tuesday e.** tous les mardis soir; **all e. (long)** toute la soirée.

eve·ning dress tenue f de soirée.

eve·ning gown robe f du soir.

e·ven·ly adv de manière égale; *(regularly)* régulièrement.

▸**even out, even up** vt égaliser.

e·vent événement m; *(in sport)* épreuve f; **in the e. of death** en cas de décès; **in any e.** en tout cas.

e·ven·tu·al adj final.

e·ven·tu·al·ly adv finalement; *(some day or other)* un jour ou l'autre.

ev·er adv jamais; **more than e.** plus que jamais; **nothing e.** jamais rien; **hardly e.** presque jamais; **the first e.** le tout premier; **e. since** *(that event etc)* depuis; **e. since then** depuis lors; **for e.** pour toujours; *(continually)* sans cesse; **e. so happy/** etc vraiment heureux/etc; **why e. not?** et pourquoi pas?

eve·ry adj chaque; **e. one** chacun, -une; **e. single one** tous or toutes (sans exception); **e. other day** tous les deux jours; **e. so often, e. now and then** de temps en temps.

eve·ry·bod·y pron tout le monde; **e. in turn** chacun or chacune à son tour.

eve·ry·day adj *(life)* de tous les jours; *(ordinary)* banal *(mpl banals)*; **in e. use** d'usage courant.

eve·ry·one pron = **everybody.**

eve·ry·place adv = **everywhere.**

eve·ry·thing pron tout; **e. I have** tout ce que j'ai.

eve·ry·where adv partout; **e. she goes** où qu'elle aille.

ev·i·dence preuve(s) f(pl); *(given by witness etc)* témoignage m; **e. of** *(wear etc)* des signes mpl de.

ev·i·dent *adj* évident (**that** que).

ev·i·dent·ly *adv* évidemment; *(apparently)* apparemment.

e·vil 1 *adj (influence, person)* malfaisant; *(deed, system)* mauvais. **2** *n* mal *m*.

e·voke *vt* évoquer.

ewe brebis *f*.

ex- *prefix* ex-; **ex-wife** ex-femme *f*.

ex·act *adj* exact; **to be e. about** sth préciser qch.

ex·act·ly *adv* exactement.

ex·ag·ger·ate *vti* exagérer.

ex·ag·ger·a·tion exagération *f*.

ex·am examen *m*.

ex·am·i·na·tion *(in school etc)* examen *m*.

ex·am·ine *vt* examiner; *(accounts, luggage)* vérifier; *(passport)* contrôler; *(question)* interroger.

ex·am·in·er examinateur, -trice *mf*.

ex·am·ple exemple *m*; **for e.** par example; **to set an e.** donner l'exemple (**to** à).

ex·ceed *vt* dépasser.

ex·cel *vi* **to e. in sth** être excellent en qch.

ex·cel·lent *adj* excellent.

ex·cept *prep* sauf, excepté; **e. for** à part; **e. that** sauf que.

ex·cep·tion exception *f*; **with the e. of** à l'exception de.

ex·cep·tion·al *adj* exceptionnel.

ex·cep·tion·al·ly *adv* exceptionnellement.

ex·cerpt extrait *m*.

ex·cess 1 *n* excès *m*; *(surplus)* excédent *m*. **2** *adj* **e. fare** supplément *m* (de billet); **e. baggage** excédent *m* de bagages.

ex·ces·sive *adj* excessif.

ex·ces·sive·ly *adv (too, too much)* excessivement; *(very)* extrêmement.

ex·change 1 *vt* échanger (**for** contre). **2** *n* échange *m*; *(of foreign currencies)* change *m*; **(telephone) e. central** *m* (téléphonique); **in e.** en échange (**for** de).

ex·cite *vt (enthuse)* passionner.

ex·cit·ed *adj (happy)* surexcité; *(nervous)* énervé; **to get e.** *(nervous, enthusiastic)* s'exciter; **to be e. about** *(new car etc)* se réjouir de.

ex·cite·ment agitation *f*; *(emotion)* vive émotion *f*.

ex·cit·ing *adj (book etc)* passionnant.

ex·claim *vti* s'exclamer (**that** que).

ex·cla·ma·tion point point *m* d'exclamation.

ex·clude *vt* exclure (**from** de).

ex·clu·sive *adj* exclusif; *(club)* fermé; **e. of wine/etc** vin/etc non compris.

ex·cur·sion excursion *f*.

ex·cuse 1 *vt* excuser (**sb for doing** qn d'avoir fait, qn de faire); *(exempt)* dispenser (**from** de). **2** *n* excuse *f*.

ex·e·cute *vt (criminal)* exécuter.

ex·e·cu·tion exécution *f*.

ex·ec·u·tive 1 *adj (job)* de cadre; *(car, plane)* de direction. **2** *n (person)* cadre *m*; **senior e.** cadre *m* supérieur; **junior e.** jeune cadre *m*; **sales e.** cadre *m* commercial.

ex·empt 1 *adj* dispensé (**from** de). **2** *vt* dispenser (**from** de).

ex·emp·tion dispense *f*.

ex·ert *vt* exercer; **to e. oneself** *(physically)* se dépenser; **don't e. yourself!** ne te fatigue pas!

ex·er·tion effort *m*.

ex·haust 1 *vt* épuiser. **2** *n* **e. (pipe)** tuyau *m* d'échappement.

ex·haust·ed *adj* épuisé; **to become e.** s'épuiser.

ex·haust·ing *adj* épuisant.

ex·hib·it 1 *vt (put on display)* exposer. **2** *n* objet *m* exposé.

ex·hi·bi·tion exposition *f*.

ex·hib·i·tor exposant, -ante *mf*.

ex·ile 1 *n (banishment)* exil *m*; *(person)* exilé, -ée *mf*. **2** *vt* exiler.

ex·ist *vi* exister; *(live)* vivre (**on** de).

ex·is·tence existence *f*; **to be in e.** exister.

ex·ist·ing adj (situation) actuel.
ex·it sortie f.
ex·or·bi·tant adj exorbitant.
ex·pand 1 vt (trade, ideas) développer; (production) augmenter; (gas, metal) dilater. **2** vi se développer; (of production) augmenter; (of gas, metal) se dilater.
ex·panse étendue f.
ex·pan·sion (of trade etc) développement m.
ex·pect vt s'attendre à; (think) penser (**that** que); (suppose) supposer (**that** que); (await) attendre; **to e. sth from sb/sth** attendre qch de qn/qch; **to e. to** compter faire; **to e. that** s'attendre à ce que (+ subjunctive); **I e. you to come** (want) je compte sur votre présence; **it was expected** c'était prévu; **she's expecting (a baby)** elle attend un bébé.
ex·pec·ta·tion attente f.
ex·pe·di·tion expédition f.
ex·pel vt (from school) renvoyer.
ex·pen·di·ture (money) dépenses fpl.
ex·pense frais mpl; **business expenses** frais mpl généraux; **at sb's e.** aux dépens de qn.
ex·pen·sive adj cher.
ex·pe·ri·ence 1 n expérience f; **he's had e. of driving** il a déjà conduit. **2** vt connaître; (difficulty) éprouver.
ex·pe·ri·enced adj expérimenté; **to be e. in** s'y connaître en.
ex·per·i·ment 1 n expérience f. **2** vi faire une expérience or des expériences.
ex·pert expert m (**on, in** en); **e. advice** le conseil d'un expert.
ex·per·tise compétence f (**in** en).
ex·pi·ra·tion date date f d'expiration.
ex·pire vi expirer.
ex·pired adj (ticket, passport etc) périmé.

ex·plain vt expliquer (**to** à; **that** que).
▸ **explain away** vt justifier.
ex·pla·na·tion explication f.
ex·plic·it adj explicite.
ex·plode vi exploser.
ex·ploit 1 vt exploiter. **2** n exploit m.
ex·plo·ra·tion exploration f.
ex·plore vt explorer; (causes etc) examiner.
ex·plor·er explorateur, -trice mf.
ex·plo·sion explosion f.
ex·plo·sive adj & n explosif (m).
ex·port 1 n exportation f. **2** vt exporter (**to** vers; **from** de).
ex·pose vt exposer (**to** à); (plot etc) révéler; (crook etc) démasquer.
ex·press 1 vt exprimer; **to e. oneself** s'exprimer. **2** adj (letter, delivery) exprès inv; (train) rapide. **3** adv (to send) par exprès or Chronopost®. **4** n (train) rapide m.
ex·pres·sion (phrase, look) expression f.
ex·press·way autoroute f.
ex·tend 1 vt (arm, business) étendre; (line, visit) prolonger (**by** de); (house) agrandir; (time limit) reculer. **2** vi s'étendre (**to** jusqu'à); (in time) se prolonger.
ex·ten·sion (for table) rallonge f; (to building) agrandissement(s) m(pl); (of phone) appareil m supplémentaire; (of office phone) poste m; **e. cord** rallonge f.
ex·ten·sive adj étendu; (repairs, damage) important.
ex·ten·sive·ly adv (very much) énormément, considérablement.
ex·tent (scope) étendue f; (size) importance f; **to a large/certain e.** dans une large/certaine mesure; **to such an e. that** à tel point que.
ex·te·ri·or adj & n extérieur (m).
ex·ter·nal adj extérieur; **for e. use** (medicine) à usage externe.
ex·tin·guish·er (fire) **e.** extincteur m.

ex·tra 1 adj supplémentaire; **one e. glass** un verre de or en plus; **to be e. (spare)** être en trop; (cost more) être en supplément; **e. charge** or **portion** supplément m. **2** adv **to pay e.** payer un supplément; **wine costs** or **is 10 euros e.** il y a un supplément de 10 euros pour le vin. **3** n (perk) à-côté m; **extras** (expenses) frais mpl supplémentaires.

ex·tra- prefix extra-.

ex·tract 1 vt extraire; (from de). **2** n extrait m.

ex·tra·cur·ric·u·lar adj extrascolaire.

ex·traor·di·nar·y adj extraordinaire.

ex·tra·spe·cial adj (occasion) très spécial.

ex·trav·a·gant adj (wasteful with money) dépenser.

ex·treme 1 adj extrême; (danger, poverty) très grand. **2** n extrême m.

ex·treme·ly adv extrêmement.

eye œil m (pl yeux); **to keep an e. on** surveiller; **to lay** or **set eyes on** voir; **to take one's eyes off sb/sth** quitter qn/qch des yeux.

eye·brow sourcil m.

eye·glass·es npl lunettes fpl.

eye·lash cil m.

eye·lid paupière f.

eye·lin·er eye-liner m.

eye shad·ow fard m à paupières.

eye·sight vue f.

F

fab·ric tissu m, étoffe f.

fab·u·lous adj (wonderful) Fam formidable.

face 1 n (of person) visage m, figure f, (of clock) cadran m; **f. down** face contre terre; (thing) tourné à l'en-

vers; **f. to f.** face à face; **to make faces** faire des grimaces. **2** vt (danger, problem etc) faire face à; (accept) accepter; (look in the face) regarder (qn) bien en face; (be opposite) être en face de; (of window) donner sur; **faced with** (problem) confronté à; **he can't f. leaving** il n'a pas le courage de partir. **3** vi (of house) être orienté (**north**/etc) au nord/etc); (be turned) être tourné (**towards** vers).

face-cloth gant m de toilette.

▸**face up to** vt (danger, problem) faire face à; (fact) accepter.

fa·cil·i·tate vt faciliter.

fa·cil·i·ties npl (for sports, cooking etc) équipements mpl; (in harbor, airport) installations fpl.

fact fait m; **as a matter of f., in f.** en fait.

fac·tor facteur m.

fac·to·ry usine f.

fac·tu·al adj basé sur les faits.

fade vi (of flower) se faner; (of light) baisser; (of color) passer; (of fabric) se décolorer.

fade (a·way) vi (of sound) s'affaiblir.

fail 1 vi échouer; (of business) faire faillite; (of health, sight) baisser; (of brakes) lâcher. **2** vt (exam) rater, échouer à; (candidate) refuser, recaler; **to f. to do** (forget) manquer de faire; (not be able) ne pas arriver à faire. **3** n **without f.** à coup sûr.

failed adj (attempt, poet) manqué.

fail·ing 1 n défaut m. **2** prep **f. that** à défaut.

fail·ure échec m; (of business) faillite f, (person) raté, -ée mf; **f. to do** incapacité f de faire.

faint 1 adj faible; (color) pâle; **I haven't got the faintest idea** je n'en ai pas la moindre idée; **to feel f.** se trouver mal. **2** vi s'évanouir.

faint·ly adv faiblement; (slightly) légèrement.

fair¹ (for trade) foire f, (for enter-

tainment) fête *f* foraine, kermesse *f*; *(for charity)* fête *f*.

fair² *adj (just)* juste; *(game, fight)* loyal; **f. enough!** très bien! ■ *(rather good)* passable; *(weather)* beau; *(price)* raisonnable; **a f. amount (of)** pas mal (de).

fair³ *adj (hair, person)* blond.

fair-haired *adj* blond.

fair·ly *adv (to treat)* équitablement; *(rather)* assez.

fair·ness justice *f*, *(of person)* impartialité *f*.

fair play fair-play *m inv*.

fair-sized *adj* assez grand.

fair·y fée *f*; **f. tale** *or* **story** conte *m* de fées.

faith foi *f*; **to have f. in sb** avoir confiance en qn.

faith·ful *adj* fidèle (**to** à).

fake 1 *n* faux *m*; *(person)* imposteur *m*. **2** *vt (document etc)* falsifier. **3** *vi* faire semblant. **4** *adj* faux (*f* fausse).

fall 1 *n* chute *f*, *(in price etc)* baisse *f* (**in** de); *(season)* automne *m*. **2** *vi** tomber; **to f. off** *or* **out of** *or* **down** **sth** tomber de qch; **to f. over** *(chair)* tomber en butant contre; *(balcony)* tomber de; **to f. ill** tomber malade.

▸**fall apart** *vi (of machine)* tomber en morceaux; *(of group)* se défaire.

▸**fall back on** *vt (as last resort)* se rabattre sur.

▸**fall behind** *vi* rester en arrière; *(in work, payments)* prendre du retard.

▸**fall down** *vi* tomber; *(of building)* s'effondrer.

▸**fall for** *vt* tomber amoureux de; *(trick)* se laisser prendre à.

▸**fall in** *vi (collapse)* s'écrouler.

▸**fall off** *vi (come off)* se détacher; *(of numbers)* diminuer.

▸**fall out** *vi (quarrel)* se brouiller (**with** avec).

▸**fall over** *vi* tomber; *(of table, vase)* se renverser.

▸**fall through** *vi (of plan)* tomber à l'eau.

false *adj* faux (*f* fausse).

fame renommée *f*.

fa·mil·iar *adj* familier (**to** à); **f. with sb** *(too friendly)* familier avec qn; **to be f. with** *(know)* connaître.

fa·mil·iar·i·ty familiarité *f* (**with** avec).

fam·i·ly famille *f*.

fa·mous *adj* célèbre (**for** pour).

fan¹ *(held in hand)* éventail *m*; *(mechanical)* ventilateur *m*.

fan² *(of person)* fan *mf*, *(of team etc)* supporter *m*; **to be a jazz/sports f.** être passionné de jazz/de sport.

fan·cy 1 *n* **I took a f. to it** j'en ai eu envie. **2** *adj (hat, button etc)* fantaisie *inv*. **3** *int* **f. (that)!** tiens (donc)!

fan·tas·tic *adj* fantastique.

fan·ta·sy *(dream)* fantasme *m*; *(imagination)* fantaisie *f*.

FAQ *(frequently asked questions)* FAQ *f*.

far 1 *adv (distance)* loin; **f. bigger/** *etc* beaucoup plus grand/*etc* (**than** que); **how f. is it to?** combien y a-t-il d'ici à?; **so f.** *(time)* jusqu'ici; **as f. as** *(place)* jusqu'à; **as f. as I know** autant que je sache; **as f. as I'm concerned** en ce qui me concerne; **f. from doing** loin de faire; **f. away** *or* **off** au loin; **by f.** de loin. **2** *adj (side, end)* autre.

far·a·way *adj (country)* lointain.

farce farce *f*.

fare *(price)* prix *m* du billet.

fare·well *int* adieu *m*.

far-fetched *adj* tiré par les cheveux.

farm 1 *n* ferme *f*. **2** *adj (worker, produce)* agricole; **f. land** terres *fpl* cultivées. **3** *vt* cultiver.

farm·er fermier, -ière *mf*.

farm·house ferme *f*.

farm·ing agriculture *f*.

farm·yard basse-cour *f*, cour *f* de ferme.

far-off *adj* lointain.

far-reach·ing *adj* de grande portée.

far·ther *adv* plus loin; **to get f. away** s'éloigner.

far·thest 1 *adj* le plus éloigné. **2** *adv* le plus loin.

fas·ci·nate *vt* fasciner.

fas·ci·nat·ing *adj* fascinant.

fas·ci·na·tion fascination *f*.

fash·ion *(style in clothes)* mode *f*; *(manner)* façon *f*; **in f.** à la mode; **out of f.** démodé.

fash·ion·a·ble *adj* à la mode; *(place)* chic *inv*.

fash·ion show présentation *f* de collections.

fast 1 *adj* rapide; **to be f.** *(of clock)* avancer (**by** de). **2** *adv (quickly)* vite; **f. asleep** profondément endormi.

fas·ten *vt* attacher (**to** à); *(door, window)* fermer (bien).

fas·ten·er *(clip)* attache *f*, *(of garment)* fermeture *f*, *(of bag)* fermoir *m*; *(hook)* agrafe *f*.

fat 1 *n* graisse *f*, *(on meat)* gras *m*. **2** *adj* gras *(f* grasse); *(cheek, salary)* gros *(f* grosse); **to get f.** grossir.

fa·tal *adj* mortel; *(mistake etc)* fatal *(mpl* fatals).

fate destin *m*, sort *m*.

fa·ther père *m*.

fa·ther-in-law, *pl* **fathers-in-law** beau-père *m*.

fa·tigue fatigue *f*.

fat·ten·ing *adj (food)* qui fait grossir.

fat·ty *adj (food)* gras *(f* grasse).

fau·cet *(tap)* robinet *m*.

fault faute *f*, *(defect)* défaut *m*; *(mistake)* erreur *f*; **it's your f.** c'est ta faute; **to find f. (with)** critiquer.

fault·y *adj* défectueux.

fa·vor 1 *n (act of kindness)* service *m*; **to do sb a f.** rendre service à qn; **to be in f. of** *(support)* être pour; *(prefer)* préférer. **2** *vt (encourage)* favoriser; *(prefer)* préférer.

fa·vor·a·ble *adj* favorable (**to** à).

fa·vor·ite *adj & n* favori, -ite *mf*, préféré, -ée *mf*.

fax 1 *n (machine)* télécopieur *m*, fax

m; *(message)* télécopie *f*, fax *m*. **2** *vt (message)* faxer; **to f. sb** envoyer une télécopie *or* un fax à qn.

fear 1 *n* crainte *f*, peur *f*, **for f. of doing** de peur de faire. **2** *vt* craindre.

fear·ful *adj (person)* apeuré; *(noise, pain)* épouvantable.

fear·less *adj* intrépide.

feast festin *m*.

feat exploit *m*.

feath·er plume *f*.

fea·ture *(of face, person)* trait *m*; *(of thing, place)* caractéristique *f*.

Feb·ru·ar·y février *m*.

fed·er·al *adj* fédéral.

fed up *adj* **to be f. up** *Fam* en avoir marre (**with** de).

fee prix *m*; **fee(s)** *(professional)* honoraires *mpl*; *(for registration)* droits *mpl*; **school** *or* **tuition fees** frais *mpl* de scolarité.

fee·ble *adj* faible.

feed* *vt* donner à manger à; *(breast-feed)* allaiter; *(bottle-feed)* donner le biberon à *(un bébé)*.

feed·back réaction(s) *f(pl)*.

feel 1 *n* toucher *m*; *(feeling)* sensation *f*. **2** *vt* *(be aware of)* sentir; *(experience)* éprouver; *(touch)* tâter; **to f. that** avoir l'impression que. **3** *vi (tired, old etc)* se sentir; **I f. hot/sleepy/etc** j'ai chaud/sommeil/etc; **she feels better** elle va mieux; **to f. like sth** *(want)* avoir envie de qch.

▸ **feel around** *vi* tâtonner; *(in pocket etc)* fouiller.

feel·ing sentiment *m*; *(physical)* sensation *f*.

▸ **feel up to** *vt* être en forme pour.

feet *see* **foot**.

fell *pt de* **fall**.

fel·low *(man)* type *m*.

fel·o·ny crime *m*.

felt¹ *pt & pp de* **feel**.

felt² feutre *m*.

felt-tip (pen) *(crayon m)* feutre *m*.

fe·male 1 adj (voice etc) féminin; (animal) femelle; **f. student** étudiante f. **2** n femme f, (animal) femelle f.

fem·i·nine adj féminin.

fence 1 n barrière f, (in race) obstacle m. **2** vi (with sword) faire de l'escrime.

fence (in) vt (land) clôturer.

fenc·ing (sport) escrime f.

fend vi **to f. for oneself** se débrouiller.

fend·er (on car) aile f.

fern fougère f.

fe·ro·cious adj féroce.

fer·ry ferry-boat m; (small, for river) bac m.

fer·tile adj (land) fertile.

fer·til·iz·er engrais m.

fes·ti·val festival m (pl -als).

fes·tiv·i·ties npl festivités fpl.

fetch[1] vt (bring) amener (qn); (object) apporter; **to (go and) f.** aller chercher.

fetch[2] vt (be sold for) rapporter.

fête fête f.

feud 1 n querelle f. **2** vi se quereller, se disputer.

fe·ver fièvre f; **to have a f.** avoir de la fièvre.

fe·ver·ish adj fiévreux.

few adj & pron peu (de); **f. towns/etc** peu de villes/etc, **a f. towns/etc** quelques villes/etc, **f. of them** peu d'entre eux; **a f.** quelques-un(e)s (of sb); **a f. of us** quelques-uns d'entre nous; **quite a f., a good f.** bon nombre (de); **a f. more books/etc** encore quelques livres/etc; **every f. days** tous les trois ou quatre jours.

few·er adj & pron moins (de) (than que).

fi·an·cé(e) fiancé, -ée mf.

fi·ber fibre f.

fi·ber·board (bois) aggloméré m.

fic·tion (works of) f. romans mpl.

fid·dle (dishonest act) Fam combine f.

▸ **fiddle (around) with** vt (pen etc) tripoter; (cars etc) bricoler.

fidg·et vi gigoter.

field champ m; (for sports) terrain m.

fierce adj féroce; (attack) furieux.

fif·teen adj & n quinze (m).

fif·teenth adj & n quinzième (mf).

fifth adj & n cinquième (mf).

fif·ti·eth adj & n cinquantième (mf).

fif·ty adj & n cinquante (m).

fig figue f.

fight 1 n bagarre f, Boxing combat m; (struggle) lutte f, (quarrel) dispute f. **2** vi* se battre (**against** contre); (struggle) lutter (**for** pour); (quarrel) se disputer. **3** vt se battre avec (qn).

▸ **fight back** vi se défendre.

fight·er (determined person) battant, -ante mf.

▸ **fight off** vt (attacker) repousser; (disease) résister à.

▸ **fight over** vt se disputer.

fig·ure[1] (numeral) chiffre m; (price) prix m; (of woman) ligne f; (diagram, person) figure f.

fig·ure[2] vt **to f. that** (guess) penser que.

▸ **figure on doing** vt compter faire.

▸ **figure out** vt arriver à comprendre; (problem) résoudre.

file (tool) lime f, (folder, information) dossier m; (computer data) fichier m; **in single f.** en file.

file (a·way) vt (document) classer.

file (down) vt limer.

▸ **file in** vi entrer à la queue leu leu.

▸ **file out** vi sortir à la queue leu leu.

fil·ing cab·i·net classeur m.

fill 1 vt remplir (**with** de); (tooth) plomber. **2** vi se remplir.

fil·let filet m.

▸ **fill in** vt (form, hole) remplir.

fill·ing 1 adj (meal) nourrissant. **2** n (in tooth) plombage m; (in food) garniture f.

▶ **fill out** vt (form) remplir.

▶ **fill up 1** vt (container, form) remplir. **2** vi se remplir; (with gas) faire le plein.

film 1 n film m; (for camera) pellicule f. **2** vt filmer.

fil·ter filtre m; **f.-tipped cigarette** cigarette f (à bout) filtre.

filth saleté f.

filth·y adj sale.

fin (of fish) nageoire f.

fi·nal 1 adj (last) dernier. **2** n (match) finale f.

fi·nal·ize vt mettre au point; (date) fixer.

fi·nal·ly adv enfin.

fi·nance 1 n finance f. **2** vt financer.

fi·nan·cial adj financier.

find 1 n trouvaille f. 2 vt* trouver; (sth or sb lost) retrouver.

▶ **find out 1** vt (secret etc) découvrir; (person) démasquer. **2** vi (inquire) se renseigner (**about** sur); **to f. out about sth** (discover) découvrir qch.

fine¹ 1 n amende f; (for driving offense) contravention f. **2** vt **to f. sb ($100/etc)** infliger une amende (de cent dollars/etc) à qn.

fine² 1 adj (thin, not coarse) fin; (very good) excellent; **he's f.** (healthy) il va bien. **2** adv (well) très bien.

fin·ger doigt m; **little f.** petit doigt m.

fin·ger·nail ongle m.

fin·ger·print empreinte f (digitale); (smudge) trace f de doigt.

fin·ger·tip bout m du doigt.

fin·ish 1 n fin f; (of race) arrivée f. **2** vt finir; **to f. doing** finir de faire. **3** vi finir; **to have finished with** ne plus avoir besoin de; (situation, person) en avoir fini avec.

fin·ished adj fini.

fin·ish line ligne f d'arrivée.

▶ **finish off** vti finir.

▶ **finish up 1** vt finir. **2** vi **to f. up in** se retrouver à; **to f. up doing** finir par faire.

Finn Finlandais, -aise mf.

Finn·ish 1 adj finlandais. **2** (language) finnois m.

fir sapin m.

fire¹ feu m; (accidental) incendie m; **to set f. to** mettre le feu à; **on f.** en feu; **(there's a) f.!** au feu!

fire² 1 vt **to f. a gun** tirer un coup de fusil or de revolver; **to f. sb** (dismiss) renvoyer qn. **2** vi tirer (**at** sur).

fire a·larm alarme f d'incendie.

fire·crack·er pétard m.

fire de·part·ment pompiers mpl.

fire en·gine voiture f de pompiers.

fire es·cape escalier m de secours.

fire·man, pl **-men** pompier m.

fire·place cheminée f.

fire sta·tion caserne f de pompiers.

fire·wood bois m de chauffage.

fire·works f. (display) feu m d'artifice.

firm 1 n entreprise. **2** adj ferme.

firm·ly adv fermement.

first 1 adj premier. **2** adv (firstly) premièrement; (for the first time) pour la première fois; **(at) f.** d'abord. **3** n premier, -ière mf; **f. (gear)** (of vehicle) première f.

first aid premiers secours mpl.

first-class 1 adj excellent; (ticket, seat) de première; (mail) ordinaire. **2** adv (to travel) en première.

first floor rez-de-chaussée m inv.

first grade cours m préparatoire.

first·ly adv premièrement.

first name prénom m.

fish 1 n inv poisson m. **2** vi pêcher.

fish·er·man, pl **-men** pêcheur m.

fish·ing pêche f; **to go f.** aller à la pêche.

fish·ing rod canne f à pêche.

fish·mar·ket poissonnerie f.

fish sticks bâtonnets mpl de poisson.

fist poing *m*.

fit¹ *adj* en bonne santé; *(in good shape)* en forme; *(suitable)* propre (**for** à; **to do** à faire); *(worthy)* digne (**for** de; **to do** de faire); *(able)* apte (**for** à; **to do** à faire); **f. to eat** bon à manger.

fit² **1** *vt (of clothes)* aller (bien) à (*qn*). **2** *vi* **this shirt fits** *(fits me)* cette chemise me va (bien).

fit³ *(attack)* accès *m*.

fit (in) 1 *vt (object)* faire entrer; **to f. sb in** *(find time to see)* prendre qn. **2** *vti* **to f. (in) sth** *(go in)* aller dans qch; **he doesn't f. in** il ne peut pas s'intégrer.

fit (on) 1 *vt* **to f. sth (on) to sth** *(put)* poser qch sur qch; *(fix)* fixer qch à qch. **2** *vti* **to f. (on) sth** *(go on sth)* aller sur qch.

fit·ness *(health)* santé *f*.

▸**fit (out) with** *vt (house etc)* équiper de.

fit·ting 1 *adj* approprié (**to** à). **2** *n (of dress)* essayage *m*; **fittings** *(in house)* installations *fpl*; **f. room** cabine *f* d'essayage.

five *adj* & *n* cinq (*m*).

fix *vt (make firm, decide)* fixer; *(mend)* réparer; *(deal with)* arranger; *(prepare, cook)* préparer.

fix·ture *Sports* rencontre *f*; **fixtures** *(in building)* installations *fpl*.

▸**fix up** *vt (trip etc)* arranger; **to f. sb up with a job**/*etc* procurer un travail/etc à qn.

fiz·zy *adj* pétillant.

flag drapeau *m*; *(on ship)* pavillon *m*.

flake *(of snow)* flocon *m*.

flake (off) *vi (of paint)* s'écailler.

flame flamme *f*; **to burst into f.**, **to go up in flames** prendre feu.

flam·ma·ble *adj* inflammable.

flan tarte *f*.

flan·nel flanelle *f*.

flap 1 *vi (of wings etc)* battre. **2** *vt* **to f. its wings** battre des ailes. **3** *n (of pocket, envelope)* rabat *m*.

▸**flare up** *vi (of fire)* prendre; *(of violence)* éclater.

flash 1 *n (of light)* éclat *m*; *(for camera)* flash *m*. **2** *vi (shine)* briller; *(on and off)* clignoter. **3** *vt (a light)* projeter; *(aim)* diriger (**on, at** sur); **to f. one's headlights** faire un appel de phares.

flash·ers *(of vehicle)* feux *mpl* de détresse.

flash·light lampe *f* électrique, lampe *f* de poche.

flask *(bottle)* bouteille *f*; *(for pocket)* flasque *f*.

flat¹ 1 *adj* plat; *(punctured)* crevé; *(deflated)* à plat; *(beer)* éventé; *(rate, fare)* fixe; **to put sth (down) f.** mettre qch à plat; **f. (on one's face)** à plat ventre. **2** *adv* **f. out** *(to work)* à toute vitesse; *(to run)* à toute vitesse. **3** *n* crevaison *f*.

flat² *(rooms)* appartement *m*.

flat·ly *adv (to deny, refuse)* catégoriquement.

flat·ten (out) *vt* aplatir.

flat·ter *vt* flatter.

fla·vor goût *m*; *(of ice cream etc)* parfum *m*.

fla·vor·ing *(in cake etc)* parfum *m*.

flaw défaut *m*.

flea puce *f*.

flea mar·ket marché *m* aux puces.

flee¹ **1** *vi* s'enfuir. **2** *vt (place)* s'enfuir de.

fleet *(of ships)* flotte *f*.

Flem·ish 1 *adj* flamand. **2** *n (language)* flamand *m*.

flesh chair *f*.

flex 1 *vt (limb)* fléchir. **2** *n (wire)* fil *m* (souple); *(for telephone)* cordon *m*.

flex·i·ble *adj* souple.

flick *(with finger)* chiquenaude *f*.

flick·er 1 *n (of eyes)* tremblement *m*; *(of flame, light)* vacillement *m*; **a f. of hope** l'ombre d'un espoir. **2** *vi (eyes)* trembler; *(flame, light)* vaciller.

▶ **flick off** *vt* enlever (d'une chiquenaude).

flight *(of bird, aircraft)* vol *m*; *(escape)* fuite *f*; **f. of stairs** escalier *m*.

flight at·ten·dant *(male)* steward *m*; *(female)* hôtesse *f* de l'air.

flim·sy *adj (light)* (trop) léger; *(thin)* (trop) mince.

fling* *vt* lancer.

flint *(for lighter)* pierre *f*.

flip 1 *n (flick)* petit coup *m*; **f. chart** tableau *m* à feuilles. **2** *vt (with finger)* donner un petit coup à; *(toss)* envoyer; **to f. a coin** jouer à pile ou face.

flip-flops *npl* tongs *fpl*.

flip·per *(of swimmer)* palme *f*.

▶ **flip through** *vt (book)* feuilleter.

float 1 *n* Fishing flotteur *m*; *(at carnival)* char *m*. **2** *vi* flotter (**on** sur).

flock 1 *n (of sheep)* troupeau *m*; *(of birds)* volée *f*. **2** *vi* venir en foule.

flood 1 *n* inondation *f*; *(of letters, tears)* flot *m*. **2** *vt (field, house etc)* inonder. **3** *vi (of river)* déborder.

▶ **flood in** *vt (of tourists etc)* affluer.

▶ **flood into** *vt (of tourists etc)* envahir *(un pays etc)*.

flood·light projecteur *m*.

floor *(ground)* sol *m*; *(wooden etc in building)* plancher *m*; *(story)* étage *m*; **on the f.** par terre; **on the first f.** au rez-de-chaussée.

floor·board planche *f*.

floor lamp lampadaire *m*.

flop 1 *vi (of play etc)* faire un four. **2** *n* four *m*.

flop·py *adj (soft)* mou *(f* molle*)*.

flop·py disk disquette *f*.

flo·rist fleuriste *mf*.

floss *(dental)* **f.** fil *m* dentaire.

flour farine *f*.

flour·ish 1 *n (gesture)* grand geste *m*; *(decoration)* fioriture *f*. **2** *vt* brandir. **3** *vi (business, economy, plant)* prospérer; *(person)* être en pleine santé.

flow 1 *vi* couler; *(of electric current, information)* circuler; *(of traffic)* s'écouler. **2** *n (of river)* courant *m*; *(of current, information)* circulation *f*.

flow chart tableau *m*.

flow·er 1 *n* fleur *f*; **in f.** en fleur(s). **2** *vi* fleurir.

flow·er bed parterre *m* de fleurs, plate-bande *f*.

flow·er shop (boutique *f* de) fleuriste *mf*.

flu grippe *f*.

flu·ent *adj* **he's f. in Russian, his Russian is f.** il parle couramment le russe.

flu·ent·ly *adv (to speak a language)* couramment.

fluff *(of material)* peluche(s) *f(pl)*; *(on floor)* moutons *mpl*.

flu·id *adj & n* fluide *(m)*.

flunk *vt (exam) Fam* être collé à.

flu·o·res·cent *adj* fluorescent.

flush *vt* **to f. the toilet** tirer la chasse d'eau.

flute flûte *f*.

flut·ter *vi (of bird)* voltiger; *(of flag)* flotter.

fly¹ *(insect)* mouche *f*.

fly² 1 *vi* voler; *(of passenger)* aller en avion; *(of flag)* flotter. **2** *vt (aircraft)* piloter; *(airline)* voyager par.

fly³ *(on pants)* braguette *f*.

▶ **fly across, fly over** *vt (country etc)* survoler.

▶ **fly away, fly off** *vi* s'envoler.

fly·ing vol *m*; *(air travel)* l'avion *m*; **f. saucer** soucoupe *f* volante.

foam écume *f*; *(on beer)* mousse *f*; **f. rubber** caoutchouc *m* mousse; **f. mattress/etc** matelas *m/etc* mousse.

fo·cus 1 *n (of attention)* centre *m*; **in f.** au point. **2** *vt (image)* mettre au point. **3** *vti* **to f. (one's atten·tion) on** se tourner vers.

fog brouillard *m*.

fog·gy *adj* **it's f.** il y a du brouillard; **f. weather** brouillard *m*.

foil *(for cooking)* papier *m* alu(minium).

fold 1 *n (in paper etc)* pli *m*. **2** *vt*

plier; (*wrap*) envelopper (**in** dans); **to f. one's arms** (se) croiser les bras. **3** *vi* (*of chair etc*) se plier.

▶**fold back, fold over 1** *vt* (*blanket etc*) replier. **2** *vi* se replier.

fold·er (*file holder*) chemise *f*.

fold·ing *adj* (*chair etc*) pliant.

▶**fold up 1** *vt* (*chair etc*) plier. **2** *vi* se plier.

folk 1 *adj* (*dance etc*) folklorique; **f. music** (musique *f*) folk *m*. **2** *npl* **folks** gens *mpl or fpl*.

fol·low 1 *vt* suivre; (*career*) poursuivre; **followed by** suivi de. **2** *vi* suivre.

▶**follow around** *vt* suivre partout.

fol·low·er partisan *m*.

fol·low·ing 1 *n* suivant. **2** *prep* à la suite de.

▶**follow through** *vt* (*plan etc*) poursuivre jusqu'au bout.

▶**follow up** *vt* (*idea, story*) creuser; (*clue*) suivre.

fond *adj* **to be (very) f. of** aimer (beaucoup).

food nourriture *f*, (*particular substance*) aliment *m*; (*for cats, dogs*) pâtée *f*.

fool 1 *n* imbécile *mf*; **to play the f.** faire l'imbécile. **2** *vt* (*trick*) rouler.

▶**fool around** *vi* faire l'imbécile; (*waste time*) perdre son temps.

fool·ish *adj* bête.

fool·ish·ly *adv* bêtement.

foot, *pl* **feet** pied *m*; (*of animal*) patte *f*, (*measure*) pied *m* (= 30,48cm); **at the f. of** (*page, stairs*) au bas de; **on f.** à pied.

foot·ball (*game*) football *m* américain; (*ball*) ballon *m* (de football américain).

foot·ball play·er joueur, -euse *mf* de football américain.

foot·bridge passerelle *f*.

foot·path sentier *m*.

foot·print empreinte *f* (de pied *or* de pas).

foot·step pas *m*.

foot·stool repose-pieds *m inv*; (*cushioned*) pouf *m*.

for *prep* pour; (*in exchange for*) contre; (*for a distance of*) pendant; **what's it f.?** ça sert à quoi?; **he was away f. a month** il a été absent pendant un mois; **he won't be back f. a month** il ne sera pas de retour avant un mois; **he's been here/I haven't seen him f. a month** il est ici/je ne l'ai pas vu depuis un mois; **I haven't seen him f. ten years** voilà dix ans que je ne l'ai pas vu; **it's f. you to say** c'est à toi de dire; **f. that to be done** pour que ça soit fait.

for·bid* *vt* interdire (**sb to do** à qn de faire); **she is forbidden to leave** il lui est interdit de partir.

force 1 *n* force *f*; **the armed forces** les forces armées. **2** *vt* forcer (*qn*) (**to do** à faire); (*door*) forcer; **forced to do** obligé *or* forcé de faire; **to f. one's way into** entrer de force dans.

fore·cast 1 *vt** prévoir. **2** *n* prévision *f*, (*of weather*) météo *f*.

fore·head front *m*.

for·eign *adj* étranger; (*trade*) extérieur; (*travel*) à l'étranger.

for·eign·er étranger, -ère *mf*.

fore·man, *pl* **-men** (*worker*) contremaître *m*.

fore·most *adj* principal.

fore·run·ner précurseur *m*.

fore·see* *vt* prévoir.

for·est forêt *f*.

for·ev·er *adv* pour toujours; (*continually*) sans cesse.

forge *vt* (*signature, money*) contrefaire; (*document*) falsifier.

▶**forge ahead** *vi* (*progress*) aller de l'avant.

for·ger·y faux *m*.

for·get* *vti* oublier (**to do** de faire).

▶**forget about** *vt* oublier.

for·get·ful *adj* **he's f.** il n'a pas de mémoire.

for·give* vt pardonner (**sb sth** qch à qn).

fork 1 n (for eating) fourchette f; (for gardening) fourche f; (in road) bifurcation f. **2** vi (of road) bifurquer.

▸**fork out** vt (money) Fam allonger.

form 1 n forme f; (document) formulaire m. **2** vt (group, basis etc) former; (habit) contracter; (an opinion) se former; **to f. part of** faire partie de. **3** vi (appear) se former.

for·mal adj (person, tone etc) cérémonieux; (stuffy) compassé; (official) officiel; **f. dress** tenue de cérémonie.

for·mal·i·ty formalité f.

for·mat 1 n format m. **2** vt Comput formater.

for·ma·tion formation f.

for·mer 1 adj (previous) ancien; (of two) premier. **2** pron **the f.** celui-là, celle-là.

for·mer·ly adv autrefois.

for·mu·la, pl **-as** or **-ae** formule f; (pl **-as**) (baby food) lait m maternisé.

fort fort m.

forth adv **and so f.** et ainsi de suite; **to walk back and f.** faire les cent pas.

forth·com·ing adj (event) à venir; (communicative) expansif (about sur); **no answer was f.** il n'y a eu aucune réponse.

for·ti·eth adj & n quarantième (mf).

for·tress forteresse f.

for·tu·nate adj (choice etc) heureux; **to be f.** (of person) avoir de la chance; **it's f. that** c'est heureux que (+ subjunctive).

for·tu·nate·ly adv heureusement.

for·tune n fortune f; **to make one's f.** faire fortune; **to have the good f. to do** avoir la chance de faire.

for·ty adj & n quarante (m).

fo·rum forum m.

for·ward 1 adv **forward(s)** en avant; **to go f.** avancer. **2** vt (letter) faire suivre; (goods) expédier.

fos·sil fossile m.

fos·ter 1 vt (child) accueillir; (hope, idea) nourrir, entretenir; (relations) favoriser. **2** adj **f. child** enfant mf placé(e) dans une famille d'accueil; **f. parents** parents mpl nourriciers.

foul 1 adj (smell, taste) infect; (language) grossier. **2** n Sports faute f.

found¹ pt & pp de **find**.

found² vt (town etc) fonder.

found·er¹ fondateur, -trice mf.

foun·der² vi (ship) sombrer; (plan, hopes) s'effondrer.

foun·tain fontaine f.

foun·tain pen stylo m à encre.

four adj & n quatre (m).

four·teen adj & n quatorze (m).

fourth adj & n quatrième (mf).

fowl volaille f.

fox renard m.

foy·er (in theater) foyer m.

frac·tion fraction f.

frac·ture 1 n fracture f. **2** vt **to f. one's leg**/etc se fracturer la jambe/etc.

frag·ile adj fragile.

frag·ment fragment m.

fra·grance parfum m.

frail adj fragile.

frame 1 n (of picture, bicycle) cadre m; (of window) châssis m; **f. of mind** humeur f. **2** vt (picture) encadrer.

frame·work structure f; **in the f. of** dans le cadre de.

franc franc m.

fran·chise (right to vote) droit m de vote; (right to sell product) franchise f.

frank adj franc (f franche).

frank·ly adv franchement.

frank·ness franchise f.

fran·tic adj (activity) frénétique; (rush) effréné; (person) hors de soi.

fran·ti·cal·ly adv comme un fou.

fraud (crime) fraude f; (person) imposteur m.

fray vi (of garment) s'effilocher.

freck·le tache f de rousseur.

freck·led adj couvert de taches de rousseur.

free 1 adj libre; (lavish) généreux (with de); **f. (of charge)** gratuit; **to get f.** se libérer; **f. to do** libre de faire; **f. of** (pain etc) débarrassé de. **2** adv **f. (of charge)** gratuitement. **3** vt (pt & pp **freed**) (prisoner) libérer; (trapped person) dégager.

free·dom liberté f; **f. from** (worry) absence f de.

free·ly adv librement; (to give) libéralement.

free-range adj (chicken) fermier; **f. eggs** œufs mpl de poules élevées en plein air.

free·way autoroute f.

freeze* 1 vi geler. **2** vt (food) congeler; (prices) bloquer.

freez·er congélateur m; (in fridge) freezer m.

▶**freeze up, freeze over** vi geler; (of window) se givrer.

freez·ing adj (weather) glacial; (hands, person) gelé; **it's f.** on gèle.

freight (goods) fret m; **f. car** wagon m de marchandises; **f. train** train m de marchandises.

French 1 adj français; (teacher) de français; (embassy) de France. **2** n (language) français m; **the F.** les Français mpl.

French bread a loaf of F. une baguette.

French fries frites fpl.

French·man, pl **-men** Français m.

French-speak·ing adj francophone.

French·wom·an, pl **-women** Française f.

fre·quent adj fréquent; **f. visitor** habitué, -ée mf (**to** de).

fre·quent·ly adv fréquemment.

fresh adj frais (f fraîche); (new)

nouveau (f nouvelle); **to get some f. air** prendre l'air.

fresh·en·er air f. désodorisant m.

▶**fresh·en up** vi faire un brin de toilette.

fret vi (worry) se faire du souci.

Fri·day vendredi m; **Good F.** Vendredi Saint.

fridge frigo m.

fried (pt & pp of **fry**) adj (fish) frit; **f. egg** œuf m sur le plat.

friend ami, -ie mf; (from school, work) camarade mf; **to be friends with sb** être ami de qn.

friend·ly adj aimable (**to** avec); **to be f. with** être ami avec.

friend·ship amitié f.

fright peur f; **to get a f.** avoir peur; **to give sb a f.** faire peur à qn.

fright·en vt effrayer.

▶**frighten away, frighten off** vt (animal, person) fair fuire.

fright·ened adj effrayé; **to be f.** avoir peur (**of** de).

fright·en·ing adj effrayant.

frill (on dress etc) volant m.

fringe frange f; **on the f. of society** en marge de la société; **f. benefits** avantages mpl en nature.

fro adv **to go to and f.** aller et venir.

frog grenouille f.

from prep de; **where are you f.?** d'où êtes-vous?; **a train f.** un train en provenance de. ▪ (time onwards) à partir de, dès; **f. today (on),** à partir d'aujourd'hui, dès aujourd'hui. ▪ (numbers, prices onwards) à partir de. ▪ (away from) à; **to take/borrow f.** prendre/emprunter à. ▪ (out of) dans; sur; **to take f.** (box) prendre dans; (table) prendre sur; **to drink f. a cup/the bottle** boire dans une tasse/à la bouteille. ▪ (according to) d'après. ▪ (cause) par. ▪ (on behalf of) de la part de; **tell her f. me** dis-lui de ma part.

front 1 n (of garment, building) devant m; (of boat, car) avant m; (of *book)* début *m*; **in f. (of)** devant; **in f.** *(ahead)* en avant; *(in race)* en tête; **in the f.** *(in vehicle)* à l'avant. **2** *adj* *(tooth)* de devant; *(part, wheel, car seat)* avant *inv*; *(row, page)* premier; **f. door** porte *f* d'entrée.

fron·tier frontière *f*.

frost gel *m*; *(on window)* givre *m*.

frost·bite gelure *f*.

▶ **frost up** *vi* (of window etc) se givrer.

frost·y *adj* *(window)* givré; **it's f.** il gèle.

froth mousse *f*.

frown *vi* froncer les sourcils.

fro·zen *adj* *(vegetables etc)* surgelé; **f. food** surgelés *mpl*.

fruit fruit *m*; **(some)** *(one piece)* un fruit; *(more than one)* des fruits; **f. drink** boisson *f* aux fruits; **f. salad** salade *f* de fruits; **f. tree** arbre *m* fruitier.

fruit·cake cake *m*.

frus·trate *vt* frustrer.

frus·trat·ed *adj* frustré.

frus·trat·ing *adj* irritant.

frus·tra·tion frustration *f*.

fry 1 *vt* faire frire. **2** *vi* frire.

fry·ing pan poêle *f* (à frire).

fudge caramel *m* mou.

fu·el combustible *m*; *(for vehicle)* carburant *m*.

fu·gi·tive fugitif, -ive *mf*.

ful·fil *vt* *(ambition)* réaliser; *(condition)* remplir; *(desire)* satisfaire.

ful·fill·ing *adj* satisfaisant.

full 1 *adj* plein **(of**); *(bus, theater etc)* complet; *(life, day)* rempli; **the f. price** le prix fort; **to pay f. fare** payer plein tarif; **to be f.** *(of person)* n'avoir plus faim; *(of hotel)* être complet; **f. name** *(on form)* nom et prénom. **2** *n* **in f.** *(to read sth etc)* en entier.

full-scale, full-size *adj* *(model)* grandeur nature *inv*.

full-time *adj & adv* à plein temps.

ful·ly *adv* entièrement.

fumes *npl* vapeurs *fpl*; *(from car exhaust)* gaz *m inv*.

fun amusement *m*; **to be f.** être très amusant; **to have (some) f.** s'amuser; **to make f. of** se moquer de; **for f.** pour le plaisir.

func·tion fonction *f*; *(meeting)* réunion *f*.

func·tion·al *adj* fonctionnel.

fund 1 *n* *(for pension etc)* caisse *f*; **funds** *(money, resources)* fonds *mpl*. **2** *vt* fournir des fonds à.

fu·ner·al enterrement *m*; **f. home** entreprise *f* de pompes funèbres.

fun·nel *(of ship)* cheminée *f*; *(for pouring)* entonnoir *m*.

fun·ny *adj* drôle; *(strange)* bizarre; **a f. idea** une drôle d'idée; **to feel f.** ne pas se sentir très bien.

fur fourrure *f*.

fu·ri·ous *adj* furieux **(with, at** contre).

fur·nace fourneau *m*.

fur·nish *vt* *(room)* meubler.

fur·nished room pièce *f* meublée.

fur·ni·ture meubles *mpl*; **a piece of f.** un meuble.

fur·ther 1 *adv* = **farther**; *(more)* davantage. **2** *adj* supplémentaire; **f. details** de plus amples détails; **a f. case** /etc un autre cas/etc.

fur·ther·more *adv* en outre.

fur·thest *adj & adv* = **farthest**.

fu·ry fureur *f*.

fuss 1 *n* chichis *mpl*; **what a f.!** quelle histoire! **2** *vi* faire des chichis.

▶ **fuss over** *vt* être aux petits soins pour.

fuss·y *adj* tatillon; *(difficult)* difficile **(about** sur).

fu·ture 1 *n* avenir *m*; *Grammar* futur *m*; **in the f.** *(one day)* un jour (futur). **2** *adj* futur; *(date)* ultérieur.

fuze *(wire)* plomb *m*, fusible *m*; *(of bomb)* amorce *f*; **to blow a f.** faire sauter un plomb; **we've blown a f.** un plomb a sauté.

fuzz·y *adj* *(picture, idea)* flou.

G

gadg·et gadget m.

Gael·ic adj & n gaélique (m).

gag 1 n (over mouth) bâillon m; (joke) gag m. **2** vt (victim) bâillonner. **3** vi (choke) s'étouffer (**on** avec).

gai·e·ty gaieté f.

gai·ly adv gaiement.

gain 1 vt (obtain) gagner; (experience) acquérir; **to g. speed/weight** prendre de la vitesse/du poids. **2** n (increase) augmentation f (**in** de); (profit) bénéfice m.

▸ **gain on** vt (catch up with) rattraper.

ga·la gala m.

ga·lax·y galaxie f.

gale grand vent m.

gal·lant adj (chivalrous) galant.

gal·ler·y galerie f, (for public) tribune f; **art g.** (private) galerie f d'art; (public) musée m d'art.

gal·li·vant Fam vadrouiller.

gal·lon gallon m.

gal·lop 1 vi galoper. **2** n galop m.

gam·ble 1 vi jouer (**on** sur; **with** avec). **2** vt jouer. **3** n coup m risqué.

gam·ble (a·way) vt (lose) perdre (au jeu).

gam·bler joueur, -euse mf.

gam·bling jeu m.

game jeu m; (of football, etc) match m; (of tennis, chess, cards) partie f; **to play a g. of** (football etc) jouer un match de; (tennis, chess, cards) faire une partie de.

game ar·cade f galerie de jeux.

gang (of children, criminals) bande f, gang m; (of workers) équipe f.

gang·ster gangster m.

▸ **gang up on** vt se mettre à plusieurs contre.

gang·way (to ship, aircraft) passerelle f.

gap (empty space) trou m; (in time) intervalle m; (in knowledge) lacune f; **the g. between** (difference) l'écart m entre.

gape vi rester bouche bée.

▸ **gape at** vt regarder bouche bée.

ga·rage garage m.

gar·bage ordures fpl; (nonsense) idioties fpl; **g. bag** sac m poubelle; **g. man** éboueur m; **g. truck** camion-benne m.

gar·ban·zo (bean) pois m chiche.

gar·den 1 n jardin m. **2** vi jardiner.

gar·den·er jardinier, -ière mf.

gar·den hose tuyau m.

gar·den·ing jardinage m.

gar·gle vi se gargariser.

gar·land guirlande f.

gar·lic ail m.

gar·ment vêtement m.

gas 1 n gaz m inv; (gasoline) essence f; **g. mask/meter/etc** masque m/compteur m/etc à gaz; **g. heat** chauffage m au gaz; **g. heater** appareil m de chauffage à gaz; **g. station** station-service f, **g. stove** cuisinière f à gaz; (portable) réchaud m à gaz. **2** vt (poison) asphyxier (qn).

gash 1 n entaille f. **2** vt entailler.

gas·o·line essence f.

gasp 1 vi to **g. (for breath)** haleter. **2** n halètement m.

gas·sy adj (drink) gazeux.

gas·works usine f à gaz.

gate (at grade crossing, field etc) barrière f, (metal) grille f, (of castle, in airport) porte f, (at stadium) entrée f; (for tickets) portillon m.

gate·crash vi s'inviter (de force).

gath·er 1 vt (people, objects) rassembler; (pick up) ramasser; (information) recueillir; **I g. that...** je crois comprendre que...; **to g. speed** prendre de la vitesse. **2** vi (of people) se rassembler.

gath·er·ing (group) réunion f.

▸ **gather round** vi (come closer) s'approcher.

gaud·y adj voyant.

gauge 1 n (instrument) jauge f. **2** vt (estimate) évaluer.

gaunt adj décharné.

gauze gaze f.

gave pt de **give**.

gay 1 n homo(sexuel). **2** n homo-(sexuel) m.

gaze 1 n regard m (fixe). **2** vi regar-der.

▸ **gaze at** vt regarder (longuement).

gear 1 n équipement m; (belong-ings) affaires fpl; (clothes) Fam vête-ments mpl; (speed in vehicle) vitesse f, **in g.** en prise; **not in g.** au point mort. **2** vt adapter (**to** à).

▸ **gear up** vt to be geared up to do être prêt à faire; **to g. oneself up for** se préparer pour.

geek Fam ringard, -e mf.

geese see **goose**.

gel gel m.

gem pierre f précieuse.

gen·der Grammar genre m.

gen·er·al 1 adj général; **in g.** en général; **the g. public** le (grand) public; **for g. use** à l'usage du pu-blic. **2** n (in army) général m.

gen·er·al·ly adv généralement.

gen·er·a·tion génération f.

gen·er·a·tor groupe m électro-gène.

gen·er·os·i·ty générosité f.

gen·er·ous adj généreux (with de); (helping) copieux.

gen·er·ous·ly adv généreusement.

gen·ius (ability, person) génie m.

gen·tle adj (person, slope etc) doux (f douce); (touch) léger; (exer-cise, speed) modéré.

gen·tle·man, pl -men monsieur m.

gen·tle·ness douceur f.

gent·ly adv doucement.

gen·u·ine adj véritable, authen-tique; (sincere) sincère.

gen·u·ine·ly adv véritablement, sincèrement.

ge·o·graph·i·cal adj géogra-phique.

ge·og·ra·phy géographie f.

ge·o·met·ric, ge·o·met·ri·cal adj géométrique.

ge·om·e·try géométrie f.

germ (in body, food etc) microbe m.

Ger·man 1 adj allemand. **2** n (per-son) Allemand, -ande mf; (lan-guage) allemand m.

Ger·man mea·sles rubéole f.

Ger·man shep·herd (dog) ber-ger m allemand.

ges·ture geste m.

get* 1 vt (obtain) obtenir; (find) trouver; (buy) acheter; (receive) re-cevoir; (catch) attraper; (bus, train) prendre; (seize) saisir; (fetch) aller chercher; (put) mettre; (derive) tirer (from de); (understand) compren-dre; (prepare) préparer; (hit with fist, stick etc) atteindre; (reputation) se faire; **I have got** j'ai; **to g. sb to do sth** faire faire qch à qn; **to g. sth built**/etc faire construire/etc qch. **2** vi (go) aller; (arrive) arriver (**to** à); (become) devenir; **to g. caught**/etc se faire prendre/etc; **to g. cleaned up** se laver; **where have you got-ten to?** où en es-tu?; **you've got to stay** (must) tu dois rester; **to g. working** se mettre à travailler.

▸ **get across 1** vt (road) traverser; (message) communiquer. **2** vi traverser.

▸ **get along** vi (manage) se dé-brouiller; (be on good terms) s'en-tendre (with avec).

▸ **get around** vi se déplacer; **to g. around to doing** se mettre à faire.

▸ **get at** vt (reach) parvenir à.

▸ **get away** vi (leave) partir; (es-cape) s'échapper.

▸ **get back 1** vt (recover) récupérer; (replace) remettre. **2** vi (return) re-venir; (move back) reculer.

▸ **get by** vi passer; (manage) se débrouiller.

▸ **get down** vti descendre.

▸ **get in 1** vt (laundry etc) rentrer;

(call for) faire venir *(qn)*. **2** *vi (enter)* entrer; *(come home)* rentrer; *(enter vehicle or train)* monter; *(of plane, train)* arriver.

▸ **get in (to)** *vt* entrer dans; *(vehicle, train)* monter dans; **to g. in (to) bed** se mettre au lit.

▸ **get off 1** *vi (leave)* partir; *(from vehicle or train)* descendre **(from** de); *(in court)* être acquitté. **2** *vt (remove)* enlever; *(send)* expédier; **to g. off a bus** descendre d'un bus.

▸ **get on 1** *vt (shoes, clothes)* mettre; *(bus, train)* monter dans. **2** *vi (progress)* marcher; *(manage)* se débrouiller; *(succeed)* réussir; *(enter bus or train)* monter; **to g. on with** *(task)* continuer.

▸ **get out 1** *vi* sortir; *(from vehicle or train)* descendre *(of* de); **to g. out of** *(danger)* se tirer de; *(habit)* perdre. **2** *vt (remove)* enlever; *(bring out)* sortir *(qch)*, faire sortir *(qn)*.

▸ **get over 1** *vt (road)* traverser; *(obstacle)* surmonter; *(fence)* franchir; *(illness)* se remettre de. **2** *vt (cross)* traverser; *(visit)* passer.

▸ **get through 1** *vi* passer; *(finish)* finir; **to g. through to sb** *(on phone)* contacter qn. **2** *vt* passer par; *(meal)* venir à bout de.

▸ **get to** *vt* **to g. sth to sb** faire parvenir qch à qn; **to g. sb to the airport** amener qn à l'aéroport.

get-to-geth-er réunion *f*.

▸ **get up 1** *vi (rise)* se lever **(from** de); **to g. up to something** *or* **to mischief** faire des bêtises. **2** *vt (bring up)* monter *(qch)*; *(wake up)* réveiller.

ghast·ly *adj (horrible)* affreux.

ghet·to, *pl* -os ghetto *m*.

ghost fantôme *m*.

gi·ant 1 *n* géant *m*. **2** *adj (tree, packet)* géant.

gid·dy *adj* **to be** *or* **feel g.** avoir le vertige; **to make g.** donner le vertige à.

gift cadeau *m*; *(talent)* don *m*.

gift·ed *adj* doué.

gift vouch·er bon-cadeau *m*.

gig *Fam (pop or rock concert)* concert *m*.

gi·ga·byte gigaoctet *m*.

gi·gan·tic *adj* gigantesque.

gig·gle 1 *vi* pouffer (de rire). **2** *n* **to get/have the giggles** attraper/ avoir le fou rire.

gills *npl (of fish)* ouïes *fpl*.

gim·mick truc *m*.

gin *(drink)* gin *m*.

gin·ger gingembre *m*.

gi·raffe girafe *f*.

girl *(jeune)* fille *f*; *(daughter)* fille *f*; **American g.** jeune Américaine *f*.

girl·friend amie *f*; *(of boy)* petite amie *f*.

girl scout éclaireuse *f*.

give* *vt* donner **(to** à); *(support)* apporter; *(a smile)* faire; *(a sigh)* pousser; *(a look)* jeter.

▸ **give away** *vt (free of charge)* donner; *(prizes)* distribuer; *(betray)* trahir *(qn)*.

▸ **give back** *vt (return)* rendre.

▸ **give in 1** *vi (surrender)* céder **(to** à). **2** *vt (hand in)* remettre.

giv·en 1 *adj (specified)* donné; **at a g. moment** à un moment donné; **to be g. to sth** *(prone to)* avoir une tendance à qch. **2** *conj (considering)* étant donné.

▸ **give out** *vt (hand out)* distribuer.

▸ **give over** *vt (devote)* consacrer **(to** à).

▸ **give up 1** *vi* abandonner. **2** *vt* abandonner; *(seat)* céder **(to** à); *(prisoner)* livrer **(to** à); **to g. up smoking** cesser de fumer.

▸ **give way** *vi (of branch, person etc)* céder **(to** à); *(in vehicle)* céder la priorité **(to** à).

glad *adj* content **(of, about** de).

glad·ly *adv* volontiers.

glam·or *(charm)* enchantement *m*; *(splendor)* éclat *m*.

glam·or·ous *adj* séduisant.

glance 1 *n* coup *m* d'œil. **2** *vi* jeter un coup d'œil **(at** à, sur).

gland glande *f*.

glare 1 *n (light)* lumière *f* éblouissante; *(look)* regard *m* furieux. **2** *vi (dazzle)* briller d'un éclat éblouissant; **to g. at sb** regarder qn avec colère.

glar·ing *adj (light)* éblouissant; *(injustice)* flagrant.

glass verre *m*; *(mirror)* miroir *m*; **a pane of g.** une vitre.

glass·es *npl (for eyes)* lunettes *fpl*.

glee joie *f*.

glen vallon *m*.

glide *vi* glisser; *(of aircraft, bird)* planer.

glid·ing *(sport)* vol *m* à voile.

glim·mer *(of hope)* lueur *f*.

glimpse aperçu *m*; **to catch** *or* **get a g. of** entrevoir.

glit·ter·ing *adj* scintillant.

globe globe *m*.

gloom *(sadness)* tristesse *f*.

gloom·y *adj* triste; *(pessimistic)* pessimiste.

glo·ri·fied *adj* **it's a g. barn**/*etc* ce n'est guère plus qu'une grange/*etc*.

glo·ri·ous *adj* glorieux; *(splendid)* magnifique.

glo·ry gloire *f*.

gloss *(shine)* brillant *m*.

gloss·y *adj (paint, finish)* brillant; *(magazine)* de luxe.

glove gant *m*.

glove box, glove com·part·ment *(in car)* boîte *f* à gants.

glow *vi (of sky, fire)* rougeoyer.

glue 1 *n* colle *f*. **2** *vt* coller (**to, on** à); **with eyes glued to** les yeux fixés sur.

glum *adj* triste.

glut *(of oil etc)* surplus *m*.

glut·ton glouton, -onne *mf*.

gnat *(insect)* moucheron *m*.

gnaw *vti* ronger.

go¹* *vi* aller (**to** à; **from** de); *(depart)* partir, s'en aller; *(disappear)* disparaître, partir; *(function)* marcher; *(become)* devenir; *(of material)* s'user; **to go well/badly** *(of event)* se passer bien/mal; **she's going to do** *(is about to, intends to)* elle va faire; **it's all gone** il n'y en a plus; **to go and get** aller chercher; **to go riding/on a trip**/*etc* faire du cheval/un voyage/*etc*; **to let go of** lâcher; **to go to a doctor**/*etc* aller voir un médecin/*etc*; **two hours/** *etc* **to go** encore deux heures/*etc*.

go², *pl* **goes** *(attempt)* coup *m*; **to have a go at (doing) sth** essayer (de faire) qch; **on the go** actif.

▸ **go about, go around 1** *vi* se déplacer; *(of news)* circuler. **2** *vt* **to know how to go about it** savoir s'y prendre.

▸ **go across** *vti (cross)* traverser.

▸ **go after** *vt (chase)* poursuivre; *(seek)* (re)chercher.

go-a·head **to get the g.** avoir le feu vert.

▸ **go ahead** *vi* avancer; *(continue)* continuer; *(start)* commencer; **go ahead!** allez-y!; **to go ahead with** *(plan etc)* poursuivre.

goal but *m*.

goal·keep·er gardien *m* de but.

▸ **go along** *vi* aller; **to go along with** *(agree)* être d'accord avec.

▸ **go around 1** *vi (turn)* tourner; *(be sufficient)* suffire. **2** *vt (corner)* tourner; *(world)* faire le tour de.

goat chèvre *f*.

▸ **go away** *vi* partir, s'en aller.

▸ **go back** *vi* retourner; *(in time)* remonter; *(step back)* reculer; **to go back on** *(promise)* revenir sur.

go-be·tween intermédiaire *mf*.

god dieu *m*; **G.** Dieu *m*.

god·daugh·ter filleule *f*.

god·fa·ther parrain *m*.

god·moth·er marraine *f*.

▸ **go down 1** *vi* descendre; *(fall down)* tomber; *(of ship)* couler; *(of sun)* se coucher; *(of price etc)* baisser. **2** *vt* **to go down the stairs/** **street** descendre l'escalier/la rue.

god·send **to be a g.** tomber à pic.

god·son filleul *m*.

goes see **go¹**.

gog·gles npl lunettes fpl (de protection, de plongée).

▸ **go in 1** vi (r)entrer; (of sun) se cacher. **2** vt **to go in a room/etc** entrer dans une pièce/etc.

▸ **go (in) for** vt s'intéresser à.

go·ing 1 n (conditions) conditions fpl; **it's slow** or **tough g.** c'est difficile. **2** adj **the g. price** le prix pratiqué (**for** pour).

go·ings-on npl activités fpl.

▸ **go into** vt (room etc) entrer dans.

gold or m; **g. watch/etc** montre/etc en or.

gold·en adj (in color) doré; (rule) d'or.

gold·fish poisson m rouge.

gold mine mine f d'or.

gold-plat·ed adj plaqué or.

golf golf m.

golf·er golfeur, -euse mf.

gone pp de **go¹**.

good 1 adj bon (f bonne); (kind) gentil; (weather) beau (f belle); (well-behaved) sage; **very g.!** (all right) très bien!; **to feel g.** se sentir bien; **g. at French/etc** bon or fort en français/etc; **to be g. with** (children) savoir s'y prendre avec; **it's a g. thing (that)...** heureusement que...; **a g. many, a g. deal (of)** beaucoup (de); **g. morning** bonjour; (on leaving) au revoir; **g. evening** bonsoir; **g. night** bonsoir; (going to bed) bonne nuit. **2** n (advantage, virtue) bien m; **for her own g.** pour son bien; **it's no g. crying/etc** ça ne sert à rien de pleurer/etc; **that's no g.** (worthless) ça ne vaut rien; (bad) ça ne va pas; **what's the g.?** à quoi bon?; **for g.** pour de bon.

good·bye int au revoir.

good-look·ing adj beau (f belle).

good·ness bonté f; **my g.!** mon Dieu!; **thank g.!** Dieu merci!; **for g.' sake!** bon sang!

goods npl marchandises fpl; (arti-

cles for sale) articles mpl.

good·will bonne volonté f.

▸ **go off** vi (leave) partir; (of alarm) se déclencher.

▸ **go on** vi continuer (**doing** à faire); (happen) se passer; (last) durer.

goose, pl **geese** oie f.

goose·ber·ry groseille f à maquereau.

goose bumps npl chair f de poule.

▸ **go out** vi sortir; (of light, fire) s'éteindre.

▸ **go over 1** vi aller (**to** à); (to enemy) passer (**to** à); **to go over to sb's** faire un saut chez qn. **2** vt examiner; (in one's mind) repasser.

gorge (ravine) gorge f.

gor·geous adj magnifique.

go·ril·la gorille m.

Gos·pel Évangile m.

gos·sip 1 n (talk) bavardage(s) m(pl); (person) commère f. **2** vi (to talk) bavarder; (ill-naturedly) se livrer à des commérages.

got pt & pp de **get**.

▸ **go through 1** vi passer. **2** vt (suffer) subir; (examine) examiner; (search) fouiller; (spend) dépenser; (wear out) user.

got·ten pp de **get**.

▸ **go under** vi (of ship, company) couler.

▸ **go up 1** vi monter; (of prices) augmenter. **2** vt **to go up the stairs/street** monter l'escalier/la rue.

gour·met gourmet m.

gov·ern 1 vt (rule) gouverner; (city) administrer; (influence) déterminer. **2** vi gouverner.

gov·ern·ment gouvernement m; (local) administration f.

gov·er·nor gouverneur m.

▸ **go with** vt (accompany) accompagner, aller avec; (colors) aller avec.

▸ **go without** vt se passer de.

gown (of woman) robe f.

grab vt **to g. (hold of)** saisir; **to g. sth from sb** arracher qch à qn.

grace (charm) grâce f.

grace·ful *adj* gracieux.

grade 1 *n* catégorie *f*; *(in exam etc)* note *f*; *(class in school)* classe *f*. **2** *vt* *(classify)* classer; *(school paper)* noter, corriger.

grade cross·ing passage *m* à niveau.

grade school école *f* primaire.

grad·u·al *adj* progressif.

gradu·al·ly *adv* progressivement.

grad·u·ate 1 *vi* obtenir son diplôme. **2** *n* diplômé, -ée *mf*.

grad·u·a·tion remise *f* des diplômes.

graf·fi·ti *npl* graffiti *mpl*.

graft 1 *n* greffe *f*. **2** *vt* greffer.

grain *(seed)* grain *m*; *(cereal)* céréales *fpl*.

gram gramme *m*.

gram·mar grammaire *f*.

gram·mar school = **grade school**.

gram·mat·i·cal *adj* grammatical.

grand *adj* *(splendid)* magnifique.

grand-dad(·dy) *Fam* papi *m*.

grand·child, *pl* -children petit(e)-enfant *mf*.

grand-daugh·ter petite-fille *f*.

grand-fa·ther grand-père *m*.

grand-ma *Fam* mamie *f*.

grand-moth·er grand-mère *f*.

grand·par·ents *npl* grands-parents *mpl*.

grand·son petit-fils *m*.

gran·ny *Fam* mamie *m*.

gra·no·la muesli *m*.

grant 1 *vt* accorder (**to** à); *(request)* accéder à; **to take sth for granted** considérer qch comme acquis; **I take it for granted that** je présume que. **2** *n* subvention *f*, *(for study)* bourse *f*.

grape grain *m* de raisin; **grapes** le raisin, les raisins *mpl*; **to eat (some) grapes** manger du raisin *or* des raisins.

grape·fruit pamplemousse *m*.

graph courbe *f*; **g. paper** papier *m* millimétré.

graph·ic *adj* graphique; **g. designer** graphiste *mf*.

graph·ics 1 *n* *(study)* art *m* graphique. **2** *npl* graphiques *mpl*.

grasp 1 *vt* *(seize, understand)* saisir. **2** *n* *(hold)* prise *f*, *(understanding)* compréhension *f*.

grass herbe *f*; *(lawn)* gazon *m*.

grass·hop·per sauterelle *f*.

grate 1 *n* *(for fireplace)* grille *f* de foyer. **2** *vt* *(cheese etc)* râper.

grate·ful *adj* reconnaissant (**to** à; **for** de); **I'm g. (to you) for your help** je vous suis reconnaissant de votre aide.

grat·er râpe *f*.

grat·i·fy·ing *adj* très satisfaisant *or* agréable.

grat·i·tude reconnaissance *f*, gratitude *f* (**for** de).

grave¹ tombe *f*.

grave² *adj* *(serious)* grave.

grav·el gravier *m*.

grave·yard cimetière *m*.

grav·i·ty *(force)* pesanteur *f*.

gra·vy jus *m* de viande.

gray *adj* gris; **to be going g.** grisonner.

graze 1 *vi* *(of cattle)* paître. **2** *vt* *(skin)* écorcher. **3** *n* *(wound)* écorchure *f*.

grease 1 *n* graisse *f*. **2** *vt* graisser.

greas·y *adj* plein de graisse; *(hair)* gras.

great *adj* grand; *(excellent)* *Fam* magnifique; **a g. deal (of)**, **a g. many** beaucoup (de); **the greatest team/etc (best)** la meilleure équipe/etc.

great-grand·fa·ther arrière-grand-père *m*.

great-grand·moth·er arrière-grand-mère *f*.

great·ly *(much)* beaucoup; *(very)* très.

greed avidité *f*; *(for food)* gourmandise *f*.

greed·y *adj* avide; *(for food)* gourmand.

Greek 1 adj grec (f grecque). **2** n Grec m, Greque f; (language) grec m.

green 1 adj vert; **to turn** or **go g.** verdir. **2** n (color) vert m; (lawn) pelouse f; **greens** légumes mpl verts.

green·house serre f; **g. effect** effet m de serre.

greet vt saluer.

greet·ing salutation f, **greetings** (for birthday, festival) vœux mpl.

gre·nade (bomb) grenade f.

grey·hound lévrier m.

grid (on map) quadrillage m; (bars) grille f.

grief chagrin m.

grieve vi **to g. for sb** pleurer qn.

grill 1 n (utensil) gril m; (dish) grillade f. **2** vti griller.

grim adj (face, future) sombre; (bad) Fam affreux.

grime crasse f.

grim·y adj crasseux.

grin 1 vi avoir un large sourire. **2** n large sourire m.

grind* vt moudre; **to g. one's teeth** grincer des dents.

grind·er coffee g. moulin m à café.

grip 1 vt saisir; (hold) tenir serré. **2** n (hold) prise f; (with hand) poigne f; **in the g. of** en proie à.

grip·ping adj (book etc) prenant.

groan 1 vi gémir. **2** n gémissement m.

gro·cer épicier, -ière mf.

gro·cer·y g. store magasin m d'alimentation; **groceries** (food) épicerie f.

groin aine f.

groom (bridegroom) marié m.

groove (slot) rainure f.

▶ **grope around** vi tâtonner.

▶ **grope for** vt chercher à tâtons.

gross adj (total) (income etc) brut.

gross·ly adv (very) extrêmement.

ground terre f, sol m; (for camping etc) terrain m; **grounds** (reasons) raisons fpl; (gardens) parc m; **on the g.** (lying, sitting) par terre.

ground meat hachis m (de viande).

ground·work préparation f.

group groupe m.

group (to·geth·er) vti (se) grouper.

grow* 1 vi (of person) grandir; (of plant, hair) pousser; (increase) augmenter, grandir; (of company, town) se développer. **2** vt (plant, crops) cultiver; (beard) laisser pousser.

▶ **grow into** vt devenir.

growl vi grogner (**at** contre).

grown adj (man, woman) adulte.

grown-up grande personne f.

▶ **grow out of** vt (clothes) devenir trop grand pour; (habit) perdre.

growth croissance f; (increase) augmentation f (**in** de); (lump) tumeur f (**on** à).

▶ **grow up** vi devenir adulte.

grub (food) Fam bouffe f.

grub·by adj sale.

grudge rancune f; **to have a g. against** garder rancune à.

gru·el·ing adj éprouvant.

grue·some adj horrible.

grum·ble vi râler, grogner (**about**, **at** contre).

grump·y adj grincheux.

grunt 1 vti grogner. **2** n grognement m.

guar·an·tee 1 n garantie f. **2** vt garantir (**against** contre; **sb that** à qn que).

guard 1 n (vigilance, soldiers) garde f; (individual person) garde m; **to keep a g. on** surveiller; **under g.** sous surveillance; **on one's g.** sur ses gardes; **on g. (duty)** de garde; **to stand g.** monter la garde. **2** vt protéger; (watch over) surveiller.

guard·i·an gardien, -enne mf; (of minor) tuteur, -trice mf; (of museum) conservateur, -trice mf; **g. angel** ange m gardien.

guess 1 n conjecture f; (intuition) intuition f; **to make a g.** (essayer de) deviner. **2** vt deviner (**that** que); (length, number) estimer; (suppose) supposer; (think) croire (**that** que).

guess·work hypothèse *f*; **by g.** au jugé.

guest invité, -ée *mf*; *(in hotel)* client, -ente *mf*; *(at meal)* convive *mf*.

guest room chambre *f* d'amis.

guid·ance conseils *mpl*.

guide 1 *n* guide *m*; **g. (book)** guide *m*. **2** *vt* guider; **guided tour** visite *f* guidée.

guide·lines *npl* indications *fpl* (à suivre).

guild association *f*.

guilt culpabilité *f*.

guilt·y *adj* coupable; **g. person** coupable *mf*.

gui·nea pig cobaye *m*.

gui·tar guitare *f*.

gui·tar·ist guitariste *mf*.

gulf *(in sea)* golfe *m*; **a g. between** un abîme entre.

gull *(bird)* mouette *f*.

gulp *(of drink)* gorgée *f*.

▸ **gulp down** *vt* avaler *(vite)*.

gum¹ *(around teeth)* gencive *f*.

gum² **1** *n* *(for chewing)* chewing-gum *m*; *(glue)* colle *f*. **2** *vt* coller.

gun pistolet *m*; *(rifle)* fusil *m*; *(firing shells)* canon *m*.

▸ **gun down** *vt* abattre.

gun·fire coups *mpl* de feu.

gun·man, *pl* -men bandit *m* armé.

gun·point **at g.** sous la menace d'une arme.

gun·pow·der poudre *f* à canon.

gun·shot coup *m* de feu.

gush (out) *vi* jaillir *(of* de).

gust **g.** *(of wind)* rafale *f* *(de* vent).

gut **1** *n* intestin *m*; **guts** *(insides)* entrailles *fpl*; *Fam (courage)* cran *m*. **2** *vt* *(poultry, fish)* étriper; *(house)* ravager.

gut·ter *(on roof)* gouttière *f*; *(in street)* caniveau *m*.

guy *Fam* type *m*.

gym gym(nastique) *f*; *(gymnasium)* gymnase *m*.

gym·nas·tics gymnastique *f*.

gy·ne·col·o·gist gynécologue *mf*.

H

hab·it habitude *f*; **to be in/get into the h. of doing** avoir/prendre l'habitude de faire.

hab·i·tat habitat *m*.

hack *vt* *(cut)* tailler.

hack·er **(computer) h.** pirate *m* informatique.

had *pt* & *pp de* **have**.

had·dock aiglefin *m*; **smoked h.** haddock *m*.

hag **(old) h.** (vieille) sorcière *f*.

hag·gle *vi* marchander; **to h. over the price** discuter le prix.

hail 1 *n* grêle *f*. **2** *vi* grêler; **it's hailing** il grêle.

hail·stone grêlon *m*.

hair *(on head)* cheveux *mpl*; *(on body, of animal)* poils *mpl*; **a h.** *(on head)* un cheveu; *(on body, of animal)* un poil.

hair·brush brosse *f* à cheveux.

hair·cut coupe *f* de cheveux; **to get a h.** se faire couper les cheveux.

hair·do, *pl* -dos *Fam* coiffure *f*.

hair·dress·er coiffeur, -euse *mf*.

hair dry·er sèche-cheveux *m inv*.

-haired *suffix* **long-/red-h.** aux cheveux longs/roux.

hair·pin épingle *f* à cheveux.

hair·rais·ing *adj* effrayant.

hair spray (bombe *f* de) laque *f*.

hair·style coiffure *f*.

hair·y *adj* *(person, animal, body)* poilu.

half 1 *n* *(pl* halves) moitié *f*, demi, -ie *mf*; **h. (of) the apple/***etc* la moitié de la pomme/*etc*; **ten and a h.** dix et demi; **ten and a h. weeks** dix semaines et demie; **to cut in h.** couper en deux. **2** *adj* demi; **h. a day, a h.-day** une demi-journée; **h. a dozen, a h.-dozen** une demi-douzaine; **at h. price** à moitié prix. **3** *adv (full etc)* à demi, à moitié; **h. past one** une heure et demie.

half-heart·ed *adj* peu enthousiaste.

half-hour demi-heure *f.*

half-time *(in game)* mi-temps *f.*

half·way *adv* à mi-chemin (**between**) entre); **to fill/etc h.** remplir/ *etc* à moitié.

hal·i·but *(fish)* flétan *m.*

hall salle *f;* **lecture h.** amphithéâtre *m.*

Hal·low·e'en Halloween *m (la veille de la Toussaint).*

hall·way entrée *f.*

halt halte *f;* **to call a h. to** mettre fin à.

halve *vt (time, expense)* réduire de moitié.

ham jambon *m;* **h. and eggs** œufs *mpl* au jambon.

ham·burg·er hamburger *m; (raw meat)* bœuf *m* haché.

ham·mer 1 *n* marteau *m.* **2** *vt (nail)* enfoncer (**into** dans).

ham·mer·ing *(defeat) Fam* raclée *f.*

ham·mock hamac *m.*

ham·per 1 *vt* gêner. **2** *n* panier *m; (laundry basket)* panier *m* à linge.

ham·ster hamster *m.*

hand¹ main *f, (of clock)* aiguille *f; Cards* jeu *m;* **to hold in one's h.** tenir à la main; **to give sb a (helping) h.** donner un coup de main à qn; **by h.** *(to make, sew etc)* à la main; **at** *or* **to h.** sous la main; **on h.** disponible; **out of h.** *(situation)* incontrôlable.

hand² *vt (give)* donner, passer (**to** à).

▸**hand around** *vt (cookies)* passer.

hand·bag sac *m* à main.

hand·book manuel *m; (guide)* guide *m.*

hand·brake frein *m* à main.

hand·cuff *vt* passer les menottes à.

hand·cuffs *npl* menottes *fpl.*

hand·ful *(group)* poignée *f.*

hand·i·cap 1 *n* handicap *m.* **2** *vt* handicaper; **to be handicapped** *(after an accident etc)* rester handicapé.

▸**hand·i·capped** *adj* handicapé.

▸**hand in** *vt* remettre.

hand·ker·chief, *pl* **-fs** mouchoir *m.*

han·dle 1 *n (of door)* poignée *f, (of knife)* manche *m, (of bucket)* anse *f, (of saucepan)* queue *f.* **2** *vt (manipulate)* manier; *(touch)* toucher à; *(vehicle)* manœuvrer; *(deal with)* s'occuper de.

han·dle·bars *npl* guidon *m.*

hand lug·gage bagages *mpl* à main.

hand·made *adj* fait à la main.

hand·out *(leaflet)* prospectus *m; (money)* aumône *f, (papers for course, workshop)* photocopies *fpl.*

▸**hand out** *vt* distribuer.

▸**hand over** *vt* remettre.

hand·rail rampe *f.*

hand·shake poignée *f* de main.

hand·some *adj* beau (*f* belle); *(profit)* considérable.

hand·writ·ing écriture *f.*

hand·y *adj* commode, pratique; *(skillful)* habile (**at doing** à faire); *(within reach)* sous la main; *(place)* accessible.

hand·y·man, *pl* **-men** bricoleur *m.*

hang¹* 1 *vt (pt & pp* **hung**) suspendre (**on, from** à); *(let dangle)* laisser pendre (**from, out of** de). **2** *vi* pendre; *(of fog)* flotter. **3** *n* **to get the h. of sth** *Fam* arriver à comprendre qch.

hang² *vt (pt & pp* **hanged**) *(criminal)* pendre (**for** pour).

han·gar hangar *m.*

▸**hang around** *vi* traîner; *(wait)* attendre.

▸**hang down** *vi* pendre.

hang·er *(coat)* **h.** cintre *m.*

hang·glid·er deltaplane® *m.*
hang·ing *adj* suspendu (**from** à).
▸**hang on** *vi* résister; *(wait)* attendre; **to h. on to** ne pas lâcher; *(keep)* garder.
▸**hang out 1** *vt (laundry)* étendre; *(flag)* arborer. **2** *vi (of tongue, shirt)* pendre.
hang·o·ver gueule *f* de bois.
▸**hang up 1** *vt (picture)* accrocher. **2** *vi (on phone)* raccrocher.
hang-up complexe *m.*
hap·pen *vi* arriver, se passer; **to h. to sb/sth** arriver à qn/qch; **I h. to know** il se trouve que je le sais; **do you h. to have…?** est-ce que par hasard vous avez…?
hap·pen·ing événement *m.*
hap·pi·ly *adv* joyeusement; *(contentedly)* tranquillement; *(fortunately)* heureusement.
hap·pi·ness bonheur *m.*
hap·py *adj* heureux (**to do** de faire; **about sth** de qch); **I'm not h. about it** ça ne me plaît pas beaucoup; **H. New Year!** bonne année!
ha·rass *vt* harceler.
ha·rass·ment harcèlement *m.*
har·bor port *m.*
hard 1 *adj (not soft, severe, difficult)* dur; **h. worker** gros travailleur *m;* **h. on sb** dur avec qn; **h. of hearing** malentendant. **2** *adv (to work, hit)* dur; *(to pull)* fort; *(to rain)* à verse; **to think h.** réfléchir bien.
hard·ball *(game)* base-ball *m;* *(ball)* balle *f* de base-ball.
hard-boiled *adj (egg)* dur.
hard cop·y *(document)* copie *f* (sur) papier.
hard-core *(group)* noyau *m.*
hard disk disque *m* dur.
hard·en *vti* durcir; **to become hardened to** s'endurcir à.
hard·ly *adv* à peine; **h. anyone** presque personne; **h. ever** presque jamais.
hard·ness dureté *f.*

hard·ship épreuve(s) *f(pl).*
hard up *adj (broke) Fam* fauché.
hard·ware *n inv* quincaillerie *f;* *(of computer)* matériel *m.*
hard·ware store quincaillerie *f.*
hard-work·ing *adj* travailleur.
hare lièvre *m.*
harm 1 *n (hurt)* mal *m;* *(wrong)* tort *m.* **2** *vt (physically)* faire du mal à; *(health, interests etc)* nuire à.
harm·ful *adj* nuisible.
harm·less *adj* inoffensif.
har·mon·i·ca harmonica *m.*
har·mo·ni·ous *adj* harmonieux.
har·mo·ny harmonie *f.*
har·ness *(for horse)* harnais *m;* *(to carry baby)* porte-bébé *m* ventral.
harp harpe *f.*
▸**harp on** *vt Fam* ne pas s'arrêter de parler de.
harsh *adj* dur, sévère; *(sound, taste)* âpre.
harshly *adv* durement.
harshness dureté *f.*
har·vest 1 *n* moisson *f;* *(of fruit)* récolte *f.* **2** *vt* moissonner; récolter.
has *see* **have.**
has·sle *Fam (trouble)* histoires *fpl;* *(aggravation)* **it's a h.** c'est casse-pieds *inv.*
haste hâte *f;* **to make h.** se hâter.
has·ten 1 *vi* se hâter (**to do** de faire). **2** *vt* hâter.
has·ti·ly *adv* à la hâte.
hast·y *adj* précipité; *(visit)* rapide.
hat chapeau *m;* *(of child)* bonnet *m;* *(cap)* casquette *f.*
hatch *vi (of chick, egg)* éclore.
hatch·back *(three-door)* trois-portes *f inv;* *(five-door)* cinq-portes *f inv.*
hate *vt* détester, haïr; **to h. doing** *or* **to do** détester faire.
hate·ful *adj* haïssable.
ha·tred haine *f.*
haul *vt (pull)* tirer.
haunt 1 *n (place)* lieu *m* de prédi-

lection; (of criminal) repaire m. **2** vt hanter.

haunt·ed adj hanté.

have* 1 vt avoir; (meal, drink etc) prendre; **to h. a party/dream** faire une fête/un rêve; **will you h...?** (some cake, tea etc) est-ce que tu veux...?; **to let sb h. sth** donner qch à qn; **you've had it!** Fam tu es fichu! **2** v aux avoir; (with 'monter', 'sortir' etc and reflexive verbs) être; **to h. decided/been** avoir décidé/été; **to h. gone** être allé; **to h. cut oneself** s'être coupé; **I've got to go, I h. to go** je dois partir; **to h. sth done** faire faire qch; **he's had his suitcase brought up** il a fait monter sa valise; **haven't I?, hasn't she?/**etc n'est-ce pas?; **no I haven't!** non!; **yes I h.!** oui!; (after negative question) si!

hav·oc ravages mpl.

hawk faucon m.

hay foin m.

hay fe·ver rhume m des foins.

hay·stack meule f de foin.

haz·ard 1 n risque m. **2** vt risquer; **to h. a guess** essayer de devenir.

haze brume f.

ha·zel·nut noisette f.

haz·y adj (weather) brumeux; (photo, idea) flou.

he pron il; (stressed) lui; **he's a happy man** c'est un homme heureux.

head n (of person, hammer etc) tête f, (leader) chef m; **it didn't enter my h.** ça ne m'est pas venu à l'esprit; **heads or tails?** pile ou face?; **per h., a h.** (each) par personne. **2** adj (salesperson etc) principal. **3** vt (group, company) être à la tête de; (list) être en tête de.

head·ache mal m de tête; **to have a h.** avoir mal à la tête.

head·band bandeau m.

▶**head for, be head·ing** or **head·ed for** vt (place) se diriger vers; (disaster) aller à.

head·ing (of chapter etc) titre m; (of subject) rubrique f.

head·light (of vehicle) phare m.

head·line (of newspaper) manchette f; **the headlines** les titres mpl.

head·mas·ter (of school) directeur m.

head·mis·tress (of school) directrice f.

head·phones npl casque m (à écouteurs).

head·quar·ters npl siège m (central); (military) quartier m général.

head·wait·er maître m d'hôtel.

head·way progrès mpl.

heal vi (of wound) se cicatriser; (of bruise) disparaître; (of bone) se ressouder.

health santé f.

health care soins mpl médicaux.

health food aliment m naturel; **h. food store** magasin m diététique.

health in·sur·ance assurance f maladie.

health·y adj (person) en bonne santé; (food, attitude etc) sain.

heap 1 n tas m; **heaps of** (money, people) Fam des tas de. **2** vt entasser.

▶**heap on** vt **to h. sth on sb** (praise) couvrir qn de qch; (insults) accabler qn de qch.

hear* 1 vt entendre; (listen to) écouter; (learn) apprendre (that que). **2** vi entendre; (get news) recevoir des nouvelles (from de); **I've heard of** or **about him** j'ai entendu parler de lui.

hear·ing (sense) ouïe f.

hear·ing aid appareil m auditif.

hearse corbillard m.

heart cœur m; **heart(s)** Cards cœur m; **by h.** par cœur.

heart at·tack crise f cardiaque.

heart·beat battement m de cœur.

heart·break·ing adj navrant.

heart·en·ing adj encourageant.

heart·y adj (appetite) gros (f grosse).

heat chaleur f; (heating) chauffage m.

heat (up) vti chauffer.

heat·er radiateur m.

heath lande f.

heat·ing chauffage m.

heat wave vague f de chaleur.

heave 1 vt (lift) soulever; (pull) tirer; (a sigh) pousser. **2** (feel sick) avoir des haut-le-cœur.

heav·en ciel m; h. knows when Dieu sait quand.

heav·i·ly adv lourdement; (to smoke, drink) beaucoup; to rain h. pleuvoir à verse.

heav·y adj lourd; (rain) fort; (traffic) dense; (smoker, drinker) grand.

heav·y·weight Boxing poids m lourd; (important person) personnage m important.

He·brew (language) hébreu m.

hec·tic adj fiévreux; (period) très agité.

hedge haie f.

hedge·hog hérisson m.

heel talon m.

heft·y adj gros (f grosse).

height hauteur f; (of person) taille f; (of success etc) sommet m; at the h. of (summer) au cœur de.

heir héritier m.

heir·ess héritière f.

held pt & pp de **hold**.

hel·i·cop·ter hélicoptère m.

hell enfer m; a h. of a lot (of) (very many, very much) Fam énormément (de); h.! Fam zut!

hel·lo! int bonjour!; (answering phone) allô!; (surprise) tiens!

helm (of boat) barre f.

hel·met casque m.

help 1 n aide f, secours m; (cleaning woman) femme f de ménage; (workers in office, store) employés, -ées mfpl; h.! au secours! **2** vt aider (do, to do à faire); to h. oneself (to) se servir (de); I can't h. laugh-

ing/etc je ne peux pas m'empêcher de rire/etc.

help·er assistant, -ante mf.

help·ful adj utile; (person) serviable.

help·ing (serving) portion f.

help·less adj (powerless) impuissant; (disabled) impotent.

▸**help out** vti aider.

hem ourlet m.

hem·i·sphere hémisphère m.

hemmed in adj enfermé; (surrounded) cerné.

hem·or·rhage hémorragie f.

hen poule f.

hep·a·ti·tis hépatite f.

her 1 pron la, l'; (after prep, 'than', 'it is') elle; (to) h. lui; I see h. je la vois; I give it to h. je le/la lui donne. **2** poss adj son, sa, pl ses.

herb herbe f; herbs (in cooking) fines herbes fpl.

herd troupeau m.

here adv ici; h. is, h. are voici; h. she is la voici; summer is h. l'été est là; h.! (answering roll call) présent!; h. (you are)! (take this) tenez!

he·red·i·ta·ry adj héréditaire.

her·mit solitaire mf.

he·ro, pl -oes héros m.

he·ro·ic adj héroïque.

her·o·in (drug) héroïne f.

her·o·ine héroïne f.

her·ring hareng m.

hers poss pron le sien, la sienne, pl les sien(ne)s; this hat is h. ce chapeau est à elle or est le sien.

her·self pron elle-même; (reflexive) se, s'; (after prep) elle.

hes·i·tant adj hésitant.

hes·i·tate vi hésiter (about sur; to do à faire).

hes·i·ta·tion hésitation f.

hey! int hé!; (calling attention) holà!

hi! int Fam salut!

hic·cups npl to have (the) h. avoir le hoquet.

hide[1]* **1** vt cacher (from à). **2** vi se cacher (from de).

hide[2] (skin) peau f.

hide-and-seek cache-cache *m inv.*

hid·e·ous *adj* horrible.

hid·e·ous·ly *adv* horriblement.

hide-out cachette *f.*

hid·ing a good h. *(beating)* une bonne raclée.

hid·ing place cachette *f.*

hi·er·ar·chy hiérarchie *f.*

hi-fi hi-fi *f inv.*

high 1 *adj* haut; *(speed)* grand; *(price, number)* élevé; *(on drugs) Fam* défoncé; **h. fever** forte fièvre *f*, **to be 16 feet h.** avoir 5 mètres de haut. **2** *adv* **h. (up)** *(to fly, throw etc)* haut. **3** *n* **an all-time h.** un nouveau record.

high·chair chaise *f* haute.

high-class *adj (service)* de premier ordre; *(building)* de luxe.

high·er *adj* supérieur (**than** à).

high·er ed·u·ca·tion enseignement *m* supérieur.

high·lands *npl* régions *fpl* montagneuses.

high·light 1 *n (of visit, day)* point *m* culminant; *(of show)* clou *m.* **2** *vt* souligner.

high·ly *adv (very)* très; *(to recommend)* chaudement; **h. paid** très bien payé.

high-pitched *adj (sound)* aigu (*f* -uë)

high-rise *adj* **h. apartment building** tour *f.*

high school *(ages 11–15)* = collège *m*; *(ages 15–18)* = lycée *m.*

high school di·plo·ma = baccalauréat *m.*

high-speed *adj* ultra-rapide; **h. train** rapide *m.*

high·way autoroute *f.*

hi·jack *vt (aircraft)* détourner.

hi·jack·er pirate *m* de l'air.

hi·jack·ing piraterie *f* aérienne; *(one incident)* détournement *m.*

hike 1 *n* excursion *f* à pied. **2** *vi* marcher à pied.

hik·er excursionniste *mf.*

hi·lar·i·ous *adj* hilarant.

hill colline *f.*

hill·side **on the h.** à flanc de colline.

hill·y *adj* accidenté.

him *pron* le, l'; *(after prep, 'than', 'it is')* lui; **(to) h.** lui; **I see h.** je le vois; **I give it to h.** je le/la lui donne.

him·self *pron* lui-même; *(reflexive)* se, s'; *(after prep)* lui.

hin·der *vt* gêner.

Hin·du 1 *n* Hindou, -oue *mf.* **2** *adj* hindou, -oue.

hinge charnière *f.*

hint 1 *n* allusion *f*; *(sign)* indication *f*; **hints** *(advice)* conseils *mpl.* **2** *vt* laisser entendre (**that** que).

▸ **hint at** *vt* faire allusion à.

hip hanche *f.*

hip·po·pot·a·mus hippopotame *m.*

hire *vt (worker)* engager, embaucher.

his 1 *poss adj* son, sa, *pl* ses. **2** *poss pron* le sien, la sienne, *pl* les sien(ne)s; **this hat is h.** ce chapeau est à lui *or* est le sien.

His·pan·ic 1 *n* Hispano-Américain, -aine *mf.* **2** *adj* hispano-américain, -aine.

hiss 1 *vti* siffler. **2** *n* sifflement *m.*

his·tor·i·c, his·tor·i·cal *adj* historique.

his·to·ry histoire *f.*

hit* **1** *vt (beat etc)* frapper; *(bump into)* heurter; *(reach)* atteindre; *(affect)* toucher. **2** *n (blow)* coup *m*; *(play, film)* succès *m*; **h. (song)** chanson *f* à succès.

hit-and-run driv·er chauffard *m.*

hitch 1 *n (snag)* problème *m.* **2** *vti* **to h. (a ride)** *Fam* faire du stop (**to** jusqu'à).

hitch-hike *vi* faire de l'auto-stop (**to** jusqu'à).

hitch-hik·er auto-stoppeur, -euse *mf.*

hitch-hik·ing auto-stop *m.*

▸ **hit (up)on** *vt (find)* tomber sur.

HIV *abbr (human immunodefi-*

ciency virus) VIH *m*, HIV *m*; **to be H. positive/negative** être séropositif/ séronégatif.

hive ruche *f*.

hoard *vt* amasser.

hoarse *adj* enroué.

hoax canular *m*.

hob·by passe-temps *m inv*.

ho·bo, *pl* -os vagabond, -onde *mf*.

hock·ey hockey *m*; **ice h.** hockey *m* sur glace.

hold 1 *n* (*grip*) prise *f*; (*of ship*) cale *f*; (*of aircraft*) soute *f*; **to get h. of** saisir; (*contact*) joindre; (*find*) trouver. **2** *vt** tenir; (*breath, interest, attention*) retenir; (*a post*) occuper; (*a record*) détenir; (*possess*) posséder; (*contain*) contenir; **to h. hands** se tenir par la main; **please h.** (*on phone*) ne quittez pas; **to be held** (*of event*) avoir lieu. **3** *vi* (*of nail, rope*) tenir; **if the rain holds off** s'il ne pleut pas.

▶**hold back** *vt* (*crowd*) contenir; (*hide*) cacher.

▶**hold down** *vt* (*price*) maintenir bas; (*job*) garder.

hold·er (*of passport*) titulaire *mf*; (*of record*) détenteur, -trice *mf*; (*container*) support *m*.

▶**hold on** *vi* attendre; (*stand firm*) tenir bon; **h. on!** (*on phone*) ne quittez pas!; **h. on (tight)** tenez bon!

▶**hold onto** *vt* (*cling to*) tenir bien; (*keep*) garder.

▶**hold out 1** *vt* offrir; (*arm*) étendre. **2** *vi* résister; (*last*) durer.

hold·up (*attack*) hold-up *m inv*; (*traffic jam*) bouchon *m*.

▶**hold up** *vt* lever; (*support*) soutenir; (*delay*) retarder; (*bank*) attaquer.

hole trou *m*.

hol·i·day (*legal*) jour *m* férié; **holidays** (*from school, work etc*) vacances *fpl*.

hol·low *adj & n* creux (*m*).

hol·ly houx *m*.

ho·ly *adj* saint; (*water*) bénit.

home 1 *n* maison *f*; (*country*) pays *m* (natal); **at h.** à la maison, chez soi; **to make oneself at h.** se mettre à l'aise; **a good h.** une bonne famille; (*retirement*) h. maison *f* de retraite; **h. life/cooking/***etc* la vie/ cuisine/*etc* familiale. **2** *adv* à la maison, chez soi; **to go** *or* **come** (**back**) **h.** rentrer; **to be h.** être rentré.

home·land patrie *f*.

home·less *adj* sans abri.

home·made *adj* (fait à la) maison *inv*.

home·sick *adj* **to be h.** (*when abroad*) avoir le mal du pays; (*in general*) être nostalgique.

home·town ville *f* natale.

home·work devoir(s) *m*(*pl*).

ho·mo·sex·u·al *adj & n* homosexuel, -elle (*mf*).

hon·est *adj* honnête; (*frank*) franc (*f* franche) (**with** avec).

hon·es·ty honnêteté *f*; (*frankness*) franchise *f*.

hon·ey miel *m*; (*person*) *Fam* chéri, -ie *mf*.

hon·ey·moon lune *f* de miel; (*trip*) voyage *m* de noces.

honk *vi* (*in vehicle*) klaxonner.

hon·or 1 *n* honneur *m*; **in h. of** en l'honneur de; **with honors** (*academic distinction*) avec mention. **2** *vt* honorer (**with** de).

hon·or·a·ble *adj* honorable.

hood capuchon *m*; (*mask of robber*) cagoule *f*; (*car or carriage roof*) capote *f*; (*of car engine*) capot *m*.

hoof, *pl* -fs *or* -ves sabot *m*.

hook crochet *m*; (*on clothes*) agrafe *f*; *Fishing* hameçon *m*; **off the h.** (*phone*) décroché.

hooked *adj* (*nose, object*) recourbé; **h. on** (*drugs, chess etc*) *Fam* accro de.

▶**hook on**, **hook up** *vt* accrocher (**to** à).

hook·y to play h. sécher (la classe).

hoo·li·gan vandale *m*.

hoop cerceau *m*.

hoot 1 *vi (of owl)* hululer. **2** *n* hululement *m*.

hop 1 *vi* sauter (à cloche-pied); *(of bird)* sautiller; **h. in!** *(in car)* montez! **2** *n* saut *m*.

hope 1 *n* espoir *m*. **2** *vi* espérer; **I h. so** j'espère que oui. **3** *vt* espérer (**to do** faire; **that** que).

▶**hope for** *vt* espérer.

hope·ful *adj* optimiste; *(promising)* prometteur; **to be h. that** avoir bon espoir que.

hope·ful·ly *(one hopes)* on espère (que).

hope·less *adj* désespéré; *(useless)* nul.

hope·less·ly *(extremely)* complètement.

hops *npl* houblon *m*.

hop·scotch marelle *f*.

ho·ri·zon horizon *m*; **on the h.** à l'horizon.

hor·i·zon·tal *adj* horizontal.

horn *(of animal)* corne *f*, *(on vehicle)* klaxon® *m*.

hor·ri·ble *adj* horrible.

hor·ri·bly *adv* horriblement.

hor·rif·ic *adj* horrible.

hor·ri·fy *vt* horrifier.

hor·ror horreur *f*.

horse cheval *m*.

horse·back on h. à cheval.

horse·pow·er cheval(-vapeur) *m*; **10 h.** 10 chevaux.

horse·ra·cing courses *fpl*.

horse·shoe fer *m* à cheval.

hose tuyau *m*; *(pantyhose)* collant *m*.

hos·pi·ta·ble *adj* accueillant.

hos·pi·tal hôpital *m*; **in the h.** à l'hôpital.

hos·pi·tal·i·ty hospitalité *f*.

hos·pi·tal·ize *vt* hospitaliser.

host hôte *m*; *(of TV show)* présentateur, -trice *mf*.

hos·tage otage *m*; **to take sb h.** prendre qn en otage.

hos·tel foyer *m*; **youth h.** auberge *f* de jeunesse.

host·ess hôtesse *f*.

hos·tile *adj* hostile (**to, towards** à).

hos·til·i·ty hostilité *f* (**to, towards** envers).

hot *adj* chaud; *(spice)* fort; **to be** or **feel h.** avoir chaud; **it's h.** *(of weather)* il fait chaud.

hot·cake crêpe *f*.

hot dog hot-dog *m*.

ho·tel hôtel *m*.

hot-wa·ter bottle bouillotte *f*.

hound *vt (pursue)* traquer.

hour heure *f*; **half an h.** une demi-heure; **a quarter of an h.** un quart d'heure.

hour·ly 1 *adj (pay)* horaire; **an h. bus/etc** un bus/etc toutes les heures. **2** *adv* toutes les heures.

house¹, *pl* **-ses** maison *f*, *(audience in theatre)* salle *f*.

house² *vt* loger; *(of building)* abriter.

house·hold famille *f*.

house·keep·er gouvernante.

house·keep·ing ménage *m (entretien)*.

House of Rep·re·sen·ta·tives Chambre *f* des représentants.

house·warm·ing to have a h. (party) pendre la crémaillère.

house·wife, *pl* **-wives** ménagère *f*.

house·work *(travaux mpl de)* ménage *m*.

hous·ing logement *m*; *(houses)* logements *mpl*.

hov·el taudis *m*.

hov·er *vi (of bird etc)* planer.

hov·er·craft aéroglisseur *m*.

how *adv* comment; **h. kind!** comme c'est gentil!; **h. do you do?** enchanté; **h. long/high is?** quelle est la longueur/hauteur de?; **h. much?, h. many?** combien?; **h. much time/etc?** combien de temps/*etc*?; **h. many apples**/*etc*? combien de pommes/*etc*?; **h. about some coffee?** du café?

how·e·ver 1 *adv* **h. big he may be** quelque grand qu'il soit; **h. she may do it** de quelque manière qu'elle le fasse. **2** *conj* cependant.

howl 1 *vi* hurler. **2** *n* hurlement *m*.

HQ *abbr* (headquarters) QG *m*.

hub·cap enjoliveur *m*.

hud·dle *vi* se blottir.

hug 1 *vt* serrer (dans ses bras). **2** *n* **to give sb a h.** serrer qn (dans ses bras).

huge *adj* énorme.

huh? *int* Fam hein?

hull (of ship) coque *f*.

hum 1 *vi* (of insect) bourdonner; (of person) fredonner. **2** *vt* (tune) fredonner.

hu·man *adj* humain; **h. being** être *m* humain.

hu·man·i·ty humanité *f*.

hum·ble *adj* humble.

hu·mid *adj* humide.

hu·mid·i·ty humidité *f*.

hu·mil·i·ate *vt* humilier.

hu·mil·i·a·tion humiliation *f*.

hu·mor·ous *adj* (book etc) humoristique; (person) plein d'humour.

hu·mor (fun) humour *m*.

hump (lump) bosse *f*.

hunch Fam intuition *f*.

hun·dred *adj & n* cent (*m*); **a h. pages** cent pages; **hundreds of** des centaines de.

hun·dredth *adj & n* centième (*mf*).

hun·ger faim *f*.

hun·gry *adj* **to be** or **feel h.** avoir faim; **to make h.** donner faim à.

hunt 1 *n* (search) recherche *f* (**for** de). **2** *vt* (animals) chasser; (pursue) poursuivre; (seek) chercher. **3** *vi* chasser.

▸ **hunt down** *vt* traquer.

hunt·er chasseur *m*.

▸ **hunt for** *vt* (re)chercher.

hunt·ing chasse *f*.

hur·dle (fence) haie *f*, (problem) obstacle *m*.

hurl *vt* lancer.

hur·ray! *int* hourra!

hur·ri·cane ouragan *m*.

hur·ry 1 *n* hâte *f*; **in a h.** à la hâte; **to be in a h.** être pressé. **2** *vi* se dépêcher (**to do** de faire); **to h. through a meal** manger à toute vitesse; **to h. towards** se précipiter vers. **3** *vt* (person) bousculer.

▸ **hurry up** *vi* se dépêcher.

hurt* 1 *vt* faire du mal à; (emotionally) faire de la peine à; (reputation etc) nuire à; **to h. sb's feelings** blesser qn. **2** *vi* faire mal. **3** *n* mal *m*.

hus·band mari *m*.

hush silence *m*.

hus·tle 1 *vt* (shove) bousculer (qn). **2** *n* **h. and bustle** tourbillon *m*.

hut cabane *f*.

hy·dro·gen hydrogène *m*.

hy·giene hygiène *f*.

hy·gi·en·ic *adj* hygiénique.

hymn cantique *m*.

hy·phen trait *m* d'union.

hy·phen·at·ed *adj* (word) à trait d'union.

hyp·no·tize *vt* hypnotiser.

hy·poc·ri·sy hypocrisie *f*.

hyp·o·crite hypocrite *mf*.

hy·poth·e·sis, *pl* **-ses** hypothèse *f*.

hys·ter·i·cal *adj* (upset) qui a une crise de nerfs; (funny) Fam désopilant.

hys·ter·i·cal·ly *adv* (to cry) sans pouvoir s'arrêter.

I

I *pron* je, j'; (stressed) moi.

ice glace *f*, (on road) verglas *m*.

ice·berg iceberg *m*.

ice-cold *adj* glacial; (drink) glacé.

ice-cream glace *f*.

ice-cream bar esquimau® *m*.

ice cube glaçon *m*.

ice-skat·ing patinage *m* (sur glace).

▸**ice up** *vi (of windshield)* givrer.

i·ci·cle glaçon *m*.

ic·ing *(on cake)* glaçage *m*.

ic·y *adj* glacé; *(weather)* glacial; *(road)* verglacé.

ID pièce *f* d'identité.

i·de·a idée *f*; **I have an i. that** j'ai l'impression que.

i·de·al 1 *adj* idéal *(mpl* -aux *or* -als). **2** *n* idéal *m (pl* -aux *or* -als).

i·de·al·ly *adv* idéalement; **i. we should stay** l'idéal, ce serait que nous restions.

i·den·ti·cal *adj* identique (**to**, **with** à).

i·den·ti·fi·ca·tion *(document)* pièce *f* d'identité.

i·den·ti·fy *vt* identifier; **to i.** (one-self) **with** s'identifier avec.

i·den·ti·ty identité *f*; **i. card** carte *f* d'identité; **i. theft** vol *m* d'identité.

id·i·om expression *f* idiomatique.

id·i·ot idiot, -ote *mf*.

id·i·ot·ic *adj* idiot.

i·dle *adj (unoccupied)* inactif; *(lazy)* paresseux.

i·dler paresseux, -euse *mf*.

i·dol idole *f*.

i·dol·ize *vt (adore)* traiter comme une idole.

i.e. *abbr* c'est-à-dire.

if *conj* si; **if he comes** s'il vient; **even if** même si; **if only I were rich** si seulement j'étais riche.

ig·loo igloo *m*.

ig·no·rance ignorance *f* (**of** de).

ig·no·rant *adj* ignorant (**of** de).

ig·nore *vt* ne prêter aucune attention à (qch); *(pretend not to recognize)* faire semblant de ne pas reconnaître (qn).

ill 1 *adj (sick)* malade; *(bad)* mauvais. **2** *n* ills maux *mpl*.

il·le·gal *adj* illégal.

il·leg·i·ble *adj* illisible.

il·lit·er·ate *adj* illettré.

ill·ness maladie *f*.

ill-treat *vt* maltraiter.

il·lu·sion illusion *f* (**about** sur).

il·lus·trate *vt* illustrer (**with** de).

il·lus·tra·tion illustration *f*.

im·age image *f*; **(public) i.** *(of firm)* image *f* de marque.

i·mag·i·nar·y *adj* imaginaire.

i·mag·i·na·tion imagination *f*.

i·mag·ine *vt* (s')imaginer (**that** que).

im·i·tate *vt* imiter.

im·i·ta·tion imitation *f*; **i. jewelry** bijoux *mpl* fantaisie.

im·mac·u·late *adj* impeccable.

im·ma·ture *adj (person)* qui manque de maturité.

im·me·di·ate *adj* immédiat.

im·me·di·ate·ly 1 *adv (at once)* tout de suite, immédiatement. **2** *conj (as soon as)* dès que.

im·mense *adj* immense.

im·mense·ly *adv* extraòrdinairement.

im·mi·grant *n & adj* immigré, -ée *(mf)*.

im·mi·gra·tion immigration *f*.

im·mi·nent *adj* imminent.

im·mor·tal *adj* immortel.

im·mune *adj (naturally)* immunisé (**to** contre); *(vaccinated)* vacciné.

im·mu·nize *vt* vacciner (**against** contre).

im·pact effet *m* (**on** sur).

im·pa·tience impatience *f*.

im·pa·tient *adj* impatient (**to do** de faire).

im·pa·tient·ly *adv* avec impatience.

im·per·a·tive *Grammar* impératif *m*.

im·per·son·ate *vt* se faire passer pour; *(on TV etc)* imiter.

im·per·son·a·tor *(on TV etc)* imitateur, -trice *mf*.

im·per·ti·nent *adj* impertinent (**to** envers).

im·pe·tus impulsion *f*.

im·ple·ment¹ *(tool)* instrument *m*; *(utensil)* ustensile *m*.

im·ple·ment² *vt* mettre en œuvre.

im·pli·ca·tion conséquence *f*; *(impact)* portée *f*.

im·plic·it *adj (implied)* implicite; *(absolute)* absolu.

im·ply *vt* laisser entendre (**that** que); *(assume)* impliquer.

im·po·lite *adj* impoli.

im·port 1 *vt* importer (**from** de). **2** *n* importation *f*.

im·por·tance importance *f*; **of no i.** sans importance.

im·por·tant *adj* important.

im·port·er importateur, -trice *mf*.

im·pose 1 *vt* imposer (**on** à); *(fine)* infliger (**on** à). **2** *vi (cause trouble)* déranger; **to i. on sb** déranger qn.

im·pos·ing *adj (building)* impressionnant.

im·po·si·tion *(inconvenience)* dérangement *m*.

im·pos·si·bil·i·ty impossibilité *f*.

im·pos·si·ble *adj* impossible (**to do** à faire); **it is i. (for us) to do it** il (nous) est impossible de le faire.

im·pos·tor imposteur *m*.

im·prac·ti·cal *adj* peu réaliste.

im·press *vt* impressionner (qn).

im·pres·sion impression *f*.

im·pres·sive *adj* impressionnant.

im·pris·on *vt* emprisonner.

im·prob·a·ble *adj* peu probable.

im·prop·er *adj (obscene)* indécent; *(inappropriate)* inopportun, peu approprié.

im·prove 1 *vt* améliorer. **2** *vi* s'améliorer; *(of business)* reprendre.

im·prove·ment amélioration *f*.

▶ **im·prove on** *vt* faire mieux que.

im·pro·vise *vti* improviser.

im·pu·dent *adj* impudent.

im·pulse impulsion *f*; **on i.** sur un coup de tête.

im·pul·sive *adj* impulsif.

im·pul·sive·ly *adv* de manière impulsive.

im·pu·ri·ty impureté *f*.

in 1 *prep* dans; **in the box/etc** dans la boîte/etc; **in an hour('s) time** dans une heure. ▪ à; **in school** à l'école; **in Paris** à Paris; **in Portugal** au Portugal; **in ink** à l'encre. ▪ en; **in summer/May/French** en été/mai/français; **in Spain** en Espagne; **in an hour** *(within that period)* en une heure; **in doing** en faisant. ▪ de; **in a soft voice** d'une voix douce; **the best in** le meilleur de. ▪ **in the morning** le matin; **one in ten** un sur dix. **2** *adv* **to be in** *(home)* être là, être à la maison; *(of train)* être arrivé; *(in fashion)* être en vogue.

in- *prefix* in-.

in·a·bil·i·ty incapacité *f* (**to do** de faire).

in·ac·ces·si·ble *adj* inaccessible.

in·ac·cu·ra·cy *(error)* inexactitude *f*.

in·ac·cu·rate *adj* inexact.

in·ad·e·qua·cy insuffisance *f*.

in·ad·e·quate *adj* insuffisant; *(person)* pas à la hauteur.

in·ap·pro·pri·ate *adj* peu approprié.

in·au·gu·rate *vt (building)* inaugurer.

in·au·gu·ra·tion inauguration *f*.

in·box *(for e-mail)* boîte *f* de réception.

Inc *abbr (Incorporated)* = SARL.

in·ca·pa·ble *adj* incapable (**of doing** de faire).

in·cense *vt* mettre en colère.

in·cen·tive encouragement *m*, motivation *f*.

inch pouce *m* (= 2,54cm).

in·ci·dent incident *m*; *(in film etc)* épisode *m*.

in·ci·dent·al·ly *(by the way)* à propos.

in·cite *vt* inciter (**to do** à faire).

in·cite·ment incitation *f*.

in·cli·na·tion *(desire)* envie *f* (**to do** de faire).

in·cline *vt (bend)* incliner; **to be inclined to do** *(feel a wish to)* avoir bien envie de faire; *(tend to)* avoir tendance à faire.

in·clude *vt (contain)* comprendre; **to be included** être compris; *(on list)* être inclus.

in·clud·ing *prep* y compris; **i. service** service *m* compris; **up to and i. Monday** jusqu'à lundi inclus.

in·clu·sive *adj* inclus; **to be i. of** comprendre.

in·come revenu *m* (**from** de); **private i.** rentes *fpl*.

in·come tax impôt *m* sur le revenu.

in·com·pat·i·ble *adj* incompatible (**with** avec).

in·com·pe·tent *adj* incompétent.

in·com·plete *adj* incomplet.

in·con·ceiv·a·ble *adj* inconcevable.

in·con·sid·er·ate *adj (remark)* irréfléchi; *(person)* pas très gentil (**towards** avec).

in·con·sis·ten·cy incohérence *f*.

in·con·sis·tent *adj* en contradiction (**with** avec).

in·con·spic·u·ous *adj* peu en évidence.

in·con·ven·ience **1** *n (bother)* dérangement *m*; *(disadvantage)* inconvénient *m*. **2** *vt* déranger, gêner.

in·con·ven·ient *adj (moment, situation etc)* gênant; *(house)* mal situé; **it's i. (for me) to** ça me dérange de.

in·cor·po·rate *vt (contain)* contenir.

in·cor·rect *adj* inexact; **you're i.** vous avez tort.

in·crease 1 *vi* augmenter; *(of effort, noise)* s'intensifier. **2** *vt* augmenter; intensifier. **3** *n* augmenta-

tion *f* (**in, of** de); *(of effort, noise)* intensification *f*; **on the i.** en hausse.

in·creas·ing *adj (amount)* croissant.

in·creas·ing·ly *adv* de plus en plus.

in·cred·i·ble *adj* incroyable.

in·cred·i·bly *adv* incroyablement.

in·cu·ba·tor *(for baby, eggs)* couveuse *f*.

in·cur *vt (expenses)* faire; *(loss)* subir.

in·cur·a·ble *adj* incurable.

in·de·cent *adj (obscene)* indécent.

in·de·ci·sive *adj* indécis.

in·deed *adv* en effet; **very good/etc i.** vraiment très bon/*etc*; **yes i.!** bien sûr!; **thank you very much i.!** merci infiniment!

in·def·i·nite *adj* indéfini.

in·def·i·nite·ly *adv* indéfiniment.

in·de·pend·ence indépendance *f*.

in·de·pend·ent *adj* indépendant (**of** de).

in·de·pend·ent·ly *adv* de façon indépendante; **i. of** indépendamment de.

in·dex 1 *n (in book)* index *m*. **2** *vt (classify)* classer.

in·dex card fiche *f*.

in·dex fin·ger index *m*.

in·dex-linked *adj* indexé (**to** sur).

In·di·an 1 *n* Indien, -ienne *mf*. **2** *adj* indien, -ienne.

in·di·cate *vt* indiquer (**that** que).

in·di·ca·tion *(sign)* indice *m*, indication *f*.

in·di·ca·tor *(instrument)* indicateur *m*; *(in vehicle)* clignotant *m*.

in·dif·fer·ence indifférence *f* (**to** à).

in·dif·fer·ent *adj* indifférent (**to** à).

in·di·ges·tion problèmes *mpl* de

digestion; **(an attack of)** i. une indigestion.

in·dig·nant *adj* indigné (**at** de).

in·dig·na·tion indignation *f*.

in·di·rect *adj* indirect.

in·di·rect·ly *adv* indirectement.

in·dis·creet *adj* indiscret.

in·dis·crim·i·nate *(random)* fait/ donné/*etc* au hasard.

in·dis·crim·i·nate·ly *adv* (**at** *random*) au hasard.

in·dis·tin·guish·a·ble *adj* indifférenciable (**from** de).

in·di·vid·u·al 1 *adj* individuel; *(specific)* particulier. **2** *n (person)* individu *m*.

indi·vid·u·al·ly *adv (separately)* individuellement.

in·door *adj (games, shoes etc)* d'intérieur; *(swimming pool)* couvert.

in·doors *adv* à l'intérieur.

in·duce *vt* persuader (**to do** de faire); *(cause)* provoquer.

in·dulge 1 *vt (person)* gâter; *(whim)* satisfaire; **to i. oneself** se faire plaisir. **2** *vi* se faire plaisir.

▶**indulge in** *vt* se permettre.

in·dul·gent *adj* indulgent (**to** envers).

in·dus·tri·al *adj* industriel; *(conflict)* du travail; **i. park** zone *f* industrielle.

in·dus·try industrie *f*.

in·ed·i·ble *adj* immangeable.

in·ef·fec·tive *adj (measure)* inefficace.

in·ef·fi·cien·cy inefficacité *f*.

in·ef·fi·cient *adj (person, measure)* inefficace.

in·ept *adj (unskilled)* peu habile (**at** à); *(incompetent)* incapable.

in·e·qual·i·ty inégalité *f*.

in·ev·i·ta·ble *adj* inévitable.

in·ev·i·ta·bly *adv* inévitablement.

in·ex·cus·a·ble *adj* inexcusable.

in·ex·pen·sive *adj* bon marché *inv*.

in·ex·pe·ri·ence inexpérience *f*.

in·ex·pe·ri·enced *adj* inexpérimenté.

in·ex·pli·ca·ble *adj* inexplicable.

in·fal·li·ble *adj* infaillible.

in·fa·mous *adj (evil)* infâme.

in·fan·cy petite enfance *f*.

in·fant petit(e) enfant *mf*, *(baby)* nourrisson *m*.

in·fan·try infanterie *f*.

in·fat·u·at·ed *adj* amoureux (**with** de).

in·fat·u·a·tion engouement *m* (**for, with** pour).

in·fect *vt* infecter; **to get infected** s'infecter.

in·fec·tion infection *f*.

in·fec·tious *adj* contagieux.

in·fer *vt* déduire (**from** de).

in·fe·ri·or *adj* inférieur (**to** à); *(goods, work)* de qualité inférieure.

in·fe·ri·or·i·ty infériorité *f*.

in·fer·nal *adj* infernal.

in·fest *vt* infester (**with** de).

in·fi·nite *adj* infini.

in·fi·nite·ly *adv* infiniment.

in·fin·i·tive *Grammar* infinitif *m*.

in·fin·i·ty infini *m*.

in·firm *adj* infirme.

in·flamed *adj (throat etc)* enflammé.

in·flam·ma·tion inflammation *f*.

in·flate *vt* gonfler.

in·fla·tion inflation *f*.

in·flex·i·ble *adj* inflexible.

in·flict *vt (a wound)* occasionner (**on** à); **to i. pain on sb** faire souffrir qn.

in·flu·ence 1 *n* influence *f*; **under the i. (of drink)** en état d'ébriété. **2** *vt* influencer.

in·flu·en·tial *adj* **to be i.** avoir une grande influence.

in·flu·en·za grippe *f*.

in·flux flot *m*.

in·fo *Fam* renseignements *mpl* (**on** sur).

in·form *vt* informer (**of** de; **that** que).

in·for·mal *adj* simple, décontracté; *(expression)* familier; *(meeting)* non-officiel.

in·for·mal·ly *adv* sans cérémonie; *(to dress)* simplement; *(to discuss)* à titre non-officiel.

in·for·ma·tion renseignements *mpl* (**about, on** sur); **a piece of i.** un renseignement.

in·form·a·tive *adj* instructif.

▸ **inform on** *vt* dénoncer.

in·fu·ri·ate *vt* exaspérer.

in·gen·ious *adj* ingénieux.

in·grat·i·tude ingratitude *f*.

in·gre·di·ent ingrédient *m*.

in·hab·it *vt* habiter.

in·hab·i·tant habitant, -ante *mf*.

in·hale *vt* aspirer.

in·her·it *vt* hériter (de).

in·her·i·tance héritage *m*.

in·hib·it *vt (hinder)* gêner; **to be inhibited** avoir des inhibitions.

in·hi·bi·tion inhibition *f*.

in·hos·pi·ta·ble *adj* peu accueillant, inhospitalier.

in·hu·man *adj* inhumain.

in·i·tial 1 *adj* premier. **2** *n* initials initiales *fpl*; *(signature)* paraphe *m*. **3** *vt* parapher.

in·i·tial·ly *adv* au début.

in·i·ti·ate *vt (reform, negotiations)* amorcer; *(quarrel)* provoquer, déclencher; *(lawsuit)* entamer; *(into society)* initier (**into** à).

in·ject *vt* injecter (**into** à).

in·jec·tion injection *f*, piqûre *f*.

in·jure *vt (physically)* blesser, faire du mal à.

in·jured 1 *adj* blessé. **2** *n* **the i.** les blessés *mpl*.

in·ju·ry blessure *f*, *(fracture)* fracture *f*, *(sprain)* foulure *f*.

in·jus·tice injustice *f*.

ink encre *f*.

in·kling (petite) idée *f*.

in·land 1 *adj* intérieur. **2** *adv* à l'intérieur.

in·laws *npl* belle-famille *f*.

in·mate *(of prison)* détenu, -ue *mf*.

inn auberge *f*.

in·ner *adj* intérieur; **the i. city** les quartiers défavorisés du centre-ville.

in·ner tube *(of tire)* chambre *f* à air.

inn·keep·er aubergiste *mf*.

in·no·cence innocence *f*.

in·no·cent *adj* innocent.

in·oc·u·late *vt* vacciner (**against** contre).

in·oc·u·la·tion vaccination *f*.

in·put *(computer operation)* entrée *f*, *(data)* données *fpl*.

in·quire 1 *vi* se renseigner (**about** sur). **2** *vt* demander; **to i. how to get to** demander le chemin de.

▸ **inquire into** *vt* faire une enquête sur.

in·quir·y demande *f* de renseignements; *(investigation)* enquête *f*.

in·quis·i·tive *adj* curieux.

in·sane *adj* fou (*f* folle).

in·san·i·ty folie *f*.

in·scrip·tion inscription *f*, *(in book)* dédicace *f*.

in·sect insecte *m*.

in·sec·ti·cide insecticide *m*.

in·se·cure *adj (not securely fixed)* mal fixé; *(uncertain)* incertain; *(person)* qui manque d'assurance.

in·sen·si·tive *adj* insensible (**to** à).

in·sen·si·tiv·i·ty insensibilité *f*.

in·sert *vt* introduire, insérer (**in, into** dans).

in·side 1 *adv* dedans, à l'intérieur. **2** *prep* à l'intérieur de. **3** *n* dedans *m*, intérieur *m*; **on the i.** à l'intérieur (**of** de); **i. out** *(socks etc)* à l'envers. **4** *adj* intérieur.

in·sid·er initié, -ée *mf*.

in·sight *(into question)* aperçu *m* (**into** de).

in·sig·nif·i·cant *adj* insignifiant.

in·sin·cere *adj* peu sincère.

in·sist 1 *vi* insister (**on doing** faire). **2** *vt (order)* insister (**that** pour que + *subjunctive*); *(declare)* affirmer (**that** que).

in·sis·tence insistance *f*; **her i. on**

seeing me l'insistance qu'elle met à vouloir me voir.
in·sis·tent *adj* to be i. insister (that pour que + *subjunctive*).
▸**insist on** *vt* (demand) exiger; (assert) affirmer.
in·so·lence insolence *f*.
in·so·lent *adj* insolent.
in·som·ni·a insomnie *f*.
in·spect *vt* contrôler.
in·spec·tion inspection *f*; (of tickets) contrôle *m*.
in·spec·tor inspecteur, -trice *mf*.
in·spi·ra·tion inspiration *f*.
in·spire *vt* inspirer (sb with sth qch à qn).
in·stall *vt* installer.
in·stall·ment (of money) acompte *m*; (of serial) épisode *m*.
in·stance (example) cas *m*; for i. par exemple.
in·stant 1 *adj* immédiat; i. coffee café *m* soluble; i. messaging messagerie *f* instantanée. **2** (moment) instant *m*.
in·stant·ly *adv* immédiatement.
in·stead *adv* plutôt; i. of (doing) sth au lieu de (faire) qch; i. of sb à la place de qn; i. (of him) à sa place.
in·stinct instinct *m*.
in·stinc·tive *adj* instinctif.
in·stinc·tive·ly *adv* instinctivement.
in·sti·tu·tion institution *f*.
in·struct *vt* (teach) enseigner (sb in sth qch à qn); to i. sb to do (order) charger qn de faire.
in·struc·tions *npl* (for use) mode *m* d'emploi; (orders) instructions *fpl*.
in·struc·tive *adj* instructif.
in·struc·tor (for skiing etc) moniteur, -trice *mf*; **driving i.** moniteur, -trice *mf* d'auto-école.
in·stru·ment instrument *m*.
in·stru·men·tal *adj* Music instrumental; **to be i. in sth** contribuer à qch.
in·suf·fi·cient *adj* insuffisant.

in·su·late *vt* (against cold and electrically) isoler.
in·su·la·tion (material) isolant *m*.
in·sult 1 *vt* insulter. **2** *n* insulte *f* (to à).
in·sur·ance assurance *f*; i. company compagnie *f* d'assurances.
in·sure *vt* assurer (against contre).
in·tact *adj* intact.
in·take (of water) prise *f*, arrivée *f*; (of food, alcohol etc) consommation *f*; (of students, recruits) admission *f*.
in·te·grate 1 *vt* intégrer. **2** *vi* s'intégrer.
in·teg·ri·ty intégrité *f*.
in·tel·lect intelligence *f*.
in·tel·lec·tu·al *adj* & *n* intellectuel, -elle (*mf*).
in·tel·li·gence intelligence *f*.
in·tel·li·gent *adj* intelligent.
in·tel·li·gi·ble *adj* compréhensible.
in·tend *vt* (gift etc) destiner (for à); to be intended to do/for sb être destiné à faire/à qn; to i. to do avoir l'intention de faire.
in·tense *adj* intense; (interest) vif.
in·ten·si·fy 1 *vt* intensifier. **2** *vi* s'intensifier.
in·ten·si·ty intensité *f*.
in·ten·sive *adj* intensif; i. care réanimation *f*.
in·tent *adj* i. on doing résolu à faire.
in·ten·tion intention *f* (of doing de faire).
in·ten·tion·al *adj* it wasn't i. ce n'était pas fait exprès.
in·ten·tion·al·ly *adv* exprès.
in·ter·act *vi* (people) communiquer.
in·ter·ac·tive *adj* interactif, -ive.
in·ter·cept *vt* intercepter.
in·ter·change (on road) échangeur *m*.
in·ter·change·a·ble *adj* interchangeable.
in·ter·com interphone *m*.

in·ter·con·nect·ed *adj (facts etc)* liés.

in·ter·course *(sexual)* rapports *mpl* sexuels.

in·ter·est 1 *n* intérêt *m; (money)* intérêts *mpl;* **to take an i.** s'intéresser à; **to be of i. to sb** intéresser qn. **2** *vt* intéresser.

in·ter·est·ed *adj* intéressé; **to be i. in sth/sb** s'intéresser à qch/qn; **I'm i. in doing** ça m'intéresse de faire.

in·ter·est·ing *adj* intéressant.

in·ter·fere *vi* se mêler des affaires d'autrui.

▸**interfere in** *vt* s'ingérer dans.

in·ter·fer·ence ingérence *f; (on radio)* parasites *mpl.*

▸**interfere with** *vt (upset)* déranger.

in·ter·im 1 *n* **in the i.** entretemps. **2** *adj* provisoire.

in·te·ri·or 1 *adj* intérieur. **2** *n* intérieur *m.*

in·ter·jec·tion *Grammar* interjection *f.*

in·ter·me·di·ar·y intermédiaire *mf.*

in·ter·me·di·ate *adj* intermédiaire; *(course)* de niveau moyen.

in·ter·mis·sion *(in theater)* entracte *m.*

in·tern *n (in office)* stagiaire *mf, (in hospital)* interne *mf.*

in·ter·nal *adj* interne; *(flight)* intérieur.

In·ter·nal Rev·e·nue Ser·vice service *m* des impôts.

in·ter·na·tion·al *adj* international.

In·ter·net **the I.** (l')Internet *m;* **on the I.** sur Internet; **I. surfer** internaute *mf.*

in·tern·ship *n (in office)* stage *m; (in hospital)* internat *m.*

in·ter·pret *vt* interpréter.

in·ter·pret·er interprète *mf.*

in·ter·ro·gate *vt* interroger.

in·ter·ro·ga·tion *(by police)* interrogatoire *m.*

in·ter·rog·a·tive *adj & n Grammar* interrogatif *(m).*

in·ter·rupt *vt* interrompre.

in·ter·rup·tion interruption *f.*

in·ter·sect 1 *vt* couper. **2** *vi* s'entrecouper.

in·ter·sec·tion *(of roads, lines)* intersection *f.*

in·ter·state autoroute *f.*

in·ter·val intervalle *m.*

in·ter·vene *vi (of person)* intervenir; *(of event)* survenir.

in·ter·ven·tion intervention *f.*

in·ter·view 1 *n* entrevue *f* (**with** avec); *(on TV etc)* interview *f.* **2** *vt* avoir une entrevue avec; *(on TV etc)* interviewer.

in·ter·view·er *(on TV etc)* interviewer *m.*

in·ti·mate *adj* intime.

in·tim·i·date *vt* intimider.

in·to *prep* dans; **to put i.** mettre dans. ▪ **en; to translate i.** traduire en; **i. pieces** en morceaux. ▪ **to be i. yoga**/*etc Fam* être à fond dans le yoga/*etc.*

in·tol·er·a·ble *adj* intolérable (**that** que + *subjunctive*).

in·tox·i·cate *vt* enivrer.

in·tox·i·cat·ed *adj* ivre.

in·tran·si·tive *adj Grammar* intransitif.

in·tri·cate *adj* complexe.

in·tro·duce *vt (bring in)* introduire (**into** dans); *(program)* présenter; **to i. sb to sb** présenter qn à qn.

in·tro·duc·tion introduction *f; (of person to person)* présentation *f;* **i. to** *(initiation)* premier contact avec.

in·trude *vi* déranger (**on sb** qn).

in·trud·er intrus, -use *mf.*

in·tru·sion *(disturbance)* dérangement *m.*

in·tu·i·tion intuition *f.*

in·un·dat·ed *adj* submergé (**with work/letters**/*etc* de travail/lettres/*etc*).

in·vade vt envahir.

in·vad·er envahisseur, -euse mf.

in·va·lid[1] malade mf; (through injury) infirme mf.

in·val·id[2] adj non valable.

in·val·u·a·ble adj inestimable.

in·va·ri·a·bly adv (always) toujours.

in·va·sion invasion f.

in·vent vt inventer.

in·ven·tion invention f.

in·ven·tor inventeur, -trice mf.

in·ven·to·ry inventaire m.

in·vest vt (money) placer, investir (in dans).

in·ves·ti·gate vt examiner; (crime) enquêter sur.

in·ves·ti·ga·tion examen m; (inquiry by journalist, police etc) enquête f (of, into sur).

in·ves·ti·ga·tor enquêteur, -euse mf.

▶ **invest in** vt placer son argent dans; (firm) investir dans.

in·vest·ment investissement m, placement m.

in·ves·tor (in shares) actionnaire mf; (saver) épargnant, -ante mf.

in·vig·or·at·ing adj stimulant.

in·vis·i·ble adj invisible.

in·vi·ta·tion invitation f.

in·vite vt inviter (to do à faire); (ask for) demander; (give occasion for) provoquer.

in·vit·ing adj engageant.

in·voice 1 n facture f. 2 vt facturer.

in·voke vt invoquer.

in·volve vt (person) mêler (in à); (entail) entraîner; **the job involves** le poste nécessite.

in·volved adj (concerned) concerné; (committed) engagé (in dans); (complicated) compliqué; (at stake) en jeu; **the person i.** la personne en question; **to be i. with sb** avoir des liens intimes avec qn.

in·volve·ment participation f (in à); (commitment) engagement m; (emotional) liaison f.

in·ward(s) adv vers l'intérieur.

IOU abbr (I owe you) reconnaissance f de dette.

IQ abbr (intelligence quotient) QI m inv.

IRA abbr (individual retirement account) plan m d'épargne retraite personnel.

i·ris (plant, of eye) iris m.

I·rish 1 npl the I. les Irlandais mpl. 2 adj irlandais.

I·rish·man, pl -men Irlandais m.

I·rish·wom·an, pl -women Irlandaise f.

i·ron 1 n fer m; (for clothes) fer m (à repasser). 2 vt (clothes) repasser.

i·ron·ic, i·ron·i·cal adj ironique.

i·ron·ing repassage m.

i·ron·ing board planche f à repasser.

i·ro·ny ironie f.

ir·ra·tion·al adj (person) peu rationnel.

ir·reg·u·lar adj irrégulier.

ir·rel·e·vance manque m de rapport.

ir·rel·e·vant adj sans rapport (to avec); **that's i.** ça n'a rien à voir.

ir·re·sist·i·ble adj irrésistible.

ir·re·spec·tive of prep sans tenir compte de.

ir·ri·gate vt irriguer.

ir·ri·ta·ble adj irritable.

ir·ri·tate vt (annoy, inflame) irriter.

ir·ri·tat·ing adj irritant.

ir·ri·ta·tion irritation f.

is see **be**.

Is·lam·ic adj islamique.

is·land île f.

i·so·late vt isoler (from de).

i·so·lat·ed adj isolé.

i·so·la·tion isolement m; **in i.** isolément.

is·sue 1 vt publier; (tickets) distribuer; (passport) délivrer; (an order) donner; (warning) lancer; (supply) fournir (with de; to à). 2 n (matter) question f; (newspaper) numéro m.

IT *abbr (information technology)* l'informatique *f*.

it *pron (subject)* il, elle; *(object)* le, la, l'; **(to) it** *(indirect object)* lui; **it's ringing** il sonne; **I've done it** je l'ai fait. ■ *(impersonal)* il; **it's snowing** il neige. ■ *(non specific)* ce, cela, ça; **who is it?** qui est-ce?; **it was Paul who…** c'est Paul qui… ■ **of it, from it, about it** en; **in it, to it, at it** y; **on it** dessus; **under it** dessous.

I·tal·ian 1 *n* Italien, -ienne *mf*; *(language)* italien *m*. **2** *adj* italien, -ienne.

i·tal·ics *npl* italique *m*.

itch 1 *n* démangeaison(s) *f(pl)*. **2** *vi* démanger; **his arm itches** son bras le démange.

itch·ing démangeaison(s) *f(pl)*.

itch·y *adj* **I have an i. hand** j'ai une main qui me démange.

i·tem *(object)* article *m*; *(matter)* question *f*; *(news)* **i.** information *f*.

its *poss adj* son, sa, *pl* ses.

it·self *pron* lui-même, elle-même; *(reflexive)* se, s'.

i·vo·ry ivoire *m*.

i·vy lierre *m*.

J

jab 1 *vt* enfoncer (**into** dans); *(prick)* piquer (*qn*) (**with sth** du bout de qch). **2** *n (blow)* coup *m*.

jack *(for car)* cric *m*; *Cards* valet *m*; **j. of all trades** homme *m* à tout faire.

jack·et veste *f*; **j. potato** pomme *f* de terre en robe des champs.

jack·ham·mer marteau *m* piqueur.

Ja·cuz·zi® Jacuzzi® *m*.

jag·ged *adj* déchiqueté.

jag·uar jaguar *m*.

jail 1 *n* prison *f*. **2** *vt* emprisonner.

jam¹ confiture *f*.

jam² 1 *n (traffic)* **j.** embouteillage *m*. **2** *vt (squeeze, make stuck)* coincer; *(street etc)* encombrer. **3** *vi (get stuck)* se coincer.

▶ **jam into** *vt* to **j. sth into sth** *(cram)* (en)tasser qch dans qch.

jammed *adj (machine etc)* coincé, bloqué; *(street etc)* encombré.

jam-packed *adj* bourré de monde.

jan·i·tor concierge *m*.

Jan·u·ar·y janvier *m*.

Jap·a·nese 1 *n* Japonais, -aise *mf*; *(language)* japonais *m*. **2** *adj* japonais, -aise.

jar pot *m*; *(large, glass)* bocal *m*.

jaun·dice jaunisse *f*.

jave·lin javelot *m*.

jaw mâchoire *f*.

jay·walk·ing = délit *m* mineur qui consiste à traverser une rue en dehors des clous ou au feu vert.

jazz jazz *m*.

jea·lous *adj* jaloux (*f* -ouse) (**of** de).

jeal·ous·y jalousie *f*.

jeans *npl* **(pair of) j.** (blue-)jean *m*.

jeep® jeep® *f*.

jeer (at) *vti* railler; *(boo)* huer.

jeer·ing *(of crowd)* huées *fpl*.

jeers *npl* huées *fpl*.

Jell-O® *inv* gelée *f*.

jel·ly *(preserve, dessert)* gelée *f*.

jeop·ard·ize *vt* mettre en danger.

jeop·ard·y danger *m*.

jerk 1 *vt* donner une secousse à. **2** *n* secousse *f*; **(stupid) j.** *Fam* crétin, -ine *mf*.

jer·sey *(garment)* maillot *m*.

jet *(plane)* avion *m* à réaction.

jet lag fatigue *f* (due au décalage horaire).

jet-lagged *adj* qui souffre du décalage horaire.

jet·ty jetée *f*.

Jew Juif *m*, Juive *f*.

jew·el bijou *m* (*pl* -oux); *(in watch)* rubis *m*.

jew·el·er bijoutier, -ière *mf*.

jew·el·ry bijoux *mpl*.

Jew·ish *adj* juif.

jig·saw j. **(puzzle)** puzzle *m*.

jin·gle *vi (of keys)* tinter.

jit·ter·y *adj* to be j. *Fam* avoir la frousse.

job *(task)* travail *m*; *(post)* poste *m*.

job·less *adj* au chômage.

jock·ey jockey *m*.

jog 1 *n (shake)* secousse *f*. 2 *vt* secouer; *(push)* pousser; *(memory)* rafraîchir. 3 *vi* faire du jogging.

john *Fam* cabinets *mpl*.

join¹ 1 *vt (put together)* joindre; *(wires, pipes)* raccorder; *(words, towns)* relier; **to j. sb** *(catch up with, meet)* rejoindre qn; *(go with)* se joindre à qn (**in doing** pour faire). 2 *vi (of roads etc)* se rejoindre; *(of objects)* se joindre. 3 *vi* raccord *m*.

join² 1 *vt (become a member of)* s'inscrire à *(club, party)*; *(firm, army)* entrer dans. 2 *vi* devenir membre.

▸**join in** 1 *vt* to join in sth prendre part à qch. 2 *vi* prendre part.

joint 1 *n (in body)* articulation *f*. 2 *adj (account)* joint; *(effort)* conjugué.

joint·ly *adv* conjointement.

joke 1 *n* plaisanterie *f*, *(trick)* tour *m*. 2 *vi* plaisanter (**about** sur).

jok·er plaisantin *m*; *Cards* joker *m*.

jol·ly *adj* gai.

jolt *vti* secouer.

jos·tle 1 *vti (push)* bousculer. 2 *vi (push each other)* se bousculer.

▸**jot down** *vt* noter.

jour·nal·ist journaliste *mf*.

jour·ney voyage *m*; *(distance)* trajet *m*.

joy joie *f*.

joy·ful *adj* joyeux.

joy·stick manche *m* à balai.

judge 1 *n* juge *m*. 2 *vti* juger.

judg·ment jugement *m*.

ju·di·cial *adj* judiciaire.

ju·do judo *m*.

jug cruche *f*, *(for milk)* pot *m*.

jug·ger·naut force *f* irrésistible.

jug·gle *vi* jongler (**with** avec).

jug·gler jongleur, -euse *mf*.

juice jus *m*.

juic·y *adj (fruit)* juteux.

Ju·ly juillet *m*.

jum·ble (up) *vt* mélanger.

jum·bo *adj* géant.

jum·bo jet gros-porteur *m*.

jump 1 *n* saut *m*; *(start)* sursaut *m*; *(increase)* hausse *f*. 2 *vi* sauter; *(start)* sursauter; **to j. off sth** sauter de qch. 3 *vt* to j. rope sauter à la corde.

jump·er *(garment)* robe-chasuble *f*.

▸**jump in, jump on** 1 *vt (train, vehicle)* monter dans. 2 *vi* monter.

jump rope corde *f* à sauter.

jump·y *adj* nerveux.

junc·tion carrefour *m*.

June juin *m*.

jun·gle jungle *f*.

jun·ior 1 *adj (younger)* plus jeune; *(in rank)* subalterne; *(doctor)* jeune. 2 *n* cadet, -ette *mf*, *(in school)* petit(e) élève *mf*.

jun·ior high (school) = collège *m* d'enseignement secondaire.

junk bric-à-brac *m* *inv*; *(metal)* ferraille *f*, *(goods)* camelote *f*, *(garbage)* ordures *fpl*. **j. food** malbouffe *f*; **j. mail** prospectus *mpl*; *(e-mail)* messages *mpl* publicitaires.

ju·ry jury *m*.

just *adv (exactly, only)* juste; **she has/had j. left** elle vient/venait de partir; **he'll (only) j. catch the bus** il aura son bus de justesse; **he j. missed it** il l'a manqué de peu; **j. as big/etc** tout aussi grand/etc (**as** que); **j. over ten** un peu plus de dix; **j. one** un(e) seul(e); **j. about** à peu près; *(almost)* presque; **j. about to do** sur le point de faire.

jus·tice justice f.
jus·ti·fi·ca·tion justification f.
jus·ti·fy vt justifier; **to be justified in doing** être fondé à faire.
▸**jut out** vi faire saillie.

K

kan·ga·roo, pl **-oos** kangourou m.
ka·ra·oke karaoké m.
ka·ra·te karaté m.
ke·bab brochette f.
keen adj (interest, emotion) vif; **k. eyesight** vue f perçante; **he's a k. athlete** c'est un passionné de sport; **to be k. on doing** (want) tenir (beaucoup) à faire.
keep* 1 vt garder; (shop, car) avoir; (diary, promise) tenir; (family) entretenir; (rule) respecter; (delay) retenir; **to k. doing** continuer à faire; **to k. sb waiting/working** faire attendre/travailler qn; **to k. sb in/out** empêcher qn de sortir/d'entrer. 2 vi (remain) rester; (of food) se garder; **to k. going** continuer; **to k. (to the) right** tenir sa droite. 3 n (food) nourriture f, subsistance f.
▸**keep away** 1 vt (person) éloigner (from de). 2 vi ne pas s'approcher (from de).
▸**keep back** 1 vt (crowd) contenir; (delay) retenir; (hide) cacher (from à). 2 vi ne pas s'approcher (from de).
▸**keep down** vt (restrict) limiter; (price) maintenir bas.
keep·er (in park, zoo) gardien, -ienne mf.
▸**keep from** vt (hide) cacher à; **to k. sb from doing** (prevent) empêcher qn de faire.
▸**keep off** vi (not go near) ne pas

s'approcher; **the rain kept off** il n'a pas plu.
▸**keep on** vt (hat, employee) garder; **to k. on doing** continuer à faire.
▸**keep up** vt i continuer (**doing sth** à faire qch); **to k. up (with sb)** (follow) suivre (qn).
ken·nel niche f.
kept pt & pp de **keep**.
ker·o·sene pétrole m (lampant).
ketch·up ketchup m.
ket·tle bouilloire f; **the k. is boiling** l'eau bout.
key 1 n clef f, (of piano, typewriter, computer) touche f. 2 adj (industry, post etc) clef (f inv).
key·board clavier m.
key ring porte-clefs m inv.
kick 1 n coup m de pied. 2 vt donner un coup de pied à. 3 vi donner des coups de pied.
▸**kick down, kick in** vt (door etc) démolir à coups de pied.
kick·off Fam coup m d'envoi.
▸**kick off** vi Sports donner le coup d'envoi.
▸**kick out** vt (throw out) Fam flanquer dehors.
kid 1 n (child) Fam gosse mf. 2 vt i (tease) Fam blaguer.
kid·nap vt kidnapper.
kid·nap·per ravisseur, -euse mf.
kid·ney rein m; (as food) rognon m.
kill vt i tuer.
kill·er tueur, -euse mf.
kill·ing (of person) meurtre m; Fam **to make a k.** se remplir les poches.
ki·lo, pl **-os** kilo m.
kil·o·gram kilogramme m.
kil·o·me·ter kilomètre m.
kin my next of k. mon plus proche parent.
kind¹ (sort) sorte f, genre m, espèce f (**of** de); **all kinds of** toutes sortes de; **what k. of drink/etc is it?** qu'est-ce que c'est comme boisson/ etc?; **k. of worried/etc** plutôt inquiet/etc.

kind² adj (pleasant) gentil (**to** avec).

kin·der·gar·ten jardin m d'enfants.

kind·ly 1 adj bienveillant. **2** adv gentiment; **k. wait** ayez la bonté d'attendre.

kind·ness gentillesse f.

king roi m.

king·dom royaume m.

ki·osk kiosque m.

kiss 1 n baiser m. **2** vt (person) embrasser; **to k. sb's hand** baiser la main de qn. **3** vi s'embrasser.

kit équipement m; (set of articles) trousse f, (do-it-yourself) **k.** kit m; **tool k.** trousse f à outils.

kitch·en cuisine f.

kite (toy) cerf-volant m.

kit·ten chaton m.

klutz Fam balourd m, -ourde mf.

knack to have a or the **k.** of doing avoir le don de faire.

knee genou m (pl genoux).

kneel* (**down**) vi s'agenouiller; **to be kneeling** (**down**) être à genoux.

knew pt of **know**.

knick·ers knickers mpl.

knife, pl knives couteau m; (penknife) canif m.

knight chevalier m; Chess cavalier m.

knit vti tricoter.

knit·ting (activity, material) tricot m; **k. needle** aiguille f à tricoter.

knob (on door etc) bouton m.

knock 1 vt (strike) frapper; (collide with) heurter; **to k. one's head on sth** se cogner la tête contre qch. **2** vi frapper. **3** n coup m; **there's a k. at the door** quelqu'un frappe; **I heard a k.** j'ai entendu frapper.

▸**knock against**, **knock into** vt (bump into) heurter.

▸**knock down** vt (vase, pedestrian etc) renverser; (house, wall etc) abattre.

knock·er (for door) marteau m.

▸**knock in** vt (nail) enfoncer.

▸**knock off** vt (person, object) faire tomber (**from** de).

▸**knock out** vt (make unconscious) assommer; (person, place etc) connaître; Boxing mettre K.-O.; (beat in competition) éliminer.

▸**knock over** vt (pedestrian, vase etc) renverser.

knot 1 n nœud m. **2** vt nouer.

know* 1 vt (facts, language etc) savoir; (person, place etc) connaître; (recognize) reconnaître (**by** à); **to k. that** savoir que; **to k. how to do** savoir faire; **I'll let you k.** je te le ferai savoir; **to k. (a lot) about** (person, event) en savoir long sur; (cars, sewing etc) s'y connaître en; **to get to k. sb** apprendre à mieux connaître qn. **2** vi savoir; **I wouldn't k.** je n'en sais rien; **I k. about that** je suis au courant; **do you k. of a good dentist/etc?** connais-tu un bon dentiste/etc?

know-how savoir-faire m inv.

know-it-all Fam je-sais-tout mf.

knowl·edge connaissance f (**of** de); (learning) connaissances fpl.

known adj connu; **well k.** (bien) connu (**that** que); **she is k. to be** on sait qu'elle est.

knuck·le articulation f (du doigt).

Ko·ran the **K.** le Coran m.

L

lab Fam labo m.

la·bel 1 n étiquette f. **2** vt (goods) étiqueter.

la·bor 1 n (work) travail m; (workers) main-d'œuvre f; **in l.** en train d'accoucher. **2** adj (market, situation) du travail.

lab·o·ra·to·ry laboratoire m.

La·bor Day fête f du travail.

la·bor·er manœuvre *m*; *(on farm)* ouvrier *m* agricole.

la·bor pro·test mouvement *m* revendicatif.

la·bor un·ion syndicat *m*.

lace *(cloth)* dentelle *f*; *(of shoe)* lacet *m*.

lace (up) *vt (shoe)* lacer.

lack 1 *n* manque *m*. 2 *vt* manquer de. 3 *vi* to be lacking manquer (**in** de).

lad gamin *m*.

lad·der échelle *f*.

la·dle louche *f*.

la·dy dame *f*; **a young l.** une jeune fille; *(married)* une jeune femme; **the ladies' room** les toilettes *fpl* pour dames.

la·dy·bug coccinelle *f*.

la·ger bière *f* blonde.

lake lac *m*.

lamb agneau *m*.

lame *adj* to be l. boiter.

lamp lampe *f*.

lamp·post réverbère *m*.

lamp·shade abat-jour *m inv.*

land 1 *n* terre *f*; *(country)* pays *m*; **(plot of) l.** terrain *m*. 2 *vi (of aircraft)* atterrir; *(of passengers)* débarquer. 3 *vt (aircraft)* poser.

land·ing *(of aircraft)* atterrissage *m*; *(at top of stairs)* palier *m*.

land·la·dy propriétaire *f*; *(of pub)* patronne *f*.

land·lord propriétaire *m*; *(of pub)* patron *m*.

land·own·er propriétaire *m* foncier.

land·scape paysage *m*.

land·slide éboulement *m*.

lane *(in country)* chemin *m*; *(in town)* ruelle *f*; *(division of road)* voie *f*.

lan·guage 1 *n (English etc)* langue *f*; *(means of expression, style)* langage *m*. 2 *adj (laboratory)* de langues; *(teacher, studies)* de langue(s).

lan·tern lanterne *f*.

lap *(of person)* genoux *mpl*; *(in race)* tour *m* (de piste).

la·pel *(of coat etc)* revers *m*.

lap·top portable *m*.

lar·ce·ny vol *m* simple.

lar·der *(storeroom)* garde-manger *m inv.*

large *adj* grand; *(in volume)* gros (*f* grosse).

large·ly *adv* en grande mesure.

large-scale *adj* de grande envergure.

lark *(bird)* alouette *f*; *(joke)* Fam rigolade *f*.

la·ser laser *m*.

last¹ 1 *adj* dernier; **next to l.** avant-dernier. 2 *adv (lastly)* en dernier lieu; *(on the last occasion)* (pour) la dernière fois; **to leave l.** sortir en dernier. 3 *n (person, object)* dernier, -ière *mf*; **the l. of the beer/etc** le reste de la bière/*etc*; **at (long) l.** enfin.

last² *vi* durer; *(endure)* tenir.

last·ly *adv* en dernier lieu, enfin.

latch loquet *m*.

late 1 *adj (not on time)* en retard (**for** à); *(meal, hour)* tardif; **he's an hour l.** il a une heure de retard; **it's l.** il est tard; **at a later date** à une date ultérieure; **at the latest** au plus tard; **of l.** dernièrement. 2 *adv (in the day, season etc)* tard; *(not on time)* en retard; **it's getting l.** il se fait tard; **later (on)** plus tard.

late·com·er retardataire *mf*.

late·ly *adv* dernièrement.

Lat·in 1 *adj* latin. 2 *n (language)* latin *m*.

La·tin A·mer·i·ca l'Amérique *f* latine.

lat·ter 1 *adj (last-named)* dernier; *(second)* deuxième. 2 *n (last)* dernier, -ière *mf*; *(second)* second, -onde *mf*.

laugh 1 *n* rire *m*. 2 *vi* rire (**at, about** de).

laugh·ter rire(s) *m(pl)*.

launch *vt (rocket, fashion etc)* lancer. 2 *n* lancement *m*.

laun·dro·mat laverie *f* automatique.

laun·dry *(place)* blanchisserie f; *(clothes)* linge m.

laun·dry de·ter·gent lessive f.

lav·a·to·ry cabinets mpl.

law loi f; *(study, profession)* droit m; **court of l.**, **l. court** cour f de justice.

lawn pelouse f, gazon m; **l. mower** tondeuse f (à gazon).

law·suit procès m.

law·yer avocat m; *(for wills, sales)* notaire m.

lay* vt *(put down)* poser; *(table)* mettre; *(blanket)* étendre (**over** sur); *(trap)* tendre; *(egg)* pondre.

▸**lay down** vt *(put down)* poser.

lay·er couche f.

▸**lay in** vt *(supplies)* faire provision de.

▸**lay off** vt *(worker)* licencier.

lay·out disposition f.

▸**lay out** vt *(garden)* dessiner; *(display)* disposer; *(money)* Fam mettre (**on** dans).

lay·per·son profane mf.

la·zy adj paresseux.

la·zy·bones Fam fainéant, -ante mf.

lead¹ 1 n vt* *(conduct)* mener, conduire (**to** à); *(team, government etc)* diriger; *(life)* mener; **to l. sb in/out/etc** faire entrer/sortir/etc qn; **to l. sb to do** amener qn à faire. **2** vi *(of street, door etc)* mener (**to** à); *(in race)* être en tête; *(in match)* mener; *(go ahead)* aller devant. **3** n *(distance or time ahead)* avance f (**over** sur); *(example)* exemple m; *(leash)* laisse f; *(electric wire)* fil m; **to be in the l.** *(in race)* être en tête; *(in match)* mener.

lead² *(metal)* plomb m; *(of pencil)* mine f.

▸**lead away**, **lead off** vt emmener.

lead·er chef m; *(of country, party)* dirigeant, -ante mf.

lead·ing adj *(main)* principal.

▸**lead on 1** vi *(go ahead)* aller devant. **2** vt *(deceive)* tromper.

▸**lead to** vt *(result in)* aboutir à; *(cause)* causer.

▸**lead up to** vt *(of street etc)* conduire à; *(precede)* précéder.

leaf, pl **leaves** feuille f; *(of book)* feuillet m.

leaf·let prospectus m; *(containing instructions)* notice f.

▸**leaf through** vt *(book)* feuilleter.

leak 1 n *(of gas etc)* fuite f. **2** vi *(of liquid, pipe etc)* fuir.

lean* 1 vi *(of object)* pencher; *(of person)* se pencher; **to l. against/on sth** *(of person)* s'appuyer contre/sur qch. **2** vt appuyer (**against** contre); **to l. one's head on/out of sth** pencher la tête sur/par qch.

▸**lean forward** vi *(of person)* se pencher (en avant).

▸**lean over** vi *(of person)* se pencher; *(of object)* pencher.

leap 1 n bond m. **2** vi* bondir.

leap year année f bissextile.

learn* 1 vt apprendre (**that** que); **to l. (how) to do** apprendre à faire. **2** vi apprendre; **to l. about** *(study)* étudier; *(hear about)* apprendre.

learn·er débutant, -ante mf.

learn·ing *(of language)* apprentissage m (**of** de).

lease 1 n bail m; **to give sb a new l. on life** redonner du tonus à qn. **2** vt louer à bail.

leash laisse f.

least 1 adj **the l.** *(smallest amount of)* le moins de; *(slightest)* le or la moindre. **2** n **the l.** le moins; **at l.** du moins; *(with quantity)* au moins. **3** adv *(to work etc)* le moins; *(with adjective)* le or la moins.

leath·er cuir m.

leave 1 n *(vacation)* congé m. **2** vt* laisser; *(go away from)* quitter; **to be left (over)** rester; **there's no bread/etc left** il ne reste plus de pain/etc; **to l. go (of)** *(release)* lâcher. **3** vi *(go away)* partir (**from** de; **for** pour).

▸**leave behind** vt *(not take)* laisser; *(in race, at school)* distancer.

▸**leave on** vt (hat, gloves) garder.
▸**leave out** vt (forget to add) oublier (de mettre); (word, line) sauter; (exclude) exclure.
lec·ture 1 n (public speech) conférence f; **to give a l.** faire une conférence. **2** vt **to l. sb** sermonner qn.
lec·tur·er conférencier, -ière mf.
leek poireau m.
left¹ pt & pp de **leave**.
left² 1 adj (side, hand etc) gauche. **2** adv à gauche. **3** n gauche f, **on** or **to the l.** à gauche (**of** de).
left-hand adj à or de gauche; **on the l. side** à gauche (**of** de).
left-hand·ed adj (person) gaucher.
left·o·vers npl restes mpl.
leg jambe f; (of dog etc) patte f; (of table) pied m; **l. (of chicken)** cuisse f (de poulet); **l. of lamb** gigot m (d'agneau).
le·gal adj légal.
le·gal·ly adv légalement.
leg·end légende f.
leg·i·ble adj lisible.
leg·is·la·tion législation f.
leg·is·la·tive adj législatif.
leg·is·la·ture (corps m) législatif m.
le·git·i·mate adj légitime.
lei·sure l. (time) loisirs mpl; **l. activities** loisirs mpl.
lem·on citron m; **tea with l.** thé m au citron.
lem·on·ade citronnade f.
lend* vt prêter (**to** à); (color, charm etc) donner (**to** à).
length longueur f; (section of rope etc) morceau m; (duration) durée f; **l. of time** temps m.
length·en vt allonger; (in time) prolonger.
length·y adj long (f longue).
le·nient adj indulgent (**to** envers).
lens lentille f; (in spectacles) verre m; (of camera) objectif m.
len·til lentille f (graine).
leop·ard léopard m.

le·o·tard collant m (de danse).
less 1 adj & n moins (de) (**than** que); **l. time/etc** moins de temps/etc; **l. than a quart/ten** (quantity, number) moins d'un litre/de dix. **2** adv moins (**than** que); **l. (often)** moins souvent; **l. and l.** de moins en moins; **one l.** un(e) de moins. **3** prep moins.
les·son leçon f.
let* vt (allow) laisser (**sb do** qn faire); **to l. sb have sth** donner qch à qn; **l. us** or **l.'s eat/etc** mangeons/ etc; **l.'s go for a stroll** allons nous promener; **l. him come** qu'il vienne.
let·down déception f.
▸**let down** vt (lower) baisser; **to l. sb down** (disappoint) décevoir qn.
▸**let in** vt (person) faire entrer; (noise, light) laisser entrer.
▸**let off** vt (firework, gun) faire partir; **to l. sb off** (not punish) ne pas punir qn; **to l. sb off doing** dispenser qn de faire.
▸**let out** vt (person) laisser sortir; (cry, secret) laisser échapper.
let·ter lettre f.
let·ter·box boîte f aux or à lettres.
let·ter o·pen·er coupe-papier m inv.
let·tuce laitue f.
▸**let up** vi (of rain etc) s'arrêter.
lev·el 1 n niveau m; (rate) taux m. **2** adj (surface) plat; (object on surface) d'aplomb; (equal in score) à égalité (**with** avec); (in height) au même niveau (**with** que).
lev·er levier m.
li·a·ble adj **to be l. to do** être capable or susceptible de faire.
li·ar menteur, -euse mf.
li·bel 1 n diffamation f. **2** vt diffamer.
lib·er·ty liberté f; **at l. to do** libre de faire.
li·brar·i·an bibliothécaire mf.
li·brar·y bibliothèque f.
lice npl poux mpl.
li·cense (document) permis m; **l.**

plate/number plaque f/numéro m d'immatriculation.

lick vt lécher.

lic·o·rice réglisse f.

lid (of box etc) couvercle m.

lie¹* vi (in flat position) s'allonger; (remain) rester; (be) être; **to be lying** (on the grass etc) être allongé.

lie² **1** vi* (tell lies) mentir. **2** n mensonge m.

▸ **lie around** vi (of objects, person) traîner.

▸ **lie down** vi s'allonger; **lying down** allongé.

life, pl **lives** vie f; **to come to l.** s'animer.

life·belt ceinture f de sauvetage.

life·boat canot m de sauvetage.

life·guard maître nageur m (sauveteur).

life in·sur·ance assurance-vie f.

life jack·et gilet m de sauvetage.

life pre·ser·ver ceinture f de sauvetage.

life·time in my l. de mon vivant.

lift **1** vt lever. **2** n (elevator) ascenseur m; **to give sb a l.** emmener qn (en voiture) (**to** à).

▸ **lift down, lift off** vt (take down) descendre (**from** de).

▸ **lift out** vt (take out) sortir (**of** de).

▸ **lift up** vt (arm, object) lever.

light¹ lumière f; (on vehicle) feu m; (vehicle headlight) phare m; **do you have a l.?** (for cigarette) est-ce que vous avez du feu?

light²* vt (match, fire, gas) allumer.

light³ adj (not dark) clair; **a l. green jacket** une veste vert clair.

light⁴ adj (in weight, quantity etc) léger; **to travel l.** voyager avec peu de bagages.

light (up) vt (room) éclairer; (cigarette) allumer.

light bulb ampoule f (électrique).

light·er (for cigarettes) briquet m; (for stove) allume-gaz m inv.

light·house phare m.

light·ing (lights) éclairage m.

light·ning (charge) foudre f; (flash of) l. éclair m.

like¹ **1** prep comme; **l. this** comme ça; **what's he l.?** comment est-il?; **to be** or **look l.** ressembler à; **what was the book l.?** comment as-tu trouvé le livre? **2** conj (as) Fam comme; **do l. I do** fais comme moi.

like² vt aimer (bien) (**to do, doing** faire); **she likes it here** elle se plaît ici; **to l. sth best** aimer mieux qch; **I'd l. to come** je voudrais (bien) or j'aimerais (bien) venir; **I'd l. some cake** je voudrais du gâteau; **would you l. an apple?** voulez-vous une pomme?; **if you l.** si vous voulez.

like·a·ble adj sympathique.

like·li·hood there's isn't much l. that il y a peu de chances que (+ subjunctive).

like·ly **1** adj probable; (excuse) vraisemblable; **it's l. (that) she'll come, she's l. to come** il est probable qu'elle viendra. **2** adv **very l.** très probablement.

like·wise adv de même.

lik·ing **l. for** (person) de la sympathie pour; (thing) du goût pour.

lil·y lis m.

limb membre m.

lime (fruit) citron m vert.

lim·it **1** n limite f (**to** à). **2** vt limiter (**to** à).

lim·ou·sine (airport shuttle) voiture-navette f.

limp **1** vi (of person) boiter. **2** n **to have a l.** boiter.

line¹ **1** n ligne f; (of poem) vers m; (wrinkle) ride f; (track) voie f; (rope) corde f; (row) rangée f; (of vehicles, people) file f; **on the l.** (phone) au bout du fil; **to stand in l.** faire la queue; **to drop a l.** (send a letter) envoyer un mot (**to** à). **2** vt **to l. the street** (of trees) border la rue; (of people) faire la haie le long de la rue.

line² vt (clothes) doubler.

lin·en (sheets etc) linge m.

lin·er (*ocean*) l. paquebot *m*.

▸**line up 1** *vt* (*children, objects*) aligner; (*arrange*) organiser. **2** *vi* s'aligner; (*of people*) faire la queue.

lin·ger *vi* (*of person*) s'attarder; (*of smell, memory*) persister; (*of doubt*) subsister.

lin·guis·tics linguistique *f*.

lin·ing (*of clothes*) doublure *f*.

link 1 *vt* (*connect*) relier; (*relate*) lier (**to** à). **2** *n* lien *m*; (*of chain*) maillon *m*; (*by road, rail*) liaison *f*.

▸**link up** *vi* (*of people etc*) s'associer; (*of roads*) se rejoindre.

li·on lion *m*.

lip lèvre *f*.

lip·stick bâton *m* de rouge; (*substance*) rouge *m* (à lèvres).

li·queur liqueur *f*.

liq·uid *n & adj* liquide (*m*).

liq·ui·date *vt* liquider.

liq·uor alcool *m*.

list 1 *n* liste *f*. **2** *vt* faire la liste de; (*names*) mettre sur la liste, inscrire; (*name one by one*) énumérer.

lis·ten (to) *vt* écouter.

lis·ten·er (*to radio*) auditeur, -trice *mf*.

▸**listen (out) for** *vt* guetter (*un bruit ou les cris etc de*).

li·ter litre *m*.

lit·er·al·ly *adv* littéralement.

lit·er·ar·y *adj* littéraire.

lit·er·a·ture littérature *f*; (*pamphlets etc*) documentation *f*.

lit·i·ga·tion litige *m*.

lit·ter (*rubbish*) détritus *m*; (*papers*) papiers *mpl*; (*young animals*) portée *f*.

lit·tle 1 *adj* (*small*) petit. **2** *adj & adv* (*not much*) peu (de); **l. time**/*etc* peu de temps/*etc*; **she eats l.** elle mange peu; **as l. as possible** le moins possible; **a l. money**/*etc* (*some*) un peu d'argent/*etc*. **3** *adv a* **l. heavy**/*etc* un peu lourd/*etc*; **to work**/*etc* **a l.** travailler/*etc* un peu; **l. by l.** peu à peu.

live¹ 1 *vi* vivre; (*reside*) habiter, vivre. **2** *vt* (*life*) mener.

live² 1 *adj* (*electric wire*) sous tension; (*switch*) mal isolé. **2** *adj & adv* (*broadcast*) en direct.

live·ly *adj* (*person, style, interest, mind*) vif; (*discussion*) animé.

▸**live off, live on** *vt* (*eat*) vivre de.

liv·er foie *m*.

▸**live through** *vt* (*experience*) vivre; (*survive*) survivre à.

liv·ing 1 *adj* (*alive*) vivant. **2** *n* vie *f*; **to make** *or* **earn a** *or* **one's l.** gagner sa vie; **the cost of l.** le coût de la vie.

liv·ing room salle *f* de séjour.

liz·ard lézard *m*.

load 1 *n* charge *f*; (*weight*) poids *m*; **a l. of, loads of** (*people, money etc*) *Fam* un tas de. **2** *vt* (*truck, gun etc*) charger (**with**).

▸**load up 1** *vt* (*car, ship etc*) charger (**with**). **2** *vi* charger la voiture, le navire *etc*.

loaf, *pl* **loaves** pain *m*.

loan 1 *n* (*money lent*) prêt *m*; (*money borrowed*) emprunt *m*. **2** *vt* (*lend*) prêter (**to** à).

lob·by (*of hotel*) hall *m*.

lob·ster homard *m*.

lo·cal *adj* local; (*regional*) régional; (*of the neighborhood*) du *or* de quartier; (*of the region*) de la région.

lo·cal·i·ty environs *mpl*.

lo·cal·ly *adv* dans le coin.

lo·cate *vt* (*find*) trouver, repérer; **to be located** être situé.

lo·ca·tion (*site*) emplacement *m*.

lock 1 *vt* (*door etc*) fermer à clef. **2** *n* (*on door etc*) serrure *f*; (*on canal*) écluse *f*; (*of hair*) mèche *f*.

▸**lock away** *vt* (*prisoner, jewels etc*) enfermer.

lock·er (*for luggage*) casier *m* de consigne automatique; (*for clothes*) vestiaire *m* (métallique).

lock·et médaillon *m*.

▸**lock in** *vt* enfermer; **to l. sb in sth** enfermer qn dans qch.

▸**lock out** *vt (accidentally)* enfermer dehors.

▸**lock up 1** *vt (house etc)* fermer à clef; *(prisoner, jewels etc)* enfermer. **2** *vi* fermer à clef.

lodge 1 *n (porter's)* loge *f*; *(hunter's)* pavillon *m*; *(in park, resort)* bâtiment *m* central. **2** *vt (accommodate)* héberger, loger; *(claim)* déposer; **to l. a complaint** porter plainte. **3** *vi (live)* loger, être logé; *(get stuck)* se loger.

lodg·er *(room and meals)* pensionnaire *mf*; *(room only)* locataire *mf*.

lodg·ing hébergement *m*; **lodgings** chambre(s) *f(pl)* meublée(s).

loft *(attic)* grenier *m*.

log *(tree trunk)* tronc *m* d'arbre; *(for fire)* bûche *f*.

log·ic logique *f*.

log·i·cal *adj* logique.

lol·li·pop sucette *f*.

lone *adj* solitaire.

lone·li·ness solitude *f*.

lone·ly *adj* solitaire.

long 1 *adj* long *(f* longue*)*; **to be 33 feet l.** avoir dix mètres de long; **to be six weeks l.** durer six semaines; **a l. time** longtemps. **2** *adv* longtemps; **has he been here l.?** il y a longtemps qu'il est ici?; **how l. ago?** il y a combien de temps?; **before l.** sous peu; **she no longer swims** elle ne nage plus; **I won't be l.** je n'en ai pas pour longtemps; **all summer l.** tout l'été; **as l. as, so l. as** *(provided that)* pourvu que *(+ subjunctive)*.

long-dis·tance *(phone call)* interurbain; *(flight)* long-courrier.

long johns caleçon *m* (long).

long-term *adj* à long terme.

look 1 *n* regard *m*; *(appearance)* air *m*; **to have a l. (at)** jeter un coup d'œil (à); **to have a l. (for)** chercher; **to have a l. around** regarder; *(walk)* faire un tour; **let me have a l.** fais voir. **2** *vi* regarder; **to l. tired/**

etc sembler *or* avoir l'air fatigué/*etc*; **you l. like** *or* **as if you're tired** on dirait que tu es fatigué; **to l. well** *or* **good** *(of person)* avoir bonne mine; **you l. good in that hat/***etc* ce chapeau/*etc* te va très bien.

▸**look around 1** *vt* visiter. **2** *vi* regarder; *(walk around)* faire un tour; *(look back)* se retourner.

▸**look at** *vt* regarder.

▸**look back** *vi* regarder derrière soi; *(remember)* regarder en arrière.

▸**look down** *vi* baisser les yeux; *(from a height)* regarder en bas.

▸**look for** *vt* chercher.

▸**look forward to** *vt (event)* attendre avec impatience; **to l. forward to doing** avoir hâte de faire.

▸**look into** *vt* examiner; *(find out about)* se renseigner sur.

▸**look (out) on to** *vt (of window etc)* donner sur.

look·out *(high place)* observatoire *m*; **to be on the l.** faire le guet; **to be on the l. for** guetter.

▸**look out** *vi (be careful)* faire attention *(for* à*)*.

▸**look over** *or* **through** *vt* examiner; *(briefly)* parcourir; *(region, town)* parcourir.

▸**look up 1** *vi* lever les yeux; *(into the air)* regarder en l'air; *(improve)* s'améliorer. **2** *vt (word)* chercher.

loom¹ métier *m* à tisser.

loom² *vi (of mountain)* apparaître indistinctement; *(of event)* paraître imminent.

loop boucle *f*.

loose 1 *adj (screw, belt, knot)* desserré; *(tooth)* branlant; *(page)* détaché; *(clothes)* flottant; *(tea etc)* au poids; *(having escaped) (animal)* l. échappé; *(prisoner)* évadé; **l. change** petite monnaie *f*; **to set** *or* **turn l.** *(dog etc)* lâcher. **2** *n* **on the l.** *(prisoner)* évadé; *(animal)* échappé.

loos·en *vt (knot, belt, screw)* desserrer.

lord seigneur *m*.

lose* 1 *vt* perdre; **to get lost** (*of person*) se perdre; **the ticket/etc got lost** on a perdu le billet/*etc*. 2 *vi* perdre.

los·er (*in contest etc*) perdant, -ante *mf*.

▸ **lose to** *vt* être battu par.

loss perte *f*.

lost *adj* perdu.

lost and found objets *mpl* trouvés.

lot a l. of, lots of beaucoup de; a l. beaucoup; **quite a l.** pas mal (of de); **such a l.** tellement (of de); **what a l. of flowers/water/etc!** regarde toutes ces fleurs/toute cette eau/*etc*!

lo·tion lotion *f*.

lot·ter·y loterie *f*.

loud 1 *adj* (*voice, music*) fort; (*noise, cry*) grand; **the radio/TV is too l.** le son de la radio/télé est trop fort. 2 *adv* (*to shout etc*) fort; **out l.** tout haut.

loud·ly *adv* (*to speak etc*) fort.

loud·speak·er haut-parleur *m*; (*for speaking to crowd*) porte-voix *m inv*.

lounge salon *m*; **teachers' l.** salle *f* des professeurs.

lous·y *adj* (*food, weather etc*) Fam infect.

love 1 *n* amour *m*; **in l.** amoureux (**with** de); **they're in l.** ils s'aiment. 2 *vt* aimer (beaucoup) (**to do, doing** faire).

love·ly *adj* agréable; (*excellent*) excellent; (*pretty*) joli; (*charming*) charmant; (*kind*) gentil.

lov·er a l. of music/*etc* un amateur de musique/*etc*.

lov·ing *adj* affectueux.

low 1 *adj* bas (*f* basse); (*speed, income, intelligence*) faible; (*opinion, quality*) mauvais; **to feel l.** être déprimé; **in a l. voice** à voix basse; **lower** inférieur (**to** à). 2 *adv* bas; **to turn down l.** baisser.

low beams (*of vehicle*) codes *mpl*.

low·er *vt* baisser; (*by rope*) descendre.

low-fat *adj* (*milk*) écrémé; (*cheese*) allégé.

loy·al *adj* fidèle (**to** à), loyal (**to** envers).

loy·al·ty loyauté *f*.

loz·enge (*tablet*) pastille *f*.

luck (*chance*) chance *f*, **bad l.** malchance *f*.

luck·i·ly *adv* heureusement.

luck·y *adj* (*person*) chanceux; (*guess, event*) heureux; **to be l.** avoir de la chance (**to do** de faire); **it's l. that** c'est une chance que; **l. charm** porte-bonheur *m inv*; **l. number/etc** chiffre *m/etc* porte-bonheur.

lu·di·crous *adj* ridicule.

lug·gage bagages *mpl*.

luke·warm *adj* tiède.

lull·a·by berceuse *f*.

lum·ber bois *m* de charpente.

lum·ber·yard dépôt *m* de bois.

lu·mi·nous *adj* lumineux.

lump morceau *m*; (*bump*) bosse *f*; (*swelling*) grosseur *f*.

lump sum somme *f* forfaitaire.

lu·na·tic fou *m*, folle *f*.

lunch déjeuner *m*; **to have l.** déjeuner; **l. break, l. hour, l. time** heure *f* du déjeuner.

lung poumon *m*.

lux·u·ri·ous *adj* luxueux.

lux·u·ry 1 *n* luxe *m*. 2 *adj* (*goods etc*) de luxe.

M

MA *abbr* = **Master of Arts**.

mac·a·ro·ni macaroni(s) *m(pl)*.

ma·chine machine *f*.

ma·chine gun (*heavy*) mitrailleuse *f*, (*portable*) mitraillette *f*.

ma·chin·e·ry machines *fpl*; *(works)* mécanisme *m*.

mack·er·el *n inv* maquereau *m*.

mad *adj* fou (*f* folle); **m. (at)** *(angry)* furieux (contre); **m. about** *(person)* fou de; *(films etc)* passionné de; **like m.** comme un fou *or* une folle.

Mad·am madame *f*; *(unmarried)* mademoiselle *f*.

made *pt & pp de* **make**.

mad·man, *pl* **-men** fou *m*.

mad·ness folie *f*.

mag·a·zine magazine *m*, revue *f*.

mag·got ver *m*.

mag·ic 1 *n* magie *f*. **2** *adj (wand etc)* magique.

mag·i·cal *adj* magique.

ma·gi·cian magicien, -ienne *mf*.

mag·is·trate magistrat *m*.

mag·net aimant *m*.

mag·nif·i·cent *adj* magnifique.

mag·ni·fy·ing glass loupe *f*.

ma·hog·a·ny acajou *m*.

maid *(servant)* bonne *f*.

mail 1 *n (system)* poste *f*; *(letters)* courrier *m*. **2** *adj (bag etc)* postal. **3** *vt (letter)* poster.

mail·box boîte *f* aux *or* à lettres.

mail·man, *pl* **-men** facteur *m*.

main¹ *adj* principal; **the m. thing is to** l'essentiel est de; **m. road** grand-route *f*.

main² water/gas **m.** conduite *f* d'eau/de gaz; **the mains** *(electricity)* le secteur.

main·land continent *m*.

main·ly *adv* surtout.

main street grand-rue *f*.

main·tain *vt (vehicle etc)* entretenir; *(law and order)* faire respecter; **to m. that** affirmer que.

main·te·nance *(of vehicle, road)* entretien *m*; *(alimony)* pension *f* alimentaire.

mai·son·ette duplex *m*.

mai·tre d' maître *m* d'hôtel.

maj·es·ty majesté *f*; **Your M.** Votre Majesté.

ma·jor 1 *adj* majeur; **a m. road** une grande route. **2** *n (officer)* commandant *m*.

ma·jor·ette majorette *f*.

ma·jor·i·ty majorité *f* (**of** de); **the m. of people** la plupart des gens.

make* 1 *vt* faire; *(tool, vehicle etc)* fabriquer; *(decision)* prendre; *(friends, salary)* se faire; *(destination)* arriver à; **to m. happy/etc** rendre heureux/etc; **to m. sb do sth** faire faire qch à qn; **to m. do** *(manage)* se débrouiller (**with** avec); **to m. do with** *(be satisfied with)* se contenter de; **to m. it** arriver; *(succeed)* réussir; **what do you m. of it?** qu'en penses-tu? **2** *n (brand)* marque *f*.

► **make for** *vt* aller vers.

► **make good** *vt (loss)* compenser; *(damage)* réparer.

► **make off** *vi (run away)* se sauver.

► **make out 1** *vt (see)* distinguer; *(understand)* comprendre; *(write)* faire *(chèque, liste)*; *(claim)* prétendre (**that** que). **2** *vi Fam* se peloter.

mak·er *(of product)* fabricant, -ante *mf*.

make-up *(for face)* maquillage *m*.

► **make up 1** *vt (story)* inventer; *(put together)* faire *(collection, liste etc)*; *(form)* former; *(loss)* compenser; *(quantity)* compléter; *(quarrel)* régler; *(one's face)* maquiller. **2** *vti* **to m. (it) up** *(of friends)* se réconcilier.

► **make up for** *vt (loss, damage)* compenser; *(lost time, mistake)* rattraper.

ma·lar·i·a malaria *f*.

male 1 *adj* mâle; *(clothes, sex)* masculin. **2** *n* mâle *m*.

mal·ice méchanceté *f*.

ma·li·cious *adj* malveillant.

mall *(shopping)* **m.** galerie *f* marchande; *(large complex)* centre *m* commercial.

ma·ma, mam·ma *Fam* maman *f*.

mam·mal mammifère *m*.

man, *pl* **men** homme *m*.

man·age 1 *vt* (run) diriger; (handle) manier; **to m. to do** (succeed) réussir à faire; (by being smart) se débrouiller pour faire; **I'll m. it** j'y arriverai. **2** *vi* (succeed) y arriver; (make do) se débrouiller (**with** avec); **to m. without sth** se passer de qch.

man·age·ment (running, managers) direction f.

man·ag·er directeur, -trice mf; (of shop, café) gérant, -ante mf.

man·ag·ing di·rec·tor PDG m.

mane crinière f.

ma·neu·ver 1 *n* manœuvre f. **2** *vti* manœuvrer.

ma·ni·ac fou m, folle f.

man·kind l'humanité f.

man·made *adj* artificiel.

man·ner (way) manière f; (behavior) attitude f; **manners** (social habits) manières fpl; **to have no manners** être mal élevé.

man·pow·er main f d'œuvre f.

man·tel·piece (shelf) cheminée f.

man·u·al 1 *adj* manuel. **2** *n* (book) manuel m.

man·u·fac·ture 1 *vt* fabriquer. **2** *n* fabrication f.

man·u·fac·tur·er fabricant, -ante mf.

ma·nure fumier m.

man·y *adj & n* beaucoup (de); **m. things** beaucoup de choses; **I don't have m.** j'en ai pas beaucoup; **m. came** beaucoup sont venus; (**a good** or **great**) **m. of** un (très) grand nombre de; **m. times** bien des fois; **as m. books/etc as** autant de livres/etc que.

map (of country, region) carte f; (of town etc) plan m.

mar·a·thon marathon m.

mar·ble marbre m; (toy) bille f.

March mars m.

march 1 *n* marche f (militaire). **2** *vi* (of soldiers) défiler.

mare jument f.

mar·ga·rine margarine f.

mar·gin (of page) marge f.

ma·rine 1 *adj* marin. **2** *n* marine m; **the M. Corps** les Marines mpl.

mark 1 *n* (symbol) marque f; (stain, trace) trace f; (token, sign) signe m; (for school exercise etc) note f; (target) but m. **2** *vt* marquer; (exam etc) corriger.

mark·er (pen) marqueur m.

mar·ket marché m.

mar·ket·ing marketing m.

▶**mark off** *vt* (area) délimiter.

mar·ma·lade confiture f d'oranges.

mar·riage mariage m.

mar·ried *adj* marié; **to get m.** se marier.

mar·row (of bone) moelle f.

mar·ry 1 *vt* épouser, se marier avec; (of priest etc) marier. **2** *vi* se marier.

marsh marais m.

mar·shal 1 *n* (in army) maréchal m; (district police officer) commissaire m; (police chief) commissaire m de police; (fire chief) capitaine m des pompiers. **2** *vt* (troops) masser, rassembler; (facts, arguments etc) rassembler.

mar·vel·ous *adj* merveilleux.

mar·zi·pan pâte f d'amandes.

mas·car·a mascara m.

mas·cot mascotte f.

mas·cu·line *adj* masculin.

mash *vt* **to m. (up)** écraser, broyer; (food) faire une purée de; **mashed potatoes** purée f (de pommes de terre).

mask masque m.

mass¹ *n* (quantity) masse f; **a m. of** (many) une multitude de; (pile) un tas de; **masses of** des masses de. **2** *adj* (protests, departure) en masse.

mass² (church service) messe f.

mas·sa·cre 1 *n* massacre m. **2** *vt* massacrer.

mas·sage 1 *n* massage m. **2** *vt* masser.

mas·seur masseur m.

mas·seuse masseuse f.

mas·sive adj (huge) énorme.
mast (of ship) mât m.
mas·ter 1 n maître m; **M. of Arts/ Science** (person) Maître m ès lettres/sciences; **M. of Ceremonies** animateur, -trice mf. **2** vt (control) maîtriser; (subject, situation) dominer; **she has mastered Latin** elle possède le latin.
mas·ter·piece chef-d'œuvre m.
mat tapis m; (of straw) natte f; (at door) paillasson m; (place) m. set m (de table).
match¹ (stick) allumette f.
match² **1** n (game) match m; (equal) égal, -ale mf; **to be a good m.** (of colors, people etc) être bien assortis. **2** vt (of clothes, color etc) aller (bien) avec; **to be well- matched** être (bien) assortis. **3** vi être assortis.
match·box boîte f d'allumettes.
match·ing adj (dress etc) assorti.
match·stick allumette f.
▶ **match up** vt (plates etc) assortir.
▶ **match up to** vt égaler; (sb's hopes or expectations) répondre à.
mate (friend) camarade mf.
ma·ter·i·al matière f; (cloth) tissu m; **material(s)** (equipment) matériel m; **building materials** matériaux mpl de construction.
ma·ter·nal adj maternel.
math maths fpl.
math·e·mat·i·cal adj mathématique.
math·e·mat·ics mathématiques fpl.
mat·i·nee (in theater) matinée f.
matt adj (paint, paper) mat.
mat·ter 1 n matière f; (subject, affair) affaire f; **what's the m. with you?** qu'est-ce que tu as?; **there's sth the m.** il y a qch qui ne va pas; **there's something the m. with my leg** j'ai quelque chose à la jambe. **2** vi importer (**to** à); **it doesn't m. if/ who**/etc peu importe si/qui/etc; **it**

doesn't m.! ça ne fait rien!
mat·tress matelas m.
ma·ture adj mûr; (cheese) fait.
max·i·mum adj & n maximum (m).
May mai m.
may v aux (pt might) (possibility) pouvoir; **he m. come** il peut arriver; **he might come** il pourrait arriver; **I m. or might have forgotten it** je l'ai peut-être oublié; **we m. or might as well go** nous ferions aussi bien de partir. ▪ (permission) pouvoir; **m. I stay?** puis-je rester?; **m. I?** vous permettez?; **you m. go** tu peux partir. ▪ (wish) **m. you be happy** (que tu) sois heureux.
may·be adv peut-être.
may·on·naise mayonnaise f.
may·or maire m.
maze labyrinthe m.
MBA abbr (Master of Business Administration) MBA m, maîtrise f de gestion.
me pron me, m'; (after prep, 'than', 'it is') moi; (to) **to me** me, m'; **she knows me** elle me connaît; **he gives (to) me** il me donne.
mead·ow pré m.
meal repas m.
mean¹ vt (signify) vouloir dire; (intend) destiner (**for** à); (result in) entraîner; **to m. to do** avoir l'intention de faire; **I m. it** je suis sérieux; **to m. sth to sb** avoir de l'importance pour qn; **I didn't m. to!** je ne l'ai pas fait exprès!
mean² adj méchant.
mean·ing sens m.
mean·ing·ful adj significatif.
mean·ing·less adj qui n'a pas de sens.
mean·ness méchanceté f.
means n(pl) (method) moyen(s) m(pl) (**to do, of doing** de faire); (wealth) moyens mpl; **by m. of** (stick etc) au moyen de; (work etc) à force de; **by all m.!** très certainement!; **by no m.** nullement.

mean·time adv & n (in the) m. entre-temps.

mean·while adv entre-temps.

mea·sles rougeole f.

meas·ure 1 n (action, amount) mesure f. **2** vt mesurer.

meas·ure·ment (of chest etc) tour m; **measurements** mesures fpl.

▸ **measure up** vt (plank etc) mesurer.

▸ **measure up to** vt (task) être à la hauteur de.

meat viande f.

me·chan·ic mécanicien, -ienne mf.

me·chan·i·cal adj mécanique.

mech·a·nism mécanisme m.

med·al médaille f.

med·al·ist to be a gold m. être médaillé d'or.

me·di·a npl the (mass) m. les médias mpl.

me·di·an (in road) refuge m.

med·i·cal adj médical; (school, studies) de médecine; (student) en médecine.

med·i·ca·tion médicaments mpl.

med·i·cine médicament m; (science) médecine f.

med·i·cine cab·i·net, med·i·cine chest (armoire f à) pharmacie f.

me·di·e·val adj médiéval.

Med·i·ter·ra·ne·an 1 adj méditerranéen. **2** n the M. la Méditerranée.

me·di·um adj moyen.

me·di·um-sized adj moyen.

meet* 1 vt (person, team) rencontrer; (person by arrangement) retrouver; (pass in street etc) croiser; (fetch) aller or venir chercher; (wait for) attendre; (be introduced to) faire la connaissance de. **2** vi (of people, teams) se rencontrer; (of people by arrangement) se retrouver; (be introduced) se connaître; (of club etc) se réunir.

meet·ing réunion f, (large) assemblée f; (between two people) rencontre f, (arranged) rendezvous m inv.

▸ **meet up** vi (of people) se rencontrer; (by arrangement) se retrouver.

▸ **meet up with** vt rencontrer; (by arrangement) retrouver.

▸ **meet with** vt (accident) avoir; (difficulty) rencontrer; (person) rencontrer; (by arrangement) retrouver.

meg·a·byte mégaoctet m.

mel·o·dy mélodie f.

mel·on melon m.

melt 1 vi fondre. **2** vt (faire) fondre.

mem·ber membre m.

mem·o, pl -os note f.

mem·o·ra·ble adj mémorable.

me·mo·ri·al 1 adj (plaque etc) commemoratif. **2** n mémorial m.

mem·o·ry mémoire f; (recollection) souvenir m; in m. of à la mémoire de; m. stick clé f USB.

men see **man**.

mend vt réparer; (clothes) raccommoder.

men·tal adj mental.

men·tal·ly adv he's m. handicapped c'est un handicapé mental; she's m. ill c'est une malade mentale.

men·tion 1 vt mentionner; not to m... sans parler de...; don't m. it! il n'y a pas de quoi! **2** n mention f.

men·u menu m.

me·ow vi (of cat) miauler.

mer·cy pitié f; at the m. of à la merci de.

mere adj simple; (only) ne...que; she's a m. child ce n'est qu'une enfant.

mere·ly adv (tout) simplement.

merge vi (blend) se mêler (with à); (of roads) se (re)joindre; (of firms) fusionner.

merg·er fusion f.

mer·it 1 n mérite m. **2** vt mériter.

mer·ry adj gai.

mer·ry-go-round (at fair) manège m.

MEETING PEOPLE

Hello, how are you?
Bonjour, comment ça va ?

Hi, how's it going?
Salut, ça va ?

Fine thank you, how are you?
Bien, merci, et vous ?

Good, and you?
Ça va, et toi/vous ?

Good morning/afternoon.
Bonjour.

Good evening.
Bonsoir.

What's your name?
Comment vous appelez-vous ?/
Comment t'appelles-tu ?

My name's Eve.
Je m'appelle Eve.

I'm Brian and this is my wife Kim.
Je suis Brian, et voici Kim, ma femme.

Nice to meet you.
Enchanté(e).

How old are you?
Quel âge avez-vous/as-tu ?

I'm 15/25 (years old).
J'ai quinze/vingt-cinq ans.

Where are you from?
D'où venez-vous/viens-tu ?

I'm from the United States./I'm American.
Je viens des États-Unis./Je suis américain(e).

Where do you live?
Où habitez-vous/habites-tu ?

I live near San Francisco.
J'habite près de San Francisco.

What do you do?
Que faites-vous/fais-tu dans la vie ?

I'm a teacher/a student.
Je suis professeur/étudiant(e).

I'm in high school.
Je suis au lycée.

I'm a stay-at-home mom.
Je suis mère au foyer.

I work for an insurance company.
Je travaille dans les assurances.

I'm retired.
Je suis à la retraite.

Do you have any brothers and sisters?
Vous avez/Tu as des frères et des sœurs ?

I've got an older sister and two little brothers.
J'ai une sœur aînée et deux petits frères.

Do you have kids?
Vous avez/Tu as des enfants ?

We have a three-year-old son named Josh.
Nous avons un fils de trois ans qui s'appelle Josh.

Are you married?
Est-ce que vous êtes/tu es marié(e) ?

I'm divorced/separated/widowed.
Je suis divorcé(e)/séparé(e)/veuf (veuve).

What do you do in your spare time?
Que faites-vous pendant votre temps libre ?/
Qu'est ce que tu fais pendant ton temps libre ?

I like reading/going to the movies.
J'aime lire/aller au cinéma.

I play basketball/do yoga.
Je joue au basket/fais du yoga.

I'm taking French classes.
Je suis des cours de français.

See you soon/later!
À bientôt/plus tard !

Have a good weekend/trip!
Bon weekend/voyage !

We should keep in touch, here's my e-mail address.
Nous devrions garder le contact, voici mon adresse e-mail.

mesh *(of net)* maille *f*.

mess *(confusion)* désordre *m*; *(dirt)* saleté *f*; **in a m.** sens dessus dessous; *(trouble)* dans le pétrin.

mes·sage message *m*.

▸ **mess around** *vi (have fun)* s'amuser; *(play the fool)* faire l'idiot.

▸ **mess around with** *vt (fiddle with)* s'amuser avec.

mes·sen·ger messager *m*; *(in office, hotel)* coursier, -ière *mf*.

▸ **mess up** *vt (ruin)* gâcher; *(dirty)* salir; *(room)* mettre sens dessus dessous.

mess·y *adj (untidy)* en désordre; *(dirty)* sale.

met·al métal *m*; **m. ladder**/*etc* échelle *f*/*etc* métallique.

met·a·phor métaphore *f*.

me·ter¹ *(device)* compteur *m*; *(parking)* **m.** parcmètre *m*.

me·ter² mètre *m*.

meth·od méthode *f*.

me·thod·i·cal *adj* méthodique.

met·ric *adj* métrique.

mice *see* mouse.

mi·cro *prefix* micro-.

mi·cro·chip puce *f*.

mi·cro·phone micro *m*.

mi·cro·scope microscope *m*.

mi·cro·wave (ov·en) four *m* à micro-ondes.

mid *adj* (in) m.-June (à) la mi-juin; **in m. air** en plein ciel.

mid·day midi *m*.

mid·dle 1 *n* milieu *m*; *(waist)* taille *f*, *(right)* **in the m. of** au (beau) milieu de; **in the m. of saying**/*etc* en train de dire/*etc*. **2** *adj* du milieu; *(class)* moyen; *(name)* deuxième.

mid·dle-aged *adj* d'un certain âge.

mid·dle-class *adj* bourgeois.

mid·night minuit *m*.

mid·se·mes·ter break vacances *fpl* scolaires.

midst in the m. of au milieu de.

mid·way *adv* à mi-chemin.

mid·wife, *pl* -wives sage-femme *f*.

might *see* may.

might·y 1 *adj (powerful)* puissant; *(great)* énorme. **2** *adv Fam* rudement.

mild *adj* doux *(f* douce); *(beer, punishment)* léger; *(medicine, illness)* bénin *(f* bénigne).

mile mile *m* (= 1,6km).

mile·age ≃ kilométrage *m*.

mil·i·ta·ry *adj* militaire.

milk 1 *n* lait *m*. **2** *adj (chocolate)* au lait; *(bottle)* à lait. **3** *vt (cow)* traire.

milk·man, *pl* -men laitier *m*.

milk·shake milk-shake *m*.

mill moulin *m*; *(factory)* usine *f*.

mil·li·me·ter millimètre *m*.

mil·lion million *m*; **a m. men**/*etc* un million d'hommes/*etc*.

mil·lion·aire millionnaire *mf*.

mime *vti* mimer.

mim·ic 1 *n* imitateur, -trice *mf*. **2** *vt* (-ck-) imiter.

mince *vt* hacher; **she doesn't m. words** elle ne mâche pas ses mots.

mind 1 *n* esprit *m*; *(sanity)* raison *f*; *(memory)* mémoire *f*; **to change one's m.** changer d'avis; **to make up one's m.** se décider; **to be on sb's m.** préoccuper qn; **to have in m.** *(person, plan)* avoir en vue. **2** *vti* faire attention à; *(look after)* garder; *(noise etc)* être gêné par; **do you m. if?** *(I smoke)* ça vous gêne si?; *(I leave)* ça ne vous fait rien si?; **I don't m.** ça m'est égal; **I wouldn't m. a cup of tea** j'aimerais bien une tasse de thé; **never m.!** ça ne fait rien!; *(don't worry)* ne vous en faites pas!

mine¹ *poss pron* le mien, la mienne, *pl* les mien(ne)s; **this hat is m.** ce chapeau est à moi *or* est le mien.

mine² *(for coal etc, explosive)* mine *f*.

min·er mineur *m*.

min·er·al *adj & n* minéral *(m)*.

min·i- *prefix* mini-.

min·i·a·ture *adj (train etc)* minia-

ture *inv*; **in m.** en miniature.
min·i·bus minibus *m.*
min·i·mum *adj & n* minimum (*m*).
min·ing 1 *n* exploitation *f* minière, extraction *f*. **2** *adj* minier.
min·is·ter (*clergyman*) pasteur *m.*
min·is·try **to enter the m.** devenir pasteur.
mi·nor *adj* (*detail, operation*) petit.
mi·nor·i·ty minorité *f.*
mint (*herb*) menthe *f*; (*candy*) bonbon *m* à la menthe; **m. tea**/*etc* thé *m*/*etc* à la menthe.
mi·nus *prep* moins; (*without*) sans.
min·ute¹ minute *f.*
mi·nute² *adj* (*tiny*) minuscule.
mir·a·cle miracle *m.*
mi·rac·u·lous *adj* miraculeux.
mir·ror miroir *m*, glace *f*; (*in vehicle*) rétroviseur *m.*
mis·be·have *vi* se conduire mal.
mis·cel·la·ne·ous *adj* divers.
mis·chief espièglerie *f*; (*malice*) méchanceté *f*; **to get into m.** faire des bêtises.
mis·chie·vous *adj* espiègle; (*harmful*) méchant, nuisible.
misdemeanor délit *m*
mi·ser avare *mf.*
mis·er·a·ble *adj* (*wretched*) misérable; (*unhappy*) malheureux.
mi·ser·ly *adj* avare.
mis·er·y souffrances *fpl*; (*sadness*) tristesse *f.*
mis·for·tune malheur *m.*
mis·hap contretemps *m.*
mis·lay* *vt* égarer.
mis·lead *vt* tromper.
mis·lead·ing *adj* trompeur.
miss¹ 1 *vt* (*train, opportunity etc*) manquer; (*not see*) ne pas voir; (*not understand*) ne pas comprendre; **he misses Paris/her** Paris/elle lui manque. **2** *vi* manquer.
miss² (*woman*) mademoiselle *f*; **Miss Brown** Mademoiselle *or* Mlle Brown.

mis·sile (*rocket*) missile *m*; (*object thrown*) projectile *m.*
mis·sing *adj* absent; (*after disaster*) disparu; (*object*) manquant; **there are two cups m.** il manque deux tasses.
mis·sion mission *f.*
▶ **miss out 1** *vt* (*leave out*) sauter. **2** *vi* rater l'occasion.
▶ **miss out on** *vt* (*opportunity etc*) rater.
mist (*fog*) brume *f*, (*on glass*) buée *f.*
mis·take 1 *n* erreur *f*, faute *f*; **to make a m.** se tromper; **by m.** par erreur. **2** *vt** (*meaning etc*) se tromper sur; **to m. sb/sth for** prendre qn/qch pour; **you're mistaken** tu te trompes.
mis·ta·ken·ly *adv* par erreur.
mis·treat *vt* maltraiter.
mis·tress maîtresse *f.*
mis·trust 1 *n* méfiance *f*. **2** *vt* se méfier de.
mist·y *adj* brumeux.
mis·un·der·stand* *vt* mal comprendre.
mis·un·der·stand·ing malentendu *m.*
mit·ten (*glove*) moufle *f.*
mix 1 *vt* mélanger, mêler; (*cake*) préparer; (*salad*) remuer. **2** *vi* se mêler; **she doesn't m.** elle n'est pas sociable.
mixed *adj* (*school*) mixte; (*chocolates etc*) assortis.
mix·er (*electric, for cooking*) mixe(u)r *m.*
mix·ture mélange *m.*
mix·up confusion *f.*
▶ **mix up** *vt* (*drink, papers etc*) mélanger; (*make confused*) embrouiller (*qn*); (*mistake*) confondre (**with** avec).
▶ **mix with** *vt* fréquenter.
moan *vi* (*groan*) gémir; (*complain*) se plaindre (**to** à; **about** de; **that** que).
mob 1 *n* foule *f*. **2** *vt* assiéger.
mo·bile *adj* mobile.

mod·el 1 n (example etc) modèle m; (fashion) m. mannequin m; (scale) m. modèle m (réduit). **2** adj (car, plane etc) modèle réduit inv; m. train train m miniature.

mod·el·ing clay pâte f à modeler.

mo·dem modem m.

mod·er·ate adj modéré.

mod·er·a·tion modération f.

mod·ern adj moderne; m. languages langues fpl vivantes.

mod·ern·ize 1 vt moderniser. **2** vi se moderniser.

mod·est adj modeste.

mod·es·ty modestie f.

mod·i·fi·ca·tion modification f.

mod·i·fy vt modifier.

moist adj humide; (sticky) moite.

mois·ture humidité f, (on glass) buée f.

mold 1 n (shape) moule m; (growth) moisissure f. **2** vt (clay etc) mouler.

mold·y adj moisi; to get m. moisir.

mole (on skin) grain m de beauté; (animal) taupe f.

mom Fam maman f.

mo·ment moment m; the m. she leaves dès qu'elle partira.

mom·my Fam maman f.

Mon·day lundi m.

mon·ey argent m.

mon·ey or·der mandat m.

mon·i·tor (computer screen) moniteur m (d'ordinateur).

monk moine m.

mon·key singe m.

mo·nop·o·lize vt monopoliser.

mo·not·o·nous adj monotone.

mo·not·o·ny monotonie f.

mon·ster monstre m.

month mois m.

month·ly 1 adj mensuel. **2** adv mensuellement.

mon·u·ment monument m.

moo vi meugler.

mood (of person) humeur f, Grammar mode m; in a good/bad m. de bonne/mauvaise humeur; to be in the m. to do être d'humeur à faire.

mood·y adj (bad-tempered) de mauvaise humeur.

moon lune f.

moon·light clair m de lune.

moor lande f.

moose inv élan m.

mop 1 n balai m (à laver). **2** vt (floor etc) essuyer.

mo·ped mobylette® f.

► **mop up** vt (liquid) éponger.

mor·al (of story) morale f.

mo·rale moral m.

more 1 adj & n plus (de) (than que); (other) d'autres; m. cars/etc plus de voitures/etc; he has m. (than you) il en a plus (que toi); a few m. months encore quelques mois; (some) m. tea/etc encore du thé/etc; m. than a quart/ten (with quantity, number) plus d'un litre/de dix; many m., much m. beaucoup plus (de). **2** adv plus (than que); m. and m. de plus en plus; m. or less plus ou moins; she doesn't have any m. elle n'en a plus.

more·o·ver adv de plus.

morn·ing matin m; (duration of morning) matinée f; in the m. le matin; (tomorrow) demain matin; at seven in the m. à sept heures du matin; every Tuesday m. tous les mardis matin.

mor·tal adj & n mortel, -elle (mf).

mort·gage prêt-logement m.

Mos·lem adj & n musulman, -ane (mf).

mosque mosquée f.

mos·qui·to, pl -oes moustique m.

moss mousse f (plante).

most 1 adj & n the m. le plus (de); I have the m. books j'ai le plus de livres; I have the m. j'en ai le plus; m. (of the) books/etc la plupart des livres/etc; m. of the cake/etc la plus grande partie du gâteau/etc; at (the very) m. tout au plus. **2** adv (le) plus; (very) très; the m. beautiful le plus beau, la plus belle (in, of de); **to talk (the) m.** parler le plus; **m. of all** surtout.

most·ly *adv* surtout.

mo·tel motel *m*.

moth papillon *m* de nuit; *(in clothes)* mite *f*.

moth·er mère *f*; **M.'s Day** la fête des Mères.

moth·er-in-law, *pl* mothers-in-law belle-mère *f*.

mo·tion 1 *n (of arm etc)* mouvement *m*. **2** *vti* **to m. (to) sb to do** faire signe à qn de faire.

mo·ti·vat·ed motivé.

mo·tive motif *m* (**for** de).

mo·tor *(engine)* moteur *m*.

mo·tor·bike moto *f*.

mo·tor·boat canot *m* automobile.

mo·tor·cy·cle motocyclette *f*.

mo·tor·cy·clist motocycliste *mf*.

mo·tor·ist automobiliste *mf*.

mount 1 *n (frame for photo)* cadre *m*. **2** *vt (horse, photo)* monter. **3** *vi (on horse)* se mettre en selle.

moun·tain montagne *f*; **m. bike** VTT *m inv*.

moun·tain·eer alpiniste *mf*.

moun·tain·eer·ing alpinisme *m*.

moun·tain·ous *adj* montagneux.

▸ **mount up** *vi (add up)* chiffrer (**to** à); *(accumulate)* s'accumuler.

mourn *vt* **to m. (for) sb, to m. the loss of sb** pleurer (la perte de) qn; **she's mourning** elle est en deuil.

mourn·ing deuil *m*; **in m.** en deuil.

mouse, *pl* mice souris *f*.

mousse mousse *f (dessert)*.

mouth, *pl* -s bouche *f*, *(of dog, lion etc)* gueule *f*, *(of river)* embouchure *f*.

mouth·wash bain *m* de bouche.

move 1 *n* mouvement *m*; *(change of house)* déménagement *m*; *(in game)* coup *m*; *(one's turn)* tour *m*; *(act)* démarche *f*; **to make a m.** *(leave)* se préparer à partir; **to get**

a m. on se remuer. **2** *vt* déplacer; *(arm, leg)* remuer; *(put)* mettre; *(transport)* transporter; *(piece in game)* jouer; **to m. sb** *(emotionally)* émouvoir qn; *(transfer in job)* muter qn. **3** *vi* bouger; *(go)* aller (**to** à); *(out of house)* déménager; *(change seats)* changer de place; *(play)* jouer; **to m. to a new house/etc** aller habiter une nouvelle maison/ *etc*; **to m. into a house** emménager dans une maison.

▸ **move along** *vi* avancer.

▸ **move around** *vi* se déplacer; *(fidget)* remuer.

▸ **move away** *vi* s'éloigner; *(to new house)* déménager.

▸ **move back 1** *vt (chair etc)* reculer; *(to its position)* remettre. **2** *vi* reculer; *(return)* retourner.

▸ **move down** *vti* descendre.

▸ **move forward** *vti* avancer.

▸ **move in** *vi (into house)* emménager.

move·ment *(action, group etc)* mouvement *m*.

▸ **move off** *vi (go away)* s'éloigner; *(of vehicle)* démarrer.

▸ **move on** *vi* avancer.

▸ **move out** *vi (out of house)* déménager.

▸ **move over 1** *vt* pousser. **2** *vi* se pousser.

mov·er déménageur *m*.

▸ **move up 1** *vt (meeting)* avancer. **2** *vi (on seats etc)* se pousser.

mov·ie film *m*; **the movies** *(art, movie theater)* le cinéma.

mov·ie cam·er·a caméra *f*.

mov·ie star vedette *f* (de cinéma).

mov·ie the·a·ter cinéma *m*.

mov·ing *adj* en mouvement; *(touching)* émouvant.

mov·ing van camion *m* de déménagement.

mow *vt (pp mown or mowed)* **to m. the lawn** tondre le gazon.

mow·er (lawn) **m.** tondeuse *f* (à gazon).

MP3 *abbr (MPEG1 Audio Layer)* M. **player** lecteur *m* MP3.

Mr Mr Brown Monsieur *or* M. Brown.

Mrs Mrs Brown Madame *or* Mme Brown.

Ms Ms Brown Madame *or* Mme Brown.

MS, MSc *abbr* = **Master of Science**.

much 1 *adj & n* beaucoup (de); **not m. time/**etc pas beaucoup de temps/etc; **I don't have m.** je n'en ai pas beaucoup; **as m. as** autant que; **as m. wine/**etc as autant de vin/etc que; **twice as m.** deux fois plus (de). **2** *adv* very **m.** beaucoup; **not (very) m.** pas beaucoup.

mud boue *f*.

mud·dle *(mix-up)* confusion *f*, *(mess)* désordre *m*; **in a m.** *(person)* désorienté; *(mind, ideas)* embrouillé. **mud·dle (up)** *vt (person, facts)* embrouiller; *(papers)* mélanger.

▸ **muddle through** *vi* se tirer d'affaire.

mud·dy *adj (water, road)* boueux; *(hands etc)* couvert de boue.

mues·li muesli *m*.

muf·fin muffin *m*.

mug[1] *(cup)* grande tasse *f*, *(beer)* **m.** chope *f*.

mug[2] *vt (in street)* agresser, attaquer.

mug·ger agresseur *m*.

mule *(male)* mulet *m*; *(female)* mule *f*.

mul·ti·cul·tur·al *adj* multiculturel.

mul·ti·ple *adj & n* multiple *(m)*.

mul·ti·plex multiplexe *m*.

mul·ti·pli·ca·tion multiplication *f*.

mul·ti·ply *vt* multiplier.

mum·ble *vti* marmotter.

mumps oreillons *mpl*.

mu·nic·i·pal *adj* municipal.

mur·der 1 *n* meurtre *m*, assassinat *m*. **2** *vt* tuer, assassiner.

mur·der·er meurtrier, -ière *mf*, assassin *m*.

mur·mur *vti* murmurer.

mus·cle muscle *m*.

mus·cu·lar *adj (arm etc)* musclé.

mu·se·um musée *m*.

mush·room champignon *m*.

mu·sic musique *f*.

mu·si·cal 1 *adj* musical; *(instrument)* de musique; **to be m.** être musicien. **2** *n* comédie *f* musicale.

mu·si·cian musicien, -ienne *mf*.

Mus·lim *adj & n* musulman, -ane *(mf)*.

mus·sel moule *f*.

must *v aux (necessity)* devoir; **you m. obey** tu dois obéir, il faut que tu obéisses. ▪ *(certainty)* devoir; **she m. be smart** elle doit être intelligente; **I m. have seen it** j'ai dû le voir.

mus·tache moustache *f*.

mus·tard moutarde *f*.

must·y to smell m. sentir le moisi.

mute 1 *adj* muet. **2** *n (person)* muet, -ette *mf*; *(on musical instrument)* sourdine *f*.

mut·ter *vti* marmonner.

mut·ton *(meat)* mouton *m*.

mu·tu·al *adj (help etc)* mutuel; *(friend)* commun.

muz·zle *(for animal)* muselière *f*.

my *poss adj* mon, ma, *pl* mes.

my·self *pron* moi-même; *(reflexive)* me, m'; *(after prep)* moi.

mys·te·ri·ous *adj* mystérieux.

mys·ter·y mystère *m*; *(novel)* roman *m* policier; *(movie)* film *m* policier.

myth mythe *m*.

N

nail *(of finger, toe)* ongle *m*; *(metal)* clou *m*; **n. file/polish** lime *f*/vernis *m* à ongles.

nail (down) *vt* clouer.

na·ïve *adj* naïf.

na·ked *adj* nu.

name 1 *n* nom *m*; *(reputation)* réputation *f*; **my n. is...** je m'appelle...; **first n.** prénom *m*; **last n.** nom *m* de famille. **2** *vt* nommer; *(date, price)* fixer; **he was named after** *or* **for** il a reçu le nom de.

name·ly *adv* à savoir.

nan·a *(grandmother) Fam* mamie *f*.

nan·ny nourrice *f*; *(grandmother) Fam* mamie *f*.

nap *(sleep)* petit somme *m*; **to have** *or* **take a n.** faire un petit somme.

nap·kin serviette *f*.

nar·ra·tive 1 *n* récit *m*. **2** *adj* narratif.

nar·row *adj* étroit.

nar·row (down) *vt (choice etc)* limiter.

nar·row·ly **he n. escaped being killed/***etc* il a failli être tué/*etc.*

nas·ti·ly *adv (to behave)* méchamment.

nas·ty *adj* mauvais; *(spiteful)* méchant (**to(wards)** avec).

na·tion nation *f*.

na·tion·al *adj* national.

na·tion·al·i·ty nationalité *f*.

na·tive 1 *adj (country)* natal *(mpl* -als); **to be an English n. speaker** avoir l'anglais comme langue maternelle. **2** *n* **to be a n. of** être originaire de.

nat·u·ral *adj* naturel; *(actor etc)* né.

nat·u·ral·ly *adv (as normal, of course)* naturellement; *(to behave etc)* avec naturel.

na·ture *(natural world, character)* nature *f*.

na·ture stud·y sciences *fpl* naturelles.

naught rien *m*.

naugh·ty *adj (child)* vilain.

nau·se·at·ing *adj* écœurant.

nau·seous *adj* **to feel n.** avoir envie de vomir.

na·val *adj* naval *(mpl* -als); *(officer)* de marine.

na·vel nombril *m*.

nav·i·gate 1 *vi* naviguer. **2** *vt (boat)* diriger.

nav·i·ga·tion navigation *f*.

na·vy 1 *n* marine *f*. **2** *adj* **n. (blue)** bleu marine *inv.*

near 1 *adv* près; **very n.** tout près; **n.** to près de; **to come n. to being killed/***etc* faillir être tué/*etc*; **n. enough** *(more or less)* plus ou moins. **2** *prep* **n. (to)** près de; **n. (to) the end** vers la fin; **to come n. sb** s'approcher de qn. **3** *adj* proche; **in the n. future** dans un avenir proche.

near·by 1 *adv* tout près. **2** *adj* proche.

near·ly *adv* presque; **she (very) n. fell** elle a failli tomber; **not n. as smart/***etc* **as** loin d'être aussi intelligent/*etc* que.

neat *adj (clothes, work)* soigné; *(room)* bien rangé.

neat·ly *adv* avec soin.

nec·es·sar·i·ly *adv* **not n.** pas forcément.

nec·es·sar·y *adj* nécessaire (**to do** *or* **de faire**); **to do what's n.** faire le nécessaire.

ne·ces·si·ty nécessité *f*.

neck cou *m*; *(of dress, horse)* encolure *f*.

neck·lace collier *m*.

nec·tar·ine nectarine *f*.

need 1 *n* besoin *m*; **to be in n. of** avoir besoin de; **there's no n. (for you)** **to do** tu n'as pas besoin de faire; **if n. be** si besoin est. **2** *vt* avoir besoin de; **her hair needs cutting** il faut qu'elle se fasse couper les cheveux; **I needn't have rushed** ce n'était pas la peine de me presser.

nee·dle aiguille *f*.

need·less·ly *adv* inutilement.

nee·dle·work couture *f*, *(object)* ouvrage *m*.

neg·a·tive 1 *adj* négatif. **2** *n (of photo)* négatif *m*; *Grammar* forme *f* négative.

ne·glect *vt* (*person, work, duty etc*) négliger; (*garden, car*) ne pas s'occuper de.

ne·glect·ed *adj* (*appearance*) négligé; (*garden, house*) mal tenu; **to feel n.** se sentir délaissé.

neg·li·gence négligence *f*.

neg·li·gent *adj* négligent.

ne·go·ti·ate *vti* (*discuss*) négocier.

ne·go·ti·a·tion négociation *f*.

neigh *vi* (*of horse*) hennir.

neigh·bor voisin, -ine *mf*.

neigh·bor·hood quartier *m*; (*neighbors*) voisinage *m*.

neigh·bor·ing *adj* voisin.

nei·ther 1 *adv* **n....nor** ni...ni; **he n. sings nor dances** il ne chante ni ne danse. **2** *conj* (*not either*) **if you won't go, n. will I** si tu n'y vas pas, je n'irai pas non plus. **3** *adj* **n. boy (came)** aucun des deux garçons (n'est venu). **4** *pron* **n. (of them)** ni l'un(e) ni l'autre.

ne·on *adj* (*lighting etc*) au néon.

neph·ew neveu *m*.

nerve nerf *m*; (*courage*) courage *m* (**to do** de faire); (*calm*) sang-froid *m*; (*cheek*) culot *m* (**to do** de faire); **you get on my nerves** tu me tapes sur les nerfs.

nerv·ous *adj* (*tense*) nerveux; (*worried*) inquiet (**about** de); (*uneasy*) mal à l'aise; **to be** *or* **feel n.** (*before exam etc*) avoir le trac.

nest nid *m*.

net 1 *n* filet *m*. **2** *adj* (*profit, weight etc*) net (*f* nette).

net·ting (*wire*) **n.** grillage *m*.

net·tle ortie *f*.

net·work réseau *m*.

neu·tral 1 *adj* neutre. **2** *n* **in n.** (*gear*) au point mort.

nev·er *adv* (*ne...*) jamais; **she n. lies** elle ne ment jamais; **n. again** plus jamais.

nev·er-end·ing *adj* interminable.

nev·er·the·less *adv* néanmoins.

new *adj* nouveau (*f* nouvelle); (*brand-new*) neuf (*f* neuve); **a n. glass/etc** (*different*) un autre verre/ *etc*; **what's n.?** *Fam* quoi de neuf?

new-born *adj* **a n. baby** un nouveau-né, une nouveau-née.

new·ly *adv* (*recently*) nouvellement.

news nouvelle(s) *f(pl)*; (*in the media*) informations *fpl*; **sports n.** (*newspaper column*) chronique *f* sportive; **a piece of n., some n.** une nouvelle; (*in the media*) une information.

news flash flash *m*.

news·let·ter bulletin *m*.

news·pa·per journal *m*.

news·stand kiosque *m* (à journaux).

next 1 *adj* prochain; (*room, house*) d'à côté; (*following*) suivant; **n. month** (*in the future*) le mois prochain; **the n. day** le lendemain; **the n. morning** le lendemain matin; (**by**) **this time n. week** d'ici (à) la semaine prochaine; **to live n. door** habiter à côté (**to** de); **n.-door neighbor** voisin *m* d'à côté. **2** *n* suivant, -ante *mf*. **3** *adv* (*afterwards*) ensuite; (*now*) maintenant; **when you come n.** la prochaine fois que tu viendras. **4** *prep* **n. to** (*beside*) à côté de.

nib (*of pen*) plume *f*.

nib·ble *vti* (*eat*) grignoter; (*bite*) mordiller.

nice *adj* (*pleasant*) agréable; (*pretty*) joli; (*kind*) gentil (**to** avec); **it's n. here** c'est bien ici; **n. and warm/etc** (*very*) bien chaud/*etc*.

nice·ly *adv* agréablement; (*kindly*) gentiment.

nick·el (*coin*) pièce *f* de cinq cents.

nick·el-and-dime-store = magasin *m* à prix unique.

nick·name surnom *m*.

niece nièce *f*.

night nuit *f*; (*evening*) soir *m*; **last n.** (*evening*) hier soir; (*night*) la nuit dernière; **to have an early/late n.** se coucher tôt/tard; **to have a good n.('s sleep)** bien dormir.

night·club boîte f de nuit.

night·gown, *Fam* **nightie** chemise f de nuit.

night·in·gale rossignol m.

night·mare cauchemar m.

night·stand table f de nuit.

night·time nuit f.

night watch·man veilleur m de nuit.

nil zéro m.

nine adj & n neuf (m).

nine·teen adj & n dix-neuf (m).

nine·ti·eth adj & n quatre-vingt-dixième (mf).

nine·ty adj & n quatre-vingt-dix (m).

ninth adj & n neuvième (mf).

nip 1 n (bite) (petite) morsure f; (drink) petit verre; (coldness) **there's a n. in the air** le fond de l'air est frais. **2** vt pincer.

nip·ple bout m de sein; (of bottle) tétine f.

ni·tro·gen azote m.

no 1 adv & n non (m inv); **no more than ten/etc** pas plus de dix/etc; **no more time/etc** plus de temps/ etc. **2** adj aucun(e); pas de; **I have no idea** je n'ai aucune idée; **no child came** aucun enfant n'est venu; **I have no time/etc** je n'ai pas de temps/etc; **of no importance/etc** sans importance/etc; **'no smoking'** 'défense de fumer'; **no way!** *Fam* pas question!; **no one = nobody.**

no·ble adj noble.

no·bod·y pron (ne...) personne; **n. came** personne n'est venue; **n.!** personne!

nod 1 vti to n. (one's head) faire un signe de tête. **2** n signe m de tête.

▸**nod off** vi s'assoupir.

noise bruit m; (of bell, drum) son m; **to make a n.** faire du bruit.

nois·i·ly adv bruyamment.

nois·y adj bruyant.

nom·i·nate vt (appoint) nommer.

nom·i·na·tion (proposal) proposition f, (appointment) nomination f.

non- prefix non-.

none pron aucun(e) mf; (in filling out a form) néant; **she has n. (at all)** elle n'en a pas (du tout); **n. (at all) came** pas un(e) seul(e) n'est venu(e); **n. of the cake/etc** pas une seule partie du gâteau/etc; **n. of the trees/etc** aucun des arbres/etc.

none·the·less adv néanmoins.

non·ex·ist·ent adj inexistant.

non·fic·tion (in library) ouvrages mpl généraux.

non·sense absurdités fpl; **that's n.** c'est absurde.

non-smok·er non-fumeur, -euse mf.

non-stick adj (pan) anti-adhésif.

non-stop 1 adj sans arrêt; (train, flight) direct. **2** adv sans arrêt; (to fly) sans escale.

noo·dles npl nouilles fpl; (in soup) vermicelle(s) m(pl).

noon midi m; **at n.** à midi.

nor conj ni; **neither you n. me/I** ni toi ni moi; **she neither drinks n. smokes** elle ne fume ni ne boit; **I do not know, n. do I care** je ne sais pas et d'ailleurs je m'en moque.

norm norme f.

nor·mal 1 adj normal. **2** n above/ below n. au-dessus/au-dessous de la normale.

nor·mal·ly adv normalement.

north 1 n nord m; (to the) n. of au nord de. **2** adj (coast) nord inv. **3** adv au nord.

North A·mer·i·can 1 n Nord-Américain, -aine mf. **2** adj nord-américain, -aine.

north·bound adj en direction du nord.

north·east n & adj nord-est (m & adj inv).

north·ern adj (coast) nord inv; (town) du nord.

north·ern·er habitant, -ante *mf* du nord.

north·ward(s) *adj & adv* vers le nord.

north·west *n & adj* nord-ouest (*m & adj inv*).

Nor·we·gian 1 *n* Norvégien, -ienne *mf*. **2** *adj* norvégien, -ienne *mf*.

nose nez *m*; her n. is bleeding elle saigne du nez.

nose·bleed saignement *m* de nez.

nos·tril *(of person)* narine *f*, *(horse)* naseau *m*.

nos·(e)y *adj* indiscret.

not *adv* (ne…) pas; he's n. there, he isn't there il n'est pas là; n. yet pas encore; why n.? pourquoi pas?; **n. one** reply/*etc* pas une seule réponse/*etc*; **n. at all** pas du tout; *(after 'thank you')* je vous en prie. ■ non; **I think/hope n.** je pense/j'espère que non; **isn't she?, don't you?**/*etc* non?

no·ta·ble *adj* notable.

no·ta·bly *adv (noticeably)* notablement; *(particularly)* notamment.

note 1 *n (comment, musical etc)* note *f*; *(money)* billet *m*; *(message)* petit mot *m*; **to make a n. of** prendre note de. **2** *vt* noter.

note·book carnet *m*; *(for school)* cahier *m*; *(computer)* portable *m*.

▸ **note down** *vt (word etc)* noter.

note·pad bloc-notes *m*.

note·pa·per papier *m* à lettres.

noth·ing *pron* (ne…) rien; he knows n. il ne sait rien; **n. to eat**/*etc* rien à manger/*etc*; **n. big**/*etc* rien de grand/*etc*; **n. much** pas grand-chose; **I've got n. to do with it** je n'y suis pour rien; **to come to n.** *(of efforts etc)* ne rien donner; **for n.** *(in vain, free of charge)* pour rien; **to have n. on** être tout nu.

no·tice 1 *n* avis *m*; *(sign)* pancarte *f*; *(poster)* affiche *f*; **to give n.** don-

ner sa démission; **to give sb (advance) n.** avertir qn *(of* de*)*; **to take n.** faire attention *(of* à*)*; **until further n.** jusqu'à nouvel ordre. **2** *vt* remarquer (that que).

no·tice·a·ble *adj* visible.

no·ti·fi·ca·tion avis *m*.

no·ti·fy *vt* avertir *(sb of sth* qn de qch*)*.

no·tion idée *f*.

no·to·ri·ous *adj* tristement célèbre; *(criminal)* notoire.

noun nom *m*.

nour·ish·ing *adj* nourrissant.

nov·el 1 *n* roman *m*. **2** *adj* nouveau *(f* nouvelle*)*.

nov·el·ist romancier, -ière *mf*.

No·vem·ber novembre *m*.

now 1 *adv* maintenant; **just n., right n.** en ce moment; **I saw her just n.** je l'ai vue à l'instant; **for n.** pour le moment; **from n. on** désormais; **before n.** avant; **n. and then** de temps à autre. **2** *conj* **n. (that)** maintenant que.

now·a·days *adv* aujourd'hui.

no·where *adv* nulle part; **n. near the house** loin de la maison; **n. near enough** loin d'être assez.

noz·zle *(hose)* jet *m*.

nu·clear *adj* nucléaire.

nude in the n. *(tout)* nu.

nudge 1 *vt* pousser du coude. **2** *n* coup *m* de coude.

nui·sance embêtement *m*; *(person)* peste *f*; **that's a n.** c'est embêtant.

numb *adj (hand etc)* engourdi.

num·ber 1 *n* nombre *m*; *(of page, house, telephone etc)* numéro *m*; **a n. of** un certain nombre de. **2** *vt (page etc)* numéroter.

nu·mer·al chiffre *m*.

nu·mer·ous *adj* nombreux.

nun religieuse *f*.

nurse 1 *n* infirmière *f*; **(male) n.** infirmier *m*. **2** *vt (take care of)* soigner; *(baby)* allaiter. **3** *vi (of baby)* téter.

nurs·er·y (*in house*) chambre f d'enfants; (*for plants*) pépinière f.

nurs·er·y rhyme chanson f enfantine.

nurs·er·y school école f maternelle.

nurs·ing home (*for elderly people*) maison f de retraite; (*for convalescents*) maison f de repos; (*for mentally ill*) maison f de santé.

nut[1] (*walnut*) noix f; (*hazelnut*) noisette f; (*peanut*) cacah(o)uète f.

nut[2] (*for bolt*) écrou m.

nut·crack·er casse-noix m inv.

nut·shell in a n. en un mot.

ny·lon 1 n nylon m; **nylons** bas mpl nylon. **2** adj (*shirt etc*) en nylon.

O

oak chêne m.

oar aviron m.

oat·meal flocons mpl d'avoine.

oats npl avoine f.

o·be·di·ence obéissance f (**to** à).

o·be·di·ent adj obéissant.

o·bey 1 vt obéir à (*qn*); **to be obeyed** être obéi. **2** vi obéir.

ob·ject[1] (*thing, aim*) objet m; *Grammar* complément m (d'objet).

ob·ject[2] vi **to o. to sth/sb** désapprouver qch/qn; **I o. to you(r) doing that** ça me gêne que tu fasses ça.

ob·jec·tion objection f.

ob·jec·tive (*aim*) objectif m.

ob·li·ga·tion obligation f.

o·blige vt (*compel*) contraindre (**sb to do** qn à faire); (*help*) rendre service à.

o·blig·ing adj serviable.

o·blique adj oblique.

ob·scene adj obscène.

ob·scure 1 adj obscur. **2** vt (*hide*) cacher; (*confuse*) obscurcir.

ob·ser·vant adj observateur.

ob·ser·va·tion observation f.

ob·serve vt observer; (*say*) remarquer (**that** que).

ob·ses·sion obsession f.

ob·sta·cle obstacle m.

ob·sti·nate adj (*person, resistance*) obstiné.

ob·struct vt (*block*) boucher; (*hinder*) gêner.

ob·tain vt obtenir.

ob·tain·a·ble adj disponible.

ob·vi·ous adj évident (**that** que).

ob·vi·ous·ly adv évidemment.

oc·ca·sion (*time, opportunity*) occasion f; (*event, ceremony*) événement m.

oc·ca·sion·al adj (*odd*) qu'on fait/voit/*etc* de temps en temps; **she drinks the o. whisky** elle boit un whisky de temps en temps.

oc·ca·sion·al·ly adv de temps en temps.

oc·cu·pant occupant, -ante mf.

oc·cu·pa·tion (*activity*) occupation f; (*job*) emploi m; (*trade*) métier m; (*profession*) profession f.

oc·cu·py vt occuper; **to keep oneself occupied** s'occuper (**doing** à faire).

oc·cur vi (*happen*) avoir lieu; (*be found*) se rencontrer; **it occurs to me that...** il me vient à l'esprit que...

oc·cur·rence (*event*) événement m.

o·cean océan m.

o'clock adv (**it's**) **three o'c.**/*etc* (il est) trois heures/*etc*.

Oc·to·ber octobre m.

oc·to·pus pieuvre f.

odd adj (*strange*) bizarre. ▪ (*number*) impair. ▪ (*left over*) **I have an o. penny** il me reste un penny; **a few o. stamps** quelques timbres (qui restent); **the o. man out** l'exception f; **sixty o.** soixante et quelques; **an o. glove**/*etc* un gant/*etc* dépareillé. ∎ qu'on fait/voit/*etc* de temps en temps; **I smoke the o. cigarette** je fume une cigarette de temps en temps; **o. jobs** menus travaux *mpl*.

odd·ly *adv* bizarrement.

odds *npl* (*in betting*) cote *f*, (*chances*) chances *fpl*; **at o.** en désaccord (**with** avec); **o. and ends** des petites choses.

o·dor odeur *f*.

of *prep* de, d' (de + le = du, de + les = des); **of the woman** de la femme; **of a book** d'un livre; **she has a lot of it** *or* **of them** elle en a beaucoup; **a friend of his** un ami à lui; **there are ten of us** nous sommes dix; **that's nice of you** c'est gentil de ta part.

off 1 *adv* (*gone away*) parti; (*light, radio etc*) éteint; (*faucet*) fermé; (*detached*) détaché; (*removed*) enlevé; (*canceled*) annulé; **6 miles o.** à 10km (d'ici *or* de là); **to be** *or* **go o.** (*leave*) partir; **a day o.** un jour de congé; **time o.** du temps libre; **5% o.** une réduction de 5%; **hands o.!** pas touche!; **to be better o.** être mieux. **2** *prep* (*from*) de; (*distant*) éloigné de; **to get o. the bus/etc** descendre du bus/*etc*; **to take sth o. the table/etc** prendre qch sur la table/*etc*; **o. New York** au large de New York.

off-col·or *adj* risqué.

of·fend *vt* froisser (*qn*); **to be offended** (**at**) se froisser (de).

of·fend·er (*criminal*) délinquant, -ante *mf*.

of·fense (*crime*) délit *m*; **to take o.** s'offenser (**at** à).

of·fen·sive *adj* (*words etc*) insultant (**to sb** pour qn); (*person*) insultant (**to sb** avec qn).

of·fer 1 *n* offre *f*; **special o.** (*in store*) promotion *f*. **2** *vt* offrir (**to do** de faire).

of·fer·ing offre *f*, (*in church*) offrande *f*.

off·hand 1 *adj* (*abrupt*) brusque, impoli. **2** *adv* (*to say, know etc*) comme ça.

of·fice (*room*) bureau *m*; (*of doctor, lawyer*) cabinet *m*; (*post*) fonction *f*; **head o.** siège *m* central; **o. building** immeuble *m* de bureaux.

of·fi·cer (*in the army etc*) officier *m*; (*police*) **o.** agent *m* (de police).

of·fi·cial 1 *adj* officiel. **2** *n* (*civil servant*) fonctionnaire *mf*.

of·fi·cial·ly *adv* officiellement.

off·spring *inv* (*children*) progéniture *f*.

of·ten *adv* souvent; **how o.?** combien de fois?; **how o. do they run?** (*train etc*) il y en a tous les combien?; **every so o.** de temps en temps.

oh! *int* oh!, ah!; **oh yes!** mais oui!; **oh yes?** ah oui?

oil 1 *n* huile *f*, (*extracted from ground*) pétrole *m*; (*fuel*) mazout *m*; **o. spill** (*event*) marée *f* noire; (*result*) nappe *f* de pétrole. **2** *vt* (*machine*) graisser.

oil·can burette *f*.

oil change (*in vehicle*) vidange *f*.

oint·ment pommade *f*.

OK, o·kay 1 *adj* (*satisfactory*) bien *inv*; (*unharmed*) sain et sauf; (*un damaged*) intact; (*without worries*) tranquille; **it's o.** ça va; **I'm o.** (*healthy*) je vais bien. **2** *adv* (*well*) bien; **o.!** (*agreement*) d'accord!

old *adj* vieux (*f* vieille); (*former*) ancien; **how o. is he?** quel âge a-t-il?; **he's ten years o.** il a dix ans; **he's older than me** il est plus âgé que moi; **an older son** un fils aîné; **the oldest son** le fils aîné; **o. man** vieillard *m*; **o. woman** vieille femme *f*; **to get** *or* **grow old(er)** vieillir; **o. age** vieillesse *f*.

old-fash·ioned *adj* démodé; (*person*) rétro *inv*.

ol·ive olive *f*; **o. oil** huile *f* d'olive.

O·lym·pic *adj* olympique; **the O. games, the Olympics** les jeux *mpl* olympiques.

om·e·let(te) omelette *f*; **cheese/** *etc* **o.** omelette au fromage/*etc*.

o·mis·sion omission *f*.

o·mit *vt* omettre.

on 1 *prep* (*position*) sur; **to put on (to)** mettre sur. ▪ (*about*) sur; **to speak on** parler sur. ▪ (*manner, means*) **on foot** à pied; **on the train/***etc* dans le train/*etc*; **to be on** (*salary*) toucher; (*team*) être membre de; **to keep** *or* **stay on** (*path etc*) suivre. ▪ (*time*) **on Monday** lundi; **on Mondays** le lundi; **on May 3rd** le 3 mai. ▪ (*+ present participle*) en; **on seeing this** en voyant ceci. **2** *adv* (*ahead*) en avant; (*in progress*) en cours; (*lid, brake*) mis; (*light, radio*) allumé; (*gas, faucet*) ouvert; **on (and on)** sans cesse; **to play/***etc* on continuer à jouer/*etc*; **what's on?** (*television*) qu'y a-t-il à la télé?; **from then on** à partir de là.

once 1 *adv* une fois; (*formerly*) autrefois; **o. a month** une fois par mois; **o. again, o. more** encore une fois; **at o.** tout de suite; **all at o.** tout à coup; (*at the same time*) à la fois. **2** *conj* une fois que.

one 1 *adj* un, une; **o. man** un homme; **o. woman** une femme; **page o.** la page un; **twenty-o.** vingt-et-un. ▪ (*only*) seul; **my o. (and only) aim** mon seul (et unique) but. ▪ (*same*) même; **on the o. bus** dans le même bus. **2** *pron* un, une; **do you want o.?** en veux-tu (un)?; **o. of them** l'un d'eux, l'une d'elles; **a big/***etc* **o.** un grand/ *etc*; **that o.** celui-là, celle-là; **the o. who** *or* **which** celui *or* celle qui; **another o.** un(e) autre. ▪ (*impersonal*) on; **o. knows** on sait; **it helps o.** ça nous *or* vous aide; **one's family** sa famille.

one·self *pron* soi-même; (*reflexive*) se, s'.

one-way *adj* (*street*) à sens unique; (*ticket*) simple.

on·ion oignon *m*.

on-line *adj* Comput en ligne.

on·look·er spectateur, -trice *mf*.

on·ly 1 *adj* seul; **the o. one** le seul, la seule; **an o. son** un fils unique. **2** *adv* seulement, ne… que; **I o. have ten** je n'en ai que dix, j'en ai dix seulement; **not o.** non seulement; **I have o. just seen it** je viens tout juste de le voir; **o. he knows** lui seul le sait. **3** *conj* (*but*) Fam seulement.

on·to *prep* = **on to**.

on·ward(s) *adv* en avant; **from that time o.** à partir de là.

o·paque *adj* opaque.

o·pen 1 *adj* ouvert; (*ticket*) open *inv*; **wide o.** grand ouvert. **2 n (out) in the o.** en plein air. **3** *vt* ouvrir. **4** *vi* (*of flower, door, eyes etc*) s'ouvrir; (*of shop, office, person*) ouvrir.

o·pen-air *adj* (*pool, market etc*) en plein air.

o·pen·ing ouverture *f*; (*career prospect*) débouché *m*.

o·pen·ly *adv* ouvertement.

o·pen-mind·ed *adj* à l'esprit ouvert.

o·pen·ness franchise *f*.

▶ **open out 1** *vt* ouvrir. **2** *vi* s'ouvrir; (*widen*) s'élargir.

▶ **open up 1** *vt* ouvrir. **2** *vi* s'ouvrir; (*open the door*) ouvrir.

op·er·a opéra *m*.

op·er·ate 1 *vi* (*of surgeon*) opérer (**on sb** qn; **for** de); (*of machine etc*) fonctionner; (*proceed*) opérer. **2** *vt* faire fonctionner; (*business*) gérer.

op·er·a·tion opération *f*; (*working*) fonctionnement *m*.

op·er·a·tor (*on phone*) standardiste *mf*.

o·pin·ion opinion *f*, avis *m*; **in my o.** à mon avis.

op·po·nent adversaire *mf*.

op·por·tu·ni·ty occasion f (**to do** de faire).

op·pose vt s'opposer à.

op·posed adj opposé (**to** à).

op·pos·ing adj (team) opposé.

op·po·site 1 adj (direction, opinion etc) opposé; (house) d'en face. **2** adv (to sit etc) en face. **3** prep o. (**to**) en face de. **4** n **the** o. **le** contraire.

op·po·si·tion opposition f (**to** à).

opt vi **to** o. **for sth** décider pour qch.

op·ti·cal adj optique.

op·ti·cian opticien, -ienne mf.

op·ti·mist to be an o. être optimiste.

op·ti·mis·tic adj optimiste.

op·tion (choice) choix m.

op·tion·al adj facultatif.

or conj ou; **he doesn't drink or smoke** il ne boit ni ne fume.

o·ral 1 adj oral. **2** n (exam) oral m.

or·ange 1 n (fruit) orange f; o. **juice** jus m d'orange. **2** adj & n (color) orange (m & adj inv).

or·ange·ade orangeade f.

or·bit orbite f.

or·chard verger m.

or·ches·tra orchestre m.

or·deal épreuve f.

or·der 1 n (command, arrangement) ordre m; (purchase) commande f, **in** o. (passport etc) en règle; **in** o. **to do** pour faire; **in** o. **that** pour que (+ subjunctive); **out of** o. (machine) en panne; (telephone) en dérangement. **2** vt order (**sb to do** à qn de faire); (meal, goods etc) commander; (taxi) appeler. **3** vi (in café etc) commander.

▸ **order around** vt commander.

or·di·nance ordonnance f.

or·di·na·ry adj (usual, commonplace) ordinaire; (average) moyen; **it's out of the** o. ça sort de l'ordinaire.

ore minerai m.

or·gan (in body) organe m; (instrument) orgue m, orgues fpl.

or·gan·ic adj (vegetables etc) biologique.

or·gan·i·za·tion organisation f.

or·gan·ize vt organiser.

or·gan·iz·er organisateur, -trice mf.

o·ri·en·tal adj oriental.

or·i·gin origine f.

o·rig·i·nal 1 adj (idea, artist etc) original; (first) premier; (copy, version) original. **2** n (document etc) original m.

o·rig·i·nal·i·ty originalité f.

o·rig·i·nal·ly adv (at first) au départ.

o·rig·i·nate vi (begin) prendre naissance (**in** dans); **to** o. **from** émaner de.

or·na·ment (on dress etc) ornement m; (vase etc) bibelot m.

or·phan orphelin, -ine mf.

or·phan·age orphelinat m.

or·tho·dox adj orthodoxe.

os·trich autruche f.

oth·er 1 adj autre; o. **doctors** d'autres médecins; **the** o. **one** l'autre mf. **2** pron **the** o. l'autre mf; (some) **others** d'autres; **some do, others don't** les uns le font, les autres ne le font pas. **3** adv o. **than** autrement que.

oth·er·wise adv autrement.

ouch! int aïe!

ought v aux (obligation, desirability) devoir; **you** o. **to leave** tu devrais partir; **I** o. **to have done it** j'aurais dû le faire; **he said he** o. **to stay** il a dit qu'il devait rester. ▪ (probability) devoir; **it** o. **to be ready** ça devrait être prêt.

ounce once f (= 28,35g).

our poss adj notre, pl nos.

ours pron le nôtre, la nôtre, pl les nôtres; **this book is** o. ce livre est à nous or est le nôtre.

our·selves pron nous-mêmes; (reflexive, after prep) nous.

EXPRESSING YOUR OPINION

What do you think?
Qu'est-ce que tu en penses/vous en pensez ?

I really like it/liked it.
Ça me plaît beaucoup/Ça m'a beaucoup plu.

It was great/beautiful!
C'était génial/beau !

It was OK.
Ce n'était pas mal.

The tour of the castle was quite interesting.
La visite du château était assez intéressante.

I love croissants/hiking.
J'adore les croissants/faire de la randonné.

I hate snow/shopping.
Je déteste la neige/faire les magasins.

I'd rather have coffee.
Je préférerais du café.

Which do you prefer?
Tu préfères/Vous préférez lequel/laquelle ?

I think she's very nice.
Je la trouve très sympa.

I agree (with you).
Je suis d'accord (avec toi/vous).

Absolutely!
Absolument !

I'm sure it'll be nice tomorrow.
Je suis sûr(e) qu'il fera beau demain.

That's true.
C'est vrai.

I've changed my mind.
J'ai changé d'avis.

I don't know.
Je ne sais pas.

Really?
Ah bon ?/C'est vrai ?

What a surprise!
Quelle surprise !

Did you like the art gallery?
Le musée d'art t'a/vous a plu ?

I don't like it/didn't like it at all.
Ça ne me plaît pas du tout/Ça ne m'a pas du tout plu.

It was a bit boring/too touristy.
C'était un peu ennuyeux/trop touristique.

The food's nothing special.
La nourriture n'a rien d'exceptionnel.

We had a great time!
On s'est éclatés !

I don't like jazz/cycling.
Je n'aime pas le jazz/faire du vélo.

This is delicious/disgusting!
C'est délicieux/dégoûtant !

I prefer small hotels to big ones.
Je préfère les petits hôtels aux grands.

I prefer the bigger/smaller one.
Je préfère le (la) plus grand(e)/le (la) plus petit(e).

I think/I don't think it's possible.
Je crois que c'est/Je ne crois pas que ce soit possible.

I disagree (with you).
Je ne suis pas d'accord (avec toi/vous).

Of course (not)!
Bien sur (que non) !

Are you sure?
Tu en es/Vous en êtes sûr(e) ?

I don't believe you.
Je ne te/vous crois pas.

I'm not sure.
Je ne suis pas sûr(e).

It depends.
Ça dépend.

That's strange!
C'est étrange/bizarre !

What a pity!
Quel dommage !

out 1 *adv (outside)* dehors; *(not at home etc)* sorti; *(light, fire)* éteint; *(news, secret)* connu; *(book)* publié; *(eliminated from game)* éliminé; **to be** *or* **go o. a lot** sortir beaucoup; **to have a day o.** sortir pour la journée; **the tide's o.** la marée est basse; **o. there** là-bas. **2** *prep* **o. of** en dehors de; *(danger, water)* hors de; *(without)* sans; **o. of pity/etc** par pitié/etc; **o. of the window** par la fenêtre; **to drink/take/copy o. of sth** boire/prendre/copier dans qch; **made o. of** *(wood etc)* fait en; **to make sth o. of a box/** *etc* faire qch avec une boîte/etc; **she's o. of town** elle n'est pas en ville; **four o. of five** quatre sur cinq; **to feel o. of place** ne pas se sentir intégré.

out·bound *adj* o. journey *or* trip aller *m*.

out·break *(of war)* début *m*; *(of violence)* éruption *f*.

out·burst *(of anger, joy)* explosion *f*.

out·come résultat *m*.

out·dat·ed *adj* démodé.

out·do* *vt* surpasser *(in en)*.

out·door *adj (pool, market)* en plein air; **o. clothes** tenue *f* pour sortir.

out·doors *adv* dehors.

out·er *adj* extérieur.

out·er space l'espace *m* (cosmique).

out·fit *(clothes)* costume *m*; *(for woman)* toilette *f*; *(toy)* panoplie *f* *(de cow-boy etc)*; **ski/etc o.** tenue *f* de ski/etc.

out·grow *vt (habit)* passer l'âge de; *(clothes)* devenir trop grand pour.

out·ing sortie *f*, excursion *f*.

out·law 1 *n* hors-la-loi *m inv.* **2** *vt* proscrire.

out·let *(market for goods)* débouché *m*.

out·line *(shape)* contour *m*.

out·look *inv (for future)* perspec-

tive(s) *f(pl)*; *(point of view)* perspective *f* *(on* sur).

out·num·ber *vt* être plus nombreux que.

out-of-date *adj (expired)* périmé; *(old-fashioned)* démodé.

out·put rendement *m*; *(computer data)* données *fpl* de sortie.

out·rage 1 *n* scandale *m*; *(anger)* indignation *f*. **2** *vt* outraged by sth indigné de qch.

out·ra·geous *(shocking)* scandaleux.

out·right *adv (to say, tell)* franchement.

out·set **at the o.** au début; **from the o.** dès le début.

out·side 1 *adv (au)* dehors; **to go o.** sortir. **2** *prep* en dehors de. **3** *n* extérieur *m*. **4** *adj* extérieur.

out·sid·er *(stranger)* étranger, -ère *mf*; *(athlete, horse etc)* outsider *m*.

out·skirts *npl* banlieue *f*.

out·stand·ing *adj* remarquable; *(problem)* non réglé; *(debt)* impayé.

out·ward *adj (sign, appearance)* extérieur.

out·ward(s) *adv* vers l'extérieur.

o·val *adj & n* ovale *(m)*.

ov·en four *m*.

ov·en mitt gant *m* isolant.

o·ver 1 *prep (on)* sur; *(above)* au-dessus de; *(on the other side of)* de l'autre côté de; **to jump/look/etc o.** **sth** sauter/regarder/etc par-dessus qch; **o. it** *(on)* dessus; *(above)* au-dessus; *(to jump etc)* par-dessus; **to be upset/etc o. sth** *(about)* avoir de la peine/etc à cause de qch; **o. the phone** au téléphone; **o. the holidays** pendant les vacances; **o. ten days** *(more than)* plus de dix jours; **men o. sixty** les hommes de plus de soixante ans; **all o. Spain** dans toute l'Espagne; **all o. the carpet** partout sur le tapis. **2** *adv (above)* (par-)dessus; **o. here** ici; **o. there** là-bas; **to come** *or* **go o.** *(visit)* passer; **to ask o.** inviter (à venir); **all o.**

(everywhere) partout; **it's (all) o.** *(finished)* c'est fini; **a pound or o.** une livre ou plus; **I have ten o.** il m'en reste dix; **o. and o. (again)** à plusieurs reprises; **o. pleased**/*etc* trop content/*etc.*

o·ver·all *adj (length etc)* total.

o·ver·alls *npl (of workman)* bleu *m* de travail; *(of child)* salopette *f*.

o·ver·board *adv* à la mer.

o·ver·charge to **o. sb for sth** faire payer qch trop cher à qn.

o·ver·coat pardessus *m*.

o·ver·come *vt (problem)* surmonter.

o·ver·do* *vt* to **o. it** ne pas y aller doucement; **don't o. it!** vas-y doucement!

o·ver·draft découvert *m*.

o·ver·due *adj (train etc)* en retard.

o·ver·eat* *vi* manger trop.

o·ver·ex·cit·ed *adj* surexcité.

o·ver·flow *vi (of river, bath etc)* déborder.

o·ver·head *adv* au-dessus.

o·ver·hear *vt (pt & pp overheard)* surprendre.

o·ver·heat *vi (of engine)* chauffer.

o·ver·joyed *adj* fou *(f* folle) de joie.

o·ver·lap 1 *vi* se chevaucher. **2** *vt* chevaucher.

ov·er·leaf *adv* au verso.

o·ver·load *vt* surcharger.

o·ver·look *vt* ne pas remarquer; *(forget)* oublier; *(ignore)* passer sur; *(of window etc)* donner sur.

o·ver·night 1 *adv* (pendant) la nuit; **to stay o.** passer la nuit. **2** *adj (train)* de nuit.

o·ver·pass *(bridge)* toboggan *m*.

o·ver·rat·ed *adj* surfait.

o·ver·seas 1 *adv (abroad)* à l'étranger. **2** *adj (visitor etc)* étranger; *(trade)* extérieur.

o·ver·sight oubli *m*.

o·ver·sleep* *vi (pt & pp overslept)* dormir trop longtemps.

o·ver·spend* *vi* dépenser trop.

o·ver·take* *vti (in vehicle)* dépasser.

o·ver·time 1 *n* heures *fpl* supplémentaires. **2** *adv* **to work o.** faire des heures supplémentaires.

o·ver·turn *vi (of car, boat)* se retourner.

o·ver·weight *adj* **to be o.** *(of person)* avoir des kilos en trop.

o·ver·whelm *vt* accabler; **overwhelmed with** *(work, offers)* submergé de.

o·ver·work 1 *n* surmenage *m*. **2** *vi* se surmener.

owe *vt (money etc)* devoir (**to** à).

ow·ing *prep* **o. to** à cause de.

owl hibou *m (pl* hiboux).

own 1 *adj* propre; **my o. house** ma propre maison. **2** *pron* **it's my (very) o.** c'est à moi (tout seul); **a house of his o.** sa propre maison; **(all) on one's o.** tout seul; **to get one's o. back** se venger. **3** *vt* posséder; **who owns this ball**/*etc*? à qui appartient cette balle/*etc*?

own·er propriétaire *mf*.

▸ **own up** *vi* avouer (**to sth** qch).

ox, *pl* **oxen** bœuf *m*.

ox·y·gen oxygène *m*.

oys·ter huître *f*.

o·zone ozone *m*; **o. layer** couche *f* d'ozone.

P

pa *Fam* papa *m*.

pace pas *m*.

Pa·cif·ic 1 *adj* pacifique. **2** *n* **the P.** le Pacifique.

pac·i·fi·er *(of baby)* sucette *f*.

pack 1 *n* paquet *m; (backpack)* sac *m* à dos; *(of wolves)* meute *f; (of cards)* jeu *m; (of lies)* tissu *m*. **2** *vt (fill)* remplir (**with** de); *(suitcase)* faire; *(object into box etc)* emballer; *(object into suitcase)* mettre dans sa valise.

pack·age paquet *m*; *Comput* progiciel *m*.

pack·age tour voyage *m* organisé.

pack·ag·ing emballage *m*.

▸**pack away** *vt (put away)* ranger.

▸**pack down** *vt (crush)* tasser.

packed *adj (bus etc)* bourré.

packed lunch panier-repas *m*.

pack·et paquet *m*.

▸**pack in 1** *vt (quit) Fam* laisser tomber.

pack·ing emballage *m*.

▸**pack into 1** *vt (cram)* entasser dans. **2** *vi (crowd into)* s'entasser dans.

▸**pack up 1** *vt (put into box)* emballer; *(give up) Fam* laisser tomber. **2** *vi Fam (stop)* s'arrêter; *(of machine)* tomber en panne.

pact pacte *m*.

pad *(of cloth etc)* tampon *m*; *(for writing etc)* bloc *m*.

pad·ded *adj (armchair etc)* rembourré.

pad·dle 1 *vi (dip one's feet)* se mouiller les pieds. **2** *n (for boat)* pagaie *f*; *(for ping-pong)* raquette *f*. **3** *vt* **to p. a canoe** pagayer.

pad·dle boat pédalo *m*.

pad·lock cadenas *m*; *(on bicycle)* antivol *m*.

page *(of book etc)* page *f*.

pain douleur *f*; *(grief)* peine *f*; **pains** *(efforts)* efforts *mpl*; **to be in p.** souffrir; **to take (great) pains to do** se donner du mal à faire.

pain·ful *adj* douloureux.

pain·kill·er calmant *m*; **on painkillers** sous calmants.

paint 1 *n* peinture *f*; **paints** *(in box, tube)* couleurs *fpl*. **2** *vti* peindre; **to p. sth blue/etc** peindre qch en bleu/*etc*.

paint·brush pinceau *m*.

paint·er peintre *m*.

paint·ing *(activity, picture)* peinture *f*.

paint strip·per décapant *m*.

pair *(two)* paire *f*; *(of people)* couple *m*.

pa·ja·mas *npl* pyjama *m*; **a pair of p.** un pyjama.

Pa·ki·sta·ni 1 *n* Pakistanais, -aise *mf*. **2** *adj* pakistanais, -aise.

pal *Fam* copain *m*, copine *f*.

pal·ace palais *m*.

pal·ate *(in mouth)* palais *m*.

pale *adj* pâle.

pal·ette *(of artist)* palette *f*.

palm *(of hand)* paume *f*; **p. (tree)** palmier *m*; **p. (leaf)** palme *f*.

pam·phlet brochure *f*.

pan casserole *f*; *(for frying)* poêle *f*.

pan·cake crêpe *f*.

pane vitre *f*.

pan·el *(of door etc)* panneau *m*; *(of judges)* jury *m*; *(of experts)* groupe *m*; **(control) p.** console *f*.

pan·ic 1 *n* panique *f*. **2** *vi* s'affoler.

pant *vi* haleter.

pant·ies *npl (female)* slip *m*.

pan·to·mime spectacle *m* de mime.

pan·try *(larder)* garde-manger *m inv*.

pants *npl (trousers)* pantalon *m*.

pant·y·hose collant *m*.

pa·per 1 *n* papier *m*; *(newspaper)* journal *m*; *(wallpaper)* papier *m* peint; *(in high school, college)* dissertation *f*; **brown p.** papier *m* d'emballage; **to put down on p.** mettre par écrit. **2** *adj (bag, towel etc)* en papier; *(cup, plate)* en carton.

pa·per·back livre *m* de poche.

pa·per clip trombone *m*.

pa·per tow·el essuie-tout *m inv*.

pap·er·work écritures *fpl*.

par *(parity)* égalité *f*; *(in golf)* par *m*; **on a p.** au même niveau (**with** de); **that's about p. for the course** c'est ce à quoi il faut s'attendre.

par·a·chute parachute *m*.

pa·rade *(procession)* défilé *m*; *(street)* avenue *f*.

par·a·dise paradis *m*.

par·a·graph paragraphe *m*; 'new p.' 'à la ligne'.

par·a·keet perruche *f*.

par·a·le·gal assistant, -ante *mf* *(d'un avocat)*.

par·al·lel *adj* parallèle (**with, to** à).

par·a·lyze *vt* paralyser.

par·a·site parasite *m*.

par·a·sol *(over table, on beach)* parasol *m*.

par·cel colis *m*, paquet *m*.

par·don 1 *n* I beg your p. je vous prie de m'excuser; *(not hearing)* vous dites?; **p.?** *(not hearing)* comment?; p. (me)! *(sorry)* pardon! **2** *vt* pardonner (**sb for sth** qch à qn).

par·ent père *m*, mère *f*, one's parents ses parents *mpl*.

par·ish paroisse *f*.

Pa·ris·ian 1 *n* Parisien, -ienne *mf*. **2** *n* parisien, -ienne.

park 1 *n* parc *m*. **2** *vt (vehicle)* garer. **3** *vi* se garer; *(remain parked)* stationner.

par·ka anorak *m*.

park·ing stationnement *m*; 'no p.' 'défense de stationner'.

park·ing en·force·ment of·fi·cer contractuel, -elle *mf*.

park·ing light *(of vehicle)* veilleuse *f*.

park·ing lot parking *m*.

park·ing me·ter parcmètre *m*.

park·ing place, parking space place *f* de parking.

park·ing tick·et contravention *f*.

par·lia·ment parlement *m*.

par·rot perroquet *m*.

pars·ley persil *m*.

pars·nip panais *m*.

part 1 *n* partie *f*, *(of machine)* pièce *f*, *(of serial)* épisode *m*; *(role)* rôle *m*; *(in hair)* raie *f*; **to take p.** participer (**in** à); **in p.** en partie; **for the most**

p. dans l'ensemble; **to be a p. of sth** faire partie de qch; **in these parts** dans ces parages. **2** *adv (partly)* en partie. **3** *vi (of friends etc)* se quitter; *(of couple)* se séparer.

par·tial *adj* partiel; **to be p. to sth** *(fond of)* Fam avoir un faible pour qch.

par·tic·i·pant participant, -ante *mf*.

par·tic·i·pate *vi* participer (**in** à).

par·tic·i·pa·tion participation *f*.

par·ti·ci·ple *Grammar* participe *m*.

par·tic·u·lar 1 *adj* particulier; *(fussy)* difficile (**about** sur); *(showing care)* méticuleux; **in p.** en particulier. **2** *npl* **particulars** détails *mpl*; **sb's particulars** les coordonnées *fpl* de qn.

par·tic·u·lar·ly *adv* particulièrement.

par·ti·tion *(in room)* cloison *f*.

part·ly *adv* en partie.

part·ner partenaire *mf*, *(in business)* associé, -ée *mf*, *(dancing)* p. cavalier, -ière *mf*.

part·ner·ship association *f*.

part·ridge perdrix *f*.

part-time *adj* & *adv* à temps partiel.

par·ty *(formal)* réception *f*, *(with friends)* soirée *f*, *(for birthday)* fête *f*, *(group)* groupe *m*; *(political)* parti *m*.

pass 1 *n (entry permit)* laissez-passer *m inv*; *(over mountains)* col *m*; Sports passe *f*; *(for transportation)* carte *f* d'abonnement. **2** *vi* passer (**to** à; **through** par); *(overtake)* dépasser; *(in exam)* être reçu (**in French/etc** en français/etc). **3** *vt* passer (**to** à); *(go past)* passer devant *(immeuble etc)*; *(vehicle)* dépasser; *(exam)* être reçu à; **to p. sb** *(in street)* croiser qn.

pass·a·ble *adj (not bad)* passable; *(road)* praticable.

pas·sage *(of text etc)* passage *m*; *(corridor)* couloir *m*.

pas·sage·way *(corridor)* couloir *m*.

▸ **pass around** *vt (cake etc)* faire passer.

▸ **pass away** *vi (die)* mourir.

pass·book livret *m* de caisse d'épargne.

▸ **pass by 1** *vi* passer (à côté). **2** *vt (building etc)* passer devant; **to p. by sb** *(in street)* croiser qn.

pas·sen·ger passager, -ère *mf*; *(on train)* voyageur, -euse *mf*.

pas·ser-by, *pl* **passers-by** passant, -ante *mf*.

pass·ing 1 *n (of time)* écoulement *m*; *(of law)* vote *m*; **in p.** en passant. **2** *adj* qui passe.

passing grade *(in school)* moyenne *f*.

pas·sion passion *f*.

pas·sion·ate *adj* passionné.

pas·sive 1 *adj* passif. **2** *n Grammar* passif *m*.

▸ **pass off** *vt* **to p. oneself off as** se faire passer pour.

▸ **pass on** *vt (message etc)* transmettre (**to** à).

▸ **pass out** *vi (faint)* s'évanouir.

▸ **pass over** *vt (ignore)* passer sur.

pass·port passeport *m*.

▸ **pass through** *vi* passer.

▸ **pass up** *vt (chance)* laisser passer.

pass·word mot *m* de passe.

past 1 *n* passé *m*; **in the p.** *(formerly)* dans le temps. **2** *adj (gone by)* passé; *(former)* ancien; **these p. months** ces derniers mois; **in the p. tense** au passé. **3** *prep (in front of)* devant; *(after)* après; *(further than)* plus loin que; **it's four o'clock p.** quatre heures passées. **4** *adv* devant; **to go p.** passer.

pas·ta pâtes *fpl*.

paste 1 *n (of meat)* pâté *m*; *(of fish)* beurre *m*; *(glue)* colle *f*. **2** *vt* coller.

pas·teur·ized *adj (milk)* pasteurisé.

pas·tille pastille *f*.

pas·time passe-temps *m inv*.

pas·try pâte *f*; *(cake)* pâtisserie *f*.

pas·ture pâturage *m*.

pat *vt (cheek etc)* tapoter; *(animal)* caresser.

patch *(for clothes)* pièce *f*, *(over eye)* bandeau *m*; *(of color)* tache *f*; **cabbage p.** carré *m* de choux; **bad p.** mauvaise période *f*.

patch (up) *vt (clothing)* rapiécer.

pat·ent¹ 1 *n* brevet *m* d'invention. **2** *vt* (faire) breveter.

pat·ent² p. (leather) cuir *m* verni.

path, *pl* **-s** sentier *m*; *(in park)* allée *f*.

pa·thet·ic *adj (results etc)* lamentable.

path·way sentier *m*.

pa·tience patience *f*; **to lose p.** perdre patience (**with sb** avec qn).

pa·tient 1 *adj* patient. **2** *n* malade *mf*, *(on doctor's or dentist's list)* patient, -ente *mf*.

pa·tient·ly *adv* patiemment.

pat·i·o, *pl* -os patio *m*.

pa·tri·ot·ic *adj* patriotique; *(person)* patriote.

pa·trol 1 *n* patrouille *f*. **2** *vi* patrouiller. **3** *vt* patrouiller dans.

pa·tron *(of charity)* patron, -onne *mf*; *(of arts)* mécène *m*; *(customer)* client, -e *mf*; **p. saint** (saint, -e *mf*) patron, -onne *mf*.

pat·tern dessin *m*; *(paper model for garment)* patron *m*.

pause 1 *n* pause *f*; *(in conversation)* silence *m*. **2** *vi* faire une pause; *(hesitate)* hésiter.

pave *vt* paver; **to p. the way for sth** ouvrir la voie à qch.

paved *adj* pavé.

pave·ment *(roadway)* chaussée *f*.

pa·vil·ion pavillon *m*.

pav·ing stone pavé *m*.

paw patte *f*.

pawn *Chess* pion *m*.

pay* 1 *n* salaire *m*; *(of workman, soldier)* paie *f*; **p. slip** bulletin *m* de paie. **2** *vt (person, sum)* payer; *(deposit)* verser; *(of investment)* rapporter; *(compliment, visit)* faire (**to** à); **to p. sb to do** *or* **for doing** payer qn pour faire; **to p. sb for sth** payer qch à qn; **to p. money into one's account** verser de l'argent sur son compte. **3** *vi* payer; **to p. a lot** payer cher.

pay·a·ble *adj* payable; **a check p. to** un chèque à l'ordre de.

▸**pay back** *vt (person, loan)* rembourser.

pay·check chèque *m* de règlement de salaire.

▸**pay for** *vt* payer.

pay·ment paiement *m*; *(of deposit)* versement *m*.

▸**pay off** *vt (debt, person)* rembourser.

▸**pay out** *vt (spend)* dépenser.

pay phone téléphone *m* public.

▸**pay up** *vti* payer.

PC¹ *abbr (personal computer)* PC *m*.

PC² *adj abbr (politically correct)* politiquement correct.

PDA *abbr (personal digital assistant)* PDA *m*.

PE *abbr (physical education)* éducation *f* physique, EPS *f*.

pea pois *m*; **(green) peas** petits pois *mpl*; **p. soup** soupe *f* aux pois.

peace paix *f*; **p. of mind** tranquillité *f* d'esprit; **in p.** en paix; **to have (some) p. and quiet** avoir la paix.

peace·ful *adj* paisible; *(demonstration)* pacifique.

peach pêche *f*.

pea·cock paon *m*.

peak 1 *n (mountain top)* sommet *m*; *(mountain)* pic *m*; **to be at its p.** être à son maximum. **2** *adj (hours, period)* de pointe.

peaked *adj Fam (ill)* patraque.

pea·nut cacah(o)uète *f*; **p. butter** beurre *m* de cacah(o)uètes.

pear poire *f*; **p. tree** poirier *m*.

pearl perle *f*.

peb·ble caillou *m* (*pl* cailloux); *(on beach)* galet *m*.

pe·can noix *f* de pécan.

peck *vti* **to p. (at)** *(of bird)* picorer *(du pain etc)*; donner un coup de bec à *(qn)*.

pe·cu·liar *adj* bizarre; *(special)* particulier (**to** à).

pe·cu·li·ar·i·ty *(feature)* particularité *f*.

ped·al 1 *n* pédale *f*. **2** *vi* pédaler. **3** *vt* **to p. a bicycle** faire marcher un vélo; *(ride)* rouler en vélo.

pe·des·tri·an piéton *m*; **p. crossing** passage *m* pour piétons; **p. street** rue *f* piétonne.

pe·do·me·ter pédomètre *m*.

peek **to have a p.** jeter un petit coup d'œil (**at** à).

peel 1 *n* épluchure(s) *f(pl)*; **a piece of p., some p.** une épluchure. **2** *vt (apple, potato etc)* éplucher. **3** *vi (of sunburnt skin)* peler; *(of paint)* s'écailler.

peel·er (potato) p. éplucheur *m*.

▸**peel off** *vt (label etc)* décoller.

peep 1 *n* coup *m* d'œil *(furtif)*. **2** *vi* **to p. (at)** regarder furtivement.

peer *vi* **to p. (at)** regarder attentivement.

peg *(for tent)* piquet *m*; *(for clothes)* pince *f* (à linge); *(for coat, hat)* patère *f*.

pen *(fountain, ballpoint)* stylo *m*; *(enclosure)* parc *m*.

pen·al·ty *(prison sentence)* peine *f*, *(fine)* amende *f*; *Sports* penalty *m*.

pen·cil crayon *m*; **in p.** au crayon.

pen·cil case trousse *f*.

▸**pencil in** *vt (note down)* noter provisoirement.

pen·cil sharp·en·er taillecrayon(s) *m inv*.

pen·e·trate *vt (substance)* pénétrer; *(forest)* pénétrer dans.

pen·guin manchot *m*.

pen·i·cil·lin pénicilline *f*.

pen·in·su·la presqu'île *f*.

pen·knife, *pl* -knives canif *m*.

pen·ni·less *adj* sans le sou.

pen·ny, *pl* **pennies** *(coin)* cent *m*; **not a p.!** pas un sou!

pen pal correspondant, -ante *mf*.
pen·sion pension *f*; (retirement)
p. retraite *f*.
pen·sion·er (old age) p. retraité,
-ée *mf*.
peo·ple 1 *npl* gens *mpl* or *fpl*, (specific persons) personnes *fpl*; **the p.**
(citizens) le peuple; **old p.** les personnes *fpl* âgées; **old p.'s home**
maison *f* de retraite; **English p.**
les Anglais *mpl*. **2** *n* (nation) peuple
m.
pep·per poivre *m*; (vegetable) poivron *m*.
pep·per·mint (flavor) menthe *f*;
(candy) bonbon *m* à la menthe.
per *prep* par; **p. year** par an; **p. person** par personne; **p. cent** pour
cent; **10 dollars p. pound** 10 dollars
la livre.
per·ceive *vt* percevoir; (notice)
remarquer.
per·cent·age pourcentage *m*.
perch 1 *n* (for bird) perchoir *m*. **2** *vi*
(of bird, person) se percher.
per·co·la·tor cafetière *f*; (in café
etc) percolateur *m*.
per·fect 1 *adj* parfait; *Grammar*
p. tense parfait *m*. **2** *n* *Grammar*
parfait *m*. **3** *vt* (technique) mettre
au point; (one's French etc) parfaire
ses connaissances en.
per·fec·tion perfection *f*.
per·fect·ly *adv* parfaitement.
per·form 1 *vt* (task, miracle) accomplir; (one's duty) remplir; (surgical operation) pratiquer (**on** sur); (a
play, piece of music) jouer. **2** *vi*
(act, play) jouer; (sing) chanter;
(dance) danser; (of machine)
fonctionner.
per·form·ance (in theater) représentation *f*; (in movie theater,
concert hall) séance *f*; (of actor, musician) interprétation *f*; (of athlete,
machine) performance *f*.
per·form·er (entertainer) artiste
mf.
per·fume parfum *m*.

per·haps *adv* peut-être; **p. not**
peut-être que non.
per·il péril *m*.
pe·ri·od période *f*; (historical)
époque *f*; (lesson) leçon *f*; (punctuation mark) point *m*; (monthly)
period(s) (of woman) règles *fpl*.
pe·ri·od·i·cal périodique *m*.
perk (in job) avantage *m* en nature.
►**perk up** *vi* (become livelier) reprendre du poil de la bête.
perm 1 *n* permanente *f*. **2** *vt* **to
have one's hair permed** se faire
une permanente.
per·ma·nent *adj* permanent; (address) fixe.
per·ma·nent·ly *adv* à titre permanent.
per·mis·sion permission *f* (**to do**
de faire); **to ask p.** demander la
permission.
per·mit 1 *vt* permettre (**sb to do** à
qn de faire). **2** *n* permis *m*; (entrance
pass) laissez-passer *m inv*.
per·pen·dic·u·lar *adj* perpendiculaire (**to** à).
per·se·cute *vt* persécuter.
per·se·cu·tion persécution *f*.
per·se·ver·ance persévérance
f.
per·se·vere *vi* persévérer (**in** dans).
per·sist *vi* persister (**in doing** à
faire; **in sth** dans qch).
per·sist·ent *adj* (person) obstiné;
(noise etc) continuel.
per·son personne *f*; **in p.** en
personne.
per·son·al *adj* personnel; (application) en personne; (friend)
intime; (life) privé; (indiscreet) indiscret.
per·son·al·i·ty personnalité *f*.
per·son·al·ly *adv* personnellement; (in person) en personne.
per·son·nel personnel *m*.
per·suade *vt* persuader (**sb to do**
qn de faire).
per·sua·sion persuasion *f*.
per·ti·nent *adj* pertinent.

pes·si·mist to be a p. être pessimiste.

pes·si·mis·tic adj pessimiste.

pest animal m or insecte m nuisible; (person) casse-pieds mf inv.

pes·ter vt harceler (with questions de questions); to p. sb to do sth/for sth harceler qn pour qu'il fasse qch/jusqu'à ce qu'il donne qch.

pet 1 n animal m (domestique); (favorite person) chouchou, -oute mf. **2** adj (dog, cat etc) domestique; (favorite) favori (f -ite).

pet·al pétale m.

pe·ti·tion (signatures) pétition f.

pet·ti·coat jupon m.

pet·ty adj (minor) petit; (mean) mesquin; **p. cash** petite caisse f.

phar·ma·cist pharmacien, -ienne mf.

phar·ma·cy pharmacie f.

phase phase f.

▸**phase in** vt introduire progressivement.

▸**phase out** vt supprimer progressivement.

PhD abbr (Doctor of Philosophy) doctorat m.

pheas·ant faisan m.

phe·nom·e·nal adj phénoménal.

phe·nom·e·non, pl -ena phénomène m.

phi·los·o·pher philosophe mf.

phil·o·soph·i·cal adj philosophique; (resigned) philosophe.

phi·los·o·phy philosophie f.

phlegm (in throat) glaires fpl.

phone 1 n téléphone m; **on the p.** au téléphone; (at other end) au bout du fil. **2** vt téléphoner à. **3** vi téléphoner.

▸**phone back** vti rappeler.

phone book annuaire m.

phone booth cabine f téléphonique.

phone call coup m de fil; **to make a p. call** téléphoner (to à).

phone numb·er numéro m de téléphone.

pho·net·ic adj phonétique.

pho·to, pl -os photo f; **to take a p. of** prendre une photo de; **to have one's p. taken** se faire prendre en photo.

pho·to·cop·i·er photocopieuse f.

pho·to·cop·y 1 n photocopie f. **2** vt photocopier.

pho·to·graph photographie f.

pho·tog·ra·pher photographe mf.

pho·to·graph·ic adj photographique.

pho·tog·ra·phy photographie f.

phrase expression f; (idiom) locution f.

phrase·book manuel m de conversation.

phys·i·cal adj physique; **p. examination** examen m médical; **p. education** éducation f physique.

phy·si·cian médecin m.

phys·ics physique f.

pi·an·ist pianiste mf.

pi·an·o, pl -os piano m.

pick 1 n **to take one's p.** faire son choix. **2** vt choisir; (flower, fruit) cueillir; (hole) faire (in dans); **to p. one's nose** se mettre les doigts dans le nez.

pick·ax pioche f.

pick·le cornichon m.

pick·led adj (onion etc) au vinaigre.

▸**pick off** vt enlever.

▸**pick on** vt s'en prendre à.

▸**pick out** vt choisir; (identify) reconnaître.

pick·pock·et pickpocket m.

▸**pick up 1** vt (sth dropped) ramasser; (fallen person or chair) relever; (person into air, weight) soulever; (a cold) attraper; (habit, accent, speed) prendre; (fetch) (passer) prendre; (find) trouver; (learn) apprendre. **2** vi (improve) s'améliorer;

(of business) reprendre; *(of patient)* aller mieux.

pic·nic pique-nique *m.*

pic·ture 1 *n* image *f*, *(painting)* tableau *m*; *(photo)* photo *f*, *(film)* film *m.* **2** *vt* *(imagine)* s'imaginer (**that** que).

pic·ture frame cadre *m.*

pic·tur·esque *adj* pittoresque.

pie *(open)* tarte *f*, *(with pastry on top)* tourte *f.*

piece morceau *m*; *(of fabric, machine, in game)* pièce *f*; *(coin)* pièce *f*; **in pieces** en morceaux; **to take to pieces** *(machine)* démonter; **a p. of news/***etc* une nouvelle/*etc*; **in one p.** intact; *(person)* indemne.

pier jetée *f.*

pierce *vt* percer *(qch).*

pier·cing 1 *adj (cry, cold)* perçant; **2** *n (for body adornment)* piercing *m.*

pig cochon *m.*

pi·geon pigeon *m.*

pi·geon·hole casier *m.*

pig·gy·back to give sb a p. porter qn sur le dos.

pig·gy·bank tirelire *f.*

pig·tail *(hair)* natte *f.*

▸ **pile 1** *n* tas *m*; *(neatly arranged)* pile *f*, **piles of** *Fam* beaucoup de. **2** *vt* entasser; *(neatly)* empiler.

piles *npl (illness)* hémorroïdes *fpl.*

pile·up *(on road)* carambolage *m.*

▸ **pile up 1** *vt* entasser; *(neatly)* empiler. **2** *vi* s'accumuler.

pill pilule *f*, **to be on the P.** prendre la pilule.

pil·lar pilier *m.*

pil·low oreiller *m.*

pil·low·case taie *f* d'oreiller.

pi·lot pilote *m.*

pim·ple bouton *m.*

pin épingle *f*, *(drawing pin)* punaise *f.*

pin (on) *vt* épingler (**to** sur, à); *(to wall)* punaiser (**to**, **on** à).

pin·a·fore *(apron)* tablier *m.*

pin·ball flipper *m*; **p. machine** flipper *m.*

pin·cers *npl (tool)* tenailles *fpl.*

pinch 1 *n (of salt)* pincée *f*, **to give sb a p.** pincer qn. **2** *vt* pincer; *(steal) Fam* piquer (**from** à).

pin·cush·ion pelote *f* (à épingles).

pine pin *m.*

pine·ap·ple ananas *m.*

pink *adj & n (color)* rose *(m).*

pink·ie petit doigt *m.*

pint pinte *f* (= 0.47 litre).

▸ **pin up** *vt (on wall)* punaiser (**on** à); *(notice)* afficher.

pi·o·neer 1 *n (settler)* pionnier, -ère *mf.* **2** *vt* **to p. sth** être le premier/la première à mettre au point qch.

pipe tuyau *m*; *(of smoker)* pipe *f*, **to smoke a p.** fumer la pipe.

pi·rate pirate *m.*

pis·ta·chi·o pistache *f.*

pis·tol pistolet *m.*

pit *(hole)* trou *m*; *(coalmine)* mine *f*; *(quarry)* carrière *f*; *(stone of fruit)* noyau *m*; *(smaller)* pépin *m.*

pitch *vt (tent)* dresser; *(ball)* lancer.

pitch-black, pitch-dark *adj* noir comme dans un four.

pitch·er *(container)* cruche *f.*

pit·y 1 *n* pitié *f*, **(what) a p.!** (quel) dommage!; **it's a p.** c'est dommage (**that** que (*+ subjunctive*); **to do** de faire). **2** *vt* plaindre.

piz·za pizza *f.*

plac·ard *(notice)* affiche *f.*

place 1 *n* endroit *m*, lieu *m*; *(house)* maison *f*; *(seat, position, rank)* place *f*; **in the first p.** en premier lieu; **to take p.** avoir lieu; **p. of work** lieu *m* de travail; **market p.** place *f* du marché; **at my p., to my p.** *(house)* chez moi; **all over the p.** partout; **to take the p. of** remplacer; **in p. of** à la place de. **2** *vt* placer; *(an order)* passer (**with sb** à qn); **to p. sb** *(identify)* remettre qn.

place mat set *m* (de table).

place set·ting couvert *m*.

plague 1 *n* peste *f*; *(nuisance)* plaie *f*. **2** *vt* harceler (**with** de).

plain[1] *adj (clear)* clair; *(simple)* simple; *(madness)* pur; *(without pattern)* uni; *(woman, man)* sans beauté; **to make it p. to sb that** faire comprendre à qn que.

plain[2] plaine *f*.

plain·ly *adv* clairement; *(frankly)* franchement.

plait 1 *n* tresse *f*. **2** *vt* tresser.

plan 1 *n* projet *m*; *(economic, of house etc)* plan *m*; **according to p.** comme prévu. **2** *vt (foresee)* prévoir; *(organize)* organiser; *(design)* concevoir; **to p. to do** *or* **doing** avoir l'intention de faire; **as planned** comme prévu.

plane *(aircraft)* avion *m*; *(tool)* rabot *m*.

plan·et planète *f*.

plane tree platane *m*.

▶ **plan for** *vt (rain, disaster)* prévoir.

plank planche *f*.

plant 1 *n* plante *f*; *(factory)* usine *f*; **house p.** plante *f* verte. **2** *vt (flower etc)* planter.

plas·ter plâtre *m*; **in p.** dans le plâtre.

plas·tic 1 *adj (object)* en plastique. **2** *n* plastique *m*.

plas·tic bag sac *m* en plastique.

plas·tic sur·ge·ry chirurgie *f* esthétique.

plas·tic wrap film *m* alimentaire.

plate *(dish)* assiette *f*; *(metal sheet)* plaque *f*.

plat·form *(at train station)* quai *m*; *(on bus etc)* plate-forme *f*; *(for speaker etc)* estrade *f*.

plau·si·ble *adj* plausible.

play 1 *n (in theater)* pièce *f* (de théâtre). **2** *vt (part, tune etc)* jouer; *(game)* jouer à; *(instrument)* jouer de; *(team)* jouer contre; *(record, CD)* passer; **to p. a part in doing/ in sth** contribuer à faire/à qch. **3** *vi* jouer (**at** à); *(of tape recorder etc)*

marcher; **what are you playing at?** qu'est-ce que tu fais?; **what's playing?** *(at movies etc)* qu'est-ce qu'on joue?

▶ **play around** *vi* jouer.

▶ **play back** *vt (tape)* réécouter.

▶ **play down** *vt* minimiser.

play·er *(in game, of instrument)* joueur, -euse *mf*; **CD/DVD p.** lecteur *m* de CD/DVD.

play·ground *(in school)* cour *f* de récréation; *(with swings etc)* terrain *m* de jeux.

play·ing card carte *f* à jouer.

play·ing field terrain *m* de jeux.

▶ **play on** *vt (feelings, fears etc)* jouer sur.

play·pen parc *m* (pour enfants).

play·school garderie *f* (d'enfants).

play·time récréation *f*.

plea *(request)* appel *m*; *Law (argument)* argument *m*; *(defense)* défense *f*.

plead 1 *vt (argue)* plaider; *(as excuse)* alléguer. **2** *vi (beg)* supplier; **to p. with sb to do sth** supplier qn de faire qch; *Law* **to p. guilty/not guilty** plaider coupable/non coupable.

pleas·ant *adj* agréable.

pleas·ant·ly *adv* agréablement.

please 1 *adv* s'il vous plaît, s'il te plaît. **2** *vt* **to p. sb** plaire à qn; *(satisfy)* contenter qn. **3** *vi* plaire; **do as you p.** fais comme tu veux.

pleased *adj* content (**with** de; **that** que (+ *subjunctive*); **to do** de faire); **p. to meet you!** enchanté!

pleas·ing *adj* agréable.

pleas·ure plaisir *m*.

pleat *(in skirt)* pli *m*.

pleat·ed *adj* plissé.

pledge 1 *n* promesse *f*. **2** *vt* promettre.

plen·ti·ful *adj* abondant.

plen·ty p. of beaucoup de; **that's p.** c'est assez.

pli·ers *npl* pince(s) *f(pl)*.

plot 1 *n* complot *m* (**against**

contre); **p. (of land)** terrain *m*. **2** *vti* comploter (**to do** de faire).

plot (out) *vt* (route) déterminer.

plow 1 *n* charrue *f*. **2** *vt* (field) labourer.

pluck *vt* (fowl) plumer; (flower) cueillir.

plug (of cotton wool) tampon *m*; (for sink, bath) bonde *f*, (electrical) fiche *f*, prise *f* (mâle); (socket) prise *f* de courant; (wall) **p.** (for screw) cheville *f*.

plug (up) *vt* boucher.

▸ **plug in** *vt* (radio etc) brancher.

plum prune *f*.

plumb·er plombier *m*.

plumb·ing plomberie *f*.

plump *adj* potelé.

plunge 1 *vt* plonger (**into** dans). **2** *vi* (dive) plonger (**into** dans); (fall) tomber (**from** de).

plu·ral 1 *adj* (form) pluriel; (noun) au pluriel. **2** *n* pluriel *m*; **in the p.** au pluriel.

plus 1 *prep* plus; **two p. two** deux plus deux. **2** *adj* **twenty p.** vingt et quelques.

p.m. *adv* de l'après-midi; (evening) du soir.

poach *vt* (egg) pocher.

PO Box boîte *f* postale.

pock·et poche *f*; **p. money/etc** argent *m/etc* de poche.

pock·et·book (handbag) sac *m* à main.

pock·et·ful **a p. of** une pleine poche de.

pock·et·knife, *pl* -knives canif *m*.

pod·cast podcast *m*.

po·em poème *m*.

po·et poète *m*.

po·et·ic *adj* poétique.

po·e·try poésie *f*.

point 1 *n* (position, score etc) point *m*; (decimal) virgule *f*, (meaning) sens *m*; (of knife etc) pointe *f*; **points** (for train) aiguillage *m*; **p. of view** point *m* de vue; **at this p. (in time)** en ce moment; **what's**

the **p.?** à quoi bon? (of waiting/ etc attendre/etc); **there's no p. (in) staying/etc** ça ne sert à rien de rester/etc. **2** *vt* (aim) pointer (**at** sur); **to p. one's finger (at)** montrer du doigt.

▸ **point at** *vt* montrer du doigt.

point·ed *adj* pointu.

point·less *adj* inutile.

▸ **point out** *vt* (show) indiquer; (mention) signaler (**that** que).

▸ **point to** *vt* (indicate) indiquer.

poi·son 1 *n* poison *m*; (of snake) venin *m*. **2** *vt* empoisonner.

poi·son·ous *adj* toxique; (snake) venimeux; (plant) vénéneux.

poke *vt* pousser (du doigt etc); (fire) tisonner; **to p. sth into sth** fourrer qch dans qch; **to p. one's head out of the window** passer la tête par la fenêtre.

▸ **poke around in** *vt* (drawer etc) fouiner dans.

pok·er (for fire) tisonnier *m*.

po·lar bear ours *m* blanc.

Pole Polonais, -aise *mf*.

pole (rod) perche *f*, (fixed) poteau *m*; (for flag) mât *m*; **North/South P.** pôle *m* Nord/Sud.

po·lice police *f*.

po·lice car voiture *f* de police.

po·lice force police *f*.

po·lice·man, *pl* -men agent *m* de police.

po·lice·wom·an, *pl* -women femme-agent *f*.

pol·i·cy (plan etc) politique *f*; (insurance) **p.** police *f* (d'assurance).

po·li·o polio *f*.

Po·lish 1 *adj* polonais. **2** *n* (language) polonais *m*.

pol·ish 1 *vt* cirer; (metal) astiquer; (rough surface) polir. **2** *n* (for shoes) cirage *m*; (for floor etc) cire *f*, (shine) vernis *m*; **to give sth a p.** faire briller qch.

▸ **polish off** *vt* (food etc) Fam avaler.

▸ **polish up** *vt* (one's French etc) perfectionner.

po·lite adj poli (**to, with** avec).
po·lite·ly adv poliment.
po·lite·ness politesse f.
po·lit·i·cal adj politique.
pol·i·ti·cian homme m/femme f politique.
pol·i·tics politique f.
poll (voting) scrutin m; **to go to the polls** aller aux urnes; **(opinion) p.** sondage m (d'opinion).
pol·len pollen m.
poll·ing place bureau m de vote.
polls urnes fpl; **to go to the p.** aller aux urnes.
pol·lute vt polluer.
pol·lu·tion pollution f.
po·lo shirt polo m.
pol·y·es·ter 1 n polyester m. 2 adj (shirt etc) en polyester.
pome·gran·ate (fruit) grenade f.
pond étang m; (artificial) bassin m.
po·ny poney m.
po·ny·tail (hair) queue f de cheval.
poo·dle caniche m.
pool (puddle) flaque f; (for swimming) piscine f; (billiards) billard m américain.
pooped adj (tired) Fam vanné.
poor 1 adj pauvre; (bad) mauvais; (weak) faible. 2 npl **the p.** les pauvres mpl.
poor·ly adv (badly) mal.
pop[1] vti (burst) crever. 2 vt (put) Fam mettre.
pop[2] 1 n (music) pop m; (drink) soda m; (father) Fam papa m. 2 adj (concert etc) pop inv.
pop·corn pop-corn m.
pope pape m.
▸ **pop in** vi entrer un instant.
▸ **pop out** vi sortir un instant.
▸ **pop over** vi faire un saut (**to** chez).
pop·py coquelicot m.
pop·si·cle® glace f à eau.
pop·u·lar adj populaire; (fashionable) à la mode; **to be p. with** plaire beaucoup à.
pop·u·lar·i·ty popularité f.

pop·u·lat·ed adj highly/sparsely/etc p. très/peu/etc peuplé; **p. by** peuplé de.
pop·u·la·tion population f.
porch porche m; (veranda) véranda f.
pork (meat) porc m.
por·ridge porridge m (bouillie de flocons d'avoine).
port (harbor) port m.
por·ta·ble adj portable, portatif.
por·ter (for luggage) porteur m.
port·fo·li·o (for documents) porte-documents m inv; (of politician) portefeuille m; (of model, artist etc) book m.
port·hole hublot m.
por·tion (share) portion f; (of train, book etc) partie f.
por·trait portrait m.
Por·tu·guese 1 adj portugais, -aise. 2 n Portugais, -aise mf; (language) portugais m.
pose 1 n (of model) pose f. 2 vi poser (**for** pour).
posh adj Fam chic inv.
po·si·tion position f; (job, circumstances) situation f; **in a p. to do** en mesure de faire.
pos·i·tive adj positif; (progress, change) réel; (answer) affirmatif; (sure) certain (**of** de; **that** que).
pos·sess vt posséder.
pos·ses·sions npl biens mpl.
pos·ses·sive adj & n Grammar possessif (m).
pos·si·bil·i·ty possibilité f.
pos·si·ble adj possible; **it is p. (for us) to do it** il (nous) est possible de le faire; **it is p. that** il est possible que (+ subjunctive), **as far as p.** autant que possible; **if p.** si possible; **as much** or **as many as p.** le plus possible.
pos·si·bly adv (perhaps) peut-être; **if you p. can** si cela t'est possible; **to do all one p. can** faire tout son possible.
post[1] (job, place) poste m.

post² *(pole)* poteau *m*; *(of door)* montant *m*.

post (up) *vt (notice etc)* afficher.

post·age tarif *m* (postal) (**to** pour).

post·age stamp timbre-poste *m*.

post·al *adj (services etc)* postal.

post·card carte *f* postale.

post·er affiche *f*; *(for decoration)* poster *m*.

post·grad·u·ate étudiant, -ante *mf* de troisième cycle.

post·man, *pl* -**men** facteur *m*.

post·mark cachet *m* de la poste.

post of·fice (bureau *m* de) poste *f*.

post·pone *vt* remettre (**for** de; **until** à).

post·pone·ment remise *f*.

pot pot *m*; *(for cooking)* marmite *f*; *(drug) Fam* hasch *m*; **pots and pans** casseroles *fpl*.

po·ta·to, *pl* -**oes** pomme *f* de terre.

po·tent *adj* puissant.

po·ten·tial 1 *adj (client, sales)* éventuel. **2** *n* **to have p.** *(of firm etc)* avoir de l'avenir.

pot·ter potier *m*.

pot·ter·y *(art)* poterie *f*; *(objects)* poteries *fpl*; **a piece of p.** une poterie.

pot·ty pot *m* (de bébé).

pouch petit sac *m*; *(of kangaroo)* poche *f*.

poul·try volaille *f*.

pounce *vi* sauter (**on** sur).

pound *(weight)* livre *f* (= 453,6g); *(money)* livre *f* (sterling); *(for cars, dogs)* fourrière *f*.

pour *vt (liquid)* verser; **to p. money into sth** investir beaucoup d'argent dans qch.

pour (down) *vi* **it's pouring (down)** il pleut à verse.

▶**pour in 1** *vt (liquid)* verser. **2** *vi (of water, rain)* entrer à flots; *(of people)* affluer.

▶**pour off** *vt (liquid)* vider.

▶**pour out 1** *vt (liquid)* verser; *(cup etc)* vider. **2** *vi (of liquid)* couler à flots; *(of people)* sortir en masse.

pov·er·ty pauvreté *f*.

pow·der 1 *n* poudre *f*. **2** *vt* **to p. one's face** se poudrer.

pow·dered *adj (milk, eggs)* en poudre; **p. sugar** sucre *m* glace.

pow·er *(ability, authority)* pouvoir *m*; *(strength, nation)* puissance *f*; *(energy)* énergie *f*; *(current)* courant *m*; **in p.** au pouvoir; **p. outage** coupure *f* de courant.

pow·er·ful *adj* puissant.

pow·er plant centrale *f* (électrique).

prac·ti·cal *adj* pratique.

prac·ti·cal joke farce *f*.

prac·ti·cal·ly *adv (almost)* pratiquement.

prac·tice 1 *n (exercise, way of proceeding)* pratique *f*; *(habit)* habitude *f*; *(sports training)* entraînement *m*; *(rehearsal)* répétition *f*; **to be out of p.** avoir perdu la pratique. **2** *vt (sports, art etc)* pratiquer; *(medicine, law)* exercer; *(flute, piano etc)* s'exercer à; *(language)* (s'exercer à) parler (**on** avec). **3** *vi* s'exercer; *(of doctor, lawyer)* exercer.

praise 1 *vt* louer (**for sth** de qch); **to p. sb for doing** louer qn d'avoir fait. **2** *n* louange(s) *f(pl)*.

prank *(trick)* farce *f*.

prawn crevette *f* (rose).

pray 1 *vi* prier; **to p. for good weather/a miracle** prier pour avoir du beau temps/pour un miracle. **2** *vt* **to p. that** prier pour que *(+ subjunctive)*.

prayer prière *f*.

preach *vti* prêcher.

pre·cau·tion précaution *f* (**of doing** de faire); **as a p.** par précaution.

pre·cede *vti* précéder.

prec·e·dent précédent *m*.

pre·ced·ing *adj* précédent.

pre·cinct *(electoral district)* cir-

conscription f; (police district) secteur m.
pre·cious adj précieux.
pre·cise adj précis; (person) minutieux.
pre·co·cious adj (child) précoce.
pred·a·tor prédateur m.
pred·e·ces·sor prédécesseur m.
pre·dic·a·ment situation f fâcheuse.
pre·dict vt prédire.
pre·dict·a·ble adj prévisible.
pre·dic·tion prédiction f.
pref·ace préface f.
pre·fer vt préférer (to à); to p. to do préférer faire.
pref·er·a·ble adj préférable (to à).
pref·er·a·bly adv de préférence.
pref·er·ence préférence f (for pour).
pre·fix préfixe m.
preg·nan·cy grossesse f.
preg·nant adj (woman) enceinte; five months p. enceinte de cinq mois.
pre·his·tor·ic adj préhistorique.
prej·u·dice préjugé m; to be full of p. être plein de préjugés.
pre·lim·i·nar·y adj préliminaire.
pre·ma·ture adj prématuré.
prem·is·es npl locaux mpl; on the p. sur les lieux.
pre·mi·um (insurance) p. prime f (d'assurance).
prep·a·ra·tion préparation f; preparations préparatifs mpl (for de).
pre·pare 1 vt préparer (sth for qch pour; sb for qn à); to p. to do se préparer à faire. 2 vt or to p. for (journey, occasion) faire des préparatifs pour; (exam) préparer.
pre·pared adj (ready) prêt (to do à faire); to be p. for sth (expect) s'attendre à qch.
prep·o·si·tion Grammar préposition f.
prep school école f préparatoire.
pre·school adj préscolaire.

pre·scribe vt (of doctor) prescrire.
pre·scrip·tion (for medicine) ordonnance f.
pres·ence présence f; in the p. of en présence de.
pres·ent[1] **1** adj (not absent) présent (at à; in dans); (year, state, job, house etc) actuel; Grammar p. tense présent m. **2** n (gift) cadeau m; Grammar (tense) présent m; at p. à présent.
pre·sent[2] vt présenter (to à); to p. sb with (gift) offrir à qn; (prize) remettre à qn.
pres·en·ta·tion présentation f; (of prize) remise f.
pres·ent·ly adv (soon) tout à l'heure; (now) à présent.
pres·er·va·tion conservation f.
pre·ser·va·tive agent m de conservation.
pre·serve 1 vt (keep) conserver. 2 n (jam) confiture f.
pre·side vi présider; to p. over or at sth présider qch.
pres·i·den·cy présidence f.
pres·i·dent président, -ente mf.
pres·i·den·tial adj présidentiel.
press[1] **1** n (newspapers, machine) presse f. **2** adj (conference etc) de presse.
press[2] **1** vt (button etc) appuyer sur; (clothes) repasser; to p. sb to do (urge) presser qn de faire. **2** vi (with finger) appuyer (on sur); (of weight) faire pression (on sur).
▸ **press down** vt (button etc) appuyer sur.
pressed adj to be p. (for time) être très bousculé.
▸ **press on** vi (carry on) continuer (with sth qch).
pres·sure pression f; the p. of work le surmenage; under p. (worker, to work) sous pression.
pres·sure cook·er cocotte-minute® f.
pre·sume vt présumer (that que).
pre·tend vti (make believe) faire

semblant (**to do** de faire; **that** que).
pre·text prétexte *m*; **on the p. of/
that** sous prétexte de/que.
pret·ty 1 *adj* joli. **2** *adv* (*rather,
quite*) assez; **p. well, p. much** (*almost*) pratiquement.
pre·vail *vi* prédominer; **to p. upon**
or **on sb to do sth** (*persuade*) persuader qn de faire qch.
pre·vent *vt* empêcher (**from doing** de faire).
pre·ven·tion prévention *f*.
pre·vi·ous *adj* précédent; (*experience*) préalable; **p. to** avant.
pre·vi·ous·ly *adv* avant.
prey proie *f*; **bird of p.** rapace *m*.
price prix *m*.
price list tarif *m*.
prick *vt* piquer (**with** avec); (*burst*)
crever.
prick·ly *adj* (*plant, beard*) piquant.
pride (*satisfaction*) fierté *f*, (*exag-
gerated*) orgueil *m*; (*self-respect*)
amour-propre *m*; **to take p. in** être
fier de; (*take care of*) prendre soin
de.
▶ **pride on** *vt* **to p. oneself on sth/
on doing** s'enorgueillir de qch/de
faire.
priest prêtre *m*.
pri·mar·i·ly *adv* essentiellement.
pri·mar·y 1 *adj* principal; **p. color**
couleur *f* primaire. **2** *n* (*election*)
(*élection f*) primaire *f*.
pri·mar·y school école *f* primaire.
prime min·is·ter premier ministre *m*.
prime numb·er nombre *m* premier.
prim·i·tive *adj* primitif.
prim·rose primevère *f*.
prince prince *m*.
prin·cess princesse *f*.
prin·ci·pal (*of school*) directeur,
-trice *mf*.
print 1 *n* (*of finger, foot etc*) empreinte *f*, (*letters*) caractères *mpl*;
(*engraving*) gravure *f*, (*photo*)

épreuve *f*, **out of p.** épuisé; **p. shop**
imprimerie *f*. **2** *vt* (*book etc*) imprimer; (*photo*) tirer; (*write*) écrire en
caractères d'imprimerie.
print·er (*of computer*) imprimante
f.
print·ing (*industry, process*) imprimerie *f*, (*print run*) tirage *m*; **p.
plant** imprimerie *f*, **p. press** presse
f d'imprimerie.
print-out (*of computer*) sortie *f* sur
imprimante.
▶ **print out** *vti* (*of computer*) imprimer.
pri·or *adj* précédent; (*experience*)
préalable.
pri·or·i·ty priorité *f* (**over** sur).
pris·on prison *f*, **in p.** en prison.
pris·on·er prisonnier, -ière *mf*; **to
take sb p.** faire qn prisonnier.
pri·va·cy intimité *f*.
pri·vate 1 *adj* privé; (*lesson, car,
secretary etc*) particulier; (*report*)
confidentiel; (*dinner etc*) intime. **2**
n (*soldier*) (*simple*) soldat *m*; **in p.**
en privé; (*to have dinner etc*) dans
l'intimité.
pri·vate·ly *adv* en privé; (*to have
dinner etc*) dans l'intimité.
prize prix *m*; (*in lottery*) lot *m*.
prize·win·ner lauréat, -ate *mf*,
(*in lottery*) gagnant, -ante *mf*.
pro¹ pro *m*; **the pros and cons** le
pour et le contre.
pro² *abbr* (*professional*) pro *mf*.
pro- *prefix* (*in favour of*) pro-.
prob·a·ble *adj* probable (**that**
que); (*convincing*) vraisemblable.
prob·a·bly *adv* probablement.
probe 1 *n* (*device*) sonde *f*, (*investigation*) enquête *f*. **2** *vt* sonder; (*investigate*) enquêter sur.
▶ **probe into** *vt* enquêter sur.
prob·lem problème *m*; **no p.!** *Fam*
pas de problème!; **to have a p. doing** avoir du mal à faire.
**prob·lem·at·ic, prob·lem·at-
·i·cal** *adj* problématique.
pro·ceed *vi* (*go*) avancer; (*act*)

procéder; *(continue)* continuer.
pro·ceeds *npl* recette *f.*
pro·cess *(method)* procédé *m* (for doing pour faire); *(chemical, economic etc)* processus *m*; **in the p. of doing** en train de faire.
pro·cessed cheese fromage *m* en tranches.
pro·ces·sion cortège *m.*
pro·duce 1 *vt (manufacture, cause etc)* produire; *(bring out)* sortir *(pistolet, mouchoir etc)*, *(passport)* présenter. **2** *n* produits *mpl.*
pro·duc·er *(of goods, film)* producteur, -trice *mf.*
prod·uct produit *m.*
pro·duc·tion production *f*, *(of play)* mise *f* en scène.
pro·duc·tive *adj* productif.
pro·duc·tiv·i·ty productivité *f.*
pro·fes·sion profession *f.*
pro·fes·sion·al 1 *adj* professionnel; *(piece of work)* de professionnel. **2** *n* professionnel, -elle *mf.*
pro·fes·sor professeur *m* (d'université).
prof·it 1 *n* profit *m*, bénéfice *m*; **to sell at a p.** vendre à profit. **2** *vi* **to p. by** *or* **from sth** tirer profit de qch.
prof·it·a·ble *adj* rentable.
pro·found *adj* profond.
pro·gram 1 *n (schedule, of computer)* programme *m*; *(broadcast)* émission *f.* **2** *vt* programmer.
prog·ress 1 *n* progrès *m(pl)*; **to make p.** faire des progrès; *(when driving etc)* bien avancer; **in p.** en cours. **2** *vi* progresser; *(of story, meeting)* se dérouler.
pro·gres·sive *adj* progressif.
pro·hib·it *vt* interdire (**sb from doing** à qn de faire).
proj·ect projet *m* (for sth pour qch); *(at school)* étude *f.*
pro·jec·tor *(for films etc)* projecteur *m.*
pro·long *vt* prolonger.
prom·i·nent *adj (person)* important.

prom·ise 1 *n* promesse *f*; **to show p.** être prometteur. **2** *vt* promettre (**sb sth, sth to sb** qch à qn; **to do** de faire; **that** que). **3** *vi* **I p.!** je te le promets!; **p.?** promis?
prom·is·ing *adj (situation)* prometteur *(f-euse)*.
pro·mote *vt* **to p. sb** *(in job etc)* donner de l'avancement à qn.
pro·mo·tion *(of person)* avancement *m.*
prompt *adj (speedy)* rapide.
prone *adj* **p. to** *(illnesses, accidents)* prédisposé à.
pro·noun pronom *m.*
pro·nounce *vt* prononcer.
pro·nun·ci·a·tion prononciation *f.*
proof *(evidence)* preuve(s) *f(pl)*.
prop 1 *n (physical support)* support *m*; *(psychological support)* soutien *m.* **2** *vt (lean)* appuyer.
prop·a·gan·da propagande *f.*
pro·pel·ler hélice *f.*
prop·er *adj (suitable, respectable)* convenable; *(downright)* véritable; *(noun, meaning)* propre; **the p. address/method/etc** *(correct)* la bonne adresse/méthode/*etc*.
prop·er·ly *adv* comme il faut, convenablement.
prop·er·ty *(building, possessions)* propriété *f.*
pro·por·tion *(ratio)* proportion *f*; *(portion)* partie *f*, **proportions** *(size)* dimensions *fpl.*
pro·por·tion·al *adj* proportionnel (**to** à).
pro·pos·al proposition *f*, *(of marriage)* demande *f* (en mariage).
pro·pose 1 *vt (suggest)* proposer (**to** à; **that** que (+ *subjunctive*)). **2** *vi* faire une demande (en mariage) (**to** à).
prop·o·si·tion proposition *f.*
props *npl (in theater)* accessoires *mpl.*
▶**prop up** *vt (ladder etc)* appuyer (**against** contre); *(one's head)* caler; *(wall)* étayer.

prose prose f.

pros·e·cute vt poursuivre (en justice).

pros·e·cu·tion (action) poursuites fpl judiciaires; **the p.** = le ministère public.

pros·pect (outlook, possibility) perspective f (of de); (future) prospects perspectives fpl d'avenir.

pros·per·i·ty prospérité f.

pros·per·ous adj riche.

pro·tect vt protéger (**from** de; **against** contre).

pro·tec·tion protection f.

pro·tec·tive adj (clothes etc) de protection.

pro·test 1 n protestation f (**against** contre); (demonstration) manifestation f. 2 vi protester (**against** contre); (of students etc) contester.

Prot·es·tant adj & n protestant, -ante (mf).

pro·test·er (student etc) contestataire mf.

pro·trac·tor (for measuring) rapporteur m.

proud adj fier (of de; **to do** de faire); (conceited) orgueilleux.

proud·ly adv fièrement; (conceitedly) orgueilleusement.

prove 1 vt prouver (**that** que). 2 vi **to p. difficult** /etc s'avérer difficile/ etc.

prov·erb proverbe m.

pro·vide vt (supply) fournir (**sb with sth** qch à qn); **to p. sb with sth** (equip) pourvoir qn de qch.

pro·vid·ed, pro·vid·ing conj **p. (that)** pourvu que (+ subjunctive).

▶ **provide for** vt pourvoir aux besoins de.

prov·ince province f; **the provinces** la province.

pro·vin·cial adj provincial.

pro·vi·sion·al adj provisoire.

pro·voke vt (annoy) agacer.

prowl (a·round) vi rôder.

prowl·er rôdeur, -euse mf.

prune 1 n pruneau m. 2 vt (tree, bush) tailler.

prun·ing shears sécateur m.

psy·chi·at·ric adj psychiatrique.

psy·chi·a·trist psychiatre mf.

psy·cho·log·i·cal adj psychologique.

psy·chol·o·gist psychologue mf.

psy·chol·o·gy psychologie f.

pub pub m.

pub·lic 1 adj public (f -ique); (library, swimming pool) municipal. 2 n public m; **in p.** en public.

pub·li·ca·tion publication f.

pub·lic·i·ty publicité f.

pub·lish vt publier; (book, author) éditer.

pub·lish·er éditeur, -trice mf.

pub·lish·ing (profession) édition f.

pud·ding pudding m; **rice p.** riz m au lait.

pud·dle flaque f (d'eau).

puff 1 n (of smoke, wind) bouffée f. 2 vi souffler.

▶ **puff at** vt (cigar etc) tirer sur.

pull 1 n **to give sth a p.** tirer qch. 2 vt tirer; (trigger) appuyer sur; (tooth) arracher; (muscle) se claquer; **to p. apart** or **to pieces** mettre en pièces. 3 vi tirer (**at, on** sur); (go, move) aller.

▶ **pull along** vt traîner (**to** jusqu'à).

▶ **pull away** 1 vt (move) éloigner; (snatch) arracher (**from** à). 2 vi (in vehicle) démarrer; **to p. away from** s'éloigner de.

▶ **pull back** 1 vi se retirer. 2 vt retirer; (curtains) ouvrir.

▶ **pull down** vt baisser; (knock down) faire tomber; (demolish) démolir.

▶ **pull in** vt (into room etc) faire entrer (de force); (crowd) attirer. 2 vi arriver; (stop in vehicle) se garer.

▶ **pull off** vt (remove) enlever.

▶ **pull on** vt (boots etc) mettre.

▶ **pull out** 1 vt (tooth, hair) arracher; (cork, pin) enlever; (from pocket

etc) tirer, sortir (**from** de). **2** *vi*
(*move out in vehicle*) déboîter;
(*withdraw*) se retirer (**from, of** de).
pull·o·ver pull(-over) *m*.

▸ **pull over 1** *vt* traîner (**to** jusqu'à);
(*knock down*) faire tomber. **2** *vi* (*in
vehicle*) se ranger (sur le côté).

▸ **pull through** *vi* s'en tirer.

▸ **pull up 1** *vt* (*socks, sleeve, collar,
shade*) remonter; (*plant,
tree*) arracher; (*chair*) approcher. **2**
vi (*in vehicle*) s'arrêter.

pulse pouls *m*.

pump 1 *n* pompe *f*; (**air**) p. (*in service station*) gonfleur *m*. **2** *vt*
pomper.

pump·kin potiron *m*, citrouille *f*.

▸ **pump up** *vt* (*mattress etc*) gonfler.

punch¹ 1 *n* (*blow*) coup *m* de poing.
2 *vt* donner un coup de poing à
(*qn*).

punch² 1 *n* (*for paper*) perforeuse *f*.
2 *vt* (*ticket*) poinçonner; (*with date*)
composter; **to p. a hole in sth** faire
un trou dans qch.

punc·tu·al *adj* (*on time*) à l'heure;
(*regularly*) ponctuel.

punc·tu·a·tion ponctuation *f*.

punc·ture 1 *n* crevaison *f*. **2** *vti*
(*burst*) crever.

pun·ish *vt* punir (**for sth** de qch;
for doing pour avoir fait).

pun·ish·ment punition *f*.

pup (*dog*) chiot *m*.

pu·pil élève *mf*; (*of eye*) pupille *f*.

pup·pet marionnette *f*.

pup·py chiot *m*.

pur·chase 1 *n* achat *m*. **2** *vt* acheter (**from sb** à qn; **for sb** à *or* pour
qn).

pur·chas·er acheteur, -euse *mf*.

pure *adj* pur.

pure·ly *adv* (*only*) strictement.

pur·ple 1 *adj* violet (*f* -ette). **2** *n*
violet *m*.

pur·pose (*aim*) but *m*; **for this p.**
dans ce but; **on p.** exprès.

pur·pose·ly *adv* exprès.

purse (*for coins*) porte-monnaie *m*

inv; (*handbag*) sac *m* à main.

pur·sue *vt* (*inquiry, aim etc*) poursuivre.

pur·suit poursuite *f*; (*of pleasure,
glory*) quête *f*; (*pastime*) occupation *f*.

push 1 *n* **to give sb/sth a p.** pousser qn/qch. **2** *vt* pousser (**to, as far
as** jusqu'à); **to p. sth into/between**
enfoncer qch dans/entre; **to p. sb
into doing** pousser qn à faire. **3** *vi*
pousser.

push (down) *vt* (*button*) appuyer
sur; (*lever*) abaisser.

▸ **push around** *vt* (*bully*) marcher
sur les pieds à.

▸ **push aside** *vt* écarter.

▸ **push away** *or* **back** *vt* repousser.

push-but·ton *adj* p. phone téléphone *m* à touches.

▸ **push on** *vi* continuer (**with sth** qch).

▸ **push over** *vt* renverser.

▸ **push through** *vt* **to p. one's way
through** se frayer un chemin (**a
crowd** à travers une foule).

▸ **push up** *vt* (*lever, sleeve, collar*)
relever; (*increase*) augmenter.

push·y *adj Fam* batailleur, -euse.

puss (*cat*) minou *m*.

put* *vt* mettre; (*money*) placer (**into** dans); (*question*) poser (**to** à);
(*say*) dire.

▸ **put across** *vt* (*message etc*) communiquer (**to** à).

▸ **put aside** *vt* (*money, object*) mettre de côté.

▸ **put away** *vt* (*book, car etc*) ranger;
(*criminal*) mettre en prison.

▸ **put back** *vt* (*replace, postpone*) remettre; (*telephone receiver*) raccrocher.

▸ **put by** *vt* (*money*) mettre de côté.

▸ **put down** *vt* (*on floor etc*) poser;
(*passenger*) déposer; (*a deposit*)
verser; (*write down*) inscrire.

▸ **put forward** *vt* (*candidate*) proposer (**for** à).

▸ **put in** *vt* (*sth into box etc*) mettre
dedans; (*insert*) introduire; (*add*)

ajouter; *(install)* installer; *(application)* faire.

▶ **put off** *vt* renvoyer (à plus tard); *(gas, radio)* fermer; **to p. sb off** dissuader qn (**doing** de faire); *(disgust)* dégoûter qn.

▶ **put on** *vt (clothes etc)* mettre; *(weight)* prendre; *(gas, radio)* mettre; *(record, cassette)* passer; *(clock)* avancer; *(lid)* mettre en place.

▶ **put out** *vt (take outside)* sortir; *(arm, leg)* étendre; *(hand)* tendre; *(gas, light)* éteindre; *(bother)* déranger.

▶ **put through** *vt (on phone)* passer qn (**to** à).

▶ **put together** *vt* mettre ensemble; *(assemble)* assembler; *(compose)* composer.

put·ty mastic *m*.

▶ **put up 1** *vi (stay)* descendre (**at a hotel** à un hôtel). **2** *vt (lift)* lever; *(window)* remonter; *(tent, statue, ladder)* dresser; *(building)* construire; *(umbrella)* ouvrir; *(picture)* mettre; *(price)* augmenter; *(candidate)* proposer (**for** à); *(guest)* loger.

▶ **put up with** *vt* supporter.

puz·zle 1 *n* mystère *m*; *(jigsaw)* puzzle *m*. **2** *vt* laisser perplexe.

puz·zled *adj* perplexe.

puz·zling *adj* curieux.

py·lon pylône *m*.

pyr·a·mid pyramide *f*.

Q

qual·i·fi·ca·tion diplôme *m*; **qualifications** *(skills)* qualités *fpl* nécessaires (**for** pour; **to do** pour faire).

qual·i·fied *adj (able)* qualifié (**to do** pour faire); *(teacher etc)* diplômé.

qual·i·fy *vt* obtenir son diplôme (**as a doctor/***etc* de médecin/*etc*); *(in sports)* se qualifier (**for** pour).

qual·i·ty qualité *f*.

quan·ti·ty quantité *f*.

quar·rel 1 *n* dispute *f*; **to pick a q.** chercher des histoires (**with sb** à qn). **2** *vi* se disputer (**with sb** avec qn).

quar·rel·ing disputes *fpl*.

quar·ry *(to extract stone etc)* carrière *f*.

quart litre *m (mesure approximative = 0.95 litre)*.

quar·ter¹ quart *m*; *(money)* quart *m* de dollar; *(of fruit)* quartier *m*; *(of school/fiscal year)* trimestre *m*; **to divide sth into quarters** diviser qch en quatre; **q. (of a) pound** quart *m* de livre; **a q. past** *or* **after nine** neuf heures et quart *or* un quart; **a q. to nine** neuf heures moins le quart.

quar·ter² *(district)* quartier *m*.

quar·ter·back quarterback *m*.

quartz *(watch etc)* à quartz.

quay quai *m*, débarcadère *m*.

queen reine *f*, Chess, Cards dame *f*.

quench *vt* **to q. one's thirst** se désaltérer.

que·ry *(question)* question *f*.

ques·tion 1 *n* question *f*; **it's out of the q.** il n'en est pas question. **2** *vt* interroger *(qn)* (**about** sur); *(doubt)* mettre *(qch)* en question.

ques·tion·a·ble *adj* discutable.

ques·tion mark point *m* d'interrogation.

ques·tion·naire questionnaire *m*.

quib·ble *vi* ergoter (**over** sur).

quiche quiche *f*.

quick 1 *adj* rapide; **be q.!** fais vite!; **to have a q. meal/***etc* manger/*etc* en vitesse. **2** *adv* vite.

quick·ly *adv* vite.

qui·et *adj (silent, peaceful)* tranquille; *(machine, vehicle)* silencieux; *(voice, sound)* doux (*f* douce); **to be** or **keep q.** (shut up) se taire; (make no noise) ne pas faire de bruit; **q.!** silence!; **to keep q. about sth** ne pas parler de qch.

qui·et·ly adv tranquillement; (not loudly) doucement; (silently) silencieusement.

quilt édredon m.

quit* **1 to q. doing** arrêter de faire. **2** vi abandonner; (resign) démissionner.

quite adv (entirely) tout à fait; (really) vraiment; (rather) assez; **q. a lot** pas mal (**of** de).

quiz, pl **quizzes** (in school) contrôle m; **q. show** jeu(-concours) m.

quo·ta quota m.

quo·ta·tion citation f; (estimate) devis m.

quo·ta·tion marks guillemets mpl; **in q.** entre guillemets.

quote **1** vt citer; (reference) rappeler; (price) indiquer. **2** vi **to q. from** citer. **3** n = **quotation**.

R

rab·bi rabbin m.

rab·bit lapin m.

ra·bies rage f.

race¹ **1** n (contest) course f. **2** vt (horse) faire courir; **to r.** (**against** or **with**) **sb** faire une course avec qn. **3** vi (run) courir.

race² (group) race f.

race·car voiture f de course.

race·car driv·er coureur m automobile.

race·horse cheval m de course.

race·track champ m de courses.

ra·cial adj racial.

ra·cial·ism, rac·ism racisme m.

rac·ing courses fpl.

ra·cist adj & n raciste (mf).

rack (for bottles, letters etc) casier m; (for drying dishes) égouttoir m; (luggage) **r.** (on bus, train) filet m à bagages.

rack·et (for tennis) raquette f; (din) vacarme m.

ra·dar radar m.

ra·di·a·tion radiation f.

ra·di·a·tor radiateur m.

rad·i·cal adj radical.

ra·di·o, pl **-os** radio f; (set) poste m de radio; **on** or **over the r.** à la radio.

ra·di·o·ac·tive adj radioactif.

rad·ish radis m.

ra·di·us, pl **-dii** (of circle) rayon m.

raf·fle tombola f.

raft (boat) radeau m.

rag (old clothing) haillon m; (for dusting etc) chiffon m; **in rags** (clothes) en loques; (person) en haillons.

rage rage f; **to fly into a r.** se mettre en rage.

rag·ged adj (clothes) en loques; (person) en haillons.

raid **1** n (military) raid m; (by police) descente f; (by thieves) hold-up m inv; **air r.** raid m aérien. **2** vt faire un raid dans; (of police) faire une descente dans; (of thieves) faire un hold-up dans.

rail (for train) rail m; (rod on balcony) balustrade f; (on stairs) rampe f; **by r.** (to travel) par le train; (to send) par chemin de fer.

rail·ing (of balcony) balustrade f; **railings** (fence) grille f.

rail·road **1** n chemin m de fer; **r.** (**track**) voie f ferrée. **2** adj (ticket) de chemin de fer; **r. line** ligne f de chemin de fer.

rain **1** n pluie f; **in the r.** sous la pluie. **2** vi pleuvoir; **it's raining** il pleut.

rain·bow arc-en-ciel m.

rain·coat imper(méable) m.

rain·y adj pluvieux.

raise **1** vt (lift) lever; (child, family, voice) élever; (salary, price) augmenter; *(question)* soulever; **to r. money** réunir des fonds. **2** *n* augmentation *f* (de salaire).

rai·sin raisin *m* sec.

rake 1 *n* râteau *m*. **2** *vt (garden)* ratisser.

rake (up) *vt (leaves)* ratisser.

ral·ly *(political)* rassemblement *m*.

▸**rally (a)round 1** *vt* venir en aide à. **2** *vi* venir en aide.

ram 1 *n (animal)* bélier *m*. **2** *vt (vehicle)* emboutir; **to r. sth into sth** enfoncer qch dans qch.

ram·ble randonnée *f*.

ramp *(slope for wheelchair etc)* rampe *f* (d'accès).

ran *pt de* **run**.

ranch ranch *m*.

ran·dom 1 *n* **at r.** au hasard. **2** *adj (choice)* (fait) au hasard; *(sample)* prélevé au hasard; **r. check** *(by police)* contrôle-surprise *m*.

range 1 *n (of gun, voice etc)* portée *f*, *(of singer's voice)* étendue *f*; *(of colors, prices, products)* gamme *f*; *(of sizes)* choix *m*; *(of mountains)* chaîne *f*; *(stove)* cuisinière *f*. **2** *vi (vary)* varier (**from** de; **to** à).

rank rang *m*.

ran·som *(money)* rançon *f*.

rape 1 *vt* violer. **2** *n* viol *m*.

rap·id *adj* rapide.

rap·id·ly *adv* rapidement.

rap·ist violeur *m*.

rare *adj* rare; *(meat)* saignant.

rare·ly *adv* rarement.

ras·cal coquin, -ine *mf*.

rash 1 *n* éruption *f*. **2** *adj* irréfléchi.

rash·ly *adv* sans réfléchir.

rasp·ber·ry framboise *f*, **r. jam** confiture *f* de framboises.

rat rat *m*.

rate 1 *n (level)* taux *m*; *(speed)* vitesse *f*, *(price)* tarif *m*; **at the r. of** à une vitesse de; *(amount)* à raison de; **at this r.** *(slow speed)* à ce train-là; **at any r.** en tout cas. **2** *vt* évaluer (**at** à); *(regard)* considérer (**as** comme); *(deserve)* mériter.

rath·er *adv (preferably, quite)* plutôt; **I'd r. stay** j'aimerais mieux rester (**than** que); **r. than leave/etc** plutôt que de partir/etc.

rat·ing *(ranking)* classement *m*; *(appraisal)* évaluation *f*, **ratings** *(for TV, radio program)* indice *m* d'écoute.

ra·tio, *pl* **-os** proportion *f*.

ra·tion 1 *n* ration *f*, **rations** *(food)* vivres *mpl*. **2** *vt* rationner.

ra·tion·al *adj (person)* raisonnable.

ra·tion·ing rationnement *m*.

rat·tle 1 *n (baby's toy)* hochet *m*. **2** *vi* faire du bruit; *(of window)* trembler. **3** *vt (shake)* secouer.

rav·en·ous *adj* **I'm r.** j'ai une faim de loup.

raw *adj (vegetable etc)* cru; *(skin)* écorché; **r. material** matière *f* première.

ray *(of light, sun)* rayon *m*.

ra·zor rasoir *m*.

re- *prefix* ré-, re-, r-.

reach 1 *vt (place, distant object, aim)* atteindre; *(gain access to)* accéder à; *(of letter)* parvenir à (qn); *(contact)* joindre (qn); *(conclusion)* arriver à; **to r. sb sth** passer qch à qn. **2** *vi* s'étendre (**to** à); *(with arm)* (é)tendre le bras (**for** pour prendre). **3** *n* portée *f*; **within r. of** à portée de; *(near)* à proximité de; **within (easy) r.** *(object)* à portée de main.

▸**reach out** *vi* (é)tendre le bras (**for** pour prendre).

re·act *vi* réagir (**against** contre; **to** à).

re·ac·tion réaction *f*.

re·ac·tor réacteur *m (nucléaire)*.

read* 1 *vt* lire; *(meter)* relever; *(of instrument)* indiquer. **2** *vi* lire; **to r. to sb** faire la lecture à qn.

▸**read aloud** *vt* lire (à haute voix).

▸**read back, read over** *vt* relire.

read·er lecteur, -trice *mf*, *(book)* livre *m* de lecture.

read·i·ly *adv (willingly)* volontiers; *(easily)* facilement.

read·ing lecture *f, (of meter)* relevé *m; (by instrument)* indication *f.*

▶ **read through** *vt* parcourir.

▶ **read up (on)** *vt* étudier.

read·y *adj* prêt (**to do** à faire; **for sth** à *or* pour qch); **to get sth/sb r.** préparer qch/qn; **to get r.** se préparer (**for sth** à *or* pour qch; **to do** à faire); **r. cash** argent *m* liquide.

read·y-made *adj* tout fait.

read·y-to-wear *adj* **r. clothes** prêt-à-porter *m inv.*

real *adj* vrai; *(life, world)* réel.

real es·tate biens *mpl* immobiliers; **r. estate agent** agent *m* immobilier.

re·al·is·tic *adj* réaliste.

re·al·i·ty réalité *f.*

re·al·ize *vt (know)* se rendre compte de; *(understand)* comprendre (**that** que).

real·ly *adv* vraiment.

Real·tor® agent *m* immobilier.

rear 1 *n (back part)* arrière *m;* **in** *or* **at the r.** à l'arrière. **2** *adj* arrière *inv;* de derrière. **3** *vt (family, animals)* élever.

rear (up) *vi (of horse)* se cabrer.

re·ar·range *vt (hair, room)* réarranger; *(plans)* changer.

rea·son 1 *n* raison *f;* **the r. for/why…** la raison de/pour laquelle…; **for no r.** sans raison. **2** *vi* raisonner.

rea·son·a·ble *adj* raisonnable.

rea·son·a·bly *adv (fairly, rather)* assez.

rea·son·ing raisonnement *m.*

▶ **reason with** *vt* raisonner.

re·as·sure *vt* rassurer.

re·as·sur·ing *adj* rassurant.

re·bel 1 *n* rebelle *mf, (against parents etc)* révolté, -ée *mf.* **2** *vi* se révolter (**against** contre).

re·bel·lion révolte *f.*

re·bound 1 *vi (of ball)* rebondir;

(of stone) ricocher. **2** *n* rebond *m;* ricochet *m.*

re·build *vt* reconstruire.

re·call *vt (remember)* se rappeler (**that** que; **doing** avoir fait); **to r. sth to sb** rappeler qch à qn.

re·ceipt *(for payment, object left etc)* reçu *m (**for** de);* **on r. of** dès réception de.

re·ceive *vt* recevoir.

re·ceiv·er *(of phone)* combiné *m;* **to pick up the r.** *(of phone)* décrocher.

re·cent *adj* récent; **in r. months** ces mois-ci.

re·cent·ly *adv* récemment.

re·cep·tion *(party, of radio etc)* réception *f,* **r. (desk)** réception *f,* accueil *m.*

re·cep·tion·ist secrétaire *mf,* réceptionniste *mf.*

re·charge *vt (battery)* recharger.

rec·i·pe recette *f (**for** de).

re·cip·i·ent *(of gift, letter)* destinataire *mf, (of award)* lauréat, -ate *mf.*

re·cite *vt (poem)* réciter; *(list)* énumérer.

reck·less *adj (rash)* imprudent.

reck·on *vt (calculate)* calculer; *(think) Fam* penser (**that** que).

▶ **reckon on** *vt (rely on)* compter sur; **to r. on doing** compter faire.

▶ **reckon with** *vt (take into account)* compter avec.

re·claim *vt (baggage at airport)* récupérer.

rec·og·nize *vt* reconnaître (**by** à).

rec·ol·lect *vt* se souvenir de; **to r. that** se souvenir que.

rec·ol·lec·tion souvenir *m.*

rec·om·mend *vt* recommander (**to** à; **for** pour); **to r. sb to do** recommander à qn de faire.

rec·om·men·da·tion recommandation *f.*

re·cord 1 *n (best performance)* record *m; (register)* registre *m; (mention)* mention *f, (background)* antécédents *mpl*; **(public) records** archives *fpl*; **to keep a r. of** noter. **2** *adj* (*time, number etc*) record *inv*. **3** *vt* (*on tape, in register*) enregistrer; (*in diary*) noter. **4** *vi* enregistrer.

re·cord·ed *adj* (*music, message, tape*) enregistré; (*TV broadcast*) en différé.

re·cord·er flûte *f* à bec; **(tape) r.** magnétophone *m*; **(video) r.** magnétoscope *m*.

re·cord·ing enregistrement *m*.

re·cov·er 1 *vt* (*get back*) retrouver. **2** *vi* (*from illness etc*) se remettre (**from** de); (*of economy*) se redresser.

rec·re·a·tion récréation *f*.

re·cruit recrue *f*.

rec·tan·gle rectangle *m*.

rec·tan·gu·lar *adj* rectangulaire.

re·cy·cle *vt* recycler.

red 1 *adj* rouge; (*hair*) roux (*f* rousse); **to turn r.** rougir; **r. light** (*traffic light*) feu *m* rouge. **2** *n* (*color*) rouge *m*; **in the r.** (*company, account*) dans le rouge, en déficit.

red-hand·ed *adj* **caught r.** pris en flagrant délit.

red·head roux *m*, rousse *f*.

red-hot *adj* brûlant.

re·di·rect *vt* (*mail*) faire suivre.

re·do* *vt* (*exercise, house etc*) refaire.

re·duce *vt* réduire (**to** à; **by** de); **at a reduced price** (*ticket, goods*) à prix réduit.

re·duc·tion réduction *f* (**in** de).

re·dun·dan·cy superfluité *f*.

re·dun·dant *adj* superflu.

reed (*plant*) roseau *m*.

reef récif *m*.

reel (*of thread, film*) bobine *f*; (*film itself*) bande *f*.

re·fec·to·ry réfectoire *m*.

re·fer *vi* **to r. to** (*mention*) faire allusion à; (*speak of*) parler de; (*apply to*) s'appliquer à. **2** *vt* **to r. sth to sb** soumettre qch à qn.

ref·e·ree 1 *n Sports* arbitre *m*. **2** *vt* arbitrer.

ref·er·ence (*in book, for job*) référence *f*; (*mention*) mention *f* (**to** de); **with r. to** concernant; **r. book** ouvrage *m* de référence.

ref·er·en·dum référendum *m*.

re·fill 1 *vt* remplir (à nouveau); (*lighter, pen*) recharger. **2** *n* recharge *f*; **a r.** (*drink*) un autre verre.

re·flect *vt* (*light etc*) refléter; **to be reflected** se refléter.

re·flec·tion (*image*) reflet *m*.

re·flex réflexe *m*.

re·form réforme *f*.

re·frain *vi* s'abstenir (**from doing** de faire).

re·fresh *vt* (*of bath, drink*) rafraîchir; (*of sleep, rest*) délasser.

re·fresh·er course cours *m* de recyclage.

re·fresh·ing *adj* (*drink*) rafraîchissant.

re·fresh·ments *npl* (*drinks*) rafraîchissements *mpl*; (*snacks*) petites choses *fpl* à grignoter.

re·frig·er·ate *vt* (*food*) conserver au frais.

re·frig·er·a·tor réfrigérateur *m*.

ref·uge refuge *m*; **to take r.** se réfugier.

ref·u·gee réfugié, -ée *mf*.

re·fund 1 *vt* rembourser. **2** *n* remboursement *m*.

re·fus·al refus *m*.

re·fuse 1 *vt* refuser (**sb sth** qch à qn; **to do** de faire). **2** *vi* refuser.

re·gain *vt* (*lost ground*) regagner; (*health, strength*) retrouver.

re·gard 1 *vt* considérer; **as regards** en ce qui concerne. **2** *n* considération *f* (**for** pour); **to have (a) high r. for sb** estimer qn; **to give one's regards to sb** transmettre son meilleur souvenir à qn.

re·gard·ing *prep* en ce qui concerne.

re·gard·less 1 *adj* **r. of** sans tenir

compte de. **2** *adv (all the same)* quand même.

reg·i·ment régiment *m*.

re·gion région *f*; **in the r. of $50/ etc** *(about)* dans les 50 dollars/ *etc*.

re·gion·al *adj* régional.

reg·is·ter 1 *n* registre *m*. **2** *vt (birth etc)* déclarer; **registered letter** lettre recommandée; **to send by registered mail** envoyer en recommandé. **3** *vi (enroll)* s'inscrire (**for a course** à un cours); *(in hotel)* signer le registre.

reg·is·tra·tion *(enrollment)* inscription *f*; **r. (number)** *(of vehicle)* numéro *m* d'immatriculation.

re·gret 1 *vt* regretter (**doing, to do** de faire; **that** que (+ *subjunctive*)). **2** *n* regret *m*.

reg·u·lar *adj (steady)* régulier; *(surface)* uni; *(usual)* habituel; *(price, size)* normal; *(listener)* fidèle.

reg·u·lar·ly *adv* régulièrement.

reg·u·late *vt (adjust)* régler; *(control)* réglementer.

reg·u·la·tions *npl (rules)* règlement *m*.

re·hears·al répétition *f*.

re·hearse 1 *vt (a play etc)* répéter. **2** *vi* répéter.

reign 1 *n* règne *m*; **in the r. of** sous le règne de. **2** *vi* régner (**over** sur).

rein·deer *inv* renne *m*.

re·in·force *vt* renforcer (**with** de).

re·in·force·ments *npl (troops)* renforts *mpl*.

reins *npl (for horse)* rênes *fpl*; *(for baby)* bretelles *fpl* de sécurité (avec laisse).

re·ject *vt* rejeter.

re·jec·tion rejet *m*; *(of candidate)* refus *m*.

re·joice *vi (celebrate)* faire la fête; *(be delighted)* se réjouir (**over** *or* **at sth** de qch).

re·lat·ed *adj (linked)* lié (**to** à); **to be r. to sb** *(by family)* être parent de qn.

► **relate to** *vt (apply to)* se rapporter à.

re·la·tion *(relative)* parent, -ente *mf*; *(relationship)* rapport *m*; **international relations** relations *fpl* internationales.

re·la·tion·ship *(in family)* lien(s) *m(pl)* de parenté; *(relations)* relations *fpl*; *(connection)* rapport *m*.

rel·a·tive 1 *n (person)* parent, -ente *mf*. **2** *adj* relatif; **r. to** en rapport avec.

rel·a·tive·ly *adv* relativement.

re·lax 1 *vt (person)* détendre; *(grip, pressure)* relâcher. **2** *vi* se détendre; **r.!** *(calm down)* du calme!

re·lax·a·tion *(rest)* détente *f*.

re·laxed *adj* décontracté.

re·lease 1 *vt (free)* libérer (**from** de); *(bomb)* lâcher; *(brake)* desserrer; *(film, record)* sortir; *(trapped person)* dégager. **2** *n (of prisoner)* libération *f*; *(of film etc)* sortie *f*; **press r.** communiqué *m* de presse.

rel·e·vant *adj* pertinent (**to** à); *(useful)* utile; **that's not r.** ça n'a rien à voir.

re·li·a·bil·i·ty fiabilité *f*; *(of person)* sérieux *m*.

re·li·a·ble *adj* fiable; *(person)* sérieux.

re·lief *(from pain etc)* soulagement *m* (**from** à); *(help)* secours *m*; *(in geography etc)* relief *m*.

re·lieve *vt (pain, person etc)* soulager; *(take over from)* relayer (qn).

re·li·gion religion *f*.

re·li·gious *adj* religieux.

rel·ish 1 *n* condiment *m*. **2** *vt (food, wine)* savourer.

re·load *vt (gun, camera)* recharger.

re·luc·tance manque *m* d'enthousiasme (**to do** de faire).

re·luc·tant *adj* peu enthousiaste (**to do** pour faire).

re·luc·tant·ly *adv* sans enthousiasme.

▶ **re·ly on** vt (count on) compter sur; (be dependent on) dépendre de.

re·main vi rester.

re·main·ing adj qui reste(nt).

re·mark 1 n remarque f. **2** vt (faire) remarquer (**that** que). **3** vi **to r. on sth** faire des remarques sur qch.

re·mark·a·ble adj remarquable (**for** par).

re·mark·a·bly adv remarquablement.

re·match Sports revanche f.

re·me·di·al adj **r. class** cours m de rattrapage.

rem·e·dy 1 n remède m. **2** vt remédier à.

re·mem·ber 1 vt se souvenir de, se rappeler; **to r. that/doing** se rappeler que/d'avoir fait; **to r. to do** penser à faire. **2** vi se souvenir, se rappeler.

re·mind vt rappeler (**sb of sth** qch à qn; **sb that** à qn que); **to r. sb to do** faire penser à qn à faire.

re·mind·er rappel m; **to give sb a r. to do** faire penser à qn à faire.

re·morse remords m(pl).

re·mote adj (far-off) lointain; (isolated) isolé; (slight) petit.

re·mote con·trol télécommande f.

re·mov·al (of clothes, stain etc) enlèvement m; (of obstacle, word) suppression f.

re·move vt (clothes, stain etc) enlever (**from sb** à qn; **from sth** de qch); (obstacle, word) supprimer.

re·new vt renouveler; (resume) reprendre; (library book) renouveler le prêt de.

rent 1 n (for house etc) loyer m. **2** vt louer.

rent·al (of house, car) location f.

▶ **rent out** vt louer.

re·or·gan·ize vt (firm etc) réorganiser.

re·pair 1 vt réparer. **2** n réparation f; **in bad r.** en mauvais état.

re·pair·man, pl -men réparateur m, dépanneur m.

re·pay vt (pt & pp repaid) (pay back) rembourser; (reward) récompenser (**for** de).

re·pay·ment (paying back) remboursement m; (rewarding) récompense f.

re·peat 1 vt répéter (**that** que); (promise, threat) réitérer; (class) redoubler; **to r. oneself** se répéter. **2** n (on TV, radio) rediffusion f.

re·peat·ed adj (attempts etc) répétés.

re·peat·ed·ly adv à maintes reprises, de nombreuses fois.

re·pel vt repousser.

rep·e·ti·tion répétition f.

re·pet·i·tive adj répétitif.

re·place vt (take the place of) remplacer (**by, with** par); (put back) remettre; (telephone receiver) raccrocher.

re·place·ment (person) remplaçant, -ante mf; (machine part) pièce f de rechange.

re·play 1 n match m rejoué; (instant or action) r. répétition f d'une séquence précédente. **2** vt (match) rejouer.

rep·li·ca copie f exacte.

re·ply 1 vti répondre (**to** à; **that** que). **2** n réponse f.

re·port 1 n (account) rapport m; (of meeting) compte rendu m; (in media) reportage m; (of pupil) bulletin m; (rumor) rumeur f. **2** vt rapporter; (announce) annoncer (**that** que); (notify) signaler (**to** à); (inform on) dénoncer (**to** à). **3** vi faire un rapport; (of journalist) faire un reportage (**on** sur); (go) se présenter (**to** à; **to sb** chez qn).

re·port card bulletin m (scolaire).

re·port·ed adj (speech) indirect.

re·port·er reporter m.

rep·re·sent vt représenter.

rep·re·sen·ta·tive représentant, -ante mf.

re·pro·duce 1 *vt* reproduire. **2** *vi* se reproduire.

re·pro·duc·tion reproduction *f.*

rep·tile reptile *m.*

re·pub·lic république *f.*

rep·u·ta·ble *adj* de bonne réputation.

rep·u·ta·tion réputation *f*; **to have a r. for being** avoir la réputation d'être.

re·quest 1 *n* demande *f* (**for** de). **2** *vt* demander (**sth from sb** qch à qn; **sb to do** à qn de faire).

re·quire *vt* (*of thing*) demander; (*of person*) avoir besoin de; **if required** s'il le faut.

re·quired *adj* **the r. qualities/***etc* les qualités/*etc* qu'il faut.

re·run (*on TV, radio*) rediffusion *f.*

res·cue 1 *vt* (*save*) sauver; (*set free*) délivrer (**from** de). **2** *n* sauvetage *m* (**of** de); (*help*) secours *m*; **to go to sb's r.** aller au secours de qn.

re·search 1 *n* recherche (**on, into** sur). **2** *vi* faire des recherches.

re·search·er chercheur, -euse *mf.*

re·sem·blance ressemblance *f* (**to** avec).

re·sem·ble *vt* ressembler à.

re·sent *vt* (*person*) en vouloir à; (*remark, criticism*) ne pas apprécier.

re·sent·ment ressentiment *m.*

res·er·va·tion (*of hotel room etc*) réservation *f*; (*doubt*) réserve *f.*

re·serve 1 *vt* réserver; (*right*) se réserver. **2** *n* nature **r.** réserve *f* naturelle; **in r.** en réserve.

re·served *adj* (*person, place*) réservé.

re·serve tank réservoir *m* de secours.

res·er·voir réservoir *m.*

re·side *vi* **to r. in New York** résider à New York.

res·i·dence (*home*) résidence *f*; (*of students*) foyer *m.*

res·i·dent habitant, -ante *mf*; (*of hotel*) pensionnaire *mf.*

res·i·den·tial *adj* (*district*) résidentiel.

re·sign 1 *vt* **to r. oneself to sth/to doing** se résigner à qch/à faire. **2** *vi* démissionner; **to r. from one's job** démissionner.

res·ig·na·tion (*from job*) démission *f.*

re·sist 1 *vt* (*attack etc*) résister à; **to r. doing sth** se retenir de faire qch; **she can't r. cakes** elle ne peut pas résister devant des gâteaux. **2** *vi* résister.

re·sis·tance résistance (**to** à).

re·sort¹ *vi* **to r. to doing** en venir à faire; **to r. to sth** avoir recours à qch. **2** *n* **as a last r.** en dernier ressort.

re·sort² (*vacation*) **r.** station *f* de vacances; **beach r.** station *f* balnéaire; **ski r.** station *f* de ski.

re·sour·ces *npl* (*wealth, means*) ressources *fpl.*

re·spect 1 *n* respect *m* (**for** pour, de); **with r. to** en ce qui concerne. **2** *vt* respecter.

re·spect·a·ble *adj* (*honorable, quite good*) respectable; (*clothes, behavior*) convenable.

re·spec·tive *adj* respectif.

re·spond *vi* répondre (**to** à); **to r. to treatment** bien réagir au traitement.

re·sponse réponse *f.*

re·spon·si·bil·i·ty responsabilité *f.*

re·spon·si·ble *adj* responsable (**for** de; **to sb** devant qn); (*job*) à responsabilités.

rest¹ *n* repos *m*; (*support*) support *m*; **to have** or **take a r.** se reposer. **2** *vi* (*relax*) se reposer; **to be resting on sth** (*of hand etc*) être posé sur qch. **3** *vt* (*lean*) appuyer (**on** sur; **against** contre).

rest² (*remaining part*) reste *m* (**of** de); **the r.** (*others*) les autres *mfpl*; **the r. of the men/***etc* les autres hommes/*etc.*

res·tau·rant restaurant *m*.

rest·ful *adj* reposant.

rest·less *adj* agité.

re·store *vt (give back)* rendre (**to** à); *(building etc)* restaurer.

re·strain *vt (person, dog)* maîtriser; *(crowd, anger)* contenir; **to r. oneself from doing sth** s'empêcher de faire qch.

re·straint *(restriction)* restriction *f*, *(moderation)* mesure *f*.

re·strict *vt* restreindre (**to** à).

re·strict·ed *adj* restreint.

re·stric·tion restriction *f*.

rest·room toilettes *fpl*.

re·sult résultat *m*; **as a r. of** par suite de.

re·sume *vti* reprendre.

ré·su·mé CV *m inv*.

re·tail 1 *adj (price, shop)* de détail. **2** *adv (to sell)* au détail.

re·tail·er détaillant, -ante *mf*.

re·tain *vt (freshness etc)* conserver.

re·take *vt (exam)* repasser.

re·tire *vi (from work)* prendre sa retraite; *(withdraw)* se retirer (**from** de; **to** à); *(go to bed)* aller se coucher.

re·tired *adj (no longer working)* retraité.

re·tir·ee retraité, -ée *mf*.

re·tire·ment retraite *f*.

re·treat 1 *n (withdrawal)* retraite *f*, *(shelter)* refuge *m*. **2** *vi* se retirer; *(of army)* battre en retraite.

re·trieve *vt (recover)* récupérer; *(of dog)* rapporter.

re·turn 1 *vi (come back)* revenir; *(go back)* retourner; *(go back home)* rentrer. **2** *vt (give back)* rendre; *(put back)* remettre; *(send back)* renvoyer. **3** *n* retour *m*; *(on investment)* rendement *m*; **tax r.** déclaration *f* de revenus; **in r.** en échange (**for** de). **4** *adj (flight etc)* (de) retour.

re·turn·a·ble *adj (bottle)* consigné.

re·veal *vt (make known)* révéler (**that** que).

rev·e·la·tion révélation *f*.

re·venge vengeance *f*; **to get one's r.** se venger (**on sb** de qn; **for sth** de qch); **in r.** pour se venger.

re·verse 1 *adj (order)* inverse. **2** *n* contraire *m*; **in r. (gear)** en marche arrière. **3** *vti* **to r. (the car)** faire marche arrière; **to r. in/out** rentrer/sortir en marche arrière.

re·vert *vi* **to r. to** revenir à.

re·view 1 *vt (book)* faire la critique de. **2** *n* critique *f*.

re·vise 1 *vt (opinion, notes, text)* réviser. **2** *vi (for exam)* réviser (**for** pour).

re·vi·sion révision *f*.

re·viv·al *(of custom, business, play)* reprise *f*, *(of fashion)* renouveau *m*.

re·vive *vt (unconscious person)* ranimer.

re·volt révolte *f*.

re·volt·ing *adj* dégoûtant.

rev·o·lu·tion révolution *f*.

rev·o·lu·tion·ar·y *adj & n* révolutionnaire *(mf)*.

re·volve *vi* tourner (**around** autour de).

re·volv·er revolver *m*.

re·volv·ing door(s) (porte *f* à) tambour *m*.

re·ward 1 *n* récompense *f* (**for** de, pour). **2** *vt* récompenser (**sb for sth** qn de *or* pour qch).

re·wind* 1 *vt (tape)* rembobiner. **2** *vi* se rembobiner.

rhet·o·ric rhétorique *f*.

rheu·ma·tism rhumatisme *m*; **to have r.** avoir des rhumatismes.

rhi·noc·er·os rhinocéros *m*.

rhu·barb rhubarbe *f*.

rhyme 1 *n* rime *f*, *(poem)* vers *mpl*. **2** *vi* rimer (**with** avec).

rhythm rythme *m*.

rhyth·mi·cal *adj* rythmé.

rib *(in body)* côte *f*.

rib·bon ruban *m*.

rice riz *m*.

rich 1 adj riche. **2** npl **the r.** les riches mpl.

rich·es npl richesses fpl.

rid adj **to get r. of** se débarrasser de.

rid·dle (puzzle) énigme f.

ride 1 n (on bicycle, by car, on horse etc) promenade f; (distance) trajet m; **to go for a r.** (in car) faire une promenade; **to take sb a r.** (in car) emmener qn en voiture. **2** vi* aller (à bicyclette/à moto/à cheval/etc) (**to** à); **to r., to go riding** (on horse) monter (à cheval). **3** vt (a particular horse) monter; (distance) faire (à cheval etc); **to r. a horse or horses** monter à cheval; **I was riding a bicycle** j'étais à bicyclette; **to r. a bicycle to** aller à bicyclette à.

rid·er (on horse) cavalier, -ière mf.

ridge crête f; (of roof) faîte m.

ri·dic·u·lous adj ridicule.

rid·ing (horseback) r. équitation f.

ri·fle fusil m.

rig (oil) r. derrick m; (at sea) plateforme f pétrolière.

right¹ 1 adj (correct) bon (f bonne); (fair) juste; (angle) droit; **to be r.** (of person) avoir raison (**to do** de faire); **the r. choice/time** le bon choix/moment; **it's the r. time** (accurate) c'est l'heure exacte; **the clock's r.** la pendule est à l'heure; **it's not r. to steal** ce n'est pas bien de voler; **to put r.** (error) corriger; **r.!** bien!; **that's r.** c'est ça. **2** adv (straight) (tout) droit; (completely) tout à fait; (correctly) juste; (well) bien; **she did r.** elle a bien fait; **r. here** ici même; **r. away, r. now** tout de suite. **3** n **r. and wrong** le bien et le mal.

right² 1 adj (hand, side etc) droit. **2** adv à droite. **3** n droite f; **on** or **to the r.** à droite (**of** de).

right³ (claim) droit m (**to do** de faire); **to have a r. to sth** avoir droit à qch.

right-hand adj à or de droite; **on the r. side** à droite (**of** de).

right-hand·ed adj (person) droitier.

right·ly adv à juste titre.

rig·id adj rigide.

rim (of cup etc) bord m.

rind (of cheese) croûte f.

ring¹ (on finger, curtain etc) anneau m; (with jewel) bague f; (of people, chairs) cercle m; Boxing ring m; **diamond r.** bague f de diamants; **to make a r. around** entourer (**with** de).

ring² **1** n (sound) sonnerie f; **to give sb a r.** (phone call) passer un coup de fil à qn. **2** vi* (of bell, phone, person) sonner. **3** vt sonner; **to r. the (door)bell** sonner (à la porte).

ring·lead·er meneur, -euse mf.

▸**ring out** vi (of bell) sonner; (of sound) retentir.

rinse 1 vt rincer; **to r. one's hands** se rincer les mains. **2** n **to give sth a r.** rincer qch.

▸**rinse out** vt rincer.

ri·ot 1 n (uprising) émeute f; (fight) bagarre f. **2** vi faire une émeute; (fight) se bagarrer.

rip 1 vt déchirer. **2** vi (of fabric) se déchirer. **3** n déchirure f.

ripe adj mûr; (cheese) fait.

rip·en vti mûrir.

rip-off Fam **it's a r.** c'est du vol organisé.

▸**rip off** vt (button etc) arracher (**from** de); **to r. sb off** Fam rouler qn.

▸**rip out** vt arracher (**from** de).

▸**rip up** vt déchirer.

rise 1 vi* (of temperature, balloon, price) monter; (of sun, curtain, person) se lever; **to r. in price** augmenter de prix. **2** n (in price etc) hausse f (**in** de); (slope in ground) montée f; **to give r. to sth** donner lieu à qch.

ris·ing 1 adj (sun) levant; (prices) en hausse. **2** n (of sun) lever m; (of prices) hausse f.

risk 1 *n* risque *m* (**of doing** de faire; **in doing** à faire); **at r.** (*person*) en danger; (*job*) menacé. **2** *vt* risquer; **she won't r. leaving** elle ne se risquera pas à partir.

risk·y *adj* risqué.

rit·u·al *adj & n* rituel (*m*).

ri·val 1 *adj* (*company etc*) rival. **2** *n* rival, -ale *mf*. **3** *vt* (*compete with*) rivaliser avec (**in** de); (*equal*) égaler (**in** en).

riv·er rivière *f*, (*flowing into sea*) fleuve *m*.

Riv·i·er·a the (*French*) R. la Côte d'Azur.

roach (*cockroach*) cafard *m*.

road *n* route *f* (**to** qui va à), (*small*) chemin *m*; (*in town*) rue *f*, (*roadway*) chaussée *f*; **across the r.** (*building etc*) en face; **by r.** par la route. **2** *adj* (*map, safety*) routier; (*accident*) de la route; **r. sign** panneau *m* (routier).

road·side bord *m* de la route; **r. bar/hotel**/*etc* bar *m*/ hôtel *m*/*etc* situé au bord de la route.

road·way chaussée *f*.

road·work travaux *mpl*.

roam *vt* parcourir; **to r. the streets** (*of child, dog etc*) traîner dans les rues.

roar 1 *vi* (*of lion*) rugir; (*of person*) hurler. **2** *n* (*of lion*) rugissement *m*.

roast 1 *vt* rôtir; (*coffee*) griller. **2** *vi* (*of meat*) rôtir. **3** *n* (*meat*) rôti *m*. **4** *adj* (*chicken etc*) rôti; **r. beef** rosbif *m*.

rob *vt* (*person*) voler; (*bank*) attaquer; (*by breaking in*) cambrioler; **to r. sb of sth** voler qch à qn.

rob·ber voleur, -euse *mf*.

rob·ber·y vol *m*.

robe (*bathrobe*) robe *f* de chambre.

rob·in rouge-gorge *m*.

ro·bot robot *m*.

rock¹ 1 *vt* (*baby, boat*) bercer. **2** *vi* (*sway*) se balancer; (*of building*) trembler. **3** *n* (*music*) rock *m*.

rock² (*substance*) roche *f*, (*boulder, rock face*) rocher *m*; (*stone*) pierre *f*, **r. face** paroi *f* rocheuse.

rock·et fusée *f*.

rock·ing chair fauteuil *m* à bascule.

rod (*wooden*) baguette *f*, (*metal*) tige *f*, (*of curtain*) tringle *f*, (*for fishing*) canne *f* (à pêche).

rogue (*dishonest*) crapule *f*, (*mischievous*) coquin, -ine *mf*.

role rôle *m*.

roll 1 *n* (*of paper etc*) rouleau *m*; (*small bread loaf*) petit pain *m*; (*of drum*) roulement *m*; (*attendance list*) cahier *m* d'appel; **to call** *or* **take the r.** faire l'appel. **2** *vi* (*of ball etc*) rouler; (*of person, animal*) se rouler. **3** *vt* rouler.

▶**roll down** *vt* (*car window etc*) baisser; (*slope*) descendre (en roulant).

roll·er (*for hair, painting etc*) rouleau *m*.

roll·er·blade 1 *n* roller *m*. **2** *vi* faire du roller.

roll·er·skate 1 *n* patin *m* à roulettes. **2** *vi* faire du patin à roulettes.

roll·ing pin rouleau *m* à pâtisserie.

▶**roll over 1** *vi* (*many times*) se rouler; (*once*) se retourner. **2** *vt* retourner.

▶**roll up** *vt* (*map, cloth*) rouler; (*sleeve, pants*) retrousser.

Ro·man 1 *n* Romain, -aine *mf*. **2** *adj* romain, -aine.

Ro·man Cath·o·lic *adj & n* catholique (*mf*).

ro·mance (*love*) amour *m*; (*affair*) aventure *f* amoureuse.

ro·man·tic *adj* romantique.

roof toit *m*; (*of tunnel, cave*) plafond *m*.

roof rack (*of car*) galerie *f*.

room (*in house etc*) pièce *f*, (*bedroom*) chambre *f*, (*large, public*) salle *f*, (*space*) place *f* (**for** pour); **men's r., ladies' r.** toilettes *fpl*.

room·mate colocataire *mf.*

room·y *adj* spacieux; *(clothes)* ample.

root racine *f*, *(origin)* origine *f*; **to take r.** *(of plant)* prendre racine.

▶ **root for** *vt Fam* encourager.

rope corde *f.*

▶ **rope off** *vt (of police etc)* interdire l'accès de.

rose *(flower)* rose *f*; **r. bush** rosier *m.*

ro·ta·tion rotation *f.*

rot (a·way) *vti* pourrir.

rot·ten *adj (fruit, weather etc)* pourri; *(bad) Fam* moche; **to feel r.** *(ill)* être mal fichu.

rough¹ *adj (surface, plank)* rugueux; *(ground)* inégal; *(brutal)* brutal; *(sea)* agité.

rough² *adj (calculation etc)* approximatif; **r. guess** approximation *f*, **r. draft** brouillon *m.*

rough·ly¹ *adv (not gently)* rudement; *(brutally)* brutalement.

rough·ly² *adv (more or less)* à peu (de choses) près.

round 1 *adj* rond. **2** *n Boxing* round *m*; *(of drinks, visits)* tournée *f*; *(of policeman)* ronde *f.*

round·a·bout *adj* indirect.

▶ **round off** *vt (meal etc)* terminer (**with** par); *(figure)* arrondir.

round trip aller (et) retour *m.*

▶ **round up** *vt (people, animals)* rassembler.

route itinéraire *m*; *(of ship, aircraft)* route *f*; **bus r.** ligne *f* d'autobus.

rou·tine routine *f.*

row¹ 1 *n (line)* rang *m*, rangée *f*; *(one behind another)* file *f*; **two days in a r.** deux jours de suite. **2** *vi (in boat)* ramer. **3** *vt (boat)* faire aller à la rame.

row² **1** *n Fam (noise)* vacarme *m*; *(quarrel)* dispute *f.* **2** *vi Fam* se disputer (**with** avec).

row·boat bateau *m* à rames.

row house maison *f* attenante aux maisons voisines.

roy·al *adj* royal.

roy·al·ty personnages *mpl* royaux.

rub *vti* frotter; *(person)* frictionner.

rub·ber caoutchouc *m*; *(eraser)* gomme *f.*

rub·ber band élastique *m.*

rub·ber boots bottes *fpl* de caoutchouc.

rub·ber stamp tampon *m.*

rub·ble décombres *mpl.*

▶ **rub down** *vt (person)* frictionner; *(wall, door)* poncer.

▶ **rub in** *vt (cream)* faire pénétrer (en massant).

▶ **rub off** *or* **out** *vt (mark)* effacer.

ru·by rubis *m.*

ruck·sack sac *m* à dos.

rud·der gouvernail *m.*

rude *adj* impoli (**to** envers); *(coarse, insolent)* grossier (**to** envers).

rude·ness impolitesse *f*, *(coarseness, insolence)* grossièreté *f.*

rug carpette *f.*

rug·by rugby *m.*

ru·in 1 *n* ruine *f*; **in ruins** *(building)* en ruine. **2** *vt (health, person etc)* ruiner; *(clothes)* abîmer.

rule 1 *n* règle *f*; **against the rule(s)** contraire au règlement; **as a r.** en règle générale. **2** *vt (country)* gouverner. **3** *vi (of king etc)* régner (**over** sur).

▶ **rule out** *vt* exclure.

rul·er *(for measuring)* règle *f*; *(king, queen etc)* souverain, -aine *mf.*

rul·ing 1 *adj (party)* au pouvoir; *(monarch)* régnant; *(class)* dirigeant. **2** *n* décision *f.*

rum rhum *m.*

rum·mage sale vente *f* de charité.

ru·mor bruit *m*, rumeur *f.*

run 1 *n (period)* période *f*, *(for skiing)* piste *f*; **to go for a r.** (aller) faire une course à pied; **on the r.** *(prisoner)* en fuite; **in the long r.** à la longue. **2** *vi** courir; *(of river, nose,* *faucet*) couler; (*of color in laundry*) déteindre; (*of play, movie*) se jouer; (*function*) marcher; **to r. down/in/***etc* descendre/entrer/*etc* en courant; **to go running** faire du jogging. **3** *vt* (*race, risk*) courir; (*temperature, errand*) faire; (*business, country etc*) diriger; (*bath*) faire couler.

▸**run across** *vt* (*meet*) tomber sur.

▸**run along** *vi* filer.

▸**run away** *vi* s'enfuir (**from** de).

▸**run down** *vt* (*pedestrian*) renverser.

rung (*of ladder*) barreau *m*.

▸**run into** *vt* (*meet*) tomber sur; (*crash into*) percuter.

run·ner (*athlete*) coureur *m*.

run·ner-up second, -onde *mf*.

run·ning 1 *n* (*on foot*) course *f*. **2** *adj* **r. water** eau *f* courante; **six days/***etc* **r.** six jours/*etc* de suite.

run·ny *adj* (*nose*) qui coule.

▸**run off** *vi* (*flee*) s'enfuir.

▸**run out** *vi* (*of inventory*) s'épuiser; (*of lease*) expirer; **to r. out of** (*time, money*) manquer de; **we've r. out of coffee** on n'a plus de café.

▸**run over** *vt* (*kill*) écraser; (*knock down*) renverser.

run·way piste *f* (d'envol).

rush 1 *vi* se précipiter (**at** sur; **towards** vers); (*hurry*) se dépêcher (**to do** de faire). **2** *vt* (*hurry*) bousculer (*qn*); **to r. sb to the hospital** transporter qn d'urgence à l'hôpital; **to r. (through) sth** (*job, meal etc*) faire/manger/*etc* qch en vitesse. **3** *n* ruée *f* (**for** vers); (*confusion*) bousculade *f*; (*hurry*) hâte *f*, **in a r.** pressé (**to do** de faire).

rush hour heure *f* de pointe.

▸**rush out** *vi* partir en vitesse.

Russian 1 *adj* russe. **2** *n* Russe *mf*; (*language*) russe *m*.

rust 1 *n* rouille *f*. **2** *vi* (se) rouiller.

rust·y *adj* (*metal, memory etc*) rouillé.

RV *abbr* (*recreational vehicle*) camping-car *m*.

rye bread pain *m* de seigle.

S

sack 1 *n* (*bag*) sac *m*; **to get the s.** (*from one's job*) se faire virer; **to give sb the s.** virer qn. **2** *vt* (*dismiss*) virer.

sa·cred *adj* sacré.

sac·ri·fice 1 *n* sacrifice *m*. **2** *vt* sacrifier (**to** à; **for** pour).

sad *adj* triste.

sad·den *vt* attrister.

sad·dle selle *f*.

sad·ly *adv* tristement; (*unfortunately*) malheureusement.

sad·ness tristesse *f*.

safe¹ *adj* (*person*) en sécurité; (*equipment, toy, animal*) sans danger; (*place, investment, method*) sûr; (*bridge, ladder*) solide; **s. (and sound)** sain et sauf; **it's s. to go out** on peut sortir sans danger; **s. from** à l'abri de.

safe² (*for money etc*) coffre-fort *m*.

safe·guard 1 *n* sauvegarde *f*. **2** *vt* sauvegarder.

safe·ly *adv* (*without accident*) sans accident; (*without risk*) sans risque; (*in a safe place*) en lieu sûr.

safe·ty sécurité *f*.

safe·ty pin épingle *f* de sûreté.

sag *vi* (*of roof, ground*) s'affaisser.

said *pt & pp de* **say**.

sail 1 *vi* naviguer; (*leave*) partir; (*as sport*) faire de la voile; **to s. around the world/an island** faire le tour du monde/d'une île en bateau. **2** *vt* (*boat*) piloter. **3** *n* voile *f*.

sail·board planche *f* (à voile).

sail·boat voilier *m*.

sail·ing navigation *f*; (*sport*) voile *f*; (*departure*) départ *m*.

sail·or marin *m*.

saint saint *m*, sainte *f*.

sake **for my/your/his/***etc* **s.** pour moi/toi/lui/*etc*; **(just) for the s. of eating/**

etc simplement pour manger/*etc.*

sal·ad salade *f*.

sal·ad bowl saladier *m*.

sal·ad dress·ing sauce *f* pour salade.

sal·a·ry *(professional)* salaire *m*, traitement *m*; *(wage)* salaire *m*.

sale vente *f*; **sale(s)** *(at reduced prices)* soldes *mpl*; **on s.** *(cheaply)* en solde; *(available)* en vente; **(up) for s.** à vendre.

sales·clerk vendeur, -euse *mf*.

sales·man, *pl* **-men** *(in store)* vendeur *m*; *(traveling)* **s.** représentant *m* (de commerce).

sales tax = TVA *f*.

sales·wom·an, *pl* **-women** vendeuse *f*; *(who travels)* représentante *f* (de commerce).

sa·li·va salive *f*.

salm·on saumon *m*.

sa·lon salon *m*.

salt 1 *n* sel *m*; **bath salts** sels *mpl* de bain. 2 *vt* saler.

salt·cel·lar, salt·sha·ker salière *f*.

salt·y *adj* salé.

sal·va·tion salut *m*; **S. Army** Armée *f* du salut.

same 1 *adj* même; **the (very) s. house as** (exactement) la même maison que. 2 *pron* **the s.** le *or* la même, *pl* les mêmes; **it's all the s. to me** ça m'est égal; **all** *or* **just the s.** tout de même; **to do the s.** en faire autant.

sam·ple 1 *n* échantillon *m*; *(of blood)* prélèvement *m*. 2 *vt* *(wine etc)* goûter.

sand 1 *n* sable *m*. 2 *vt* *(road)* sabler.

san·dal sandale *f*.

sand·cas·tle château *m* de sable.

sand·pa·per papier *m* de verre.

sand·wich sandwich *m*; **cheese/** *etc* **s.** sandwich au fromage/*etc*; **s. shop** sandwicherie *f*.

sand·y *adj* *(beach)* de sable; *(road)* sablonneux.

san·i·tar·y nap·kin serviette *f* hygiénique.

San·ta Claus le père Noël.

sar·dine sardine *f*.

sat *pt & pp de* sit.

satch·el cartable *m*.

sat·el·lite satellite *m*.

sat·in satin *m*.

sat·is·fac·tion satisfaction *f*.

sat·is·fac·to·ry *adj* satisfaisant.

sat·is·fy *vt* satisfaire (**qn**); **to s. oneself that** s'assurer que; **satisfied (with)** satisfait (de).

sat·is·fy·ing *adj* satisfaisant.

sat·su·ma *(fruit)* mandarine *f*, satsuma *f*.

sat·u·rate *vt* *(soak)* tremper; **saturated fats** graisses *fpl* saturées.

Sat·ur·day samedi *m*.

sauce sauce *f*, *(stewed fruit)* compote *f*; **tomato s.** sauce *f* tomate.

sauce·pan casserole *f*.

sau·cer soucoupe *f*.

sau·na sauna *m*.

sau·sage saucisse *f*, *(dried, for slicing)* saucisson *m*.

save 1 *vt* *(rescue)* sauver (**from** de); *(keep)* garder; *(money, time)* économiser; *(stamps)* collectionner; **to s. sb from doing** empêcher qn de faire; **that will s. him the trouble of going** ça lui évitera d'y aller. 2 *n* *Sports* arrêt *m*.

▸**save up** 1 *vt* *(money)* économiser. 2 *vi* faire des économies (**for sth, to buy sth** pour acheter qch).

sav·ings *npl* *(money)* économies *fpl*.

sav·ings and loan = société *f* de crédit immobilier.

sav·ings bank caisse *f* d'épargne.

saw[1] 1 *n* scie *f*. 2 *vt** scier.

saw[2] *pt de* see.

saw·dust sciure *f*.

▸**saw off** *vt* scier.

sax·o·phone saxophone *m*.

say* *vt* dire (**to** à; **that** que); *(of dial etc)* marquer; **to s. again** répéter; **(let's) s. tomorrow** disons demain; **that is to s.** c'est-à-dire.

say·ing proverbe *m*.

scab (of wound) croûte f.

scaf·fold·ing échafaudage m.

scald vt ébouillanter.

scale (of map, wages etc) échelle f; (on fish) écaille f; (in music) gamme f.

scales npl (for weighing) balance f; (bathroom) s. pèse-personne m.

scal·lion oignon m vert.

scan 1 vt (text, graphics) passer au scanner; (scrutinize) scruter; (glance at) parcourir. **2** n échographie f; to have a s. passer une échographie.

scan·dal scandale m; (gossip) médisances fpl.

Scan·di·na·vi·an 1 n Scandinave mf. **2** adj scandinave.

scan·ner scanner m.

scar cicatrice f.

scarce adj rare.

scarce·ly adv à peine.

scare vt faire peur à.

scare·crow épouvantail m.

scared adj effrayé; to be s. (stiff) avoir (très) peur.

scarf, pl **scarves** (long) écharpe f; (square, for women) foulard m.

scar·let fe·ver scarlatine f.

scar·y adj it's s. ça fait peur.

scat·ter 1 vt (crowd, clouds etc) disperser; (throw around) éparpiller (papiers etc). **2** vi (of crowd) se disperser.

sce·nar·i·o scénario m.

scene (setting, fuss, part of play or movie) scène f; (of crime, accident) lieu m; (view) vue f.

scen·er·y paysage m; (for play or movie) décor(s) m(pl).

scent (fragrance, perfume) parfum m.

sched·ule 1 n (of work etc) programme m; (timetable) horaire m; on s. (on time) à l'heure; according to s. comme prévu. **2** vt (to plan) prévoir; (event) fixer le programme de.

sched·uled adj (planned) prévu; (service, flight) régulier.

scheme plan m (to do pour faire); (dishonest trick) combine f.

schmuck Fam andouille f.

schol·ar (learned person) érudit, -ite mf.

schol·ar·ship (grant) bourse f (d'études).

school 1 n école f; (teaching, lessons) classe f; in or at s. à l'école; public s. école f publique; summer s. cours mpl d'été. **2** adj (year etc) scolaire.

school·boy écolier m.

school·girl écolière f.

school·teach·er (primary) instituteur, -trice mf; (secondary) professeur m.

sci·ence science f; to study s. étudier les sciences.

sci·ence fic·tion science-fiction f.

sci·en·tif·ic adj scientifique.

sci·en·tist scientifique mf; savant m.

scis·sors npl ciseaux mpl.

scold vt gronder (for doing pour avoir fait).

scone petit pain m au lait.

scoot·er (child's) trottinette f; (motorcycle) scooter m.

scope (range) étendue f; (limits) limites fpl; s. for sth/for doing (opportunity) des possibilités fpl de qch/de faire.

scorch vt roussir.

score¹ 1 n (in sports) score m; (at cards) marque f; (music) partition f. **2** vt (point, goal) marquer. **3** vi (point) marquer un point; (goal) marquer un but; (count points) marquer les points.

score² a s. (of) une vingtaine (de).

scorn mépris m.

Scot Écossais, -aise mf.

Scotch (whisky) scotch m.

scotch (tape)® scotch® m.

Scots·man, pl -men Écossais m.

Scots·wom·an, pl -women Écossaise f.

Scot·tish adj écossais.

scoun·drel vaurien m.

scout (boy) s. scout m; **girl s.** éclaireuse f.

scram·ble 1 vi to s. up a hill gravir une colline en s'aidant des mains. **2** vt (message) brouiller; **scrambled eggs** œufs mpl brouillés. **3** n (rush) bousculade f.

scrap 1 n petit morceau m (**of** de); (of information) fragment m; (metal) ferraille f; **scraps** (food) restes mpl. **2** vt se débarrasser de; (vehicle) mettre à la ferraille; (plan) abandonner.

scrap·book album m (pour collages etc).

scrape 1 vt racler; (skin, knee etc) érafler. **2** vi to s. against sth frotter contre qch. **3** n (on skin) éraflure f.

▸**scrape away, scrape off** vt (mud etc) racler.

▸**scrape through** vi (in exam) réussir de justesse.

▸**scrape together** vt (money, people) réunir (difficilement).

scrap met·al ferraille f.

scrap pa·per (papier m) brouillon m.

scratch 1 n (mark, injury) éraflure f; **to start from s.** (re)partir de zéro; **it isn't up to s.** ce n'est pas au niveau. **2** vt (arm etc that itches) gratter; (skin, furniture etc) érafler; (one's name) graver (**on** sur). **3** vi (relieve an itch) se gratter.

scratch·card carte f à gratter.

scratch pa·per (for draft) (papier m) brouillon m.

scream 1 vti crier; **to s. at sb** crier après qn. **2** n cri m (perçant).

screen écran m; (folding) s. paravent m.

screw 1 n vis f. **2** vt visser (**to** à).

screw an·chor cheville f.

▸**screw down** vt visser.

screw·driv·er tournevis m.

▸**screw on** vt visser.

scrib·ble vti griffonner.

script (of movie) scénario m; (of play) texte m.

scrub vt nettoyer (à la brosse); (pan) récurer.

scrub brush brosse f dure.

scu·ba div·ing plongée f sous-marine.

sculp·tor sculpteur m.

sculp·ture (art, object) sculpture f.

scum (on liquid) écume f; Fam (people) racaille f.

sea mer f; (out) at s. en mer; by s. par mer; by or beside the sea au bord de la mer.

sea·food fruits mpl de mer.

sea·front bord m or front m de mer.

sea·gull mouette f.

seal 1 n (animal) phoque m; (mark, design) sceau m; (of wax) cachet m (de cire). **2** vt (document, container) sceller; (envelope) cacheter; (with putty) boucher.

sea li·on otarie f.

▸**seal off** vt (of police etc) interdire l'accès de.

seam (in cloth) couture f.

search 1 n recherche f (**for** de); (of person, place) fouille f; **in s. of** à la recherche de. **2** vt (person, place) fouiller (**for** pour trouver); **to s. (through) one's papers**/etc chercher qch dans ses papiers/etc. **3** vi chercher; **to s. for sth** chercher qch.

sea·shell coquillage m.

sea·shore bord m de la mer.

sea·sick adj to be s. avoir le mal de mer.

sea·sick·ness mal m de mer.

sea·side bord m de la mer.

sea·son 1 n saison f. **2** vt (food) assaisonner.

sea·son·al adj saisonnier.

sea·son·ing assaisonnement m.

sea·son tick·et abonnement m.

seat 1 *n* siège *m*; *(on train, bus)* banquette *f*; *(in theater)* fauteuil *m*; *(place)* place *f*; **to take** *or* **have a s.** s'asseoir; **the room seats 50** la salle a 50 places (assises); **be seated!** asseyez-vous!

seat belt ceinture *f* de sécurité.

seat·ed *adj (sitting)* assis.

seat·ing *(seats)* places *fpl* assises.

sea·weed algue(s) *f(pl)*.

sec·ond[1] **1** *adj* deuxième, second; **every s. week** une semaine sur deux; **in s. (gear)** en second. **2** *vt* **to come s.** se classer deuxième. **3** *n (person, object)* deuxième *mf*, second, -onde *mf*.

sec·ond[2] *(part of minute)* seconde *f*.

sec·ond·ar·y *adj* secondaire.

sec·ond-class *adj (ticket)* de seconde (classe); *(mail)* non urgent.

sec·ond·hand *adj & adv (not new)* d'occasion.

sec·ond·ly *adv* deuxièmement.

se·cret *adj & n* secret *(m)*; **in s.** en secret.

sec·re·tar·y secrétaire *mf*; *(cabinet official)* ministre *m*; **S. of State** Ministre des Affaires étrangères.

se·cret·ly *adv* en secret, secrètement.

sec·tion *(of town, book etc)* partie *f*, *(of machine, furniture)* élément *m*; *(in store)* rayon *m*; **the sports/etc s.** *(of newspaper)* la page des sports/ etc.

sec·u·lar *adj (music, art)* profane; *(education, school)* laïque.

se·cure 1 *adj (person, valuables)* en sûreté; *(place)* sûr; *(solid)* solide; *(door, window)* bien fermé. **2** *vt (fasten)* attacher; *(window etc)* bien fermer.

se·cure·ly *adv (firmly)* solidement; *(safely)* en sûreté.

se·cu·ri·ty sécurité *f*, *(for loan)* caution *f*.

se·dan berline *f*.

se·da·tion under s. sous calmants.

sed·a·tive calmant *m*.

see* *vti* voir; **we'll s.** on verra (bien); **I saw him run(ning)** je l'ai vu courir; **s. you (later)!** à tout à l'heure!; **s. you (soon)!** à bientôt!; **to s. that** *(take care that)* veiller à ce que (+ *subjunctive*); *(check)* s'assurer que.

▶**see about** *vt* s'occuper de; *(consider)* songer à.

seed graine *f*, *(in grape)* pépin *m*.

see·ing *conj* **s. (that)** vu que.

seek* *vt* chercher (**to do** à faire); *(ask for)* demander (**from** à).

seem *vi* sembler (**to do** faire); **it seems that** *(impression)* il semble que (+ *subjunctive or indicative*); *(rumor)* il paraît que (+ *indicative*); **it seems to me that** il me semble que (+ *indicative*).

seem·ing·ly *adv* apparemment.

▶**see off** *vt* accompagner *(qn)*.

▶**see out** *vt* raccompagner *(qn)*.

see·saw *(jeu m de)* bascule *f*.

▶**see through** *vt* **to s. sth through** *(carry out)* mener qch à bien; **to s. through sb** voir dans le jeu de qn; **$20 should s. me through** 20 dollars devraient me suffire.

▶**see to** *vt (deal with)* s'occuper de; *(mend)* réparer; **to see to it that** veiller à ce que (+ *subjunctive*); *(check)* s'assurer que.

seg·ment segment *m*; *(of orange)* quartier *m*.

seize *vt* saisir; *(power, land)* s'emparer de.

sel·dom *adv* rarement.

se·lect *vt* choisir (**from** parmi); *(candidates, players etc)* sélectionner.

se·lec·tion sélection *f*.

se·lec·tive *adj* sélectif.

self-as·sur·ance assurance *f*.

self-as·sured *adj* sûr de soi.

self-con·fi·dence assurance *f*.

self-con·fi·dent *adj* sûr de soi.

self-con·scious *adj* gêné.

self-con·trol maîtrise *f* de soi.

self-de·fense légitime défense f.

self-em·ployed adj qui travaille à son compte.

self-ev·i·dent adj évident.

self-ish adj égoïste.

self-re·spect amour-propre m.

self-righ·teous adj suffisant.

self-serv·ice n & adj libre-service (m inv).

sell* 1 vt vendre; **to have** or **be sold out of sth** n'avoir plus de qch. 2 vi (of product) se vendre.

sell·er vendeur, -euse mf.

se·mes·ter semestre m.

sem·i- prefix demi-, semi-.

sem·i·cir·cle demi-cercle m.

sem·i·co·lon point-virgule m.

sem·i·de·tached house maison f jumelle.

sem·i·fi·nal demi-finale f.

sem·i·nar séminaire m.

sem·i·trail·er semi-remorque m.

sem·o·li·na semoule f.

sen·a·tor sénateur m.

send* vt envoyer (**to** à); **to s. sb for sth/sb** envoyer qn chercher qch/qn.

▸**send away, send off** 1 vt envoyer (**to** à); (dismiss) renvoyer. 2 vi **to s. away** or **off for sth** commander qch (par courrier).

▸**send back** vt renvoyer.

send·er expéditeur, -trice mf.

▸**send for** vt (doctor etc) faire venir; (by mail) commander (par courrier).

▸**send in** vt (form etc) envoyer; (person) faire entrer.

▸**send on** vt (letter, luggage) faire suivre.

▸**send out** vt (invitation etc) envoyer; (from room etc) faire sortir (qn); **to s. out for** (meal) envoyer chercher.

▸**send up** vt (luggage) faire monter.

sen·ior 1 adj (older) plus âgé; (position, rank) supérieur. 2 n aîné, -ée mf; (in school) grand m, grande f,

étudiant, -ante mf de dernière année.

sen·ior high (school) = lycée m.

sen·sa·tion sensation f.

sen·sa·tion·al adj (terrific) Fam sensationnel.

sense 1 n (meaning) sens m; **s. of smell** odorat m; **a s. of** (shame etc) un sentiment de; **to have a s. of hu·mor** avoir de l'humour; **to have (good) s.** avoir du bon sens; **to have the s. to do** avoir l'intelligence de faire; **to make s.** (of story) avoir un sens, tenir debout. 2 vt sentir (intuitivement) (**that** que).

sense·less adj (stupid) insensé.

sen·si·ble adj (wise) raisonnable.

sen·si·tive adj sensible (**to** à); (skin) délicat; (touchy) susceptible (**about** à propos de).

sen·tence 1 n Grammar phrase f; (punishment, in prison) peine f. 2 vt **to s. sb to 3 years (in prison)** condamner qn à 3 ans de prison.

sen·ti·ment sentiment m.

sen·ti·ment·al adj sentimental.

sep·a·rate 1 adj (distinct) séparé; (independent) indépendant; (different) différent. 2 vt séparer (**from** de). 3 vi se séparer (**from** de).

sep·a·rate·ly adv séparément.

sep·a·ra·tion séparation f.

Sep·tem·ber septembre m.

se·quence (order) ordre m; (series) succession f.

se·quin paillette f.

ser·geant sergent m; (in police force) brigadier m.

se·ri·al (story, film) feuilleton m.

se·ries inv série f.

se·ri·ous adj sérieux; (illness, mistake) grave.

se·ri·ous·ly adv sérieusement; (ill) gravement; **to take s.** prendre au sérieux.

ser·vant (in house etc) domestique mf.

serve vt servir (**to sb** à qn; **sb with**

sth qch à qn); *(of train, bus etc)* desservir *(un village etc)*; **(it) serves you right!** ça t'apprendra!

▸**serve up** *vt (meal etc)* servir.

serv·ice 1 *n* service *m*; *(machine or vehicle repair)* révision *f*; **s. charge** *(in restaurant)* service *m*. **2** *vt (machine, vehicle)* réviser.

ser·vice ar·e·a *(on highway)* aire *f* de service.

ser·vice sta·tion station-service *f*.

ses·sion séance *f*.

set 1 *n (of keys, tools etc)* jeu *m*; *(of stamps, numbers)* série *f*; *(of people)* groupe *m*; *(in mathematics)* ensemble *m*; *(of books)* collection *f*; *(scenery)* décor *m*; *(hairstyle)* mise *f* en plis; *Tennis* set *m*; **chess s.** jeu *m* d'échecs. **2** *adj (time, price etc)* fixe; **the s. menu** le plat du jour; **s. on doing** résolu à faire; **to be s. on sth** vouloir qch à tout prix; **all s.** *(ready)* prêt (**to do** pour faire). **3** *vt* (put)* mettre; *(date, limit etc)* fixer; *(record)* établir; *(mechanism, clock)* régler; *(alarm clock)* mettre (**for** pour); *(arm etc in plaster)* plâtrer; *(task)* donner (**for sb** à qn); *(trap)* tendre; **to have one's hair s.** se faire faire une mise en plis. **4** *vi (of sun)* se coucher; *(of jelly)* prendre.

▸**set about** *vt* **to s. about sth/about doing** *(begin)* se mettre à qch/à faire.

set·back revers *m*.

▸**set back** *vt (clock)* retarder.

▸**set down** *vt (object)* déposer.

▸**set forward** *vt (clock)* avancer.

▸**set off 1** *vt (bomb)* faire exploser; *(mechanism)* déclencher. **2** *vi (leave)* partir.

▸**set out 1** *vt (display, explain)* exposer (**to** à); *(arrange)* disposer. **2** *vi (leave)* partir; **to s. out to do** entreprendre de faire.

set·tee canapé *m*.

set·ting *(surroundings)* cadre *m*.

set·tle 1 *vt (decide, arrange, pay)* régler; *(date)* fixer; **that's (all) settled** c'est décidé. **2** *vi (live)* s'installer.

▸**settle down** *vi (in chair or house)* s'installer; *(calm down)* se calmer; *(in one's lifestyle)* se ranger.

set·tle·ment *(agreement)* accord *m*.

set·tler colon *m*.

▸**settle (up) with** *vt (pay)* régler.

▸**set up 1** *vt (tent)* dresser; *(business)* créer. **2** *vi* **to s. up shop** monter une affaire.

sev·en *adj & n* sept *(m)*.

sev·en·teen *adj & n* dix-sept *(m)*.

sev·enth *adj & n* septième *(mf)*.

sev·en·ti·eth *adj & n* soixante-dixième *(mf)*.

sev·en·ty *adj & n* soixante-dix *(m)*; **s.-one** soixante et onze.

sev·er·al *adj & pron* plusieurs (**of** d'entre).

se·vere *adj (tone etc)* sévère; *(winter)* rigoureux; *(test)* dur.

sew* *vti* coudre.

sew·er égout *m*.

sew·ing couture *f*.

sew·ing ma·chine machine *f* à coudre.

▸**sew on** *vt (button)* (re)coudre.

▸**sew up** *vt (tear)* (re)coudre.

sex 1 *n* sexe *m*; *(activity)* relations *fpl* sexuelles; **to have s. with sb** coucher avec qn. **2** *adj (education, life etc)* sexuel.

sex·u·al *adj* sexuel.

sex·y *adj* sexy *inv*.

sh! *int* chut!

shab·by *adj (room etc)* minable.

shade ombre *f*; *(of colour)* ton *m*; *(of lamp)* abat-jour *m inv*; **(window) s.** store *m*; **in the s.** à l'ombre.

shad·ow ombre *f*.

shad·y *adj (place)* ombragé.

shaft *(of tool)* manche *m*; *(in mine)* puits *m*; *(of elevator)* cage *f*; *(of light)* rayon *m*.

shake 1 vt secouer; (bottle) agiter; (upset) bouleverser; **to s. one's head** (say no) secouer la tête; **to s. hands with sb** serrer la main à qn; **we shook hands** nous nous sommes serré la main. **2** vi trembler (**with** de).

shall v aux (future) **I s. come, I'll come** je viendrai; **we s. not come, we shan't come** nous ne viendrons pas. ▪ (question) **s. I leave?** veux-tu que je parte?; **s. we leave?** on part?

shal·low adj (water, river etc) peu profond.

shame (feeling, disgrace) honte f; **it's a s.** c'est dommage (**to do** de faire); **it's a s. (that)** c'est dommage que (+ subjunctive); **what a s.!** (quel) dommage!

shame·ful adj honteux.

sham·poo 1 n shampooing m. **2** vt **to s. sb's hair** faire un shampooing à qn.

shan't = **shall not**.

shape forme f; **in (good) s.** (fit) en (pleine) forme; **to stay in s.** se maintenir en forme; **to be in good/bad s.** (of vehicle etc) être en bon/mauvais état; (of business) marcher bien/mal; **to take s.** (of plan, book etc) prendre forme; (progress well) avancer.

-shaped suffix pear-s./etc en forme de poire/etc.

share 1 n part f (**of**, in de); (of stock) action f. **2** vt (meal, opinion etc) partager (**with** avec); (characteristic) avoir en commun.

share·hold·er actionnaire mf.

▸ **share in** vt avoir sa part de.

▸ **share out** vt partager, répartir (**among** entre).

shark requin m.

sharp 1 adj (knife etc) tranchant; (pointed) pointu; (point, pain) aigu (f -uë); (bend) brusque. **2** adv **five o'clock/etc s.** cinq heures/etc pile.

sharp·en vt (knife) aiguiser; (pencil) tailler.

sharp·ly adv (suddenly) brusquement.

shat·ter 1 vt (door, arm etc) fracasser; (glass) faire voler en éclats. **2** vi fracasser; (of glass) voler en éclats.

shave 1 vt (person, head) raser; **to s. off one's beard** se raser la barbe. **2** vi se raser. **3** n **to have a s.** se raser.

shav·er rasoir m électrique.

shav·ing cream crème f à raser.

shav·ing kit trousse f de toilette (d'homme).

shawl châle m.

she pron elle; **she's a happy woman** c'est une femme heureuse.

shed¹ (in garden) abri m (de jardin); (for goods or machines) hangar m.

shed² vt (lose) perdre; (tears) répandre.

sheep inv mouton m.

sheep·skin peau f de mouton.

sheer adj (utter) pur; (cliff) à pic; (stockings, fabric) extra fin.

sheet (on bed) drap m; (of paper) feuille f; (of glass, ice) plaque f.

shelf, pl **shelves** étagère f; (in shop) rayon m.

shell 1 n (of egg etc) coquille f; (of tortoise) carapace f; (seashell) coquillage m; (explosive) obus m. **2** vt (peas) écosser.

shell·fish (oysters etc) fruits mpl de mer.

shel·ter 1 n abri m; **to take s.** se mettre à l'abri (**from** de). **2** vt abriter (**from** de). **3** vi s'abriter.

shelv·ing rayonnage(s) m(pl).

shep·herd berger m.

sher·iff shérif m.

sher·ry sherry m.

shield n bouclier m; (screen) écran m. **2** vt protéger (**from** de).

shift 1 n (change) changement m (**of**, in de); (period of work) poste m; (workers) équipe f; **gear s.** levier m de vitesse. **2** vt (move) bouger; **to s. gear(s)** changer de vitesse. **3** vi bouger.

shin tibia *m.*

shine 1 *vi** briller. **2** *vt (polish)* faire briller; **to s. a light on sth** éclairer qch. **3** *n (on shoes, cloth)* brillant *m.*

shin·y *adj* brillant.

ship navire *m*, bateau *m*; **by s.** en bateau.

ship·ping *(traffic)* navigation *f.*

ship·wreck naufrage *m.*

ship·wrecked *adj* naufragé; **to be s.** faire naufrage.

ship·yard chantier *m* naval.

shirt chemise *f*, *(of woman)* chemisier *m*; *(of sportsman)* maillot *m.*

shiv·er 1 *vi* frissonner (**with** de). **2** *n* frisson *m.*

shock 1 *n (emotional, physical)* choc *m*; **(electric) s.** décharge *f* (électrique); **suffering from s., in s.** en état de choc. **2** *vt (offend)* choquer; *(surprise)* stupéfier.

shock ab·sorb·er amortisseur *m.*

shock·ing *adj* affreux; *(outrageous)* scandaleux.

shoe chaussure *f*, soulier *m.*

shoe·lace lacet *m.*

shoe pol·ish cirage *m.*

shoe re·pair shop cordonnerie *f.*

shoe store magasin *m* de chaussures.

shoot* 1 *vt (kill)* tuer (d'un coup de feu); *(wound)* blesser (d'un coup de feu); *(execute)* fusiller; *(gun)* tirer un coup de; *(film)* tourner. **2** *vi (with gun)* tirer (**at** sur).

▸ **shoot ahead** *vi (rush)* avancer à toute vitesse.

shoot·ing *(shots)* coups *mpl* de feu; *(murder)* meurtre *m.*

▸ **shoot off** *vi (rush)* partir à toute vitesse.

▸ **shoot up** *vi (of price)* monter en flèche.

shop 1 *n* magasin *m*; *(small)* boutique *f*; **at the flower s.** chez le fleuriste. **2** *vi* faire ses courses (**at** chez).

shop·keep·er commerçant, -ante *mf.*

shop·ping to go s. faire des courses.

shop·ping bag sac *m* à provisions.

shop·ping dis·trict quartier *m* commerçant.

shop·ping mall centre *m* commercial.

shore *(of sea, lake)* rivage *m*; *(coast)* côte *f.*

short 1 *adj* court; *(person, distance)* petit; **a s. time** *or* **while (ago)** (il y a) peu de temps; **to be s. of money/time** être à court d'argent/de temps; **we're s. ten men** il nous manque dix hommes; **to be s. for sth** *(of name)* être l'abréviation de qch. **2** *adv* **to cut s.** *(hair)* couper court; *(visit etc)* raccourcir; *(person)* couper la parole à; **to get** *or* **run s.** manquer (**of** de).

short·age manque *m.*

short·cut raccourci *m.*

short·en *vt (dress, text etc)* raccourcir.

short·ly *adv (soon)* bientôt; **s. after** peu après.

shorts *npl* **(a pair of) s.** un short.

short·sight·ed *adj* myope.

short-term *adj* à court terme.

shot *(from gun)* coup *m*; *(with camera)* prise *f* de vues.

shot·gun fusil *m* (de chasse).

should *v aux (ought to)* **you s. do it** vous devriez le faire; **I s. have stayed** j'aurais dû rester; **that s. be Paul** ça doit être Paul. ▪ *(would)* **it's strange she s. say no** il est étrange qu'elle dise non. ▪ *(possibility)* **if he s. come** s'il vient.

shoul·der épaule *f*, **(hard) s.** *(of highway)* bas-côté *m.*

shoul·der bag sac *m* à bandoulière.

shout 1 *n* cri *m.* **2** *vti* crier; **to s. to sb to do** crier à qn de faire.

▸ **shout at** *vt (scold)* crier après.

shout·ing (*shouts*) cris *mpl*.
▸**shout out** *vti* crier.
shove 1 *n* poussée *f*; **to give a s.
(to)** pousser. **2** *vt* pousser; (*put*)
Fam fourrer. **3** *vi* pousser.
shov·el 1 *n* pelle *f*. **2** *vt* (*snow etc*)
enlever à la pelle.
show 1 *n* (*in theater*) spectacle *m*;
(*at movies*) séance *f*; **the Auto S.** le
Salon de l'Automobile; **on s.** (*painting etc*) exposé. **2** *vt** montrer (**to** à;
that que); (*in exhibition*) exposer;
(*movie*) passer; (*indicate*) indiquer;
to s. sb to the door reconduire qn.
3 *vi* (*be visible*) se voir; (*of movie*)
passer.
▸**show around** *vt* faire visiter; **to s.
sb around the house** faire visiter la
maison à qn.
show·er (*bath*) douche *f*; (*of rain*)
averse *f*.
▸**show in** *vt* (*visitor*) faire entrer.
show·ing (*of movie*) séance *f*.
show·off crâneur, -euse *mf*.
▸**show off** *vi* crâner.
▸**show out** *vt* (*visitor*) reconduire.
▸**show up 1** *vi* (*of person*) arriver. **2**
vt (*embarrass*) mettre (*qn*) dans
l'embarras.
shrimp crevette *f* (grise).
shrink* *vi* (*of clothes*) rétrécir.
shrub arbuste *m*.
shrug *vt* **to s. one's shoulders**
hausser les épaules.
shud·der *vi* frémir (**with** de).
shuf·fle *vt* (*cards*) battre.
shush! *int* chut!
shut* **1** *vt* fermer. **2** *vi* (*of door
etc*) se fermer; (*of shop etc*)
fermer.
▸**shut down** *vti* fermer.
▸**shut in** *vt* enfermer.
▸**shut off** *vt* (*gas etc*) fermer; (*engine*) arrêter; (*isolate*) isoler.
▸**shut out** *vt* (*light*) empêcher d'entrer; **to s. sb out** (*accidentally*) enfermer qn dehors.
shut·ter (*on window*) volet *m*; (*of
store*) rideau *m* (métallique).

shut·tle *s.* (*service*) navette *f*;
space s. navette spatiale.
▸**shut up 1** *vt* (*house etc*) fermer;
(*lock up*) enfermer (*personne, objet
précieux*). **2** *vi* (*be quiet*) se taire.
shy *adj* timide.
shy·ness timidité *f*.
sick 1 *adj* malade; **to be s.** (*vomit*)
vomir; **off s.** en congé de maladie;
to feel s. avoir mal au cœur; **to be
s. (and tired) of sth/sb** *Fam* en
avoir marre de qch/qn. **2** *npl* **the s.**
les malades *mpl*.
sick·ness maladie *f*.
side côté *m*; (*of hill, animal*) flanc
m; (*of road, river*) bord *m*; (*team*)
équipe *f*; **at** *or* **by the s. of** à côté
de; **at** *or* **by my s.** à côté de moi, à
mes côtés; **s. by s.** l'un à côté de l'autre; **to move to one s.** s'écarter; **on
this s.** de ce côté; **on the other s.** de
l'autre côté; **to take sides with sb**
se ranger du côté de qn; **on our s.**
de notre côté.
side·board buffet *m*.
side·burns *npl* pattes *fpl*.
side·walk trottoir *m*.
side·ways *adv & adj* de côté.
sid·ing (*for train*) voie *f* d'évite-
ment; (*of wall*) parement *m* (extérieur).
siege siège *m*; **under s.** assiégé.
sieve tamis *m*; (*for liquids*) passoire
f.
sift *vt* (*flour etc*) tamiser.
sigh 1 *n* soupir *m*. **2** *vi* soupirer.
sight vue *f*; (*thing seen*) spectacle
m; **to lose s. of** perdre de vue; **to
catch s. of** apercevoir; **by s.** de
vue; **in s.** (*target etc*) en vue; **out of
s.** caché; **the (tourist) sights** les at-
tractions *fpl* touristiques.
sight·see·ing to go s. faire du
tourisme.
sign 1 *n* signe *m*; (*notice*) panneau
m; (*over shop, inn*) enseigne *f*; **no
s. of** aucune trace de. **2** *vti* (*with
signature*) signer.
sig·nal 1 *n* signal *m*; (*of vehicle*) cli-

gnotant *m*; **traffic signals** feux *mpl* de signalisation. **2** *vi* faire signe (**to** à); **to s. (left/right)** *(in car)* mettre son clignotant (à gauche/à droite).

sig·na·ture signature *f.*

sig·nif·i·cant *adj (important, large)* important.

sig·nif·i·cant·ly *adv* sensiblement.

sig·ni·fy *vt* signifier.

▸**sign in** *vi (in hotel etc)* signer le registre.

▸**sign on, sign up** *vi (of soldier, worker)* s'engager; *(for course)* s'inscrire (**for** à).

sign·post poteau *m* indicateur.

si·lence 1 *n* silence *m*; **in s.** en silence. **2** *vt* faire taire.

si·lent *adj* silencieux; *(movie)* muet (*f* muette); **to keep s.** garder le silence (**about** sur).

si·lent·ly *adv* silencieusement.

silk soie *f.*

sill *(of window)* rebord *m.*

sil·ly *adj* bête; **to do something s.** faire une bêtise.

sil·ver 1 *n* argent *m*; *(plates etc)* argenterie *f.* **2** *adj (spoon etc)* en argent; **s. paper** papier *m* d'argent.

sil·ver-plat·ed *adj* plaqué argent.

sil·ver·ware *inv* argenterie *f.*

sim·i·lar *adj* semblable (**to** à).

sim·i·lar·i·ty ressemblance *f* (**to** avec).

sim·ple *adj* simple.

sim·pli·fy *vt* simplifier.

sim·ply *adv (plainly, merely)* simplement; *(absolutely)* absolument.

si·mul·ta·ne·ous *adj* simultané.

si·mul·ta·ne·ous·ly *adv* simultanément.

sin péché *m.*

since 1 *prep* depuis. **2** *conj* depuis que; *(because)* puisque; **s. she's been here** depuis qu'elle est ici; **it's a year s.** I saw him ça fait un an que je ne l'ai pas vu. **3** *adv* **(ever) s.** depuis.

sin·cere *adj* sincère.

sin·cere·ly *adv* sincèrement; **yours s.** *(in letter)* veuillez croire à mes sentiments dévoués.

sin·cer·i·ty sincérité *f.*

sing* *vti* chanter.

sing·er chanteur, -euse *mf.*

sin·gle *adj* seul; *(room, bed)* pour une personne; *(unmarried)* célibataire; **not a s. book/etc** pas un seul livre/*etc*; **every s. day** tous les jours sans exception.

Sin·gle Mar·ket Marché *m* unique.

▸**single out** *vt* choisir.

sin·gu·lar 1 *adj (form)* singulier; *(noun)* au singulier. **2** *n* singulier *m*; **in the s.** au singulier.

sin·is·ter *adj* sinistre.

sink¹ *(in kitchen)* évier *m*; *(washbasin)* lavabo *m.*

sink*² *vi (of ship, person etc)* couler.

▸**sink (down) into** *vt (mud)* s'enfoncer dans; *(armchair)* s'affaler dans.

sip *vi* boire à petites gorgées.

sir monsieur *m*; **S.** *(title)* sir.

si·ren *(of factory etc)* sirène *f.*

sis·ter sœur *f.*

sit* 1 *vi* s'asseoir; **to be sitting** être assis; **she was sitting reading** elle était assise à lire. **2** *vt (child on chair etc)* asseoir.

sit (for) *vt (exam)* se présenter à.

▸**sit around** *vi* traîner; *(do nothing)* ne rien faire.

▸**sit down 1** *vi* s'asseoir; **to be sitting down** être assis. **2** *vt* asseoir *(qn).*

site *(position)* emplacement *m*; **(building) s.** chantier *m.*

sit·ting room salon *m.*

sit·u·ate *vt* situer; **to be situated** être situé, se situer.

sit·u·a·tion situation *f.*

▸**sit up (straight)** *vi* s'asseoir (bien droit).

six adj & n six (m).
six·teen adj & n seize (m).
sixth adj & n sixième (mf).
six·ti·eth adj & n soixantième (mf).
six·ty adj & n soixante (m).
size (of person, clothes, packet etc) taille f; (measurements) dimensions fpl; (of town, sum) importance f; (of shoes, gloves) pointure f; (of shirt) encolure f; (of chest) hip/chest s. tour m de hanches/de poitrine.
skate 1 n patin m. 2 vi patiner.
skate·board planche f (à roulettes).
skat·er patineur, -euse mf.
skat·ing patinage m; to go s. faire du patinage.
skat·ing rink (ice-skating) patinoire f.
skel·e·ton squelette m.
sketch 1 n (drawing) croquis m; (comic play) sketch m. 2 vi faire un or des croquis.
skew·er (for meat etc) broche f; (for kebab) brochette f.
ski 1 n ski m. 2 vi faire du ski.
skid 1 vi déraper; to s. into sth déraper et heurter qch. 2 n dérapage m.
ski·er skieur, -euse mf.
ski·ing 1 n ski m. 2 adj (school, clothes, etc) de ski.
ski lift remonte-pente m.
skill habileté f (at à); (technique) technique f.
skilled adj habile.
skilled work·er ouvrier, -ière mf qualifié(e).
skill·ful adj habile (at doing à faire; at sth à qch).
skim milk lait m écrémé.
skin peau f.
skin div·ing plongée f sous-marine.
skin·ny adj maigre.
skip 1 vi (hop) sautiller; (with rope) sauter à la corde. 2 vt (miss) sauter (repas, classe etc).
skirt jupe f.

skull crâne m.
sky ciel m.
sky·scrap·er gratte-ciel m inv.
slack adj (knot, spring) lâche; to be s. (of rope) avoir du mou; (in office etc) être calme.
slack·en vt (rope) relâcher.
slacks npl pantalon m.
slam 1 vt (door, lid) claquer. 2 vi (of door) claquer. 3 n claquement m.
slang argot m.
slant 1 n inclinaison f. 2 vi (of roof) être en pente.
slap 1 n tape f; (on face) gifle f. 2 vt (person) donner une tape à; to s. sb's face gifler qn; to s. sb's bottom donner une fessée à qn.
slate ardoise f.
slaugh·ter 1 vt massacrer; (animal) abattre. 2 n massacre m; (of animal) abattage m.
slave esclave mf.
►**slave away** vi se crever (au travail).
slav·er·y esclavage m.
sled luge f; (horse-drawn) traîneau m.
sleep 1 n sommeil m; to get some s. dormir. 2 vi* dormir; (spend the night) coucher; to go or get to s. s'endormir.
sleep·er (bed in train) couchette f; (train) m couchettes.
sleep·ing adj (asleep) endormi.
sleep·ing bag sac m de couchage.
sleep·ing car wagon-lit m.
sleep·ing pill somnifère m.
sleep·y adj to be s. (of person) avoir sommeil.
sleet 1 n neige f fondue. 2 vi it's sleeting il tombe de la neige fondue.
sleeve (of shirt etc) manche f; (of record) pochette f; long-/short-sleeved à manches longues/courtes.
sleigh traîneau m.
slen·der adj (person) svelte;

(wrist, neck etc) fin; *(hope, chance)* maigre, faible.

slept *pt & pp de* **sleep**.

slice tranche *f.*

slice (up) *vt* couper (en tranches).

slide 1 *n (in playground)* toboggan *m; (film)* diapositive *f.* **2** *vi* glisser. **3** *vt (letter etc)* glisser (**into** dans); *(table, chair etc)* faire glisser.

slid·ing door porte *f* à glissière *or* coulissante.

slight *adj (noise, mistake etc)* léger, petit; *(chance)* faible; **the slightest thing** la moindre chose; **not in the slightest** pas le moins du monde.

slight·ly *adv* légèrement.

slim 1 *adj* mince. **2** *vi* maigrir.

sling *(for arm)* écharpe *f,* **in a s.** en écharpe.

slip 1 *n (mistake)* erreur *f, (woman's undergarment)* combinaison *f,* **a s. of paper** un bout de papier. **2** *vi* glisser. **3** *vt (slide)* glisser (qch) (**to** à; **into** dans).

▸**slip away** *vi* s'esquiver.

slip·cov·er *(on furniture)* housse *f.*

▸**slip in** *vi* entrer furtivement.

▸**slip into** *vt (room etc)* se glisser dans; *(bathrobe etc)* mettre, passer.

▸**slip off** *vt (garment)* enlever.

▸**slip on** *vt (garment)* mettre.

▸**slip out** *vi* sortir furtivement; *(for a moment)* sortir (un instant).

slip·per pantoufle *f.*

slip·per·y *adj* glissant.

▸**slip up** *vi (make a mistake)* gaffer.

slit *(opening)* fente *f, (cut)* coupure *f.*

slo·gan slogan *m.*

slope 1 *n* pente *f, (of mountain)* versant *m; (of skiing)* piste *f.* **2** *vi (of ground, roof etc)* être en pente.

slop·ing *adj* en pente.

slot *(slit)* fente *f, (groove)* rainure *f.*

slot ma·chine distributeur *m* automatique; *(for gambling)* machine *f* à sous.

slow 1 *adj* lent; **to be s.** *(of clock,*

watch) retarder; **to be five minutes s.** retarder de cinq minutes; **in s. motion** au ralenti. **2** *adv* lentement.

▸**slow down, slow up** *vti* ralentir.

slow·ly *adv* lentement; *(bit by bit)* peu à peu.

slow-poke *Fam* tortue *f.*

slug limace *f.*

slum *(house)* taudis *m;* **the slums** les quartiers *mpl* pauvres.

slump 1 *n (in sales, prices etc)* baisse *f* soudaine; *(economic depression)* crise *f.* **2** *vi (sales, prices, person)* s'effondrer; *(morale)* baisser soudainement.

sly *(cunning)* rusé.

smack 1 *n* claque *f;* gifle *f;* (*on bottom*) fessée *f.* **2** *vt (person)* donner une claque à; **to s. sb's face** gifler qn; **to s. sb's bottom** donner une fessée à qn.

small 1 *adj* petit. **2** *adv (to cut, chop)* menu.

small·pox petite vérole *f.*

smart `*adj (fashionable, elegant)* élégant; *(clever)* intelligent.

smash 1 *vt (break)* briser; *(shatter)* fracasser. **2** *vi* se briser.

smash·ing *adj Fam* formidable.

▸**smash into** *vt (of vehicle)* (r)entrer dans.

smash-up collision *f.*

smell 1 *n* odeur *f,* **(sense of) s.** odorat *m.* **2** *vt** sentir. **3** *vi (stink)* sentir (mauvais); *(have a smell)* avoir une odeur; **to s. of smoke/etc** sentir la fumée/etc.

smell·y *adj* qui sent mauvais, qui pue; **to be s.** sentir mauvais, puer.

smile 1 *n* sourire *m.* **2** *vi* sourire (**at** sb à qn).

smock blouse *f.*

smoke 1 *n* fumée *f,* **to have a s.** fumer une cigarette/etc. **2** *vti* fumer; **'no smoking'** 'défense de fumer'; **smoking compartment** compartiment *m* fumeurs.

smok·er fumeur, -euse *mf, (train*

compartment) compartiment *m* fumeurs.

smooth *adj (surface, skin etc)* lisse; *(flight)* agréable.

▸**smooth down, smooth out** *vt (dress, hair etc)* lisser.

smug·gle *vt* passer (en fraude).

smug·gler contrebandier, -ière *mf*.

smug·gling contrebande *f*.

snack *(meal)* casse-croûte *m inv*; **snacks** *(things to eat)* petites choses *fpl* à grignoter; *(candies)* friandises *fpl*; **to eat a s. or snacks** grignoter.

snack bar snack(-bar) *m*.

snail escargot *m*.

snake serpent *m*.

snap 1 *vt (break)* casser (avec un bruit sec). **2** *vi* se casser net. **3** *n (fastener)* bouton-pression *m*.

snap(·shot) photo *f*.

snatch *vt* saisir *(d'un geste vif)*; **to s. sth from sb** arracher qch à qn.

sneak·er basket *m*.

sneer *vi* ricaner.

sneeze 1 *vi* éternuer. **2** *n* éternuement *m*.

sniff *vti* **to s. (at)** renifler.

snip (off) *vt* couper.

snook·er snooker *m (sorte de jeu de billard)*.

snore *vi* ronfler.

snor·ing ronflements *mpl*.

snout museau *m*.

snow 1 *n* neige *f*. **2** *vi* neiger; **it's snowing** il neige.

snow·ball boule *f* de neige.

snow·drift congère *f*.

snow·flake flocon *m* de neige.

snow·man bonhomme *m* de neige.

snow·plow chasse-neige *m inv*.

snow·storm tempête *f* de neige.

so 1 *adv (to such a degree)* si, tellement *(that* que); *(thus)* ainsi; **so that** *(purpose)* pour que *(+ subjunctive)*; *(result)* si bien que *(+ indicative)*; **so as to do** pour faire; **I**

think so je le pense; **if so** si oui; **is that so?** c'est vrai?; **so am I, so do I/etc** moi aussi; **so much** *(to work etc)* tant *(that* que); **so much courage/etc** tant de courage/*etc*; **so many** tant; **so many books/etc** tant de livres/*etc*; **ten or so** environ dix; **and so on** et ainsi de suite. **2** *conj (therefore)* donc; **so what?** et alors?

soak 1 *vt (drench)* tremper *(qn)*; *(laundry, food)* faire tremper. **2** *vi (of laundry etc)* tremper.

soaked (through) *adj (person)* trempé jusqu'aux os.

soak·ing *adj & adv* **s. (wet)** trempé.

▸**soak up** *vt* absorber.

soap savon *m*.

soap pow·der lessive *f*.

soap·y *adj* savonneux.

sob 1 *n* sanglot *m*. **2** *vi* sangloter.

so·ber *adj* **he's s.** *(not drunk)* il n'est pas ivre.

soc·cer football *m*.

so·cial *adj* social; **s. club** club *m*; **s. evening** soirée *f*; **to have a good s. life** sortir beaucoup; **s. security** *(pension)* pension *f* de retraite; **s. services, S. Security** = Sécurité *f* sociale; **s. worker** assistant, -ante *mf* social(e).

so·cial·ist *adj & n* socialiste *(mf)*.

so·ci·e·ty société *f*.

sock chaussette *f*.

sock·et *(for electric plug)* prise *f* de courant.

so·da (pop) soda *m*.

so·da (wa·ter) eau *f* gazeuse.

so·fa canapé *m*; **s. bed** canapé-lit *m*.

soft *adj (gentle, not stiff)* doux *(f* douce); *(butter, ground)* mou *(f* molle); **s. drink** boisson *f* non alcoolisée.

soft·ball = sorte de base-ball.

soft·en 1 *vt (object)* ramollir; *(skin)* adoucir. **2** *vi (object)* ramollir; *(skin)* s'adoucir.

soft·ly *adv* doucement.

soft·ware *inv* logiciel *m*.

soil sol *m*, terre *f*.

so·lar *adj* solaire.

sol·dier soldat *m*.

sole *(of shoe)* semelle *f*; *(of foot)* plante *f*; *(fish)* sole *f*, **lemon s.** limande *f*.

sol·emn *adj (formal)* solennel; *(serious)* grave.

sol·id 1 *adj (car, meal etc)* solide; *(wall, line)* plein; *(gold)* massif; **s. line** ligne *f* continue. 2 *n* solide *m*.

sol·i·dar·i·ty solidarité *f*.

so·lo *adj & n* solo *(m)*.

so·lu·tion solution *f* (**to** de).

solve *vt (problem)* résoudre.

sol·vent 1 *n* solvant *m*. 2 *adj (financially)* solvable.

some 1 *adj (amount, number)* du, de la, des; **s. wine** du vin; **s. water** de l'eau; **s. dogs** des chiens; **s. pretty flowers** de jolies fleurs. ▪ *(unspecified)* un, une; **s. man (or other)** un homme (quelconque); ▪ *(a few)* quelques; *(a little)* un peu de. 2 *pron (number)* quelques-un(e)s *(of* de). ▪ *(a certain quantity)* en; **I want s.** j'en veux.

some·bod·y *pron* = **someone**.

some·day *adv* un jour.

some·how *adv* d'une manière ou d'une autre; *(for some reason)* on ne sait pourquoi.

some·one *pron* quelqu'un; **s. small/etc** quelqu'un de petit/etc.

some·place *adv* quelque part.

som·er·sault culbute *f*.

some·thing *pron* quelque chose; **s. awful/etc** quelque chose d'affreux/etc; **s. of a liar/etc** un peu menteur/etc.

some·time *adv* un jour.

some·times *adv* quelquefois.

some·what *adv* quelque peu.

some·where *adv* quelque part.

son fils *m*.

song chanson *f*.

son-in-law, *pl* **sons-in-law** gendre *m*.

soon *adv* bientôt; *(quickly)* vite; *(early)* tôt; **s. after** peu après; **as s. as she leaves** aussitôt qu'elle partira; **no sooner had he spoken than** à peine avait-il parlé que; **I'd sooner leave** je préférerais partir; **I'd just as s. leave** j'aimerais autant partir; **sooner or later** tôt ou tard.

soot suie *f*.

soothe *vt (pain, nerves)* calmer.

sore 1 *adj (painful)* douloureux; *(angry) Fam* fâché (**at** contre); **she has a s. throat** elle a mal à la gorge. 2 *n* plaie *f*.

sor·row chagrin *m*.

sor·ry *adj* **to be s.** *(regret)* être désolé (**to do** de faire); **I'm s. she can't come** je regrette qu'elle ne puisse pas venir; **I'm s. about the delay** je m'excuse pour ce retard; **s.!** pardon!; **to feel** *or* **be s. for sb** plaindre qn.

sort¹ sorte *f*, espèce *f* (**of** de); **all sorts of** toutes sortes de; **what s. of drink/etc is it?** qu'est-ce que c'est comme boisson/etc?

sort² *vt (papers etc)* trier.

▸ **sort out** *vt (classify, select)* trier; *(separate)* séparer (**from** de); *(tidy)* ranger; *(problem)* régler.

soul âme *f*.

sound¹ 1 *n* son *m*; *(noise)* bruit *m*; **I don't like the s. of it** ça ne me plaît pas du tout. 2 *vt (bell, alarm etc)* sonner; **to s. one's horn** klaxonner. 3 *vi (of bell etc)* sonner; *(seem)* sembler; **to s. like** sembler être; *(resemble)* ressembler à.

sound² 1 *adj (healthy)* sain; *(good, reliable)* solide. 2 *adv* **s. asleep** profondément endormi.

sound·proof *vt* insonoriser.

soup soupe *f*, potage *m*.

sour *adj* aigre.

source source *f*.

south 1 *n* sud *m*; **(to the) s. of** au sud de. 2 *adj (coast)* sud *inv* 3 *adv* au sud.

south·bound *adj* en direction du sud.

south·east n & adj sud-est (m & adj inv).

south·ern adj (town) du sud; (coast) sud inv.

south·ern·er habitant, -ante mf du sud.

south·ward(s) adj & adv vers le sud.

south·west n & adj sud-ouest (m & adj inv).

sou·ve·nir (object) souvenir m.

sow* vt (seeds) semer.

space (gap, emptiness, atmosphere) espace m; (period) période f; (for parking) place f; **to take up s.** (room) prendre de la place.

space heat·er radiateur m d'appoint.

▸**space out** vt espacer.

space·ship engin m spatial.

space·suit combinaison f spatiale.

spa·cious adj spacieux.

spade bêche f; (of child) pelle f; **spade(s)** Cards pique m.

spa·ghet·ti spaghetti(s) mpl.

spam (e-mail) messages mpl publicitaires, pourriels mpl; **a s. e-mail** un message publicitaire, un pourriel.

span 1 n (of hand, wing) envergure f; (of arch) portée f; (of bridge) travée f; (duration) durée m. 2 vt (river etc) enjamber; (period of time etc) couvrir.

Span·iard Espagnol, -ole mf.

Span·ish 1 adj espagnol. 2 n (language) espagnol m.

spank vt donner une fessée à.

spank·ing fessée f.

spare 1 adj (extra) de trop; (clothes) de rechange; (wheel) de secours; (bed, room) d'ami; **s. time** loisirs mpl. 2 n **s.** (part) pièce f détachée. 3 vt (do without) se passer de (qn, qch); **to s. sb** (details etc) épargner à qn; (time) accorder à qn; (money) donner à qn.

spark étincelle f.

spar·kle vi (of diamond, star) étinceler.

spar·kling adj (wine, water) pétillant.

spark·plug bougie f.

spar·row moineau m.

speak* 1 vi parler (**about, of** de); **English-/French-speaking** qui parle anglais/français. 2 vt (language) parler; (say) dire.

speak·er (public) orateur m; (loudspeaker) haut-parleur m; (of stereo system) enceinte f.

▸**speak up** vi parler plus fort.

spear lance f.

spe·cial 1 adj spécial; (care, attention) (tout) particulier. 2 n **today's s.** (in restaurant) le plat du jour.

spe·cial·ist spécialiste mf (**in** de).

spe·cial·ize vi se spécialiser (**in** dans).

spe·cial·ly adv spécialement.

spe·cial·ty spécialité f.

spe·cies inv espèce f.

spe·cif·ic adj précis.

spec·i·fi·ca·tion spécification f.

spec·i·men (example, person) spécimen m.

spec·ta·cle spectacle m; **spectacles** (glasses) lunettes fpl.

spec·tac·u·lar adj spectaculaire.

spec·ta·tor spectateur, -trice mf.

spec·trum spectre m; (range) gamme f.

spec·u·late vi s'interroger; (financially) spéculer; **to s. that** conjecturer que.

speech (talk, lecture) discours m (**on, about** sur); (power of language) parole f; (spoken language) langage m.

speed 1 n (rate) vitesse f; (quickness) rapidité f; **s. limit** limitation f de vitesse. 2 vi* (drive too fast) aller trop vite.

speed·boat vedette f.

speed·om·e·ter compteur m (de vitesse).

▸**speed* up 1** vt accélérer. **2** vi (of person) aller plus vite.

spell¹ (period) (courte) période f; (magic) charme m; **cold s.** vague f de froid.

spell*² vt (write) écrire; (say aloud) épeler; (of letters) former (mot); **how is it spelled?** comment cela s'écrit-il?

spell·ing orthographe f.

spend* 1 vt (money) dépenser (on pour); (time etc) passer (on sth sur qch; doing à faire). **2** vi dépenser.

sphere sphère f.

spice 1 n épice f. **2** vt épicer.

spic·y adj (food) épicé.

spi·der araignée f; **s.'s web** toile f d'araignée.

spike pointe f.

spill* 1 vt répandre, renverser. **2** vi se répandre, se renverser (on, over sur).

▸**spill out 1** vt (empty) vider (café, verre etc). **2** vi (of coffee etc) se renverser.

▸**spill over** vi déborder.

spin* vt (wheel etc) faire tourner; (washing) essorer.

spin·ach (food) épinards mpl.

spin (a·round) vi (of dancer, wheel etc) tourner.

spine (of back) colonne f vertébrale.

spi·ral spirale f.

spire flèche f.

spir·its npl (drinks) alcool m.

spir·i·tu·al adj spirituel.

spit 1 vti* cracher. **2** n (for meat) broche f.

spite in s. of malgré.

spite·ful adj malveillant.

splash 1 vt éclabousser (with de; over sur). **2** n (mark) éclaboussure f.

splash (a·round) vi (in river, mud) patauger; (in bath) barboter.

splen·did adj splendide.

splin·ter (in finger) écharde f.

split 1 n fente f; (tear) déchirure f. **2** vt* (break apart) fendre; (tear) déchirer.

split (up) 1 vt (group) diviser; (money, work) partager (between entre). **2** vi (of group) se diviser (in-to en); (because of disagreement) se séparer.

spoil* vt gâter; (damage, ruin) abîmer; (child, dog etc) gâter.

spoke (of wheel) rayon m.

spoke, spo·ken pt & pp de **speak**.

spokes·man, pl -men porte-parole m inv (for, of de).

sponge éponge f.

sponge cake gâteau m de Savoie.

▸**sponge down** vt to s. oneself down se laver à l'éponge.

spon·sor 1 vt sponsoriser. **2** n sponsor mf.

spon·ta·ne·ous adj spontané.

spool bobine f.

spoon cuillère f.

spoon·ful cuillerée f.

sport sport m; sports (in general) sport m; **my favorite s.** mon sport préféré; **to play sports** faire du sport; **sports club** club m sportif; **sports car/jacket/ground** voiture f/veste f/terrain m de sport.

sports·man, pl -men sportif m.

sports·wom·an, pl -women sportive f.

spot¹ (stain, mark) tache f; (dot) point m; (place) endroit m; **on the s.** sur place.

spot² vt (notice) apercevoir.

spot·less adj (clean) impeccable.

spot·light (in theater etc) projecteur m; (for photography) spot m.

spot·ted adj (animal) tacheté.

spouse époux, -ouse mf.

spout (of teapot etc) bec m.

sprain 1 n foulure f. **2** vt to s. one's ankle/wrist se fouler la cheville/le poignet.

spray 1 n (can) bombe f; **hair s.** laque f à cheveux. **2** vt (liquid, surface) vaporiser; (plant) arroser;

(car) peindre à la bombe.

spread 1 *vt* (stretch, open out)* étendre; *(legs, fingers)* écarter; *(distribute)* répandre (**over** sur); *(paint, payment, visits)* étaler; *(news, germs)* propager. **2** *vi (of fire)* s'étendre; *(of news, epidemic)* se propager. **3** *n (paste)* pâte *f* (à tartiner); **cheese s.** fromage *m* à tartiner.

▸**spread out 1** *vt (stretch, open out)* étendre; *(legs, fingers)* écarter; *(distribute)* répandre; *(paint, payment, visits)* étaler. **2** *vi (of people)* se disperser.

spring¹ 1 *n (metal device)* ressort *m.* **2** *vi* (leap)* bondir.

spring² *(season)* printemps *m;* **in (the) s.** au printemps.

spring³ *(of water)* source *f.*

spring·board tremplin *m.*

spring on·ion oignon *m* vert.

spring·time printemps *m.*

sprin·kle *vt (sand etc)* répandre (**on, over** sur); **to s. with water, to s. water on** asperger d'eau; **to s. with** *(sugar, salt, flour)* saupoudrer de.

sprin·kler *(in garden)* arroseur *m.*

sprout (**Brussels**) **s.** chou *m (pl* choux) de Bruxelles.

spur *(of horse rider)* éperon *m.*

spurt (**out**) *vi (of liquid)* jaillir.

spy espion, -onne *mf.*

spy·ing espionnage *m.*

▸**spy on** *vt* espionner.

square 1 *n* carré *m; (in town)* place *f; (for drawing right angles)* équerre *f.* **2** *adj* carré; *(meal)* solide.

squash 1 *vt (crush)* écraser; *(squeeze)* serrer. **2** *n (game)* squash *m; (vegetable)* courge *f.*

squat (**down**) *vi* s'accroupir.

squeak *vi (of door)* grincer; *(of shoe)* craquer.

squeal 1 *vi* pousser des cris aigus. **2** *n* cri *m* aigu.

squeeze 1 *vt* presser; **to s. sb's hand** serrer la main à qn. **2** *vi (force oneself)* se glisser (**through/into/**

etc par/dans/*etc).* **3** *n (pressure)* pression *f; (hug)* étreinte; **to give sth a s.** presser qch; **a s. of lemon** quelques gouttes de citron.

▸**squeeze in** *vi (of person)* trouver un peu de place.

▸**squeeze into** *vt* **to s. sth into sth** faire rentrer qch dans qch.

▸**squeeze out** *vt (juice etc)* faire sortir (**from** de).

▸**squeeze up** *vi* se serrer (**against** contre).

squint 1 *n* **to have a s.** loucher. **2** *vi* loucher; *(in the sunlight etc)* plisser les yeux.

squir·rel écureuil *m.*

squirt 1 *vt (liquid)* faire gicler. **2** *vi* gicler.

stab *vt (with knife)* poignarder.

sta·bil·i·ty stabilité *f.*

sta·ble¹ *adj* stable.

sta·ble² écurie *f.*

stack *(heap)* tas *m;* **stacks of** *Fam* un *or* des tas de.

stack (**up**) *vt* entasser.

sta·di·um stade *m.*

staff personnel *m; (of school)* professeurs *mpl; (of army)* état-major *m.*

stag cerf *m.*

stage¹ 1 *n (platform)* scène *f.* **2** *vt (play)* monter.

stage² *(phase, of journey)* étape *f.*

stage·coach diligence *f.*

stag·ger *vi* chanceler.

stain 1 *vt (to mark)* tacher (**with** de). **2** *n* tache *f.*

stained glass win·dow vitrail *m (pl* vitraux).

stain·less steel *adj (knife etc)* en inox.

stain re·mov·er détachant *m.*

stair·case escalier *m.*

stairs *npl* escalier *m.*

stake *(post)* pieu *m.*

stale *adj (bread etc)* rassis *(f* rassie).

stalk¹ *(of plant)* tige *f.*

stalk² *vt (animal)* traquer; *(celebrity)* harceler.

stalk·er = admirateur obsessionnel.

stall 1 n (in market) étal m (pl étals); (for newspapers, flowers) kiosque m. **2** vti (of car engine) caler.

stam·mer vti bégayer.

stamp 1 n (for postage, instrument) timbre m; (mark) cachet m. **2** vt (document) tamponner; (letter) timbrer; **self-addressed stamped envelope** enveloppe f timbrée à votre adresse. **3** vti **to s. (one's feet)** taper des pieds.

stance position f.

stand 1 n (support) support m; (at exhibition) stand m; (for spectators) tribune f; **news/flower s.** kiosque m à journaux/à fleurs. **2** vt* (pain, person etc) supporter; (put) mettre (debout); **to s. a chance** avoir une chance. **3** vi être or se tenir (debout); (get up) se lever; (remain) rester (debout); (be situated) se trouver.

stan·dard 1 n norme f; (level) niveau m; **standards (of behavior)** principes mpl; **s. of living** niveau m de vie; **up to s.** (of work etc) au niveau. **2** adj (model, size) standard inv.

▸**stand around** vi traîner.

▸**stand aside** vi s'écarter.

▸**stand back** vi reculer.

stand·by adj (ticket) sans garantie.

▸**stand by 1** vi rester là (sans rien faire); (be ready) être prêt. **2** vt (friend) rester fidèle à.

▸**stand for** vt (mean) signifier, représenter; (put up with) supporter.

▸**stand in for** vt remplacer.

stand·ing adj debout inv.

▸**stand out** vi ressortir (**against** sur).

stand·point point m de vue.

stand·still **to bring to a s.** immobiliser; **to come to a s.** s'immobiliser.

▸**stand up 1** vt mettre debout. **2** vi se lever.

▸**stand up for** vt défendre.

▸**stand up to** vt résister à (qch); (defend oneself) tenir tête à (qn).

sta·ple 1 n (for paper etc) agrafe f. **2** vt agrafer.

sta·pler agrafeuse f.

star 1 n étoile f; (person) vedette f. **2** vi (of actor) être la vedette (**in** de). **3** vt (of movie) avoir pour vedette.

stare 1 n regard m (fixe). **2** vi **to s.** **at** fixer (du regard).

Star-Span·gled Ban·ner (flag) drapeau m américain; (hymn) hymne m national américain.

start¹ 1 n commencement m, début m; (of race) départ m; (lead) avance f (**on** sur); **to make a s.** commencer. **2** vt commencer; **to s. doing** or **to do** commencer à faire. **3** vi commencer (**with sth** par qch; **by doing** par faire); **starting from** (price etc) à partir de.

start² vi (jump) sursauter.

start (off or **out)** vi partir (**for** pour).

start (up) 1 vt (engine, vehicle) mettre en marche; (business) fonder. **2** vi (of engine, vehicle) démarrer.

start·er (in vehicle) démarreur m.

star·tle vt (make jump) faire sursauter.

▸**start on** vt commencer.

star·va·tion faim f.

starve vi souffrir de la faim; (die) mourir de faim; **I'm starving!** (hungry) je meurs de faim!

state¹ (condition) état m; **S.** (nation etc) État m; **the States** Fam les États-Unis mpl.

state² vt déclarer (**that** que); (time, date) fixer.

state·ment déclaration f; (bank) **s.** relevé m de compte.

states·man, pl **-men** homme m d'État.

stat·ic 1 adj statique. **2** n (on radio)

parasites *mpl*; *(electricity)* électricité *f* statique.

sta·tion *(for trains)* gare *f*; *(underground)* station *f*; **(police) s.** commissariat *m* (de police); **bus s.** gare *f* routière; **radio s.** station *f* de radio; **service** *or* **gas s.** station-service *f*.

sta·tion·ar·y *adj (vehicle)* à l'arrêt.

sta·tion·er·y articles *mpl* de bureau.

sta·tion·er·y store papeterie *f*.

sta·tion·mas·ter chef *m* de gare.

sta·tion wag·on break *m*, commerciale *f*.

sta·tis·tic *(fact)* statistique *f*.

stat·ue statue *f*.

stay 1 *n (visit)* séjour *m*. **2** *vi* rester; *(reside)* loger; *(visit)* séjourner; **to s. put** ne pas bouger.

▸ **stay away** *vi* ne pas s'approcher (**from** de); **to s. away from** *(school etc)* ne pas aller à.

▸ **stay in** *vi* rester à la maison; *(of nail, screw)* tenir.

▸ **stay out** *vi* rester dehors; *(not come home)* ne pas rentrer.

▸ **stay out of** *vt (not interfere in)* ne pas se mêler de.

▸ **stay up** *vi* ne pas se coucher; *(of fence etc)* tenir; **to s. up late** se coucher tard.

stead·i·ly *adv (gradually)* progressivement; *(regularly)* régulièrement; *(without stopping)* sans arrêt.

stead·y *adj* stable; *(hand)* sûr; *(progress, speed)* régulier; **s. (on one's feet)** solide sur ses jambes.

steak steak *m*, bifteck *m*.

steal* *vti* voler (**from sb** à qn).

steam 1 *n* vapeur *f*; *(on glass)* buée *f*. **2** *vt (food)* cuire à la vapeur.

steam·roll·er rouleau *m* compresseur.

steel acier *m*.

steep *adj (stairs, slope etc)* raide; *(hill, path)* escarpé; *(price)* excessif.

stee·ple clocher *m*.

steer *vt (vehicle, ship, person)* diriger (**towards** vers).

steer·ing wheel volant *m*.

stem *(of plant)* tige *f*.

step 1 *n* pas *m*; *(of stairs)* marche *f*; *(on train, bus)* marchepied *m*; *(doorstep)* pas *m* de la porte; *(action)* mesure *f*. **(flight of) steps** escalier *m*; *(outdoors)* perron *m*; **(pair of) steps** *(ladder)* escabeau *m*. **2** *vi (walk)* marcher (**on** sur).

▸ **step aside** *vi* s'écarter.

▸ **step back** *vi* reculer.

step·broth·er demi-frère *m*.

step·daugh·ter belle-fille *f*.

step·fa·ther beau-père *m*.

▸ **step forward** *vi* faire un pas en avant.

▸ **step into** *vt (car etc)* monter dans.

▸ **step out of** *vt (car etc)* descendre de.

step·lad·der escabeau *m*.

step·mo·ther belle-mère *f*.

▸ **step over** *vt (obstacle)* enjamber.

step·sis·ter demi-sœur *f*.

step·son beau-fils *m*.

▸ **step up** *vt (increase)* augmenter; *(quicken)* accélérer.

ster·e·o 1 *n (pl -os) (equipment)* chaîne (stéréo *inv*). **2** *adj* stéréo *inv*.

ster·il·ize *vt* stériliser.

ster·ling *(currency)* sterling *m inv*; **s. silver** argent *m* fin; **the pound s.** la livre sterling.

stew ragoût *m*.

stew·ard *(on plane, ship)* steward *m*.

stew·ard·ess hôtesse *f*.

stewed fruit compote *f*.

stick¹ bâton *m*; *(for walking)* canne *f*.

stick*²* 1 *vt (glue)* coller; *(put)* *Fam* mettre, fourrer; **to s. sth into sth** fourrer qch dans qch. **2** *vi* coller (**to** à); *(of food in pan)* attacher (**to** dans); *(of drawer etc)* se coincer, être coincé.

stick·er autocollant *m*.

▸ **stick on** vt (stamp) coller.

▸ **stick out 1** vt (tongue) tirer. **2** vi (of petticoat etc) dépasser.

▸ **stick up** vt (notice) afficher.

▸ **stick up for** vt défendre.

stick·y adj collant; (label) adhésif.

stiff adj raide; (leg etc) ankylosé; (brush) dur; **to have a s. neck** avoir le torticolis; **to feel s.** être courbaturé.

sti·fle vi **it's stifling** on étouffe.

still[1] adv encore, toujours; (even) encore; (nevertheless) tout de même.

still[2] adj (not moving) immobile; (calm) calme; **to keep** or **stand s.** rester tranquille.

stim·u·late vt stimuler.

sting 1 vti* (of insect, ointment etc) piquer. **2** n piqûre f.

stin·gy adj avare.

stink* vi puer; **to s. of smoke/**etc empester la fumée/etc.

▸ **stink up** vt (room) empester.

stir vt (coffee, leaves etc) remuer.

stir·rup étrier m.

stitch point m; (in knitting) maille f; (in wound) point m de suture.

stitch (up) vt (sew) coudre; (repair) recoudre.

stock 1 n (supply) provision f; (soup) bouillon m; **stock(s)** (securities) valeurs fpl (boursières); **in s.** en magasin, en stock; **out of s.** épuisé; **the S. Market** la Bourse. **2** vt (sell) vendre.

stock·ing bas m.

stock·pile 1 n réserve f. **2** vt faire des réserves de.

▸ **stock up** vi s'approvisionner (**with** de, en).

stock·y adj trapu.

sto·len pp of **steal**.

stom·ach (for digestion) estomac m; (front of body) ventre m.

stom·ach·ache mal m de ventre; **to have a s.** avoir mal au ventre.

stone pierre f; (pebble) caillou m; (pl cailloux); (in fruit) noyau m.

stood pt & pp de **stand**.

stool tabouret m.

stop 1 n (place, halt) arrêt m; (for plane, ship) escale f; **bus s.** arrêt m d'autobus; **to put a s. to sth** mettre fin à qch; **s. sign** (on road) stop m. **2** vt arrêter; (end) mettre fin à; (prevent) empêcher (**from doing** faire). **3** vi s'arrêter; (of pain, conversation etc) cesser; (stay) rester; **to s. eating/**etc s'arrêter de manger/etc; **to s. snowing/**etc cesser de neiger/etc; **'no stopping (no standing)'** (street sign) 'arrêt interdit'.

▸ **stop by** vi passer (**sb's** chez qn).

stop·light (on vehicle) stop m.

stop·off, stop·o·ver halte f.

▸ **stop off, stop over** vi (on trip) s'arrêter.

stop·per bouchon m.

▸ **stop up** vt (sink, pipe etc) boucher.

stop·watch chronomètre m.

store (supply) provision f; (warehouse) entrepôt m; (shop) magasin m.

store (a·way) vt (furniture) entreposer.

store (up) vt (in warehouse etc) stocker; (for future use) mettre en réserve.

store·keep·er commerçant, -ante mf.

store·room (in house) débarras m; (in office, store) réserve f.

stork cigogne f.

storm tempête f; (thunderstorm) orage m.

storm·y adj orageux.

sto·ry[1] histoire f; (newspaper article) article m; (plot) intrigue f; **short s.** nouvelle f.

sto·ry[2] (of building) étage m.

stove (for cooking) cuisinière f; (portable) réchaud m; (for heating) poêle m.

straight 1 adj droit; (hair) raide; (route) direct; (tidy) en ordre; (frank) franc (f franche). **2** adv (to *walk etc)* droit; *(directly)* tout droit; *(to drink whisky etc)* sec; **s. away** tout de suite; **s. ahead** *or* **on** tout droit.

straight·en *vt (wire, tie, picture)* redresser; *(hair)* défriser; *(room, papers)* ranger.

▶ **straighten out** *vt (problem)* résoudre.

straight·for·ward *adj (easy, clear)* simple.

strain 1 *n (tiredness)* fatigue *f*; *(mental)* tension *f* nerveuse. **2** *vt (eyes)* fatiguer; *(voice)* forcer; **to s. one's back** se faire mal au dos.

strain·er passoire *f*.

strand *(of wool)* brin *m*; *(of hair)* mèche *f*.

strand·ed *adj* en rade.

strange *adj (odd)* étrange; *(unknown)* inconnu.

strang·er *(unknown)* inconnu, -ue *mf*; *(person from outside)* étranger, -ère *mf*.

stran·gle *vt* étrangler.

strap sangle *f*, courroie *f*; *(on dress)* bretelle *f*; *(on watch)* bracelet *m*; *(on sandal)* lanière *f*.

strap (down *or* **in)** *vt* attacher *(avec une courroie).*

straw paille *f*; **a (drinking) s.** une paille.

straw·ber·ry 1 *n* fraise *f*. **2** *adj (ice-cream)* à la fraise; *(jam)* de fraises; *(tart)* aux fraises.

streak *(line)* raie *f*; *(of color)* strie *f*; *(of paint)* traînée *f*.

stream *(brook)* ruisseau *m*; *(flow)* flot *m*.

street rue *f*; **s. door** porte *f* d'entrée.

street·car *(tram)* tramway *m*.

street lamp, street light réverbère *m*.

street map plan *m* des rues.

strength force *f*; *(health, energy)* forces *fpl*; *(of wood etc)* solidité *f*.

strength·en *vt* renforcer.

stress 1 *n (mental)* stress *m*; *(emphasis)* & *Grammar* accent *m*; **under s.** stressé. **2** *vt* insister sur;

(word) accentuer; **to s. that** souligner que.

stressed *adj (person)* stressé.

stretch 1 *vt (rope, neck)* tendre; *(shoe, rubber)* étirer; **to s. one's legs** se dégourdir les jambes. **2** *vi (of person, elastic)* s'étirer. **3** *n (area)* étendue *f*.

stretch (out) 1 *vt (arm, leg)* étendre; **to s. (out) one's arm** *(reach out)* tendre le bras *(to take* pour prendre).* **2** *vi (of plain etc)* s'étendre.

stretch·er brancard *m*.

strict *adj* strict.

strict·ly *adv* strictement; **s. forbidden** formellement interdit.

strict·ness sévérité *f*.

stride (grand) pas *m*, enjambée *f*.

▶ **stride* along/out/***etc vi* avancer/sortir/*etc* à grands pas.

strike*¹ *vt (hit, impress)* frapper; *(collide with)* heurter; *(a match)* frotter; *(of clock)* sonner *(l'heure)*; **it strikes me that** il me semble que *(+ indicative).*

strike² *(of workers)* grève *f*; **to go on s.** se mettre en grève *(***for** pour obtenir).*

▶ **strike out 1** *vt (cross out)* rayer, barrer. **2** *vi* **to s. out at sb** essayer de frapper qn.

strik·er *(worker)* gréviste *mf*.

strik·ing *adj (impressive)* frappant.

string ficelle *f*; *(of parka, apron)* cordon *m*; *(of violin, racket etc)* corde *f*; *(of pearls)* collier *m*.

strip *(piece)* bande *f*; **(thin) s.** *(of metal etc)* lamelle *f*.

strip (off) *vi* se déshabiller.

stripe rayure *f*.

striped *adj* rayé.

strip mall = centre *m* commercial qui longe une route.

strive *vi* **to s. to do sth** s'efforcer de faire qch.

stroke 1 *n (movement)* coup *m*; *(illness)* hémorragie *f* cérébrale; **(swimming) s.** nage *f*; **a s. of luck** un coup de chance. **2** vt (beard, cat etc) caresser.

stroll 1 n promenade f. **2** vi se promener.

stroll·er (for baby) poussette f.

strong adj fort; (shoes, chair etc) solide.

struc·ture structure f; (building) construction f.

strug·gle 1 n (fight) lutte f (**to do** pour faire). **2** vi (fight) lutter, se battre (**with** avec); (thrash around) se débattre; **to s. to do** (try hard) s'efforcer de faire; (have difficulty) avoir du mal à faire.

stub (of cigarette etc) bout m; (of ticket, check) talon m, souche f.

stub·born adj (person) entêté.

stub·born·ness entêtement m.

▶ **stub out** vt (cigarette) écraser.

stuck (pt & pp of stick) adj (caught, jammed) coincé.

stud (for collar) bouton m de col.

stu·dent 1 n étudiant, -ante mf; (at school) élève mf; **music/etc s.** étudiant, -ante en musique/etc. **2** adj (life, protest) étudiant; (restaurant, housing) universitaire.

stu·di·o, pl -os (of artist etc) studio m; **s. apartment** studio m.

stud·y 1 n étude f; (office) bureau m. **2** vt (learn, observe) étudier. **3** vi étudier; **to s. to be a doctor/etc** faire des études de médecine/etc; **to s. for an exam** préparer un examen.

stuff 1 n (things) trucs mpl; (possessions) affaires fpl; **it's good s.** c'est bon. **2** vt (fill) bourrer (**with** de); (cushion etc) rembourrer (**with** avec); (put) fourrer (**into** dans); (chicken etc) farcir.

stuffed (up) adj (nose) bouché.

stuff·ing (for chicken etc) farce f.

stuff·y adj (room etc) mal aéré; **it smells s.** ça sent le renfermé.

stum·ble vi trébucher (**over** sur).

stump (of tree) souche f.

stun vt (with punch etc) étourdir.

stunned adj (amazed) stupéfait (**by** par).

stun·ning adj (astounding) stupéfiant; (beautiful) superbe.

stu·pid adj stupide; **a s. thing** une stupidité; **s. fool** idiot, -ote mf.

stu·pid·i·ty stupidité f.

stur·dy adj robuste.

stut·ter 1 vi bégayer. **2** n **to have a s.** être bègue.

sty (for pigs) porcherie f.

style style m; (fashion) mode f; (design of dress etc) modèle m; (of hair) coiffure f.

styl·ish adj chic inv.

sub·ject (matter) & Grammar sujet m; (at school, university) matière f; (citizen) ressortissant, -ante mf.

sub·junc·tive Grammar subjonctif m.

sub·ma·rine sous-marin m.

sub·scrib·er abonné, -ée mf.

▶ **sub·scribe to** vt (take out subscription) s'abonner à (journal etc); (be a subscriber) être abonné à (journal etc).

sub·scrip·tion (to newspaper etc) abonnement m.

sub·side vi (of ground) s'affaisser.

sub·si·dy subvention f.

sub·stance substance f.

sub·stan·tial adj important; (meal) copieux.

sub·sti·tute produit m de remplacement; (person) remplaçant, -ante mf (**for** de).

sub·ti·tle sous-titre m.

sub·tle adj subtil.

sub·tract vt soustraire (**from** de).

sub·trac·tion soustraction f.

sub·urb banlieue f; **the suburbs** la banlieue.

sub·ur·ban adj (train etc) de banlieue.

sub·way métro m.

suc·ceed vi réussir (**in doing** à faire; **in sth** dans qch).

suc·cess succès m, réussite f; **he**

was a s. il a eu du succès; **it was a s.** c'était réussi.

suc·cess·ful adj (effort etc) couronné de succès; (firm) prospère; (candidate in exam) admis; (writer, film etc) à succès; **to be s.** réussir (in dans; in an exam à un examen; in doing à faire).

suc·cess·ful·ly adv avec succès.

suc·ces·sion succession f, série f, ten days in s. dix jours consécutifs.

suc·ces·sive adj successif.

suc·ces·sor successeur m (to de).

such 1 adj tel, telle; **s. a car**/etc une telle voiture/etc, **s. happiness**/etc tant de bonheur/etc, **s. as** comme, tel que. **2** adv (so very) si; (in comparisons) aussi; **s. a large helping** une si grosse portion; **s. a kind woman as you** une femme aussi gentille que vous.

suck vt sucer.

suck (up) vi (with straw) aspirer.

sud·den adj soudain; **all of a s.** tout à coup.

sud·den·ly adv subitement.

suds npl (soap) **s.** mousse f de savon.

sue 1 vt poursuivre (en justice). **2** vi engager des poursuites judiciaires.

suede 1 n daim m. **2** adj de daim.

suf·fer 1 vi souffrir (from de). **2** vt (loss) subir; (pain) ressentir.

suf·fer·er victime f, AIDS **s.** malade mf du SIDA.

suf·fer·ing souffrance(s) f(pl).

suf·fi·cient adj (quantity) suffisant; **s. money**/etc suffisamment d'argent/etc.

suf·fi·cient·ly adv suffisamment.

suf·fix suffixe m.

suf·fo·cate vti étouffer.

sug·ar 1 n sucre m; **granulated/lump s.** sucre cristallisé/en morceaux. **2** vt sucrer.

sug·ar bowl sucrier m.

sug·gest vt (propose) suggérer, proposer (**to** à; **doing** de faire; **that**

que (+ subjunctive)); (imply) suggérer.

sug·ges·tion suggestion f.

su·i·cide suicide m; **to commit s.** se suicider; **s. bombing** attentat-suicide m.

suit¹ (man's) costume m; (woman's) tailleur m; Cards couleur f, **flying/diving/ski s.** combinaison f de vol/plongée/ski.

suit² vt (please, be acceptable to) convenir à; (of dress, color etc) aller (bien) à; **it suits me to stay** ça m'arrange de rester; **suited to** (job, activity) fait pour.

suit·a·ble adj qui convient (**for** à), convenable (**for** pour); (dress, color) qui va (bien).

suit·case valise f.

suite (rooms) suite f; (furniture) mobilier m.

sulk vi bouder.

sul·len adj maussade.

sum (amount of money, total) somme f; (calculation) calcul m.

sum·ma·rize vt résumer.

sum·ma·ry résumé m.

sum·mer 1 n été m; **in (the) s.** en été. **2** adj d'été; **s. vacation** grandes vacances fpl.

sum·mer·time été m.

sum·mon vt (meeting, person) convoquer; (aid) appeler à; (to court etc) citer.

sum·mons 1 n (to court etc) assignation f à comparaître. **2** vt (to court etc) assigner à comparaître.

▶**summon up** vt **to s. up one's courage/strength** rassembler son courage/ses forces.

▶**sum up** vti (facts etc) résumer.

sun soleil m; **in the s.** au soleil; **the sun is shining** il fait (du) soleil.

sun·bathe vi prendre un bain de soleil, se faire bronzer.

sun·burn coup m de soleil.

sun·burned, sun·burnt adj brûlé par le soleil.

sun·dae glace f aux fruits.

SUGGESTIONS, INVITATIONS AND DESIRES

What do you want to do?
Qu'est-ce que tu veux/vous voulez faire ?

Do you want to go to a restaurant?
Tu veux/Vous voulez allez au restaurant ?

How about going for a walk?
Et si on allait faire une promenade ?

Let's meet at noon/outside the movie theater.
On se retrouve à midi/devant le cinéma ?

I don't want to go to the art gallery.
Je ne veux pas aller au musée d'art.

I feel like an ice-cream.
J'ai envie d'une glace.

What would you rather do?
Qu'est-ce que tu préfères/vous préférez faire ?

I'd like to learn French.
J'aimerais apprendre le français.

I don't mind.
Ça m'est égal.

I'd love to!
Avec plaisir !

I don't feel like it.
Je n'en ai pas envie.

Are you free tomorrow night?
Est-ce que tu es/vous êtes libre demain soir ?

That's very kind of you.
C'est très gentil.

Shall we go for a coffee?
On va prendre un café ?

Would you like to go for a drink?
Ça te/vous dit d'aller boire un verre ?

Let's go for a swim!
Allons nous baigner !

I'd like to go to the beach.
J'aimerais aller à la plage.

I'd rather go shopping.
Je préférerais faire les magasins.

I don't feel like going to the market.
Je n'ai pas envie d'aller au marché.

I think we should leave around 6.30.
Je propose qu'on parte vers six heures et demie.

I wouldn't mind living here.
J'aimerais bien habiter ici.

It's up to you.
C'est comme tu veux/vous voulez.

That's a good idea.
C'est une bonne idée.

I'm sorry, I can't.
Je suis désolé(e), je ne peux pas.

I'm afraid I already have plans.
Je regrette, j'ai déjà quelque chose de prévu.

Thank you for inviting me.
Merci de m'avoir invité.

Sun·day dimanche *m*.

sun·glass·es *npl* lunettes *fpl* de soleil.

sun·lamp lampe *f* à bronzer.

sun·light (lumière *f* du) soleil *m*.

sun·ny *adj* (*day etc*) ensoleillé; **it's s.** il fait (du) soleil; **s. periods** *or* **intervals** éclaircies *fpl*.

sun·rise lever *m* du soleil.

sun·roof toit *m* ouvrant.

sun·set coucher *m* du soleil.

sun·shine soleil *m*.

sun·stroke insolation *f*.

sun·tan bronzage *m*; **s. lotion/oil** crème *f*/huile *f* solaire.

sun·tanned *adj* bronzé.

su·per *adj Fam* sensationnel.

su·perb *adj* superbe.

su·per·fi·cial *adj* superficiel.

su·per·glue colle *f* extra-forte.

su·per·in·ten·dent (*of apartment building*) gardien, -enne *mf*; (**police**) **s.** = commissaire *mf* (de police).

su·pe·ri·or *adj* supérieur (**to** à).

su·pe·ri·or·i·ty supériorité *f*.

su·per·mar·ket supermarché *m*.

su·per·mo·del top model *m*.

su·per·sti·tion superstition *f*.

su·per·sti·tious *adj* superstitieux.

su·per·vise *vt* (*person, work*) surveiller; (*office, research*) diriger.

su·per·vi·sor surveillant, -ante *mf*; (*in office*) chef *m* de service; (*in store*) chef *m* de rayon.

sup·per dîner *m*; (*late-night*) souper *m*; **to have s.** dîner; (*late at night*) souper.

sup·ple *adj* souple.

sup·ple·ment 1 *n* supplément *m*. **2** *vt* compléter.

sup·ply 1 *vt* fournir; (*with electricity, gas, water*) alimenter (**with** en); (*equip*) équiper (**with** de); **to s. sb with sth, to s. sth to sb** fournir qch à qn. **2** *n* (*stock*) provision *f*, (**food**) **supplies** vivres *mpl*.

sup·port 1 *vt* (*bear weight of, help, encourage*) soutenir; (*be in favor of*) être en faveur de; (*family etc*) subvenir aux besoins de. **2** *n* (*help*) soutien *m*; (*object*) support *m*.

sup·port·er partisan *m*; (*in sport*) supporter *m*.

sup·pose *vti* supposer (**that** que); **I'm supposed to work** *or* **be working** je suis censé travailler; **he's supposed to be rich** on le dit riche; **I s. (so)** je pense; **you're tired, I s.** vous êtes fatigué, je suppose; **s. we go** (*suggestion*) si nous partions; **s.** *or* **supposing you're right** supposons que tu aies raison.

sup·press *vt* (*feelings, smile, revolution*) supprimer; (*news, truth, evidence*) faire disparaître.

sure *adj* sûr (**of** de; **that** que); **she's s. to accept** il est sûr qu'elle acceptera; **to make s. of sth** s'assurer de qch; **be s. to do it!** ne manquez pas de le faire!

sure·ly *adv* sûrement; **s. he didn't refuse?** (*I hope*) il n'a tout de même pas refusé?

surf 1 *vt* **to s. the Net** naviguer sur Internet. **2** *vi* (*as sport*) faire du surf.

sur·face surface *f*; **s. area** superficie *f*; **s. mail** courrier *m* par voie normale.

surf·board planche *f* (de surf).

surf·ing surf *m*; **to go s.** faire du surf.

surge 1 *n* (*increase*) augmentation *f*, (*of anger, pity*) accès *m*. **2** *vi* **to s. forward** (*people*) se ruer en avant.

sur·geon chirurgien, -enne *mf*.

sur·ger·y **to have s.** avoir une opération (**for** pour).

sur·gi·cal *adj* chirurgical.

sur·name nom *m* de famille.

sur·plus 1 *n* surplus *m*. **2** *adj* en surplus.

sur·prise 1 *n* surprise *f*; **to take sb by s.** prendre qn au dépourvu. **2** *adj* (*visit etc*) inattendu. **3** *vt* (*astonish*) étonner, surprendre.

sur·prised *adj* surpris (**that** que (+ *subjunctive*); **at sth** de qch); **I'm s. to see you** je suis surpris de te voir.

sur·pris·ing *adj* surprenant.

sur·ren·der *vi* se rendre (**to** à).

sur·round *vt* entourer (**with** de); *(of army, police)* encercler; **surrounded by** entouré de.

sur·round·ing *adj* environnant.

sur·round·ings *npl* environs *mpl*; *(setting)* cadre *m*.

sur·veil·lance surveillance *f*.

sur·vey enquête *f*; *(of opinion)* sondage *m*.

sur·vey·or *(of land)* géomètre *m*.

sur·vive 1 *vi* survivre. **2** *vt* survivre à.

sur·vi·vor survivant, -ante *mf*.

sus·pect 1 *n* suspect, -ecte *mf*. **2** *vt* soupçonner (**that** que; **of sth** de qch; **of doing** d'avoir fait).

sus·pend *vt* *(postpone, dismiss)* suspendre; *(student)* renvoyer; *(driver's license)* retirer.

sus·pend·ers *npl* bretelles *fpl*.

sus·pense *(in book etc)* suspense *m*.

sus·pen·sion *(of vehicle)* suspension *f*.

sus·pi·cion soupçon *m*.

sus·pi·cious *adj* *(person)* méfiant; *(behavior)* suspect; **s.(-looking)** suspect; **to be s. of** se méfier de.

SUV *abbr* *(sport-utility vehicle)* quatre-quatre *m* ou *f*.

swal·low 1 *vti* avaler. **2** *n (bird)* hirondelle *f*.

▸**swallow down** *vt* avaler.

swamp marécage *m*.

swan cygne *m*.

swap 1 *n* échange *m*. **2** *vt* échanger (**for** contre); **to s. seats** changer de place. **3** *vi* échanger.

swarm *(of bees etc)* essaim *m*.

sway *vi* se balancer.

swear* 1 *vt* *(promise)* jurer (**to do** de faire; **that** que). **2** *vi* *(curse)* jurer (**at** contre).

swear·word gros mot *m*.

sweat 1 *n* sueur *f*. **2** *vi* transpirer, suer; **I'm sweating** je suis en sueur.

sweat·er pull *m*.

sweat·shirt sweat-shirt *m*.

Swede Suédois, -oise *mf*.

Swed·ish 1 *adj* suédois. **2** *n (language)* suédois *m*.

sweep* 1 *vt (with broom)* balayer; *(chimney)* ramoner. **2** *vi* balayer.

▸**sweep aside** *vt* écarter.

▸**sweep away** *vt (leaves etc)* balayer; *(carry off)* emporter.

▸**sweep out** *vt (room etc)* balayer.

▸**sweep up** *vt* balayer.

sweet *adj (not sour)* doux (*f* douce); *(tea, coffee etc)* sucré; *(child, house, cat)* mignon (*f* mignonne); *(kind)* aimable.

sweet·corn maïs *m*.

sweet·en *vt (tea etc)* sucrer.

sweet·ly *adv (kindly)* aimablement; *(agreeably)* agréablement.

swell* (up) *vi (of hand, leg etc)* enfler; *(of wood, dough)* gonfler.

swell·ing enflure *f*.

swerve *vi (of vehicle)* faire une embardée.

swift 1 *adj* rapide. **2** *n (bird)* martinet *m*.

swim 1 *n* **to go for a s.** se baigner. **2** *vi** nager; *(as sport)* faire de la natation; **to go swimming** aller nager. **3** *vt (crawl etc)* nager.

swim meet *(competition)* concours *m* de natation.

swim·mer nageur, -euse *mf*.

swim·ming natation *f*.

swim·ming pool piscine *f*.

swim·ming trunks slip *m* de bain.

swim·suit maillot *m* de bain.

swing 1 *n (in playground etc)* balançoire *f*. **2** *vi* (sway)* se balancer. **3** *vt (arms etc)* balancer.

▸**swing around** *vi (turn)* virer; *(of person)* se retourner (vivement).

Swiss 1 *adj* suisse. **2** *n inv* Suisse *m*, Suissesse *f*; **the S.** les Suisses *mpl*.

switch 1 *n* (*electric*) bouton *m* (électrique). **2** *vt* (*money, employee*) transférer (**to** à); (*exchange*) échanger (**for** contre); **to s. places** *or* **seats** changer de place.

▸ **switch off** *vt* (*lamp, gas etc*) éteindre; (*engine*) arrêter.

▸ **switch on** *vt* (*lamp, gas etc*) mettre, allumer; (*engine*) mettre en marche.

swol·len (*pp of* **swell**) *adj* (*leg etc*) enflé; (*stomach*) gonflé.

sword épée *f*.

syl·la·ble syllabe *f*.

syl·la·bus programme *m* (scolaire).

sym·bol symbole *m*.

sym·bol·ic *adj* symbolique.

sym·pa·thet·ic *adj* (*showing pity*) compatissant; (*understanding*) compréhensif.

sym·pa·thize *vi* **I s.** (**with you**) (*pity*) je suis désolé (pour vous); (*understanding*) je vous comprends.

sym·pa·thy (*pity*) compassion *f*; (*understanding*) compréhension *f*; (*when sb dies*) condoléances *fpl*.

sym·pho·ny symphonie *f*.

symp·tom symptôme *m*.

syn·a·gogue synagogue *f*.

syn·o·nym synonyme *m*.

sy·ringe seringue *f*.

syr·up sirop *m*.

sys·tem système *m*; (*human body*) organisme *m*; (*order*) méthode *f*.

T

tab (*cloth etc flap*) patte *f*.

ta·ble (*furniture, list*) table *f*; bedside t. table *f* de chevet; **to lay** *or* **set/clear the t.** mettre/débarrasser la table.

ta·ble·cloth nappe *f*.

ta·ble·mat (*of cloth*) napperon *m*; (*hard*) dessous-de-plat *m inv*.

ta·ble·spoon = cuillère *f* à soupe.

ta·ble·spoon·ful = cuillerée *f* à soupe.

tab·let (*pill*) comprimé *m*.

tack (*nail*) petit clou *m*; (*thumbtack*) punaise *f*.

tack·le *vt* (*problem etc*) s'attaquer à; *Rugby, Football* plaquer; *Soccer* tacler.

tack·y *adj* (*remark etc*) de mauvais goût.

tact tact *m*.

tact·ful *adj* **to be t.** (*of person*) avoir du tact.

tac·tic **a t.** une tactique; **tactics** la tactique.

taf·fy caramel *n* (*dur*).

tag (*label*) étiquette *f*.

tail (*of animal etc*) queue *f*.

tai·lor tailleur *m*.

take* *vt* prendre; (*prize*) remporter; (*exam*) passer; (*subtract*) soustraire (**from** de); (*tolerate*) supporter; (*bring*) amener (*qn*) (**to** à); (*by car*) conduire (*qn*) (**to** à); **to t. sth to sb** (ap)porter qch à qn; **to t. sb (out) to the theater/** *etc* emmener qn au théâtre/*etc*; **to t. sth with one** emporter qch; **to t. sb home** ramener qn; **it takes courage/***etc* il faut du courage/*etc* (**to do** pour faire); **it took me an hour to do it** j'ai mis une heure à le faire.

▸ **take after** *vt* ressembler à.

▸ **take along** *vt* (*object*) emporter; (*person*) emmener.

▸ **take apart** *vt* (*machine*) démonter.

▸ **take away** *vt* (*thing*) emporter; (*person*) emmener; (*remove*) enlever; (*subtract*) soustraire (**from** de).

▸ **take back** *vt* reprendre; (*return*) rapporter; (*accompany*) ramener (*qn*) (**to** à).

▶ **take down** *vt (object)* descendre; *(notes)* prendre.

▶ **take in** *vt (chair, car etc)* rentrer; *(include)* inclure; *(understand)* comprendre; *(deceive) Fam* rouler.

tak·en *adj (seat)* pris.

take·off *(of aircraft)* décollage *m*.

▶ **take off 1** *vt (remove)* enlever; *(lead away)* emmener; *(subtract)* déduire (**from** de). **2** *vi (of aircraft)* décoller.

▶ **take on** *vt (work, staff, passenger)* prendre.

take·out 1 *adj (meal)* à emporter; *(restaurant)* qui fait des plats à emporter. **2** *n (food)* plat *m* à emporter.

▶ **take out** *vt (from pocket etc)* sortir; *(stain)* enlever; *(tooth)* arracher; *(insurance)* prendre.

take·o·ver *(of company etc)* rachat *m*; **t. bid** OPA *f*.

▶ **take over 1** *vt (company etc)* racheter; **to t. over sb's job** remplacer qn. **2** *vi* prendre la relève (**from** de); *(permanently)* prendre la succession (**from** de).

▶ **take up** *vt (carry up)* monter; *(space, time)* prendre; *(hobby)* se mettre à.

tak·ings *npl* recette *f*.

tale *(story)* conte *m*.

tal·ent talent *m*; **to have a t. for** avoir du talent pour.

tal·ent·ed *adj* doué.

talk 1 *n* propos *mpl*; *(gossip)* bavardage(s) *m(pl)*; *(conversation)* conversation *f*; *(lecture)* exposé *m* (**on** sur); **talks** pourparlers *mpl*; **to have a t. with sb** parler avec qn; **there's t. of** on parle de. **2** *vi* parler (**to** à; **with** avec; **about, of** de). **3** *vt (nonsense)* dire; **to t. sb into doing/out of doing** persuader qn de faire/de ne pas faire.

talk·a·tive *adj* bavard.

▶ **talk over** *vt* discuter (de).

tall *adj (person)* grand; *(tree,* *house)* haut; **how t. are you?** combien mesures-tu?

tam·bou·rine tambourin *m*.

tame 1 *adj (animal)* apprivoisé. **2** *vt* apprivoiser.

tam·pon tampon *m* hygiénique.

tan 1 *n (suntan)* bronzage *m*. **2** *vti* bronzer.

tan·ger·ine mandarine *f*.

tan·gled *adj* enchevêtré.

tank *(storing liquid or gas)* réservoir *m*; *(vehicle)* char *m*; **(fish) t.** aquarium *m*.

tank·er (oil) **t.** *(ship)* pétrolier *m*.

tap 1 *n (for water)* robinet *m*; *(blow)* petit coup *m*. **2** *vti (hit)* frapper légèrement.

tape¹ *n (of cloth, paper)* ruban *m*; **(adhesive) t.** ruban *m* adhésif. **2** *vt (stick)* coller *(avec du ruban adhésif)*.

tape² **1** *n (for sound or video recording)* bande *f* (magnétique/vidéo). **2** *vt (a movie etc)* enregistrer, magnétoscoper; *(music, voice)* enregistrer; *(event)* faire une cassette de. **3** *vi* enregistrer.

tape meas·ure mètre *m* (à) ruban.

tape re·cord·er magnétophone *m*.

tar goudron *m*.

tar·get cible *f*; *(objective)* objectif *m*.

tar·iff *(list of prices)* tarif *m*; *(at customs)* tarif *m* douanier.

tar·pau·lin bâche *f*.

tart *(pie)* *(open)* tarte *f*; *(with pastry* *on top)* tourte *f*.

tar·tan *adj (skirt etc)* écossais.

task travail *m*.

taste 1 *n* goût *m*. **2** *vt (eat, drink)* goûter à; *(make out the taste of)* sentir (le goût de). **3** *vi* **to t. of** or **like sth** avoir un goût de qch; **to t. delicious/etc** avoir un goût délicieux/etc.

tast·y *adj* savoureux.

tat·tered *adj (clothes)* en lambeaux.

tat·tle *vi* rapporter (**on** sur).

tat·tle·tale *Fam* rapporteur, -euse *mf*.

tat·too 1 *n* (*pl* -oos) (*on body*) tatouage *m*. **2** *vt* tatouer.

tax 1 *n* (*on goods*) taxe *f*; (*on income*) impôt *m*, contributions *fpl*; **t. free** (*goods*) non taxé; **t. collector** percepteur *m* d'impôt. **2** *vt* (*goods*) taxer; (*person, company*) imposer.

tax·a·ble *adj* imposable.

tax·i taxi *m*; **t. stand** station *f* de taxis.

tax·pay·er contribuable *mf*.

TB tuberculose *f*.

tea thé *m*; **to have t.** prendre le thé; **t. party** thé *m*; **t. set** service *m* à thé.

tea·bag sachet *m* de thé.

teach*1 *vt* apprendre (**sb sth** qch à qn; **that** que); (*in school etc*) enseigner (**sb sth** qch à qn); **to t. sb (how) to do** apprendre à qn à faire. **2** *vi* enseigner.

teach·er professeur *m*; (*in primary school*) instituteur, -trice *mf*.

teach·ing enseignement *m*; **t. staff** personnel *m* enseignant.

tea·cup tasse *f* à thé.

team équipe *f*.

▸**team up** *vi* faire équipe (**with** avec).

tea·pot théière *f*.

tear¹ 1 *n* (*rip*) déchirure. **2** *vt* déchirer.

tear² (*in eye*) larme *f*, **in tears** en larmes.

▸**tear off, tear out** *vt* (*with force*) arracher; (*receipt, stamp etc*) détacher.

▸**tear up** *vt* (*letter etc*) déchirer.

tease *vt* taquiner.

tea·spoon petite cuillère *f*, cuillère *f* à café.

tea·spoon·ful cuillerée *f* à café.

tech·ni·cal *adj* technique.

tech·ni·cian technicien, -ienne *mf*.

tech·nique technique *f*.

tech·no·log·i·cal *adj* technologique.

tech·nol·o·gy technologie *f*.

ted·dy bear ours *m* (en peluche).

teen·age *adj* (*boy, girl, behavior*) adolescent; (*magazine, fashion*) pour adolescents.

teen·ag·er adolescent, -ente *mf*.

tee-shirt tee-shirt *m*.

teeth *see* **tooth**.

tee·tot·al·er = personne *f* qui ne boit jamais d'alcool.

tele- *prefix* télé-.

tel·e·com·mu·ni·ca·tions *npl* télécommunications *fpl*.

tel·e·gram télégramme *m*.

tel·e·graph pole poteau *m* télégraphique.

tel·e·phone 1 *n* téléphone *m*; **on the t.** (*speaking*) au téléphone. **2** *adj* (*call, line etc*) téléphonique; (*number*) de téléphone; **t. booth** cabine *f* téléphonique; **t. directory** annuaire *m* du téléphone. **3** *vi* téléphoner. **4** *vt* **to t. sb** téléphoner à qn.

tel·e·scope télescope *m*.

tel·e·vise *vt* retransmettre à la télévision.

tel·e·vi·sion télévision *f*; **on t.** à la télévision; **t. set** téléviseur *m*.

tell* 1 *vt* dire (**sb sth** qch à qn; **that** que); (*story*) raconter; (*distinguish*) distinguer (**from** de); (*know*) savoir; **to t. sb to do** dire à qn de faire; **to t. the difference** voir la différence. **2** *vi* **to t. of** *or* **about sth/sb** parler de qch/qn; **to t. on sb** rapporter sur qn.

tell·er (*bank*) **t.** guichetier, -ière *mf* (*de banque*).

▸**tell off** *vt* disputer.

tem·per **to lose one's t.** se mettre en colère; **in a bad t.** de mauvaise humeur.

tem·per·a·ture température *f*, **to have a t.** avoir de la température.

tem·ple (*building*) temple *m*.

tem·po·rar·i·ly *adj* temporairement.

tem·po·rar·y *adj* provisoire;

USING THE TELEPHONE

Hello?
Allô ?

Hi Claire, it's Alex.
Salut Claire, c'est Alex (à l'appareil).

Hello, could you put me through to Customer Services, please?
Bonjour, pouvez-vous me passer le service clientèle, s'il vous plaît ?

Can I speak to Julie Rey, please? This is Steve Brown from CPS.
Est-ce que je peux parler à Julie Rey, s'il vous plaît ? C'est Steve Brown de la part de CPS.

Speaking!
C'est moi !

Could you repeat that/spell it?
Pourriez-vous répéter/l'épeler ?

Hold the line please, I'll put you through.
Ne quittez pas, je vous le/la passe.

The line's busy, would you like to hold?
Ça sonne occupé, voulez-vous patienter ?

Would you like to leave a message?
Voulez-vous laisser un message ?

No thanks, I'll call back later.
Non merci, je rappellerai plus tard.

Can you ask him/her to call me back as soon as possible?
Pouvez-vous lui demander de me rappeler dès que possible ?

My number is 42-35-59-01.
Mon numéro est le quarante-deux, trente-cinq, cinquante-neuf, zéro-un.

Thank you for calling.
Merci d'avoir appelé.

Can I take your number?
Je peux avoir votre/ton numéro ?

I'll text you later.
Je vous/t'envoie un SMS plus tard.

I don't have many minutes left.
Il ne me reste plus beaucoup de crédit.

You've got the wrong number.
Vous vous êtes trompé(e) de numéro.

I can barely hear you.
Je vous/t'entends très mal.

Is there a payphone around here?
Est-ce qu'il y a une cabine téléphonique par ici ?

Hello, Alan Wright speaking?
Allô, Alan Wright à l'appareil ?

Good morning/afternoon, Staff Solutions!
Staff Solutions, bonjour !

Who's calling, please?
C'est de la part de qui ?

Just a moment, I'll get him/her.
Un instant, je vais le/la chercher.

I'm afraid she's in a meeting/she's not in.
Je regrette, elle est en réunion/elle n'est pas là.

There's no reply.
Ça ne répond pas.

Please leave a message after the tone.
Veuillez laisser un message après le bip.

Can you tell him/her I called?
Vous pouvez lui dire que j'ai appelé ?

The French read out phone numbers in pairs of digits.

Talk to you later!
On s'appelle !

You can reach me on my cell.
Vous pouvez/Tu peux me joindre sur mon portable.

I can't get a signal in here.
Je ne capte pas ici.

I need to charge my cellphone.
J'ai besoin de recharger mon portable.

Sorry, I must have the wrong number.
Désolé(e), j'ai dû me tromper de numéro.

We got cut off.
On a été coupés.

I'd like to call collect.
Je voudrais appeler en PCV.

(job) temporaire; *(secretary)* intérimaire.

tempt *vt* tenter; **tempted to do** tenté de faire.

temp·ta·tion tentation *f.*

tempt·ing *adj* tentant.

ten *adj & n* dix *(m).*

ten·an·cy location *f; (period)* occupation *f.*

ten·ant locataire *mf.*

tend *vi* **to t. to do** avoir tendance à faire.

ten·den·cy tendance *f* **(to do à** faire).

ten·der *adj (soft, loving)* tendre; *(painful)* sensible.

ten·nis tennis *m;* **table t.** tennis *m* de table; **t. court** court *m* (de tennis); **t. shoes** (chaussures *fpl* de) tennis *fpl.*

tense 1 *adj (person, muscle, situation)* tendu. **2** *n (of verb)* temps *m.*

ten·sion tension *f.*

tent tente *f.*

tenth *adj & n* dixième *(mf).*

term *(word)* terme *m; (period)* période *f; (semester)* semestre *m;* **terms** *(conditions)* conditions *fpl; (prices)* prix *mpl;* **on good/bad terms** en bons/mauvais termes *(with avec).*

ter·mi·nal (air) t. aérogare *f; (computer)* **t.** terminal *m* (d'ordinateur).

ter·mi·nate 1 *vt (work, project)* terminer; *(contract)* résilier; *(pregnancy)* interrompre. **2** *vi* se terminer.

ter·race *(next to house etc)* terrasse *f.*

ter·ri·ble *adj* affreux.

ter·ri·bly *adv (badly, very)* affreusement.

ter·ri·fic *adj Fam (excellent, very great)* formidable.

ter·ri·fy *vt* terrifier; **to be terrified of** avoir très peur de.

ter·ri·fy·ing *adj* terrifiant.

ter·ri·to·ry territoire *m.*

ter·ror terreur *f.*

ter·ror·ist *n & adj* terroriste *(mf).*

test 1 *vt (try)* essayer; *(product, machine)* tester; *(pupil)* interroger; *(of doctor)* examiner *(les yeux etc); (analyze)* analyser *(le sang etc).* **2** *n* essai *m; (of product)* test *m; (in school)* interrogation *f,* test *m; (by doctor)* examen *m; (of blood etc)* analyse *f;* **eye t.** examen *m* de la vue.

tes·ta·ment testament *m; (tribute)* preuve *f;* **Old/New T.** Ancien/ Nouveau Testament.

tes·ti·mo·ny témoignage *m.*

test tube éprouvette *f.*

test-tube ba·by bébé-éprouvette *m.*

text 1 *n* texte *m;* **t. (message)** SMS *m,* texto *m.* **2** *vt (send text message to)* envoyer un SMS *or* un texto à.

text·book manuel *m* (scolaire).

tex·tile *adj & n* textile *(m).*

tex·ture texture *f.*

than *conj* que; **happier t.** plus heureux que. ▪ *(with numbers)* de; **more t. six** plus de six.

thank 1 *vt* remercier **(for sth** pour qch; **for doing** d'avoir fait); **t. you!** merci!; **no t. you!** (non) merci! **2** *n* **thanks** remerciements *mpl;* **(many) thanks!** merci (beaucoup)!; **thanks to** *(because of)* grâce à.

thank·ful *adj* reconnaissant **(for** de).

Thanks·giv·ing (day) = 4ème jeudi de novembre, fête commémorant la première action de grâce des colons anglais.

that 1 *conj* que; **to say t.** dire que. **2** *rel pron (subject)* qui; *(object)* que; *(after prep)* lequel, laquelle, *pl* lesquel(le)s; **the boy t. left** le garçon qui est parti; **the book t. I read** le livre que j'ai lu; **the carpet t. I put it on** le tapis sur lequel je l'ai mis; **the house t. she told me about** la maison dont elle m'a parlé; **the**

day/moment t. le jour/moment où.
3 *dem adj* (*pl see* **those**) ce, cet (*before vowel or mute h*), cette; (*opposed to 'this'*) ce … + -là; **t. day** ce jour; ce jour-là; **t. girl** cette fille; cette fille-là. **4** *dem pron* (*pl see* **those**) ça, cela; **t. (one)** celui-là *m*, celle-là *f*; **give me t.** donne-moi ça *or* cela; **t.'s right** c'est juste; **who's t.?** qui est-ce?; **t.'s the house** c'est la maison; (*pointing*) voilà la maison; **t. is (to say)** c'est-à-dire. **5** *adv* (*so*) si; **not t. good** pas si bon; **t. much** (*to cost etc*) (au)tant que ça.

thaw 1 *n* dégel *m*. **2** *vi* dégeler; (*of snow*) fondre; (*of food*) décongeler; **it's thawing** ça dégèle. **3** *vt* (*food*) (faire) décongeler.

the le, l', la, *pl* les; **t. roof** le toit; **t. man** l'homme; **t. moon** la lune; **t. boxes** les boîtes; **of t., from t.** du, de l', de la, *pl* des; **to t., at t.** au, à l', à la, *pl* aux.

the·a·ter théâtre *m*.

theft vol *m*.

their *poss adj* leur, *pl* leurs.

theirs *poss pron* le leur, la leur, *pl* les leurs; **this book is t.** ce livre est à eux *or* est le leur.

them *pron* les; (*after prep, 'than', 'it is'*) eux *mpl*, elles *fpl*; **(to) t.** leur; **I see t.** je les vois; **I give (to) t.** je leur donne; **ten of t.** dix d'entre eux/elles; **all of t. came** tous sont venus, toutes sont venues; **I like all of t.** je les aime tous/toutes.

them·selves *pron* eux-mêmes *mpl*, elles-mêmes *fpl*, (*reflexive*) se, s'; (*after prep*) eux *mpl*, elles *fpl*.

then 1 *adv* (*at that time*) à cette époque-là; (*just a moment ago*) à ce moment-là; (*next*) ensuite; **from t. on** dès lors; **before t.** avant cela; **until t.** jusque-là. **2** *conj* (*therefore*) donc.

the·o·ry théorie *f*.

the·ra·py thérapie *f*.

there *adv* là; (**down** *or* **over**) **t.** là-bas; **on t.** là-dessus; **t. is, t. are** il y a; (*pointing*) voilà; **t. he is** le voilà; **that man t.** cet homme-là.

there·fore *adv* donc.

ther·mom·e·ter thermomètre *m*.

Ther·mos® thermos® *m or f*.

ther·mo·stat thermostat *m*.

these 1 *dem adj* (*sing see* **this**) ces; (*opposed to 'those'*) ces … + -ci; **t. men** ces hommes; ces hommes-ci. **2** *dem pron* (*sing see* **this**) **t. (ones)** ceux-ci *mpl*, celles-ci *fpl*; **t. are my friends** ce sont mes amis.

the·sis, *pl* **-ses** thèse *f*.

they *pron* ils *mpl*, elles *fpl*; (*stressed*) eux *mpl*, elles *fpl*; **t. are doctors** ce sont des médecins. ■ (*people in general*) on; **t. say** on dit.

thick 1 *adj* épais (*f* épaisse). **2** *adv* (*to spread*) en couche épaisse.

thick·en 1 *vt* épaissir. **2** *vi* (*of fog etc*) s'épaissir; (*of cream etc*) épaissir.

thick·ly *adv* (*to spread*) en couche épaisse.

thick·ness épaisseur *f*.

thief, *pl* **thieves** voleur, -euse *mf*.

thigh cuisse *f*.

thim·ble dé *m* (à coudre).

thin 1 *adj* (*slice, paper etc*) mince; (*person, leg*) maigre; (*soup*) peu épais (*f* épaisse). **2** *adv* (*to spread*) en couche mince.

thin (down) *vt* (*paint etc*) diluer.

thing chose *f*; **one's things** (*belongings*) ses affaires *fpl*; **it's a good t. (that)** heureusement que.

think* **1** *vi* penser (**about, of** à); **to t. (carefully)** réfléchir (**about, of** à); **to t. of doing** penser à faire; **she doesn't t. much of it** ça ne lui dit pas grand-chose. **2** *vt* penser (**that** que); **I t. so** je pense que oui; **what do you t. of him?** que penses-tu de lui?

▸ **think over** *vt* réfléchir à.

▸ **think up** *vt* inventer.

thin·ly *adv* (*to spread*) en couche mince.

third 1 *adj* troisième. **2** *n* troisième

mf; **a t.** *(fraction)* un tiers. **3** *adv* **to come t.** se classer troisième.

third·ly *adv* troisièmement.

thirst soif *f.*

thirst·y *adj* **to be** *or* **feel t.** avoir soif; **to make sb t.** donner soif à qn.

thir·teen *adj & n* treize *(m).*

thir·teenth *adj & n* treizième *(mf).*

thir·ti·eth *adj & n* trentième *(mf).*

thir·ty *adj & n* trente *(m).*

this 1 *dem adj (pl see* these) ce, cet *(before vowel or mute h)*, cette; *(opposed to 'that')* ce… + ci; **t. book** ce livre; ce livre-ci; **t. photo** cette photo; cette photo-ci. **2** *dem pron (pl see* these) ceci; **t. (one)** celui-ci *m*, celle-ci *f*; **give me t.** donne-moi ceci; **t. is Paul** c'est Paul; *(pointing)* voici Paul. **3** *adv* **t. high** *(pointing)* haut comme ceci; **t. far** jusqu'ici.

thong *(underwear)* string *m*; *(sandal)* tong *f.*

thorn épine *f.*

thor·ough *adj (careful)* minutieux; *(knowledge, examination)* approfondi; **to give sth a t. clean/ etc** nettoyer/*etc* qch à fond.

thor·ough·ly *adv (completely)* tout à fait; *(carefully)* avec minutie; *(to know, clean etc)* à fond.

those 1 *dem adj (sing see* that) ces; *(opposed to 'these')* ces… + -là; **t. men** ces hommes; ces hommes-là. **2** *dem pron (sing see* that) **t. (ones)** ceux-là *mpl*, celles-là *fpl*; **t. are my friends** ce sont mes amis.

though 1 *conj (even)* **t.** bien que *(+ subjunctive)*; **as t.** comme si. **2** *adv (however)* cependant.

thought *(pt & pp of* think) pensée *f*; *(careful)* **t.** réflexion *f.*

thought·ful *adj (considerate)* gentil, attentionné.

thought·less *adj (towards others)* pas très gentil; *(absentminded)* étourdi.

thou·sand *adj & n* mille *(m & adj inv)*; **a t. pages** mille pages; **two t.**

pages deux mille pages; **thousands of** des milliers de.

thread 1 *n (yarn)* fil *m.* **2** *vt (needle, beads)* enfiler.

threat menace *f.*

threat·en *vt* menacer *(to do* de faire; **with sth** de qch).

threat·en·ing *adj* menaçant.

three *adj & n* trois *(m).*

thresh·old seuil *m.*

threw *pt de* throw.

thrill frisson *m.*

thrilled *adj* ravi *(with sth* de qch; **to do** de faire).

thrill·er film *m*/roman *m* à suspense.

thrill·ing *adj* passionnant.

thrive *vi (person, business, plant)* prospérer; **to t. on sth** avoir besoin de qch pour s'épanouir.

thriv·ing *adj* prospère.

throat gorge *f.*

throne trône *m.*

through 1 *prep (place)* à travers; *(window, door)* par; *(time)* pendant; *(means)* par; **to go** *or* **get t.** *(forest etc)* traverser; *(hole etc)* passer par; *(wall etc)* passer à travers. **2** *adv* à travers; **to let t.** laisser passer; **to be t.** *(finished)* avoir fini; **t. to** *or* **till** jusqu'à; **I'll put you t. (to him)** *(on phone)* je vous le passe.

through·out 1 *prep* **t. the neighborhood/***etc* dans tout le quartier/ *etc*; **t. the day/***etc* pendant toute la journée/*etc*. **2** *adv (everywhere)* partout; *(all the time)* tout le temps.

throw* *vt* jeter *(to, at* à); *(party)* donner.

▸ **throw away** *vt (unwanted object)* jeter.

▸ **throw out** *vt (unwanted object)* jeter; *(expel)* mettre à la porte.

▸ **throw up** *vti (vomit) Fam* rendre.

thrust 1 *vt** **t. sth into sth** enfoncer qch dans qch. **2** *n (movement)* mouvement *m* en avant; *(of argument etc)* idée *f* principale.

thud bruit *m* sourd.
thug voyou *m*.
thumb pouce *m*.
thumb·tack punaise *f*.
thun·der 1 *n* tonnerre *m*. **2** *vi* tonner; **it's thundering** il tonne.
thun·der·storm orage *m*.
Thurs·day jeudi *m*.
thus *adv* ainsi.
tick (off) *vt* (*on list etc*) cocher.
tick·et billet *m*; (*for bus, subway, cloakroom*) ticket *m*; (*price*) t. étiquette *f*.
tick·et col·lec·tor contrôleur, -euse *mf*.
tick·et of·fice guichet *m*.
tick·le *vt* chatouiller.
tick·lish *adj* chatouilleux.
tic-tac-toe morpion *m* (*jeu*).
tide marée *f*.
ti·di·ly *adv* (*to put away*) soigneusement.
ti·dy *adj* (*place, toys etc*) bien rangé; (*clothes, hair*) soigné; (*person*) ordonné; (*in appearance*) soigné.
tidy (up *or* **away)** *vt* ranger.
tie 1 *n* (*around neck*) cravate *f*; (*game*) match *m* nul. **2** *vt* (*fasten*) attacher (**to** à); (*a knot*) faire (**in** à); (*shoe*) lacer.
▸ **tie down** *vt* attacher.
▸ **tie up** *vt* attacher (**to** à); (*person*) ligoter.
ti·ger tigre *m*.
tight 1 *adj* (*clothes fitting too closely*) (trop) étroit; (*drawer, lid*) dur; (*knot, screw*) serré; (*rope, wire*) raide. **2** *adv* (*to hold, shut*) bien; (*to squeeze*) fort.
tight·en (up) *vt* (*bolt, screw*) (res)serrer; (*security*) renforcer.
tight·ly *adv* (*to hold*) bien; (*to squeeze*) fort.
tights *npl* collant(s) *m(pl)*.
tile 1 *n* (*on roof*) tuile *f*; (*on wall or floor*) carreau *m*. **2** *vt* (*wall, floor*) carreler.
till 1 *prep & conj* = **until**. **2** *n* (*for*

money) caisse *f* (enregistreuse).
tilt *vti* pencher.
tim·ber bois *m* (de construction).
time 1 *n* temps *m*; (*point in time*) moment *m*; (*period in history*) époque *f*; (*on clock*) heure *f*; (*occasion*) fois *f*; **some/most of the t.** une partie/la plupart du temps; **all of the t.** tout le temps; **in a year's t.** dans un an; **it's t. (to do)** il est temps (de faire); **to have a good t.** s'amuser; **to have a hard t. doing** avoir du mal à faire; **in t.** (*to arrive*) à temps; **from t. to t.** de temps en temps; **what t. is it?** quelle heure est-il?; **on t.** à l'heure; **at the same t.** en même temps (**as** que); (*simultaneously*) à la fois; **for the t. being** pour le moment; **one at a t.** un à un. **2** *vt* (*athlete etc*) chronométrer; (*activity*) minuter; (*choose the time of*) choisir le moment de.
tim·er (*device*) minuteur *m*; (*built into appliance*) programmateur *m*; (*plugged into socket*) prise *f* programmable.
time·ta·ble horaire *m*; (*of activities*) emploi *m* du temps.
tim·id *adj* (*afraid*) craintif; (*shy*) timide.
tim·ing **what good t.!** ça tombe bien!
tin (*metal*) étain *m*; (*coated steel or iron*) fer-blanc *m*; (*can*) boîte *f*.
tin·foil papier *m* (d')alu.
ti·ny *adj* tout petit.
tip 1 *n* (*end*) bout *m*; (*pointed*) pointe *f*; (*money*) pourboire *m*; (*advice*) conseil *m*. **2** *vt* (*waiter etc*) donner un pourboire à.
tip (out) *vt* (*liquid, load*) déverser (**into** dans).
tip·toe **on t.** sur la pointe des pieds.
▸ **tip up, tip over 1** *vt* (*tilt*) pencher; (*overturn*) faire basculer. **2** *vi* (*tilt*) pencher; (*overturn*) basculer.
tire[1] **1** *vt* fatiguer. **2** *vi* se fatiguer.
tire[2] pneu *m* (*pl* pneus).

tired vt fatigué; **to be t. of sth/sb/ doing** en avoir assez de qch/de qn/ de faire.

tired·ness fatigue f.

▶ **tire out** vt épuiser.

tir·ing adj fatigant.

tis·sue (handkerchief etc) mouchoir m en papier.

ti·tle titre m.

to prep à; (towards) vers; (of attitude) envers; (right up to) jusqu'à; **give it to him** donne-le-lui; **to France** en France; **to Portugal** au Portugal; **to the butcher(s)/etc** chez le boucher/etc; **the road to Paris** la route de Paris; **the train to Paris** le train pour Paris; **kind/cruel to sb** gentil/cruel envers qn; **it's ten (minutes) to one** il est une heure moins dix. ▪ (with infinitive) **to say/do/etc** dire/faire/etc; **(in order) to** pour. ▪ (with adjective) de; à; **happy/etc to do** heureux/etc de faire; **it's easy/difficult to do** c'est facile/difficile à faire.

toad crapaud m.

toad·stool champignon m (vénéneux).

toast 1 n pain m grillé; **piece** or **slice of t.** tranche f de pain grillé, toast m. **2** vt (faire) griller.

toast·er grille-pain m inv.

to·bac·co tabac m.

to·bac·co store (bureau m de) tabac m.

to·bog·gan luge f.

to·day adv aujourd'hui.

tod·dler enfant mf (en bas âge).

toe orteil m.

toe·nail ongle m du pied.

tof·fee caramel m (dur).

to·geth·er adv ensemble; (at the same time) en même temps; **t. with** avec.

toi·let (room) toilettes fpl; (bowl, seat) cuvette f or siège m des cabinets; **to go to the t.** aller aux toilettes.

toi·let pa·per papier m hygiénique.

toi·let·ries npl articles mpl de toilette.

toi·let wa·ter (perfume) eau f de toilette.

to·ken (for subway etc) jeton m.

told pt & pp de **tell**.

tol·er·ance tolérance f.

tol·er·ant adj tolérant (**of** à l'égard de).

tol·er·ate vt tolérer.

toll (fee) péage m; **t. road/bridge** route f/pont m à péage.

toll-free num·ber = numéro m vert.

to·ma·to, pl **-oes** tomate f.

tomb tombeau m.

to·mor·row adv demain; **t. morning** demain matin; **the day after t.** après-demain.

ton tonne f (= 907kg); **tons of** (lots of) Fam des tonnes de.

tone ton m; (dial) **t.** tonalité f.

tongs npl pince f.

tongue langue f.

ton·ic t. (water) Schweppes® m; **gin and t.** gin-tonic m.

to·night adv (this evening) ce soir; (during the night) cette nuit.

tonne = **ton**.

ton·sil amygdale f.

ton·sil·li·tis to have t. avoir une angine.

too adv trop; (also) aussi; (moreover) en plus; **t. tired to play** trop fatigué pour jouer; **t. hard to solve** trop difficile à résoudre; **t. much, t. many** trop; **t. much salt/t. many people/etc** trop de sel/gens/etc; **one t. many** un de trop.

took pt de **take**.

tool outil m.

tooth, pl **teeth** dent f.

tooth·ache mal m de dents; **to have a t.** avoir mal aux dents.

tooth·brush brosse f à dents.

tooth·paste dentifrice m.

tooth·pick cure-dent m.

top¹ n (of mountain, tower, tree) sommet m; (of wall, ladder, page, *garment)* haut *m; (of table)* dessus *m; (of list)* tête *f; (of bottle, tube)* bouchon *m; (bottle cap)* capsule *f; (of saucepan)* couvercle *m; (of pen)* capuchon *m;* **at the t. of the class** le premier de la classe; **on t.** of sur. **2** *adj (drawer, shelf)* du haut; *(step, layer)* dernier; *(in competition)* premier; *(maximum)* maximum; **on the t. floor** au dernier étage; **at t. speed** à toute vitesse.

top² (spinning) **t.** toupie *f.*

top·ic sujet *m.*

▸ **top up** *vt (glass)* remplir; *(coffee, tea)* remettre.

torch torche *f.*

tor·ment *vt (annoy)* agacer.

tor·na·do, *pl* -oes tornade *f.*

tor·toise tortue *f.*

tor·toise-shell écaille *f.*

tor·ture **1** *n* torture *f.* **2** *vt* torturer.

toss **1** *vt (throw)* jeter (**to** à); **to t. a coin** jouer à pile ou face. **2** *vi* **let's t.** jouons à pile ou face.

to·tal *adj & n* total *(m).*

to·tal·ly *adv* totalement.

touch **1** *n (contact)* contact *m; (sense)* toucher *m;* **in t. with sb** en contact avec qn; **to get in t.** se mettre en contact. **2** *vt* toucher. **3** *vi (of lines, hands etc)* se toucher; **don't t.!** n'y or ne touche pas!

touch·down *(of plane)* atterrissage *m; (in football)* essai *m.*

▸ **touch down** *vi (of aircraft)* atterrir.

touch·y *adj* susceptible.

tough *adj (meat)* dur; *(sturdy)* solide; *(strong)* fort; *(difficult, harsh)* dur.

tour **1** *n (journey)* voyage *m; (visit)* visite *f; (by artist etc)* tournée *f* **2** *vt* visiter.

tour·ism tourisme *m.*

tour·ist **1** *n* touriste *mf.* **2** *adj* touristique.

tour·ist (in·for·ma·tion) of·fice syndicat *m* d'initiative.

tour·na·ment tournoi *m.*

tow *vt (car, boat)* remorquer; *(trailer)* tracter.

to·ward(s) *prep* vers; *(of feelings)* envers; **cruel/etc t. sb** cruel/etc envers qn.

tow·el serviette *f* (de toilette); *(for dishes)* torchon *m.*

tow·er tour *f.*

town ville *f;* **in t., (in)to t.** en ville.

town coun·cil conseil *m* municipal.

town hall mairie *f.*

town-house maison *f* mitoyenne (en ville).

town-ship canton *m.*

tow truck dépanneuse *f.*

tox·ic *adj* toxique.

toy **1** *n* jouet *m.* **2** *adj (gun)* d'enfant; *(house, car)* miniature.

toy-shop magasin *m* de jouets.

trace **1** *n* trace *f* (**of** de). **2** *vt (with tracing paper)* (dé)calquer; *(find)* retrouver.

trac·ing pa·per papier-calque *m inv.*

track *(of animal, sports stadium etc)* piste *f; (of record)* plage *f; (for train)* voie *f; (path)* chemin *m; (racetrack)* champ *m* de courses; **tracks** *(of wheels)* traces *fpl;* **on the right t.** sur la bonne voie.

track shoe *(running shoe)* jogging *m.*

track·suit survêtement *m.*

trac·tor tracteur *m.*

trac·tor-trail·er semi-remorque *m.*

trade **1** *n* commerce *m; (job)* métier *m.* **2** *vi* faire du commerce (**with** avec); *(swap)* échanger; **to t. places** changer de place. **3** *vt* échanger (**for** contre).

trade-in *(car etc)* reprise *f.*

trade-mark marque *f* de fabrique; **(registered) t.** marque déposée.

trad·er commerçant, -ante *mf,* marchand, -ante *mf.*

trade un·ion syndicat *m.*

trad·ing commerce *m.*

tra·di·tion tradition *f.*

tra·di·tion·al *adj* traditionnel.

traf·fic circulation *f, (air, sea, rail)* trafic *m.*

traf·fic jam embouteillage *m.*

traf·fic laws Code *m* de la route.

traf·fic lights *npl* feux *mpl* (de signalisation); *(when red)* feu *m* rouge.

traf·fic sign panneau *m* de signalisation.

trag·e·dy tragédie *f.*

trag·ic *adj* tragique.

trail 1 *n (of smoke, blood etc)* traînée *f.* **2** *vti (on the ground etc)* traîner.

trail·er *(for car)* remorque *f, (caravan)* camping-car *m;* **t. park** = terrain aménagé pour les camping-cars.

train[1] train *m; (underground)* rame *f;* **to go** or **come by t.** prendre le train; **t. set** petit train *m;* **t. ticket** billet *m* de train; **t. station** gare *f;* **t. tracks** voie *f* ferrée.

train[2] **1** *vt (teach)* former (**to do** à faire); *(in sport)* entraîner; *(animal, child)* dresser (**to do** à faire). **2** *vi* recevoir une formation (**as a doctor/** *etc* de médecin/*etc*); *(of athlete)* s'entraîner.

trained *adj (skilled)* qualifié; *(nurse, engineer)* diplômé.

train·ee stagiaire *mf.*

train·er *(of athlete, sportsperson, racehorse)* entraîneur, -euse *mf, (of animal)* dresseur, -euse *mf.*

train·ing formation *f, (in sports)* entraînement *m.*

trai·tor traître *m.*

tramp clochard, -arde *mf.*

tran·quil·iz·er tranquillisant *m.*

trans·fer 1 *vt (person, goods etc)* transférer (**to** à). **2** *n* transfert *m* (**to** à); *(image)* décalcomanie *f.*

trans·fu·sion (blood) t. transfusion *f* (sanguine).

tran·sis·tor t. (radio) transistor *m.*

tran·sit transit *m;* **in t.** en transit.

tran·si·tive *adj Grammar* transitif.

trans·late *vt* traduire (**from** de; **in·to** en).

trans·la·tion traduction *f.*

trans·la·tor traducteur, -trice *mf.*

trans·mis·sion transmission *f.*

trans·mit *vt* transmettre.

trans·par·ent *adj* transparent.

trans·plant greffe *f.*

trans·port 1 *vt* transporter. **2** *n* transport *m* (**of** de); **means of t.** moyen *m* de transport; **public t.** les transports en commun.

trap 1 *n* piège *m.* **2** *vt (animal)* prendre (au piège); *(jam)* coincer; *(cut off by snow etc)* bloquer (**by** par).

trap door trappe *f.*

trash *(nonsense)* sottises *fpl; (junk)* bric-à-brac *m inv; (waste)* ordures *fpl.*

trash·can poubelle *f.*

trash·y *adj (book, movie)* nul; *(goods)* de mauvaise qualité.

trav·el 1 *vi* voyager. **2** *vt (country, distance)* parcourir. **3** *n* travel(s) voyages *mpl;* **t. agent** agent *m* de voyages; **t. guide** guide *m.*

trav·el·er voyageur, -euse *mf.*

trav·el·er's check chèque *m* de voyage.

trav·el·ing voyages *mpl.*

trav·el sick·ness *(in car)* mal *m* de la route; *(in aircraft)* mal *m* de l'air.

tray plateau *m.*

treach·er·ous *adj (road, conditions)* très dangereux.

tread* *vi* marcher (**on** sur).

treas·ure trésor *m.*

treas·ur·er trésorier, -ère *mf.*

treat 1 *vt* traiter; *(consider)* considérer (**as** comme). **2** *n (special)* **t.** petit extra *m;* **to give sb a (special) t.** donner une surprise à qn.

treat·ment traitement *m.*

treb·le *vti* tripler.

tree arbre *m.*

trem·ble *vi* trembler (**with** de).

tre·men·dous *adj (huge)* énorme; *(dreadful)* affreux; *Fam (marvellous)* formidable.

trench tranchée *f.*

trend·y *adj Fam* branché.

tri·al *(in court)* procès *m;* **to go or be on t.** être jugé, passer en jugement.

tri·an·gle triangle *m.*

tri·an·gu·lar *adj* triangulaire.

tribe tribu *f.*

trib·ute *(mark of respect)* hommage *m;* **to pay t. to** rendre hommage à.

trick 1 *n (joke, of magician etc)* tour *m; (clever method)* astuce *f;* **to play a t. on sb** jouer un tour à qn. **2** *vt* tromper.

trick·le 1 *n (of liquid)* filet *m.* **2** *vi* dégouliner.

trick·y *adj (problem etc)* difficile.

tri·cy·cle tricycle *m.*

trig·ger *(of gun)* gâchette *f.*

trim *vt* couper (un peu).

trip *(journey)* voyage *m; (outing)* excursion *f.*

trip (over or up) *vi* trébucher; **to t. over sth** trébucher contre qch.

tri·ple *vti* tripler.

▶**trip up** *vt* faire trébucher.

tri·umph 1 *n* triomphe *m* (**over** sur). **2** *vi* triompher (**over** de).

triv·i·al *adj (unimportant)* insignifiant.

trol·ley *(streetcar)* tramway *m.*

trom·bone trombone *m.*

troop·er *(soldier)* soldat *m* de cavalerie; *(policeman)* gendarme *m.*

troops *npl* troupes *fpl.*

tro·phy coupe *f,* trophée *m.*

trop·i·cal *adj* tropical.

trot 1 *n* trot *m.* **2** *vi* trotter.

trou·ble 1 *n (difficulty)* ennui(s) *m(pl); (effort)* peine *f, (disorder, illness)* troubles *mpl;* **to be in t.** avoir des ennuis; **to get into t.** s'attirer des ennuis (**with** avec); **to go to the t. of doing, take the t. to do** se donner la peine de faire. **2** *vt (inconvenience)* déranger; *(worry, annoy)* ennuyer.

trou·sers *npl* pantalon *m;* **a pair of t.,** **some t.** un pantalon.

trout truite *f.*

tru·ant **to play t.** sécher (la classe).

truck camion *m.*

truck driv·er, truck·er camionneur *m; (over long distances)* routier *m.*

true *adj* vrai; *(accurate)* exact; **t. to** *(one's promise etc)* fidèle à; **to come t.** se réaliser.

trump (card) atout *m.*

trum·pet trompette *f.*

trunk *(of tree, body)* tronc *m; (of elephant)* trompe *f; (case)* malle *f; (of vehicle)* coffre *m;* **trunks** *(for swimming)* slip *m* de bain.

trust 1 *n (faith)* confiance *f* (**in** en). **2** *vt (person, judgment)* avoir confiance en; **to t. sb with sth, to t. sth to sb** confier qch à qn.

truth vérité *f.*

try 1 *vt* essayer (**to do, doing** faire); **to t. one's luck** tenter sa chance. **2** *vi* essayer; **to t. hard** faire un gros effort. **3** *n (attempt)* essai *m;* **to give sth/a t.** essayer qch.

try (out) *vt (car, method etc)* essayer; *(person)* mettre à l'essai.

try·ing *adj (person)* difficile.

▶**try on** *vt (clothes, shoes)* essayer.

T-shirt tee-shirt *m.*

tub *(basin)* baquet *m; (bath)* baignoire *f.*

tube tube *m.*

▶**tuck in** *vt (shirt, blanket)* rentrer; *(person in bed)* border.

Tues·day mardi *m.*

tuft touffe *f.*

tug *vti* tirer (**at** sur).

tug(·boat) remorqueur *m.*

tu·i·tion enseignement *m; (lessons)* leçons *fpl.*

tu·lip tulipe *f.*

tum·ble dégringolade *f.*

tum·ble (down) *vi* dégringoler.
tum·ble dry·er sèche-linge *m inv.*
tum·bler *(glass)* gobelet *m.*
tum·my *Fam* ventre *m.*
tu·mor tumeur *f.*
tu·na (fish) thon *m.*
tune 1 *n* air *m*; **in t./out of t.** *(instrument)* accordé/désaccordé; **to sing in t./out of t.** chanter juste/faux. **2** *vt (instrument)* accorder; *(engine)* régler.
tun·ing *(of engine)* réglage *m.*
tun·nel tunnel *m.*
tur·ban turban *m.*
tur·key dindon *m*, dinde *f*; *(as food)* dinde *f.*
turn 1 *n (movement, in game)* tour *m*; *(in road)* tournant *m*; **to take turns** se relayer; **it's your t.** *(to play)* c'est à toi *or* (à) ton tour (de jouer). **2** *vt* tourner; *(mattress, pancake)* retourner; **to t. sth red**/*etc* rendre qch rouge/*etc*; **she's turned twenty** elle a vingt ans passés. **3** *vi (of wheel etc)* tourner; *(turn head or body)* se (re)tourner; *(become)* devenir; **to t. red**/*etc* devenir rouge/*etc.*
▸ **turn around 1** *vt (head, object)* tourner; *(vehicle)* faire faire demi-tour à. **2** *vi (of person)* se retourner.
▸ **turn away 1** *vt (eyes)* détourner; *(person)* renvoyer. **2** *vi* se détourner.
▸ **turn back** *vi* retourner.
▸ **turn down** *vt (gas, radio etc)* baisser; *(offer, person)* refuser.
▸ **turn into** *vt* **to t. sb into sth** *(change)* changer qn en qch; **to t. into sb/sth** se changer en qn/qch.
tur·nip navet *m (plante).*
▸ **turn off** *vt (light, radio etc)* éteindre; *(faucet)* fermer; *(machine)* arrêter.
▸ **turn on** *vt (light, radio etc)* mettre; *(faucet)* ouvrir; *(machine)* mettre en marche.

▸ **turn out 1** *vt (light)* éteindre. **2** *vi (happen)* se passer.
▸ **turn over 1** *vt (page)* tourner. **2** *vi (of vehicle, person)* se retourner.
turn·pike autoroute *f* à péage.
▸ **turn up 1** *vt (radio, light etc)* mettre plus fort; *(collar)* remonter. **2** *vi (arrive)* arriver.
tur·tle tortue *f*; **sea t.** tortue *f* de mer.
tur·tle·neck *(sweater)* col *m* roulé.
tusk défense *f.*
tu·tor 1 *n* précepteur, -trice *mf.* **2** *vt* donner des cours particuliers à.
TV télé *f.*
tweez·ers *npl* pince *f* à épiler.
twelfth *adj & n* douzième *(mf).*
twelve *adj & n* douze *(m).*
twen·ti·eth *adj & n* vingtième *(mf).*
twen·ty *adj & n* vingt *(m).*
twice *adv* deux fois; **t. as heavy**/*etc* deux fois plus lourd/*etc.*
twig brindille *f.*
twi·light crépuscule *m.*
twin jumeau *m*, jumelle *f*; **t. brother** frère *m* jumeau; **t. sister** sœur *f* jumelle; **t. beds** lits *mpl* jumeaux.
twine *(grosse)* ficelle *f.*
twin·kle *vi (of star)* scintiller.
twirl 1 *vt* faire tournoyer. **2** *vi* tournoyer.
twist 1 *vt (wire, arm etc)* tordre; *(roll)* enrouler **(around** autour de); *(knob)* tourner; **to t. one's ankle** se tordre la cheville. **2** *n (turn)* tour *m*; *(in road)* zigzag *m.*
▸ **twist off** *vt (lid)* dévisser.
two *adj & n* deux *(m)*; **t.-way traffic** circulation *f* dans les deux sens.
type¹ *(sort)* genre *m*, type *m.*
type² 1 *n (print)* caractères *mpl.* **2** *vti (write)* taper (à la machine).
typed *adj* tapé à la machine.
type·writ·er machine *f* à écrire.
typ·i·cal *adj* typique **(of** de); **that's t. (of him)!** c'est bien lui!
typ·ist dactylo *f.*

U

UFO abbr (unidentified flying object) OVNI m.

ug·li·ness laideur f.

ug·ly adj laid.

ul·cer ulcère m.

ul·ti·mate adj (last) final; (supreme, best) absolu.

um·brel·la parapluie m; (over table, on beach) parasol m.

um·pire arbitre m.

ump·teen adj Fam je ne sais combien de, des tas de.

un- prefix in-, peu, non, sans.

un·a·ble adj to be u. to do être incapable de faire; **he's u. to swim** il ne sait pas nager.

un·ac·cept·a·ble adj inacceptable.

un·ac·cus·tomed to be u. to sth/to doing ne pas être habitué à qch/à faire.

u·nan·i·mous adj unanime.

u·nan·i·mous·ly adv à l'unanimité.

un·at·trac·tive adj (idea, appearance) peu attrayant; (ugly) laid.

un·a·vail·a·ble adj (person) qui n'est pas disponible; (product) épuisé.

un·a·void·a·ble adj inévitable.

un·a·void·a·bly adv inévitablement; (delayed) pour une raison indépendante de sa volonté.

un·a·ware adj to be u. of sth ignorer qch; **to be u. that** ignorer que.

un·a·wares adv to catch sb u. prendre qn au dépourvu.

un·bear·a·ble adj insupportable.

un·be·liev·a·ble adj incroyable.

un·break·a·ble adj incassable.

un·but·ton vt déboutonner.

un·cer·tain adj incertain (about,

of de); **it's u. whether** il n'est pas certain que (+ subjunctive); **I'm u. whether to stay** je ne sais pas très bien si je dois rester.

un·cer·tain·ty incertitude f.

un·changed adj inchangé.

un·cle oncle m.

un·clear adj (meaning) qui n'est pas clair; (result) incertain; **it's u. whether** on ne sait pas très bien si.

un·com·fort·a·ble adj (chair etc) inconfortable; (uneasy) mal à l'aise.

un·com·mon adj rare.

un·con·nect·ed adj (facts etc) sans rapport (with avec).

un·con·scious adj (person) sans connaissance.

un·con·sti·tu·tion·al adj inconstitutionnel.

un·con·vinc·ing adj peu convaincant.

un·co·op·er·a·tive adj peu coopératif.

un·cork vt (bottle) déboucher.

un·cov·er vt découvrir.

un·dam·aged adj (goods) en bon état.

un·de·cid·ed adj (person) indécis (about sur).

un·de·ni·a·ble adj incontestable.

un·der 1 prep sous; (less than) moins de; (according to) selon; **children u. nine** les enfants de moins de neuf ans; **u. the circumstances** dans les circonstances; **u. there** là-dessous; **u. it** dessous. **2** adv au-dessous.

un·der- prefix sous-.

un·der·charge vt **I undercharged him (for it)** je ne (le) lui ai pas fait payer assez.

un·der·clothes npl sous-vêtements mpl.

un·der·done adj pas assez cuit.

un·der·es·ti·mate vt sous-estimer.

un·der·go* vt subir.

un·der·grad·u·ate étudiant, -ante *mf* (qui prépare la licence).

un·der·ground *adj* souterrain; **u. passage** passage souterrain.

un·der·line *vt (word etc)* souligner.

un·der·mine *vt* saper.

un·der·neath 1 *prep* sous. **2** *adv* (en) dessous; **the book u.** le livre d'en dessous. **3** *n* dessous *m.*

un·der·pants *npl* slip *m.*

un·der·pass *(on highway)* passage *m* inférieur.

un·der·shirt tricot *m* de corps; *(woman's)* chemise *f* (américaine).

un·der·stand* *vti* comprendre.

un·der·stand·a·ble *adj* compréhensible.

un·der·stand·ing 1 *n* compréhension *f*, *(agreement)* accord *m*; *(sympathy)* entente *f*. **2** *adj (person)* compréhensif.

un·der·stood *adj (agreed)* entendu.

un·der·take* *vt* entreprendre (**to do** de faire).

un·der·tak·er entrepreneur *m* de pompes funèbres.

un·der·tak·ing *(task)* entreprise *f.*

un·der·wa·ter 1 *adj* sous-marin. **2** *adv* sous l'eau.

un·der·wear sous-vêtements *mpl*, *(underpants)* slip *m.*

un·do* *vt* défaire.

un·done *adj* **to come u.** *(of knot etc)* se défaire.

un·doubt·ed·ly *adv* sans aucun doute.

un·dress 1 *vi* se déshabiller. **2** *vt* déshabiller; **to get undressed** se déshabiller.

un·eas·y *adj (ill at ease)* mal à l'aise.

un·em·ployed 1 *adj* au chômage. **2** *n* **the u.** les chômeurs *mpl.*

un·em·ploy·ment chômage *m*; *(payment)* allocation *f* de chômage; **to go on u.** s'inscrire au chômage.

un·em·ploy·ment of·fice = agence *f* nationale pour l'emploi, ANPE *f.*

un·e·ven *adj* inégal.

un·e·vent·ful *adj (trip etc)* sans histoires.

un·ex·pect·ed *adj* inattendu.

un·ex·pect·ed·ly *adv* à l'improviste; *(suddenly)* subitement.

un·fair *adj* injuste (**to sb** envers qn).

un·fair·ly *adv* injustement.

un·fair·ness injustice *f.*

un·faith·ful *adj* infidèle (**to** à).

un·fa·mil·iar *adj* inconnu; **to be u. with sth** ne pas connaître qch.

un·fash·ion·a·ble *adj (subject etc)* démodé; *(restaurant etc)* peu chic *inv.*

un·fas·ten *vt* défaire.

un·fa·vor·a·ble *adj* défavorable.

un·fin·ished *adj* inachevé.

un·fit *adj* en mauvaise santé; *(in bad shape)* pas en forme; *(unsuitable)* impropre (**for** à; **to do** à faire); *(unworthy)* indigne (**for** de; **to do** de faire); *(unable)* inapte (**for** à; **to do** à faire).

un·fold *vt* déplier.

un·for·get·ta·ble *adj* inoubliable.

un·for·giv·a·ble *adj* impardonnable.

un·for·tu·nate *adj* malheureux; **you were u.** tu n'as pas eu de chance.

un·for·tu·nate·ly *adv* malheureusement.

un·friend·ly *adj* froid, peu aimable (**to** avec).

un·fur·nished *adj* non meublé.

un·grate·ful *adj* ingrat.

un·hap·pi·ness tristesse *f.*

un·hap·py *adj (sad)* malheureux; **u. with** *or* **about sth** mécontent de qch.

un·harmed *adj (person)* indemne.

un·health·y *adj (climate etc)* malsain; *(person)* en mauvaise santé.

un·help·ful *adj (person)* peu serviable.

un·hook *vt (picture, curtain)* décrocher; *(dress)* dégrafer.

un·hurt *adj* indemne.

un·hy·gi·en·ic *adj* pas très hygiénique.

u·ni·form uniforme *m*.

un·im·por·tant *adj* peu important.

un·in·hab·it·ed *adj* inhabité.

un·in·jured *adj* indemne.

un·in·ten·tion·al *adj* involontaire.

un·in·ter·est·ing *adj (book etc)* peu intéressant.

un·ion 1 *n* union *f*; *(labor union)* syndicat *m*. **2** *adj* syndical; **u. member** syndiqué, -ée *mf*.

u·nique *adj* unique.

u·nit unité *f*; *(of furniture etc)* élément *m*; *(team)* groupe *m*.

u·nite 1 *vt* unir; *(country, party)* unifier. **2** *vi (of students etc)* s'unir.

u·ni·ver·sal *adj* universel.

u·ni·verse univers *m*.

u·ni·ver·si·ty 1 *n* université *f*; **at u.** à l'université. **2** *adj* universitaire; *(student)* d'université.

un·just *adj* injuste.

un·kind *adj* peu gentil (**to sb** avec qn).

un·know·ing·ly *adj* inconsciemment.

un·known *adj* inconnu.

un·lead·ed *adj (gasoline)* sans plomb.

un·less *conj* à moins que (+ *subjunctive*); **u. she comes** à moins qu'elle ne vienne.

un·like *prep* **u. me, she…** à la différence de moi, elle…; **that's u. him** ça ne lui ressemble pas.

un·like·ly *adj* peu probable; *(unbelievable)* incroyable; **she's u. to win** il est peu probable qu'elle gagne.

un·lim·it·ed *adj* illimité.

un·list·ed *adj (phone number)* sur la liste rouge.

un·load *vt* décharger.

un·lock *vt* ouvrir *(avec une clef)*.

un·luck·i·ly *adv* malheureusement.

un·luck·y *adj (person)* malchanceux; *(number etc)* qui porte malheur; **you're u.** tu n'as pas de chance.

un·made *adj (bed)* défait.

un·mar·ried *adj* célibataire.

un·nec·es·sar·y *adj* inutile.

un·no·ticed *adj* **to go u.** passer inaperçu.

un·oc·cu·pied *adj (house)* inoccupé; *(seat)* libre.

un·pack 1 *vt (suitcase)* défaire; *(goods, belongings)* déballer. **2** *vi* défaire sa valise.

un·paid *adj (bill, sum)* impayé; *(work, worker)* bénévole.

un·pleas·ant *adj* désagréable (**to sb** avec qn).

un·plug *vt (appliance)* débrancher.

un·pop·u·lar *adj* peu populaire; **to be u. with sb** ne pas plaire à qn.

un·pre·dict·a·ble *adj* imprévisible; *(weather)* indécis.

un·pre·pared *adj* **to be u. for sth** *(not expect)* ne pas s'attendre à qch.

un·rea·son·a·ble *adj* qui n'est pas raisonnable.

un·rec·og·niz·a·ble *adj* méconnaissable.

un·re·lat·ed *adj (facts etc)* sans rapport (**to** avec).

un·re·li·a·ble *adj (person)* peu sûr; *(machine)* peu fiable.

un·rest agitation *f*.

un·roll 1 *vt* dérouler. **2** *vi* se dérouler.

un·safe *adj (place, machine etc)* dangereux; *(person)* en danger.

un·sat·is·fac·to·ry *adj* peu satisfaisant.

un·screw *vt* dévisser.

un·skilled work·er ouvrier, -ière *mf* non qualifié(e).

un·sta·ble adj instable.

un·stead·i·ly adv (to walk) d'un pas mal assuré.

un·stead·y adj (hand, step) mal assuré; (table, ladder etc) instable.

un·suc·cess·ful adj (attempt etc) vain; (candidate) malheureux; **to be u.** ne pas réussir (**in doing** à faire).

un·suc·cess·ful·ly adv en vain.

un·suit·a·ble adj qui ne convient pas (**for** à).

un·suit·ed adj **u. to** (job, activity) peu fait pour.

un·sure adj incertain (**of, about** de).

un·tan·gle vt démêler.

un·ti·dy adj (clothes, hair) peu soigné; (room) en désordre; (person) désordonné; (in appearance) peu soigné.

un·tie vt (person, hands) détacher; (knot, parcel) défaire.

un·til 1 prep jusqu'à; **u. then** jusque-là; **I didn't come u. yesterday** je ne suis venu qu'hier; **not u. tomorrow** pas avant demain. 2 conj jusqu'à ce que (+ subjunctive); **do nothing u. I come** ne fais rien avant que j'arrive.

un·true adj faux (f fausse).

un·used adj (new) neuf (f neuve).

un·u·su·al adj exceptionnel; (strange) étrange.

un·u·su·al·ly adv exceptionnellement.

un·veil vt dévoiler.

un·want·ed adj non désiré.

un·well adj indisposé.

un·will·ing adj **he's u. to do** il ne veut pas faire.

un·will·ing·ly adv à contrecœur.

un·wor·thy adj indigne (**of** de).

un·wrap vt ouvrir.

un·zip vt ouvrir (la fermeture éclair® de).

up 1 adv en haut; (in the air) en l'air; (out of bed) levé, debout; **to come** or **go up** monter; **prices are up** les prix ont augmenté; **up there** là-haut; **further** or **higher up** plus

haut; **up to** (as far as) jusqu'à; **it's up to you to do it** c'est à toi de le faire; **that's up to you** ça dépend de toi; **what are you up to?** que fais-tu?; **to walk up and down** marcher de long en large. 2 prep (a hill) en haut de; (a tree) dans; (a ladder) sur; **to go up** (hill, stairs) monter.

up·date vt mettre à jour.

up·grade 1 vt (improve) améliorer; (promote) promouvoir; (software) mettre à jour. 2 n (of software) mise f à jour.

up·hill adv **to go u.** monter.

up·hold vt maintenir.

up·on prep sur.

up·per adj supérieur.

up·right adj & adv (straight) droit.

up·roar vacarme m, tapage m.

up·scale adj haut de gamme.

up·set 1 vt* (stomach, routine etc) déranger; **to u. sb** (make sad) peiner qn; (offend) vexer qn. 2 adj (sad) peiné; (offended) vexé; (stomach) dérangé; **to have an u. stomach** avoir l'estomac dérangé.

up·side down adv à l'envers.

up·stairs 1 adv en haut; **to go u.** monter (l'escalier). 2 adj (people, room) du dessus.

up-to-date adj moderne; (information) à jour; (well-informed) au courant (**on** de).

up·town les quartiers mpl résidentiels.

up·ward(s) adv vers le haut; **upwards of five euros** cinq euros et plus.

urge vt **to u. sb to do** conseiller vivement à qn de faire.

ur·gen·cy urgence f.

ur·gent adj urgent.

ur·gent·ly adv d'urgence.

u·rine urine f.

us pron nous; (to) us nous; **she sees us** elle nous voit; **he gives (to) us** il nous donne; **all of us** nous tous; **let's** or **let us eat!** mangeons!

us·age usage m.

use 1 n usage m, emploi m; **to make u. of sth** se servir de qch; **not in u.** hors d'usage; **to be of u.** être utile; **it's no u. crying/etc** ça ne sert à rien de pleurer/etc; **what's the u. of worrying/etc?** à quoi bon s'inquiéter/etc? **2** vt se servir de, utiliser (**as** comme; **to do, for doing** pour faire); **it's used to do** or **for doing** ça sert à faire; **it's used as** ça sert de.

use (up) vt (fuel) consommer; (supplies) épuiser; (money) dépenser.

used 1 adj (secondhand) d'occasion. **2** v aux **I u. to sing/etc** avant, je chantais/etc. **3** adj **u. to sth/to doing** habitué à qch/à faire; **to get u. to** s'habituer à.

use·ful adj utile (**to** à); **to come in u.** être utile.

use·ful·ness utilité f.

use·less adj inutile; (person) nul.

us·er (of road) usager m; (of machine, dictionary) utilisateur, -trice mf.

us·er-friend·ly adj convivial.

u·su·al adj habituel; **as u.** comme d'habitude.

u·su·al·ly adv d'habitude.

u·ten·sil ustensile m.

u·til·i·ty (public) u. service m public.

ut·ter 1 adj complet; (idiot) parfait. **2** vt (a cry) pousser; (a word) dire.

ut·ter·ly adv complètement.

U-turn (in vehicle) demi-tour m.

V

va·can·cy (post) poste m vacant; (room) chambre f libre.

va·cant adj (room, seat) libre; **v. lot** terrain m vague.

va·ca·tion vacances fpl; **on v.** en vacances.

va·ca·tion·er vacancier, -ière mf.

vac·ci·nate vt vacciner.

vac·ci·na·tion vaccination f.

vac·cine vaccin m.

vac·u·um vt (carpet etc) passer à l'aspirateur.

vac·u·um clean·er aspirateur m.

vague adj vague; (outline) flou.

vague·ly adv vaguement.

vain adj in v. en vain.

val·id adj (ticket etc) valable.

val·ley vallée f.

val·u·a·ble 1 adj (object) de (grande) valeur. **2** npl **valuables** objets mpl de valeur.

val·ue valeur f; **it's good v. (for money)** ça a un bon rapport qualité/prix.

valve (of machine) soupape f; (in pipe, tube, heart) valve f.

van camionnette f, fourgonnette f; (large) camion m.

van·dal vandale mf.

van·dal·ize vt saccager.

va·nil·la 1 n vanille f. **2** adj (ice cream) à la vanille.

van·ish vi disparaître.

var·i·a·ble adj & n variable (f).

var·i·ant variante f.

var·ied adj varié.

va·ri·e·ty variété f; **a v. of reasons/etc** diverses raisons/etc; **v. show** spectacle m de variétés.

var·i·ous adj divers.

var·nish 1 vt vernir. **2** n vernis m.

var·y vti varier.

vase vase m.

Vas·e·line® vaseline f.

vast adj vaste.

VCR abbr (video cassette recorder) magnétoscope m.

veal (meat) veau m.

veg·e·ta·ble légume m.

veg·e·tar·i·an adj & n végétarien, -ienne (mf).

veg·e·ta·tion végétation f.

ve·hi·cle véhicule m.

veil voile m.

vein (in body) veine f.

vel·vet **1** *n* velours *m*. **2** *adj* de velours.

vend·ing ma·chine distributeur *m* automatique.

ven·dor vendeur, -euse *mf*.

ve·ne·tian blind store *m* vénitien.

ven·ti·la·tion *(in room)* aération *f*.

ven·ture **1** *vt* hasarder; **to v. to do sth** se hasarder à faire qch. **2** *vi* **to v. out of doors** se risquer à sortir. **3** *n* entreprise *f* (hasardeuse).

ven·ue *(meeting place)* lieu *m* (de rendez-vous); *(for concert etc)* salle *f*.

verb verbe *m*.

ver·bal *adj* verbal.

ver·dict verdict *m*.

verse *(part of song)* couplet *m*; *(poetry)* poésie *f*; **in v.** en vers.

ver·sion version *f*.

ver·sus *prep* contre.

ver·ti·cal *adj* vertical.

ver·y **1** *adv* très; **v. much** beaucoup; **at the v. latest** au plus tard. **2** *adj* *(actual)* même; **his** *or* **her v. brother** son frère même.

vest *(waistcoat)* gilet *m*.

vet vétérinaire *mf*.

vet·er·an *(of war)* ancien combattant *m*; *(experienced person)* vétéran *m*.

vet·er·i·nar·i·an vétérinaire *mf*.

vi·a *prep* par.

vi·brate *vi* vibrer.

vi·bra·tion vibration *f*.

vic·ar pasteur *m*.

vice vice *m*; *(tool)* étau *m*.

vi·cious *adj* *(spiteful)* méchant; *(violent)* brutal.

vic·tim victime *f*; **to be the v. of** être victime de.

vic·to·ry victoire *f*.

vid·e·o **1** *n* *(cassette)* cassette *f*; **on v.** sur cassette. **2** *adj* *(game, camera etc)* vidéo *inv*. **3** *vt* *(event)* faire une (vidéo)cassette de.

vid·e·o·cas·sette vidéocassette *f*; **v. recorder** magnétoscope *m*.

vid·e·o game jeu *m* vidéo.

vid·e·o·tape cassette *f* vidéo.

view vue *f*; **to come into v.** apparaître; **in my v.** à mon avis; **in v. of** compte tenu de.

view·er *(person)* téléspectateur, -trice *mf*.

view·find·er viseur *m*.

view·point point *m* de vue.

vil·la villa *f*.

vil·lage village *m*.

vil·lag·er villageois, -oise *mf*.

vil·lain scélérat *m*; *(in movie, play)* méchant, -ante *mf*.

vin·e·gar vinaigre *m*.

vine·yard vignoble *m*.

vi·o·lence violence *f*.

vi·o·lent *adj* violent.

vi·o·lent·ly *adv* violemment.

vi·o·lin violon *m*.

VIP *abbr* (very important person) VIP *mf*.

vir·gin vierge *f*.

vir·tu·al *adj* quasi; **v. reality** réalité *f* virtuelle.

vir·tue *(goodness)* vertu *f*; *(advantage)* mérite *m*; **by v. of** en vertu de.

vi·rus virus *m*.

vi·sa visa *m*.

vise étau *m*.

vis·i·ble *adj* visible.

vis·it **1** *n* visite *f*, *(stay)* séjour *m*. **2** *vt* *(place)* visiter; **to v. sb** rendre visite à qn; *(stay with)* faire un séjour chez qn. **3** *vi* être en visite.

vis·it·ing hours heures *fpl* de visite.

vis·i·tor visiteur, -euse *mf*, *(guest)* invité, -ée *mf*.

vi·tal *adj* essentiel; **it's v. that** il est essentiel que (+ *subjunctive*).

vi·ta·min vitamine *f*.

viv·id *adj* vif; *(description)* vivant.

vo·cab·u·lar·y vocabulaire *m*.

vo·ca·tion·al *adj* profesionnel, -elle.

vod·ka vodka *f*.

voice voix *f*; **at the top of one's v.** à tue-tête.

voice·mail *(service)* messagerie f vocale; *(message)* message m vocal.

vol·ca·no, *pl* -oes volcan m.

volt·age voltage m.

vol·ume *(book, capacity, loudness)* volume m.

vol·un·tar·y *adj* volontaire; *(unpaid)* bénévole.

vol·un·teer 1 n volontaire mf. **2** vi se proposer (**for sth** pour qch; **to do** pour faire).

vom·it vti vomir.

vote 1 n vote m. **2** vi voter; **to v. Republican** voter républicain.

vot·er électeur, -trice mf.

vouch·er *(for meal, gift etc)* chèque m.

vow·el voyelle f.

voy·age voyage m (par mer).

vul·gar adj vulgaire.

W

wad *(of money etc)* liasse f; *(of cotton wool)* tampon m.

wad·dle vi se dandiner.

▶ **wade through** vt *(mud, water etc)* patauger dans.

wad·ing pool *(small, inflatable)* piscine f gonflable.

▶ **wad up** vt *(paper)* chiffonner.

wa·fer gaufrette f.

waf·fle gaufre f.

wag vti *(tail)* remuer.

wage(·s) n(pl) salaire m.

wage earn·er salarié, -ée mf.

wag·on *(horse-drawn)* charrette f, chariot m.

waist taille f; **stripped to the w.** torse nu.

waist·coat gilet m.

wait 1 n attente f. **2** vi attendre; **to w. for sb/sth** attendre qn/qch; **w.**

until I've gone, **w. for me to go** attends que je sois parti; **to keep sb waiting** faire attendre qn.

▶ **wait behind** vi rester.

wait·er garçon m (de café).

wait·ing attente f.

wait·ing room salle f d'attente.

wait·ress serveuse f.

wait·staff serveurs mpl.

▶ **wait up** vi veiller; **to w. up for sb** attendre le retour de qn avant de se coucher.

wake* (up) 1 vi se réveiller. **2** vt réveiller.

walk 1 n promenade f; *(shorter)* (petit) tour m; *(path)* allée f; **to go for a w.** faire une promenade; *(shorter)* faire un (petit) tour; **to take for a w.** *(child)* emmener se promener; *(baby, dog)* promener; **five minutes' w. (away)** à cinq minutes à pied. **2** vi marcher; *(stroll)* se promener; *(go on foot)* aller à pied. **3** vt *(distance)* faire à pied; *(take for a walk)* promener *(chien)*.

▶ **walk away** vi s'éloigner (**from** de).

walk·er *(for pleasure)* promeneur, -euse mf.

▶ **walk in** vi entrer.

walk·ing stick canne f.

Walk·man®, *pl* Walkmans baladeur m.

▶ **walk off** vi s'en aller; **to walk off with sth** *(steal)* partir avec qch.

▶ **walk out** vi *(leave)* partir.

wall mur m; *(of cabin, tunnel)* paroi f.

wal·let portefeuille m.

wall·pa·per 1 n papier m peint. **2** vt tapisser.

wall-to-wall car·pet(·ing) moquette f.

wal·nut *(nut)* noix f.

wal·rus *(animal)* morse m.

wan·der (a·round) vi errer; *(stroll)* flâner.

want vt vouloir (**to do** faire); *(ask for)* demander *(qn)*; *(need)* avoir besoin de; **I w. him to go** je veux qu'il parte; **you're wanted** on vous demande.

WAP *abbr (Wireless Application Protocol)* WAP *m*.

war guerre *f*; **at w.** en guerre (**with** avec).

ward *(in hospital)* salle *f*.

war·den directeur, -trice *mf*.

ward·robe *(built-in)* penderie *f*; *(free-standing)* armoire *f*.

ware·house, *pl* -ses entrepôt *m*.

warm 1 *adj* chaud; **to be** *or* **feel w.** avoir chaud; **it's (nice and) w.** *(of weather)* il fait (agréablement) chaud. **2** *vt (person, food etc)* réchauffer.

warmth chaleur *f*.

▸**warm up 1** *vt (person, food etc)* réchauffer. **2** *vi (of person, room, engine)* se réchauffer; *(of food, water)* chauffer.

warn *vt* avertir (**that** que); **to w. sb against sth** mettre qn en garde contre qch; **to w. sb against doing** conseiller à qn de ne pas faire.

warn·ing avertissement *m*; *(advance notice)* (pré)avis *m*; *(hazard)* **w. flashers** *(of vehicle)* feux *mpl* de détresse.

war·rant 1 *n (legal order)* mandat *m*. **2** *vt (justify)* justifier.

war·ran·ty *(for goods)* garantie *f*.

war·ri·or guerrier, -ère *mf*.

war·ship navire *m* de guerre.

wart verrue *f*.

war·time **in w.** en temps de guerre.

was *pt de* **be**.

wash 1 *n* **to give sth a w.** laver qch; **in the w.** *(of dirty clothes)* au sale. **2** *vt* laver; **to w. one's hands** se laver les mains.

wash·a·ble *adj* lavable.

▸**wash away, wash off, wash out 1** *vt (stain)* faire partir (en lavant). **2** *vi* partir (au lavage).

wash·ba·sin lavabo *m*.

wash·cloth gant *m* de toilette.

wash·ing *(act)* lavage *m*.

wash·ing ma·chine machine *f* à laver.

▸**wash out** *(bowl etc)* laver.

wash·room toilettes *fpl*.

▸**wash up** *vi (wash hands and face)* se laver.

wasp guêpe *f*.

waste 1 *n* gaspillage *m*; *(of time)* perte *f*. **2** *vt (money, food etc)* gaspiller; *(time, opportunity)* perdre.

waste·pa·per vieux papiers *mpl*.

waste·pa·per bas·ket corbeille *f* (à papier).

watch 1 *n (small clock)* montre *f*. **2** *vt* regarder; *(be careful of)* faire attention à. **3** *vi* regarder.

watch·band bracelet *m* de montre.

watch (o·ver) *vt (suspect, baby etc)* surveiller.

▸**watch out for** *vt (wait for)* guetter.

▸**watch out** *vi (take care)* faire attention (**for** à); **w. out!** attention!

wa·ter 1 *n* eau *f*; **w. pistol** pistolet *m* à eau. **2** *vt (plant etc)* arroser.

wa·ter·col·or *(picture)* aquarelle *f*; *(paint)* couleur *f* pour aquarelle.

wa·ter·cress cresson *m* (de fontaine).

▸**water down** *vt (wine etc)* couper (d'eau).

wa·ter·fall chute *f* d'eau.

wa·ter·front bord *m* *or* front *m* de mer.

wa·ter·ing can arrosoir *m*.

wa·ter·mel·on pastèque *f*.

wa·ter·proof *adj (material)* imperméable.

wa·ter ski·ing ski *m* nautique.

wa·ter·tight *adj* étanche.

wave 1 *n (of sea)* vague *f*; *(in hair)* ondulation *f*; **medium/short w.** *(on radio)* ondes *fpl* moyennes/courtes; **long w.** grandes ondes *fpl*, ondes *fpl* longues. **2** *vi (with hand)* faire signe (de la main); **to w. to sb** *(greet)* saluer qn de la main. **3** *vt (arm, flag etc)* agiter.

wave·length longueur *f* d'ondes.

wav·y *adj (hair)* ondulé.

wax 1 *n* cire *f.* **2** *vt* cirer; **to have one's legs waxed** se faire épiler les jambes (à la cire).

wax pa·per papier *m* sulfurisé.

way¹ *n (path)* chemin *m* (**to** de); *(direction)* sens *m*; *(distance)* distance *f*; **all the w., the whole w.** *(to talk etc)* pendant tout le chemin; **this w.** par ici; **that w.** par là; **which w.?** par où?; **to lose one's w.** se perdre; **the w. there** l'aller *m*; **the w. back** le retour; **the w. in** l'entrée *f*, **the w. out** la sortie; **on the w.** en route (**to** pour); **to be** *or* **stand in sb's w.** être sur le chemin de qn; **to get out of the w.** s'écarter; **a long w. (away** *or* **off)** très loin. **2** *adv (behind etc)* très loin; **w. ahead** très en avance (**of** sur).

way² *(manner)* façon *f*, *(means)* moyen *m*; **(in) this w.** de cette façon; **no w.!** *Fam* pas question!

we *pron* nous; **we teachers** nous autres professeurs.

weak *adj* faible; *(tea, coffee)* léger.

weak·en 1 *vt* affaiblir. **2** *vi* faiblir.

weak·ness faiblesse *f*, *(fault)* point *m* faible.

wealth richesse(s) *f(pl)*.

wealth·y *adj* riche.

weap·on arme *f.*

wear¹ *vt (have on body)* porter; *(put on)* mettre. **2** *n* **w. (and tear)** usure *f.*

▸ **wear off** *vi (of color, effect etc)* disparaître.

▸ **wear out 1** *vt (clothes etc)* user; *(person)* épuiser. **2** *vi* s'user.

wea·ry *adj* fatigué.

wea·sel belette *f.*

weath·er temps *m*; **what's the w. like?** quel temps fait-il?; **it's nice w.** il fait beau; **under the w.** *(ill)* patraque.

weath·er fore·cast, weather report météo *f.*

weave* *vt (cloth)* tisser.

web *(of spider)* toile *f*; **the W.** le Web; **w. page** page *f* web; **w. site** site *m* web.

web·cam webcam *m.*

wed·ding mariage *m.*

wed·ding ring alliance *f.*

Wednes·day mercredi *m.*

weed mauvaise herbe *f.*

week semaine *f*; **a w. from tomorrow** demain en huit.

week·day jour *m* de semaine.

week·end week-end *m*; **over the w.** ce week-end.

week·ly 1 *adj* hebdomadaire. **2** *adv* toutes les semaines. **3** *n (magazine)* hebdomadaire *m.*

weep* *vi* pleurer.

weigh *vti* peser.

weight poids *m*; **by w.** au poids; **to put on w.** grossir; **to lose w.** maigrir.

weird *adj (odd)* bizarre.

wel·come 1 *adj* **to be w.** *(warmly received, of person)* être bien reçu; **w.!** bienvenue!; **to make sb (feel) w.** faire bon accueil à qn; **you're w.!** *(after 'thank you')* il n'y a pas de quoi!; **some coffee/a break would be w.** un café/une pause ne ferait pas de mal. **2** *n* accueil *m*. **3** *vt* accueillir; *(warmly)* faire bon accueil à.

weld *vt* souder.

wel·fare to be on w. vivre d'allocations.

well¹ *(for water)* puits *m*; **(oil) w.** puits *m* de pétrole.

well² 1 *adv* bien; **w. done!** bravo!; **as w.** *(also)* aussi; **as w. as** aussi bien que; **as w. as two cats, he has a dog** en plus de deux chats, il a un chien. **2** *adj* bien *inv*; **she's w.** *(healthy)* elle va bien; **to get w.** se remettre. **3** *int* eh bien!; **huge, w., very big** énorme, enfin, très grand.

well-be·haved *adj* sage.

well-be·ing bien-être *m.*

well-in·formed *adj* bien informé.

well-known *adj* (bien) connu.

well-man·nered *adj* bien élevé.

well-off *adj* riche.

well-to-do *adj* aisé.

Welsh 1 *adj* gallois. **2** *n (language)*
gallois *m*; **the W.** les Gallois *mpl*.

Welsh·man, *pl* **-men** Gallois *m*.

Welsh·wom·an, *pl* **-women** Gal-
loise *f*.

went *pt de* **go**[1].

were *pt de* **be**.

west 1 *n* ouest *m*; **(to the) w. of** à
l'ouest de. **2** *adj* (coast) ouest *inv*. **3**
adv à l'ouest.

west·bound *adj* en direction de
l'ouest.

west·ern 1 *adj* (coast) ouest *inv*;
(culture etc) occidental. **2** *n (film)*
western *m*.

west·ward(s) *adj & adv* vers
l'ouest.

wet 1 *adj* mouillé; *(damp, rainy)* humide; *(day, month)* de pluie; **'w.
paint'** 'peinture fraîche'; **to get w.**
se mouiller; **to make w.** mouiller;
it's w. *(raining)* il pleut. **2** *vt*
mouiller.

whale baleine *f*.

wharf quai *m*, débarcadère *m*.

what 1 *adj* quel, quelle, *pl* quel(-
le)s; **w. book?** quel livre?; **w. a fool!**
quel idiot! **2** *pron (in questions)*
qu'est-ce qui; *(object)* qu'est-ce
que; *(after prep)* quoi; **w.'s happen-
ing?** qu'est-ce qui se passe?; **w.
does he do?** qu'est-ce qu'il fait?,
que fait-il?; **w. is it?** qu'est-ce que
c'est?; **w.'s that book?** c'est quoi, ce
livre?; **w.!** *(surprise)* quoi!; **w.'s it
called?** comment ça s'appelle?; **w.
for?** pourquoi?; **w. about me?** et
moi?; **w. about leaving?** si on par-
tait? **3** *pron (indirect, relative)*
ce qui; *(object)* ce que; **I know w. will
happen/w. she'll do** je sais ce qui
arrivera/ce qu'elle fera; **w. I need**
ce dont j'ai besoin.

what·ev·er 1 *adj* **w. (the) mis-
take/etc** quelle que soit l'erreur/
etc; **no chance w.** pas la moindre
chance; **nothing w.** rien du tout. **2**
pron (no matter what) quoi que (+
subjunctive); **w. you do** quoi que tu
fasses; **w. is important** tout ce qui
est important; **do w. you want** fais
tout ce que tu veux.

wheat blé *m*.

wheel 1 *n* roue *f*; **at the w.** *(driving)*
au volant. **2** *vt* pousser.

wheel·bar·row brouette *f*.

wheel·chair fauteuil *m* roulant.

when 1 *adv* quand. **2** *conj* quand;
w. I finish, w. I've finished quand
j'aurai fini; **w. I saw him** *or* **w. I'd
seen him, I left** après l'avoir vu, je
suis parti; **the day/moment w.** le
jour/moment où.

when·ev·er *conj* quand; *(each
time that)* chaque fois que.

where 1 *adv* où; **w. are you from?**
d'où êtes-vous? **2** *conj* (là) où; **I
found it w. she'd left it** je l'ai trouvé
là où elle l'avait laissé; **the place/
house w.** l'endroit/la maison où.

where·a·bouts 1 *adv* où (donc).
2 *n his* **w.** l'endroit *m* où il est.

where·as *conj* alors que.

where·by *adv* par quoi.

wher·ev·er *conj* **w. you go** partout où tu iras; **I'll go w. you like**
j'irai (là) où vous voudrez.

wheth·er *conj* si; **I don't know w.
to leave** je ne sais pas si je dois partir; **w. she does it or not** qu'elle le
fasse ou non.

which 1 *adj (in questions etc)* quel,
quelle, *pl* quel(le)s; **w. hat?** quel
chapeau?; **in w. case** auquel cas. **2**
rel pron (subject) qui; *(object)* que;
(after prep) lequel, laquelle, *pl* les-
quel(le)s; *(after clause)* ce qui; *(object)* ce que; **the house w. is old** la
maison qui est vieille; **the book w. I like** le
livre que j'aime; **the table w. I put it
on** la table sur laquelle je l'ai mis;
the film of w. le film dont; **she's**

sick, w. is sad elle est malade, ce qui est triste; **he lies, w. I don't like it** il ment, ce que je n'aime pas. **3** *pron* **w. (one)** *(in questions)* lequel, laquelle, *pl* lesquel(le)s; **w. (one) of us?** lequel *or* laquelle d'entre nous *or* de nous? ■ **w. (one)** *(the one that)* celui qui, celle qui, *pl* ceux qui, celles qui; *(object)* celui *etc* que; **show me w. (one) is red** montrez-moi celui *or* celle qui est rouge; **I know w. (ones) you want** je sais ceux *or* celles que vous désirez.

which·ev·er *adj & pron* **w. book/ etc** *or* **w. of the books/etc you buy** quel que soit le livre/*etc* que tu achètes; **take w. books interest you** prenez les livres qui vous intéressent; **take w. (one) you like** prends celui *or* celle que tu veux; **w. (ones) remain** ceux *or* celles qui restent.

while 1 *conj* (*when*) pendant que; *(although)* bien que (+ *subjunctive*); *(as long as)* tant que; *(whereas)* tandis que; **while eating/etc** en mangeant/*etc*. **2** *n* **a w.** un moment; **all the w.** tout le temps.

whim caprice *m*.

whine *vi* gémir.

whip 1 *n* fouet *m*. **2** *vt* fouetter.

▶**whip out** *vt* sortir brusquement.

whirl (a·round) *vi* tourbillonner.

whisk 1 *n* (*for eggs etc*) fouet *m*. **2** *vt* fouetter.

whisk·ers *npl* (*of cat*) moustaches *fpl*.

whis·key whisky *m*.

whis·per 1 *vti* chuchoter. **2** *n* chuchotement *m*.

whis·tle 1 *n* sifflement *m*; *(object)* sifflet *m*; **to blow the** *or* **one's w.** siffler. **2** *vti* siffler.

white 1 *adj* blanc (*f* blanche); **to turn w.** blanchir; **w. man** blanc *m*; **w. woman** blanche *f*. **2** *n* (*color, of egg*) blanc *m*.

white·wash *vt* (*wall*) badigeonner.

▶**whizz past** *vi* passer à toute vitesse.

who *pron* qui; **w. did it?** qui (est-ce qui) a fait ça?

who·ev·er *pron* qui que ce soit qui; *(object)* qui que ce soit que; **this man, w. he is** cet homme, quel qu'il soit.

whole 1 *adj* entier; *(intact)* intact; **the w. time/village/etc** tout le temps/village/*etc*; **the w. thing** le tout. **2** *n* **on the w.** dans l'ensemble.

whole·sale 1 *adj* (*price*) de gros. **2** *adv* (*to sell*) au prix de gros; *(in bulk)* en gros.

whole·sal·er grossiste *mf*.

whole-wheat *adj* (*bread*) complet.

whol·ly *adv* entièrement.

whom *pron* (*object*) que; *(in questions and after prep)* qui; **of w.** dont.

whoop·ing cough coqueluche *f*.

whose *poss pron & adj* à qui, de qui; **w. book is this?** à qui est ce livre?; **w. daughter are you?** de qui es-tu la fille?; **the woman w. book I have** la femme de qui j'ai le livre.

why 1 *adv* pourquoi; **w. not?** pourquoi pas? **2** *conj* **the reason w. they...** la raison pour laquelle ils....

wick mèche *f* (*de bougie*).

wick·ed *adj* (*evil*) méchant; *(mischievous)* malicieux.

wick·er 1 *n* osier *m*. **2** *adj* (*basket etc*) en osier.

wide 1 *adj* large; *(choice, variety)* grand; **to be three yards w.** avoir trois mètres de large. **2** *adv* (*to open*) tout grand.

wide-a·wake *adj* éveillé.

wide·ly *adv* (*to travel*) beaucoup.

wid·en 1 *vt* élargir. **2** *vi* s'élargir.

wide·spread *adj* (*très*) répandu.

wid·ow veuve *f*.

wid·ow·er veuf *m*.

width largeur *f*.

wife, *pl* **wives** femme *f*.

wig perruque *f.*

wild *adj (animal, flower etc)* sauvage.

wil·der·ness désert *m.*

wild·life nature *f.*

wild·ly *adv (cheer)* frénétiquement; *(guess)* au hasard.

will¹ *v aux* he will come, he'll come *(future tense)* il viendra; you will not come, you won't come tu ne viendras pas; you'll come, w. you? tu viendras, n'est-ce pas?; **w. you have a cup of tea?** veux-tu prendre un thé?; **w. you be quiet!** veux-tu te taire!; **I w.!** *(yes)* oui!

will² volonté *f, (legal document)* testament *m;* **ill w.** mauvaise volonté *f,* **against one's w.** à contrecœur.

will·ing *adj (helper, worker)* de bonne volonté; **to be w. to do** vouloir bien faire.

will·ing·ly *adv (with pleasure)* volontiers; *(voluntarily)* volontairement.

will·ing·ness bonne volonté *f,* his or her w. to do son empressement *m* à faire.

wil·low saule *m.*

win 1 *n* victoire *f.* 2 *vi** gagner. 3 *vt (money, prize, race)* gagner.

wind¹ vent *m.*

wind²* 1 *vt (roll)* enrouler (**around** autour de); *(clock)* remonter. **2** *vi (of river, road)* serpenter.

wind·break·er blouson *m.*

wind·mill moulin *m* à vent.

win·dow fenêtre *f, (pane, in vehicle or train)* vitre *f, (in store)* vitrine *f, (counter)* guichet *m;* **to go w. shopping** faire du lèche-vitrines.

win·dow box jardinière *f.*

win·dow-pane vitre *f.*

win·dow screen grillage *m.*

win·dow-sill *(inside)* appui *m* de (la) fenêtre; *(outside)* rebord *m* de (la) fenêtre.

wind·shield pare-brise *m inv;* **w. wiper** essuie-glace *m.*

wind·surf·ing to go w. faire de la planche (à voile).

wind·y *adj* it's w. *(of weather)* il y a du vent.

wine vin *m;* **w. bottle** bouteille *f* à vin; **w. list** carte *f* des vins.

wine-glass verre *m* à vin.

wing aile *f.*

wink 1 *vi* faire un clin d'œil (**at, to** à). 2 *n* clin *m* d'œil.

win·ner gagnant, -ante *mf; (of argument, fight)* vainqueur *m.*

win·ning 1 *adj (number, horse etc)* gagnant; *(team)* victorieux. **2** *n* **winnings** gains *mpl.*

win·ter 1 *n* hiver *m;* **in (the) w.** en hiver. 2 *adj* d'hiver.

win·ter·time hiver *m.*

wipe *vt* essuyer; **to w. one's feet / hands** s'essuyer les pieds/les mains.

▸ **wipe off, wipe up** *vt (liquid)* essuyer.

wip·er *(in vehicle)* essuie-glace *m.*

wire fil *m.*

wire·less *adj* sans fil.

wir·ing *(electrical)* installation *f* électrique.

wis·dom sagesse *f.*

wise *adj (in knowledge)* sage; *(advisable)* prudent.

wish 1 *vt* souhaiter, vouloir (**to do** faire); **I w. (that) you could help me/could have helped me** je voudrais que/j'aurais voulu que vous m'aidiez; **I w. I hadn't done that** je regrette d'avoir fait ça; **if you w.** si tu veux; **I w. you a happy birthday** je vous souhaite un bon anniversaire; **I w. I could** si seulement je pouvais. **2** *vi* **to w. for sth** souhaiter qch. **3** *n (specific)* souhait *m; (general)* désir *m;* **best wishes** *(on greeting card)* meilleurs vœux *mpl; (in letter)* amitiés *fpl;* **send him** or **her my best wishes** fais-lui mes amitiés.

wit *(humor)* esprit *m; (person)* homme *m*/femme *f* d'esprit; **wits**

(intelligence) intelligence f; **to be at one's wits' end** ne plus savoir que faire.

witch sorcière f.

with prep avec; **come w. me** viens avec moi; **w. no hat/etc** sans chapeau/etc. ▪ *(at the house etc of)* chez; **she's staying w. me** elle loge chez moi. ▪ *(cause)* de; **to jump w. joy** sauter de joie. ▪ *(instrument, means)* avec, de; **to write w. a pen** écrire avec un stylo; **to fill w.** remplir de. ▪ *(description)* à; **w. blue eyes** aux yeux bleus.

with·draw* 1 vt retirer. 2 vi se retirer (**from** de).

with·draw·al retrait m.

with·er vi *(of plant etc)* se flétrir.

with·hold* vt *(permission, help)* refuser (**from** à); *(decision)* différer; *(money)* retenir (**from** de); *(information)* cacher (**from** à).

with·in prep *(place, box etc)* à l'intérieur de; **w. 6 miles (of)** *(less than)* à moins de 10 km (de); *(inside an area of)* dans un rayon de 10 km (de); **w. a month** *(to return etc)* avant un mois; *(to finish sth)* en moins d'un mois.

with·out prep sans; **w. a tie/etc** sans cravate/etc; **w. doing** sans faire.

wit·ness 1 n *(person)* témoin m. 2 vt *(accident etc)* être (le) témoin de.

wob·bly adj *(table, tooth)* branlant.

wolf, pl **wolves** loup m.

wom·an, pl **women** femme f; **women's** *(clothes etc)* féminin.

won·der 1 n *(it's)* **no w.** ce n'est pas étonnant *(that* que *(+ subjunctive)).* 2 vt se demander *(if* si; *why* pourquoi). 3 vi *(think)* réfléchir; **I was just wondering** je réfléchissais.

won·der·ful adj merveilleux.

won't = will not.

wood *(material, forest)* bois m.

wood·en adj de or en bois.

wood·work *(school subject)* menuiserie f.

wool laine f.

wool·en 1 adj en laine. 2 n **woolens** lainages mpl.

word mot m; *(spoken, promise)* parole f; **words** *(of song etc)* paroles fpl; **to have a w. with sb** parler à qn; *(advise, criticize)* avoir un mot avec qn; **in other words** autrement dit.

word·ing termes mpl.

word pro·cess·ing traitement m de texte.

wore pt de **wear**.

work 1 n travail m; *(product, book etc)* œuvre f, *(building or repair work)* travaux mpl; **out of w.** au chômage; **a day off w.** un jour de congé; **he's off w.** il n'est pas allé travailler; **the works** *(of clock etc)* le mécanisme. 2 vi travailler; *(of machine etc)* marcher; *(of drug)* agir. 3 vt *(machine)* faire marcher; **to get worked up** s'exciter.

▸**work at, work on** vt *(improve)* travailler.

work·bench établi m.

work·er travailleur, -euse mf; *(manual)* ouvrier, -ière mf, **(office)** w. employé, -ée mf (de bureau).

work·force main-d'œuvre f.

work·ing adj **w. class** classe f ouvrière; **in w. order** en état de marche.

work·man, pl -**men** ouvrier m.

▸**work on** vt *(book, problem etc)* travailler à.

work·out séance f d'entraînement.

▸**work out** 1 vi *(succeed)* marcher; *(do exercises)* s'entraîner; **it works out at 50 euros** ça fait 50 euros. 2 vt calculer; *(problem)* résoudre; *(scheme)* préparer; *(understand)* comprendre.

work·shop atelier m.

world 1 n monde m; **all over the w.** dans le monde entier. 2 adj *(war etc)* mondial; *(champion, cup, record)* du monde.

world·wide *adj* mondial.

worm ver *m*.

worn (*pp of* **wear**) *adj* (*clothes etc*) usé.

worn-out *adj* (*object*) complètement usé; (*person*) épuisé.

wor·ri·some *adj* inquiétant.

wor·ry 1 *n* souci *m*. **2** *vi* s'inquiéter (**about sth** de qch; **about sb** pour qn). **3** *vt* inquiéter; **to be worried** être inquiet.

worse 1 *adj* pire, plus mauvais (**than** que); **to get w.** se détériorer; **he's getting w.** (*in health*) il va de plus en plus mal. **2** *adv* plus mal (**than** que); **to be w. off** aller moins bien financièrement.

wors·en *vti* empirer.

wor·ship *vt* (*person, god*) adorer.

worst 1 *adj* pire, plus mauvais. **2** *adv* (**the**) **w.** le plus mal. **3** *n* **the w. (one)** le *or* la pire, le *or* la plus mauvais(e); **at w.** au pire.

worth 1 *n* valeur *f*; **to buy 50 dollars w. of gas** acheter pour 50 dollars d'essence. **2** *adj* **to be w. sth** valoir qch; **how much** *or* **what is it w.?** ça vaut combien?; **the movie's w. seeing** le film vaut la peine d'être vu; **it's w. (one's) while** ça (en) vaut la peine; **it's w. (while) waiting** ça vaut la peine d'attendre.

worth·while *adj* (*activity*) qui vaut la peine; (*book, movie*) qui vaut la peine d'être lu/vu; (*plan, contribution*) valable; (*cause*) louable.

wor·thy *adj* **w. of sth/sb** digne de qch/qn.

would *v aux* **I w. stay, I'd stay** (*conditional tense*) je resterais; **he w. have done it** il l'aurait fait; **w. you help me, please?** voulez-vous m'aider, s'il vous plaît?; **w. you like some tea?** voudriez-vous (prendre) du thé?; **I w. see her every day** (*in the past*) je la voyais chaque jour.

wound 1 *vt* blesser; **the wounded** les blessés *mpl*. **2** *n* blessure *f*.

wrap (up) 1 *vt* envelopper; (*par-*

cel) emballer. **2** *vti* **to w. (oneself) up** (*dress warmly*) se couvrir. **3** *n* plastic w. film *m* plastique.

wrap·per (*of candy*) papier *m*.

wrap·ping (*action, material*) emballage *m*; **w. paper** papier *m* d'emballage.

wreath, *pl* **-s** couronne *f*.

wreck 1 *n* (*ship*) épave *f*; (*sinking*) naufrage *m*; (*train etc*) train *m* etc accidenté; (*accident*) accident *m*. **2** *vt* détruire.

wrench (*tool*) clef *f* (à écrous), clef *f* à molette.

wres·tle *vi* lutter (**with sb** avec qn).

wres·tler lutteur, -euse *mf*; (*no holds barred*) catcheur, -euse *mf*.

wres·tling (*sport*) lutte *f*; (*no holds barred*) catch *m*.

wring* (out) *vt* (*clothes by hand*) tordre.

wrin·kle (*on skin*) ride *f*.

wrist poignet *m*.

wrist·watch montre *f*.

write* *vti* écrire.

▸ **write away for, write off for** *vt* (*details etc*) écrire pour.

▸ **write back** *vi* répondre.

▸ **write down** *vt* noter.

▸ **write off** *vt* (*debt*) annuler.

▸ **write out** *vt* écrire; (*copy*) recopier.

writ·er auteur *m* (**of** de); (*literary*) écrivain *m*.

writ·ing (*handwriting*) écriture *f*; **to put sth (down) in w.** mettre qch par écrit; **some w.** (*on page*) quelque chose d'écrit.

writ·ing desk secrétaire *m*.

writ·ing pad bloc *m* de papier à lettres; (*for notes*) bloc-notes *m*.

writ·ing pa·per papier *m* à lettres.

wrong 1 *adj* (*sum, idea etc*) faux (*f* fausse); (*direction, time etc*) mauvais; (*unfair*) injuste; **to be w.** (*of person*) avoir tort (**to do** de faire); (*mistaken*) se tromper; **it's w. to swear/etc** c'est mal de jurer/*etc*; **the clock's w.** la pendule n'est pas

à l'heure; **something's w.** quelque chose ne va pas; **something's w. with the phone** le téléphone ne marche pas bien; **something's w. with her arm** elle a quelque chose au bras; **what's w. with you?** qu'est-ce que tu as?; **the w. way around** or **up** à l'envers. **2** adv mal; **to go w.** (of plan) mal tourner. **3** n to be in the w. être dans son tort.
wrong·ly adv (incorrectly) mal.

X

X·mas Fam Noël m.
X-ray 1 n (photo) radio(graphie) f, (beam) rayon m X; **to have an X-ray** passer une radio. **2** vt radiographier.

Y

yacht yacht m.
yard (of farm, school etc) cour f, (for storage) dépôt m; (measure) yard m (= 91,44cm).
yarn (thread) fil m.
yawn 1 vt bâiller. **2** n bâillement m.
year an m, année f; **school/fiscal y.** année f scolaire/fiscale; **this y.** cette année; **in the y. 1992** en (l'an) 1992; **he's ten years old** il a dix ans; **New Y.** Nouvel An; **New Year's Day** le jour de l'An; **New Year's Eve** la Saint-Sylvestre.
year·ly adj annuel.
yeast levure f.
yell hurlement m.
yell (out) vti hurler.

▶ **yell at** vt (scold) crier après.
yel·low adj & n (color) jaune (m).
yes adv oui; (contradicting negative question) si.
yes·ter·day adv hier; **y. morning** hier matin; **the day before y.** avant-hier.
yet 1 adv encore; (already) déjà; **she hasn't come (as) y.** elle n'est pas encore venue; **has he come y.?** est-il déjà arrivé? **2** conj (nevertheless) pourtant.
yield vi **'y.'** (road sign) 'cédez la priorité'.
yo·gurt yaourt m.
yolk jaune m (d'œuf).
you pron (polite form singular) vous; (familiar form singular) tu; (polite and familiar form plural) vous; (object) vous; te, t'; pl vous; (after prep, 'than', 'it is') vous; toi; pl vous; **(to) y.** vous; te, t'; pl vous; **y. are** vous êtes; tu es; **I see y.** je vous vois; je te vois; **y. teachers** vous autres professeurs; **y. idiot!** espèce d'imbécile! ■ (indefinite) on; (object) vous; te, t'; pl vous; **y. never know** on ne sait jamais.
young 1 adj jeune; **my young(er) brother** mon (frère) cadet; **his** or **her youngest brother** le cadet de ses frères; **the youngest son** le cadet. **2** n (of animals) petits mpl; **the y.** (people) les jeunes mpl.
young·ster jeune mf.
your poss adj (polite form singular, polite and familiar form plural) votre, pl vos; (familiar form singular) ton, ta, pl tes; (one's) son, sa, pl ses.
yours poss pron le vôtre, la vôtre, pl les vôtres; (familiar form singular) le tien, la tienne, pl les tien(ne)s; **this book is y.** ce livre est à vous or est le vôtre; ce livre est à toi or est le tien.
your·self pron (polite form) vous-même; (familiar form) toi-même; (reflexive) vous; te, t'; (after prep) vous; toi.

your·selves *pron pl* vous-mêmes; *(reflexive, after prep)* vous.

youth jeunesse *f*, *(young man)* jeune *m*; **y. center** maison *f* des jeunes.

Z

ze·bra zèbre *m*.

ze·ro, *pl* -os zéro *m*.

zig·zag 1 *n* zigzag *m*. **2** *adj* en zigzag. **3** *vi* zigzaguer.

zip (up) *vt* fermer (avec une fermeture éclair®).

zip code code *m* postal; *(geographic area)* division *f* postale.

Zip® drive *Comput* lecteur *m* Zip®.

zip·per fermeture *f* éclair®.

zit *(pimple) Fam* bouton *m*.

zone zone *f*.

zoo, *pl* zoos zoo *m*.

zuc·chi·ni, *pl* -ni *or* -nis courgette *f*.

French verb conjugations

Regular verbs

	-ER Verbs	**-IR Verbs**	**-RE Verbs**
Infinitive	*donn / er*	*fin / ir*	*vend / re*
1 Present	je donne	je finis	je vends
	tu donnes	tu finis	tu vends
	il donne	il finit	il vend
	nous donnons	nous finissons	nous vendons
	vous donnez	vous finissez	vous vendez
	ils donnent	ils finissent	ils vendent
2 Imperfect	je donnais	je finissais	je vendais
	tu donnais	tu finissais	tu vendais
	il donnait	il finissait	il vendait
	nous donnions	nous finissions	nous vendions
	vous donniez	vous finissiez	vous vendiez
	ils donnaient	ils finissaient	ils vendaient
3 Past historic	je donnai	je finis	je vendis
	tu donnas	tu finis	tu vendis
	il donna	il finit	il vendit
	nous donnâmes	nous finîmes	nous vendîmes
	vous donnâtes	vous finîtes	vous vendîtes
	ils donnèrent	ils finirent	ils vendirent
4 Future	je donnerai	je finirai	je vendrai
	tu donneras	tu finiras	tu vendras
	il donnera	il finira	il vendra
	nous donnerons	nous finirons	nous vendrons
	vous donnerez	vous finirez	vous vendrez
	ils donneront	ils finiront	ils vendront
5 Subjunctive	je donne	je finisse	je vende
	tu donnes	tu finisses	tu vendes
	il donne	il finisse	il vende
	nous donnions	nous finissions	nous vendions
	vous donniez	vous finissiez	vous vendiez
	ils donnent	ils finissent	ils vendent
7 Present participle	donnant	finissant	vendant
8 Past participle	donné	fini	vendu

Note The conditional is formed by adding the following endings to the infinitive: -ais, -ais, -ait, -ions, -iez, -aient. Final 'e' is dropped in infinitives ending '-re'.

Spelling anomalies of -er verbs

Verbs in **-ger** (eg **manger**) take an extra **e** before endings beginning with **o** or **a**: *Present* je mange, nous mangeons; *Imperfect* je mangeais, nous mangions; *Past historic* je mangeai, nous mangeâmes; *Present participle* mangeant. Verbs in **-cer** (eg **commencer**) change **c** to **ç** before endings beginning with **o** or **a**: *Present* je commence, nous commençons; *Imperfect* je commençais, nous commencions; *Past historic* je commençai, nous commençâmes; *Present participle* commençant. Verbs containing mute **e** in their penultimate syllable fall into two groups. In the first (eg **mener, peser, lever**), **e** becomes **è** before an unpronounced syllable in the present and subjunctive, and in the future and conditional tenses (eg je mène, ils mèneront). The second group contains most verbs ending in **-eler** and **-eter** (eg **appeler, jeter**). These verbs change **l** to **ll** and **t** to **tt** before an unpronounced syllable (eg j'appelle, ils appelleront; je jette, ils jetteront). However, the following four verbs in **-eler** and **-eter** fall into the first group in which **e** changes to **è** before an unpronounced syllable (eg je pèle, ils pèleront; j'achète, ils achèteront): **geler, peler; acheter, haleter**. Derived verbs (eg **dégeler, racheter**) are conjugated in the same way. Verbs containing **é** in their penultimate syllable change **é** to **è** before the unpronounced endings of the present and subjunctive only (eg je cède but je céderai). Verbs in **-yer** (eg **essuyer**) change **y** to **i** before an unpronounced syllable in the present and subjunctive, and in the future and conditional tenses (eg j'essuie, ils essuieront). In verbs in **-ayer** (eg **balayer**), **y** may be retained before mute **e** (eg je balaie or balaye, ils balaieront or balayeront).

Irregular verbs

Listed below are those verbs considered to be the most useful. Forms and tenses not given are fully derivable, such as the third person singular of the present tense which is normally formed by substituting 't' for the final 's' of the first person singular, eg 'crois' becomes 'croit', 'dis' becomes 'dit'. Note that the endings of the past historic fall into three categories, the 'a' and 'i' categories shown at *donner*, and at *finir* and *vendre*, and the 'u' category which has the following endings: -us, -ut, -ûmes, -ûtes, -urent. Most of the verbs listed below form their past historic with 'u'. The imperfect may usually be formed by adding -ais, -ait, -ions, -iez, -aient to the stem of the first person plural of the present tense, eg 'je buvais' etc may be derived from 'nous buvons' (stem 'buv-' and ending '-ons'); similarly, the present participle may generally be formed by substituting -ant for -ons (eg buvant). The future may usually be formed by adding -ai, -as, -a, -ons, -ez, -ont to the infinitive or to an infinitive without final 'e' where the ending is -re (eg conduire). The imperative usually has the same forms as the second persons singular and plural and first person plural of the present tense.

1 = Present 2 = Imperfect 3 = Past historic 4 = Future
5 = Subjunctive 6 = Imperative 7 = Present participle
8 = Past participle n = nous v = vous † verbs conjugated with **être** only.

Irregular French verbs

abattre	*like* **battre**
† **s'abstenir**	like **tenir**
accourir	*like* **courir**
accueillir	*like* **cueillir**
acquérir	1 j'acquiers, n acquérons 2 j'acquérais 3 j'acquis 4 j'acquerrai 5 j'acquière 7 acquérant 8 acquis
admettre	*like* **mettre**
† **aller**	1 je vais, tu vas, il va, n allons, v allez, ils vont 4 j'irai 5 j'aille, nous allions, ils aillent 6 va, allons, allez (*but note* vas-y)
apercevoir	*like* **recevoir**
apparaître	*like* **connaître**
appartenir	*like* **tenir**
apprendre	*like* **prendre**
asseoir	1 j'assieds, il assied, n asseyons, ils asseyent 2 j'asseyais 3 j'assis 4 j'assiérai 5 j'asseye 7 asseyant 8 assis
atteindre	1 j'atteins, n atteignons, ils atteignent 2 j'atteignais 3 j'atteignis 4 j'atteindrai 5 j'atteigne 7 atteignant 8 atteint
avoir	1 j'ai, tu as, il a, n avons, v avez, ils ont 2 j'avais 3 j'eus 4 j'aurai 5 j'aie, il ait, n ayons, ils aient 6 aie, ayons, ayez 7 ayant 8 eu
battre	1 je bats, il bat, n battons 5 je batte
boire	1 je bois, n buvons, ils boivent 2 je buvais 3 je bus 5 je boive, n buvions 7 buvant 8 bu
bouillir	1 je bous, n bouillons, ils bouillent 2 je bouillais 3 *not used* 5 je bouille 7 bouillant
combattre	*like* **battre**
commettre	*like* **mettre**
comprendre	*like* **prendre**
conclure	1 je conclus, n concluons, ils concluent 5 je conclue
conduire	1 je conduis, n conduisons 3 je conduisis 5 je conduise 8 conduit
connaître	1 je connais, il connaît, n connaissons 3 je connus 5 je connaisse 7 connaissant 8 connu
conquérir	*like* **acquérir**
consentir	*like* **conduire**
contenir	*like* **tenir**
contraindre	*like* **atteindre**
contredire	*like* **dire** *except* 1 v contredisez
convaincre	*like* **vaincre**
convenir	*like* **tenir**
coudre	1 je couds, il coud, n cousons, ils cousent 3 je cousis 5 je couse 7 cousant 8 cousu

(3)

French verb conjugations

courir	1 je cours, n courons 3 je courus 4 je courrai 5 je coure 8 couru
couvrir	1 je couvre, n couvrons 2 je couvrais 5 je couvre 8 couvert
craindre	*like* **atteindre**
croire	1 je crois, n croyons, ils croient 2 je croyais 3 je crus 5 je croie, n croyions 7 croyant 8 cru
cueillir	1 je cueille, n cueillons 2 je cueillais 4 je cueillerai 5 je cueille 7 cueillant
cuire	1 je cuis, n cuisons 2 je cuisais 3 je cuisis 5 je cuise 7 cuisant 8 cuit
débattre	*like* **battre**
décevoir	*like* **recevoir**
découvrir	*like* **couvrir**
décrire	*like* **écrire**
déduire	*like* **conduire**
défaire	*like* **faire**
déplaire	*like* **plaire**
déteindre	*like* **atteindre**
détruire	*like* **conduire**
† **devenir**	*like* **tenir**
devoir	1 je dois, n devons, ils doivent 2 je devais 3 je dus 4 je devrai 5 je doive, n devions 6 *not used* 7 devant 8 dû, due, *pl* dus, dues
dire	1 je dis, n disons, v dites 2 je disais 3 je dis 5 je dise 7 disant 8 dit
disparaître	*like* **connaître**
dissoudre	1 je dissous, n dissolvons 2 je dissolvais 5 je dissolve 7 dissolvant 8 dissous, dissoute
distraire	1 je distrais, n distrayons 2 je distrayais 3 *none* 5 je distraie 7 distrayant 8 distrait
dormir	*like* **mentir**
éclore	1 il éclôt, ils éclosent 8 éclos
écrire	1 j'écris, n écrivons 2 j'écrivais 3 j'écrivis 5 j'écrive 7 écrivant 8 écrit
élire	*like* **lire**
émettre	*like* **mettre**
émouvoir	1 j'émeus, n émouvons, ils émeuvent 2 j'émouvais 3 j'émus (*rare*) 4 j'émouvrai 5 j'émeuve, n émouvions 8 ému
endormir	*like* **mentir**
enfreindre	*like* **atteindre**
† **s'enfuir**	*like* **fuir**
entretenir	*like* **tenir**
envoyer	4 j'enverrai
éteindre	*like* **atteindre**
être	1 je suis, tu es, il est, n sommes, v êtes, ils sont 2 j'étais 3 je fus 4 je serai 5 je sois, n soyons, ils soient 6 sois, soyons, soyez 7 étant 8 été

exclure	*like* **conclure**
extraire	*like* **distraire**
faillir	*(defective)* 3 je faillis 4 je faillirai 8 failli
faire	1 je fais, n faisons, v faites, ils font 2 je faisais 3 je fis 4 je ferai 5 je fasse 7 faisant 8 fait
falloir	*(impersonal)* 1 il faut 2 il fallait 3 il fallut 4 il faudra 5 il faille 6 *none* 7 *none* 8 fallu
frire	*(defective)* 1 je fris, tu fris, il frit 4 je frirai *(rare)* 6 fris *(rare)* 8 frit *(for other persons and tenses use* faire frire*)*
fuir	1 je fuis, n fuyons, ils fuient 2 je fuyais 3 je fuis 5 je fuie 7 fuyant 8 fui
haïr	1 je hais, il hait, n haïssons
inscrire	*like* **écrire**
instruire	*like* **conduire**
interdire	*like* **dire** *except* 1 v interdisez
interrompre	*like* **rompre**
intervenir	*like* **tenir**
introduire	*like* **conduire**
joindre	*like* **atteindre**
lire	1 je lis, n lisons 2 je lisais 3 je lus 5 je lise 7 lisant 8 lu
maintenir	*like* **tenir**
mentir	1 je mens, n mentons 2 je mentais 5 je mente 7 mentant
mettre	1 je mets, n mettons 2 je mettais 3 je mis 5 je mette 7 mettant 8 mis
moudre	je mouds, il moud, n moulons 2 je moulais 3 je moulus 5 je moule 7 moulant 8 moulu
† mourir	1 je meurs, n mourons, ils meurent 2 je mourais 3 je mourus 4 je mourrai 5 je meure, n mourions
† naître	1 je nais, il naît, n naissons 2 je naissais 3 je naquis 4 je naîtrai 5 je naisse 7 naissant 8 né
nuire	1 je nuis, n nuisons 2 je nuisais 3 je nuisis 5 je nuise 7 nuisant 8 nui
obtenir	*like* **tenir**
offrir	*like* **couvrir**
ouvrir	*like* **couvrir**
paître	*(defective)* 1 il paît 2 il paissait 3 *none* 4 il paîtra 5 il paisse 7 paissant 8 *none*
paraître	*like* **connaître**
parcourir	*like* **courir**
† partir	*like* **mentir**
† parvenir	*like* **tenir**
peindre	*like* **atteindre**
permettre	*like* **mettre**
plaindre	*like* **atteindre**
plaire	1 je plais, il plaît, n plaisons 2 je plaisais 3 je plus 5 je plaise 7 plaisant 8 plu
pleuvoir	*(impersonal)* 1 il pleut 2 il pleuvait 3 il plut 4 il pleuvra 5 il pleuve 6 *none* 7 pleuvant 8 plu
poursuivre	*like* **suivre**

French verb conjugations

pouvoir	1 je peux *or* je puis, tu peux, il peut, n pouvons, ils peuvent 2 je pouvais 3 je pus 4 je pourrai 5 je puisse 6 *not used* 7 pouvant 8 pu
prédire	*like* **dire** *except* 1 v prédisez
prendre	1 je prends, il prend, n prenons, ils prennent 2 je prenais 3 je pris 5 je prenne 7 prenant 8 pris
prescrire	*like* **écrire**
pressentir	*like* **mentir**
prévenir	*like* **tenir**
prévoir	*like* **voire** *except* 4 je prévoirai
produire	*like* **conduire**
promettre	*like* **mettre**
† **provenir**	*like* **tenir**
rabattre	*like* **battre**
recevoir	1 je reçois, n recevons, ils reçoivent 2 je recevais 3 je reçus 4 je recevrai 5 je reçoive, n recevions, ils reçoivent 7 recevant 8 reçu
reconduire	*like* **conduire**
reconnaître	*like* **connaître**
reconstruire	*like* **conduire**
recoudre	*like* **coudre**
recouvrir	*like* **couvrir**
recueillir	*like* **cueillir**
redire	*like* **dire**
réduire	*like* **conduire**
refaire	*like* **faire**
rejoindre	*like* **atteindre**
relire	*like* **lire**
reluire	*like* **nuire**
rendormir	*like* **mentir**
renvoyer	*like* **envoyer**
† **repartir**	*like* **mentir**
repentir	*like* **mentir**
reprendre	*like* **prendre**
reproduire	*like* **conduire**
résoudre	1 je résous, n résolvons 2 je résolvais 3 je résolus 5 je résolve 7 résolvant 8 résolu
ressentir	*like* **mentir**
resservir	*like* **mentir**
ressortir	*like* **mentir**
restreindre	*like* **atteindre**
retenir	*like* **tenir**
† **revenir**	*like* **tenir**
revivre	*like* **vivre**
revoir	*like* **voir**
rire	1 je ris, n rions 2 je riais 3 je ris 5 je rie, n riions 7 riant 8 ri
rompre	*regular except* 1 il rompt
satisfaire	*like* **faire**

French verb conjugations

savoir	1 je sais, n savons, il savent 2 je savais 3 je sus 4 je saurai 5 je sache 6 sache, sachons, sachez 7 sachant 8 su
sentir	*like* **mentir**
servir	*like* **mentir**
sortir	*like* **mentir**
souffrir	*like* **couvrir**
sourire	*like* **rire**
soustraire	*like* **distraire**
soutenir	*like* **tenir**
† **se souvenir**	*like* **tenir**
suffire	1 je suffis, n suffisons 2 je suffisais 3 je suffis 5 je suffise 7 suffisant 8 suffi
suivre	1 je suis, n suivons 2 je suivais 3 je suivis 5 je suive 7 suivant 8 suivi
surprendre	*like* **prendre**
survivre	*like* **vivre**
taire	1 je tais, n taisons 2 je taisais 3 je tus 5 je taise 7 taisant 8 tu
teindre	*like* **atteindre**
tenir	1 je tiens, n tenons, ils tiennent 2 je tenais 3 je tins, tu tins, il tint, n tînmes, v tîntes, ils tinrent 4 je tiendrai 5 je tienne 7 tenant 8 tenu
traduire	*like* **conduire**
traire	*like* **distraire**
transmettre	*like* **mettre**
vaincre	1 je vaincs, il vainc, n vainquons 2 je vainquais 3 je vainquis 5 je vainque 7 vainquant 8 vaincu
valoir	1 je vaux, il vaut, n valons 2 je valais 3 je valus 4 je vaudrai 5 je vaille 6 *not* used 7 valant 8 valu
† **venir**	*like* **tenir**
vivre	1 je vis, n vivons 2 je vivais 3 je vécus 5 je vive 7 vivant 8 vécu
voir	1 je vois, n voyons 2 je voyais 3 je vis 4 je verrai 5 je voie, n voyions 7 voyant 8 vu
vouloir	1 je veux, il veut, n voulons, ils veulent 2 je voulais 3 je voulus 4 je voudrai 5 je veuille 6 veuille, veuillons, veuillez 7 voulant 8 voulu

Countries and regions

Africa *(African)*	Afrique f *(africain)*
South/North Africa *(South/North African)*	Afrique du Sud/Nord *(sud-/nord-africain)*
Algeria *(Algerian)*	Algérie f *(algérien)*
America *(American)*	Amérique f *(américain)*
South/North America *(South/North American)*	Amérique du Sud/Nord *(sud-/nord-américain)*
Argentina *(Argentinian)*	Argentine f *(argentin)*
Asia *(Asian)*	Asie f *(asiatique)*
Australia *(Australian)*	Australie f *(australien)*
Austria *(Austrian)*	Autriche f *(autrichien)*
Belgium *(Belgian)*	Belgique f *(belge)*
Brazil *(Brazilian)*	Brésil m *(brésilien)*
Canada *(Canadian)*	Canada m *(canadien)*
Caribbean (the) *(Caribbean)*	Antilles fpl (les) *(antillais)*
China *(Chinese)*	Chine f *(chinois)*
CIS *(abbr* Commonwealth of Independent States)	CEI f *(abrév* Communauté des États Indépendants)
Cuba *(Cuban)*	Cuba m *(cubain)*
Cyprus *(Cypriot)*	Chypre f *(c(h)ypriote)*
Czech Republic *(Czech)*	République f tchèque *(tchèque)*
Denmark *(Danish)*	Danemark m *(danois)*
Egypt *(Egyptian)*	Égypte f *(égyptien)*
England *(English)*	Angleterre f *(anglais)*
Europe *(European)*	Europe f *(européen)*
Finland *(Finnish)*	Finlande f *(finlandais)*
France *(French)*	France f *(français)*
Germany *(German)*	Allemagne f *(allemand)*
Great Britain *(British)*	Grande-Bretagne f *(britannique)*
Greece *(Greek)*	Grèce f *(grec)*
Holland *(Dutch)*	Pays-Bas mpl *(néerlandais)*
Hungary *(Hungarian)*	Hongrie f *(hongrois)*
India *(Indian)*	Inde f *(indien)*
Indonesia *(Indonesian)*	Indonésie f *(indonésien)*
Iran *(Iranian)*	Iran m *(iranien)*
Iraq *(Iraqi)*	Irak m *(irakien)*
Ireland *(Irish)*	Irlande f *(irlandais)*
Israel *(Israeli)*	Israël m *(israélien)*

Countries and regions

Italy *(Italian)*	Italie *f (italien)*
Jamaica *(Jamaican)*	Jamaïque *f (jamaïcain)*
Japan *(Japanese)*	Japon *m (japonais)*
Kenya *(Kenyan)*	Kenya *m (kényan)*
Korea *(Korean)*	Corée *f (coréen)*
South/North Korea	Corée du Sud/Nord
(South/North Korean)	*(sud-nord-coréen)*
Lebanon *(Lebanese)*	Liban *m (libanais)*
Libya *(Libyan)*	Libye *f (libyen)*
Luxembourg *(Luxembourgish)*	Luxembourg *m (luxembourgeois)*
Malaysia *(Malaysian)*	Malaisie *(malais)*
Mexico *(Mexican)*	Mexique *m (mexicain)*
Morocco *(Moroccan)*	Maroc *m (marocain)*
New Zealand	Nouvelle-Zélande *f (néo-zélandais)*
Nigeria *(Nigerian)*	Nigéria *m (nigérian)*
Norway *(Norwegian)*	Norvège *f (norvégien)*
Pakistan *(Pakistani)*	Pakistan *m (pakistanais)*
Philippines *(Filipino)*	Philippines *fpl (philippin)*
Poland *(Polish)*	Pologne *f (polonais)*
Portugal *(Portuguese)*	Portugal *m (portugais)*
Romania *(Romanian)*	Roumanie *f (roumain)*
Russia *(Russian)*	Russie *f (russe)*
Saudi Arabia *(Saudi)*	Arabie *f Saoudite (saoudien)*
Scotland *(Scottish)*	Écosse *f (écossais)*
Slovakia *(Slovak)*	Slovaquie *(slovaque)*
Spain *(Spanish)*	Espagne *f (espagnol)*
Sweden *(Swedish)*	Suède *f (suédois)*
Switzerland *(Swiss)*	Suisse *f (suisse)*
Syria *(Syrian)*	Syrie *f (syrien)*
Thailand *(Thai)*	Thaïlande *f (thaïlandais)*
Tunisia *(Tunisian)*	Tunisie *f (tunisien)*
Turkey *(Turkish)*	Turquie *f (turc)*
United Kingdom *(British)*	Royaume-Uni *m (britannique)*
United States *(American)*	États-Unis *mpl (américain)*
Vietnam *(Vietnamese)*	Viêt-nam *m (vietnamien)*
Wales *(Welsh)*	Pays *m* de Galles *(gallois)*
West Indies *(West Indian)*	Antilles *fpl (antillais)*

Français – Anglais

French – English

A

a *voir* **avoir**.

à *prép* (à + le = **au** [o], à + les = **aux** [o]) *(direction: lieu)* to; *(temps)* till, to; **aller à Paris** to go to Paris; **de 3 à 4 h** from 3 till *ou* to 4 (o'clock). ▪ *(position: lieu)* at, in; *(surface)* on; *(temps)* at; **être au bureau/à la ferme/au jardin/à Paris** to be at *ou* in the office/on *ou* at the farm/in the garden/in Paris; **à 8 h** at 8 (o'clock); **à mon arrivée** on (my) arrival; **à lundi!** see you (on) Monday! ▪ *(description)* **l'homme à la barbe** the man with the beard; **verre à liqueur** liqueur glass. ▪ *(attribution)* **donner qch à qn** to give sth to sb, to give sb sth. ▪ *(devant infinitif)* **apprendre à lire** to learn to read; **travail à faire** work to do; **maison à vendre** house for sale. ▪ *(appartenance)* **c'est (son livre) à lui** it's his (book); **c'est à vous de** *(décider, protester etc)* it's up to you to; *(lire, jouer etc)* it's your turn to. ▪ *(prix)* for; **pain à un euro** loaf for one euro. ▪ *(poids)* by; **vendre au poids** to sell by weight. ▪ *(moyen, manière)* **à bicyclette** by bicycle; **à la main** by hand; **à pied** on foot; **au crayon** in pencil; **au galop** at a gallop; **deux à deux** two by two. ▪ *(appel)* **au voleur!** (stop) thief!

abaisser *vt* to lower.

abaisser (s') *vpr (barrière)* to lower; *(température)* to drop.

abandon *m (de sportif)* withdrawal; **à l'a.** in a neglected state.

abandonner 1 *vt (travail)* to give up; *(endroit)* to desert. **2** *vi (sportif)* to withdraw.

abasourdi, -ie *adj* stunned.

abat-jour *m inv* lampshade.

abattoir *m* slaughterhouse.

abattre* *vt (mur)* to knock down; *(arbre)* to cut down; *(animal)* to slaughter; *(avion)* to shoot down; *(personne)* to shoot.

abattre (s') *vpr* **s'a. sur** *(pluie)* to come down on; *(tempête)* to hit.

abattu, -ue *adj (mentalement)* dejected; *(physiquement)* exhausted.

abbaye *f* abbey.

abbé *m (prêtre)* priest.

abcès *m* abscess.

abdomen *m* stomach, abdomen.

abeille *f* bee.

aberrant, -ante *adj* absurd.

abîmer *vt* to ruin.

abîmer (s') *vpr* to get ruined.

aboiement *m* bark; **aboiements** barking.

abolir *vt* to abolish.

abominable *adj* terrible.

abondance *f* **une a. de** plenty of.

abondant, -ante *adj* plentiful.

abonné, -ée *mf (à un journal, au téléphone)* subscriber.

abonnement *m* subscription; *(carte d')a.* (de train) season pass.

abonner (s') *vpr* to subscribe, to take out a subscription (à to).

abord (d') *adv* first.

abordable *adj (prix, marchandises)* affordable.

abordage *m (assaut)* boarding.

aborder 1 *vi* to land. **2** *vt (personne)* to approach; *(problème)* to tackle; *(navire)* to board.

aboutir *vi* to succeed; **a. à** to lead to; **n'a. à rien** to come to nothing.

aboyer *vi* to bark.

abréger *vt (récit)* to shorten.

abreuvoir *m (récipient)* drinking trough.

abréviation *f* abbreviation.

abri *m* shelter; **a. (de jardin)** (garden) shed; **à l'a. de** *(vent)* sheltered from; *(besoin)* safe from; **sans a.** homeless.

abricot *m* apricot.

abricotier *m* apricot tree.

abriter *vt* to shelter.

abriter (s') *vpr* to (take) shelter.

abrupt, -e *adj (pente etc)* steep.

abrutir *vt (télévision)* to stupefy, to numb; *(travail)* to exhaust.

absence *f* absence.

absent, -ente 1 *adj* absent, away. **2** *mf* absentee.

absenter (s') *vpr* to go away (**de** from).

absolu, -ue *adj* absolute.

absolument *adv* absolutely.

absorbant, -ante *adj (papier)* absorbent; *(travail, lecture)* absorbing.

absorber *vt* to absorb.

abstenir* (s') *vpr* to refrain (**de faire** from doing).

absurde *adj* absurd.

absurdité *f* absurdity; **dire des absurdités** to talk nonsense.

abus *m* abuse; *(de nourriture)* over-indulgence (**de** in).

abuser *vi* to go too far; **a. de** *(situation, personne)* to take unfair advantage of; *(friandises)* to over-indulge in.

acajou *m* mahogany.

accabler *vt* to overwhelm (**de** with).

accalmie *f* lull.

accéder *vi* **a. à** *(lieu)* to reach.

accélérateur *m* accelerator.

accélérer *vi* to accelerate.

accélérer (s') *vpr* to speed up.

accent *m* accent; *(sur une syllabe)* stress.

accepter *vt* to accept; **a. de faire** to agree to do.

accès *m* access (**à** to); *(de folie, colère, toux)* fit; *(de fièvre)* bout; **'a. interdit'** 'no entry'.

accessoires *mpl (de voiture etc)* accessories; *(de théâtre)* props.

accident *m* accident; **a. d'avion/ de train** plane/train crash.

accidentel, -elle *adj* accidental.

acclamations *fpl* cheers.

acclamer *vt* to cheer.

accolade *f (embrassade)* embrace; *(signe)* curly bracket.

accommoder *vt (assaisonner)* to prepare.

accompagnateur, -trice *mf (musical)* accompanist; *(d'un groupe)* guide.

accompagnement *m (musical)* accompaniment.

accompagner *vt (personne)* to go *ou* come with; *(chose, musique)* to accompany.

accomplir *vt* to carry out.

accord *m* agreement; *(musical)* chord; **tomber d'a.** to reach an agreement; **être d'a.** to agree (**avec** with); **d'a.!** all right!

accordéon *m* accordion.

accorder *vt (donner)* to grant; *(instrument)* to tune; *(verbe)* to make agree.

accorder (s') *vpr (s'entendre)* to get along.

accotement *m (of road)* shoulder.

accouchement *m* delivery.

accoucher *vi* to give birth (**de** to).

accouder (s') *vpr* **s'a. à** *ou* **sur** to lean on *(with one's elbows).*

accoudoir *m* armrest.

accourir* *vi* to come running.

accoutumer (s') *vpr* to get accustomed (**à** to).

accroc *m* tear (**à** in).

accrochage *m (de voitures)* minor collision.

accrocher *vt (déchirer)* to catch; *(fixer)* to hook; *(suspendre)* to hang up *(on a hook)*; *(heurter)* to hit.

accrocher (s') *vpr (se cramponner)* to cling (**à** to); *(ne pas céder)* to persevere.

accroissement *m* increase (**de** in).

accroître *vt,* **s'accroître** *vpr* to increase.

accroupi, -ie *adj* squatting.

accroupir (s') *vpr* to squat (down).

accueil *m* welcome.

accueillant, -ante *adj* welcoming.

accueillir* *vt* to welcome.

accumuler *vt*, **s'accumuler** *vpr* to pile up.

accusation *f* accusation; *(au tribunal)* charge.

accusé, -ée *mf* accused; *(à la cour d'assises)* defendant.

accuser *vt* to accuse *(de* of*)*; *(rendre responsable)* to blame *(de* for*)*.

acharnement *m* (stubborn) determination.

acharner (s') *vpr* **s'a. sur** *(attaquer)* to lay into; **s'a. à faire** to struggle to do.

achat *m* purchase; **faire des achats** to go shopping.

acheter *vti* to buy; **a. à qn** to buy from sb; *(pour qn)* to buy for sb.

acheteur, -euse *mf* buyer; *(dans un magasin)* shopper.

achever *vt* to finish (off); **a. de faire qch** *(personne)* to finish doing sth; **a. qn** *(tuer)* to finish sb off.

acide 1 *adj* sour. **2** *m* acid.

acier *m* steel.

acné *f* acne.

acompte *m* deposit.

acquéreur *m* purchaser.

acquérir* *vt (acheter)* to purchase; *(obtenir)* to acquire.

acquisition *f (achat)* purchase.

acquittement *m (d'un accusé)* acquittal.

acquitter *vt (dette)* to pay; *(accusé)* to acquit.

acquitter (s') *vpr* **s'a. envers qn** to repay sb.

acrobate *mf* acrobat.

acrobatie(s) *f(pl)* acrobatics.

acrobatique *adj* acrobatic.

acte *m (action, de pièce de théâtre)* act.

acteur, -trice *mf* actor, actress.

actif, -ive 1 *adj* active. **2** *m Grammaire* active.

action *f* action; *(en Bourse)* share, stock.

actionnaire *mf* shareholder.

activer *vt (feu)* to boost.

activer (s') *vpr (se dépêcher) Fam* to get a move on.

activité *f* activity.

actualité *f (événements)* current affairs; **actualités** *(à la télévision etc)* news.

actuel, -elle *adj (présent)* present; *(contemporain)* topical.

actuellement *adv* at the present time.

adaptateur *m* adapter.

adaptation *f* adjustment; *(de roman)* adaptation.

adapter *vt* to adapt; *(ajuster)* to fit *(à* to*)*.

adapter (s') *vpr* **s'a. à** *(s'habituer)* to adapt to, to adjust to; *(tuyau etc)* to fit.

additif *m* additive.

addition *f* addition; *(au restaurant)* check.

additionner *vt* to add *(à* to*)*; *(nombres)* to add up.

adepte *mf* follower.

adéquat, -ate *adj* appropriate; *(quantité)* adequate.

adhérent, -ente *mf* member.

adhérer *vi* **a. à** *(coller)* to stick to; *(s'inscrire)* to join.

adhésif, -ive *adj & m* adhesive.

adieu, -x *int & m* farewell.

adjectif *m* adjective.

adjoint, -ointe *mf* assistant; **a. au maire** deputy mayor.

adjuger *vt* **a. qch à qn** *(prix, contrat)* to award sth to sb; *(aux enchères)* to knock sth down to sb.

admettre* *vt (laisser entrer, accueillir, reconnaître)* to admit; *(autoriser, tolérer)* to allow; *(candidat)* to pass; **être admis à** *(examen)* to have passed.

administratif, -ive *adj* administrative.

administration *f* administration; **l'A.** *(service public)* the Civil Service.

administrer *vt (gérer, donner)* to administer.

admirable *adj* admirable.
admirateur, -trice *mf* admirer.
admiratif, -ive *adj* admiring.
admiration *f* admiration.
admirer *vt* to admire.
admissible *adj (tolérable)* acceptable, admissible; **candidat a.** =
candidate who has qualified for the
oral examination.
admission *f* admission (**à, dans**
to).
adolescent, -ente *mf* adolescent, teenager.
adopter *vt* to adopt.
adoptif, -ive *adj (fils, patrie)*
adopted.
adoption *f* adoption.
adorable *adj* adorable.
adoration *f* worship.
adorer *vt* to love, to adore (**faire**
doing); *(dieu)* to worship.
adosser (s') *vpr* to lean back (**à**
against).
adoucir *vt (voix, traits)* to tone
down.
adoucir (s') *vpr (temps)* to turn
milder.
adresse *f (domicile)* address; *(habileté)* skill.
adresser *vt (lettre)* to send; *(compliment, remarque)* to address; **a. la**
parole à to speak to.
adresser (s') *vpr* **s'a. à** to speak
to; *(aller trouver)* to go and see;
(bureau) to (go and) ask at; *(être*
destiné à) to be aimed at.
adroit, -oite *adj* skillful.
ADSL *m abrév (asymmetric digital*
subscriber line) broadband.
adulte *mf* adult, grown-up.
adverbe *m* adverb.
adversaire *mf* opponent.
aération *f* ventilation.
aérer *vt* to air (out).
aérien, -ienne *adj (photo)* aerial;
attaque/transport aérien(ne) air
attack/transport.
aérobic *m* aerobics.
aérogare *f* air terminal.

aéroglisseur *m* hovercraft.
aéroport *m* airport.
aérosol *m* aerosol.
affaiblir *vt,* **s'affaiblir** *vpr* to weaken.
affaire *f (question)* matter; **affaires**
business; *(effets)* things; **avoir a. à**
to have to deal with; **c'est mon a.**
that's my business; **faire une bonne**
a. to get a bargain.
affamé, -ée *adj* starving.
affection *f (attachement)* affection.
affectueux, -euse *adj* affectionate, loving.
affichage *m* **panneau d'a.** billboard.
affiche *f* poster.
afficher *vt (affiche)* to stick up.
affirmatif, -ive *adj (ton, réponse)*
positive, affirmative.
affirmation *f* assertion.
affirmer *vt* to assert.
affliger *vt* to distress.
affluence *f* crowd; **heure(s) d'a.**
rush hour(s).
affluent *m* tributary.
affolant, -ante *adj* terrifying.
affolement *m* panic.
affoler *vt* to drive crazy.
affoler (s') *vpr* to panic.
affranchir *vt (lettre)* to stamp.
affranchissement *m (tarif)*
postage.
affreux, -euse *adj* horrible.
affront *m* insult; **faire un a. à** to
insult.
affrontement *m* confrontation.
affronter *vt* to confront; *(mauvais*
temps, difficultés etc) to brave.
affûter *vt* to sharpen.
afin 1 *prép* **a. de** (+ *infinitif)* in order to. **2** *conj* **a. que** (+ *subjonctif)*
so that.
africain, -aine 1 *adj* African. **2** *mf*
A. African.
agaçant, -ante *adj* irritating.
agacer *vt* to irritate.
âge *m* age; **quel â. as-tu?** how old

are you?; **d'un certain â.** middle-aged; **le moyen â.** the Middle Ages.

âgé, -ée *adj* elderly; **â. de six ans** six years old; **enfant â. de six ans** six-year-old child.

agence *f* agency; *(succursale)* branch office; **a. immobilière** real estate office.

agenda *m* appointment book.

agenouiller (s') *vpr* to kneel (down); **être agenouillé** to be kneeling (down).

agent *m* agent; **a. (de police)** police officer; **a. immobilier** real estate agent.

agglomération *f* built-up area; *(ville)* town.

aggloméré *n* fiberboard.

aggravation *f (de maladie)* aggravation; *(de situation)* worsening.

aggraver *vt,* **s'aggraver** *vpr (situation, maladie)* to get worse; *(état de santé)* to deteriorate; *(difficultés)* to increase.

agile *adj* agile.

agilité *f* agility.

agir *vpr* to act.

agir (s') *vpr* **il s'agit d'argent/***etc* it's a question *ou* matter of money/ *etc;* **de quoi s'agit-il?** what is it?, what's it about?

agitation *f (de la mer)* roughness; *(d'une personne)* restlessness.

agité, -ée *adj (mer)* rough; *(personne)* restless.

agiter *vt (remuer)* to stir; *(secouer)* to shake; *(brandir)* to wave.

agiter (s') *vpr (enfant)* to fidget.

agneau, -x *m* lamb.

agrafe *f* hook; *(pour papiers)* staple.

agrafer *vt (robe)* to do up; *(papiers)* to staple.

agrafeuse *f* stapler.

agrandir *vt* to enlarge.

agrandir (s') *vpr* to expand.

agrandissement *m (de ville)* expansion; *(de maison)* extension; *(de photo)* enlargement.

agréable *adj* pleasant.

agréer *vt* **veuillez a. (l'expression de) mes salutations distinguées** *(dans une lettre)* sincerely yours.

agresser *vt* to attack.

agresseur *m* attacker; *(dans la rue)* mugger.

agressif, -ive *adj* aggressive.

agression *f (dans la rue)* mugging.

agressivité *f* aggressiveness.

agricole *adj* **ouvrier/machine a.** farm worker/machine; **travaux agricoles** farm work.

agriculteur *m* farmer.

agriculture *f* farming.

aguets (aux) *adv* on the look-out.

ah! *int* ah!, oh!

ai *voir* **avoir**.

aide 1 *f* help; **à l'a. de** with the aid of. **2** *mf (personne)* assistant.

aider *vt* to help (**à faire** to do).

aider (s') *vpr* **s'a. de** to make use of.

aïe! *int* ouch!

aie(s), aient *voir* **avoir**.

aigle *m* eagle.

aigre *adj* sour.

aigu, -uë *adj (douleur)* acute; *(dents)* sharp; *(voix)* shrill.

aiguillage *m (pour train)* switches.

aiguille *f (à coudre, de pin)* needle; *(de montre)* hand.

aiguiller *vt (train)* to switch.

aiguilleur *m* signalman; **a. du ciel** air-traffic controller.

aiguiser *vt* to sharpen.

ail *m* garlic.

aile *f* wing; *(de moulin à vent)* sail; *(d'automobile)* fender.

ailier *m Sport* wing.

aille(s), aillent *voir* **aller**[1].

ailleurs *adv* somewhere else; **d'a.** *(du reste)* anyway.

aimable *adj (gentil)* kind; *(sympathique)* likeable.

aimant *m* magnet.

aimanter *vt* to magnetize.

aimer *vt* to love; **a. (bien)** *(apprécier)* to like, to be fond of; **a. faire**

to like doing *ou* to do; **a. mieux** to prefer.

aimer (s') *vpr* ils s'aiment they're in love.

aîné, -ée 1 *adj (de deux frères etc)* elder, older; *(de plus de deux)* eldest, oldest. **2** *mf (de deux)* elder *ou* older (child); *(de plus de deux)* eldest *ou* oldest (child).

ainsi *adv (comme ça)* (in) this *ou* that way; **a. que** as well as; **et a. de suite** and so on.

air¹ *m* air; *(mélodie)* tune; **en plein a.** in the open (air), outdoors; **ficher en l'a.** *Fam (jeter)* to chuck, to pitch; *(gâcher)* to mess up; **en l'a.** *(jeter)* (up) in the air; *(paroles)* empty.

air² *m (expression)* look; **avoir l'a.** to look, to seem; **avoir l'a. de** to look like.

aire *f* area; **a. de stationnement** parking area.

aisance *f (facilité)* ease; *(prospérité)* affluence.

aise *f* à l'a. *(dans un vêtement etc)* comfortable; *(dans une situation)* at ease; **mal à l'a.** uncomfortable.

aisé, -ée *adj (facile)* easy; *(riche)* comfortably off.

aisselle *f* armpit.

ait *voir* **avoir**.

ajourner *vt* to postpone; *(après le début de la séance)* to adjourn.

ajout *m* addition (à to).

ajouter *vti* to add (à to).

ajuster *vt (pièce, salaires)* to adjust; **a. à** *(adapter)* to fit to.

alaise *f* (waterproof) undersheet.

alarme *f (signal)* alarm; **a. antivol/ d'incendie** burglar/fire alarm.

alarmer *vt* to alarm.

album *m (de timbres etc)* album.

alcool *m* alcohol; *(spiritueux)* spirits; **a. à 90°** rubbing alcohol.

alcoolique *adj & mf* alcoholic.

alcoolisé, -ée *adj* alcoholic.

alcootest® *m* breath test; *(appareil)* Breathalyzer®.

alentours *mpl* surroundings.

alerte *f* alarm; **en état d'a.** on the alert.

alerter *vt* to warn.

algèbre *f* algebra.

algérien, -ienne 1 *adj* Algerian. **2** *mf* A. Algerian.

algue(s) *f(pl)* seaweed.

alibi *m* alibi.

aliéné, -ée *mf* insane person.

alignement *m* alignment.

aligner *vt*, **s'aligner** *vpr* to line up.

aliment *m* food.

alimentaire *adj* **ration/etc a.** food rations/etc; **produits alimentaires** foods.

alimentation *f (action)* feeding; *(régime)* diet; *(nourriture)* food; **magasin d'a.** grocery store.

alimenter *vt (nourrir)* to feed.

allaiter *vti* to breastfeed.

allécher *vt* to tempt.

allée *f (de parc etc)* path; *(de cinéma, supermarché etc)* aisle.

allégé, -ée *adj (fromage etc)* low-fat.

alléger *vt* to make lighter.

allemand, -ande 1 *adj* German. **2** *mf* A. German. **3** *m (langue)* German.

aller¹* *vi (aux être)* to go; **a. à** *(convenir à)* to suit; **a. avec** *(vêtement)* to go with; **a. bien/mieux** *(personne)* to be well/better; **il va savoir/etc** he'll know/etc, he's going to know/etc; **il va partir** he's about to leave, he's going to leave; **va voir!** go and see!; **comment vas-tu?, (comment) ça va?** how are you?; **ça va!** all right!, fine!; **allez-y!** go on!, go ahead!; **allez! au lit!** come on *ou* go on to bed!

aller² *m* outward journey; **a. (simple)** one-way (ticket); **a. (et) retour** round-trip (ticket).

aller (s'en) *vpr* to go away; *(tache)* to come out.

allergie *f* allergy.

allergique *adj* allergic (à to).

alliance *f (anneau)* wedding ring; *(de pays)* alliance.

allié, -ée *mf* ally.

allier *vt* to combine (**à** with); *(pays)* to ally (**à** with).

allier (s') *vpr (pays)* to become allied (**à** with, to).

allô! *int* hello!

allocation *f* allowance, benefit; **a. (de) chômage** unemployment benefit; **allocations familiales** child benefit.

allongé, -ée *adj (étiré)* elongated.

allonger 1 *vt (bras)* to stretch out; *(jupe)* to lengthen. **2** *vi (jours)* to get longer.

allonger (s') *vpr* to stretch out.

allouer *vt* **a. qch à qn** *(ration)* to allocate sb sth; *(indemnité)* to grant sb sth.

allumage *m (de voiture)* ignition.

allumer *vt (feu, cigarette, gaz)* to light; *(électricité)* to turn *ou* switch on.

allumer (s') *vpr (lumière)* to come on.

allumette *f* match.

allure *f (vitesse)* pace; *(de véhicule)* speed; *(air)* look.

allusion *f* allusion; **faire a. à** to refer to.

alors *adv (en ce cas-là)* so; **a. que** *(tandis que)* whereas.

alouette *f* (sky)lark.

alourdir *vt* to weigh down.

alourdir (s') *vpr* to become heavy *ou* heavier.

Alpes (les) *fpl* the Alps.

alphabet *m* alphabet.

alphabétique *adj* alphabetical.

alpinisme *m* mountain climbing.

alpiniste *mf* mountain climber.

alterner *vti* to alternate.

altitude *f* height.

alu *m* **papier (d')a.** tinfoil.

aluminium *m* aluminum; **papier a.** tinfoil.

amabilité *f* kindness.

amaigri, -ie *adj* thin(ner).

amaigrissant *adj* **régime a.** (weight-loss) diet.

amande *f* almond.

amant *m* lover.

amarrer *vt* to moor.

amarres *fpl* moorings.

amas *m* heap, pile.

amasser *vt,* **s'amasser** *vpr* to pile up.

amateur *m (d'art etc)* lover; *(sportif)* amateur; **une équipe a.** an amateur team.

ambassade *f* embassy.

ambassadeur, -drice *mf* ambassador.

ambiance *f* atmosphere.

ambigu, -uë *adj* ambiguous.

ambitieux, -euse *adj* ambitious.

ambition *f* ambition.

ambulance *f* ambulance.

ambulant, -ante *adj* traveling.

âme *f* soul.

amélioration *f* improvement.

améliorer *vt,* **s'améliorer** *vpr* to improve.

aménagement *m (disposition)* fitting out; *(transformation)* conversion.

aménager *vt (arranger)* to fit out (**en** as); *(transformer)* to convert (**en** into).

amende *f* fine.

amener *vt* to bring.

amer, -ère *adj* bitter.

américain, -aine 1 *adj* American. **2** *mf* **A.** American.

amertume *f* bitterness.

ameublement *m* furniture.

ami, -ie *mf* friend; *(de la nature etc)* lover (**de** of); **petit a.** boyfriend; **petite amie** girlfriend.

amical, -e, -aux *adj* friendly.

amincir *vt* to make thin *or* thinner; **cette robe t'amincit** that dress makes you look thinner.

amiral, -aux *m* admiral.

amitié *f* friendship.

amonceler (s') *vpr* to pile up.

amont (en) *adv* upstream.

amorce *f (de pêcheur)* bait; *(de pistolet d'enfant)* cap.

amortir *vt (coup)* to cushion; *(bruit)* to deaden.

amortisseur m shock absorber.

amour m love; **pour l'a. de** for the sake of.

amoureux, -euse 1 mf lover. **2** adj **a. de qn** in love with sb.

amour-propre m self-respect.

amovible adj removable.

amphithéâtre m (romain) amphitheater; (à l'université) lecture hall.

ample adj (vêtement) full, ample.

amplement adv fully, amply; **c'est a. suffisant** it's more than enough.

ampleur f (de robe) fullness.

amplificateur m amplifier.

amplifier vt (son, courant) to amplify.

ampoule f (électrique) (light) bulb; (aux pieds etc) blister; (de médicament) phial.

amputer vt to amputate.

amusant, -ante adj amusing.

amusement m amusement.

amuser vt to entertain.

amuser (s') vpr to enjoy oneself, to have fun; **s'a. avec** to play with; **s'a. à faire** to amuse oneself doing.

amygdales fpl tonsils.

an m year; **il a dix ans** he's ten (years old); **Nouvel A.** New Year.

analogue adj similar.

analphabète adj & m illiterate.

analyse f analysis.

analyser vt to analyze.

ananas m pineapple.

anarchie f anarchy.

anatomie f anatomy.

ancêtre m ancestor.

anchois m anchovy.

ancien, -ienne adj old; (meuble) antique; (qui n'est plus) former; (antique) ancient; (dans une fonction) senior.

anciennement adv formerly.

ancienneté f (âge) age; (expérience) seniority.

ancre f anchor.

ancrer vt to anchor.

andouille f Fam fool; **espèce d'a.!** (you) fool!

âne m (animal) donkey; (personne) ass.

anéantir vt to wipe out.

anecdote f anecdote.

ânesse f female donkey.

anesthésie f anesthesia; **a. générale** general anesthetic.

anesthésier vt to anesthetize.

ange m angel.

angine f throat infection.

anglais, -aise 1 adj English. **2** mf **A.** Englishman, Englishwoman; **les A.** the English. **3** m (langue) English.

angle m angle; (de rue) corner.

anglophone 1 adj English-speaking. **2** mf English speaker.

angoissant, -ante adj distressing.

angoisse f (great) anxiety, anguish.

angoisser (s') vpr to get anxious.

anguille f eel.

animal, -e, -aux m & adj animal.

animateur, -trice mf (de télévision) emcee; (de club) leader, organizer.

animation f (des rues) activity; (de réunion) liveliness.

animé, -ée adj lively.

animer vt (débat) to lead; (soirée) to liven up; (mécanisme) to drive.

animer (s') vpr (rue etc) to come to life.

anis m aniseed.

ankylosé, -ée adj stiff.

anneau, -x m ring.

année f year; **bonne a.!** Happy New Year!

annexe f (bâtiment) annex(e).

anniversaire m (d'événement) anniversary; (de naissance) birthday.

annonce f (publicitaire) advertisement; **petites annonces** classified advertisements.

annoncer vt to announce; (vente) to advertise.

annoncer (s') vpr **s'a. pluvieux/difficile/etc** to look rainy/difficult/etc.

annuaire *m (téléphonique)* directory, phone book.

annuel, -elle *adj* yearly.

annulaire *m* ring finger.

annulation *f* cancelation.

annuler *vt* to cancel.

ânonner *vt* to stumble through.

anonymat *m* anonymity; **garder l'a.** to remain anonymous.

anonyme 1 *adj* anonymous. **2** *mf* anonymous person.

anorak *m* parka.

anorexie *f* anorexia.

anormal, -e, -aux *adj* abnormal.

anse *f (de tasse etc)* handle.

Antarctique (l') *m* the Antarctic.

antécédent *m Grammaire* antecedent; **antécédents** *(de personne)* past record; **antécédents médicaux** medical history.

antenne *f (de radio, d'insecte)* antenna.

antérieur, -eure *adj (précédent)* former; *(placé devant)* front.

antibiotique *m* antibiotic.

antibrouillard *adj & m (phare)* **a.** fog light.

antichoc *adj inv* shockproof.

anticipé, -ée *adj (retraite, retour)* early; *(paiement)* advance.

anticorps *m* antibody.

antilope *f* antelope.

antipathique *adj* disagreeable.

antiquaire *mf* antique dealer.

antique *adj* ancient.

antiquité *f (temps, ancienneté)* antiquity; *(objet ancien)* antique.

antivol *m* anti-theft device.

anxiété *f* anxiety.

anxieux, -euse *adj* anxious.

août *m* August.

apaisant, -ante *adj* soothing.

apaiser *vt (personne)* to calm; *(douleur)* to soothe.

apercevoir* *vt* to see; *(brièvement)* to catch a glimpse of.

apercevoir (s') *vpr* **s'a. de** to realize.

aperçu *m (idée)* general idea.

apéritif *m* aperitif.

aphte *m* mouth ulcer.

apitoyer (s') *vpr* **s'a. sur son sort** to feel sorry for oneself.

aplanir *vt (terrain)* to level; *(difficulté)* to iron out, to smooth out.

aplati, -ie *adj* flat.

aplatir *vt* to flatten (out).

aplomb (d') *adv (meuble etc)* level, straight.

apostrophe *f (signe)* apostrophe.

apparaître* *vi* to appear.

appareil *m (électrique)* appliance; *(téléphonique)* telephone; *(avion)* aircraft; *(dentaire)* braces; *(digestif)* system; **a. (photo)** camera.

apparemment *adv* apparently.

apparence *f* appearance.

apparent, -ente *adj* apparent; *(visible)* conspicuous, noticeable.

apparition *f* appearance; *(spectre)* apparition.

appartement *m* apartment.

appartenance *f (de groupe)* belonging (à to); *(de parti)* membership (à of).

appartenir* *vi* to belong (à to).

appât *m* bait.

appâter *vt* to lure.

appauvrir (s') *vpr* to become impoverished.

appauvrissement *m* impoverishment.

appel *m (cri)* call; *(en justice)* appeal; **faire l'a.** to call the roll; **faire a.** à to call upon.

appeler *vt (personne, nom etc)* to call; *(en criant)* to call out to *(sb)*; **a. à l'aide** to call for help.

appeler (s') *vpr* to be called; **il s'appelle Paul** his name is Paul.

appellation *f (nom)* term; **a. contrôlée** *(de vin)* guaranteed vintage.

appendicite *f* appendicitis.

appétissant, -ante *adj* appetizing.

appétit *m* appetite (**de** for); **bon a.!** enjoy your meal!

applaudir *vti* to applaud.
applaudissements *mpl* applause.
application *f* application.
applique *f* wall lamp.
appliqué, -ée *adj* painstaking.
appliquer (s') *vpr* s'a. à (*un travail*) to apply oneself to; (*concerner*) to apply to; s'a. à faire to take pains to do.
appoint *m* faire l'a. to give the exact money.
apporter *vt* to bring.
appréciation *f* (*de professeur*) comment (sur on).
apprécier *vt* (*aimer, percevoir*) to appreciate.
appréhender *vt* (*craindre*) to dread (de faire doing).
apprendre* *vti* (*étudier*) to learn; (*événement, fait*) to hear of; (*nouvelle*) to hear; a. à faire to learn to do; a. qch à qn to teach sb sth; (*informer*) to tell sb sth; a. à qn à faire to teach sb to do; a. que to learn that; (*être informé*) to hear that.
apprenti, -ie *mf* apprentice.
apprentissage *m* apprenticeship; (*d'une langue*) learning (de of).
apprêter (s') *vpr* to get ready (à faire to do).
apprivoisé, -ée *adj* tame.
apprivoiser *vt* to tame.
approcher 1 *vt* (*chaise etc*) to draw up (de to); (*personne*) to come ou get close to, to approach. **2** *vi* to draw near(er), to get close(r) (de to).
approcher (s') *vpr* to come ou get near(er) (de to); il s'est approché de moi he came up to me.
approfondir *vt* (*trou*) to dig deeper; (*question*) to go into thoroughly.
approprier (s') *vpr* to take, to help oneself to.
approuver *vt* to approve.
approvisionner (s') *vpr* to get one's supplies (de of).

approximatif, -ive *adj* approximate.
appui *m* support; (*pour coude etc*) rest.
appuyer 1 *vt* (*soutenir*) to support; a. qch sur (*poser*) to rest sth on. **2** *vi* a. sur to rest on; (*bouton*) to press.
appuyer (s') *vpr* s'a. sur to lean on, to rest on.
après 1 *prép* (*temps*) after; (*espace*) beyond; a. un an after a year; a. le pont beyond the bridge; a. avoir mangé after eating. **2** *adv* after(-wards); l'année d'a. the following year.
après (d') *prép* according to.
après-demain *adv* the day after tomorrow.
après-midi *m ou f inv* afternoon.
après-rasage, *pl* après-rasages *m* aftershave.
après-shampooing *m inv* conditioner.
après-ski, *pl* après-skis *m* snowboot.
apte *adj* capable (à of).
aptitudes *fpl* aptitude (pour for).
aquarelle *f* watercolor.
aquarium *m* aquarium.
aquatique *adj* aquatic.
arabe 1 *adj* Arab. **2** *mf* A. Arab. **3** *adj & m* (*langue*) Arabic; chiffres arabes Arabic numerals.
arachide *f* peanut.
araignée *f* spider.
arbitre *m* Football, Boxe referee; Tennis umpire.
arbitrer *vt* Football, Boxe to referee; Tennis to umpire.
arbre *m* tree.
arbuste *m* (small) shrub.
arc *m* (*arme*) bow; (*voûte*) arch; (*de cercle*) arc.
arcades *fpl* arcade, arches.
arc-en-ciel, *pl* arcs-en-ciel *m* rainbow.
arche *f* (*voûte*) arch.
archer *m* archer.

archiplein, -pleine *adj* jam-packed.

architecte *m* architect.

architecture *f* architecture.

archives *fpl* records.

Arctique (l') *m* the Arctic.

ardent, -ente *adj (passionné)* ardent.

ardeur *f (énergie)* enthusiasm.

ardoise *f* slate.

are *m* = 100 square meters.

arène *f (pour taureaux)* bullring; **arènes** *(romaines)* amphitheater.

arête *f (de poisson)* bone; *(de cube)* edge, ridge.

argent *m (métal)* silver; *(monnaie)* money; **a. comptant** cash.

argenterie *f* silverware.

argile *f* clay.

argot *m* slang.

argument *m* argument.

argumenter *vi* to argue.

arithmétique *f* arithmetic.

armature *f (de lunettes, tente)* frame.

arme *f* arm, weapon; **a. à feu** firearm.

armée *f* army; **a. de l'air** air force.

armement(s) *m(pl)* arms.

armer *vt (personne)* to arm (**de** with); *(fusil)* to cock.

armer (s') *vpr* to arm oneself (**de** with).

armoire *f (penderie)* wardrobe, closet; **a. à pharmacie** medicine chest *ou* cabinet.

armure *f* armor.

arobase *f* = **arrobas**.

aromate *m (herbe)* herb; *(épice)* spice.

arôme *m (goût)* flavor; *(odeur)* (pleasant) smell.

arracher *vt (clou, dent, cheveux, page)* to pull out; *(plante)* to pull up; **a. qch à qn** to snatch sth from sb.

arranger *vt (chambre, visite etc)* to fix up; *(voiture, texte)* to put right; **ça m'arrange** that suits me.

arranger (s') *vpr* to come to an agreement; *(finir bien)* to turn out fine; **s'a. pour faire** to manage to do.

arrestation *f* arrest.

arrêt *m (halte, endroit)* stop; *(action)* stopping; **temps d'a.** pause; **sans a.** constantly; **'a. interdit'** *(panneau de signalisation)* 'no stopping (no standing)'.

arrêté *m* order.

arrêter 1 *vt* to stop; *(voleur etc)* to arrest. **2** *vi* to stop; **il n'arrête pas de critiquer/etc** he's always criticizing/*etc*.

arrêter (s') *vpr* to stop (**de faire** doing).

arrière 1 *adv* **en a.** *(marcher)* backwards; *(rester)* behind. **2** *m & adj inv* rear, back; **faire marche a.** to reverse, to back. **3** *m Sport* (full)back.

arrière-boutique, *pl* **arrière-boutiques** *f* back (room) *(of a shop)*.

arrière-goût, *pl* **arrière-goûts** *m* aftertaste.

arrière-grand-mère, *pl* **arrière-grands-mères** *f* great-grandmother.

arrière-grand-père, *pl* **arrière-grands-pères** *m* great-grandfather.

arrière-pays *m inv* hinterland.

arrière-pensée, *pl* **arrière-pensées** *f* ulterior motive.

arrière-plan, *pl* **arrière-plans** *m* background; **à l'a.** in the background.

arrivage *m* shipment.

arrivée *f* arrival; **ligne d'a.** finish line.

arriver *vi (aux être)* to arrive; *(survenir)* to happen; **a. à** to reach; **a. à faire** to manage to do; **il m'arrive d'oublier/etc** I (sometimes) forget/*etc*.

arrobas *m* at sign.

arrogant, -ante *adj* arrogant.

arrondir *vt (chiffre, angle)* to round off.

arrondissement *m (d'une ville)* district.

arrosage *m* watering.

arroser *vt (terre)* to water.

arrosoir *m* watering can.

art *m* art.

artère *f* artery; *(rue)* main road.

artichaut *m* artichoke.

article *m (de presse, de commerce, en grammaire)* article; **articles de toilette** toiletries.

articulation *f (de membre)* joint; **a. (du doigt)** knuckle.

articuler *vt (mot etc)* to articulate.

artifice *m* **feu d'a.** firework display.

artificiel, -elle *adj* artificial.

artisan *m* craftsman.

artisanal, -e, -aux *adj* **objet a.** object made by craftsmen.

artisanat *m* craft industry.

artiste *mf* artist.

artistique *adj* artistic.

as¹ *voir* avoir.

as² *m (carte, champion)* ace.

ascenseur *m* elevator.

ascension *f* ascent; **l'A.** Ascension Day.

asiatique 1 *adj* Asian. **2** *mf* **A.** Asian.

asile *m (abri)* shelter.

aspect *m (air)* appearance.

asperge *f* asparagus.

asperger *vt* to spray (**de** with).

asphyxie *f* suffocation.

asphyxier *vt* to suffocate.

aspirateur *m* vacuum cleaner; **passer (à) l'a.** to vacuum.

aspirer *vt (liquide)* to suck up.

aspirine *f* aspirin.

assaisonnement *m* seasoning.

assaisonner *vt* to season.

assassin *m* murderer.

assassinat *m* murder.

assassiner *vt* to murder.

assaut *m* onslaught; **prendre d'a.** to (take by) storm.

assemblée *f (personnes réunies)* gathering; *(parlement)* assembly.

assembler *vt* to put together.

assembler (s') *vpr* to gather.

asseoir* (s') *vpr* to sit (down).

assez *adv* enough; **a. de pain/gens** enough bread/people; **j'en ai a.** I've had enough; **a. grand/etc (suffisamment)** big/etc enough (**pour faire** to do); **a. fatigué/etc (plutôt)** fairly *ou* quite tired/etc.

assiéger *vt (magasin, vedette)* to mob.

assiette *f* plate; **a. anglaise** (assorted) cold cuts.

assis, -ise *(pp of asseoir) adj* sitting (down).

assises *fpl* **(cour d')a.** court of assizes.

assistance *f (assemblée)* audience; *(aide)* assistance.

assistant, -ante *mf* assistant; **assistant(e) social(e)** social worker; **assistante maternelle** *(dans une garderie)* daycare worker; *(à domicile)* babysitter.

assister 1 *vt (aider)* to help. **2** *vi* **a. à** *(réunion, cours etc)* to attend; *(accident)* to witness.

association *f* association.

associé, -ée *mf* partner.

associer (s') *vpr* to associate (**à** with).

assoiffé, -ée *adj* thirsty.

assombrir (s') *vpr (ciel)* to cloud over.

assommer *vt (personne)* to knock unconscious.

assorti, -ie *adj (objet semblable)* matching; *(bonbons)* assorted; **a. de** accompanied by.

assortiment *m* assortment.

assortir *vt,* **s'assortir** *vpr* to match.

assoupir (s') *vpr* to doze off.

assouplir *vt (corps)* to limber up, to stretch.

assouplissement *m* **exercices d'a.** stretching exercises.

assourdir *vt* to deafen.

assourdissant, -ante *adj* deafening.

assumer vt (tâche, rôle) to assume, to take on; (risque) to take.

assurance f (aplomb) self-assurance; (contrat) insurance.

assuré, -ée adj (succès) guaranteed; (air, personne) confident. 2 mf policyholder.

assurer vt (par un contrat) to insure; (travail) to carry out; **a. à qn que** to assure sb that; **a. qn de qch** to assure sb of sth.

assurer (s') vpr s'a. to insure oneself (contre against); **s'a. que/de** to make sure that/of.

astérisque m asterisk.

asthmatique adj & mf asthmatic.

asthme m asthma.

asticot m maggot.

astiquer vt to polish.

astre m star.

astrologie f astrology.

astronaute mf astronaut.

astronomie f astronomy.

astuce f (pour faire qch) knack, trick.

astucieux, -euse adj clever.

atelier m (d'ouvrier etc) workshop; (de peintre) studio.

athée 1 adj atheistic. 2 mf atheist.

athlète mf athlete.

athlétique adj athletic.

athlétisme m athletics.

atlantique 1 adj Atlantic. 2 m l'A. the Atlantic.

atlas m atlas.

atmosphère f atmosphere.

atome m atom.

atomique adj (bombe etc) atomic.

atout m trump (card).

atroce adj atrocious.

atrocités fpl atrocities.

attabler (s') vpr to sit down at the table.

attachant, -ante adj (enfant etc) likeable.

attaché-case, pl **attachés-cases** m attaché case, briefcase.

attacher vt (lier) to tie (up) (à to); (boucler, fixer) to fasten.

attacher (s') vpr s'a. à qn to become attached to sb.

attaquant, -ante mf attacker.

attaque f attack.

attaquer vti to attack.

attaquer (s') vpr s'a. à to attack.

attarder (s') vpr (en chemin) to dawdle.

atteindre* vt to reach; être atteint de (maladie) to be suffering from.

attelage m (crochet) hook (for towing).

atteler vt (bêtes) to harness; (remorque) to hook up.

attendre 1 vt to wait for; **elle attend un bébé** she's expecting a baby. **2** vi to wait; **a. que qn vienne** to wait for sb to come; **faire a. qn** to keep sb waiting; **en attendant** meanwhile; **en attendant que** (+ subjonctif) until.

attendre (s') vpr s'a. à to expect.

attendrir (s') vpr to be moved (sur).

attendrissant, -ante adj moving.

attentat m attempt on sb's life; **a. (à la bombe)** (bomb) attack.

attentat-suicide m suicide bombing.

attente f wait(ing); **salle d'a.** waiting room.

attentif, -ive adj (personne) attentive; (travail, examen) careful.

attention f attention; **faire a. à** to pay attention to; **a.!** watch out!, be careful!; **a. à la voiture!** watch out for the car!

attentionné, -ée adj considerate.

attentivement adv attentively.

atténuer vt (effet) to reduce; (douleur) to ease.

atténuer (s') vpr (douleur) to ease.

atterrir vi to land.

atterrissage m landing.

attestation f (document) certificate.

attester *vt* to testify to; **a. que...** to testify that...

attirant, -ante *adj* attractive.

attirer *vt* to attract; *(attention)* to draw (**sur** to).

attitude *f* attitude.

attraction *f* attraction.

attraper *vt (ballon, maladie, voleur, train etc)* to catch; *(accent, contravention etc)* to pick up; **se laisser a.** *(duper)* to get taken in.

attrayant, -ante *adj* attractive.

attribuer *vt (donner)* to assign (**à** to); *(décerner)* to award (**à** to).

attribut *m* attribute.

attrister *vt* to sadden.

attroupement *m* (disorderly) crowd.

attrouper *vt*, **s'attrouper** *vpr* to gather.

au *voir* **à, le**.

aube *f* dawn.

auberge *f* inn; **a. de jeunesse** youth hostel.

aubergine *f* eggplant.

aucun, -une 1 *adj* no, not any; **il n'a a. talent** he has no talent, he doesn't have any talent; **a. professeur n'est venu** no teacher has come. **2** *pron* none, not any; **il n'en a a.** he has none (at all), he doesn't have any (at all).

audace *f (courage)* daring.

audacieux, -euse *adj* daring.

au-delà 1 *adv* beyond; **100 euros mais pas a.** 100 euros but no more. **2** *prép* **a. de** beyond.

au-dessous 1 *adv* below, under; *(à l'étage inférieur)* downstairs. **2** *prép* **a. de** under, below.

au-dessus 1 *adv* above, over; *(à l'étage supérieur)* upstairs. **2** *prép* **a. de** above; *(âge, température, prix)* over.

audience *f (entretien)* audience; *(de tribunal)* hearing; **l'a. est suspendue** the case is adjourned.

audio *adj inv* audio.

auditeur, -trice *mf* listener; **les**

auditeurs the audience.

auditoire *m* audience.

auge *f (feeding)* trough.

augmentation *f* increase (**de** in, of); **a. de salaire** (pay) raise.

augmenter *vti* to increase (**de** by).

aujourd'hui *adv* today.

auparavant *adv (avant)* before(-hand); *(d'abord)* first.

auprès de *prép* by, close to.

auquel *voir* **lequel**.

aura, aurai(t) *etc voir* **avoir**.

auriculaire *m* pinkie, little finger.

aurore *f* dawn.

ausculter *vt* to examine *(with a stethoscope)*.

aussi *adv (comparaison)* as; **a. sage que** as wise as. ▪ *(également)* too, also, as well; **moi a.** so do/can/am/ etc I. ▪ *(tellement)* so; **un repas a. délicieux** so delicious a meal, such a delicious meal.

aussitôt *adv* immediately; **a. que** as soon as; **a. levé, il partit** as soon as he was up, he left.

australien, -ienne *adj* Australian. **2** *mf* **A.** Australian.

autant *adv* **a. de...que** *(quantité)* as much...as; *(nombre)* as many... as. ▪ **a. de** *(tant de)* so much; *(nombre)* so many. ▪ **a. (que)** *(souffrir, lire etc)* as much (as); **en faire a.** to do the same; **j'aimerais a. aller au cinéma** I'd just as soon go to the movies.

autel *m* altar.

auteur *m (de livre)* author; *(de chanson)* composer.

authentique *adj* genuine.

auto *f* car; **autos tamponneuses** bumper cars.

autobus *m* bus.

autocar *m* bus, coach.

autocollant *m* sticker.

auto-école *f* driving school.

autographe *m* autograph.

automatique *adj* automatic.

automatiquement *adv* automatically.

automne *m* autumn, fall.

automobile *f & adj* car, automobile.

automobiliste *mf* motorist, driver.

autonome *adj (région)* autonomous, self-governing; *(personne)* self-sufficient.

autoradio *m* car radio.

autorisation *f* permission.

autoriser *vt* to permit (**à faire** to do).

autoritaire *adj* authoritarian.

autorité *f* authority.

autoroute *f* highway.

auto-stop *m* hitchhiking; **faire de l'a.** to hitchhike.

auto-stoppeur, -euse *mf* hitchhiker.

autour 1 *adv* around. 2 *prép* **a. de** around.

autre *adj & pron* other; **un a. livre** another book; **un a.** another (one); **d'autres** others; **d'autres médecins** other doctors; **d'autres questions?** any other questions?; **quelqu'un/ personne/rien d'a.** someone/no one/nothing else; **a. chose/part** something/somewhere else; **qui/ quoi d'a.?** who/what else?; **l'un l'a., les uns les autres** each other; **l'un et l'a.** both (of them); **l'un ou l'a.** either (of them); **ni l'un ni l'a.** neither (of them); **les uns...les autres** some...others; **d'un moment à l'a.** any moment.

autrefois *adv* in the past.

autrement *adv* differently; *(sinon)* otherwise.

autrichien, -ienne 1 *adj* Austrian. 2 *mf* **A.** Austrian.

autruche *f* ostrich.

aux *voir* **à, le**.

auxiliaire *adj & m (verbe)* **a.** auxiliary (verb).

auxquel(le)s *voir* **lequel**.

aval (en) *adv* downstream.

avalanche *f* avalanche.

avaler *vti* to swallow.

avance *f* **à l'a., d'a.** in advance; **en a.** *(arriver, partir)* early; *(avant l'horaire prévu)* ahead (of time); **en a. sur** ahead of; **avoir une heure d'a.** *(train etc)* to be an hour early.

avancement *m (de personne)* promotion.

avancer 1 *vt (date)* to move up; *(main, chaise)* to move forward; *(travail)* to speed up. 2 *vi* to advance, to move forward; *(montre)* to be fast.

avancer (s') *vpr* to move forward.

avant 1 *prép* before; **a. de voir** before seeing; **a. qu'il (ne) parte** before he leaves; **a. tout** above all. 2 *adv* before; **en a.** *(mouvement)* forward; *(en tête)* ahead; **la nuit d'a.** the night before. 3 *m & adj inv* front. 4 *m (joueur)* forward.

avantage *m* advantage.

avantager *vt* to favor.

avantageux, -euse *adj (offre)* attractive; *(prix)* reasonable.

avant-bras *m inv* forearm.

avant-dernier, -ière *adj & mf* last but one.

avant-hier *adv* the day before yesterday.

avant-première, *pl* avant-premières *f* preview.

avant-veille *f* **l'a. (de)** two days before.

avare 1 *adj* miserly, stingy. 2 *mf* miser.

avarice *f* miserliness, avarice.

avarie *f* damage; **subir une a.** to be damaged.

avarié, -ée *adj (aliment)* rotting, rotten.

avec *prép* with; *(envers)* to(wards); **et a. ça?** *(dans un magasin)* anything else?

avenir *m* future; **à l'a.** in future.

aventure *f* adventure.

aventurer (s') *vpr* to venture.

aventurier, -ière *mf* adventurer.

avenue *f* avenue.

avérer (s') *vpr (se révéler)* to prove

to be; **il s'avère que...** it turns out that...

averse f shower.

avertir vt (mettre en garde) to warn; (informer) to notify.

avertissement m warning; notification.

avertisseur m (klaxon®) horn; **a. d'incendie** fire alarm.

aveu, -x m confession.

aveugle 1 adj blind. **2** mf blind man, blind woman; **les aveugles** the blind.

aveugler vt to blind.

aveuglette (à l') adv **chercher qch à l'a.** to grope for sth.

aviateur, -trice mf airman, airwoman.

aviation f (armée de l'air) air force; (avions) aircraft inv; **l'a.** (activité) flying; **base d'a.** air base.

avide adj (cupide) greedy; (passionné) eager (**de** for).

avion m aircraft inv, (air)plane; **a. à réaction** jet; **a. de ligne** airliner; **par a.** (lettre) airmail; **en a., par a.** (voyager) by plane, by air.

aviron m oar; **l'a.** (sport) rowing.

avis m opinion; (communiqué) notice; **à mon a.** in my opinion; **changer d'a.** to change one's mind.

avocat, -ate 1 mf attorney. **2** m (fruit) avocado.

avoine f oats.

avoir* 1 v aux to have; **je l'ai vu** I've seen him. **2** vt (posséder) to have; (obtenir) to get; **qu'est-ce que tu as?** what's the matter with you?; **il n'a qu'à essayer** all he has to do is try; **a. faim/chaud/**etc to be ou feel hungry/hot/etc; **a. cinq ans** to be five (years old); **j'en ai pour dix minutes** this will take me ten minutes. **3** (locution) **il y a** there is, pl there are; **il y a six ans** six years ago; (voir **il**).

avortement m abortion.

avouer vt to confess (**que** that).

avril m April.

axe m (ligne) axis; (essieu) axle; **grands axes** (routes) main roads.

ayant, ayez, ayons voir **avoir**.

azote m nitrogen.

azure m (sky) blue; **la Côte d'A.** the (French) Riviera.

B

baby-foot m inv foosball.

bac 1 m (bateau) ferry(boat); (cuve) tank. **2** abrév = **baccalauréat**.

baccalauréat m = high school diploma.

bâche f tarpaulin.

bachelier, -ière mf holder of the baccalauréat.

bâcher vt to cover over (with a tarpaulin).

bâcler vt Fam to botch (up).

badaud, -aude mf onlooker.

badigeonner vt (mur) to whitewash; (écorchure) to coat, to paint.

bafouiller vti to stammer.

bagage m piece of baggage; **bagages** baggage.

bagarre f fight(ing).

bagarrer (se) vpr to fight.

bagnole f Fam car.

bague f (anneau) ring.

baguette f stick; (de chef d'orchestre) baton; (pain) (long thin) loaf; **baguettes** (de tambour) drumsticks; (pour manger) chopsticks; **b. (magique)** (magic) wand.

baie¹ f (de côte) bay.

baie² f (fruit) berry.

baignade f (bain) bath, swim; (endroit) swimming place.

baigner 1 vt to bathe. **2** vi **b. dans** (aliment) to be steeped in.

baigner (se) vpr to go swimming.

baigneur, -euse 1 mf bather, swimmer. **2** m (poupée) baby doll.

baignoire *f* bath (tub).

bail, *pl* **baux** *m* lease; **ça fait un b. que je ne l'ai pas vu** *Fam* I haven't seen him for ages.

bâillement *m* yawn.

bâiller *vi* to yawn.

bâillon *m* gag.

bâillonner *vt* to gag.

bain *m* bath; **prendre un b. de soleil** to sunbathe; **salle de bain(s)** bathroom; **être dans le b.** *Fam* to have gotten into the swing of things; **b. de bouche** mouthwash.

baiser *m* kiss.

baisse *f* fall, drop (**de** in); **en b.** falling.

baisser 1 *vt* to lower, to drop; *(tête)* to bend; *(radio, chauffage)* to turn down. **2** *vi* to go down, to drop.

baisser (se) *vpr* to bend down.

bal, *pl* **bals** *m* ball; *(populaire)* dance.

balade *f Fam* walk; *(en auto)* drive.

balader (se) *vpr Fam (à pied)* to (go for a) walk; **se b. (en voiture)** to go for a drive.

baladeur *m* Walkman®.

balai *m* broom; **manche à b.** broomstick.

balance *f* (pair of) scales.

balancer *vt* to sway; *(lancer) Fam* to pitch; *(se débarrasser de) Fam* to chuck, to pitch.

balancer (se) *vpr* to swing (from side to side).

balançoire *f (suspendue)* swing.

balayer *vt* to sweep (up); *(enlever)* to sweep away.

balayette *f* (hand)brush.

balayeur, -euse 1 *mf (personne)* roadsweeper. **2** *f (véhicule)* road-sweeper.

balbutier *vti* to stammer.

balcon *m* balcony.

baleine *f* whale.

balisage *m* beacons.

balise *f (pour naviguer)* beacon.

baliser *vt* to mark with beacons.

ballast *m* ballast.

balle *f (de tennis, golf etc)* ball; *(projectile)* bullet.

ballerine *f* ballerina.

ballet *m* ballet.

ballon *m (jouet d'enfant, appareil)* balloon; *(sports)* ball; **b. de football** soccer ball.

ballot *m* bundle.

ballottage *m (scrutin)* second ballot.

balnéaire *adj* **station b.** beach resort.

balustrade *f* (hand)rail.

bambin *m* tiny tot.

bambou *m* bamboo.

ban *m (applaudissements)* round of applause; **un (triple) b. pour…** three cheers for…

banal, -e, -als *adj (objet, gens)* ordinary; *(idée)* trite, banal; **pas b.** unusual.

banane *f* banana.

banc *m (siège)* bench; **b. de sable** sandbank.

bancaire *adj* **compte b.** bank account.

bancal, -e, -als *adj (meuble)* wobbly.

bandage *m* bandage.

bande¹ *f (de terrain, papier etc)* strip; *(de film)* reel; *(rayure)* stripe; *(pansement)* bandage; *(sur la chaussée)* line; **b. d'arrêt d'urgence** shoulder; **b. (magnétique)** tape; **b. vidéo** videotape; **b. dessinée** comic strip.

bande² *f (groupe)* gang.

bande-annonce, *pl* **bandes-annonces** *f* preview.

bandeau, -x *m (sur les yeux)* blindfold; *(pour la tête)* headband.

bander *vt (blessure)* to bandage; *(yeux)* to blindfold.

banderole *f (sur montants)* banner.

bandit *m* robber.

bandoulière *f (de sac)* shoulder strap; **en b.** slung across the shoulder.

banlieue f la b. the outskirts (of town).

banque f bank; (activité) banking; **b. électronique** e-banking.

banquette f (de véhicule, train) seat.

banquier m banker.

banquise f ice floe.

baptême m christening, baptism.

baptiser vt (enfant) to christen, to baptize.

baquet m tub, basin.

bar m (lieu, comptoir) bar.

baraque f hut, shack.

baraquement m (makeshift) huts.

baratin m Fam (verbiage) waffle; (de séducteur) sweet talk; (de vendeur) sales patter.

barbare adj (cruel) barbaric.

barbe f beard; **se faire la b.** to shave; **quelle b.!** Fam what a bore!

barbecue m barbecue.

barbelé adj **fil de fer b.** barbed wire.

barbiche f goatee.

barboter vi to splash around.

barbouillage m smear(ing); (gribouillage) scribble, scribbling.

barbouiller vt (salir) to smear; (gribouiller) to scribble.

barbu, -ue adj bearded.

barème m (de notes, de salaires, de prix) scale; (pour calculer) ready reckoner.

baril m barrel; **b. de poudre** powder keg.

barman, pl -men ou -mans m bartender.

baromètre m barometer.

baron m baron.

baronne f baroness.

barque f (small) boat.

barquette f (de fruit) punnet; (de plat cuisiné) container.

barrage m (sur une route) roadblock; (sur un fleuve) dam.

barre f bar; (de bateau) helm; (trait) stroke.

barreau, -x m (de fenêtre) bar; (d'échelle) rung.

barrer vt (route etc) to block; (mot, phrase) to cross out.

barrette f barrette.

barricade f barricade.

barricader vt to barricade.

barricader (se) vpr to barricade oneself (in).

barrière f (porte) gate; (clôture) fence; (obstacle) barrier.

barrique f (large) barrel.

bas, basse 1 adj low. **2** adv low; (parler) in a whisper; **plus b.** further ou lower down. **3** m (de côte, page, mur etc) bottom; **tiroir/etc du b.** bottom drawer/etc, **en b.** down (below); (par l'escalier) downstairs; **en ou au b. de** at the bottom of.

bas m (chaussette) stocking.

bas-côté m roadside, verge, shoulder.

bascule f weighing machine; (jeu d'enfant) seesaw.

basculer vti to topple over.

base f base; bases (d'un argument, accord etc) basis; **salaire de b.** base pay; **à b. de lait/citron** milk-/lemon-based.

baser vt to base (sur on).

basket(-ball) m basketball.

baskets fpl (chaussures) sneakers.

basque 1 adj Basque. **2** mf B. Basque.

basse voir bas.

basse-cour, pl basses-cours f farmyard.

bassin m pond; (rade) dock; (du corps) pelvis; **b. houiller** coalfield.

bassine f bowl.

bataille f battle.

batailleur, -euse 1 mf fighter. **2** adj fond of fighting, belligerent.

bateau, -x m boat; (grand) ship.

bateau-mouche, pl bateaux-mouches m river boat (on the Seine).

bâtiment m building; (navire) vessel; **le b.** (industrie) the construction industry.

bâtir *vt* to build; **bien bâti** well-built.

bâton *m* stick; *(d'agent)* baton; **b. de rouge** lipstick; **donner des coups de b. à qn** to beat sb (with a stick).

battante *adj f* **pluie b.** driving rain.

battement *m* beat(ing); *(de paupières)* blink(ing); *(délai)* interval; **b. de cœur** heartbeat.

batterie *f* battery; **la b.** *(d'un orchestre)* the drums.

batteur *m (d'orchestre)* drummer.

battre* **1** *vt* to beat. **2** *vi* to beat; **b. des mains** to clap (one's hands); **b. des paupières** to blink; **b. des ailes** *(oiseau)* to flap its wings.

battre (se) *vpr* to fight.

baume *m* balm.

bavard, -arde *adj* talkative.

bavardage *m* chatting.

bavarder *vi* to chat.

bave *f* drool.

baver *vi* to drool; **en b.** *Fam* to have a rough time of it.

bavoir *m* bib.

bavure *f (tache)* smudge.

bazar *m (magasin)* bazaar; *(désordre)* mess.

BD *f abrév (bande dessinée)* comic strip.

beau *(or* **bel** *before vowel or mute* h*),* **belle,** *pl* **beaux, belles** *adj* beautiful, attractive; *(voyage, temps etc)* fine, lovely; **au b. milieu** right in the middle; **j'ai b. crier/**etc it's no use (my) shouting/*etc.*

beaucoup *adv (lire etc)* a lot; **aimer b.** to like very much *ou* a lot; **b. de** *(livres etc)* many, a lot of; *(courage etc)* a lot of; **pas b. d'argent/**etc not much money/*etc*; **j'en ai b.** *(quantité)* I have a lot; *(nombre)* I have lots; **b. plus** much more; many more (**que** than).

beau-fils, *pl* **beaux-fils** *m (gendre)* son-in-law; *(après remariage)* stepson.

beau-frère, *pl* **beaux-frères** *m* brother-in-law.

beau-père, *pl* **beaux-pères** *m (père du conjoint)* father-in-law; *(après remariage)* stepfather.

beauté *f* beauty.

beaux-arts *mpl* fine arts; **école des b., les B.** art school.

beaux-parents *mpl* parents-in-law.

bébé *m* baby.

bec *m (d'oiseau)* beak; *(de cruche)* spout; **coup de b.** peck.

bécane *f Fam* bike.

bêche *f* spade.

bêcher *vt (cultiver)* to dig.

becquée *f* **donner la b. à** *(oiseau)* to feed.

bedonnant, -ante *adj* potbellied.

bégayer *vi* to stutter.

bègue **1** *mf* stutterer. **2** *adj* **être b.** to stutter.

beige *adj & m* beige.

beignet *m (pâtisserie)* fritter; *(rond)* donut.

bel *voir* **beau**.

bêler *vi* to bleat.

belette *f* weasel.

belge **1** *adj* Belgian. **2** *mf* **B.** Belgian.

bélier *m* ram.

belle *voir* **beau**.

belle-famille, *pl* **belles-familles** *f* in-laws.

belle-fille, *pl* **belles-filles** *f (épouse du fils)* daughter-in-law; *(après remariage)* stepdaughter.

belle-mère, *pl* **belles-mères** *f (mère du conjoint)* mother-in-law; *(après remariage)* stepmother.

belle-sœur, *pl* **belles-sœurs** *f* sister-in-law.

belliqueux, -euse *adj (agressif)* aggressive.

bénédiction *f* blessing.

bénéfice *m (gain)* profit; *(avantage)* benefit.

bénéficiaire **1** *mf (de chèque)* payee. **2** *adj (entreprise)* profit-making; *(compte)* in credit.

bénéficier *vi* to benefit (**de** from).
bénéfique *adj* beneficial.
bénévolat *m* voluntary work.
bénévole 1 *adj* voluntary. **2** *mf* volunteer.
bénin, -igne *adj (accident, opération)* minor; *(tumeur)* benign.
bénir *vt* to bless; *(remercier)* to give thanks to.
bénit, -ite *adj (pain)* consecrated; **eau bénite** holy water.
benjamin, -ine *mf* youngest child.
benne *f (de camion)* (movable) container; **camion à b. basculante** dump truck.
BEP *m abrév (brevet d'études professionnelles)* = vocational diploma taken at 18.
béquille *f (canne)* crutch; *(de moto)* stand.
berceau, -x *m* cradle.
bercer *vt (balancer)* to rock; *(apaiser)* to soothe, to lull.
berceuse *f* lullaby.
béret *m* beret.
berge *m (rive)* (raised) bank.
berger *m* shepherd; **b. allemand** German shepherd.
bergère *f* shepherdess.
bergerie *f* sheepfold.
berline *f (voiture)* sedan.
berner *vt* to fool.
besogne *f* job, task.
besoin *m* need; **avoir b. de** to need.
bestiole *f (insecte)* bug.
bétail *m* livestock.
bête[1] *f* animal; *(insecte)* bug; **b. noire** pet peeve.
bête[2] *adj* stupid.
bêtement *adv* stupidly; **tout b.** quite simply.
bêtise *f* stupidity; *(action, parole)* stupid thing.
béton *m* concrete; **mur/etc en b.** concrete wall/etc.
betterave *f* beet.
beurre *m* butter.

beurrer *vt* to butter.
beurrier *m* butter dish.
biais *m* **regarder qn de b.** to look sideways at sb; **par le b. de** through.
bibelot *m* (small) ornament, trinket.
biberon *m* (feeding) bottle.
bible *f* bible; **la B.** the Bible.
bibliothécaire *mf* librarian.
bibliothèque *f* library; *(meuble)* bookcase.
bic® *m* ballpoint.
biceps *m (muscle)* biceps.
biche *f* doe.
bicyclette *f* bicycle.
bidon 1 *m* (jerry) can. **2** *adj inv* Fam phoney.
bidonville *m* shantytown.
bidule *m (chose)* Fam whatchamacallit.
bien 1 *adv* well; **b. fatigué/souvent/etc (très)** very tired/often/etc; **merci b.!** thanks very much!; **b.! fine!, right!; b. des fois/des gens/etc** lots of *ou* many times/people/etc; **je l'ai b. dit (intensif)** I *did* say so; **tu as b. fait** you did right; **c'est b. fait (pour lui)** it serves him right. **2** *adj inv (convenable, compétent etc)* fine. **3** *m (avantage)* good; *(chose)* possession; **ça te fera du b.** it will do you good; **pour ton b.** for your own good; **le b. et le mal** good and evil.
bien-être *m* wellbeing.
bienfaisant, -ante *adj* beneficial.
bien que *conj* (+ subjonctif) although.
bientôt *adv* soon; **à b.!** see you soon!; **il est b. midi/etc** it's nearly twelve/etc.
bienveillant, -ante *adj* kind.
bienvenu, -ue 1 *adj* welcome. **2** *f* welcome; **souhaiter la bienvenue à** to welcome.
bière *f* beer; **b. pression** draft beer.
bifteck *m* steak.
bifurcation *f (route etc)* fork.

bifurquer *vi* to fork.

bigoudi *m* (hair) roller.

bijou, -x *m* jewel.

bijouterie *f* (commerce) jewelry store, jeweler's.

bijoutier, -ière *mf* jeweler.

bilan *m* (financier) balance sheet; (résultat) outcome; (d'un accident) (casualty) toll; **b. de santé** check-up; **déposer le b.** to file for bankruptcy.

bile *f* bile; **se faire de la b.** *Fam* to worry.

bilingue *adj* bilingual.

billard *m* (jeu) billiards; (table) billiard table.

bille *f* (d'enfant) marble; **stylo à b.** ballpoint (pen).

billet *m* ticket; **b. (de banque)** bill; **b. aller, b. simple** one-way ticket; **b. aller-retour** round trip ticket; **b. électronique** e-ticket.

billeterie *f* (lieu) ticket office; **b. automatique** (de billet de transport) ticket machine.

biologie *f* biology.

biologique *adj* biological; (légumes etc) organic.

biotechnologie *f* biotechnology.

bip *m* beeper.

biscotte *f* Melba toast.

biscuit *m* cookie.

bise¹ *f* (vent) north wind.

bise² *f* (baiser) Fam kiss; **faire la b. à qn** to kiss sb on both cheeks.

bison *m* (American) buffalo.

bisou *m* Fam kiss.

bissextile *adj f* année b. leap year.

bistouri *m* scalpel.

bistro(t) *m* Fam bar.

bitume *m* (revêtement) asphalt.

bizarre *adj* peculiar, odd.

blague *f* (plaisanterie, farce) joke; **b. à part** seriously.

blaguer *vi* to be joking.

blaireau, -x *m* (animal) badger; (brosse) shaving brush.

blâmer *vt* to criticize, to blame.

blanc, blanche 1 *adj* white;

(page) blank. **2** *mf* (personne) white person. **3** *m* (couleur) white; (de poulet) breast; (espace) blank; **b. (d'œuf)** (egg) white; **laisser en b.** to leave blank; **chèque en b.** blank check; **donner carte blanche à qn** to give sb free rein.

blancheur *f* whiteness.

blanchir *vi* to turn white.

blanchisserie *f* (lieu) laundry.

blatte *f* (cock)roach.

blé *m* wheat.

blême *adj* sickly pale; **b. de colère** livid.

blêmir *vi* to turn pale.

blessant, -ante *adj* hurtful.

blessé, -ée *mf* casualty.

blesser *vt* to injure, to hurt; (avec un couteau, une balle etc) to wound; (offenser) to hurt.

blesser (se) *vpr* se **b. le** *ou* au **bras/etc** to hurt one's arm/etc.

blessure *f* injury; wound.

bleu, -e 1 *adj* (mpl bleus) blue. **2** *m* (pl bleus) (couleur) blue; (contusion) bruise; (vêtement) overalls.

blindé, -ée *adj* (voiture etc) armored; **porte blindée** reinforced steel door; **une vitre blindée** bullet-proof glass.

bloc *m* block; (de papier) pad; **à b.** (visser etc) tight.

bloc-notes, *pl* **blocs-notes** *m* writing pad.

blog *m* blog.

blogueur, -euse *mf* blogger.

blond, -onde 1 *adj* fair(-haired), blond. **2** *mf* fair-haired *ou* blond person; **(bière) blonde** beer.

bloquer *vt* (obstruer) to block; (coincer) to jam; (roue) to lock; (prix) to freeze.

bloquer (se) *vpr* to jam; (roue) to lock.

blottir (se) *vpr* to crouch; (dans son lit) to snuggle in; **se b. contre** to snuggle up to.

blouse *f* (tablier) smock.

blouson *m* windbreaker.

bobine f reel, spool.

bocal, -aux m glass jar; (à poissons) bowl.

bœuf, pl **-fs** m ox (pl oxen); (viande) beef.

boire* vti to drink; **offrir à b. à qn** to offer sb a drink.

bois m wood; (de construction) timber; **en** ou **de b.** wooden; **b. de chauffage** firewood.

boisé, -ée adj wooded.

boisson f drink.

boîte f box; (de conserve) can; **b. aux** ou **à lettres** mailbox. ▪ (entreprise) Fam firm; **b. de nuit** nightclub; **b. de réception** (pour e-mails) in-box.

boiter vi to limp.

boîtier m (de montre) case.

bol m bowl; **un b. d'air** a breath of fresh air.

bombardement m bombing; shelling.

bombarder vt to bomb; (avec des obus) to shell.

bombe f bomb; (de laque etc) spray.

bon¹, bonne adj good; (qui convient) right; (apte) fit; **b. anniversaire!** happy birthday!; **le b. choix/moment** the right choice/time; **b. à manger** fit to eat; **c'est b. à savoir** it's worth knowing; **croire b. de** to think it wise to; **b. en français/etc** good at French/etc; **un b. moment** (intensif) a good while; **pour de b.** really (and truly); **ah b.?** is that so?

bon² m (billet) coupon, voucher.

bonbon m candy.

bond m leap.

bondé, -ée adj packed.

bondir vi to leap.

bonheur m happiness; (chance) good luck; **par b.** luckily.

bonhomme, pl **bonshommes** m fellow; **b. de neige** snowman.

bonjour m & int good morning; (après-midi) good afternoon; **donner le b. à, dire b. à** to say hello to.

bonne¹ voir **bon**.

bonne² f maid.

bonnet m (de ski etc) cap; (de femme, d'enfant) bonnet, hat.

bonsoir m & int (en rencontrant qn) good evening; (en quittant qn) goodbye; (au coucher) good night.

bonté f kindness.

bord m (rebord) edge; (rive) bank; **au b. de la mer** at the beach; **au b. de la route** by the roadside; **b. du trottoir** curb; **à bord (de)** (avion, bateau) on board.

border vt (vêtement) to edge; (lit, personne) to tuck in; **b. la rue/etc** (maisons, arbres) to line the street/ etc.

bordereau, -x m (de livraison etc) note.

bordure f border.

borne f boundary mark; **b. kilométrique** = milestone.

borné, -ée adj (personne) narrow-minded; (esprit) narrow.

bosse f (dans le dos) hump; (enflure, de terrain) bump.

bosser vi Fam to work (hard).

bossu, -ue 1 adj hunchbacked. **2** mf hunchback.

botte f (chaussure) boot; (de fleurs etc) bunch.

bottine f (ankle) boot.

bouc m billy goat; (barbe) goatee.

boucan m Fam din, row; **faire du b.** to kick up a row.

bouche f mouth; **b. de métro** métro entrance; **b. d'égout** drain opening.

bouché, -ée adj j'ai le nez b. my nose is stuffed up.

bouchée f mouthful.

boucher¹ vt (évier etc) to stop up; (bouteille) to cork; (vue, rue etc) to block.

boucher², -ère m butcher.

boucher (se) vpr se b. le nez to hold one's nose.

boucherie f butcher's (shop).

bouchon m stopper; (de liège)

cork; (de tube, bidon) cap; (embouteillage) traffic jam.

boucle f (de ceinture) buckle; **b.
d'oreille** earring; **b. (de cheveux)**
curl.

bouclé, -ée adj (cheveux) curly.

boucler 1 vt (attacher) to fasten;
(cheveux) to curl. 2 vi to be curly.

bouclier m shield.

bouder vi to sulk.

boudin m blood sausage.

boue f mud.

bouée f buoy; **b. de sauvetage**
lifebuoy.

boueux, -euse adj muddy.

bouffe f (nourriture) Fam grub.

bouffée f (de fumée) puff.

bouffer vti (manger) Fam to eat.

bougeoir m candlestick.

bouger vti to move.

bougie f candle; (d'automobile)
spark plug.

bouillie f porridge.

bouillir* vi to boil.

bouilloire f kettle.

bouillon m (aliment) broth;
(bulles) bubbles.

bouillonner vi to bubble.

boulanger, -ère mf baker.

boulangerie f baker's (shop).

boule f ball; **boules** (French) bowling game; **b. de neige** snowball.

bouleau, -x m (silver) birch.

bouledogue m bulldog.

boulet m **b. de canon** cannonball.

boulette f (de papier) ball; (de
viande) meatball.

boulevard m boulevard.

bouleversant, -ante adj (per-
turbant) distressing; (émouvant)
deeply moving.

bouleversement m upheaval.

bouleverser vt (déranger) to turn
upside down; (perturber) to distress; (émouvoir) to move deeply.

boulimie f bulimia.

boulon m bolt.

boulot m Fam (emploi) job; (travail) work.

bouquet m (de fleurs) bunch.

bouquin m Fam book.

bourdon m (insecte) bumblebee.

bourdonnement m buzzing.

bourdonner vi to buzz.

bourg m (small) market town.

bourgeois, -oise adj & mf
middle-class (person).

bourgeon m bud.

bourgeonner vi to bud.

bourrasque f squall, gust of wind.

bourré, -ée adj (ivre) Fam wasted.

bourrer vt to stuff, to cram (**de**
with); (pipe) to fill.

bourse f (sac) purse; (d'études)
grant, scholarship; **la B.** the Stock
Exchange.

bousculade f jostling.

bousculer vt (heurter, pousser) to
jostle.

boussole f compass.

bout m end; (de langue, canne,
doigt) tip; (de papier, pain, ficelle)
piece; **un b. de temps** a little while;
au b. d'un moment after a moment;
à b. exhausted; à b. de souffle out
of breath.

bouteille f bottle; (de gaz) cylinder.

boutique f shop.

bouton m (bourgeon) bud; (au visage etc) pimple; (de vêtement, de
machine) button; (de porte, télévision) knob.

bouton-d'or, pl **boutons-d'or** m
buttercup.

boutonner vt, **se boutonner** vpr
to button (up).

boutonnière f buttonhole.

bouton-pression, pl **boutons-
pression** m snap (fastener).

box, pl **boxes** m (garage) garage fa-
cility; (de cheval) stall; (au bureau)
cubicle.

boxe f boxing.

boxer vi to box.

boxeur m boxer.

boycotter vt to boycott.

BP f abrév (boîte postale) PO Box.

bracelet m bracelet; (de montre) strap, band.

braconner vi to poach.

braconnier m poacher.

braguette f (de pantalon) fly.

brailler vti to bawl.

braise(s) f(pl) embers.

brancard m (civière) stretcher.

branchages mpl (cut) branches.

branche f (d'arbre) branch; (de compas) arm, leg.

branchement m connection.

brancher vt to plug in.

brandir vt to flourish.

branlant, -ante adj (table etc) wobbly, shaky.

braquer 1 vt (arme etc) to point (sur at). **2** vi to turn the steering wheel, to steer.

bras m arm; **b. dessus b. dessous** arm in arm; **à b. ouverts** with open arms.

brasier m blaze.

brassard m armband.

brasse f (nage) breaststroke.

brasserie f (usine) brewery; (café) brasserie.

brassière f (de bébé) undershirt.

brave adj & m brave (man).

bravement adv bravely.

bravo 1 int bravo. **2** m cheer.

bravoure f bravery.

break m (voiture) station wagon.

brebis f ewe.

brèche f gap.

bredouille adj rentrer b. to come back empty-handed.

bredouiller vti to mumble.

bref, brève 1 adj brief, short. **2** adv (enfin) b. in a word.

bretelle f strap; (d'accès) access road; **bretelles** (pour pantalon) suspenders.

breton, -onne 1 adj Breton. **2** mf B. Breton.

brevet m diploma; **b. (des collèges)** = exam at end of junior high school; **b. (d'invention)** patent.

bricolage m (passe-temps) do-it-yourself.

bricoler 1 vi to do odd jobs. **2** vt (fabriquer) to put together.

bricoleur, -euse mf handyman, handywoman.

bride f bridle.

brider vt to hold in ou back.

bridés adj avoir les yeux bridés to have slanting eyes.

brièvement adv briefly.

brièveté f shortness, brevity.

brigand m robber; (enfant) rascal.

brillamment adv brilliantly.

brillant, -ante 1 adj (luisant) shining; (astiqué) shiny; (couleur) bright; (doué) brilliant. **2** m shine; (couleur) brightness.

briller vi to shine; faire b. (meuble) to polish (up).

brin m (d'herbe) blade; (de corde, fil) strand; (de muguet) spray.

brindille f twig.

brioche f brioche (light sweet bun).

brique f brick; (de lait, jus de fruit) carton.

briquet m (cigarette) lighter.

brise f breeze.

briser vt, se briser vpr to break.

britannique 1 adj British. **2** mf B. Briton; les Britanniques the British.

broc m pitcher, jug.

brocante f (commerce) second-hand trade (in furniture etc).

brocanteur, -euse mf second-hand dealer (in furniture etc).

broche f (pour rôtir) spit; (bijou) brooch.

brochet m pike.

brochette f (tige) skewer; (plat) kebab.

brochure f brochure, booklet.

brocolis mpl broccoli.

broder vt to embroider (de with).

broderie f embroidery.

bronches fpl bronchial tubes.

bronchite f bronchitis.

bronzage m (sun)tan.

bronze m bronze.

bronzer 1 vt to tan. **2** vi to get (sun)tanned.

bronzer (se) *vpr* se (faire) b. to sunbathe, to get a (sun)tan.

brosse *f* brush; **b. à dents** toothbrush.

brosser *vt* to brush.

brosser (se) *vpr* se b. les dents/cheveux to brush one's teeth/hair.

brouette *f* wheelbarrow.

brouhaha *m* hubbub.

brouillard *m* fog; **il y a du b.** it's foggy.

brouiller *vt (œufs)* to scramble; **b. la vue à qn** to blur sb's vision.

brouiller (se) *vpr (temps)* to cloud over; *(vue)* to get blurred; *(amis)* to fall out (**avec** with).

brouillon *m* rough draft.

broussailles *fpl* bushes.

brousse *f* la b. the bush.

brouter *vti* to graze.

broyer *vt* to grind.

brugnon *m* nectarine.

bruine *f* drizzle.

bruit *m* noise, sound; *(nouvelle)* rumor; **faire du b.** to make noise.

brûlant, -ante *adj (objet, soleil)* burning (hot).

brûlé *m* odeur de b. smell of burning.

brûler *vti* to burn; **b. un feu (rouge)** to go through the lights.

brûler (se) *vpr* to burn oneself.

brûlure *f* burn.

brume *f* mist, haze.

brumeux, -euse *adj* misty, hazy.

brun, brune 1 *adj* brown; *(cheveux)* dark, brown; *(personne)* dark-haired. **2** *m (couleur)* brown. **3** *mf* dark-haired person.

brunir *vi* to turn brown; *(cheveux)* to get darker.

brushing *m* blow-dry.

brusque *adj (manière, personne)* abrupt; *(subit)* sudden.

brusquement *adv* suddenly.

brusquerie *f* abruptness.

brut *adj (pétrole)* crude; *(poids, salaire)* gross.

brutal, -e, -aux *adj (violent)* brutal; *(enfant)* rough.

brutaliser *vt* to ill-treat.

brutalité *f* brutality.

brute *f* brute.

bruyamment *adv* noisily.

bruyant, -ante *adj* noisy.

BTS *m abrév (brevet de technicien supérieur)* = advanced vocational training certificate.

bu, bue *pp of* **boire**.

bûche *f* log.

bûcheron *m* lumberjack.

bûcheur, -euse *mf Fam* grind.

budget *m* budget.

buée *f* mist.

buffet *m (armoire)* sideboard; *(table, repas)* buffet.

buisson *m* bush.

bulldozer *m* bulldozer.

bulle *f* bubble; *(de BD)* balloon.

bulletin *m (météo)* report; *(scolaire)* report card; **b. de paie** pay slip; **b. de vote** ballot paper.

bureau, -x *m (table)* desk; *(lieu)* office; **b. de change** foreign exchange office, bureau de change; **b. de tabac** tobacco store.

burette *f* oilcan.

bus *m* bus.

buste *m (torse)* chest; *(sculpture)* bust.

but *m (objectif)* aim, goal; *Sport* goal.

buté, -ée *adj* obstinate.

buter *vi* b. contre to stumble over.

butoir *m (de porte)* stop(per).

butte *f* mound.

buvard *m* blotting paper.

buvette *f* refreshment bar.

buveur, -euse *mf* drinker.

C

ça *pron dém (abrév de cela) (pour désigner)* that; *(plus près)* this; *(sujet indéfini)* it, that; **ça m'amuse que...** it amuses me that...; **où/quand/comment/etc ça?** where?/

when?/how?/*etc*; **ça va (bien)?** how's it going?; **ça va!** fine!, OK!; **ça alors!** (*surprise, indignation*) I'll be!, how about that!; **c'est ça** that's right.
cabane *f* hut, cabin; (*à outils*) shed; (*à lapins*) hutch.
cabine *f* (*de bateau*) cabin; (*téléphonique*) phone booth *ou* box; (*à la piscine*) cubicle; **c. (de pilotage)** cockpit; (*d'un grand avion*) flight deck; **c. d'essayage** fitting room.
cabinet *m* (*de médecin*) office; (*de ministre*) department; **cabinets** (*toilettes*) bathroom, men's/ladies' room; **c. de toilette** (*small*) bathroom; **c. de travail** study.
câble *m* cable; (*cordage*) rope; **la télévision par c.** cable television.
cabosser *vt* to dent.
cabrer (se) *vpr* (*cheval*) to rear (up).
cacah(o)uète *f* peanut.
cacao *m* cocoa.
cachalot *m* sperm whale.
cache-cache *m inv* hide-and-seek.
cache-nez *m inv* scarf, muffler.
cacher *vt* to hide (à from); **je ne cache pas que...** I don't hide the fact that...
cacher (se) *vpr* to hide.
cachet *m* (*de la poste*) postmark; (*comprimé*) tablet.
cacheter *vt* to seal.
cachette *f* hiding place; **en c.** in secret.
cachot *m* dungeon.
cactus *m* cactus.
cadavre *m* corpse.
caddie® *m* (supermarket) cart.
cadeau, -x *m* present, gift.
cadenas *m* padlock.
cadence *f* (*vitesse*) rate; **en c.** in time.
cadet, -ette 1 *adj* (*de deux frères etc*) younger; (*de plus de deux*) youngest. **2** *mf* (*de deux*) younger (child); (*de plus de deux*) youngest (child); (*sportif*) junior.

cadran *m* (*de téléphone*) dial; (*de montre*) face.
cadre *m* (*de photo, vélo etc*) frame; (*décor*) setting; (*sur un imprimé*) box; (*chef*) executive, manager.
cadrer 1 *vt* (*photo*) to center. **2** *vi* (*correspondre*) to tally (**avec** with).
cafard *m* (*insecte*) (cock)roach; **avoir le c.** to feel blue; **ça me donne le c.** it depresses me.
café *m* coffee; (*bar*) café; **c. au lait, c. crème** coffee with milk; **c. noir, c. nature** black coffee; **c. soluble** *ou* **instantané** instant coffee; **tasse de c.** cup of black coffee.
cafétéria *f* cafeteria.
cafetière *f* coffeepot; (*électrique*) percolator.
cage *f* cage; (*d'escalier*) well; *Sport* goal (area).
cageot *m* crate, box.
cagnotte *f* (*caisse commune*) kitty; (*de jeux*) pool.
cagoule *f* ski mask; (*de bandit, moine*) hood.
cahier *m* exercise book; **c. de brouillon** scratch pad; **c. d'appel** roll (*in school*).
cahot *m* jolt, bump.
cailler *vti* (*sang*) to clot; (*lait*) to curdle; **faire c.** (*lait*) to curdle.
caillot *m* (blood) clot.
caillou, -x *m* stone.
caisse *f* case, box; (*guichet*) cash desk; (*de supermarché*) checkout; (*tambour*) drum; **c. (enregistreuse)** till, cash register; **c. d'épargne** savings bank.
caissier, -ière *mf* cashier; (*de supermarché*) checkout assistant.
cake *m* fruit cake.
calcaire *adj* (*eau*) hard.
calciné, -ée *adj* charred.
calcul *m* calculation; (*discipline*) arithmetic.
calculatrice *f* calculator.
calculer *vt* to calculate.
cale *f* (*pour maintenir*) wedge; (*de bateau*) hold.

caleçon *m* underpants; **c. de bain** bathing trunks.

calendrier *m* calendar.

calepin *m* notebook.

caler 1 *vt (meuble etc)* to wedge; *(appuyer)* to prop (up). **2** *vti (moteur)* to stall.

calfeutrer *vt* to draftproof.

calfeutrer (se) *vpr* **se c.** *(chez soi)* to shut oneself away.

calibre *m (diamètre)* caliber; *(d'œuf)* grade.

califourchon (à) *adv* astride; **se mettre à c. sur** to straddle.

câlin, -ine 1 *adj* affectionate. **2** *m* cuddle.

calmant *m (pour la nervosité)* sedative; *(pour la douleur)* painkiller; **sous calmants** *(pour la nervosité)* under sedation; *(pour la douleur)* on painkillers.

calme 1 *adj* calm. **2** *m* calm(ness); **du c.!** keep quiet!; *(pas de panique)* keep calm!; **dans le c.** *(travailler, étudier)* in peace and quiet.

calmer *vt (douleur)* to soothe; *(inquiétude)* to calm; **c. qn** to calm sb (down).

calmer (se) *vpr* to calm down.

calomnie *f (en paroles)* slander; *(par écrit)* libel.

calorie *f* calorie.

calque *m (dessin)* tracing; **(papier-)c.** tracing paper.

camarade *mf* friend; **c. de jeu** playmate.

camaraderie *f* friendship.

cambouis *m* (dirty) oil.

cambrer (se) *vpr* to arch one's back.

cambriolage *m* burglary.

cambrioler *vt* to burglarize.

cambrioleur, -euse *mf* burglar.

camelote *f* junk.

camembert *m* Camembert (cheese).

caméra *f* (TV *ou* film) camera.

caméscope® *m* camcorder.

camion *m* truck.

camion-benne, *pl* **camions-bennes** *m* garbage truck.

camionnette *f* van.

camp *m* camp; **feu de c.** campfire; **lit de d. camp** bed; **dans mon c.** *(jeu)* on my side.

campagnard, -arde *mf* countryman, countrywoman.

campagne *f* country(side); *(électorale, militaire etc)* campaign; **à la c.** in the country.

camper *vi* to camp.

campeur, -euse *mf* camper.

camping *m* camping; *(terrain)* camp(ing) site.

camping-car *m* camper.

canadien, -ienne 1 *adj* Canadian. **2** *mf* C. Canadian.

canal, -aux *m (pour bateaux)* canal.

canalisation *f (de gaz etc)* mains.

canaliser *vt (foule)* to channel.

canapé *m (siège)* sofa, couch, settee.

canapé-lit, *pl* **canapés-lits** *m* sofa bed.

canard *m* duck.

canari *m* canary.

cancer *m* cancer.

cancéreux, -euse *mf* cancer sufferer.

candidat, -ate *mf* candidate; **être** *ou* **se porter c. à** to apply for.

candidature *f* application; *(aux élections)* candidacy; **poser sa c.** to apply (à for).

cane *f* (female) duck.

caneton *m* duckling.

canette *f (de bière)* (small) bottle.

caniche *m* poodle.

canicule *f* heatwave.

canif *m* penknife.

canine *f* canine (tooth).

caniveau, -x *m* gutter *(in street)*.

canne *f (walking) stick; **c. à pêche** fishing rod.

cannelle *f* cinnamon.

cannibale *mf* cannibal.

canoë *m* canoe; *(sport)* canoeing.

canon *m* (big) gun; *(de fusil etc)* barrel.

canot *m* boat; **c. de sauvetage** lifeboat; **c. pneumatique** rubber dinghy.

canoter *vi* to go boating.

cantine *f* canteen; *(à l'école)* cafeteria.

cantique *m* hymn.

cantonnier *m* road mender.

caoutchouc *m* rubber; **balle/etc en c.** rubber ball/etc.

CAP *m abrév (certificat d'aptitude professionnelle)* technical and vocational diploma.

cap *m (pointe de terre)* cape; *(direction)* course; **mettre le c. sur** to steer a course for.

capable *adj* capable, able; **c. de faire** able to do, capable of doing.

capacité *f* ability; *(contenance)* capacity.

cape *f* cape; *(grande)* cloak.

capitaine *m* captain.

capitale *f (lettre, ville)* capital.

capitulation *f* surrender.

capituler *vi* to surrender.

capot *m (de véhicule)* hood.

capote *f (de véhicule)* (convertible) top.

caprice *m (passing)* whim.

capricieux, -euse *adj* temperamental.

capsule *f (spatiale)* capsule; *(de bouteille)* cap.

capter *vt (signal, radio)* to pick up.

captiver *vt* to fascinate.

capture *f* capture.

capturer *vt* to capture.

capuche *f* hood.

capuchon *m* hood; *(de stylo)* cap.

car 1 *conj* because, for. **2** *m* bus, coach; **c. de police** police van.

carabine *f* rifle; **c. à air comprimé** airgun.

caractère[1] *m (lettre)* character; **petits caractères** small letters; **caractères d'imprimerie** capitals.

caractère[2] *m (tempérament, na-*ture*)* character; **avoir bon c.** to be good-natured.

caractéristique *adj & f* characteristic.

carafe *f* decanter.

carambolage *m* pileup *(of vehicles)*.

caramel *m* caramel; *(bonbon dur)* taffy.

carapace *f* shell.

caravane *f (pour camper)* trailer.

carbone *m* **(papier) c.** carbon (paper).

carbonisé, -ée *adj (nourriture)* burnt to a cinder.

carburant *m* fuel.

carburateur *m* carburetor.

carcasse *f* carcass; *(d'immeuble etc)* frame, shell.

cardiaque *adj* **être c.** to have a weak heart; **crise/problème c.** heart attack/trouble.

cardinal, -aux 1 *adj (nombre, point)* cardinal. **2** *m* cardinal.

caressant, -ante *adj* loving.

caresse *f* caress.

caresser *vt* to stroke.

cargaison *f* cargo.

cargo *m* cargo boat.

carie *f* la **c. (dentaire)** tooth decay; **une c.** a cavity.

cariée *adj f* **dent c.** decayed *ou* bad tooth.

carillon *m (cloches)* chimes; *(horloge)* chiming clock.

caritatif, -ive *adj* charitable.

carlingue *f (d'avion)* cabin.

carnaval, *pl* **-als** *m* carnival.

carnet *m* notebook; *(de timbres, chèques, adresses)* book; **c. de notes** report card.

carotte *f* carrot.

carpe *f* carp.

carpette *f* rug.

carré, -ée *adj & m* square.

carreau, -x *m (vitre)* (window) pane; *(pavé)* tile; *Cartes (couleur)* diamonds; **à carreaux** *(nappe etc)* check.

carrefour *m* crossroads.

carrelage m (sol) tiled floor.

carrément adv (dire etc) bluntly; (complètement) downright.

carrière f (terrain) quarry; (métier) career.

carrosse m (horse-drawn) carriage.

carrosserie f body(work).

carrure f build.

cartable m satchel.

carte f card; (routière) map; (menu) menu; **c. (postale)** (post)card; **c. à jouer** playing card; **c. à gratter** scratchcard; **jouer aux cartes** to play cards; **c. de visite** business card; **c. de crédit** credit card; **c. des vins** wine list; **c. grise** vehicle registration document.

carton m cardboard; (boîte) cardboard box.

cartonné adj livre c. hardback.

cartouche f cartridge; (de cigarettes) carton.

cas m case; **en tout c.** in any case; **en aucun c.** on no account; **en c. de besoin** if need be; **en c. d'accident** in the event of an accident; **en c. d'urgence** in an emergency; **au c. où elle tomberait** if she should fall; **pour le c. où il pleuvrait** in case it rains.

casanier, -ière adj stay-at-home.

cascade f waterfall; (de cinéma) stunt.

cascadeur, -euse mf stunt man, stunt woman.

case f pigeonhole; (de tiroir) compartment; (d'échiquier etc) square; (de fomulaire) box; (hutte) hut, cabin.

caserne f barracks; **c. de pompiers** fire station.

casier m pigeonhole; (fermant à clef) locker; **c. à bouteilles/à disques** bottle/record rack; **c. judiciaire** criminal record.

casino m casino.

casque m helmet; (de coiffeur) (hair)-dryer; **c. (à écouteurs)** headphones.

casqué, -ée adj helmeted.

casquette f (coiffure) cap.

casse-cou mf inv (personne) daredevil.

casse-croûte m inv snack.

casse-noisettes m inv, **casse-noix** m inv nutcracker(s).

casse-pieds mf inv (personne) Fam pain.

casser 1 vt to break; (noix) to crack; **elle me casse les pieds** Fam she's getting on my nerves. **2** vi, **se casser** vpr to break; **se c. la figure** (tomber) Fam to take a spill.

casserole f (sauce) pan.

casse-tête m inv (problème) headache; (jeu) puzzle.

cassette f (audio) cassette; (vidéo) video (cassette); **sur c.** (film) on video.

cassis m (fruit) blackcurrant; (obstacle) dip (across road).

castor m beaver.

catalogue m catalog.

catastrophe f disaster; **atterrir en c.** to make an emergency landing.

catastrophique adj disastrous.

catch m (all-in) wrestling.

catcheur, -euse mf wrestler.

catéchisme m catechism.

catégorie f category.

cathédrale f cathedral.

catholique adj & mf Catholic.

cauchemar m nightmare.

cause f cause; **à c. de** because of, on account of.

causer 1 vt (provoquer) to cause. **2** vi (bavarder) to chat (**de** about).

caution f (d'appartement) deposit; (d'un détenu) bail; (personne) guarantor; (appui) backing.

cavalier, -ière mf rider; (pour danser) partner.

cave f cellar.

caveau, -x m (burial) vault.

caverne f cave.

cavité f hollow.

CCP m abrév (compte chèque post-

al) Post Office checking account.
ce[1] (**c'** *before e and é*) *pron dém* it,
that; **c'est toi/bon**/*etc* it's *ou* that's
you/good/*etc*; **c'est mon médecin**
he's my doctor; **ce sont eux qui...**
they are the ones who...; **c'est à elle
de jouer** it's her turn to play; **est-ce
que tu viens?** are you coming? ■
ce que, ce qui what; **je sais ce qui
est bon/ce que tu veux** I know
what is good/what you want; **ce
que c'est beau!** it's so beautiful!
ce[2], **cette**, *pl* **ces** (**ce** *becomes* **cet**
before a vowel or mute h) *adj dém*
this, that, *pl* these, those; **(+ ci)** this,
pl these; **(+ là)** that, *pl* those; **cet
homme** this/that man; **cet
homme-ci** this man; **cet homme-là**
that man.
ceci *pron dém* this.
céder 1 *vt* to give up (**à** to). **2** *vi*
(*personne*) to give in (**à** to);
(*branche, chaise etc*) to give way.
cédille *f Grammaire* cedilla.
CEI *f abrév (Communauté d'États In-
dépendants)* CIS.
ceinture *f* belt; (*taille*) waist; **c. de
sécurité** seatbelt; **c. de sauvetage**
life preserver.
cela *pron dém (pour désigner)* that;
(*sujet indéfini*) it, that; **c. m'attriste
que...** it saddens me that...;
quand/comment/*etc* **c.?** when?/
how?/*etc*.
célèbre *adj* famous.
célébrer *vt* to celebrate.
célébrité *f* fame.
céleri *m (en branches)* celery.
célibataire 1 *adj* single, unmarried. **2** *m* bachelor. **3** *f* unmarried
woman.
cellophane® *f* cellophane®.
cellule *f* cell.
celui, celle, *pl* **ceux, celles** *pron
dém* the one, *pl* those, the ones; **c.
de Jean** Jean's (one); **ceux de Jean**
Jean's (ones). ■ **(+ ci)** this one, *pl*
these (ones) (*dont on vient de parler*) the latter; **(+ là)** that one, *pl*

those (ones); the former; **ceux-ci
sont gros** these (ones) are big.
cendre *f* ash.
cendrier *m* ashtray.
censé, -ée *adj* être c. faire qch to
be supposed to do sth.
censure *f (activité)* censorship;
(*comité*) board of censors. ■
censurer *vt (film)* to censor.
cent *adj & m* hundred; **c. pages** a *ou*
one hundred pages; **cinq pour c.**
five percent.
centaine *f* une c. a hundred (or so);
des centaines de hundreds of.
centenaire 1 *adj* hundred-year-
old; **être c.** to be a hundred. **2** *mf*
centenarian. **3** *m (anniversaire)*
centenary.
centième *adj & mf* hundredth.
centigrade *adj* centigrade.
centime *m* centime.
centimètre *m* centimeter; (*ruban*)
tape measure.
central, -e, -aux 1 *adj* central. **2**
m c. **(téléphonique)** (telephone)
exchange.
centrale *f (usine)* power plant.
centre *m* center; **c. commercial**
shopping mall.
centre-ville *m inv* downtown
area.
cependant *conj* however, yet.
céramique *f (matière)* ceramic;
de c. ceramic.
cerceau, -x *m* hoop.
cercle *m* circle.
cercueil *m* coffin.
céréale *f* cereal.
cérémonie *f* ceremony.
cerf *m* deer.
cerf-volant, *pl* **cerfs-volants** *m*
kite.
cerise *f* cherry.
cerisier *m* cherry tree.
cerne *m* ring.
cerner *vt* to surround; **avoir les
yeux cernés** to have rings under
one's eyes.
certain[1], **-aine** *adj (sûr)* certain,

sure; **c'est c. que tu réussiras** you're certain *ou* sure to succeed; **je suis c. de réussir** I'm certain *ou* sure I'll succeed; **être c. de qch** to be certain *ou* sure of sth.

certain², -aine *adj (difficile à fixer)* certain; **un c. temps** a certain (amount of) time.

certainement *adv* certainly.

certains *pron pl* some (people).

certificat *m* certificate.

certifier *vt* to certify.

certitude *f* certainty; **avoir la c. que** to be certain that.

cerveau, -x *m* brain; **rhume de c.** head cold.

cervelle *f* brain; *(plat)* brains.

ces *voir* **ce².**

CES *m abrév (collège d'enseignement secondaire)* = (junior) high school.

cesse *f* **sans c.** constantly.

cesser *vti* to stop; **faire c.** to put a stop to; **il ne cesse (pas) de parler** he doesn't stop talking.

cessez-le-feu *m inv* ceasefire.

c'est-à-dire *conj* that is (to say).

cet, cette *voir* **ce².**

ceux *voir* **celui.**

chacun, -une *pron* each (one), every one; *(tout le monde)* everyone.

chagrin *m* grief; **avoir du c.** to be very upset.

chahut *m* racket.

chahuter *vi* to create a racket.

chahuteur, -euse *mf* rowdy.

chaîne *f* chain; *(de télévision)* channel; *(de montagnes)* chain, range; **travail à la c.** assembly-line work; **c. hi-fi** hi-fi system.

chaînette *f* (small) chain.

chair *f* flesh; **(couleur) c.** flesh-colored; **en c. et on os** in the flesh; **la c. de poule** goose pimples *ou* bumps; **c. à saucisses** sausage meat.

chaise *f* chair; **c. longue** deckchair; **c. haute** high-chair.

châle *m* shawl.

chalet *m* chalet.

chaleur *f* heat; *(douce)* warmth.

chaleureux, -euse *adj* warm.

chaloupe *f (bateau)* launch.

chalumeau, -x *m* blowtorch.

chalutier *m* trawler.

chamailler (se) *vpr* to squabble.

chambouler *vt Fam* to make topsy-turvy.

chambre *f* (bed)room; **c. à coucher** bedroom; *(mobilier)* bedroom suite *ou* set; **c. à air** *(de pneu)* inner tube; **c. de commerce** chamber of commerce; **c. d'amis** guest room; **garder la c.** to stay indoors.

chameau, -x *m* camel.

chamois *m* peau de c. chamois.

champ *m* field; **c. de bataille** battlefield; **c. de courses** racetrack.

champagne *m* champagne.

champignon *m* mushroom.

champion, -onne *mf* champion.

championnat *m* championship.

chance *f* luck; *(probabilité, occasion)* chance; **avoir de la c.** to be lucky; **c'est une c. que** it's lucky that.

chanceler *vi* to stagger.

chanceux, -euse *adj* lucky.

chandail *m* (thick) sweater.

chandelier *m* candlestick.

chandelle *f* candle; **en c.** *(tir)* straight into the air.

change *m (de devises)* exchange.

changement *m* change.

changer *vti* to change; **c. qn en** to change sb into; **ça la changera de ne pas travailler** it'll be a change for her not to be working; **c. de train/voiture/etc** to change trains/one's car/*etc*; **c. de vitesse/sujet** to change gear/the subject.

changer (se) *vpr* to change (one's clothes).

chanson *f* song.

chant *m* singing; *(chanson)* song; **c. de Noël** Christmas carol.

chantage *m* blackmail.

chanter 1 *vi* to sing; *(coq)* to crow;

si ça te chante *Fam* if you feel like it. **2** *vt* to sing.

chanteur, -euse *mf* singer.

chantier *m* (building) site; **c. naval** shipyard, dockyard.

chantilly *f* whipped cream.

chantonner *vti* to hum.

chaos *m* chaos.

chapeau, -x *m* hat.

chapelet *m* rosary; **un c. de** *(saucisses etc)* a string of.

chapelle *f* chapel.

chapelure *f* breadcrumbs.

chapiteau, -x *m* (de cirque) big top; *(pour expositions etc)* marquee, tent.

chapitre *m* chapter.

chaque *adj* each, every.

char *m* (romain) chariot; (de carnaval) float; **c. (d'assaut)** tank.

charade *f* (énigme) riddle.

charbon *m* coal; **c. de bois** charcoal.

charcuterie *f* pork butcher's shop; *(aliments)* cooked pork meats.

charcutier, -ière *mf* pork butcher.

chardon *m* thistle.

charge *f* (poids) load; *(fardeau)* burden; **à la c. de qn** *(personne)* dependent on sb; *(frais)* payable by sb; **prendre en c.** to take charge of.

chargé, -ée *adj* (véhicule, arme etc) loaded; *(journée)* busy.

chargement *m* loading; *(objet)* load.

charger *vt* to load; *(soldats, batterie)* to charge; **c. qn de** *(travail etc)* to entrust sb with; **c. qn de faire** to instruct sb to do.

charger (se) *vpr* **se c. de** *(enfant, travail etc)* to take charge of.

chargeur *m* (pour batterie, portable) charger.

chariot *m* (à bagages etc) cart.

charité *f* (secours) charity.

charmant, -ante *adj* charming.

charme *m* charm; *(magie)* spell.

charmer *vt* to charm.

charnière *f* hinge.

charpente *f* frame(work).

charpentier *m* carpenter.

charrette *f* cart.

charrier *vt* (transporter) to cart; *(rivière)* to carry along *(sand etc)*.

charrue *f* plow.

charter *m* charter (flight).

chasse¹ *f* hunting, hunt; **c. à courre** hunting; **avion de c.** fighter plane; **faire la c. à** to hunt for.

chasse² *f* **c. d'eau** toilet flush; **tirer la c.** to flush the toilet.

chasse-neige *m inv* snowplow.

chasser 1 *vt* (animal) to hunt; *(personne, odeur)* to chase away; *(mouche)* to brush away. **2** *vi* to hunt.

chasseur, -euse *mf* hunter.

châssis *m* frame; *(d'automobile)* chassis.

chat *m* cat; **pas un c.** not a soul; **c. perché** *(jeu)* tag.

châtaigne *f* chestnut.

châtaignier *m* chestnut tree.

châtain *adj inv* (chestnut) brown.

château, -x *m* castle; *(palais)* palace; **c. fort** fortified castle; **c. d'eau** water tower.

châtiment *m* punishment.

chaton *m* kitten.

chatouiller *vt* to tickle.

chatouilleux, -euse *adj* ticklish.

chatte *f* (she-)cat.

chatterton *m* electrician's tape.

chaud, chaude 1 *adj* hot; *(doux)* warm. **2** *m* **avoir c.** to be hot; *(doux)* to be warm; **il fait c.** it's hot; **être au c.** to be in the warm.

chaudement *adv* warmly.

chaudière *f* boiler.

chauffage *m* heating.

chauffant, -ante *adj* (couverture) electric; **plaque chauffante** hot plate.

chauffard *m* reckless driver.

chauffé, -ée *adj* (piscine etc) heated.

chauffe-eau *m inv* water heater.

chauffer 1 *vt* to heat (up). **2** *vi* to heat (up); *(moteur)* to overheat.

chauffeur *m* driver; *(employé)* chauffeur.

chaume *m (pour toiture)* thatch; **toit de c.** thatched roof.

chaumière *f* thatched cottage.

chaussée *f* road(way).

chausse-pied, *pl* **chausse-pieds** *m* shoehorn.

chausser *vt* **c. qn** to put shoes on (to) sb; **c. du 40** to take a size 40 shoe.

chausser (se) *vpr* to put on one's shoes.

chaussette *f* sock.

chausson *m* slipper; *(de danse)* shoe.

chaussure *f* shoe.

chauve 1 *adj* bald. **2** *mf* bald person.

chauve-souris, *pl* **chauves-souris** *f (animal)* bat.

chauvin, -ine 1 *adj* chauvinistic. **2** *mf* chauvinist.

chaux *f* lime.

chavirer *vti* to capsize.

chef *m* leader, head; **c. d'entreprise** head of (a) company; **c. de gare** stationmaster; **c. d'orchestre** conductor; **en c.** *(commandant, rédacteur)* in chief.

chef-d'œuvre, *pl* **chefs-d'œuvre** *m* masterpiece.

chef-lieu, *pl* **chefs-lieux** *m* chief town *(of a département)*.

chemin *m* road, path; *(trajet, direction)* way; **beaucoup de c. à faire** a long way to go; **se mettre en c.** to set out.

chemin de fer *m* railroad.

cheminée *f* fireplace; *(encadrement)* mantelpiece; *(sur le toit)* chimney; *(de navire)* funnel.

cheminot *m* railroad employee.

chemise *f* shirt; *(cartonnée)* folder; **c. de nuit** *(de femme)* nightgown; *(d'homme)* nightshirt.

chemisette *f* short-sleeved shirt.

chemisier *m* blouse.

chêne *m* oak.

chenil *m* kennel.

chenille *f* caterpillar.

chèque *m* check; **c. de voyage** traveler's check.

chèque-repas, *pl* **chèques-repas** *m* meal voucher.

chéquier *m* checkbook.

cher, chère *adj (aimé)* dear (à to); *(coûteux)* expensive; **payer c.** *(objet)* to pay a lot for; *(erreur etc)* to pay dearly for.

chercher *vt* to look for; *(dans un dictionnaire)* to look up; **aller c.** to (go and) fetch *ou* get; **c. à faire** to attempt to do.

chercheur, -euse *mf* research worker.

chéri, -ie 1 *adj* dearly loved. **2** *mf* darling.

cherté *f* high cost.

chétif, -ive *adj* puny.

cheval, -aux *m* horse; **à c.** on horseback; **faire du c.** to go horseback riding; **chevaux de bois** merry-go-round.

chevalier *m* knight.

chevaline *adj f* **boucherie c.** horse butcher's (shop).

chevelure *f* (head of) hair.

chevet *m* **table/livre de c.** bedside table/book; **au c. de** at the bedside of.

cheveu, -x *m* **un c.** a hair; **cheveux** hair; **tiré par les cheveux** farfetched.

cheville *f* ankle; *(pour vis)* (wall) plug.

chèvre *f* goat.

chevreau, -x *m (petit de la chèvre)* kid.

chez *prép* **c. qn** at sb's house/apartment/etc; **il est c. Jean/c. le médecin** he's at Jean's (place)/at the doctor's; **il va c. Jean/c. le médecin** he's going to Jean's (place)/to the doctor's; **c. moi, c. nous** at home; **je vais c. moi** I'm going home; **une habitude c. elle** a habit with her; **c.**

Mme Dupont *(adresse)* care of Mme Dupont.

chic 1 *adj inv* smart; *(gentil) Fam* nice. **2** *int* c. **(alors)!** great! **3** *m* style.

chicorée *f (à café)* chicory; *(pour salade)* endive.

chien *m* dog; **un mal de c.** an awful lot of trouble; **temps de c.** rotten weather.

chien-loup, *pl* **chiens-loups** *m* wolfhound.

chienne *f* dog, bitch.

chiffon *m* rag; **c. (à poussière)** dust cloth.

chiffonner *vt* to crumple.

chiffre *m* figure, number; *(romain, arabe)* numeral; **c. d'affaires** sales.

chimie *f* chemistry.

chimique *adj* chemical.

chimpanzé *m* chimpanzee.

chinois, -oise 1 *adj* Chinese. **2** *mf* **C.** Chinese man, Chinese woman, Chinese *inv*; **les C.** the Chinese. **3** *m (langue)* Chinese.

chiot *m* puppy.

chipoter *vi (contester)* to quibble *(sur* about).

chips *mpl (potato)* chips.

chirurgical, -e, -aux *adj* surgical.

chirurgie *f* surgery.

chirurgien *m* surgeon.

choc *m (d'objets, émotion)* shock.

chocolat *m* chocolate; **c. à croquer** bittersweet chocolate; **c. au lait** milk chocolate.

chocolaté, -ée *adj* chocolate-flavored.

chœur *m (chanteurs, nef)* choir; **en c.** (all) together.

choisir *vt* to choose, to pick.

choix *m* choice; *(assortiment)* selection.

cholestérol *m* cholesterol.

chômage *m* unemployment; **au c.** unemployed.

chômer *vi* to be unemployed.

chômeur, -euse *mf* unemployed person; **les chômeurs** the unemployed.

choquant, -ante *adj* shocking.

choquer *vt* to shock.

chorale *f* choral society.

chose *f* thing; **monsieur C.** Mr What's-his-name.

chou, -x *m* cabbage; **choux de Bruxelles** Brussels sprouts.

choucroute *f* sauerkraut.

chouette 1 *f* owl. **2** *adj Fam* super, great.

chou-fleur, *pl* **choux-fleurs** *m* cauliflower.

choyer *vt* to pamper.

chrétien, -ienne *adj & mf* Christian.

chrome *m* chrome.

chromé, -ée *adj* chrome-plated.

chronique *f (à la radio)* report; *(dans le journal)* column.

chronomètre *m* stopwatch.

chronométrer *vt* to time.

chrysanthème *m* chrysanthemum.

chuchotement *m* whisper(ing).

chuchoter *vti* to whisper.

chut! *int* sh!, shush!

chute *f* fall; **c. d'eau** waterfall; **c. de neige** snowfall; **c. de pluie** rainfall.

chuter *vi (diminuer)* to fall, to drop; *(tomber) Fam* to fall.

ci 1 *adv* par-ci par-là here and there. **2** *pron dém* **comme ci comme ça** so so.

cible *f* target.

cicatrice *f* scar.

cicatrisation *f* healing (up).

cicatriser *vt,* **se cicatriser** *vpr* to heal up *(leaving a scar).*

cidre *m* cider.

Cie *abrév (compagnie)* Co.

ciel *m (pl* **ciels)** sky; *(pl* **cieux)** *(paradis)* heaven.

cierge *m* candle.

cigale *f (insecte)* cicada.

cigare *m* cigar.

cigarette *f* cigarette.

cigogne *f* stork.

ci-joint, -jointe 1 *adj* le document c. the enclosed document. **2** *adv* **vous trouverez c. copie de…** please find enclosed a copy of…

cil *m* (eye)lash.

cime *f (d'un arbre)* top; *(d'une montagne)* peak.

ciment *m* cement.

cimenter *vt* to cement.

cimetière *m* cemetery.

ciné *m Fam* movies.

cinéaste *m* movie maker.

ciné-club *m* film club.

cinéma *m (art, industrie)* movies; *(bâtiment)* movie theater; **faire du c.** to make movies.

cinéphile *mf* movie enthusiast.

cinglé, -ée *adj Fam* crazy.

cinq *adj & m* five.

cinquantaine *f* about fifty.

cinquante *adj & m* fifty.

cinquantième *adj & m* fiftieth.

cinquième *adj & mf* fifth.

cintre *m* coathanger.

cirage *m* (shoe) polish.

circonférence *f* circumference.

circonflexe *adj Grammaire* circumflex.

circonstance *f* circumstance; **pour la c.** for this occasion.

circonstanciel, -ielle *adj Grammaire* adverbial.

circuit *m (électrique, sportif etc)* circuit; *(voyage)* tour.

circulaire 1 *adj* circular. **2** *f (lettre)* circular.

circulation *f* circulation; *(automobile)* traffic.

circuler *vi* to circulate; *(véhicule, train)* to travel; *(passant)* to walk around; *(rumeur)* to go around; **faire c.** *(piétons etc)* to move on.

cire *f* wax.

ciré *m (vêtement)* oilskins.

cirer *vt* to polish.

cirque *m* circus.

ciseau, -x *m* chisel; **(une paire de) ciseaux** (a pair of) scissors.

citadin, -ine *mf* city dweller.

citation *f* quotation.

cité *f* city; **c. universitaire** (university) dormitory complex.

citer *vt* to quote.

citerne *f (réservoir)* tank.

citoyen, -enne *mf* citizen.

citoyenneté *f* citizenship.

citron *m* lemon; **c. pressé** (fresh) lemon juice.

citronnade *f* lemonade.

citrouille *f* pumpkin.

civière *f* stretcher.

civil, -e 1 *adj* civil; *(non militaire)* civilian; **année civile** calendar year. **2** *m* civilian; **en c.** *(policier)* in plain clothes.

civilisation *f* civilization.

civilisé, -ée *adj* civilized.

civique *adj* civic; **instruction c.** civics.

clair, -e 1 *adj (distinct, limpide, évident)* clear; *(éclairé)* light; *(pâle)* light(-colored); **bleu/vert c.** light blue/green. **2** *adv (voir)* clearly. **3** *m* **c. de lune** moonlight.

clairement *adv* clearly.

clairière *f* clearing.

clairon *m* bugle.

clairsemé, -ée *adj* sparse.

clairvoyant, -ante *adj* perceptive.

clandestin, -ine *adj (journal, mouvement)* underground; **passager c.** stowaway.

claque *f* smack, slap.

claquement *m (de porte)* slam(ming).

claquer 1 *vt (porte)* to slam, to bang. **2** *vi (porte)* to slam, to bang; *(coup de feu)* to ring out; **c. des mains** to clap one's hands; **elle claque des dents** her teeth are chattering.

claquer (se) *vpr* **se c. un muscle** to tear a muscle.

claquettes *fpl* tap dancing; **faire des c.** to do tap dancing.

clarinette *f* clarinet.

clarté *f* light; *(précision)* clarity.

classe f class; **aller en c.** to go to school.

classement m classification; filing; grading; *(rang)* place; *(en sport)* placing.

classer vt to classify; *(papiers)* to file; *(candidats)* to grade.

classer (se) vpr **se c. premier** to come first.

classeur m *(meuble)* filing cabinet; *(portefeuille)* (loose leaf) binder.

classique adj classical.

clavicule f collarbone.

clavier m keyboard.

clé, clef f key; *(outil)* wrench; **fermer à c.** to lock; **sous c.** under lock and key; **c. de contact** ignition key; **c. USB** memory stick.

clémentine f tangerine.

clergé m clergy.

clic m *(avec une souris)* click.

cliché m *(de photo)* negative.

client, -ente mf customer; *(d'un avocat)* client; *(d'un médecin)* patient; *(d'hôtel)* guest.

clientèle f customers; *(d'un avocat, d'un médecin)* practice.

cligner vi **c. des yeux** to blink; *(fermer à demi)* to squint; **c. de l'œil** to wink.

clignotant m *(de voiture)* turn signal.

clignoter vi to blink; *(lumière)* to flicker.

climat m climate.

climatisation f air conditioning.

climatisé, -ée adj air-conditioned.

clin d'œil m wink; **en un c.** in no time (at all).

clinique f *(private)* clinic.

cliquer vi to click (**sur** on); **c. deux fois** to double-click.

clochard, -arde mf down-and-out, tramp.

cloche f bell.

cloche-pied (à) adv **sauter à c.** to hop on one foot.

clocher m bell tower; *(en pointe)* steeple.

clochette f (small) bell.

cloison f partition.

clone m clone.

cloner vt to clone.

clope m ou f Fam smoke, cigarette.

clopin-clopant adv **aller c.** to hobble.

cloque f blister.

clos, close adj closed.

clôture f *(barrière)* fence.

clôturer vt to enclose.

clou m nail; **les clous** *(passage)* crosswalk.

clouer vt to nail; **cloué au lit** confined to bed.

clouté, -ée adj *(pneus)* studded; **passage c.** crosswalk.

clown m clown.

club m *(association)* club.

cm abrév *(centimètre)* cm.

coaguler vti, **se coaguler** vpr to clot.

coalition f coalition.

cobaye m guinea pig.

coca mf *(Coca-Cola®)* Coke®.

cocaïne f cocaine.

coccinelle f ladybug.

cocher[1] vt to tick (off), to check (off).

cocher[2] m coachman.

cochon, -onne 1 m pig; **c. d'Inde** guinea pig. **2** mf *(personne sale)* (dirty) pig.

cochonnerie f *(chose sans valeur)* trash; *(obscénité)* smutty remark; **manger des cochonneries** to eat junk food.

cocorico int & m cock-a-doodle-doo.

cocotier m coconut palm.

cocotte f casserole; **c. minute®** pressure cooker.

code m code; **codes, phares c.** low beams; **C. de la route** traffic laws.

cœur m heart; *(couleur)* Cartes hearts; **au c. de** *(ville, hiver etc)* in the middle ou heart of; **par c.**

by heart; **avoir mal au c.** to feel sick; **avoir le c. gros** to have a heavy heart; **avoir bon c.** to be kind-hearted; **de bon c.** (offrir) willingly; (rire) heartily.

coffre m chest; (de banque) safe; (de voiture) trunk.

coffre-fort, pl **coffres-forts** m safe.

coffret m (à bijoux etc) box.

cogner vti to knock, to bang.

cogner (se) vpr **se c. la tête**/etc to knock ou bang one's head/etc; **se c. à qch** to knock ou bang into sth.

cohabiter vi to live together; **c. avec qn** to live with sb.

cohérent, -ente adj (discours) coherent; (attitude) consistent.

cohue f crowd.

coiffer vt **c. qn** to do sb's hair.

coiffer (se) vpr to do one's hair.

coiffeur, -euse mf hairdresser.

coiffure f hat; (arrangement) hair-style.

coin m (angle) corner; (endroit) spot; **du c.** (magasin etc) local; **dans le c.** in the (local) area.

coincé, -ée adj stuck.

coincer vt (mécanisme etc) to jam.

coincer (se) vpr to get stuck ou jammed; **se c. le doigt** to get one's finger stuck.

coïncidence f coincidence.

coing m quince.

col m collar; (de montagne) pass; **c. roulé** turtleneck.

colère f anger; **une c.** a fit of anger; **en c.** angry (**contre** with); **se mettre en c.** to lose one's temper.

coléreux, -euse adj quick-tempered.

colique f diarrhea.

colis m parcel.

collaboration f collaboration.

collaborer vi collaborate (**à** on).

collant, -ante 1 adj (papier) sticky; (vêtement) skin-tight. **2** m pantyhose; (opaque) tights; (de danse) leotard.

colle f glue; (blanche) paste.

collecte f (quête) collection.

collectif, -ive adj collective; **billet c.** group ticket.

collection f collection.

collectionner vt to collect.

collectionneur, -euse mf collector.

collectivité f (groupe) community.

collège m = (junior) high school.

collégien, -enne mf = (junior) high school student.

collègue mf colleague.

coller vt to stick; (à la colle transparente) to glue; (à la colle blanche) to paste; (affiche) to stick up; (papier peint) to hang; (mettre) Fam to stick; **c. contre** (nez, oreille etc) to press against.

collier m (bijou) necklace; (de chien) collar.

colline f hill.

collision f collision; **entrer en c. avec** to collide with.

colocataire mf roommate.

colombe f dove.

colonel m colonel.

colonie f colony; **c. de vacances** summer camp.

colonne f column; **c. vertébrale** spine.

coloré, -ée adj colorful; (verre, liquide) colored.

colorer vt to color.

coloriage m album de coloriages coloring book.

colorier vt (dessin) to color (in).

coloris m (nuance) shade.

colosse m giant.

colza m (plante) rape.

coma m coma; **dans le c.** in a coma.

combat m fight.

combatif, -ive adj eager to fight; (instinct, esprit) fighting.

combattant m fighter, brawler.

combattre* vti to fight.

combien 1 adv (quantité) how much; (nombre) how many; **c. de** (temps, argent etc) how much;

(gens, livres etc) how many. ■ *(à quel point)* how; **c. y a-t-il d'ici à…?** how far is it to…? **2** *m inv* **le c. sommes-nous?** *Fam* what is the date?; **tous les c.?** *Fam* how often?

combinaison *f* combination; *(vêtement de femme)* slip; *(de mécanicien)* overalls; **c. de vol/plongée/ski** flying/diving/ski suit; **c. spatiale** spacesuit.

combiné *m (de téléphone)* receiver.

combiner *vt (assembler)* to combine.

comble 1 *m* **le c. de** *(la joie etc)* the height of; **c'est un ou le c.!** that's the limit! **2** *adj (bondé)* packed.

combler *vt (trou etc)* to fill; **c. son retard** to make up lost time.

combustible *m* fuel.

comédie *f* comedy; **c. musicale** musical; **jouer la c.** to put on an act, to pretend.

comédien *m* actor.

comédienne *f* actress.

comestible *adj* edible.

comique *adj (amusant)* funny; *(acteur etc)* comic.

comité *m* committee.

commandant *m (d'un navire)* captain; **c. de bord** *(d'un avion)* captain.

commande *f (achat)* order; **sur c.** to order; **les commandes** *(d'un avion etc)* the controls.

commandement *m (autorité)* command.

commander 1 *vt* to command; *(acheter)* to order. **2** *vi* **c. à qn de faire** to command sb to do.

comme 1 *adv & conj* like; **c. moi** like me; **c. cela** like that; **qu'as-tu c. vins?** what kind of wines do you have? ■ as; **blanc c. neige** (as) white as snow; **c. si** as if; **c. pour faire** as if to do; **c. par hasard** as if by chance. **2** *adv (exclamatif)* **regarde c. il pleut!** look how (hard) it's raining!; **c. c'est petit!** how

small it is! **3** *conj (temps, cause)* as; **c. elle entrait** as she was coming in.

commencement *m* beginning, start.

commencer *vti* to begin, to start (**à faire** to do, doing; **par** with; **par faire** by doing; **pour c.** to begin with.

comment *adv* how; **c. le sais-tu?** how do you know?; **c.?** *(répétition, surprise)* what?; **c. est-il?** what is he like?; **c. faire?** what's to be done?; **c. t'appelles-tu?** what's your name?; **c. allez-vous?** how are you?

commentaire *m (remarque)* comment; *(de radio, de télévision)* commentary.

commerçant, -ante *mf* merchant; **rue commerçante** shopping street.

commerce *m* trade, commerce; *(magasin)* store, business; **dans le c.** *(objet)* (on sale) in stores.

commercial, -e, -aux *adj* commercial.

commère *f* gossip.

commettre* *vt (délit etc)* to commit; *(erreur)* to make.

commissaire *m* **c. (de police)** police chief.

commissariat *m* **c. (de police)** (central) police station.

commission *f (course)* errand; *(pourcentage)* commission (**sur** on); **faire les commissions** to go shopping, to run the errands.

commode 1 *adj (pratique)* handy. **2** *f* chest of drawers, dresser.

commun, -une *adj (collectif, habituel etc)* common; *(frais, cuisine)* shared; **ami c.** mutual friend; **en c.** in common; **avoir ou mettre en c.** to share.

communautaire *adj (de la CE)* Community; **vie c.** community life.

communauté *f (collectivité)* community; **la C.** *(économique)* **européenne** the European (Economic) Community; **la C. des États in-**

dépendants the Commonwealth of Independent States.

commune f commune.

communication f communication; **c. (téléphonique)** (telephone) call.

communier vi to receive (Holy) Communion.

communion f (Holy) Communion.

communiqué m (official) statement; (publicitaire) message; **c. de presse** press release.

communiquer vti to communicate.

communiste adj & mf communist.

compact, -e adj dense.

compagne f friend; (épouse) companion.

compagnie f (présence, société) company; **tenir c. à qn** to keep sb company.

compagnon m companion; **c. de jeu** playmate; **c. de travail** co-worker.

comparable adj comparable.

comparaison f comparison (avec with).

comparaître* vi (devant tribunal) to appear (**devant** before).

comparer vt to compare (**à** to, with).

compartiment m compartment.

compas m compass.

compatir vi to sympathize.

compatriote mf compatriot.

compenser 1 vt to compensate for. **2** vi to compensate.

compétence f competence.

compétent, -ente adj competent.

compétition f competition; (épreuve sportive) event; **de c.** (esprit, sport) competitive.

complaisance f kindness.

complaisant, -ante adj kind.

complément m Grammaire complement.

complet, -ète 1 adj complete;

(train, hôtel etc) full; (aliment) whole. **2** m suit.

complètement adv completely.

compléter vt to complete; (somme) to make up.

complexe 1 adj complex. **2** m (sentiment, construction) complex.

complication f complication.

complice m accomplice.

compliment m compliment; **mes compliments!** congratulations!

complimenter vt to compliment (**sur, pour** on).

compliqué, -ée adj complicated.

compliquer vt to complicate.

compliquer (se) vpr to get complicated.

complot m plot.

comploter vti to plot (**de faire** to do).

comportement m behavior.

comporter (se) vpr to behave; (joueur, voiture) to perform.

composé, -ée adj & m (mot, en chimie etc) compound; **temps c.** compound tense; Grammaire **passé c.** perfect (tense).

composer vt to make up, to compose; (numéro) to dial; **être composé de** to be made up ou composed of.

composer (se) vpr se **c. de** to be made up ou composed of.

compositeur, -trice mf composer.

composter vt (billet) to cancel.

compote f sauce; **c. de pommes** applesauce.

compréhensible adj understandable.

compréhensif, -ive adj (personne) understanding.

comprendre* vt to understand; (comporter) to include; **je n'y comprends rien** I don't understand anything about it.

comprendre (se) vpr **ça se comprend** that's understandable.

comprimé m tablet.

comprimer *vt* to compress.

compris, -ise *adj (inclus)* included (**dans** in); **tout c.** (all) inclusive; **y c.** including.

compromettre* *vt (personne)* to compromise; *(sécurité)* to jeopardize.

comptabilité *f (comptes)* accounts; *(science)* bookkeeping, accounting; *(service)* accounts department.

comptable *mf* bookkeeper; *(expert)* accountant.

comptant 1 *adj* **argent c.** (hard) cash. **2** *adv* **payer c.** to pay (in) cash.

compte *m* account; *(calcul)* count; *(nombre)* (right) number; **avoir un c. en banque** to have a bank(ing) account; **c. courant** checking account; **c. à rebours** countdown; **tenir c. de** to take into account; **c. tenu de** considering; **se rendre c. de** to realize; **à son c.** *(travailler)* for oneself; *(s'installer)* on one's own; **en fin de c.** all things considered.

compte-gouttes *m inv* dropper; *Fig* **au c.** a little at a time.

compter 1 *vt (calculer)* to count; **c. faire** to expect to do; *(avoir l'intention de)* to intend to do; **c. qch à qn** *(facturer)* to charge sb for sth. **2** *vi (calculer, avoir de l'importance)* to count; **c. sur** to rely on.

compte rendu *m* report; *(de livre, film)* review.

compteur *m* meter; **c. (de vitesse)** speedometer; **c. (kilométrique)** odometer.

comptoir *m (de magasin)* counter; *(de café)* bar; *(de bureau)* (reception) desk.

comte *m* count.

comtesse *f* countess.

concentré, -ée 1 *adj (lait)* condensed; *(attentif)* concentrating (hard). **2** *m* **c. de tomates** tomato purée.

concentrer *vt*, **se concentrer** *vpr* to concentrate.

concerner *vt* to concern.

concert *m* concert.

concerter (se) *vpr* to consult each other.

concessionnaire *mf* (authorized) dealer.

concevoir *vt* to conceive.

concierge *mf* caretaker, janitor.

concitoyen, -enne *mf* fellow citizen.

conclure* *vti* to conclude (**que** that).

conclusion *f* conclusion.

concombre *m* cucumber.

concordant, -ante *adj* in agreement.

concorder *vi* to agree; **c. avec** to match.

concours *m (examen)* competitive examination; *(jeu)* competition; **c. hippique** horse show.

concret, -ète *adj* concrete.

concrétiser *vt (rêve)* to realize; *(projet)* to carry out.

conçu, -ue *adj* **c. pour faire/pour qn** designed to do/for sb; **bien c.** *(maison etc)* well designed.

concubinage *m* cohabitation; **vivre en c.** to cohabit.

concurrence *f* competition; **faire c. à** to compete with.

concurrencer *vt* to compete with.

concurrent, -ente *mf* competitor.

condamnation *f* sentence; *(censure)* condemnation.

condamné, -ée *mf* condemned man/woman.

condamner *vt* to condemn; *(accusé)* to sentence (**à** to); *(porte)* to block up; **c. à une amende** to fine.

condition *f* condition; **conditions** *(clauses, tarifs)* terms; **à c. de faire, à c. que l'on fasse** providing *ou* provided (that) one does.

conditionné *adj* à air c. *(pièce etc)* air-conditioned.

conditionnel *m Grammaire* conditional.

condoléances *fpl* sympathy.

conducteur, -trice *mf* driver.

conduire* *vt (voiture)* to lead; *(voiture)* to drive; *(eau)* to carry; **c. qn à** *(accompagner)* to take sb to.

conduire (se) *vpr* to behave.

conduite *f* behavior; *(de voiture)* driving (**de** of); *(d'eau, de gaz)* main.

cône *m* cone.

confection *f* making (**de** of); **vêtements de c.** ready-to-wear clothes.

confectionner *vt* to make.

conférence *f* conference.

confesser *vt*, **se confesser** *vpr* to confess.

confession *f* confession.

confettis *mpl* confetti.

confiance *f* trust; **faire c. à qn, avoir c. en qn** to trust sb; **c. en soi** (self-)confidence.

confiant, -ante *adj* trusting; *(sûr de soi)* confident.

confidence *f (secret)* confidence; **faire une c. à qn** to confide in sb.

confidentiel, -ielle *adj* confidential.

confier *vt* **c. qch à qn** *(enfant, objet)* to give sb sth to take care of; **c. un secret/etc à qn** to confide a secret/etc to sb.

confier (se) *vpr* **se c. à qn** to confide in sb.

confirmation *f* confirmation.

confirmer *vt* to confirm (**que** that).

confiserie *f* candy store; **confiseries** *(produits)* candy.

confiseur, -euse *mf* confectioner.

confisquer *vt* to confiscate (**à qn** from sb).

confit *adj* **fruits confits** candied fruit.

confiture *f* jelly.

conflit *m* conflict.

confondre *vt (choses, personnes)* to mix up, to confuse; **c. avec** to mistake for.

conformément *adv* **c. à** in accordance with.

confort *m* comfort.

confortable *adj* comfortable.

confrère *m* colleague.

confus, -use *adj* confused; *(gêné)* embarrassed; **je suis c.!** *(désolé)* I'm terribly sorry!

confusion *f* confusion; *(gêne, honte)* embarrassment.

congé *m (vacances)* vacation; **c. de maladie** sick leave; **congés payés** paid vacation.

congélateur *m* freezer, deep-freeze.

congeler *vt* to freeze.

congère *f* snowdrift.

congrès *m* congress.

conjoint *m* spouse.

conjonction *f Grammaire* conjunction.

conjoncture *f* circumstances.

conjugaison *f* conjugation.

conjugal, -e, -aux *adj (bonheur)* marital; *(vie)* married; *(devoir)* conjugal.

conjuguer *vt (verbe)* to conjugate.

connaissance *f* knowledge; *(personne)* acquaintance; **connaissances** knowledge (**en** of); **faire la c. de qn, faire c. avec qn** to meet sb; **perdre c.** to lose consciousness; **sans c.** unconscious.

connaître *vt* to know; *(rencontrer)* to meet; **nous nous connaissons déjà** we've met before; **s'y c. à** *ou* **en qch** to know (all) about sth.

connu, -ue *(pp of* connaître*) adj (célèbre)* well-known.

conquérant, -ante *mf* conqueror.

conquérir* *vt* to conquer.

conquête *f* conquest; **faire la c. de** to conquer.

consacrer *vt (temps, vie etc)* to devote (**à** to).

FAIRE CONNAISSANCE

Bonjour, comment ça va?
Hello, how are you?

Salut, ça va ?
Hi, how's it going?

Bien, merci, et vous ?
Fine thank you, how are you?

Ça va, et toi ?
Good, and you?

Bonjour.
Good morning/afternoon.

Bonsoir.
Good evening.

Comment vous appelez-vous ?/
Comment t'appelles-tu ?
What's your name?

Je m'appelle Marie.
My name's Marie.

Je m'appelle Paul, et voici Nicole,
ma femme.
I'm Paul and this is my wife Nicole.

Enchanté(e).
Pleased to meet you.

Quel âge avez-vous/as-tu ?
How old are you?

J'ai quinze/vingt-cinq ans.
I'm 15/25 (years old).

D'où venez-vous/viens-tu?
Where are you from?

Je viens de France./Je suis français(e).
I'm from France./I'm French.

Où habitez-vous/habites-tu ?
Where do you live?

J'habite près de Bordeaux.
I live near Bordeaux.

Que faites-vous/fais-tu dans la vie ?
What do you do?

Je suis professeur/étudiant(e).
I'm a teacher/a student.

Je suis au lycée.
I'm in high school.

Je suis mère au foyer.
I'm a stay-at-home mom.

Je travaille dans les assurances.
I work for an insurance company.

Je suis à la retraite.
I'm retired.

Vous avez/Tu as des frères et des sœurs ?
Do you have any brothers and sisters?

J'ai une sœur aînée et deux petits frères.
I've got an older sister and two little brothers.

Vous avez/Tu as des enfants ?
Do you have kids?

Nous avons un fils de trois ans qui
s'appelle Luc.
We have a three-year-old son named Luc.

Est-ce que vous êtes/tu es marié(e) ?
Are you married?

Je suis divorcé(e)/séparé(e)/veuf (veuve).
I'm divorced/separated/widowed.

Que faites-vous pendant votre temps
libre ?/
Qu'est-ce que tu fais pendant ton temps
libre ?
What do you do in your spare time?

J'aime lire/aller au cinéma.
I like reading/going to the movies.

Je joue au basket/fais du yoga.
I play basketball/do yoga.

Je suis des cours de français.
I'm taking French classes.

À bientôt/plus tard !
See you soon/later!

Bon weekend/voyage !
Have a good weekend/trip!

Nous devrions garder le contact, voici mon adresse e-mail.
We should keep in touch, here's my e-mail address.

consacrer (se) *vpr* se c. à to devote oneself to.

conscience *f (psychologique)* consciousness; *(morale)* conscience; **avoir/prendre c. de** to be/become conscious *ou* aware of; **c. professionnelle** conscientiousness.

consciencieux, -euse *adj* conscientious.

conscient, -ente *adj* c. de aware of.

conseil[1] *m* un c. a piece of advice; **des conseils** advice.

conseil[2] *m (assemblée)* council; **c. d'administration** board of directors; **c. des ministres** *(réunion)* cabinet meeting.

conseiller *vt* to advise; **c. qch à qn** to recommend sth to sb; **c. à qn de faire** to advise sb to do.

conseiller, -ère *mf (expert)* consultant, adviser; *(d'un conseil)* councilor; **c. municipal** city councilman/councilwoman.

consentement *m* consent.

consentir* *vi* c. à to consent to.

conséquence *f* consequence.

conservation *f* preservation.

conservatoire *m* school *(of music, drama)*.

conserve *f* conserves canned food; **de** *ou* **en c.** canned; **mettre en c.** to can.

conserver *vt* to keep; *(fruits, vie, tradition etc)* to preserve.

conserver (se) *vpr (aliment)* to keep.

considérable *adj* considerable.

considération *f (respect)* regard, esteem; **prendre qch en c.** to take sth into consideration.

considérer *vt* to consider (**que** that; **comme** to be).

consigne *f (instruction)* orders; *(de gare)* baggage check; *(somme)* deposit; **c. automatique** baggage lockers.

consigner *vt (bouteille etc)* to charge a deposit on.

consistant, -ante *adj (sauce etc)* thick; *(repas)* solid.

consister *vi* c. en/dans to consist of/in; **c. à faire** to consist in doing.

consolation *f* comfort.

console *f* console.

consoler *vt* to comfort, to console (**de** for).

consoler (se) *vpr* se c. de *(la mort de qn etc)* to get over.

consolider *vt* to strengthen.

consommateur, -trice *mf* consumer; *(au café)* customer.

consommation *f* consumption; *(boisson)* drink.

consommer 1 *vt (aliment etc)* to consume. **2** *vi (au café)* to drink; **c. beaucoup/peu** *(véhicule)* to get good/bad mileage.

consonne *f* consonant.

conspirateur, -trice *mf* conspirator.

conspiration *f* plot.

conspirer *vi* to plot (**contre** against).

constamment *adv* constantly.

constat *m* (official) report.

constatation *f* observation.

constater *vt* to note, to observe (**que** that); *(enregistrer)* to record.

consternation *f* distress.

consterner *vt* to distress.

constipé, -ée *adj* constipated.

constituer *vt (composer)* to make up; *(représenter)* to represent; **constitué de** made up of.

constituer (se) *vpr* se c. prisonnier to give oneself up.

constitution *f* constitution; *(composition)* composition.

constructeur *m (bâtisseur)* builder; *(fabricant)* maker (**de** of); **c. automobile** car manufacturer.

construction *f* construction; **matériaux/jeu de c.** construction materials/set.

construire* *vt* to build.

consul *m* consul.

consulat *m* consulate.

consultation f consultation; **cabinet de c.** (doctor's) office.

consulter vt, **se consulter** vpr to consult.

contact m contact; *(toucher)* touch; *(de voiture)* ignition; **être en c. avec** to be in touch ou contact with; **entrer en c. avec** to come into contact with; **mettre/couper le c.** *(dans une voiture)* to turn on/off the ignition; **lentilles** ou **verres de c.** contact lenses.

contacter vt to contact.

contagieux, -euse adj contagious, infectious.

contagion f infection.

conte m tale; **c. de fée** fairy tale.

contempler vt to gaze at.

contemporain, -aine adj & mf contemporary.

contenance f *(d'un récipient)* capacity.

contenir* vt to contain; *(avoir comme capacité)* to hold.

content, -ente adj pleased, happy (**de faire** to do; **de qn/qch** with sb/sth); **c. de soi** self-satisfied.

contenter vt to satisfy, to please.

contenter (se) vpr **se c. de** to be content ou happy with.

contenu m *(de récipient)* contents.

conter vt *(histoire etc)* to tell.

contestable adj debatable.

contestataire mf protester.

contestation f protest.

contesté, -ée adj *(théorie, dirigeant)* controversial.

contester 1 vi *(étudiants etc)* to protest. **2** vt to protest against.

conteur, -euse mf storyteller.

contexte m context.

continent m continent; *(opposé à une île)* mainland.

continu, -ue adj continuous.

continuel, -elle adj continual.

continuellement adv continually.

continuer 1 vt to continue, to carry on (**à** ou **de faire** doing). **2** vi to continue, to go on.

contour m outline.

contourner vt *(colline etc)* to go around.

contraceptif, -ive adj & m contraceptive.

contracter vt, **se contracter** vpr to contract.

contractuel, -elle mf parking enforcement officer.

contradiction f contradiction.

contradictoire adj contradictory; *(théories)* conflicting.

contraindre* vt to compel (**à faire** to do).

contrainte f compulsion.

contraire 1 adj opposite; **c. à** contrary to. **2** m opposite; **au c.** on the contrary.

contrairement adv **c. à** contrary to.

contrariant, -ante adj *(action etc)* annoying; *(personne)* difficult.

contrarier vt *(projet etc)* to spoil; *(personne)* to annoy.

contrariété f annoyance.

contraste m contrast.

contrat m contract.

contravention f *(pour stationnement interdit)* (parking) ticket.

contre prép & adv against; *(en échange de)* (in exchange) for; **échanger c.** to exchange for; **fâché c.** angry with; **six voix c. deux** six votes to two; **Nîmes c. Arras** *(match)* Nîmes versus Arras; **un médicament c.** *(toux etc)* medicine for; **par c.** on the other hand; **tout c.** qch/qn close to sth/sb.

contre- préfixe counter-.

contre-attaque f counterattack.

contrebande f *(fraude)* smuggling; **de c.** *(tabac etc)* smuggled; **passer qch en c.** to smuggle sth.

contrebandier, -ière mf smuggler.

contrebas (en) adv & prép (down) below; **en c. de** below.

contrebasse f *(instrument)* double bass.

contrecarrer vt to thwart.

contrecœur (à) *adv* reluctantly.

contrecoup *m* repercussions.

contredire* *vt* to contradict.

contredire (se) *vpr* **se c.** to contradict oneself.

contrefaçon *f (pratique)* counterfeiting; *(produit)* fake.

contre-jour (à) *adv* against the (sun)light.

contremaître *m* foreman.

contre-plaqué *m* plywood.

contretemps *m* hitch.

contribuable *mf* taxpayer.

contribuer *vi* to contribute (**à** to).

contribution *f* contribution; *(impôt)* tax.

contrôle *m* inspection, check(ing) (**de** of); *(des prix, de la qualité)* control; *(maîtrise)* control.

contrôleur, -euse *mf (de train)* conductor; *(au quai)* ticket collector; *(de bus)* conductor.

contrordre *m* change of orders.

contusion *f* bruise.

convaincant, -ante *adj* convincing.

convaincre* *vt* to convince (**de** of); **c. qn de faire** to persuade sb to do.

convaincu, -ue *adj (certain)* convinced (**de** of).

convalescence *f* convalescence; **être en c.** to convalesce.

convalescent, -ente 1 *mf* convalescent. **2** *adj* **être c.** to convalesce.

convenable *adj* suitable; *(correct)* decent.

convenablement *adv* suitably; decently.

convenir* *vi* **c. à** *(être fait pour)* to be suitable for; *(plaire à, aller à)* to suit; **ça convient** *(date etc)* that's suitable, that suits me/us/*etc.*

convention *f (accord)* agreement; *(règle)* convention.

convenu, -ue *adj (prix etc)* agreed.

conversation *f* conversation.

convertir *vt* to convert (**à** to; **en** into).

conviction *f (certitude)* conviction.

convive *mf* guest *(at table)*.

convivial, -e, -aux *adj* convivial; *(système informatique)* user-friendly.

convocation *f (lettre)* (written) notice to attend.

convoi *m (véhicules)* convoy.

convoquer *vt* to summon (**à** to).

coopération *f* cooperation.

coopérer *vi* to cooperate (**à** in; **avec** with).

coordonnées *fpl (adresse, téléphone)* contact details.

copain *m Fam (camarade)* pal; *(petit ami)* boyfriend; **être c. avec** to be pals with.

copeau, -x *m (de bois)* shaving.

copie *f* copy; *(devoir, examen)* paper.

copier *vti* to copy (**sur** from).

copieux, -euse *adj* plentiful.

copine *f Fam (camarade)* pal; *(petite amie)* girlfriend; **être c. avec** to be pals with.

copropriété *f* **(immeuble en) c.** condominium.

coq *m* rooster.

coque *f (de navire)* hull; *(de noix)* shell; *(fruit de mer)* cockle; **œuf à la c.** soft-boiled egg.

coquelicot *m* poppy.

coqueluche *f* whooping cough.

coquet, -ette *adj (chic)* stylish, chic.

coquetier *m* egg cup.

coquetterie *f (élégance)* style, elegance.

coquillage *m (mollusque)* shellfish; *(coquille)* shell.

coquille *f* shell; **c. Saint-Jacques** scallop.

coquin, -ine *adj* mischievous.

cor *m (instrument)* horn; *(au pied)* corn.

corail, -aux *m* coral.

Coran m le C. the Koran.

corbeau, -x m crow.

corbeille f basket; **c. à papier** waste paper basket.

corbillard m hearse.

corde f rope; (plus mince) cord; (de raquette, violon etc) string; **c. à linge** clothesline; **c. à sauter** jump rope.

cordial, -e, -aux adj warm.

cordon m (de tablier, sac etc) string; (de rideau) cord.

cordon-bleu, pl **cordons-bleus** m cordon-bleu cook.

cordonnerie f shoe repair shop.

cordonnier m shoe repairman.

coriace adj tough.

corne f (de chèvre etc) horn; (de cerf) antler; (matière, instrument) horn.

corneille f crow.

cornet m (de glace) cornet, cone; **c. (de papier)** (paper) cone.

cornichon m (concombre) pickle.

corps m body; **lutter c. à c.** to fight hand-to-hand; **prendre c.** (projet) to take shape.

correct, -e adj (exact, décent) correct.

correctement adv correctly.

correcteur, -trice 1 adj verres correcteurs corrective lenses. **2** mf (d'examen) examiner; (en typographie) proofreader. **3** m **c. d'orthographe** spellchecker.

correction f correction; (punition) beating; (exactitude, décence) correctness; **la c. de** (devoirs, examen) the marking of.

correspondance f correspondence; (de train, d'autocar) connection, transfer.

correspondant, -ante 1 adj corresponding. **2** mf (d'un adolescent etc) pen pal; (au téléphone) caller.

correspondre vi to correspond (à to, with); (écrire) to correspond (avec with).

corrida f bullfight.

corriger vt to correct; (devoir) to mark; **c. qn de** (défaut) to cure sb of.

corrompu, -ue adj corrupt.

corsage m (chemisier) blouse.

cortège m procession; **c. officiel** (automobiles) motorcade.

corvée f chore.

cosmonaute mf cosmonaut.

cosmos m (univers) cosmos; (espace) outer space.

cosse f (de pois etc) pod.

costaud, -aude adj Fam brawny.

costume m (déguisement) costume; (complet) suit.

costumé adj bal c. costume ball.

côte f side; (de mouton) chop; (de veau) cutlet; (montée) hill; (littoral) coast; **c. à c.** side by side.

côté m side; (direction) way; **de l'autre c.** on the other side (**de** of); (direction) the other way; **du c. de** (vers, près de) towards; **de c.** (mettre de l'argent etc) to one side; (regarder) sideways; **à c.** nearby; (pièce) in the other room; (maison) next door; **à c. de** next to, beside; (comparaison) compared to; **à mes côtés** by my side.

coteau, -x m (small) hill.

côtelette f (d'agneau, de porc) chop; (de veau) cutlet.

côtier, -ière adj coastal.

cotisation f (de club) dues.

cotiser vi (à un cadeau, pour la retraite) to contribute (**à** to; **pour** towards).

cotiser (se) vpr to club together (**pour acheter** to buy).

coton m cotton; **c. (hydrophile)** absorbent cotton.

cou m neck.

couchage m sac de c. sleeping bag.

couchant adj (soleil) setting.

couche f (épaisseur) layer; (de peinture) coat; (linge de bébé) diaper.

couché, -ée adj être c. to be in

bed; *(étendu)* to be lying (down).
couche-culotte, *pl* **couches-culottes** *f* disposable diaper.
coucher 1 *vt* to put to bed; *(héberger)* to put up; *(allonger)* to lay (down *ou* out). **2** *vi* to sleep (**avec** with).
coucher (se) *vpr* to go to bed; *(s'allonger)* to lie flat *ou* down; *(soleil)* to set.
couchette *f (de train)* sleeper, sleeping berth; *(de bateau)* bunk.
coucou *m (oiseau)* cuckoo; *(fleur)* cowslip.
coude *m* elbow; **se serrer les coudes** to help one another; **c. à c.** side by side; **coup de c.** nudge; **pousser du c.** to nudge.
coudre* *vti* to sew.
couette *f* duvet, down comforter.
couler¹ *vi (eau etc)* to flow; *(robinet, nez, sueur)* to run; *(fuir)* to leak.
couler² *vti (bateau, nageur)* to sink.
couleur *f* color; *Cartes* suit; **couleurs** *(teint)* color; **de c.** colored; **photo/etc en couleurs** color photo/etc; **téléviseur c. ou en couleurs** color TV set.
couleuvre *f* (grass) snake.
coulisses *fpl* **dans les c.** in the wings, backstage.
couloir *m* corridor; *(de circulation, d'une piste)* lane.
coup *m* blow, knock; *(léger)* tap; *(choc moral)* blow; *(de fusil etc)* shot; *(de crayon, d'horloge)* stroke; *(aux échecs etc)* move; *(fois)* *Fam* time; **donner des coups à** to hit; **c. de brosse** brush(-up); **c. de chiffon** wipe (with a rag); **c. de sonnette** ring (on a bell); **c. de dents** bite; **c. de chance** stroke of luck; **tenter le c.** *Fam* to give it a try; **tenir le c.** to hold out; **sous le c. de** *(émotion)* under the influence of; **après c.** afterwards; **tué sur le c.** killed outright; **à c. sûr** for sure; **tout à c., tout d'un c.** suddenly; **d'un seul c.** all at once; **du c.** *(de ce fait)* as a result.

coupable 1 *adj* guilty (**de** of). **2** *mf* guilty person, culprit.
coupant, -ante *adj* sharp.
coupe *f (trophée)* cup; *(à boire)* goblet; *(de vêtement etc)* cut; **c. de cheveux** haircut.
coupe-ongles *m inv* (fingernail) clippers.
coupe-papier *m inv* letter opener.
couper 1 *vt* to cut; *(arbre)* to cut down; *(téléphone)* to cut off; *(courant etc)* to switch off; *(morceler)* to cut up; *(croiser)* to cut across; **c. la parole à qn** to cut sb short. **2** *vi* to cut; **ne coupez pas!** *(au téléphone)* hold on!
couper (se) *vpr (routes)* to intersect; **se c. au doigt** to cut one's finger.
couple *m* pair, couple.
couplet *m* verse.
coupure *f* cut; *(de journal)* clipping; **c. d'électricité** blackout, power outage.
cour *f* court(yard); *(de roi)* court; **c. (de récréation)** playground.
courage *m* courage; **bon c.!** good luck!
courageux, -euse *adj* courageous.
couramment *adv (parler)* fluently; *(souvent)* frequently.
courant, -ante 1 *adj (fréquent)* common; *(eau)* running; *(modèle, taille)* standard. **2** *m (de l'eau, électrique)* current; **c. d'air** draft; **coupure de c.** blackout, power outage; **être/mettre au c.** to know/tell (**de** about).
courbature *f* ache; **avoir des courbatures** to be aching (all over).
courbaturé, -ée *adj* aching (all over).
courbe 1 *adj* curved. **2** *f* curve.
courber *vti* to bend.
coureur *m* runner; *(cycliste)* cyclist; *(automobile)* racecar driver.
courgette *f* zucchini.

courir* 1 *vi* to run; *(se hâter)* to rush; *(à bicyclette, en auto)* to race; **le bruit court que...** there's a rumor going around that... 2 *vt (risque)* to run; *(épreuve sportive)* to run (in); *(danger)* to face.

couronne *f* crown; *(de fleurs)* wreath.

couronnement *m (de roi etc)* coronation.

couronner *vt* to crown.

courriel *m Can* e-mail.

courrier *m* mail; **c. électronique** e-mail.

courroie *f* strap; *(de transmission)* belt.

cours *m* course; *(d'une monnaie etc)* rate; *(leçon)* class; *(série de leçons)* course; **c. d'eau** river, stream; **en c.** *(travail)* in progress; *(année)* current; **en c. de route** on the way; **au c. de** during.

course[1] *f (action)* run(ning); *(épreuve de vitesse)* race; **courses** *(de chevaux)* races; **cheval de c.** racehorse; **voiture de c.** racecar.

course[2] *f (commission)* errand; **courses** *(achats)* shopping; **faire une c.** to run an errand; **faire les courses** to go shopping.

coursier, -ière *mf* messenger.

court, courte 1 *adj* short. 2 *adv (couper, s'arrêter)* short; **à c. de** *(argent etc)* short of. 3 *m Tennis* court.

court-circuit, *pl* **courts-circuits** *m* short-circuit.

couscous *m* couscous.

cousin, -ine *mf* cousin.

coussin *m* cushion.

coût *m* cost; **le c. de la vie** the cost of living.

couteau, -x *m* knife.

coûter *vti* to cost; **ça coûte combien?** how much does it cost?; **coûte que coûte** at all costs.

coûteux, -euse *adj* costly, expensive.

coutume *f* custom; **avoir c. de**

faire to be accustomed to doing.

couture *f* sewing; *(métier)* dressmaking; *(raccord)* seam.

couturier *m* fashion designer.

couturière *f* dressmaker.

couvée *f (oiseaux)* brood.

couvent *m* convent.

couver 1 *vt (œufs)* to sit on. 2 *vi (poule)* to brood.

couvercle *m* lid, cover.

couvert *m (set of)* cutlery; **mettre le c.** to set *ou* lay the table.

couvert, -erte *adj* covered (**de** with, in); *(de ciel)* overcast.

couverture *f (de lit)* blanket; *(de livre etc)* cover.

couveuse *f* incubator.

couvrir* *vt* to cover (**de** with).

couvrir (se) *vpr (s'habiller)* to wrap up; *(ciel)* to cloud over.

cow-boy *m* cowboy.

crabe *m* crab.

crachat *m* spit, spittle.

cracher 1 *vi* to spit. 2 *vt* to spit (out).

crachin *m (fine)* drizzle.

craie *f* chalk.

craindre* *vt* to be afraid of, to fear; *(chaleur, froid)* to be sensitive to; **c. de faire** to be afraid of doing; **ne craignez rien** don't be afraid.

crainte *f* fear.

craintif, -ive *adj* timid.

crampe *f* cramp.

cramponner (se) *vpr* **se c. à** to hold on to, to cling to.

crampons *mpl (de chaussures)* cleats.

cran *m (entaille)* notch; *(de ceinture)* hole; **couteau à c. d'arrêt** switchblade; **c. de sûreté** safety catch.

crâne *m* skull.

crapaud *m* toad.

craquement *m* snapping *ou* cracking (sound).

craquer *vi (branche)* to snap; *(bois sec)* to crack; *(sous la dent)* to crunch; *(se déchirer)* to split, to rip;

(personne) to break down.
crasse *f* filth.
crasseux, -euse *adj* filthy.
cratère *m* crater.
cravate *f* tie.
crawl *m (nage)* crawl.
crayon *m* pencil; **c. de couleur** colored pencil; *(en cire)* crayon; **c. à bille** ballpoint (pen).
crayonner *vt* to pencil.
créancier, -ière *mf* debtor.
création *f* creation; **1000 créations d'emplois** 1000 new jobs.
créature *f* creature.
crèche *f (de Noël)* crib; *(pour bébé)* daycare (center).
crédit *m* credit; **à c.** on credit; **faire c.** *(prêter)* to give credit (**à** to).
créditeur *adj* **compte c.** account in credit.
créer *vt* to create.
crémaillère *f* **pendre la c.** to have a house-warming (party).
crématorium *m* crematorium.
crème *f* cream; *(dessert)* cream dessert; **c. Chantilly** whipped cream; **c. glacée** ice cream; **c. à raser** shaving cream; **c. anglaise** custard sauce.
créneau, -x *m* **faire un c.** to parallel park.
crêpe *f* pancake, crepe.
crépiter *vi* to crackle.
crépu, -ue *adj* frizzy.
crépuscule *m* twilight, dusk.
cresson *m* (water)cress.
crête *f (de montagne etc)* crest.
creuser *vt* to dig.
creuser (se) *vpr* **se c. la tête** to rack one's brains.
creux, -euse 1 *adj* hollow; *(estomac)* empty; **assiette creuse** soup plate. **2** *m* hollow; *(de l'estomac)* pit.
crevaison *f (de pneu)* flat.
crevasse *f (trou)* crevice.
crevé, -ée *adj (fatigué) Fam* worn out; *(mort) Fam* dead.
crever 1 *vi (bulle etc)* to burst; *(pneu)* to go flat; *(mourir) Fam* to

die. **2** *vt* to burst; *(œil)* to put out.
crevette *f (grise)* shrimp; *(rose)* prawn.
cri *m (de joie, surprise)* cry, shout; *(de peur)* scream; *(de douleur)* cry; *(appel)* call, cry.
cric *m (de voiture)* jack.
crier 1 *vi* to shout (out), to cry (out); *(de peur)* to scream; **c. après qn** *Fam* to shout at sb. **2** *vt (injure, ordre)* to shout (out).
crime *m* crime; *(assassinat)* murder.
criminel, -elle 1 *adj* criminal. **2** *mf* criminal; *(assassin)* murderer.
crinière *f* mane.
crise *f* crisis; *(accès)* attack; *(de colère etc)* fit; **c. cardiaque** heart attack.
crisper *vt (visage)* to make tense; *(poing)* to clench.
cristal, -aux *m* crystal.
critique 1 *adj* critical. **2** *f (reproche)* criticism.
critiquer *vt* to criticize.
croc *m (dent)* fang.
croche-pied *m* **faire un c. à qn** to trip sb up.
crochet *m* hook; *(aiguille)* crochet hook; *(travail)* crochet; **faire qch au c.** to crochet sth; **faire un c.** *(personne)* to make a detour.
crochu, -ue *adj (nez)* hooked.
crocodile *m* crocodile.
croire* 1 *vt* to believe; *(estimer)* to think, to believe (**que** that); **j'ai cru la voir** I thought I saw her. **2** *vi* to believe (**à, en** in).
croisement *m (de routes)* crossroads.
croiser *vt (jambes, ligne etc)* to cross; **c. qn** to pass *ou* meet sb.
croiser (se) *vpr (voitures etc)* to pass (each other); *(routes)* to cross.
croisière *f* cruise.
croissance *f* growth.
croissant, -ante 1 *adj (nombre)* growing. **2** *m* crescent; *(pâtisserie)* croissant.

croix f cross.

croque-monsieur m inv = toasted cheese and ham sandwich.

croquer vti to crunch.

croquis m sketch.

crosse f (de fusil) butt.

crotte f (de lapin etc) droppings, dung.

crottin m (horse) dung.

crouler vi (édifice) to crumble; **c. sous le travail** to be snowed under with work.

croustillant, -ante adj (pain) crusty.

croustiller vi to be crusty.

croûte f (de pain etc) crust; (de fromage) rind; (de plaie) scab.

croûton m crust (at end of loaf).

croyant, -ante 1 adj être c. to be a believer. **2** mf believer.

CRS abrév mpl (Compagnies républicaines de sécurité) riot police.

cru¹, crue pp of **croire**.

cru², crue adj (aliment etc) raw.

cruauté f cruelty (envers to).

cruche f pitcher, jug.

crudités fpl assorted raw vegetables.

cruel, -elle adj cruel (envers, avec to).

crustacés mpl shellfish.

cube 1 m cube; **cubes** (jeu) building blocks. **2** adj (mètre etc) cubic.

cueillette f picking; (fruits cueillis) harvest.

cueillir* vt to pick.

cuiller, cuillère f spoon; **petite c., c. à café** teaspoon; **c. à soupe** soup spoon, tablespoon.

cuillerée f spoonful; **c. à café** teaspoonful; **c. à soupe** tablespoonful.

cuir m leather.

cuire* 1 vt to cook; (à l'eau) to boil; **c. (au four)** to bake; (viande) to roast. **2** vi to cook; (à l'eau) to boil; (au four) to bake; (viande) to roast; **faire c.** to cook.

cuisine f (pièce) kitchen; (art, aliments) cooking; **faire la c.** to cook,

to do the cooking; **livre de c.** cook book.

cuisiner vti to cook.

cuisinier, -ière 1 mf cook. **2** f (appareil) stove, range.

cuisse f thigh; (de poulet) leg.

cuisson m cooking.

cuit, cuite (pp of **cuire**) adj cooked; **bien c.** well done.

cuivre m (rouge) copper; (jaune) brass.

culbute f (saut) somersault; (chute) (backward) tumble.

culbuter vi to tumble over (backwards).

cul-de-sac, pl **culs-de-sac** m dead end.

culot m (d'ampoule, de lampe) base; (audace) Fam nerve.

culotte f (de femme) (pair of) panties; **culottes (courtes)** knickers.

culpabiliser vt **c. qn** to make sb feel guilty.

culte m (de dieu) worship; (religion) form of worship.

cultivateur, -trice mf farmer.

cultivé, -ée adj (personne) cultivated.

cultiver vt (terre) to farm; (plantes) to grow.

cultiver (se) upr to improve one's mind.

culture f culture; (agriculture) farming; (de légumes) growing.

culturel, -elle adj cultural.

cupide adj avaricious.

cure f (course of) treatment, cure.

curé m (parish) priest.

cure-dent m toothpick.

curer vt (fossé etc) to clean out.

curieux, -euse 1 adj (bizarre) curious; (indiscret) inquisitive, curious (de about). **2** mf inquisitive person; (badaud) onlooker.

curiosité f curiosity.

curriculum (vitae) m inv résumé.

curseur m (d'ordinateur) cursor.

cuve f (réservoir) tank.

cuvette f (récipient) basin, bowl; (des toilettes) bowl.

CV m abrév (curriculum vitae) résumé.

cycle m (série) cycle.

cyclisme m cycling.

cycliste mf cyclist; **course c.** cycling ou bicycle race; **champion c.** cycling champion.

cyclomoteur m moped.

cyclone m cyclone.

cygne m swan.

cylindre m cylinder.

cylindrée f (engine) capacity.

cylindrique adj cylindrical.

cymbale f cymbal.

cyprès m (arbre) cypress.

D

dactylo f (personne) typist; (action) typing.

daim m fallow deer; (cuir) suede.

dallage m paving.

dalle f paving stone.

dallé, -ée adj paved.

dame f lady; (mariée) married lady; Échecs, Cartes queen; (au jeu de dames) king; **(jeu de) dames** checkers.

damier m checkerboard.

dandiner (se) vpr to waddle.

danger m danger; **en d.** in danger; **mettre en d.** to endanger; **en cas de d.** in an emergency; **en d. de mort** in peril of death; **'d. de mort'** (panneau) 'danger'; **être sans d.** to be safe.

dangereusement adv dangerously.

dangereux, -euse adj dangerous (**pour** to).

danois, -oise 1 adj Danish. **2** mf **D.** Dane. **3** m (langue) Danish.

dans prép in; (changement de lieu) into; (à l'intérieur de) inside; **entrer d.** to go in(to); **boire/prendre/etc d.** to drink/take/etc from ou out of; **d. deux jours/etc (temps futur)** in two days/etc; **d. les dix euros/etc** about ten euros/etc.

danse f dance; (art) dancing.

danser vti to dance.

danseur, -euse mf dancer.

date f date; **en d. du...** dated the...; **d. d'expiration** expiry date; **d. limite** deadline.

dater 1 vt (lettre etc) to date. **2** vi **d. de** to date from; **à d. de** as from.

datte f (fruit) date.

dauphin m dolphin.

davantage adv (quantité) more; (temps) longer; **d. de temps/etc** more time/etc; **d. que** more than; longer than.

de¹ (**d'** before a vowel or mute h; **de + le = du, de + les = des**) prép (complément d'un nom) of; **les rayons du soleil** the rays of the sun; **le livre de Paul** Paul's book; **un pont de fer** an iron bridge; **une augmentation d'impôts/etc** an increase in taxes/etc. ▪ (complément d'un adjectif) **digne de** worthy of; **heureux de** happy to; **content de qch/qn** pleased with sth/sb. ▪ (complément d'un verbe) **parler de** to speak of ou about; **décider de faire** to decide to do. ▪ (provenance: lieu & temps) from; **mes amis du village** my friends from the village. ▪ (agent) **accompagné de** accompanied by. ▪ (moyen) **armé de** armed with; **se nourrir de** to live on. ▪ (manière) **d'une voix douce** in ou with a gentle voice. ▪ (cause) **mourir de faim** to die of hunger. ▪ (temps) **travailler de nuit** to work by night; **six heures du matin** six o'clock in the morning. ▪ (mesure) **avoir ou faire six mètres de haut** to be 20 feet high; **homme de trente ans** thirty-year-old man; **ga-**

LA DATE ET L'HEURE

On est quel jour aujourd'hui ?
What day is it today?

On est vendredi.
It's Friday.

On est le combien aujourd'hui ?
What's today's date?

On est le quinze avril deux mille huit.
It's April 15th, 2008.

On est le mercredi douze avril.
It's Wednesday April 12th.

Demain c'est jeudi.
It's Thursday tomorrow.

Je suis né(e) en mille neuf cent quatre-vingt.
I was born in 1980.

Je suis venu(e) à Paris il y a quelques années.
I came to Paris a few years ago.

Vous restez jusqu'à quand ?
How long are you staying?

Nous partons dimanche/le huit.
We leave on Sunday/the 8th.

Nous sommes arrivés le weekend dernier.
We got here last weekend.

J'ai attendu toute la journée.
I waited all day.

À samedi !
See you on Saturday!

À la semaine prochaine !
See you next week!

Prenez-le trois fois par jour.
Take it three times a day.

Je les vois toutes les deux semaines.
I see them every two weeks.

Quelle heure est-il ?
What's the time?

Il est deux heures.
It's 2 o'clock.

Il est presque midi/minuit.
It's nearly midday/midnight.

Il est quatre heures et demie/quatre heures trente.
It's half past four/four-thirty.

Il est sept heures moins le quart.
It's a quarter to seven.

Il est sept heures vingt.
It's twenty after seven.

Je me lève à 6h.
I get up at 6 a.m.

Je me couche à 22h.
I go to bed at 10 p.m.

Je serai là vers huit heures.
I'll be there about eight.

On se retrouve dans une demi-heure.
I'll meet you in half an hour.

Mon avion a eu deux heures de retard.
My plane was two hours late.

Je suis en avance/en retard/à l'heure.
I'm early/late/on time.

Je n'ai pas le temps (de...).
I don't have time (to...).

C'est l'heure de partir.
It's time to go.

gner quinze euros de l'heure to earn fifteen euros an hour.

de² *art partitif* some; **elle boit du vin** she drinks (some) wine; **il ne boit pas de vin** *(négation)* he doesn't drink (any) wine; **des fleurs** (some) flowers; **de jolies fleurs** (some) pretty flowers; **il y en a six de tués** *(avec un nombre)* there are six dead.

dé *m* *(à jouer)* dice; *(à coudre)* thimble; **jouer aux dés** to play dice.

déballer *vt* to unpack.

débarbouiller (se) *vpr* to wash one's face.

débarquement *m* *(de passagers)* landing; *(de marchandises)* unloading.

débarquer 1 *vt* *(passagers)* to land; *(marchandises)* to unload. **2** *vi* *(passagers)* to land.

débarras *m* storeroom; **bon d.!** *Fam* good riddance!

débarrasser *vt* *(table etc)* to clear (**de** of); **d. qn de** *(ennemi, soucis etc)* to rid sb of; *(manteau etc)* to relieve sb of.

débarrasser (se) *vpr* **se d. de** to get rid of.

débat *m* discussion, debate.

débattre* *vt* to discuss, to debate.

débattre (se) *vpr* to struggle (to get free).

débile 1 *adj* *(esprit, enfant etc)* weak; *Fam* idiotic. **2** *mf Fam* idiot.

débit *m* *(vente)* sales; *(compte)* debit; *(de fleuve)* flow; **d. de boissons** bar, café.

débiter *vt* *(découper)* to cut up (**en** into); *(vendre)* to sell; *(compte)* to debit.

débiteur, -trice 1 *mf* debtor. **2** *adj* **compte d.** debit account.

déblayer *vt* *(terrain, décombres)* to clear.

débloquer *vt* *(mécanisme)* to unjam; *(crédits)* to release.

déboîter 1 *vt* *(tuyau)* to disconnect; *(os)* to dislocate. **2** *vi* *(véhi-*

cule) to pull out, to change lanes.

déborder 1 *vi* *(fleuve, liquide)* to overflow; **l'eau déborde du vase** the water is overflowing the vase. **2** *vt* *(dépasser)* to go beyond; **débordé de travail** snowed under with work.

débouché *m* *(carrière)* opening; *(marché pour produit)* outlet.

déboucher *vt* *(bouteille)* to open, to uncork; *(lavabo, tuyau)* to unclog.

débourser *vti* to pay out.

debout *adv* standing (up); **mettre d.** *(planche etc)* to stand up, to put upright; **se mettre d.** to stand *ou* get up; **rester d.** to remain standing; **être d.** *(levé)* to be up; **d.!** get up!

déboutonner *vt* to unbutton, to undo.

débraillé, -ée *adj* *(tenue etc)* slovenly, sloppy.

débrancher *vt* to unplug, to disconnect.

débrayer *vi* *(conducteur)* to depress the clutch.

débris *mpl* fragments; *(restes)* remains; *(détritus)* garbage.

débrouillard, -arde *adj* smart, resourceful.

débrouiller (se) *vpr* to manage (**pour faire** to do).

début *m* start, beginning; **au d.** at the beginning.

débutant, -ante *mf* beginner.

débuter *vi* to start, to begin.

décaféiné, -ée *adj* decaffeinated.

décalage *m* *(écart)* gap; **d. horaire** time difference.

décalcomanie *f* *(image)* decal.

décaler *vt* to shift.

décalquer *vt* *(dessin)* to trace.

décapant *m* cleaning agent; *(pour enlever la peinture)* paint stripper.

décaper *vt* *(métal)* to clean; *(surface peinte)* to strip.

décapiter *vt* to behead.

décapotable *adj (voiture)* convertible.

décapsuler *vt* d. une bouteille to take the top off a bottle.

décapsuleur *m* bottle-opener.

décéder *vi* to die.

déceler *vt (trouver)* to detect.

décembre *m* December.

décemment *adv* decently.

décennie *f* decade.

décent, -ente *adj (convenable)* decent.

déception *f* disappointment.

décerner *vt (prix)* to award.

décès *m* death.

décevant, -ante *adj* disappointing.

décevoir* *vt* to disappoint.

déchaîné, -ée *adj (foule)* wild.

déchaîner *vt* d. les rires to cause an outburst of laughter; d. la colère to arouse anger.

déchaîner (se) *vpr (tempête, rires)* to break out; *(foule)* to run riot; *(personne)* to fly into a rage.

décharge *f* d. (publique) (garbage) dump; d. (électrique) (electric) shock.

déchargement *m* unloading.

décharger *vt* to unload; *(batterie)* to discharge.

décharger (se) *vpr (batterie)* to go dead.

déchausser (se) *vpr* to take one's shoes off.

déchet *m* déchets *(restes)* waste; il y a du d. there's some waste.

déchiffrer *vt* to decipher.

déchiqueter *vt* to tear to shreds.

déchirer *vt (page etc)* to tear (up); *(vêtement)* to tear; *(ouvrir)* to tear open.

déchirer (se) *vpr (robe etc)* to tear.

déchirure *f* tear.

décidé, -ée *adj (air, ton)* determined; d. à faire determined to do.

décidément *adv* undoubtedly.

décider 1 *vt (opération)* to decide on; d. que to decide that. **2** *vi* d. de faire to decide to do.

décider (se) *vpr* se d. à faire to make up one's mind to do.

décimal, -e, -aux *adj* decimal.

décimètre *m* decimeter; **double d.** ruler.

décisif, -ive *adj* decisive.

décision *f* decision; *(fermeté)* determination.

déclaration *f* declaration; *(de vol etc)* notification; *(commentaire)* statement; d. de revenus tax return.

déclarer *vt* to declare (que that); *(vol etc)* to notify.

déclarer (se) *vpr (incendie)* to break out.

déclencher *vt (mécanisme, réaction)* to trigger, to start (off); *(attaque)* to launch.

déclencher (se) *vpr (alarme etc)* to go off.

déclic *m (bruit)* click.

déclin *m* decline; être en d. to be in decline.

décoiffer *vt* d. qn to mess up sb's hair.

décollage *m (d'avion)* takeoff.

décoller 1 *vi (avion)* to take off. **2** *vt (timbre)* to unstick.

décoller (se) *vpr* to come unstuck.

décolleté, -ée 1 *adj (robe)* lowcut. **2** *m (de robe)* low neckline.

décolorer (se) *vpr* to fade.

décombres *mpl* rubble.

décongeler 1 *vt* (faire) d. *(aliment)* to thaw. **2** *vi* to thaw.

déconseiller *vt* d. qch à qn to advise sb against sth; d. à qn de faire to advise sb against doing.

décontracté, -ée *adj (ambiance, personne)* relaxed; *(vêtement)* casual.

décontracter (se) *vpr* to relax.

décor *m (théâtre, paysage)* scenery; *(d'intérieur)* decoration.

décorateur, -trice *mf* (interior) decorator.

décoratif, -ive *adj* decorative.

décoration *f* decoration.

décorer *vt* (*maison, soldat*) to decorate (**de** with).

découdre *vt* to unstitch.

découdre (se) *vpr* to come unstitched.

découpage *m* (*image*) cutout.

découper *vt* (*viande*) to carve; (*article*) to cut out.

découragement *m* discouragement.

décourager *vt* to discourage.

décourager (se) *vpr* to get discouraged.

découvert *m* (*d'un compte*) overdraft.

découverte *f* discovery.

découvrir (se) *vpr* (*dans son lit*) to push the bedcovers off; (*ciel*) to clear (up); (*enlever son chapeau*) to remove one's hat.

décrasser *vt* (*nettoyer*) to clean.

décrire* *vt* to describe.

décroché *adj* (*téléphone*) off the hook.

décrocher *vt* (*détacher*) to unhook; (*tableau*) to take down; **d. (le téléphone)** to pick up the phone.

décrocher (se) *vpr* (*tableau*) to fall down.

décrotter *vt* to clean (the mud off).

déçu, -ue (*pp of* décevoir) *adj* disappointed.

déculotter (se) *vpr* to take off one's pants.

dédaigner *vt* to scorn, to despise.

dédaigneux, -euse *adj* scornful.

dédain *m* scorn.

dedans 1 *adv* inside; **en d.** on the inside; **tomber d.** (*trou*) to fall in (it); **je me suis fait rentrer d.** (*accident de voiture*) someone crashed into me. **2** *m* **le d.** the inside.

dédommagement *m* compensation.

dédommager *vt* to compensate (**de** for).

déduction *f* deduction.

déduire* *vt* (*soustraire*) to deduct (**de** from).

déesse *f* goddess.

défaillance *f* (*évanouissement*) fainting fit; (*faiblesse*) weakness; (*panne*) failure; **avoir une d.** (*s'évanouir*) to faint; (*faiblir*) to feel weak.

défaire* *vt* (*nœud etc*) to undo.

défaire (se) *vpr* to come undone.

défait *adj* (*lit*) unmade.

défaite *f* defeat.

défaut *m* (*faiblesse*) fault; (*de fabrication*) defect.

défavorable *adj* unfavorable (**à** to).

défavorisé, -ée *adj* (*milieu*) underprivileged.

défavoriser *vt* to put at a disadvantage.

défectueux, -euse *adj* faulty, defective.

défendre¹ *vt* (*protéger*) to defend.

défendre² *vt* (*interdire*) **d. à qn de faire** to forbid sb to do; **d. qch à qn** to forbid sb sth.

défendre (se) *vpr* to defend oneself.

défense¹ *f* (*protection*) defense; (*d'éléphant*) tusk.

défense² *f* (*interdiction*) **'d. de fumer'** 'no smoking'; **'d. (absolue) d'entrer'** '(strictly) no entry'.

défenseur *m* defender.

défi *m* challenge; **lancer un d. à qn** to challenge sb.

déficitaire *adj* (*budget*) in deficit; (*entreprise*) loss-making; (*compte*) in debit.

défier *vt* to challenge (**à** to); **d. qn de faire** to challenge sb to do.

défiguré, -ée *adj* disfigured.

défilé *m* (*militaire*) parade; (*gorge*) pass.

défiler *vi* (*soldats*) to march.

définir *vt* to define; **article défini** *Grammaire* definite article.

définitif, -ive *adj* final, definitive.

définition *f* definition; (*de mots croisés*) clue.

définitivement adv (partir, exclure) for good.

défoncé, -ée adj (route) bumpy; (drogué) Fam high.

défoncer vt (porte, mur) to smash in, to knock down; (trottoir, route) to dig up.

déformé, -ée adj misshapen; **chaussée déformée** uneven road surface, bumpy road.

déformer vt to put out of shape.

déformer (se) vpr to lose its shape.

défouler (se) vpr to let off steam.

défricher vt (terrain) to clear.

défroisser vt to smooth out.

défunt, -unte 1 adj (mort) departed; **mon d. mari** my late husband. **2** mf **le d., la défunte** the deceased.

dégagé, -ée adj (ciel) clear.

dégagement m (action) clearing; Football kick (down the field); **itinéraire de d.** alternative route (to ease traffic congestion).

dégager 1 vt (table etc) to clear (de of); (odeur) to give off; **d. qn de** (décombres etc) to pull sb out of. **2** vi Football to clear the ball (down the field); **dégagez!** get lost!

dégager (se) vpr (ciel) to clear; **se d. de** (personne) to pull oneself free from (rubble); (odeur) to come out of (room).

dégainer vti (arme) to draw.

dégarni, -ie adj bare; **front d.** receding hairline.

dégarnir vt (arbre de Noël) to take down the decorations from.

dégarnir (se) vpr (crâne) to go bald.

dégâts mpl damage.

dégel m thaw.

dégeler vti to thaw (out).

dégivrer vt (réfrigérateur) to defrost.

déglingué, -ée adj falling to pieces.

dégonfler vt (pneu) to deflate.

dégonfler (se) vpr (pneu) to deflate; (se montrer lâche) Fam to chicken out.

dégouliner vt to trickle.

dégourdi, -ie 1 adj (malin) smart. **2** mf smart boy/girl.

dégourdir (se) vpr se **d. les jambes** to stretch one's legs.

dégoût m disgust; **avoir du d. pour qch** to have a (strong) dislike for sth.

dégoûtant, -ante adj disgusting.

dégoûté, -ée adj disgusted (de with, by); **il n'est pas d.** (difficile) he's not fussy.

dégoûter vt to disgust; **d. qn de qch** to (be enough to) make sb sick of sth.

dégrader (se) vpr (situation) to deteriorate.

degré m (angle, température) degree.

dégringolade f tumble.

dégringoler vi to tumble (down).

déguerpir vi to clear out, to make tracks.

dégueulasse adj Fam disgusting.

déguisement m disguise; (de bal costumé) costume.

déguiser vt to disguise; **d. qn (en)** (costumer) to dress sb up (as).

déguiser (se) vpr to dress oneself up (en as).

déguster vt (goûter) to taste.

dehors 1 adv out(side); **en d.** on the outside; **en d. de la maison** outside the house; **en d. de la ville** out of town; **au-d. (de), au d. (de)** outside. **2** m (extérieur) outside.

déjà adv already; **elle l'a d. vu** she's seen it before, she's already seen it; **quand partez-vous, d.?** when did you say you were leaving?

déjeuner 1 vi (à midi) to have lunch; (le matin) to have breakfast. **2** m lunch; **petit d.** breakfast.

delà adv **au-d. (de), au d. (de)** beyond.

délabré, -ée adj dilapidated.

délacer vt (chaussures) to undo, to untie.

délai m time limit; **sans d.** without delay; **dernier d.** final date.

délasser (se) vpr to relax.

délayer vt (mélanger) to mix (with liquid).

délégation f delegation.

délégué, -ée mf delegate.

délibérer vi (se consulter) to deliberate (**de** about).

délicat, -ate adj (santé, travail) delicate; (geste) tactful; (exigeant) particular.

délicatement adv (doucement) delicately.

délicatesse f (tact) tact.

délice m delight.

délicieux, -euse adj (plat) delicious.

délier vt to undo.

délier (se) vpr (paquet) to come undone.

délimiter vt (terrain) to mark off.

délinquant, -ante mf delinquent.

délirer vi (dire n'importe quoi) to rave.

délit m offense.

délivrer vt (prisonnier) to release, to (set) free; (billet) to issue.

déloger vt to drive out.

deltaplane® m hang glider.

déluge m flood; (de pluie) downpour.

demain adv tomorrow; **à d.!** see you tomorrow!

demande f request (**de qch for** sth); **demandes d'emploi** positions wanted.

demander vt to ask for; (nécessiter) to require; **d. le chemin/l'heure** to ask the way/the time; **d. qch à qn** to ask sb for sth; **d. à qn de faire** to ask sb to do; **ça demande du temps** it takes time; **être très demandé** to be in great demand.

demander (se) vpr to wonder (**pourquoi** why; **si** if).

demandeur, -euse mf d. d'emploi job seeker.

démangeaison f itch; **avoir des démangeaisons** to be itching.

démanger vti to itch; **son bras le démange** his arm itches.

démaquillant m cleanser.

démaquiller (se) vpr to take off one's make-up.

démarche f walk; **faire des démarches** to go through the process (**pour faire** of doing).

démarrage m start.

démarrer vi (moteur) to start (up); (voiture) to move off.

démarreur m starter.

démasquer vt to expose.

démêler vt (cheveux) to untangle.

déménagement m move, moving; **camion de d.** moving van.

déménager vi to move.

déménageur m mover.

démesuré, -ée adj excessive.

démettre (se) vpr se d. le pied/etc to dislocate one's foot/etc.

demeure f (belle maison) mansion.

demeurer vi (aux être) (rester) to remain; (aux avoir) (habiter) to live.

demi, -ie 1 adj half; **une heure et demie** an hour and a half; (horloge) half past one. **2** adv (**à**) **d. plein**/etc half-full/etc. **3** m (verre) (half-pint) glass of beer.

demi-cercle m semicircle.

demi-douzaine f une d. (de) half a dozen.

demi-finale f semifinal.

demi-frère m stepbrother.

demi-heure f une d. a half-hour, half an hour.

demi-journée f half-day.

demi-pension f breakfast and one meal.

demi-pensionnaire mf day student.

démission f resignation.

démissionner vt to resign.

demi-sœur f stepsister.

demi-tarif *adj inv (billet)* half-price.

demi-tour *m (en voiture)* U-turn; **faire d.** *(à pied)* to turn back; *(en voiture)* to make a U-turn.

démocratie *f* democracy.

démocratique *adj* democratic.

démodé, -ée *adj* old-fashioned.

demoiselle *f (célibataire)* single woman; **d. d'honneur** *(à un mariage)* bridesmaid.

démolir *vt (maison)* to demolish, to knock down.

démolition *f* demolition.

démonstratif, -ive *adj & m Grammaire* demonstrative.

démonstration *f* demonstration, proof.

démonter *vt (mécanisme)* to take apart; *(tente)* to take down.

démonter (se) *vpr* to come apart, to come down.

démontrer *vt* to show.

démoraliser *vt* to demoralize.

démoraliser (se) *vpr* to become demoralized.

déneiger *vt* to clear of snow.

dénicher *vt (trouver)* to dig up.

dénombrer *vt* to count.

dénoncer *vt* **d. qn** *(au professeur)* to tell on sb (à to).

dénoncer (se) *vpr* to own up (à to).

dénouement *m (de livre)* ending; *(de pièce de théâtre)* dénouement; *(d'affaire)* outcome.

dénouer *vt (corde)* to undo, to untie.

dénouer (se) *vpr (nœud)* to come undone ou untied.

denrées *fpl* **d. alimentaires** foods.

dense *adj* dense.

dent *f* tooth *(pl* teeth); *(de fourchette)* prong; **faire ses dents** *(enfant)* to be teething; **coup de d.** bite.

dentaire *adj* dental.

dentelle *f* lace.

dentier *m* (set of) false teeth.

dentifrice *m* toothpaste.

dentiste *mf* dentist.

déodorant *m* deodorant.

dépannage *m* (emergency) repair.

dépanner *vt (voiture)* to repair.

dépanneur *m (de télévision)* repairman; *(de voiture)* roadside mechanic.

dépanneuse *f (voiture)* tow truck.

départ *m* departure; *(d'une course)* start; **ligne de d.** starting post; **au d.** at the start.

départager *vt* to decide between.

département *m* department.

départementale *adj f* **route d.** secondary road.

dépassé, -ée *adj (démodé)* outdated; *(incapable)* unable to cope.

dépasser 1 *vt (véhicule)* to overtake; **d. qn** *(en hauteur)* to be taller than sb; *(surclasser)* to be ahead of sb. **2** *vi (clou etc)* to stick out.

dépêcher (se) *vpr* to hurry (up).

dépeigné, -ée *adj* **être d.** to have untidy hair.

dépendre *vi* to depend (**de** on, upon).

dépense *f (frais)* expense.

dépenser *vt (argent)* to spend.

dépenser (se) *vpr* to exert oneself.

dépensier, -ière *adj* wasteful.

dépilatoire *adj* **crème d.** hair-removing cream.

dépister *vt (criminel)* to track down; *(maladie)* to detect.

dépit *m* **en d. de** in spite of; **en d. du bon sens** *(mal)* atrociously.

déplacé, -ée *adj (mal à propos)* out of place.

déplacement *m (voyage)* (business) trip.

déplacer *vt* to shift, to move.

déplacer (se) *vpr (voyager)* to travel (around).

déplaire* *vi* **ça me déplaît** I don't like it.

dépliant *m (prospectus)* leaflet.

déplier *vt*, **se déplier** *vpr* to unfold.

déplorable *adj* regrettable, deplorable.

déplorer *vt (regretter)* to deplore; **d. que** (+ *subjonctif*) to regret that.

déployer *vt (ailes)* to spread.

déporter *vt (dévier)* to carry (off course).

déposer *vt (poser)* to put down; *(laisser)* to leave; *(plainte)* to lodge; *(ordures)* to dump; **d. qn** *(en voiture)* to drop sb (off).

déposer (se) *vpr (poussière)* to settle.

dépôt *m (d'ordures)* dump; *(dans une bouteille)* deposit.

dépotoir *m* garbage dump.

dépouillé, -ée *adj (arbre)* bare.

dépression *f* depression; **d. nerveuse** nervous breakdown.

déprimé, -ée *adj* depressed.

déprimer *vt* to depress.

depuis 1 *prép* since; **d. lundi** since Monday; **d. qu'elle est partie** since she left; **j'habite ici d. un mois** I've been living here for a month; **d. quand êtes-vous là?** how long have you been here?; **d. Paris** from Paris. **2** *adv* since (then).

député *m (à l'Assemblée Nationale)* = Congressman, Congresswoman.

déraciner *vt (arbre)* to uproot.

déraillement *m* derailment.

dérailler *vi (train)* to jump the rails.

dérangement *m* **en d.** *(téléphone)* out of order.

déranger *vt (affaires)* to disturb, to upset; **d. qn** to disturb *ou* bother sb; **ça vous dérange si je fume?** do you mind if I smoke?

déranger (se) *vpr (se déplacer)* to bother to come *ou* go; **ne te dérange pas!** don't bother!

dérapage *m* skid.

déraper *vi* to skid.

déréglé, -ée *adj* out of order.

dérégler *vt (télévision etc)* to put out of order.

dérégler (se) *vpr (montre etc)* to go wrong.

dériver *vi (bateau)* to drift.

dernier, -ière 1 *adj* last; *(mode)* latest; *(étage)* top; **en d.** last. **2** *mf* last (person *ou* one); **ce d.** the latter; **être le d. de la classe** to be (at the) bottom of the class.

dernièrement *adv* recently.

dérober *vt (voler)* to steal (**à** from).

dérouiller (se) *vpr* se d. les jambes to stretch one's legs.

dérouler *vt (tapis)* to unroll; *(fil)* to unwind.

dérouler (se) *vpr (événement)* to take place.

derrick *m* oil rig.

derrière 1 *prép & adv* behind; **assis d.** *(dans une voiture)* sitting in the back; **par d.** *(attaquer)* from behind. **2** *m* back; *(fesses)* behind; **pattes de d.** hind legs.

des *voir* de[1,2], **le**.

dès *prép* from; **d. le début** (right) from the start; **d. qu'elle viendra** as soon as she comes.

désabusé, -ée *adj* disillusioned.

désaccord *m* disagreement.

désaccordé, -ée *adj (violon etc)* out of tune.

désaffecté, -ée *adj (gare etc)* disused.

désagréable *adj* unpleasant.

désaltérer *vt* **d. qn** to quench sb's thirst.

désaltérer (se) *vpr* to quench one's thirst.

désapprobation *f* disapproval.

désapprouver *vt* to disapprove of.

désarmement *m (de nation)* disarmament.

désarmer *vt* to disarm.

désastre *m* disaster.

désastreux, -euse *adj* disastrous.

désavantage *m* disadvantage.

désavantager *vt* to handicap.

desceller (se) *vpr* to come loose.

descendre 1 *vi (aux être)* to come *ou* go down; *(d'un train)* to get off; *(d'un arbre)* to climb down (de from); *(thermomètre)* to fall; *(marée)* to go out; **d. de cheval** to dismount; **d. en courant** to run down. **2** *vt (aux avoir) (escalier)* to come *ou* go down; *(objet)* to bring *ou* take down.

descente *f (d'avion etc)* descent; *(pente)* slope; **d. de lit** *(tapis)* bedside rug.

description *f* description.

désemparé, -ée *adj (personne)* at a loss.

désenchanté, -ée *adj* disillusioned.

désenfler *vi* to go down.

déséquilibre (en) *adv (meuble)* unsteady.

déséquilibrer *vt* to throw off balance.

désert, -erte *adj* deserted; **île déserte** desert island.

désert *m* desert.

désespérant, -ante *adj (enfant)* hopeless.

désespéré, -ée *adj (personne)* in despair; *(situation)* hopeless; *(efforts)* desperate.

désespérer *vt* to drive to despair.

désespoir *m* despair.

déshabiller *vt*, **se déshabiller** *vpr* to undress.

désherbant *m* weed killer.

désherber *vti* to weed.

désigner *vt (montrer)* to point to; *(élire)* to appoint; *(signifier)* to indicate.

désinfectant *m* disinfectant.

désinfecter *vt* to disinfect.

désintéresser (se) *vpr* **se d. de qch** to lose interest in sth.

désinvolte *adj (dégagé)* casual; *(insolent)* offhand.

désir *m* desire.

désirer *vt* to want; **je désire que tu viennes** I want you to come.

désister (se) *vpr* to withdraw.

désobéir *vi* to disobey; **d. à qn** to disobey sb.

désobéissant, -ante *adj* disobedient.

désobligeant, -ante *adj* disagreeable.

désodorisant *m* air freshener.

désolé, -ée *adj* **être d.** *(navré)* to be sorry (**que** (+ *subjonctif*) that; **de faire** to do).

désoler *vt* to upset (very much).

désordonné, -ée *adj (personne)* messy, untidy.

désordre *m (dans une chambre)* mess; *(dans une classe)* disturbance; **en d.** messy, untidy.

désorganisé, -ée *adj* disorganized.

désormais *adv* from now on.

desquel(le)s *voir* **lequel**.

dessécher (se) *vpr (plante)* to wither; *(peau)* to get dry.

desserrer *vt (ceinture)* to loosen; *(poing)* to open; *(frein)* to release.

desserrer (se) *vpr* to come loose.

dessert *m* dessert.

desservir *vt (table)* to clear; **le car dessert ce village** the bus stops at this village.

dessin *m* drawing; **d. (humoristique)** cartoon; **d. animé** *(film)* cartoon; **école de d.** art school.

dessinateur, -trice *mf* drawer; **d. humoristique** cartoonist.

dessiner *vt* to draw.

dessous **1** *adv* under(neath), below; **en d.** under(neath); **par-d.** *(passer)* under(neath). **2** *m* underside, underneath; **drap de d.** bottom sheet; **les gens du d.** the people downstairs.

dessous-de-plat *m inv* tablemat.

dessus **1** *adv (marcher, monter)* on it; *(passer)* over it; **par-d.** *(sauter)* over (it). **2** *m* top; **drap de d.** top sheet; **les gens du d.** the people upstairs.

dessus-de-lit *m inv* bedspread.

destin *m* fate.

destinataire *mf* addressee.

destination *f (lieu)* destination; **à d. de** *(train)* to, for.

destiner *vt* **d. qch à qn** to intend sth for sb.

destruction *f* destruction.

désuet, -ète *adj* obsolete.

détachant *m* stain remover.

détacher¹ *vt (ceinture)* to undo; *(personne)* to untie; *(ôter)* to take off.

détacher² *vt (linge)* to remove the stains from.

détacher (se) *vpr (chien)* to break loose; *(se dénouer)* to come undone; **se d. (de qch)** *(fragment)* to come off (sth).

détail¹ *m* detail; **en d.** in detail.

détail² *m* **de d.** *(magasin, prix)* retail; **vendre au d.** to sell retail.

détaillant, -ante *mf* retailer.

détaillé, -ée *adj (récit etc)* detailed.

détaler *vi* to run off.

détecteur *m* detector.

détective *m* **d. (privé)** *(private)* detective.

déteindre* *vi (couleur)* to run; **ton tablier bleu a déteint sur ma chemise** the blue of your apron has come off on my shirt.

détendre *vt* **d. qn** to relax sb.

détendre (se) *vpr (se reposer)* to relax; *(corde etc)* to slacken.

détendu, -ue *adj* relaxed; *(ressort etc)* slack.

détenir* *vt (record, pouvoir, titre, prisonnier)* to hold; *(secret, objet volé)* to be in possession of.

détente *f (repos)* relaxation.

détenu, -ue *mf* prisoner.

détergent *m* detergent.

détérioration *f* deterioration (**de** in).

détériorer (se) *vpr* to deteriorate.

déterminant, -ante *adj* decisive.

déterminer *vt (préciser)* to determine.

déterrer *vt* to dig up.

détester *vt* to hate (**faire** doing, to do).

détonation *f* explosion.

détour *m (crochet)* detour.

détourné, -ée *adj (chemin)* roundabout, indirect.

détournement *m (d'avion)* hijacking.

détourner *vt (dévier)* to divert; *(tête)* to turn (away); *(avion)* to hijack; **d. les yeux** to look away.

détourner (se) *vpr* to turn away; **se d. de** *(chemin)* to stray from.

détraqué, -ée *adj* out of order.

détraquer *vt (mécanisme)* to put out of order.

détraquer (se) *vpr (machine)* to break down.

détresse *f* distress; **en d.** *(navire)* in distress.

détritus *mpl* garbage.

détroit *m* strait(s).

détruire* *vt* to destroy.

dette *f* debt; **avoir des dettes** to be in debt.

deuil *m (vêtements)* mourning; **en d.** in mourning.

deux *adj & m* two; **d. fois** twice; **tous (les) d.** both.

deuxième *adj & mf* second.

deuxièmement *adv* secondly.

deux-pièces *m inv (maillot de bain)* bikini.

deux-points *m inv Grammaire* colon.

deux-roues *m inv* two-wheeled vehicle.

dévaler 1 *vt (escalier)* to race down. **2** *vi (tomber)* to tumble down.

dévaliser *vt* to rob.

devancer *vt* to get *ou* be ahead of.

devant 1 *prép & adv* in front (of); **d. (l'hôtel/etc)** in front (of the hotel/ etc); **passer d. (l'église/etc)** to go past (the church/etc); **assis d.** *(dans une voiture)* sitting in the front. **2** *m* front; **roue de d.** front wheel; **patte de d.** foreleg.

devanture f (vitrine) shop ou store window.

dévaster vt to ruin, to devastate.

développement m development; (de photos) developing; **en plein d.** (entreprise, pays) growing fast.

développer vt, **se développer** to develop.

devenir* vi (aux être) to become; **qu'est-il devenu?** what's become of him?

déverser vt, **se déverser** vpr (liquide) to pour out (**dans** into).

déviation f (itinéraire provisoire) detour.

dévier 1 vt (circulation) to divert. **2** vi (de sa route) to veer (off course).

deviner vt to guess.

devinette f riddle.

devis m estimate (of cost of work to be done).

devise f (légende) motto; **devises** (argent) (foreign) currency.

dévisser vt to unscrew.

dévisser (se) vpr (bouchon) to unscrew; (se desserrer) to come loose.

dévoiler vt (secret) to disclose.

devoir*¹ v aux (nécessité) **je dois refuser** I must refuse, I have (got) to refuse; **j'ai dû refuser** I had to refuse. ▪ (probabilité) **il doit être tard** it must be late; **elle a dû oublier** she must have forgotten; **il ne doit pas être bête** he can't be stupid. ▪ (obligation) **tu dois apprendre tes leçons** you must study your lessons; **il aurait dû venir** he should have come; **vous devriez rester** you should stay. ▪ (événement prévu) **elle doit venir** she's supposed to be coming, she's due to come.

devoir*² **1** vt (argent etc) to owe (**à** to). **2** m (obligation) duty; (exercice) exercise; **devoirs** (à faire à la maison) homework; **d. sur table** exam(ination) in class.

dévorer vt (manger) to eat up.

dévoué, -ée adj (soldat etc) dedicated.

dévouement m dedication.

dévouer (se) vpr **se d. (pour qn)** to sacrifice oneself (for sb).

diabète m diabetes.

diabétique mf diabetic.

diable m devil; **habiter au d.** to live miles from anywhere.

diagnostic m diagnosis.

diagonale f diagonal (line); **en d.** diagonally.

dialecte m dialect.

dialogue m conversation; (de film) dialogue.

diamant m diamond.

diamètre m diameter.

diapositive, Fam diapo f (color) slide.

diarrhée f diarrhea.

dictature f dictatorship.

dictée f dictation.

dicter vt to dictate (**à** to).

dictionnaire m dictionary.

dicton m saying.

diesel adj & m (moteur) **d.** diesel (engine).

diète f (jeûne) **à la d.** on a diet.

diététique adj **produit d.** health food.

dieu, -x m god; **D.** God.

différence f difference (**de** in).

différent, -ente adj different (**de** than, from, to).

difficile adj difficult; (exigeant) fussy; **d. à faire** difficult to do; **il nous est d. de** it's difficult for us to.

difficulté f difficulty; **en d.** in a difficult situation.

diffuser vt (émission) to broadcast.

digérer vti to digest.

digestif, -ive 1 adj digestive. **2** m after-dinner liqueur.

digestion f digestion.

digne adj **d. de** worthy of.

digue f dike; (en bord de mer) sea wall.

dilater vt, **se dilater** vpr to expand.

diligence f (véhicule) stagecoach.

dimanche m Sunday.

dimension f dimension.

diminuer 1 vt to reduce. **2** vi (réserves) to decrease; (jours) to get shorter; (prix) to drop.

diminutif m (prénom) nickname.

diminution f reduction, decrease (de in).

dinde f turkey.

dindon m turkey (cock).

dîner 1 vi to have dinner; (au Canada, en Belgique) to have lunch. **2** m dinner.

dînette f (jouet) doll's dinner service ou set.

dinosaure m dinosaur.

diphtongue f diphthong.

diplôme m certificate, diploma.

diplômé, -ée 1 adj qualified; (de l'université) **être d. (de)** to be a graduate (of). **2** mf holder of a diploma; (de l'université) graduate.

dire* vt (mot) to say; (vérité, secret, heure) to tell; **d. des bêtises** to talk nonsense; **d. qch à qn** to tell sb sth, to say sth to sb; **d. à qn que** to tell sb that, to say to sb that; **d. à qn de faire** to tell sb to do; **on dirait un château/du Mozart** it looks like a castle/sounds like Mozart; **ça ne me dit rien** (envie) I don't feel like it; (souvenir) it doesn't ring a bell.

dire (se) vpr ça ne se dit pas you don't say that.

direct, -e 1 adj direct; **train d.** fast train. **2** m (émission) live.

directement adv directly.

directeur, -trice mf director; (d'école) principal.

direction f (sens) direction; **en d. de** (train) to, for; **sous la d. de** (orchestre) conducted by; **la d.** (équipe dirigeante) the management.

dirigeable adj & m (ballon) **d.** airship, dirigible.

dirigeant m (de parti etc) leader; (d'entreprise, club) manager.

diriger vt (société) to run; (parti, groupe) to lead; (véhicule) to steer; (orchestre) to conduct; (arme etc) to point (**vers** towards).

diriger (se) vpr **se d. vers** (lieu) to make one's way towards.

dis, disant voir **dire**.

discipline f (règle) discipline.

discipliné, -ée adj well-disciplined.

discipliner (se) vpr to discipline oneself.

disco f disco.

discontinu, -ue adj (ligne) broken; (bruit) intermittent.

discothèque f (club) disco(theque).

discours m speech.

discret, -ète adj (personne) discreet.

discrètement adv discreetly.

discrétion f discretion.

discrimination f discrimination.

discussion f discussion; (conversation) talk; **pas de d.!** no argument!

discuter vi (parler) to talk (**de** about); (répliquer) to argue; **d. sur qch** to discuss sth.

dise(nt) etc voir **dire**.

disjoncter vi (circuit électrique) to fuze.

disloquer (se) vpr (meuble) to fall apart.

disparaître* vi to disappear; (être porté manquant) to be reported missing.

disparition f disappearance.

disparu, -ue adj (soldat) missing.

dispense f exemption.

dispenser vt **d. qn de** (obligation) to exempt sb from.

disperser vt (objets) to scatter.

disperser (se) vpr (foule) to disperse.

disponible adj (article, place etc) available.

disposé, -ée *adj* bien d. in a good mood; **d. à faire** prepared to do.

disposer 1 *vt (objets)* to arrange. **2** *vi* **d. de qch** to make use of sth.

disposer (se) *vpr* se d. à faire to prepare to do.

dispositif *m (mécanisme)* device.

disposition *f* arrangement; **à la d. de qn** at sb's disposal; **prendre ses dispositions** to make arrangements.

disproportionné, -ée *adj* disproportionate.

dispute *f* quarrel.

disputer *vt (match)* to play; *(rallye)* to compete in; **d. qn** *(gronder)* Fam to tell sb off.

disputer (se) *vpr* to quarrel (avec with).

disqualifier *vt (équipe)* to disqualify.

disque *m* disk; **d. compact** compact disk.

disquette *f (d'ordinateur)* floppy (disk), diskette.

dissertation *f (au lycée etc)* essay.

dissimuler *vt, se dissimuler (cacher)* to hide (à from).

dissipé, -ée *adj (élève)* unruly.

dissiper *vt (brouillard)* to dispel; **d. qn** to distract sb.

dissiper (se) *vpr (brume)* to lift; *(élève)* to misbehave.

dissolvant *m* solvent; *(pour vernis à ongles)* nail polish remover.

dissoudre* *vt, se dissoudre vpr* to dissolve.

dissuader *vt* to dissuade (de qch from sth; de faire from doing).

distance *f* distance; **à deux mètres de d.** seven feet apart.

distancer *vt* to leave behind.

distinct, -incte *adj* distinct.

distinctement *adv* clearly.

distinguer *vt* to distinguish; *(voir)* to make out; **d. le blé de l'orge** to tell wheat from barley.

distinguer (se) *vpr* se d. de to be distinguishable from.

distraction *f* amusement; *(étourderie)* absent-mindedness.

distraire* *vt (divertir)* to entertain.

distraire (se) *vpr* to amuse oneself.

distrait, -aite *adj* absent-minded.

distribuer *vt (donner)* to hand out; *(courrier)* to deliver; *(cartes)* to deal.

distributeur *m* **d. (automatique)** vending machine; **d. de billets** ticket machine; *(de banque)* automatic teller machine, ATM.

distribution *f* distribution; *(du courrier)* delivery.

dit, dite, dites *voir* dire.

divan *m* couch.

divergent, -ente *adj (lignes)* divergent; *(opinions)* differing.

divers, -erses *adj pl (distincts)* varied; *(plusieurs)* various.

diversifier *vt, se diversifier vpr* to diversify.

divertir *vt* to entertain.

divertir (se) *vpr* to enjoy oneself.

divertissement *m* entertainment.

diviser *vt, se diviser vpr* to divide (en into).

division *f* division.

divorce *m* divorce.

divorcé, -ée 1 *adj* divorced. **2** *mf* divorcee.

divorcer *vi* to get divorced.

dix *adj & m* ten.

dix-huit *adj & m* eighteen.

dixième *adj & mf* tenth.

dix-neuf *adj & m* nineteen.

dix-sept *adj & m* seventeen.

dizaine *f* une d. (de) about ten.

docile *adj* docile.

docker *m* docker.

docteur *m* doctor.

doctorat *m* doctorate, = PhD.

document *m* document.

documentaire *m (film)* documentary.

documentaliste *mf (à l'école)* (school) librarian.

documentation *f (documents)* documentation.

documenter (se) *vpr* to collect information.

dodo *m (langage enfantin)* **faire d.** to sleep.

doigt *m* finger; **d. de pied** toe; **petit d.** little finger, pinkie.

dois, doit, doive(nt) *voir* **devoir**[1,2].

dollar *m* dollar.

domaine *m (terres)* estate.

dôme *m* dome.

domestique 1 *adj (animal)* domestic; **travaux domestiques** housework. **2** *mf* servant.

domicile *m* home; **livrer à d.** to deliver (to the house).

domination *f* domination.

dominer 1 *vt* to dominate. **2** *vi (être le plus fort)* to dominate.

domino *m* domino; **dominos** *(jeu)* dominoes.

dommage *m* **c'est d.!** it's a pity *ou* a shame! **(que** + *subjonctif* that); **dommages** *(dégâts)* damage.

dompter *vt (animal)* to tame.

dompteur, -euse *mf (de lions)* lion tamer.

DOM-TOM *mpl abrév (départements et territoires d'outre-mer)* = French overseas departments and territories.

don *m (cadeau, aptitude)* gift; *(charité)* donation.

donc *conj (par conséquent)* so; **asseyez-vous d.!** won't you sit down!

donjon *m* keep.

données *fpl (information)* data.

donner 1 *vt* to give; *(récolte)* to produce; *(sa place)* to give up; *(cartes)* to deal; **d. un coup à** to hit; **d. à réparer** to take (in) to be repaired; **ça donne soif/faim** it makes you thirsty/hungry. **2** *vi* **d. sur** *(fenêtre)* to overlook; *(porte)* to open onto.

donner (se) *vpr* **se d. du mal** to go to a lot of trouble (**pour faire** to do).

dont *pron rel (= de qui, duquel, de quoi etc) (personne)* of whom; *(chose)* of which; *(appartenance: personne, chose)* whose; **une mère d. le fils est malade** a mother whose son is ill; **la fille d. il est fier** the daughter he is proud of *ou* of whom he is proud; **la façon d.** the way in which.

doper (se) *vpr* to take drugs.

doré, -ée *adj (objet)* gilt, gold; *(couleur)* golden.

dorénavant *adv* from now on.

dorer *vt (objet)* to gild.

dorer (se) *vpr* **se d. au soleil** to sunbathe.

dormir* *vi* to sleep.

dortoir *m* dormitory.

dos *m (de personne, d'animal)* back; **à d. d'âne** (riding) on a donkey; **'voir au d.'** *(verso)* 'see over'.

dose *f* dose.

dossier *m (de siège)* back; *(papiers)* file.

doter *vt (équiper)* to equip (**de** with); **doté d'une grande intelligence** endowed with great intelligence.

douane *f* customs.

douanier *m* customs officer.

doublage *m (de film)* dubbing.

double 1 *adj & adv* double. **2** *m* **le d. (de)** *(quantité)* twice as much (as), double; **je l'ai en d.** I have two of them.

doubler 1 *vt (vêtement)* to line; *(film)* to dub. **2** *vti (augmenter)* to double; *(en voiture)* to overtake.

doublure *f (étoffe)* lining.

douce *voir* **doux**.

doucement *adv (délicatement)* gently; *(à voix basse)* softly; *(lentement)* slowly.

douceur *f (de miel)* sweetness; *(de peau)* softness; *(de temps)* mildness.

douche *f* shower.

doucher *vt* **d. qn** to give sb a shower.

doucher (se) *vpr* to take a shower.

doué, -ée *adj* gifted (**en** at); *(intelligent)* clever.

douillet, -ette *adj (lit)* soft, cozy; **tu es d.** *(délicat)* you're such a baby.

douleur *f (mal)* pain; *(chagrin)* sorrow.

douloureux, -euse *adj* painful.

doute *m* doubt; **sans d.** probably, no doubt.

douter *vi* to doubt.

douter (se) *vpr* se d. de qch to suspect sth; **je m'en doute** I would think so.

douteux, -euse *adj (peu certain)* doubtful; *(louche, médiocre)* dubious.

doux, douce *adj (miel etc)* sweet; *(peau)* soft; *(temps)* mild.

douzaine *f* dozen; *(environ)* about twelve; **une d. d'œufs**/etc a dozen eggs/etc.

douze *adj & m* twelve.

douzième *adj & mf* twelfth.

dragée *f* sugared almond.

dragon *m (animal)* dragon.

draguer *vt (rivière)* to dredge; *(personne)* Fam to come on to.

dramatique *adj* dramatic; **film d.** drama.

drame *m* drama; *(catastrophe)* tragedy.

drap *m (de lit)* sheet; **d. housse** fitted sheet; **d. de bain** bath towel.

drapeau, -x *m* flag.

dressage *m* training.

dresser *vt (échelle)* to put up; *(animal)* to train.

dresser (se) *vpr (personne)* to stand up; *(montagne)* to stand.

dribbler *vti Sport* to dribble.

drogue *f* une d. *(stupéfiant)* a drug; **la d.** drugs.

drogué, -ée *mf* drug addict.

droguer (se) *vpr* to take drugs.

droguerie *f* hardware store.

droit¹ *m (privilège)* right (**de faire** to do); *(d'inscription etc)* fee(s); **le d.** *(science)* law; **avoir d. à** to be entitled to.

droit², droite 1 *adj (route etc)* straight; *(vertical)* upright; *(angle)* right. **2** *adv* straight; **tout d.** straight ahead.

droit³, droite *adj (côté etc)* right.

droite *f* la d. *(côté)* the right (side); **à d.** *(tourner)* (to the) right; *(rouler etc)* on the right; **de d.** *(fenêtre etc)* right-hand; **à d. de** on *ou* to the right of.

droitier, -ière *adj & mf* right-handed (person).

drôle *adj* odd, strange; **d. d'air/de type** strange look/guy.

drôlement *adv (extrêmement)* terribly.

du *voir* de¹'², le.

dû, due *(pp of* devoir¹'²*) adj* d. à due to.

duc *m* duke.

duchesse *f* duchess.

duel *m* duel.

dune *f* (sand) dune.

duplex *m* duplex.

duquel *voir* lequel.

dur, -e 1 *adj (substance)* hard; *(difficile)* hard, tough; *(hiver, personne, ton)* harsh; *(œuf)* hard-boiled. **2** *adv (travailler)* hard.

durable *adj* lasting.

durant *prép* during.

durcir *vti,* se durcir *vpr* to harden.

durée *f (de film etc)* length.

durer *vi* to last; **ça dure depuis** it's been going on for *ou* since.

dureté *f* hardness; *(de ton etc)* harshness.

duvet *m (d'oiseau)* down; *(sac)* sleeping bag.

DVD *m abrév (digital video disk, digital versatile disk)* DVD.

dynamique *adj* dynamic.

dynamite *f* dynamite.

dynamo *f* dynamo.

dyslexique *adj & mf* dyslexic.

E

eau, -x f water; **e. douce/salée** fresh/salt water; **e. de Cologne** cologne; **tomber à l'e.** (projet) to fall through.

eau-de-vie, pl **eaux-de-vie** f brandy.

ébahi, -ie adj astounded.

ébaucher vt (tableau, roman) to rough out.

ébéniste m cabinet-maker.

éblouir vt to dazzle.

éboueur m garbage collector.

ébouillanter (s') vpr to scald oneself.

éboulement m landslide.

ébouler (s') vpr (falaise) to crumble; (roches) to fall.

ébouriffé, -ée adj (cheveux) disheveled.

ébranler vt to shake; (santé) to weaken.

ébranler (s') vpr (train etc) to move off.

ébrécher vt (assiette) to chip.

ébruiter vt, **s'ébruiter** vpr (nouvelle) to spread.

ébullition f **être en é.** (eau) to be boiling.

écaille f (de poisson) scale; (de tortue) shell; (pour lunettes) tortoiseshell; (de peinture) flake.

écailler vt (poisson) to scale; (huitre) to shell.

écailler (s') vpr (peinture) to flake (off), to peel.

écarlate adj scarlet.

écarquiller vt **é. les yeux** to open one's eyes wide.

écart m (intervalle) gap; (embardée) swerve; (différence) difference (**de** in; **entre** between); **à l'é.** out of the way; **à l'é. de** away from.

écarté, -ée adj (endroit) remote;

les jambes **écartées** with legs apart.

écarter vt (objets) to move apart; (jambes, rideaux) to open; **é. qch de qch** to move sth away from sth; **é. qn de** (exclure) to keep sb out of.

écarter (s') vpr (s'éloigner) to move away (**de** from).

échafaud m scaffold.

échafaudage m (de peintre etc) scaffold(ing).

échalote f shallot.

échancré, -ée adj low-cut.

échange m exchange; **en é.** in exchange (**de** for).

échanger vt to exchange (**contre** for).

échangeur m (autoroute) interchange.

échantillon m sample.

échapper vi **é. à qn** to escape from sb; **é. à la mort** to escape death; **son nom m'échappe** her name escapes me.

échapper (s') vpr (s'enfuir) to escape (**de** from); (gaz, eau) to escape.

écharde f splinter.

écharpe f scarf; (de maire) sash; **en é.** (bras) in a sling.

échauffer (s') vpr (sportif) to warm up.

échec m failure; les **échecs** (jeu) chess; **é.!** check!; **é. et mat!** checkmate!

échelle f (marches) ladder; (dimension) scale; **faire la courte é. à qn** to give sb a leg up ou a boost.

échelon m (d'échelle) rung; (de fonctionnaire) grade.

échiquier m chessboard.

écho m (d'un son) echo.

échographie f (ultrasound) scan; **passer une é.** to have a scan.

échouer vi to fail; **é. à** (examen) to fail.

échouer (s') vpr (navire) to run aground.

éclabousser *vt* to splash (**de** with).

éclaboussure *f* splash.

éclair *m (lumière)* flash; *(d'orage)* flash of lightning.

éclairage *m (de pièce etc)* lighting.

éclaircie *f (durée)* sunny interval.

éclaircir *vt (couleur etc)* to make lighter; *(mystère)* to clear up.

éclaircir (s') *vpr (ciel)* to clear (up); *(situation)* to become clear.

éclaircissement *m* explanation.

éclairé, -ée *adj* bien/mal é. well/badly lit.

éclairer *vt (pièce etc)* to light (up); **é. qn** *(avec une lampe)* to give sb some light.

éclairer (s') *vpr (visage)* to brighten up; *(situation)* to become clear; **s'é. à la bougie** to use candlelight.

éclaireur, -euse *mf* boy/girl scout.

éclat[1] *m (de la lumière)* brightness; *(de phare)* glare.

éclat[2] *m (de verre ou de bois)* splinter; *(de rire)* (out)burst.

éclatant, -ante *adj (lumière, succès)* brilliant.

éclatement *m (de ballon etc)* bursting; *(de bombe)* explosion.

éclater *vi (ballon etc)* to burst; *(bombe)* to go off; *(verre)* to shatter; *(guerre, incendie)* to break out; *(orage)* to break; **é. de rire** to burst out laughing; **é. en sanglots** to burst into tears.

éclore* *vi (œuf)* to hatch.

éclosion *f* hatching.

écluse *f (de canal)* lock.

écœurant, -ante *adj* disgusting, sickening.

écœurer *vt* **é. qn** to make sb feel sick.

école *f* school; **à l'é.** in *ou* at school; **aller à l'é.** to go to school.

écolier, -ière *mf* schoolboy, schoolgirl.

écologiste *mf* environmentalist.

économe *adj* thrifty.

économie *f* economy; **économies** *(argent)* savings; **une é. de temps** time saved; **faire des économies** to save (up).

économique *adj (bon marché)* economical.

économiser *vti* to economize (**sur** on).

écorce *f (d'arbre)* bark; *(de fruit)* peel, skin.

écorcher *vt (érafler)* to scrape; **é. les oreilles** to grate on one's ears.

écorcher (s') *vpr* to scrape oneself.

écorchure *f* scrape.

écossais, -aise 1 *adj* Scottish; *(tissu)* tartan; *(whisky)* Scotch. **2** *mf* **E.** Scot.

écosser *vt (pois)* to shell.

écoulement *m (de liquide)* flow; *(de temps)* passage.

écouler (s') *vpr (eau)* to flow out; *(temps)* to pass.

écourter *vt (séjour)* to cut short; *(texte, tige)* to shorten.

écouter 1 *vt* to listen to. **2** *vi* to listen.

écouteur *m (de téléphone)* earpiece; **écouteurs** *(casque)* earphones.

écran *m* screen; **le petit é.** television.

écrasant, -ante *adj* overwhelming.

écraser *vt* to crush; *(cigarette)* to put *ou* stub out; *(piéton)* to run over; **se faire é.** to get run over.

écraser (s') *vpr* to crash (**contre** into).

écrémé *adj (lait)* skim.

écrevisse *f* crayfish.

écrier (s') *vpr* to exclaim (**que** that).

écrire* **1** *vt* to write; *(en toutes lettres)* to spell; **é. à la machine** to type. **2** *vi* to write.

écrire (s') *vpr (mot)* to be spelled *ou* spelt.

écrit *m* **par é.** in writing.

écriteau, -x m notice, sign.

écriture f writing.

écrivain m author, writer.

écrou m (de boulon) nut.

écrouler (s') vpr to collapse.

écueil m reef; (obstacle) pitfall.

écuelle f bowl.

écume f (de mer etc) foam.

écureuil m squirrel.

écurie f stable.

écusson m (en étoffe) badge.

édifice m building.

édifier vt to erect.

éditer vt to publish.

éditeur, -trice mf publisher.

édition f (livre, journal) edition; (métier) publishing.

édredon m eiderdown.

éducateur, -trice mf educator.

éducatif, -ive adj educational.

éducation f education; **avoir de l'é.** to have good manners.

éduquer vt to educate.

effacer vt to rub out, to erase; (en lavant) to wash out; (avec un chiffon) to wipe away.

effarant, -ante adj astounding.

effaroucher vt to scare away.

effectif m (de classe etc) total number.

effectivement adv actually.

effectuer vt (expérience etc) to carry out; (trajet etc) to make.

effet m effect (sur on); **faire de l'e.** (remède) to be effective; **en e.** indeed, in fact; **sous l'e. de la colère** in anger.

efficace adj (mesure etc) effective; (personne) efficient.

efficacité f (de mesure etc) effectiveness; (de personne) efficiency.

effilocher (s') vpr to fray.

effleurer vt to skim, to touch (lightly).

effondrer (s') vpr to collapse.

efforcer (s') vpr s'e. de faire to try (hard) to do.

effort m effort; **sans e.** (réussir etc) effortlessly.

effrayant, -ante adj frightening.

effrayer vt to frighten, to scare.

effronté, -ée adj (personne) impudent.

effroyable adj dreadful.

égal, -e, aux 1 adj equal (à to); (uniforme, régulier) even; **ça m'est é.** I don't care. **2** mf (personne) equal.

également adv (aussi) also, as well.

égaler vt to equal.

égaliser vi to equalize.

égalité f equality; (régularité) evenness; **à é. (de score)** even, equal (in points).

égard m à l'é. de (envers) towards.

égarer vt (objet) to mislay.

égarer (s') vpr to lose one's way.

égayer vt (pièce) to brighten up; **é. qn** to cheer sb up.

église f church.

égoïste 1 adj selfish. **2** mf selfish person.

égorger vt to cut the throat of.

égout m sewer; **eaux d'é.** sewage.

égoutter 1 vt to drain. **2** vi, s'égoutter vpr to drain; (linge) to drip.

égouttoir m (dish) drainer.

égratigner vt to scratch.

égratignure f scratch.

eh! int hey!; **eh bien!** well!

élaborer vt (plan, idée) to develop.

élan m (vitesse) momentum; (impulsion) impulse; **prendre son é.** to get a running start.

élancer (s') vpr (bondir) to leap ou rush (forward).

élargir (s') vpr (route etc) to widen.

élastique 1 adj (objet) elastic. **2** m (lien) elastic ou rubber band.

électeur, -trice mf voter.

élection f election.

électoral, -e, -aux adj campagne électorale election campaign.

électricien m electrician.

électricité f electricity.

électrique *adj* electric.

électrocuter *vt* to electrocute.

électroménager 1 *adj m* **appareil é.** household electrical appliance. **2** *m* household appliances.

électronique *adj* electronic.

électrophone *m* record player.

élégance *f* elegance; **avec é.** elegantly.

élégant, -ante *adj* elegant.

élément *m* element; *(de meuble)* unit; **éléments** *(notions)* rudiments.

élémentaire *adj* basic; *(cours, école etc)* elementary.

éléphant *m* elephant.

élevage *m* breeding, raising.

élève *mf* pupil.

élevé, -ée *adj (haut)* high; **bien/ mal é.** well/bad-mannered.

élever *vt (prix, voix etc)* to raise; *(enfant)* to bring up, to raise; *(animal)* to breed, to raise.

élever (s') *vpr (prix, ton etc)* to rise; **s'é. à** *(prix)* to amount to.

éleveur, -euse *mf* breeder.

éliminatoire *adj & f (épreuve)* é. heat.

éliminer *vt* to eliminate.

élire* *vt* to elect (à to).

elle *pron (sujet)* she; *(chose, animal)* it; **elles** they. ▪ *(complément)* her; *(chose, animal)* it; **elles** them.

elle-même *pron* herself; *(chose, animal)* itself; **elles-mêmes** themselves.

éloigné, -ée *adj (lieu)* far away; *(date)* distant; **é. de** *(village etc)* far (away) from.

éloigner *vt (chose, personne)* to move *ou* go away (**de** from).

e-mail *m* e-mail; **envoyer un e.** to send an e-mail (**à** to).

émail, -aux *m* enamel.

emballage *m (action)* packing; wrapping; *(caisse)* packaging; *(papier)* wrapping (paper).

emballer *vt (dans une caisse etc)* to pack; *(dans du papier)* to wrap

(up); **e. qn** *(passionner)* Fam to thrill sb.

emballer (s') *vpr (personne)* Fam to get carried away; *(cheval)* to bolt.

embarcadère *m* quay, wharf.

embarcation *f (small)* boat.

embardée *f (sudden)* swerve.

embarquement *m (de passagers)* boarding.

embarquer 1 *vt (passagers)* to take on board; *(marchandises)* to load (up). **2** *vi,* **s'embarquer** *vpr* to (go on) board.

embarras *m (gêne)* embarrassment.

embarrassant, -ante *adj (paquet)* cumbersome; *(question)* embarrassing.

embarrasser *vt* **e. qn** to be in sb's way; *(question etc)* to embarrass sb.

embarrasser (s') *vpr* **s'e. de** to burden oneself with.

embaucher *vt (ouvrier)* to hire.

embellir 1 *vt (pièce, personne)* to make more attractive. **2** *vi (personne)* to grow more attractive.

embêtant, -ante *adj* annoying, boring.

embêtement *m* trouble.

embêter *vt (agacer)* to bother; *(ennuyer)* to bore.

embêter (s') *vpr* Fam to get bored.

emboîter *vt,* **s'emboîter** *vpr (tuyau(x))* to fit together.

embouchure *f (de fleuve)* mouth.

embourber (s') *vpr* to get bogged down.

embouteillage *m* traffic jam.

embouteillé, -ée *adj (rue)* congested.

emboutir *vt (voiture)* to crash into.

embranchement *m (de voie)* junction.

embrasser *vt (donner un baiser à)* to kiss.

embrasser (s') *vpr* to kiss (each other).

embrayage *m* (*de véhicule*) clutch.

embrocher *vt* to skewer.

embrouiller *vt* (*fils*) to tangle (up); (*papiers etc*) to mix up; **e. qn** to confuse sb

embrouiller (s') *vpr* to get confused (**dans** in, with).

embuscade *f* ambush.

émerger *vi* to emerge (**de** from).

émerveiller *vt* to amaze, to fill with wonder.

émetteur *m* (*poste*) é. transmitter.

émettre* *vt* (*lumière, son etc*) to give out; (*message, radio*) to broadcast; (*timbre, monnaie*) to issue.

émeute *f* riot.

émietter *vt*, **émietter (s')** *vpr* to crumble.

émigrer *vi* to emigrate.

émission *f* (*de radio etc*) broadcast; (*diffusion*) transmission; (*de timbre, monnaie*) issue.

emmanchure *f* arm hole.

emmêler *vt* to tangle (up).

emménager *vi* (*dans un logement*) to move in; **e. dans** to move into.

emmener *vt* to take (**à** to); **e. qn en promenade** to take sb for a walk.

emmitoufler (s') *vpr* to wrap (oneself) up.

émotif, -ive *adj* emotional.

émotion *f* emotion; (*trouble*) excitement; **une é.** (*peur*) a scare.

émouvant, -ante *adj* moving.

émouvoir* *vt* to move, to touch.

empailler *vt* to stuff.

empaqueter *vt* to pack.

emparer (s') *vpr* s'**e. de** to take, to grab.

empêchement *m* **j'ai eu un e.** something's come up at the last minute.

empêcher *vt* to prevent, to stop (**de faire** (from) doing).

empêcher (s') *vpr* s'**e. de faire qch** to stop oneself from doing sth;

elle ne peut pas s'**e. de rire** she can't help laughing.

empereur *m* emperor.

empester **1** *vt* (*tabac etc*) to stink of; **e. qn** to stink sb out. **2** *vi* to stink.

empiler *vt*, **empiler (s')** *vpr* to pile up (**sur** on).

empire *m* empire.

empirer *vi* to worsen, to get worse.

emplacement *m* site; (*de stationnement*) place.

emplir *vt*, **emplir (s')** *vpr* to fill (**de** with).

emploi *m* (*usage*) use; (*travail*) job, employment; **e. du temps** schedule; **sans e.** (*au chômage*) unemployed.

employé, -ée *mf* employee; (*de bureau, banque*) clerk, employee.

employer *vt* (*utiliser*) to use; **e. qn** to employ sb.

employer (s') *vpr* (*expression*) to be used.

employeur, -euse *mf* employer.

empoigner *vt* to grab.

empoisonner *vt* to poison.

empoisonner (s') *vpr* to poison oneself; (*par accident*) to be poisoned.

emporter *vt* (*prendre*) to take (away) (**avec soi** with one); (*entraîner*) to carry away; (*par le vent*) to blow off *ou* away.

emporter (s') *vpr* to lose one's temper (**contre** with).

empreinte *f* mark; **e. (digitale)** fingerprint; **e. (de pas)** footprint.

empresser (s') *vpr* s'**e. de faire** to hasten to do.

emprisonner *vt* to jail.

emprunt *m* (*argent etc*) loan.

emprunter *vt* (*argent*) to borrow (**à** from); (*route*) to use.

ému, -ue *adj* moved; (*attristé*) upset.

en¹ *prép* (*lieu*) in; (*direction*) to; **être/aller en France** to be in/go to France. ■ (*temps*) in; **en février** in February; **d'heure en heure** from hour to hour. ■ (*moyen, état etc*) by; in; on; **en avion** by plane; **en groupe** in a group; **en congé** on leave *ou* vacation. ▪ *(matière)* in; **en bois** in wood; **chemise en nylon** nylon shirt; **c'est en or** it's (made of) gold. ▪ *(comme)* **en cadeau** as a present. ▪ *(+ participe présent)* **en mangeant**/*etc* while eating/*etc*; **en apprenant que** on hearing that; **en souriant** smiling, with a smile. ▪ *(transformation)* into; **traduire en** to translate into.

en² *pron & adv* *(= de là)* from there; **j'en viens** I've just come from there. ▪ *(= de ça, lui etc)* **il en est content** he's pleased with it/him/them; **en parler** to talk about it; **en mourir** to die of *ou* from it. ▪ *(partitif)* some; **j'en ai** I have some.

encadrer *vt (tableau)* to frame; *(entourer d'un trait)* to circle *(word)*.

encaisser *vt (argent, loyer etc)* to collect.

enceinte¹ *adj (femme)* pregnant; **e. de six mois** six months pregnant.

enceinte² *f* enclosure; **dans l'e. de** within; **e. (acoustique)** speaker.

encens *m* incense.

encercler *vt* to surround.

enchaîner *vt* to chain (up); *(idées etc)* to link (up).

enchaîner (s') *vpr (idées etc)* to be linked (up).

enchanté, -ée *adj (ravi)* delighted *(de* with; *que* (+ *subjonctif)* that); **e. (de faire votre connaissance)!** pleased to meet you!

enchantement *m* delight; **comme par e.** as if by magic.

enchanter *vt (ravir)* to delight.

enchanteur *m* magician.

enchère *f(offre)* bid; **vente aux enchères** auction; **mettre qch aux enchères** to put sth up for auction, to auction sth.

enclos *m* enclosure.

encoche *f* nick *(à* in).

encolure *f* neck; *(tour du cou)* collar (size).

encombrant, -ante *adj (paquet)* bulky.

encombrement *m (d'objets)* clutter; *(de rue)* traffic jam.

encombrer *vt (pièce etc)* to clutter up *(de* with); *(rue)* to congest *(de* with); **e. qn** to hamper sb.

encore *adv (toujours)* still; **e. là** still here. ▪ *(avec négation)* yet; **pas e.** not yet. ▪ *(de nouveau)* again; **essaie e.** try again. ▪ *(de plus)* **e. un café** another coffee, one more coffee; **e. une fois** (once) again, once more; **e. un** another (one), one more; **e. du pain** (some) more bread; **e. quelque chose** something else; **qui/quoi e.?** who/what else? ▪ *(avec comparatif)* even, still; **e. mieux** even better, still better.

encourageant, -ante *adj* encouraging.

encouragement *m* encouragement.

encourager *vt* to encourage *(à faire* to do).

encrasser *vt* to clog up (with dirt).

encre *f* ink; **e. de Chine** India ink.

encrier *m* inkpot.

encyclopédie *f* encyclopedia.

endettement *m* debts.

endetter (s') *vpr* to get into debt.

endive *f* chicory, endive.

endommager *vt* to damage.

endormi, -ie *adj* asleep, sleeping.

endormir* *vt* to put to sleep.

endormir (s') *vpr* to fall asleep, to go to sleep.

endroit *m (lieu)* place; **à l'e.** *(vêtement)* right side out.

endurant, -ante *adj* tough.

endurcir *vt* **e. qn** to harden sb.

endurcir (s') *vpr* **s'e. à** to become hardened to *(pain etc).*

endurer *vt* to endure.

énergie *f* energy.

énergique *adj* energetic; *(remède)* powerful; *(mesure, ton)* forceful.

énergiquement *adv* energetically.

énervé, -ée *adj* on edge.

énerver *vt* é. qn (*irriter*) to get on sb's nerves; (*rendre énervé*) to make sb nervous.

énerver (s') *vpr* to get worked up.

enfance *f* childhood.

enfant *m* child (*pl* children); **e. en bas âge** infant; **e. de chœur** altar boy.

enfantin, -ine *adj* (*voix, joie*) child-like; (*simple*) easy.

enfer *m* hell; **d'e.** (*bruit etc*) infernal; **à un train d'e.** at breakneck speed.

enfermer *vt* to lock up; **s'.e. dans** (*chambre etc*) to lock oneself (up) in.

enfiler *vt* (*aiguille*) to thread; (*perles etc*) to string; (*vêtement*) to pull on.

enfin *adv* (*à la fin*) finally, at last; (*en dernier lieu*) lastly; **e. bref** in a word; **(mais) e.!** for heaven's sake!

enflammer *vt* to set fire to; (*allumette*) to light; (*irriter*) to inflame (*throat etc*).

enflammer (s') *vpr* to catch on fire.

enfler *vti* to swell.

enflure *f* swelling.

enfoncer **1** *vt* (*clou*) to knock in, to hammer in; (*porte, voiture*) to smash in; **e. dans qch** (*couteau, mains etc*) to plunge into sth. **2** *vi*, **s'enfoncer** *vpr* (*s'enliser*) to sink (**dans** into).

enfouir *vt* to bury.

enfreindre* *vt* to infringe.

enfuir* (s') *vpr* to run away *ou* off (**de** from).

enfumer *vt* (*pièce*) to fill with smoke.

engagé, -ée *adj* (*écrivain*) politically committed.

engagement *m* (*promesse*) commitment; (*dans une compéti-*

tion) entry; **prendre l'e.** de to undertake to.

engager *vt* (*discussion, combat*) to start; **e. qn** (*embaucher*) to hire sb.

engager (s') *vpr* (*dans l'armée*) to enlist; (*sportif*) to enter (**pour** for); (*action, jeu*) to start; **s'e. à faire** to undertake to do.

engelure *f* chilblain.

engin *m* machine; **e. spatial** spaceship.

englober *vt* to include.

engloutir *vt* (*nourriture*) to wolf down; (*faire disparaître*) to swallow up.

engouffrer (s') *vpr* s'e. dans to sweep *ou* rush into.

engourdir (s') *vpr* to go numb.

engrais *m* fertilizer; (*naturel*) manure.

engraisser **1** *vt* (*animal*) to fatten (up). **2** *vi* to get fat.

engrenage *m* gears.

engueuler *vt* e. qn *Fam* to give sb hell.

énigme *f* riddle.

enivrer (s') *vpr* to get drunk (**de** on).

enjambée *f* stride.

enjamber *vt* to step over; (*pont etc*) to span (*river etc*).

enjeu, -x *m* (*mise*) stake; (*de pari, de guerre*) stakes.

enjoliveur *m* hubcap.

enjoué, -ée *adj* playful.

enlaidir **1** *vt* to make ugly. **2** *vi* to grow ugly.

enlèvement *m* (*d'enfant*) kidnapping.

enlever *vt* to take away (**à qn** from sb); (*vêtement*) to take off; (*tache*) to take out; (*enfant etc*) to kidnap.

enlever (s') *vpr* (*tache*) to come out.

enliser (s') *vpr* to get bogged down (**dans** in).

enneigé, -ée *adj* (*montagne, route*) snow-covered; (*bloqué par la neige*) snowed in.

enneigement *m* bulletin d'e. snow report.

ennemi, -ie 1 *mf* enemy. **2** *adj* pays/soldat e. enemy country/ soldier.

ennui *m* boredom; **un e.** *(tracas)* trouble; **l'e., c'est que** the annoying thing is that.

ennuyé, -ée *adj (air)* bored; **je suis e.** that bothers me.

ennuyer *vt (agacer, préoccuper)* to bother; *(fatiguer)* to bore.

ennuyer (s') *vpr* to get bored.

ennuyeux, -euse *adj* boring; *(contrariant)* annoying.

énoncer *vt* to state.

énorme *adj* enormous, huge.

énormément *adv* enormously; **e. de** an enormous amount of.

énormité *f (d'une demande, d'un crime, d'une somme)* enormity; *(faute)* glaring mistake.

enquête *f (de police)* investigation; *(judiciaire)* inquiry; *(sondage)* survey.

enquêter *vi* to investigate; **e. sur** to investigate.

enquêteur, -euse *mf* investigator.

enragé, -ée *adj (chien)* rabid; *(furieux)* furious.

enregistrement *m (des bagages)* check-in; *(sur bande etc)* recording.

enregistrer 1 *vt (par écrit, sur bande etc)* to record; **(faire) e.** *(bagages)* to check. **2** *vi* to record; **ça enregistre** it's recording.

enrhumer (s') *vpr* to catch a cold.

enrichir (s') *vpr* to get rich.

enrobé, -ée *adj* e. de chocolat chocolate-covered.

enroué, -ée *adj* hoarse.

enrouler *vt* to wind; *(tapis)* to roll up.

enrouler (s') *vpr* s'e. dans *(couvertures)* to wrap oneself up in.

ensanglanté, -ée *adj* bloodstained.

enseignant, -ante *mf* teacher.

enseigne *f* sign; **e. lumineuse** neon sign.

enseignement *m* education; *(action, métier)* teaching.

enseigner 1 *vt* to teach; **e. qch à qn** to teach sb sth. **2** *vi* to teach.

ensemble 1 *adv* together. **2** *m (d'objets)* set; *(vêtement féminin)* outfit; **l'e. du personnel** the whole staff; **l'e. des enseignants** all of the teachers; **dans l'e.** on the whole; **d'e.** *(vue etc)* general.

ensevelir *vt* to bury.

ensoleillé, -ée *adj* sunny.

ensuite *adv (puis)* next; *(plus tard)* afterwards.

entaille *f (fente)* notch; *(blessure)* gash.

entailler *vt (bois)* to notch; *(peau)* to gash.

entamer *vt (pain, peau etc)* to cut (into); *(bouteille etc)* to start (on).

entasser, s'entasser *vpr (objets)* to pile up; **(s')e. dans** *(passagers etc)* to crowd *ou* pile into.

entendre *vt* to hear; **e. parler de** to hear of; **e. dire que** to hear (it said) that.

entendre (s') *vpr (être d'accord)* to agree (**sur** on); **s'e. (avec qn)** to get on (with sb).

entendu, -ue *adj (convenu)* agreed; **e.!** all right!; **bien e.** of course.

entente *f (accord)* agreement; **(bonne) e.** *(amitié)* good relationship.

enterrement *m* burial; *(funérailles)* funeral.

enterrer *vt* to bury.

entêté, -ée *adj* stubborn.

entêtement *m* stubbornness; *(à faire qch)* persistence.

entêter (s') *vpr* to persist (**à faire** in doing).

enthousiasme *m* enthusiasm.

enthousiasmer *vt* to fill with enthusiasm.

enthousiasmer (s') *vpr* s'e.

pour to be ou get enthusiastic about.

enthousiaste adj enthusiastic.

entier, -ière 1 adj (total) whole; (intact) intact; **le pays tout e.** the whole country. **2** m **en e.** completely.

entièrement adv entirely.

entonnoir m (ustensile) funnel.

entorse f sprain.

entortiller vt **e. qch autour de qch** to wrap sth around sth.

entourage m circle of family and friends.

entourer vt to surround (de with); **entouré de** surrounded by.

entracte m (au théâtre) intermission.

entraide f mutual aid.

entraider (s') vpr to help each other.

entrain m **plein d'e.** lively.

entraînant, -ante adj (musique) lively.

entraînement m (sportif) training.

entraîner vt to carry away; (causer) to bring about; (emmener de force) to drag (sb) (away); (athlète etc) to train (**à** for).

entraîner (s') vpr (sportif) to train.

entraîneur m (d'athlète) coach.

entre prép between; **l'un d'e. vous** one of you.

entrebâillé, -ée adj slightly open.

entrebâiller vt to open slightly.

entrechoquer (s') vpr to chink.

entrecôte f (filleted) rib steak.

entrée f (action) entry; (porte) entrance; (accès) admission (**de** to); (vestibule) entrance hall; (billet) ticket (for admission); (plat) first course; (en informatique) input; **à son e.** as he/she came in; **'e. interdite'** 'no entry'; **'e. libre'** 'admission free'.

entreposer vt to store.

entrepôt m warehouse.

entreprendre* vt to undertake (**de faire** to do).

entrepreneur m (en bâtiment) contractor.

entreprise f company, firm.

entrer vi (aux être) to go in; (venir) to come in; **e. dans** (pièce) to come ou go into; (arbre etc) to crash into; **faire/laisser e. qn** to show/let sb in.

entre-temps adv meanwhile.

entretenir* vt to maintain; **e. sa forme** to stay in shape.

entretenir (s') vpr **s'e. de** to talk about (**avec** with).

entretien m maintenance; (dialogue) conversation; (entrevue) interview.

entrevoir* vt (rapidement) to catch a glimpse of; (pressentir) to foresee.

entrevue f interview.

entrouvert, -erte adj half-open.

énumération f list(ing).

énumérer vt to list.

envahir vt to invade; (herbe etc) to overrun (garden).

envahisseur m invader.

enveloppe f (pour lettre) envelope; **e. timbrée à votre adresse** self-addressed stamped envelope.

envelopper vt to wrap (up) (**dans** in).

envers 1 prép toward(s), to. **2** m **à l'e.** (chaussette) inside out; (pantalon) back to front; (la tête en bas) upside down.

envie f (jalousie) envy; (désir) desire; **avoir e. de qch** to want sth; **j'ai e. de faire** I feel like doing.

envier vt to envy (**qch à qn** sb sth).

environ adv (à peu près) about.

environnant, -ante adj surrounding.

environnement m environment.

environner vt to surround.

environs mpl surroundings; **aux environs de** around.

envisager *vt* to consider (**de faire** doing).

envoi *m* sending; *(paquet)* package; **coup d'e.** *Sport* kick-off.

envoler (s') *vpr (oiseau)* to fly away; *(avion)* to take off; *(chapeau etc)* to blow away.

envoyé, -ée *mf (reporter)* correspondent.

envoyer* *vt* to send; *(lancer)* to throw.

épais, -aisse *adj* thick.

épaisseur *f* thickness.

épaissir *vti,* **s'épaissir** *vpr* to thicken.

épanoui, -ie *adj* in full bloom; *(visage)* beaming.

épanouir (s') *vpr* to blossom; *(visage)* to beam.

épargne *f (action, vertu)* saving; *(sommes)* savings.

épargner *vt (argent)* to save; *(ennemi etc)* to spare; **e. qch à qn** *(ennuis etc)* to spare sb sth.

éparpiller *vt,* **s'éparpiller** *vpr* to scatter.

épatant, -ante *adj* marvelous.

épaule *f* shoulder.

épauler *vt (fusil)* to raise (to one's shoulder); **é. qn** *(aider)* to back sb up.

épave *f* wreck.

épée *f* sword.

épeler *vt (mot)* to spell.

éperon *m* spur.

épi *m (de blé etc)* ear.

épice *f* spice.

épicé, -ée *adj* spicy.

épicer *vt* to spice.

épicerie *f* grocery store; *(produits)* groceries.

épicier, -ière *mf* grocer.

épidémie *f* epidemic.

épiler (s') *vpr* to remove unwanted hair; **s'é. les jambes à la cire** to wax one's legs.

épinards *mpl* spinach.

épine *f (de plante)* thorn.

épineux, -euse *adj* thorny.

épingle *f* pin; **é. de nourrice** safety pin; **é. à linge** clothes pin; **é. à cheveux** hairpin.

épisode *m* episode.

épithète *f (adjectif)* attribute.

éplucher *vt (carotte, pomme etc)* to peel.

épluchure *f* peeling.

éponge *f* sponge.

éponger *vt* to sponge.

époque *f (date)* time; *(historique)* age.

épouse *f* wife.

épouser *vt* **é. qn** to marry sb.

épousseter *vt* to dust.

épouvantable *adj* terrifying; *(mauvais)* appalling.

épouvantail *m* scarecrow.

épouvante *f* terror; **film d'é.** horror movie.

épouvanter *vt* to terrify.

époux *m* husband.

épreuve *f (examen)* test; *(sportive)* event; *(malheur)* ordeal.

éprouvant, -ante *adj (pénible)* trying.

éprouver *vt* to test; *(sentiment etc)* to feel.

éprouvette *f* test tube; **bébé-é.** test-tube baby.

épuisant, -ante *adj* exhausting.

épuisé, -ée *adj* exhausted; *(marchandise)* out of stock.

épuiser *vt* to exhaust.

épuiser (s') *vpr (réserves)* to run out; **s'é. à faire** to exhaust oneself doing.

équateur *m* equator.

équation *f* equation.

équerre *f (pour tracer)* square.

équilibre *m* balance; **tenir** *ou* **mettre en é.** to balance **(sur** on); **perdre l'é.** to lose one's balance.

équilibrer *vt (budget)* to balance.

équipage *m* crew.

équipe *f* team; *(d'ouvriers)* crew; **é. de secours** search party.

équipement *m* equipment; *(de camping, ski)* gear.

équiper vt to equip (**de** with).

équipier, -ière mf team member.

équitable adj fair.

équitation f (horseback) riding.

équivalent, -ente adj & m equivalent.

équivaloir* vi é. à qch to be equivalent to sth.

érafler vt to scrape, to scratch.

éraflure f scrape, scratch.

errer vi to wander.

erreur f mistake.

éruption f (de boutons) rash.

es voir être.

escabeau, -x m stepladder.

escadrille f (groupe d'avions) flight.

escalade f climbing.

escalader vt to climb.

escale f faire e. à (avion) to stop (over) at; (navire) to put in at.

escalier m stairs; **e. roulant** escalator.

escalope f escalope (thin slice of meat).

escargot m snail.

escarpé, -ée adj steep.

esclavage m slavery.

esclave mf slave.

escorte f escort.

escorter vt to escort.

escrime f fencing.

escrimeur, -euse mf fencer.

escroc m crook.

espace m space; **e. vert** garden, park.

espacer vt to space out.

espagnol, -ole 1 adj Spanish. **2** mf E. Spaniard. **3** m (langue) Spanish.

espèce f (race) species; (genre) kind, sort; **e. d'idiot!** you fool!

espèces fpl (argent) cash; **en e.** in cash.

espérance f hope.

espérer 1 vt to hope for; **e. que** to hope that; **e. faire** to hope to do. **2** vi to hope.

espiègle adj mischievous.

espion, -onne mf spy.

espionnage m spying.

espionner vt to spy on.

espoir m hope; **sans e.** (cas etc) hopeless.

esprit m spirit; (intellect) mind; (humour) wit; **venir à l'e. de qn** to cross sb's mind.

Esquimau, -de, -aux mf Eskimo.

esquiver vt to dodge.

essai m (épreuve) test; (tentative) try, attempt.

essaim m swarm (of bees etc).

essayage m (de costume) fitting.

essayer vt to try (**de faire** to do); (vêtement) to try on.

essence f gas.

essentiel, -ielle 1 adj essential. **2** m l'e. the main thing.

essentiellement adv essentially.

essieu, -x m axle.

essor m (d'oiseau) flight; (de pays, d'entreprise) rapid growth; **en plein e.** booming; **prendre son e.** to take off.

essorer vt (dans une essoreuse) to spin-dry; (dans une machine à laver) to spin.

essoufflé, -ée adj out of breath.

essuie-glace, pl essuie-glaces m windshield wiper.

essuie-mains m inv (hand) towel.

essuyer vt to wipe.

est¹ voir être.

est² m & adj inv east; **d'e.** (vent) east(erly); **de l'e.** eastern.

estime f regard.

estimer vt (objet) to value; (juger) to consider (**que** that); **e. qn** to have a high regard for sb.

estimer (s') vpr s'e. heureux/etc to consider oneself happy/etc.

estivant, -ante mf vacationer.

estomac m stomach.

estrade f platform.

estropier vt to cripple.

estuaire m estuary.

et conj and; **vingt et un** twenty-one.

étable f cowshed.

établi m (work)bench.

établir vt (installer) to set up; (plan, liste) to draw up.

établir (s') upr (habiter) to settle.

établissement m establishment; **é. scolaire** school.

étage m (d'immeuble) floor; **à l'é.** upstairs; **au premier é.** on the second floor.

étagère f shelf.

étais, était etc voir **être**.

étalage m (vitrine) display window.

étaler vt to lay out; (en vitrine) to display; (beurre etc) to spread.

étanche adj watertight; (montre) waterproof.

étang m pond.

étant voir **être**.

étape f stage; (lieu) stop(over).

État m (nation) State; **homme d'É.** statesman.

état m (condition) state; **en bon é.** in good condition; **être en é. de faire** to be up to doing.

étau, -x m vise.

été¹ pp de **être**.

été² m summer; **en é.** in (the) summer.

éteindre* 1 vt (feu etc) to put out; (lampe etc) to turn ou switch off. **2** vi to switch off.

éteindre (s') upr (feu) to go out.

éteint, -einte adj (feu, bougie) out; (lampe) off.

étendre vt (nappe) to spread (out); (linge) to hang out; **é. le bras/etc** to stretch out one's arm/etc.

étendre (s') upr (personne) to stretch out; (plaine) to stretch; (feu) to spread.

étendu, -ue adj (forêt etc) extensive; (personne) stretched out.

étendue f (importance) extent; (surface) area.

éterniser (s') upr (débat) to drag on endlessly; (visiteur) Fam to stay for ever.

éternité f eternity.

éternuement m sneeze.

éternuer vi to sneeze.

êtes voir **être**.

étinceler vi to sparkle.

étincelle f spark.

étiqueter vt to label.

étiquette f label.

étirer (s') upr to stretch (oneself).

étoffe f material.

étoile f star; **à la belle é.** (out) in the open.

étoilé, -ée adj (ciel) starry.

étonnant, -ante adj surprising.

étonnement m surprise.

étonner vt to surprise.

étonner (s') upr to be surprised (**de qch** at sth; **que** (+ subjonctif) that).

étouffant, -ante adj (air) stifling.

étouffer 1 vt (tuer) to suffocate, to smother; (bruit) to muffle; (feu) to smother; **é. qn** (chaleur) to stifle sb. **2** vi on étouffe! it's stifling!

étouffer (s') upr (en mangeant) to choke (**sur, avec** on).

étourderie f thoughtlessness; **une é.** a thoughtless blunder.

étourdi, -ie adj thoughtless.

étourdir vt to stun; (vertige) to make dizzy.

étourdissant, -ante adj (bruit) deafening.

étourdissement m (malaise) dizzy spell.

étrange adj strange, odd.

étranger, -ère 1 adj (d'un autre pays) foreign; (non familier) strange (**à** to). **2** mf foreigner; (inconnu) stranger; **à l'é.** abroad; **de l'é.** from abroad.

étrangler vt (tuer) to strangle.

étrangler (s') upr to choke.

être* 1 vi to be; **il est tailleur** he's a tailor; **est-ce qu'elle vient?** is she coming?; **il vient, n'est-ce pas?** he's coming, isn't he?; **est-ce qu'il aime le thé?** does he like tea?; **nous sommes dix** there are ten of us; **nous sommes le dix** today is the tenth (of the month); **il a été à Paris** he has been to Paris. **2** *v aux (avec venir, partir etc)* to have; **elle est arrivée** she has arrived. **3** *m* **ê. humain** human being.

étrennes *fpl* New Year's gift.

étrier *m* stirrup.

étroit, -oite *adj* narrow; *(vêtement)* tight; **être à l'é.** to be cramped.

étroitement *adv (surveiller etc)* closely.

étude *f* study; *(salle)* study hall; **à l'é.** *(projet)* under consideration; **faire des études de** *(médecine etc)* to study.

étudiant, -ante *mf & adj* student.

étudier *vti* to study.

étui *m (à lunettes etc)* case.

eu, eue *pp of* **avoir**.

euh! *int* hem!, er!

euro *m (monnaie)* euro.

euro- *préfixe* Euro-.

européen, -enne 1 *adj* European. **2** *mf* **E.** European.

eux *pron (sujet)* they; *(complément)* them; *(réfléchi, emphase)* themselves.

eux-mêmes *pron* themselves.

évacuer *vt* to evacuate.

évadé, -ée *mf* escaped prisoner.

évader (s') *vpr* to escape *(de from)*.

évaluer *vt* to estimate; *(bien)* to value.

Évangile *m* Gospel.

évanouir (s') *vpr* to faint, to pass out.

évanouissement *m* blackout.

évasion *f* escape *(de from)*.

éveiller *vt (susciter)* to arouse.

événement *m* event.

éventail *m* fan; *(choix)* range.

éventrer *vt (sac, oreiller)* to rip open; *(animal)* to open up.

éventuel, -elle *adj* possible.

éventuellement *adv* possibly.

évêque *m* bishop.

évidemment *adv* obviously.

évident *adj* obvious *(que* that); *(facile) Fam* easy.

évier *m* (kitchen) sink.

éviter *vt* to avoid *(de faire* doing); **é. qch à qn** to spare sb sth.

évoluer *vi (changer)* to develop; *(société, situation)* to evolve; *(se déplacer)* to move around.

ex- *préfixe* ex-; **ex-mari** ex-husband.

exact, -e *adj (précis)* exact, accurate; *(juste, vrai)* correct.

exactement *adv* exactly.

exactitude *f (expression précise)* accuracy; *(justesse)* correctness.

ex æquo *adv* **être classés e.** to tie.

exagération *f* exaggeration.

exagéré, -ée *adj* excessive.

exagérer *vti* to exaggerate.

examen *m* examination; *(bac etc)* exam(ination).

examinateur, -trice *mf* examiner.

examiner *vt* to examine.

exaspérer *vt (personne)* to exasperate.

excédent *m* **e. de bagages** excess baggage.

excellent, -ente *adj* excellent.

excepté *prép* except.

exception *f* exception; **à l'e. de** except (for).

exceptionnel, -elle *adj* exceptional.

exceptionnellement *adv* exceptionally.

excès *m* excess; **e. de vitesse** speeding.

excessif, -ive *adj* excessive.

excitant, -ante *adj Fam* exciting.

excitation *f* excitement.

excité, -ée *adj* excited.

exciter *vt* to excite.

exclamation *f* exclamation.

exclamer (s') *vpr* to exclaim.

exclure* *vt* to exclude *(de* from).

excursion *f* trip, outing; *(à pied)* hike.

excuse *f (prétexte)* excuse; **excuses**

(regrets) apology; **faire des excuses** to apologize (**à** to).

excuser *vt* to excuse (**qn d'avoir fait, qn de faire** sb for doing).

excuser (s') *vpr* to apologize (**de** for; **auprès de** to).

exécuter *vt (travail etc)* to carry out; *(jouer)* to perform; **e. qn** *(tuer)* to execute sb.

exécution *f (mise à mort)* execution.

exemplaire *m* copy.

exemple *m* example; **par e.** for example; **donner l'e.** to set an example (**à** to).

exercer *vt (muscles, droits)* to exercise.

exercer (s') *vpr* to practice (**à qch** sth; **à faire** doing).

exercice *m* exercise; **faire de l'e.** to (take) exercise.

exigeant, -eante *adj* demanding.

exigence *f* demand.

exiger *vt* to demand (**de** from; **que** (+ *subjonctif*) that).

exiler (s') *vpr* to go into exile.

existence *f* existence.

exister *vi* to exist; **il existe** there is, *pl* there are.

exorbitant, -ante *adj* exorbitant.

expédier *vt (envoyer)* to send off.

expéditeur, -trice *mf* sender.

expédition *f (envoi)* dispatch; *(voyage)* expedition.

expérience *f (connaissance)* experience; *(scientifique)* experiment; **faire l'e. de qch** to experience sth.

expérimenté, -ée *adj* experienced.

expérimenter *vt (remède, vaccin)* to try out (**sur** on).

expert *m* expert (**en** on, in).

expirer *vi* to breathe out; *(mourir)* to pass away.

explicatif, -ive *adj* explanatory.

explication *f* explanation; *(mise au point)* discussion.

expliquer *vt* to explain (**à** to; **que** that).

expliquer (s') *vpr (discuter)* to talk things over (**avec** with).

exploit *m* feat, exploit.

exploitation *f (agricole)* farm.

exploiter *vt (champs)* to farm; *(profiter de)* to exploit.

explorateur, -trice *mf* explorer.

exploration *f* exploration.

explorer *vt* to explore.

exploser *vi* to explode.

explosif *m* explosive.

explosion *f* explosion.

exportateur, -trice 1 *mf* exporter. **2** *adj* exporting.

exportation *f* export.

exporter *vt* to export (**vers** to; **de** from).

exposé, -ée *adj* **e. au sud**/*etc* facing south/*etc*.

exposer *vt* to expose (**à** to); *(tableau etc)* to exhibit; *(vie)* to risk.

exposer (s') *vpr* **s'e. à** to expose oneself to.

exposition *f (salon)* exhibition.

exprès *adv* on purpose; *(spécialement)* specially.

express *m inv (train)* express; *(café)* espresso.

expression *f (phrase, mine)* expression.

exprimer *vt* to express.

exprimer (s') *vpr* to express oneself.

expulser *vt* to expel (**de** from); *(joueur)* to send off.

exquis, -ise *adj (nourriture)* delicious.

exténué, -ée *adj* exhausted.

extérieur, -e 1 *adj* outside; *(surface)* outer, external; *(signe)* outward. **2** *m* outside; **à l'e. (de)** outside.

extérioriser *vt* to express.

externe *mf (élève)* day student.

extincteur *m* fire extinguisher.

extra- *préfixe* extra-.
extraire* *vt* to extract (**de** from).
extrait *m* extract.
extraordinaire *adj* extraordinary.
extrême *adj & m* extreme.
extrêmement *adv* extremely.
extrémité *f* end.

F

fable *f* fable.
fabricant, -ante *mf* manufacturer.
fabrication *f* manufacture.
fabriquer *vt* to make; *(en usine)* to manufacture; **qu'est-ce qu'il fabrique?** *Fam* what's he up to?
fabuleux, -euse *adj* fabulous.
fac *f abrév (faculté)* university.
façade *f (de bâtiment)* front.
face *f* face; *(de cube etc)* side; **en f.** opposite; **en f. de** opposite, facing; *(en présence de)* in front of, face to face with; **f. à un problème** faced with a problem; **regarder qn en f.** to look sb in the face; **f. à** face to face.
fâché, -ée *adj (air)* angry; *(amis)* on bad terms.
fâcher *vt* to anger.
fâcher (se) *vpr* to get angry (**contre** with); **se f. avec qn** to fall out with sb.
facile *adj* easy; **c'est f. à faire** it's easy to do; **il nous est f. de** it's easy for us to do.
facilement *adv* easily.
facilité *f* easiness; *(à faire qch)* ease.
faciliter *vt* to make easier.
façon *f* way; **la f. dont elle parle** the way (in which) she talks; **f. (d'agir)** behavior; **façons** *(manières)* manners; **de toute f.** anyway; **à ma f.** my way.
facteur *m* mailman, postal carrier.
factrice *f* postal carrier.
facture *f* bill, invoice.
facturer *vt* to bill, to invoice.
facultatif, -ive *adj* optional.
faculté *f* university; **à la f.** at the university, at school.
fade *adj (nourriture)* bland.
faible 1 *adj* weak; *(bruit)* faint; *(vent)* slight; **f. en anglais/*etc*** poor at English/*etc*. **2** *m* **avoir un f. pour** to have a soft spot for.
faiblement *adv* weakly; *(légèrement)* slightly; *(éclairer)* faintly.
faiblesse *f* weakness; faintness; slightness.
faiblir *vi (forces)* to weaken.
faïence *f (matière)* earthenware; **faïences** *(objets)* earthenware.
faillir* *vi* **il a failli tomber** he almost fell.
faillite *f* **faire f.** to go bankrupt.
faim *f* hunger; **avoir f.** to be hungry; **donner f. à qn** to make sb hungry.
fainéant, -ante *mf* lazy bones.
faire* **1** *vt (bruit, faute, gâteau etc)* to make; *(devoir, ménage etc)* to do; *(rêve)* to have; *(sourire)* to give; *(promenade, chute)* to take; **ça fait dix mètres/euros** *(mesure, prix)* it's *ou* that's ten metres/euros; **qu'a-t-il fait (de)?** what's he done (with)?; **que f.?** what should I/you/we/*etc* do?; **f. du tennis/*etc*** to play tennis/*etc*, **f. l'idiot** to play the fool; **ça ne fait rien** that doesn't matter. **2** *vi (agir)* to do; *(paraître)* to look; **il fait vieux** he looks old; **elle ferait bien de partir** she'd do well to leave; **il fait beau/froid/*etc*** it's sunny/cold/*etc*, **ça fait deux ans que je ne l'ai pas vu** I haven't seen him for two years; **ça fait un an que je suis là** I've been here for a year. **3** *v aux* (+ *infinitif*) **f. construire une maison** to have *ou* get a house built; **f. crier/*etc* qn** to make sb shout/*etc*,

se f. obéir/*etc* to be obeyed/*etc*; se f. tuer/*etc* to get *ou* be killed/*etc*.

faire (se) *vpr* se f. des amis to make friends; se f. vieux/*etc* to get old/*etc*; il se fait tard it's getting late; se f. à to get used to; ne t'en fais pas! don't worry!

faire-part *m inv* announcement.

fais, fait, faites *voir* **faire**.

faisable *adj* feasible.

faisan *m* pheasant.

faisceau, -x *m* (*rayons*) beam.

fait, faite (*pp of* **faire**) **1** *adj* (*fromage*) ripe; (*yeux*) made up; tout f. ready made; c'est bien f.! it serves you right! **2** *m* event; (*réalité*) fact; prendre sur le f. to catch red-handed; f. divers news item; au f. by the way; en f. in fact.

falaise *f* cliff.

falloir* *v i* il faut qch/qn I/you/we/*etc* need sth/sb; il lui faut un stylo he/she needs a pen; il faut partir I/you/we/*etc* have to go; il faut que je parte I have to go; il faudrait qu'elle reste she ought to stay; il faut un jour it takes a day (*pour* faire to do).

fameux, -euse *adj* famous; (*excellent*) first-class.

familial, -e, -aux *adj* (*atmosphère, ennuis*) family; (*entreprise*) family-run.

familiariser (se) *vpr* to familiarize oneself (*avec* with).

familiarité *f* familiarity (*avec* with).

familier, -ière *adj* familiar (à to); f. avec qn (over)familiar with sb; animal f. pet.

familièrement *adv* (*parler*) informally.

famille *f* family; en f. with one's family.

fan *m* fan.

fana *mf* être f. de to be crazy about.

fané, -ée *adj* faded.

faner (se) *vpr* to fade.

fanfare *f* (*orchestre*) brass band.

fantaisie *f* (*caprice*) whim; (de) f. (*bouton etc*) novelty.

fantastique *adj* fantastic.

fantôme *m* ghost.

faon *m* fawn.

FAQ *f abrév* (*foire aux questions*) FAQ.

farce¹ *f* practical joke.

farce² *f* (*viande*) stuffing.

farceur, -euse *mf* practical joker.

farcir *vt* to stuff.

fardeau, -x *m* burden.

farine *f* flour.

farouche *adj* (*animal*) easily scared; (*violent*) fierce.

fascination *f* fascination.

fasciner *vt* to fascinate.

fasse(s), fassent *etc voir* **faire**.

fatal, -e, -als *adj* fatal; (*inévitable*) inevitable.

fatalement *adv* inevitably.

fatigant, -ante *adj* tiring; (*ennuyeux*) tiresome.

fatigue *f* tiredness.

fatigué, -ée *adj* tired (de of).

fatiguer *vt* to tire.

fatiguer (se) *vpr* to get tired (de of).

fauché, -ée *adj Fam* (*flat*) broke.

faucher *vt* (*herbe*) to mow; (*blé*) to reap.

faucon *m* hawk.

faufiler (se) *vpr* to edge one's way (*dans* through, into).

fausse *voir* **faux**.

fausser *vt* (*réalité, résultat*) to distort.

faut *voir* **falloir**.

faute *f* mistake; (*responsabilité*) fault; (*péché*) sin; c'est ta f. it's your fault.

fauteuil *m* armchair; f. roulant wheelchair.

fautif, -ive *adj* (*personne*) at fault; (*erroné*) faulty.

fauve *m* wild animal, big cat.

faux, fausse 1 *adj* false; (*pas exact*) wrong; (*monnaie*) forged. **2** *adv* (*chanter*) out of tune.

faux *f* scythe.
faux-filet *m* sirloin.
faveur *f* en f. de in aid *ou* favor of.
favorable *adj* favorable (à to).
favori, -ite *adj & mf* favorite.
favoriser *vt* to favor.
fax *m (appareil, message)* fax.
faxer *vt (message)* to fax.
fée *f* fairy.
féerique *adj* fairy(-like).
feinte *f (ruse)* ruse.
fêler *vt,* se fêler *vpr* to crack.
félicitations *fpl* congratulations (pour on).
féliciter *vt* to congratulate (qn de *ou* sur sb on).
fêlure *f* crack.
femelle *adj & f (animal)* female.
féminin, -ine *adj (prénom etc)* female; *(trait, pronom etc)* feminine; *(mode, revue etc)* women's.
femme *f* woman *(pl* women); *(épouse)* wife; f. médecin woman doctor; f. de ménage cleaning woman.
fendre *vt (bois etc)* to split.
fendre (se) *vpr* to crack.
fenêtre *f* window.
fente *f* slit.
fer *m* iron; barre de f. iron bar; f. forgé wrought iron; f. à cheval horseshoe; f. à repasser iron *(for clothes)*; santé de f. cast-iron constitution.
fera, ferai(t) *etc voir* faire.
fer-blanc, *pl* fers-blancs *m* tin.
férié *adj* jour f. holiday.
ferme¹ *f* farm.
ferme² 1 *adj* firm; *(pas, voix)* steady. 2 *adv (travailler, boire)* hard.
fermé, -ée *adj (porte etc)* closed, shut; *(route etc)* closed; *(gaz etc)* off.
fermement *adv* firmly.
fermer 1 *vt* to close, to shut; *(gaz etc)* to turn *ou* switch off; *(vêtement)* to do up; f. (à clef) to lock. 2 *vi,* se fermer *vpr* to close, to shut.

fermeté *f* firmness.
fermeture *f* closing; *(heure)* closing time; f. éclair® zipper.
fermier, -ière *mf* farmer.
féroce *adj* fierce, savage.
feront *voir* faire.
ferraille *f* scrap metal, old iron; mettre à la f. to scrap.
ferrée *adj* f voie f. railroad; *(rails)* track.
ferroviaire *adj* compagnie f. railroad company.
fertile *adj* fertile.
fesse *f* buttock; les fesses one's behind.
fessée *f* spanking.
festin *m (banquet)* feast.
festival, *pl* -als *m* festival.
fête *f (civile)* holiday; *(religieuse)* feast (day); *(entre amis)* party; f. foraine fair, carnival; f. de famille family celebration; c'est sa f. it's his/her saint's *ou* feast day; f. des Mères Mother's Day; jour de f. holiday; faire la f. to have a good time.
fêter *vt* to celebrate.
feu, -x *m* fire; *(de réchaud)* burner; feux de détresse (hazard) warning flashers; f. rouge red light; *(objet)* traffic lights; mettre le f. à to set fire to; en f. on fire; faire du f. to light *ou* make a fire; avez-vous du f.? have you got a light?; à f. doux on low heat; au f.! fire!; coup de f. *(bruit)* gunshot.
feuillage *m* leaves.
feuille *f* leaf; *(de papier etc)* sheet; f. d'impôt tax form; f. de paye pay slip.
feuilleter *vt* to flip through; pâte feuilletée puff pastry *ou* paste.
feuilleton *m* serial.
feutre *m* crayon f. felt-tip (pen).
février *m* February.
fiabilité *f* reliability.
fiable *adj* reliable.
fiançailles *fpl* engagement.
fiancé *m* fiancé.
fiancée *f* fiancée.

fiancer (se) *vpr* to get engaged (**avec** to).

ficeler *vt* to tie up.

ficelle *f* string.

fiche *f* (*carte*) index card; (*papier*) form.

fiche(r) *vt* (*pp* **fichu**) *Fam* **f. le camp** to shove off; **fiche-moi la paix!** leave me alone!

fiche(r) (se) *vpr* **se f. de qn** to make fun of sb; **je m'en fiche!** I don't give a damn!

fichier *m* card index.

fichu, -ue *adj* **c'est f.** (*abîmé*) *Fam* it's had it.

fidèle *adj* faithful (**à** to); (*client*) regular.

fidélité *f* fidelity, faithfulness.

fier (se) *vpr* **se f. à** to trust.

fier, fière *adj* proud (**de** of).

fièrement *adv* proudly.

fierté *f* pride.

fièvre *f* fever; **avoir de la f.** to have a temperature *ou* a fever.

fiévreux, -euse *adj* feverish.

figer *vti*, **se figer** *vpr* to congeal.

figue *f* fig.

figurant, -ante *mf* (*de film*) extra.

figure *f* (*géométrique*) figure.

figurer *vi* to appear.

figurer (se) *vpr* to imagine.

fil¹ *m* thread; **f. dentaire** dental floss.

fil² *m* (*métallique*) wire; **sans f.** wireless; **f. de fer** wire; **passer un coup de f. à qn** to call sb (up).

file *f* line; (*couloir*) lane; **f. d'attente** line; **en f. (indienne)** in single file.

filer 1 *vt* **f. qn** (*suivre*) to shadow sb. **2** *vi* (*partir*) to rush off; (*aller vite*) to speed along.

filet *m* (*à bagages*) rack; (*d'eau*) trickle; (*de poisson*) fillet; **f. (à provisions)** string bag.

filiale *f* subsidiary (company).

filière *f* (*voie obligée*) channels; (*domaine d'études*) field of study; (*organisation clandestine*) net-work; **suivre la f. normale** to go through the official channels.

fille *f* girl; (*parenté*) daughter; **petite f.** (*little ou young*) girl; **jeune f.** girl, young lady.

fillette *f* little girl.

filleul *m* godson.

film *m* movie, film; (*pellicule*) film; **f. plastique** plastic wrap.

filmer *vt* to film.

fils *m* son.

filtre *m* filter; (**à bout**) **f.** (*cigarette*) (filter-)tipped; (**bout**) **f.** filter tip.

filtrer *vt* to filter.

fin *f* end; **mettre f. à** to put an end to; **prendre f.** to come to an end; **sans f.** endless; **à la f.** in the end; **f. mai** at the end of May.

fin, fine 1 *adj* (*pointe etc*) fine; (*peu épais*) thin; (*esprit, oreille*) sharp. **2** *adv* (*couper etc*) finely.

final, -e, -aux *ou* **-als** *adj* final.

finale *f* final.

finalement *adv* finally.

finance *f* finance.

financement *m* financing.

financer *vt* to finance.

financier, -ière *adj* financial.

finir *vt* to finish; **f. de faire** to finish doing; (*cesser*) to stop doing; **f. par faire** to end up doing; **c'est fini** it's over.

finlandais, -aise 1 *adj* Finnish. **2** *mf* F. Finn.

finnois *m* (*langue*) finnish.

fisc *m* = Internal Revenue.

fissure *f* crack.

fissurer (se) *vpr* to crack.

fixe *adj* fixed; **idée f.** obsession; **regard f.** stare.

fixement *adv* **regarder f.** to stare at.

fixer *vt* (*attacher*) to fix (**à** to); (*date etc*) to fix; **f. (du regard)** to stare at; **être fixé** (*décidé*) to be decided.

flacon *m* (small) bottle.

flair *m* (*d'un chien etc*) (sense of) smell; (*intuition*) insight.

flairer vt to smell.

flamand, -ande 1 adj Flemish. **2** m (langue) Flemish.

flamber vi to burn.

flamme f flame; **en flammes** on fire.

flan m (dessert) custard tart, baked custard.

flanc m side.

flâner vi to stroll.

flaque f puddle.

flash, pl **flashes** m (de photographie) flash(light); (dispositif) flash(gun); (d'informations) (news)-flash.

flatter vt to flatter.

flatterie f flattery.

fléau, -x m (catastrophe) scourge.

flèche f arrow; (d'église) spire; **monter en f.** (prix) to shoot up.

flécher vt to mark (with arrows).

fléchette f dart; **fléchettes** (jeu) darts.

fléchir 1 vt (membre) to flex. **2** vi (poutre) to sag.

flétrir vt, **se flétrir** vpr to wither.

fleur f flower; (d'arbre) blossom; **en fleur(s)** in flower; **à fleurs** (tissu) flowered, flowery.

fleuri, -ie adj in bloom; (tissu) flowered, flowery.

fleurir vi to flower; (arbre) to blossom.

fleuriste mf florist.

fleuve m river.

flexible adj pliable.

flic m Fam cop.

flipper m (jeu) pinball; (appareil) pinball machine.

flocon m (de neige) flake.

flot m (de souvenirs etc) flood; **à f.** afloat; **les flots** the waves.

flotte f (de bateaux) fleet; (pluie) Fam rain; (eau) Fam water.

flotter vi to float; (drapeau) to fly.

flotteur m Pêche float.

flou, -e adj fuzzy, blurred.

fluide adj & m fluid.

fluo adj inv (couleur etc) luminous, fluorescent.

fluorescent, -ente adj fluorescent.

flûte 1 f flute; (verre) champagne glass. **2** int heck!

foi f faith; **être de bonne/mauvaise f.** to be/not to be (completely) sincere.

foie m liver.

foin m hay.

foire f fair.

fois f time; **une f.** once; **deux f.** twice; **chaque f. que** whenever; **une f. qu'il sera arrivé** once he has arrived; **à la f.** at the same time; **des f.** sometimes; **une f. pour toutes** once and for all.

fol voir **fou**.

folie f madness.

folklore m folklore.

folklorique adj musique f. folk music.

folle voir **fou**.

foncé, -ée adj (couleur) dark.

foncer vi (aller vite) to tear along; **f. sur qn** to charge at sb.

fonction f function; **la f. publique** public ou civil service.

fonctionnaire mf civil servant.

fonctionnement m working.

fonctionner vi (machine etc) to work; **faire f.** to operate.

fond m (de boîte, jardin etc) bottom; (de salle etc) back; (arrière-plan) background; **au f. de** at the bottom of; at the back of; **f. de teint** foundation (makeup); **à f.** (connaître etc) thoroughly.

fonder vt (ville etc) to found.

fondre 1 vt to melt; (métal) to melt down; **faire f.** (sucre etc) to dissolve. **2** vi to melt; (sucre etc) to dissolve; **f. en larmes** to burst into tears.

fonds mpl (argent) funds.

font voir **faire**.

fontaine f fountain.

fonte f (des neiges) melting; (fer) cast iron.

football *m* soccer; **f. américain** football.

footballer, -euse *mf* soccer player.

footing *m* jogging.

force *f* force; *(physique, morale)* strength; **ses forces** one's strength; **de f.** by force; **à f. de lire/***etc* through reading/*etc*, after much reading/*etc*.

forcément *adv* obviously; **pas f.** not necessarily.

forcer *vt (porte etc)* to force; **f. qn à faire** to force sb to do.

forcer (se) *vpr* to force oneself (**à faire** to do).

forêt *f* forest.

forfait *m* **déclarer f.** to withdraw from the game.

formalité *f* formality.

format *m* size.

formation *f* education, training.

forme *f (contour)* shape, form; **en f. de poire/***etc* pear/*etc*-shaped; **en (pleine) f.** in good shape *ou* form.

formel, -elle *adj (absolu)* formal.

former *vt* to form; *(apprenti etc)* to train.

former (se) *vpr (apparaître etc)* to form.

formidable *adj* terrific, tremendous.

formulaire *m (feuille)* form.

formule *f* formula; *(phrase)* (set) expression; **f. de politesse** polite form of address.

fort, forte 1 *adj* strong; *(pluie, mer)* heavy; *(voix, radio)* loud; *(fièvre)* high; *(élève)* bright; **f. en** *(maths etc)* good at; **c'est plus f. qu'elle** she can't help it. **2** *adv (frapper, pleuvoir)* hard; *(parler)* loud(ly); *(serrer)* tight; **sentir f.** to have a strong smell.

fort *m* fort.

forteresse *f* fortress.

fortifiant *m* tonic.

fortune *f* fortune; **faire f.** to make one's fortune.

fosse *f (trou)* pit; *(tombe)* grave.

fossé *m* ditch.

fou *(or* **fol** *before vowel or mute h),* **folle 1** *adj (succès, temps)* tremendous; **f. de** *(musique etc)* crazy about; **f. de joie** wildly happy. **2** *mf* madman, madwoman. **3** *m Echecs* bishop; **faire le f.** to play the fool.

foudre *f* **la f.** lightning.

foudroyant, -ante *adj (succès etc)* staggering.

foudroyer *vt (tuer)* to electrocute.

fouet *m* whip; *(de cuisine)* whisk.

fouetter *vt* to whip; *(œufs)* to whisk.

fougère *f* fern.

fouiller 1 *vt (personne, maison etc)* to search. **2** *vi* **f. dans** *(tiroir etc)* to search through.

fouillis *m* jumble, mess.

foulard *m* (head)scarf.

foule *f* crowd; **une f. de** *(objets etc)* a mass of.

fouler (se) *vpr* **se f. la cheville/***etc* to sprain one's ankle/*etc*.

foulure *f* sprain.

four *m* oven.

fourche *f (embranchement)* fork.

fourchette *f (pour manger)* fork.

fourgon *m* van; *(mortuaire)* hearse.

fourgonnette *f* (small) van.

fourmi *f* ant; **avoir des fourmis** to have pins and needles (**dans** in).

fourneau, -x *m (poêle)* stove.

fournée *f* batch.

fournir *vt* to supply; *(effort)* to make; **f. qch à qn** to supply sb with sth.

fournisseur *m (commerçant)* supplier; **f. d'accès** access provider.

fournitures *fpl* **f. de bureau** office supplies; **f. scolaires** school stationery.

fourré, -ée *adj (gant etc)* furlined.

fourrer *vt Fam (mettre)* to stick.

fourre-tout *m inv (sac)* carryall.

fourrière *f (lieu)* pound.

fourrure f fur.
foyer m (maison, famille) home; (résidence de jeunes etc) hostel.
fracas m din.
fracasser vt, **se fracasser** vpr to smash.
fraction f fraction.
fracture f fracture; **se faire une f. au bras**/etc to fracture one's arm/etc.
fracturer vt (porte etc) to break (open).
fracturer (se) vpr **se f. la jambe**/etc to fracture one's leg/etc.
fragile adj fragile.
fragment m fragment.
fraîcheur f freshness; (du temps) coolness.
frais, fraîche 1 adj fresh; (temps) cool; (boisson) cold; **servir f.** (vin etc) to serve chilled. **2 m il fait f.** it's cool; **mettre au f.** to put in a cool place; (au frigo) to refrigerate.
frais mpl expenses; **à mes f.** at my (own) expense.
fraise f strawberry.
framboise f raspberry.
franc, franche adj (personne etc) frank; **coup f.** Football free kick; Basket-ball foul shot.
franc m (monnaie) franc.
français, -aise 1 adj French. **2** mf F. Frenchman, Frenchwoman; **les F.** the French. **3** m (langue) French.
franchement adv frankly; (vraiment) really.
franchir vt (fossé) to jump (over), to clear; (frontière etc) to cross; (porte) to go through; (distance) to cover.
franchise f frankness.
francophone mf French speaker.
frange f (de cheveux) bangs.
frappant, -ante adj striking.
frapper 1 vt to hit, to strike; **f. qn** (surprendre) to strike sb. **2** vi (à la porte etc) to knock (**à** at); **f. du pied** to stamp (one's foot).
fraternel, -elle adj fraternal, brotherly.

fraude f (à un examen) cheating; (crime) fraud; **passer qch en f.** to smuggle sth.
frauder vi (à un examen) to cheat (**à** on).
frayer (se) vpr **se f. un passage** to clear a way (**à travers, dans** through).
frayeur f fright.
fredonner vt to hum.
freezer m freezer.
frein m brake; **donner un coup de f.** to brake.
freinage m braking.
freiner vi to brake.
frêle adj frail.
frémir vi (trembler) to shudder (**de** with).
fréquemment adv frequently.
fréquent, -ente adj frequent.
fréquenter vt (école, église) to attend; **f. qn** to see sb.
fréquenter (se) vpr to see each other.
frère m brother.
friandises fpl candy.
fric m (argent) Fam cash.
frictionner vt to rub (down).
frigidaire® m refrigerator.
frigo m fridge.
frileux, -euse adj sensitive to cold.
frire* vti to fry; **faire f.** to fry.
frisé, -ée adj curly.
friser vti (cheveux) to curl.
frisson m (de froid) shiver; (de peur etc) shudder.
frissonner vi (de froid) to shiver; (de peur etc) to shudder (**de** with).
frit, frite (pp of frire) adj fried.
frites fpl French fries.
friteuse f (deep) fryer.
froid, froide 1 adj cold. **2** m cold; **avoir/prendre f.** to be/catch cold; **il fait f.** it's cold.
froisser (se) vpr (tissu) to crumple; (personne) to take offense (**de** at).
frôler vt (toucher) to brush against.
fromage m cheese; **f. blanc** soft white cheese.

fromagerie f (magasin) cheese shop.

froncer vt f. les sourcils to frown.

front m forehead, brow; (de bataille) front.

frontière f border.

frotter vti to rub; (pour nettoyer) to scrub.

frousse f Fam fear; **avoir la f.** to be scared.

fruit m fruit; **des fruits, les fruits** fruit; **fruits de mer** seafood.

fruitier adj **arbre f.** fruit tree.

frustré, -ée adj frustrated.

fuel m (fuel) oil.

fugitif, -ive mf fugitive.

fugue f faire une f. (enfant) to run away.

fuir* vi to run away; (gaz, robinet etc) to leak.

fuite f flight (de from); (de gaz etc) leak; **en f.** on the run; **prendre la f.** to run away ou off.

fulgurant, -ante adj (progrès) spectacular; (douleur) shooting.

fumé, -ée adj smoked.

fumée f smoke; (vapeur) fumes.

fumer 1 vi to smoke; (liquide brûlant) to steam. **2** vt to smoke.

fumeur, -euse mf smoker; **compartiment fumeurs** smoking compartment.

fumier m manure.

funérailles fpl funeral.

fur et à mesure (au) adv as one goes along; **au f. que** as.

fureur f fury; **faire f.** (mode etc) to be all the rage.

furie f fury.

furieux, -euse adj furious (contre with, at); (vent) raging.

furoncle m boil.

fuseau, -x m (pantalon) ski pants; **f. horaire** time zone.

fusée f rocket.

fusible m fuse.

fusil m rifle, gun; (de chasse) shotgun; **coup de f.** gunshot.

fusillade f (tirs) gunfire.

fusiller vt (exécuter) to shoot; **f. qn du regard** to glare at sb.

fusion f (de métal) melting; (en physique) fusion; **métal en f.** molten metal. ■ (de sociétés) merger.

fusionner vti (sociétés) to merge.

fût m (tonneau) barrel, cask.

futé, -ée adj cunning.

futile adj (personne) frivolous; (prétexte) trivial.

futur, -ure adj & m future.

G

gâcher vt to spoil; (argent etc) to waste.

gâchette f trigger.

gâchis m (gaspillage) waste.

gadget m gadget.

gaffe f Fam (maladresse) gaffe; **faire une g.** to put one's foot in it. ■ **faire g.** to be careful.

gag m gag.

gage m (garantie) security; **mettre en g.** to pawn.

gagnant, -ante 1 adj winning. **2** mf winner.

gagner 1 vt to earn; (par le jeu) to win; (atteindre) to reach; **g. une heure/etc** to save an hour/etc. **2** vi to win.

gai, -e adj cheerful.

gaiement adv cheerfully.

gaieté f cheerfulness.

gain m **un g. de temps** a saving of time; **gains** (salaire) earnings; (au jeu) winnings.

gaine f (sous-vêtement) girdle; (étui) sheath.

gala m gala.

galant, -ante adj gallant.

galerie f gallery; (porte-bagages) roof rack.

galet m pebble.

galette f *(gâteau)* butter cookie; *(crêpe)* buckwheat pancake; **g. des Rois** = Twelfth Night cake.

gallois, -oise 1 *adj* Welsh. **2** *mf* **G.** Welshman, Welshwoman. **3** *m (langue)* Welsh.

galon m *(ruban)* braid; *(de soldat)* stripe.

galop m gallop; **aller au g.** to gallop.

galoper *vi* to gallop.

gambade f leap.

gambader *vi* to leap around.

gamelle f *Fam* pan; *(de chien)* bowl; *(d'ouvrier)* lunch box.

gamin, -ine *mf (enfant)* kid.

gamme f *(de notes)* scale; *(série)* range.

gangster m gangster.

gant m glove; **g. de toilette** face-cloth; **boîte à gants** glove compartment.

ganté, -ée *adj (main)* gloved; *(personne)* wearing gloves.

garage m garage.

garagiste *mf* garage mechanic.

garantie f guarantee; **garantie(s)** *(d'assurance)* cover.

garantir *vt* to guarantee (**contre** against); **g. à qn que** to assure ou guarantee sb that.

garçon m boy; *(jeune homme)* young man; **g. (de café)** waiter.

garde 1 m guard; **g. du corps** bodyguard. **2** f *(d'enfants, de bagages etc)* care (**de** of); **avoir la g. de** to be in charge of; **prendre g.** to pay attention (**à qch** to sth); **prendre g. de ne pas faire** to be careful not to do; **mettre en g.** to warn (**contre** against); **mise en g.** warning; **de g.** on duty; **monter la g.** to stand guard; **sur ses gardes** on one's guard; **chien de g.** watchdog.

garde-chasse, *pl* gardes-chasses *m* gamekeeper.

garder *vt* to keep; *(vêtement)* to keep on; *(surveiller)* to watch (over); *(enfant)* to take care of; **g. la chambre** to stay in one's room.

garder (se) *vpr (aliment)* to keep.

garderie f daycare center.

garde-robe, *pl* garde-robes f wardrobe.

gardien, -ienne *mf (d'immeuble etc)* caretaker, janitor; *(de prison)* (prison) guard; *(de zoo, parc)* keeper; *(de musée)* attendant, guard; **g. de but** goalkeeper.

gare f station; **g. routière** bus station.

garer *vt* to park; *(au garage)* to put in the garage.

garer (se) *vpr* to park.

garnement m rascal.

garnir *vt (équiper)* to outfit, to equip (**de** with); *(magasin)* to stock; *(orner)* to trim (**de** with).

garniture f *(de légumes)* garnish.

gars m fellow, guy.

gas-oil m diesel (oil).

gaspillage m waste.

gaspiller *vt* to waste.

gâté, -ée *adj (dent etc)* bad.

gâteau, -x m cake; **g. de riz** rice pudding; **g. sec** cookie.

gâter *vt* to spoil.

gâter (se) *vpr (aliment, dent)* to go bad; *(temps, situation)* to get worse.

gâteux, -euse *adj* senile.

gauche 1 *adj* left. **2** f la g. *(côté)* the left (side); **à g.** *(tourner)* (to the) left; *(marcher etc)* on the left; **de g.** *(fenêtre etc)* left-hand; **à g. de** on ou to the left of.

gaucher, -ère *adj & mf* left-handed (person).

gaufre f waffle.

gaufrette f wafer.

Gaulois *mpl* les G. the Gauls.

gaver (se) *vpr* to stuff oneself (**de** with).

gaz m inv gas; **réchaud à g.** gas stove.

gaze f gauze.

gazeux, -euse *adj (boisson, eau)* fizzy, carbonated.

gazinière f gas stove.

gazole *m* diesel (oil).

gazon *m* grass, lawn.

géant, -ante *adj & mf* giant.

gel *m* frost.

gelée *f* frost; **g. blanche** ground frost. ▪ *(de fruits)* jelly.

geler *vti* to freeze; **il gèle** it's freezing.

gémir *vi* to groan.

gémissement *m* groan.

gênant, -ante *adj (objet)* cumbersome; *(situation)* awkward; *(bruit)* annoying.

gencive *f* gum.

gendarme *m* gendarme.

gendarmerie *f (local)* police headquarters.

gendre *m* son-in-law.

gêne *f (trouble physique)* discomfort; *(confusion)* embarrassment.

gêné, -ée *adj (mal à l'aise)* awkward.

gêner *vt* to bother; *(troubler)* to embarrass; *(mouvement)* to hamper; *(circulation)* to hold up; **g. qn** *(par sa présence)* to be in sb's way.

général, -e, -aux 1 *adj* general; **en g.** in general. **2** *m (officier)* general.

généralement *adv* generally.

généraliste *mf (médecin)* family doctor.

génération *f* generation.

généreusement *adv* generously.

généreux, -euse *adj* generous (**de** with).

générique *m (de film)* credits.

générosité *f* generosity.

génial, -e, -aux *adj* brilliant.

génie *m* genius.

genou, -x *m* knee; **à genoux** kneeling (down); **se mettre à genoux** to kneel (down); **sur ses genoux** on one's lap.

genre *m (espèce)* kind, sort; *(d'un nom)* gender.

gens *mpl* people; **jeunes g.** young people; *(hommes)* young men.

gentil, -ille *adj* nice; **g. avec qn** nice *ou* kind to sb; **sois g.** *(sage)* be good.

gentillesse *f* kindness.

gentiment *adv* kindly; *(sagement)* nicely.

géographie *f* geography.

géographique *adj* geographical.

géomètre *m* surveyor.

géométrie *f* geometry.

géométrique *adj* geometric(al).

gerbe *f (de blé)* sheaf; *(de fleurs)* bunch.

gercer *vti*, **se gercer** *vpr* to chap.

gerçure *f* **avoir des gerçures aux mains/lèvres** to have chapped hands/lips.

gérer *vt* to manage.

germe *m (microbe)* germ; *(de plante)* seed.

germer *vi (graine)* to start to grow; *(pomme de terre)* to sprout.

geste *m* gesture; **ne pas faire un g.** not to make a move.

gesticuler *vi* to gesticulate.

gestion *f (action)* management.

gibier *m (animaux etc)* game.

giboulée *f* shower.

gicler *vi (liquide)* to spurt; **faire g.** to spurt.

gifle *f* slap (in the face).

gifler *vt* **g. qn** to slap sb.

gigantesque *adj* gigantic.

gigaoctet *m* gigabyte.

gigot *m* leg of mutton *ou* lamb.

gigoter *vi* to wriggle, to fidget.

gilet *m* cardigan; *(de costume)* vest; **g. de sauvetage** life jacket.

girafe *f* giraffe.

giratoire *adj* **sens g.** traffic circle.

girouette *f* weather vane.

gitan, -ane *mf* (Spanish) gipsy.

gîte *m (abri)* resting place; **g. rural** gîte, = self-catering holiday cottage or apartment.

givre *m* frost.

givré, -ée *adj* frost-covered.

glace *f (eau gelée)* ice; *(crème glacée)* ice cream; *(vitre)* window; *(miroir)* mirror.

glacé, -ée *adj (eau, main etc)* icy.
glacer *vt* to chill.
glacial, -e, -aux *adj* icy.
glacier *m (vendeur)* ice-cream seller.
glacière *f* icebox.
glaçon *m* ice cube.
gland *m* acorn.
glande *f* gland.
glissant, -ante *adj* slippery.
glisser 1 *vi (involontairement)* to slip; *(volontairement) (sur la glace etc)* to slide; *(coulisser) (tiroir etc)* to slide; **ça glisse** it's slippery. **2** *vt* to slip (**dans** into).
glissière *f* **porte à g.** sliding door.
global, -e, -aux *adj* total, global.
globe *m* globe.
gloire *f* glory.
glorieux, -euse *adj* glorious.
gloussement *m* cluck(ing).
glousser *vi* to cluck.
glouton, -onne 1 *adj* greedy. **2** *mf* glutton.
gluant, -ante *adj* sticky.
goal *m* goalkeeper.
gobelet *m (de plastique, papier)* cup.
godet *m* pot.
golf *m* golf; *(terrain)* golf course.
golfe *m* gulf, bay.
golfeur, -euse *mf* golfer.
gomme *f (à effacer)* eraser.
gommer *vt (effacer)* to rub out, to erase.
gond *m* hinge.
gonflable *adj* inflatable.
gonflé, -ée *adj* swollen.
gonfler 1 *vt (pneu)* to pump up; *(en soufflant)* to blow up. **2** *vi*, **se gonfler** *vpr* to swell.
gonfleur *m* (air) pump.
gorge *f* throat; *(vallée)* gorge.
gorgée *f* mouthful *(of wine etc)*; **petite g.** sip.
gorille *m* gorilla.
gosier *m* throat.
gosse *mf (enfant)* *Fam* kid.
gouache *f* gouache.

goudron *m* tar.
goudronner *vt* to tar.
goulot *m (de bouteille)* neck; **boire au g.** to drink from the bottle.
gourde *f* water bottle.
gourdin *m* club, cudgel.
gourmand, -ande 1 *adj* (over)-fond of food; **g. de** fond of. **2** *mf* hearty eater.
gourmandise *f* (over)fondness for food.
gourmet *m* gourmet.
gourmette *f* identity bracelet.
gousse *f* **g. d'ail** clove of garlic.
goût *m* taste; **de bon g.** in good taste; **sans g.** tasteless.
goûter 1 *vt* to taste; **g. à qch** to taste (a little of) sth. **2** *vi* to have an afternoon snack. **3** *m* afternoon snack.
goutte *f* drop.
gouttelette *f* droplet.
goutter *vi* to drip (**de** from).
gouttière *f (d'un toit)* gutter.
gouvernail *m* rudder; *(barre)* helm.
gouvernement *m* government.
gouverner *vti* to govern.
grâce 1 *f* grace; *(avantage)* favor. **2** *prép* **g. à** thanks to.
gracieux, -euse *adj (élégant)* graceful.
grade *m* rank.
gradin *m* tier (of seats).
graffiti *mpl* graffiti.
grain *m* grain; *(de café)* bean; *(de poussière)* speck; **g. de beauté** mole; *(sur le visage)* beauty spot.
graine *f* seed.
graisse *f* fat; *(pour machine)* grease; **graisses saturées** saturated fats.
graisser *vt* to grease.
graisseux, -euse *adj (vêtement etc)* greasy.
grammaire *f* grammar; **livre de g.** grammar (book).
gramme *m* gram.
grand, grande 1 *adj* big, large;

(en hauteur) tall; *(chaleur, découverte etc)* great; *(bruit)* loud; *(différence)* big, great; **g. frère/etc** *(plus âgé)* big brother/etc; **il est g. temps** it's high time (**que** that). **2** *adv* **g. ouvert** wide-open; **ouvrir g.** to open wide.

grand-chose *pron* **pas g.** not much.

grandeur *f (importance)* greatness; *(dimension)* size; **g. nature** life-size.

grandiose *adj* imposing.

grandir *vi* to grow.

grand-mère, *pl* **grands-mères** *f* grandmother.

grand-père, *pl* **grands-pères** *m* grandfather.

grand-route, *pl* **grands-routes** *f* main road.

grands-parents *mpl* grandparents.

grange *f* barn.

graphique *m* graph.

grappe *f* cluster; **g. de raisin** bunch of grapes.

gras, grasse 1 *adj* fat; *(aliment)* fatty; *(graisseux)* greasy; **matières grasses** fat. **2** *m (de viande)* fat.

gratin *m* **macaronis/chou-fleur au g.** macaroni and/cauliflower with cheese.

gratitude *f* gratitude.

gratte-ciel *m inv* skyscraper.

gratter *vt* to scrape; *(avec les ongles etc)* to scratch; **ça me gratte** it itches.

gratter (se) *vpr* to scratch oneself.

gratuit, -uite *adj* free.

gratuitement *adv* free (of charge).

gravats *mpl* rubble.

grave *adj* serious; *(voix)* deep; **ce n'est pas g.!** it's not important!; **accent g.** grave accent.

gravement *adv* seriously.

graver *vt (sur métal etc)* to engrave; *(sur bois)* to carve.

graveur *m* engraver.

gravier *m* gravel.

gravillons *mpl* gravel.

gravir *vt* to climb *(with effort)*.

gravité *f (de situation etc)* seriousness.

gravure *f (image)* print.

grec, grecque 1 *adj* Greek. **2** *mf* **G.** Greek. **3** *m (langue)* Greek.

greffe *f (de peau, d'arbre)* graft; *(d'organe)* transplant.

greffer *vt (peau etc)* to graft (**à** on to); *(organe)* to transplant.

grêle *f* hail.

grêler *vi* to hail.

grêlon *m* hailstone.

grelot *m* (small round) bell *(that jingles)*.

grelotter *vi* to shiver (**de** with).

grenade *f (fruit)* pomegranate; *(projectile)* grenade.

grenadine *f* pomegranate syrup, grenadine.

grenier *m* attic.

grenouille *f* frog.

grève *f* strike; **g. de la faim** hunger strike; **se mettre en g.** to go (out) on strike.

gréviste *mf* striker.

gribouiller *vti* to scribble.

gribouillis *m* scribble.

grièvement *adv* **g. blessé** seriously injured.

griffe *f (ongle)* claw; *(de couturier)* (designer) label.

griffer *vt* to scratch.

griffonner *vt* to scribble.

grignoter *vti* to nibble.

gril *m* grill.

grillade *f (viande)* grill.

grillage *m* window screen, chicken wire.

grille *f (clôture)* railing.

grille-pain *m inv* toaster.

griller 1 *vt (viande)* to grill; *(pain)* to toast; **g. un feu rouge** to run a red light. **2** *vi* **mettre à g.** to put on the grill.

grillon *m (insecte)* cricket.

grimace *f* faire des grimaces/la g. to make faces/a face.

grimacer *vi* to make faces *ou* a face.

grimpant, -ante *adj* climbing.

grimper 1 *vi* to climb (**à qch** up sth). **2** *vt* to climb.

grincement *m* creaking; *(des dents)* grinding.

grincer *vi* to creak; **g. des dents** to grind one's teeth.

grincheux, -euse *adj* grumpy.

grippe *f* flu.

grippé, -ée *adj* être g. to have (the) flu.

gris, grise 1 *adj* gray. **2** *m* gray.

grisaille *f* grayness.

grisâtre *adj* grayish.

grisonnant, -ante *adj (cheveux, personne)* graying.

grognement *m* growl; *(d'un cochon)* grunt.

grogner *vi* to growl (**contre** at); *(cochon)* to grunt.

grognon, -onne *adj* grumpy.

grommeler *vti* to mutter.

grondement *m* growl; *(de tonnerre)* rumble.

gronder 1 *vi* to growl; *(tonnerre)* to rumble. **2** *vt* to scold, to tell off.

groom *m* bellboy.

gros, grosse 1 *adj* big; *(gras)* fat; *(épais)* thick; *(effort, progrès)* great; *(somme)* large; *(averse, rhume)* heavy; **g. mot** swearword. **2** *adv* en g. roughly; *(écrire)* in big letters; *(vendre)* wholesale.

groseille *f* (white *ou* red) currant.

grossesse *f* pregnancy.

grosseur *f* size; *(tumeur)* lump.

grossier, -ière *adj* rough; *(personne)* rude (**envers** to).

grossièrement *adv* roughly; *(répondre)* rudely.

grossièreté *f* roughness; *(insolence)* rudeness; *(mot)* rude word.

grossir *vi* to put on weight.

grossiste *mf* wholesaler.

grotte *f* cave, grotto.

grouiller *vi* to be swarming (**de** with).

groupe *m* group.

grouper *vt*, **se grouper** *vpr* to group (together).

grue *f* crane.

grumeau, -x *m* lump.

gruyère *m* gruyère (cheese).

guenilles *fpl* rags (and tatters).

guenon *f* female monkey.

guêpe *f* wasp.

guère *adv* (ne)...g. hardly; **il ne sort g.** he hardly goes out.

guéri, -ie *adj* cured, better.

guérir 1 *vt* to cure (**de** of). **2** *vi* to recover (**de** from).

guérison *f* recovery.

guerre *f* war; **en g.** at war (**avec** with).

guerrier, -ière *mf* warrior.

guet *m* faire le g. to be on the lookout.

guetter *vt* to be on the lookout for.

gueule *f* mouth.

gui *m* mistletoe.

guichet *m* ticket office; *(de banque etc)* window.

guichetier, -ière *mf (de banque etc)* teller; *(à la gare)* ticket agent.

guide *m (personne, livre)* guide.

guider *vt* to guide.

guidon *m* handlebar(s).

guignol *m (spectacle)* = Punch and Judy show.

guillemets *mpl* quotation marks; **entre g.** in quotation marks.

guirlande *f* garland.

guitare *f* guitar.

guitariste *mf* guitarist.

gymnase *m* gymnasium.

gymnastique *f* gymnastics.

gynécologue *mf* gynecologist.

H

habile *adj* skillful (**à qch** at sth; **à faire** at doing).

habileté *f* skill.

habillé, -ée *adj* dressed (**de** in; **en** as a).

habiller *vt* to dress (**de** in).

habiller (s') *vpr* to dress, to get dressed; *(avec élégance)* to dress up.

habitable *adj (maison)* fit to live in.

habitant, -ante *mf (de pays etc)* inhabitant; *(de maison)* occupant.

habitation *f* house.

habité, -ée *adj (région)* inhabited; *(maison)* occupied.

habiter 1 *vi* to live (**à, en, dans** in). **2** *vt (maison etc)* to live in.

habits *mpl (vêtements)* clothes.

habitude *f* habit; **avoir l'h. de qch/faire** to be used to sth/doing; **d'h.** usually; **comme d'h.** as usual.

habitué, -ée *mf* regular.

habituel, -elle *adj* usual.

habituellement *adv* usually.

habituer *vt* **h. qn à** to accustom sb to.

habituer (s') *vpr* to get accustomed (**à** to).

hache *f* ax.

hacher *vt* to chop (up); *(avec un appareil)* to grind.

hachis *m* ground meat.

haie *f (clôture)* hedge; **course de haies** *(coureurs)* hurdle race.

haine *f* hatred.

haïr *vt* to hate.

haleine *f* breath; **hors d'h.** out of breath.

haleter *vi* to pant.

hall *m (de gare)* main hall; *(de maison)* hall(way).

halle *f* (covered) market; **les halles** the central food market.

hallucinant, -ante *adj* extraordinary.

halte 1 *f (arrêt)* stop. **2** *int* stop!

haltères *mpl* weights.

hamac *m* hammock.

hameçon *m* (fish) hook.

hamster *m* hamster.

hanche *f* hip.

handicap *m (physique, mental)* disability, handicap.

handicapé, -ée 1 *adj* disabled, handicapped. **2** *mf* disabled person, handicapped person.

hangar *m* shed; *(pour avions)* hangar.

hanté, -ée *adj* haunted.

harassé, -ée *adj (fatigué)* exhausted.

harceler *vt (importuner)* to harass; *(insister auprès de)* to pester.

hardi, -ie *adj* bold.

hareng *m* herring.

hargneux, -euse *adj* bad-tempered.

haricot *m (blanc)* (haricot) bean; *(vert)* green bean.

harmonica *m* harmonica.

harmonie *f* harmony.

harmonieux, -euse *adj* harmonious.

harnais *m* harness.

harpe *f* harp.

hasard *m* le h. chance; **un h.** a coincidence; **par h.** by chance; **au h.** at random; **à tout h.** just in case.

hasardeux, -euse *adj* risky.

hâte *f* haste; **à la h.** in a hurry; **avoir h. de faire** to be eager to do.

hâter (se) *vpr* to hurry (**de faire** to do).

hausse *f* rise (**de** in); **en h.** rising.

haut, haute 1 *adj* high; *(de taille)* tall; **à haute voix** aloud; **h. de 5 mètres** 16 feet high *ou* tall. **2** *adv (voler etc)* high (up); *(parler)* loud; **tout h.** *(lire etc)* aloud; **h. placé** *(personne)* in a high position. **3** *m* top; **en h. de** at the top of; **en h.** *(loger)* upstairs; *(regarder)* up; *(mettre)* on (the) top;

avoir 5 mètres de h. to be 16 feet high *ou* tall.

hautain, -aine *adj* haughty.

hauteur *f* height.

haut-parleur *m* loudspeaker.

hayon *m (porte)* hatchback.

hé! *int (appel)* hey!

hebdomadaire *adj & m* weekly.

héberger *vt* to put up.

hectare *m* hectare *(= 2,47 acres).*

hein! *int Fam* eh!

hélas! *int* unfortunately.

hélice *f* propeller.

hélicoptère *m* helicopter.

helvétique *adj* Swiss.

hémorragie *f* hemorrhage; **h. cérébrale** stroke.

hennir *vi* to neigh.

hépatite *f* hepatitis.

herbe *f* grass; *(pour soigner etc)* herb; **mauvaise h.** weed; **fines herbes** herbs.

hérisser (se) *vpr (poils)* to bristle (up).

hérisson *m* hedgehog.

héritage *m (biens)* inheritance.

hériter *vti* to inherit (**qch de qn** sth from sb); **h. de qch** to inherit sth.

héritier *m* heir.

héritière *f* heiress.

hermétique *adj* airtight.

héroïne *f (femme)* heroine; *(drogue)* heroin.

héroïque *adj* heroic.

héros *m* hero.

hésitant, -ante *adj* hesitant; *(pas, voix)* unsteady.

hésitation *f* hesitation; **avec h.** hesitantly.

hésiter *vi* to hesitate (**sur** over, about; **à faire** to do).

hêtre *m (arbre, bois)* beech.

heu! *int* er!

heure *f* hour; *(moment)* time; **quelle h. est-il?** what time is it?; **il est six heures** it's six (o'clock); **six heures moins cinq** five to six; **six heures cinq** five after *ou* past six; **à l'h.** *(arriver)* on time; **dix kilomè-** **tres à l'h.** six miles an hour; **de bonne h.** early; **tout à l'h.** *(futur)* later; *(passé)* a moment ago; **heures supplémentaires** overtime; **l'h. de pointe** *(circulation etc)* rush hour.

heureusement *adv (par chance)* fortunately.

heureux, -euse 1 *adj* happy; *(chanceux)* lucky; **h. de qch/de voir qn** happy *ou* glad about sth/to see sb. **2** *adv (vivre etc)* happily.

heurter *vt* to hit.

heurter (se) *vpr* **se h. à** to bump into, to hit.

hexagone *m* hexagon; **l'H.** France.

hibou, -x *m* owl.

hier *adv & m* yesterday; **h. soir** last night.

hi-fi *adj inv & f inv* hi-fi.

hilarant, -ante *adj* hilarious.

hippodrome *m* racetrack.

hippopotame *m* hippopotamus.

hirondelle *f* swallow.

hisser (se) *vpr* to heave oneself up.

histoire *f* history; *(récit, mensonge)* story; **des histoires** *(ennuis)* trouble; **sans histoires** *(voyage etc)* uneventful.

historique *adj* historical; *(lieu, événement)* historic.

hiver *m* winter.

HLM *m ou f abrév (habitation à loyer modéré)* = low-income housing.

hocher *vt* **h. la tête** *(pour dire oui)* to nod one's head; *(pour dire non)* to shake one's head.

hochet *m (jouet)* rattle.

hockey *m* hockey; **h. sur glace** ice hockey.

hold-up *m inv (attaque)* holdup.

hollandais, -aise 1 *adj* Dutch. **2** *mf* H. Dutchman, Dutchwoman; **les H.** the Dutch. **3** *m (langue)* Dutch.

homard *m* lobster.

homme *m* man *(pl men)*; **l'h.** *(espèce)* man(kind); **des vête-**

ments d'h. men's clothes; **h. d'affaires** businessman.

homosexuel, -elle *adj & mf* homosexual.

honnête *adj* honest; *(satisfaisant)* decent.

honnêtement *adv* honestly; decently.

honnêteté *f* honesty.

honneur *m* honor; **en l'h. de** in honor of; **faire h. à** *(sa famille etc)* to be a credit to; *(repas)* to do justice to.

honorable *adj* honorable; *(convenable)* respectable.

honoraires *mpl* fees.

honte *f* shame; **avoir h.** to be *ou* feel ashamed (**de qch** of sth; **de faire** to do, of doing).

honteux, -euse *adj* ashamed; *(scandaleux)* shameful.

hôpital, -aux *m* hospital; **à l'h.** in the hospital.

hoquet *m* **avoir le h.** to have (the) hiccups.

horaire *m* timetable.

horizon *m* horizon; **à l'h.** on the horizon.

horizontal, -e, -aux *adj* horizontal.

horloge *f* clock.

horreur *f* horror; **faire h. à** to disgust; **avoir h. de** to hate.

horrible *adj* horrible.

horriblement *adv* horribly.

horrifiant, -ante *adj* horrifying.

horrifié, -ée *adj* horrified.

hors *prép* **h. service** out of order; **h. de** out of.

hors-bord *m inv* speedboat.

hors-d'œuvre *m inv* *(à table)* hors d'oeuvre, appetizer.

hors-taxe *adj inv* duty-free.

hospitaliser *vt* to hospitalize.

hospitalité *f* hospitality.

hostile *adj* hostile (**à** to, towards).

hostilité *f* hostility (**envers** to, towards).

hôte **1** *m (qui reçoit)* host. **2** *mf (invité)* guest.

hôtel *m* hotel; **h. de ville** city hall.

hôtesse *f* hostess; **h. (de l'air)** flight attendant.

hotte *f* basket *(carried on back)*.

houleux, -euse *adj (mer)* rough; *(réunion)* stormy.

hourra! *int* hurray!

housse *f* (protective) cover.

HT *abrév (hors taxe)* before tax, exclusive of tax.

hublot *m* porthole.

huées *fpl* boos.

huile *f* oil.

huit *adj & m* eight; **h. jours** a week.

huitième *adj & mf* eighth.

huître *f* oyster.

humain, -aine *adj* human.

humanité *f* humanity.

humble *adj* humble.

humblement *adv* humbly.

humecter *vt* to moisten.

humeur *f* mood; *(caractère)* temperament; **bonne h.** *(gaieté)* good humor; **de bonne/mauvaise h.** in a good/bad mood.

humide *adj* damp.

humidité *f* humidity; *(plutôt froide)* damp(ness).

humiliation *f* humiliation.

humilier *vt* to humiliate.

humoristique *adj* humorous.

humour *m* humor; **avoir de l'h.** to have a sense of humor.

hurlement *m (d'un loup, du vent)* howl; *(d'une personne)* scream.

hurler **1** *vi (loup, vent)* to howl; *(personne)* to scream. **2** *vt* to scream.

hydrater *vt (peau)* to moisturize.

hygiène *f* hygiene.

hygiénique *adj* hygienic; **papier h.** toilet paper.

hymne *m* **h. national** national anthem.

hypermarché *m* hypermarket.

hypocrisie *f* hypocrisy.

hypocrite **1** *adj* hypocritical. **2** *mf* hypocrite.

hypothèse *f (supposition)* assumption.

I

iceberg *m* iceberg.

ici *adv* here; **par i.** *(passer)* this way; *(habiter)* around here; **jusqu'i.** *(temps)* up to now; *(lieu)* as far as this *ou* here; **d'i. peu** before long.

idéal, -e, -aux *ou* **-als** *adj & m* ideal.

idée *f* idea; **changer d'i.** to change one's mind.

identifier *vt* to identify.

identifier (s') *vpr* s'i. **à** *ou* **avec** to identify (oneself) with.

identique *adj* identical (**à** to, with).

identité *f* identity; **carte d'i.** identity card, ID card.

idiot, -ote 1 *adj* silly. **2** *mf* idiot.

idiotie *f* **une i.** a silly thing.

idole *m* idol.

igloo *m* igloo.

ignifugé, -ée *adj* fireproof(ed).

ignoble *adj* vile.

ignorance *f* ignorance.

ignorant, -ante *adj* ignorant (**de** of).

ignorer *vt* not to know; **i. qn** to ignore sb.

il *pron (personne)* he; *(chose, animal)* it; **il pleut** it's raining; **il y a** there is; *pl* there are; **il y a six ans** six years ago; **il y a une heure qu'il travaille** he's been working for an hour; **qu'est-ce qu'il y a?** what's the matter?

île *f* island.

illégal, -e, -aux *adj* illegal.

illettré, -ée *adj* illiterate.

illisible *adj (écriture)* illegible.

illuminer *vt*, **s'illuminer** *vpr* to light up.

illusion *f* illusion; **se faire des illusions** to delude oneself (**sur** about).

illustration *f* illustration.

illustré *m* comic.

illustrer *vt* to illustrate (**de** with).

ils *pron* they.

image *f* picture; *(dans une glace)* reflection.

imaginaire *adj* imaginary.

imagination *f* imagination.

imaginer *vt*, **s'imaginer** *vpr* to imagine (**que** that).

imbattable *adj* unbeatable.

imbécile *mf* idiot.

imbécilité *f (état)* imbecility; **une i.** *(action, parole)* an idiotic thing.

imbuvable *adj* undrinkable.

imitateur, -trice *mf (artiste)* impersonator.

imitation *f* imitation.

imiter *vt* to imitate; **i. qn** *(pour rire)* to mimic sb; *(faire comme)* to do the same as sb.

immangeable *adj* inedible.

immatriculation *f* registration.

immédiat, -ate *adj* immediate.

immédiatement *adv* immediately.

immense *adj* immense.

immeuble *m* building; *(d'habitation)* apartment building; *(de bureaux)* office building.

immigration *f* immigration.

immigré, -ée *adj & mf* immigrant.

immobile *adj* still.

immobilier, -ère 1 *adj* **marché i.** property market. **2** *m* **l'i.** real estate.

immobiliser *vt* to bring to a stop.

immobiliser (s') *vpr* to come to a stop.

immonde *adj (sale)* foul; *(ignoble, laid)* vile.

immortel, -elle *adj* immortal.

immuable *adj* immutable, unchanging.

impair, -e *adj (nombre)* odd.

impardonnable *adj* unforgivable.

imparfait *m (temps)* Grammaire imperfect.

impartial, -e, -aux *adj* fair, un- biased.

impasse *f* dead end.

impassible *adj* impassive.

impatience *f* impatience.

impatient, -ente *adj* impatient (**de** faire to do).

impatienter (s') *vpr* to get impa- tient.

impeccable *adj (propre)* imma- culate.

impératif *m Grammaire* imperative.

imperméable 1 *adj (tissu)* water- proof. **2** *m* raincoat.

impitoyable *adj* ruthless.

implanter (s') *vpr* to become established.

impoli, -ie *adj* rude.

impolitesse *f* rudeness.

importance *f* importance; **ça n'a pas d'i.** it doesn't matter.

important, -ante 1 *adj* impor- tant; *(quantité etc)* big. **2** *m* **l'i., c'est de** the important thing is to.

importateur, -trice 1 *adj* im- porting. **2** *mf* importer.

importation *f* import; **d'i.** *(arti- cle)* imported.

importer 1 *vi* **n'importe qui/ quoi/où/quand/comment** any- one/anything/anywhere/anytime/ anyhow. **2** *vt* to import (**de** from).

imposer *vt* to impose (**à** on).

impossibilité *f* impossibility.

impossible *adj* impossible (**à** **faire** to do); **il (nous) est i. de le faire** it is impossible (for us) to do it.

impôt *m* tax; **i. sur le revenu** in- come tax; **(service des) impôts** tax authorities.

impression *f* impression.

impressionnant, -ante *adj* im- pressive.

impressionner *vt (émouvoir)* to make a strong impression on.

imprévisible *adj* unforeseeable.

imprévu, -ue *adj* unexpected.

imprimante *f (d'ordinateur)* prin- ter.

imprimé *m* printed form.

imprimer *vt (livre etc)* to print.

imprimerie *f* printing plant.

improviser *vti* to improvize.

improviste (à l') *adv* unexpec- tedly.

imprudence *f* carelessness, fool- ishness; **commettre une i.** to do something foolish.

imprudent, -ente *adj* careless, foolish.

impuissant, -ante *adj* helpless.

impulsif, -ive *adj* impulsive.

inabordable *adj (prix)* prohibitive.

inacceptable *adj* unacceptable.

inachevé, -ée *adj* unfinished.

inadapté, -ée *adj (socialement)* maladjusted; *(physiquement, men- talement)* handicapped; *(matériel)* unsuitable (**à** for).

inadmissible *adj* unacceptable, inadmissible.

inanimé, -ée *adj (mort)* lifeless; *(évanoui)* unconscious.

inaperçu, -ue *adj* **passer i.** to go unnoticed.

inapte *adj (intellectuellement)* un- suited (**à** for); *(médicalement)* unfit (**à** for).

inattendu, -ue *adj* unexpected.

inattention *f* lack of attention; **un moment d'i.** a moment of distrac- tion.

inauguration *f* inauguration.

inaugurer *vt* to inaugurate.

incapable *adj* **i. de faire qch** unable to do sth.

incapacité *f (impossibilité)* inabili- ty (**de** faire to do); *(invalidité)* dis- ability; **être dans l'i. de faire qch** to be unable to do sth.

incarner *vt* to embody.

incassable *adj* unbreakable.

incendie *m* fire.

incendier *vt* to set fire to.

incertain, -aine *adj* uncertain; *(temps)* unsettled.

incertitude *f* uncertainty.

incessamment *adv* very soon.

incessant, -ante adj continual.
inchangé, -ée adj unchanged.
incident m incident.
incisive f incisor (tooth).
inciter vt to encourage (**à faire** to do).
incliner vt (courber) to bend; (pencher) to tilt.
incliner (s') vpr (se courber) to bow (down).
inclure vt to include; (dans un courrier) to enclose (**dans** with).
inclus, -use adj inclusive; **jusqu'à lundi i.** up to and including Monday.
incohérent, -ente adj (propos) incoherent; (histoire) inconsistent.
incolore adj colorless; (vernis) clear.
incommoder vt to bother.
incomparable adj matchless.
incompatible adj incompatible.
incompétent, -ente adj incompetent.
incomplet, -ète adj incomplete.
incompréhensible adj incomprehensible.
inconnu, -ue 1 adj unknown (**à** to). **2** mf (étranger) stranger.
inconscient, -ente adj unconscious (**de** of); (imprudent) thoughtless.
inconsolable adj heartbroken, cut up.
incontestable adj undeniable.
inconvenant, -ante adj improper.
inconvénient m drawback.
incorrect, -e adj (grossier) impolite.
incroyable adj incredible.
inculpé, -ée mf **l'i.** the accused.
inculper vt to charge (**de** with).
inculte adj (terre, personne) uncultivated.
incurable adj incurable.
indécis, -ise adj (hésitant) undecided.
indéfini, -ie adj indefinite.
indéfiniment adv indefinitely.

indemne adj unhurt.
indemnisation f compensation.
indemnité f compensation; (allocation) allowance.
indépendance f independence.
indépendant, -ante adj independent (**de** of).
indescriptible adj indescribable.
indéterminé, -ée adj (date, heure) unspecified; (raison) unknown.
index m (doigt) index finger, forefinger.
indicatif m (à la radio) theme song ou music; (téléphonique) area code; Grammaire indicative.
indication f (piece of) information; **indications** (pour aller quelque part) directions.
indice m (dans une enquête) clue.
indien, -ienne 1 adj Indian. **2** mf **I.** Indian.
indifférence f indifference (**à** to).
indifférent, -ente adj indifferent (**à** to).
indigestion f (attack of) indigestion.
indignation f indignation.
indigne adj (personne) unworthy; (conduite) shameful; **i. de qn/qch** unworthy of sb/sth.
indigner (s') vpr to be ou become indignant (**de** at).
indiquer vt (montrer) to show; (dire) to tell; **i. du doigt** to point to ou at.
indirect, -e adj indirect.
indirectement adv indirectly.
indiscipliné, -ée adj unruly.
indiscret, -ète adj inquisitive.
indiscrétion f indiscretion.
indispensable adj essential.
indisponible adj unavailable.
indistinct, -incte adj unclear.
individu m individual.
individuel, -elle adj individual.
indolore adj painless.
indulgent, -ente adj indulgent (**envers** to).

industrialisé, -ée *adj* industrialized.

industrie *f* industry.

industriel, -elle *adj* industrial.

inédit, -ite *adj (texte)* unpublished.

inefficace *adj (mesure etc)* ineffective; *(personne)* inefficient.

inégal, -e, -aux *adj (parts, lutte)* unequal; *(sol, humeur)* uneven; *(travail)* inconsistent.

inépuisable *adj* inexhaustible.

inespéré, -ée *adj* unhoped-for.

inestimable *adj* priceless.

inévitable *adj* inevitable, unavoidable.

inexact, -e *adj* inaccurate.

inexcusable *adj* inexcusable.

inexplicable *adj* inexplicable.

inexpliqué, -ée *adj* unexplained.

infaillible *adj* infallible.

infarctus *m* un i. a coronary.

infatigable *adj* tireless.

infect, -e *adj (odeur)* foul; *(café etc)* vile.

infecter (s') *upr* to get infected.

infection *f* infection; *(odeur)* stench.

inférieur, -e *adj* lower; *(qualité etc)* inferior (**à** to); **l'étage i.** the floor below.

infériorité *f* inferiority.

infernal, -e, -aux *adj* infernal.

infesté, -ée *adj* i. de requins/etc shark/etc-infested.

infidèle *adj* unfaithful (**à** to).

infiltrer (s') *upr (liquide)* to seep (through) (**dans** into).

infini, -ie 1 *adj* infinite. **2** *m* infinity.

infiniment *adv (regretter, remercier)* very much.

infinitif *m Grammaire* infinitive.

infirme *adj & mf* disabled (person).

infirmerie *f* sick room, sickbay.

infirmier *m* male nurse.

infirmière *f* nurse.

inflammable *adj* (in)flammable.

inflammation *f* inflammation.

inflation *f* inflation.

inflexible *adj* inflexible.

influence *f* influence.

influencer *vt* to influence.

informaticien, -enne *mf* computer scientist.

information *f* information; *(nouvelle)* piece of news; **les informations** the news.

informatique *f (science)* computer science, IT; *(technique)* data processing.

informatisé, -ée *adj* computerized.

informer *vt* to inform (**de** of, about; **que** that).

informer (s') *upr* to inquire (**de** about; **si** if, whether).

infraction *f* offense.

infusion *f* herbal *ou* herb tea.

ingénieur *m* engineer.

ingénieux, -euse *adj* ingenious.

ingrat, -ate *adj* ungrateful (**envers** to).

ingratitude *f* ingratitude.

ingrédient *m* ingredient.

inhabitable *adj* uninhabitable.

inhabité, -ée *adj* uninhabited.

inhabituel, -elle *adj* unusual.

inhumain, -aine *adj* inhuman.

inimaginable *adj* unimaginable.

ininflammable *adj* non-flammable.

ininterrompu, -ue *adj* continuous.

initiale *f (lettre)* initial.

initier (s') *upr* s'i. à qch to start learning sth.

injecter *vt* to inject.

injection *f* injection.

injure *f* insult.

injurier *vt* to insult.

injuste *adj (contraire à la justice)* unjust; *(non équitable)* unfair.

injustice *f* injustice.

inlassable *adj* untiring.

innocence *f* innocence.

innocent, -ente 1 *adj* innocent (**de** of). **2** *mf* innocent person.

innombrable *adj* countless.

inoccupé, -ée *adj* unoccupied.

inoffensif, -ive *adj* harmless.

inondation *f* flood.

inonder *vt* to flood.

inoubliable *adj* unforgettable.

inouï, -ïe *adj* incredible.

inox® *m* stainless steel.

inoxydable *adj* **acier i.** stainless steel.

inqualifiable *adj* unspeakable.

inquiet, -iète *adj* worried (**de** about).

inquiétant, -ante *adj* worrying.

inquiéter *vt* to worry.

inquiéter (s') *vpr* s'i. (**de**) to worry (about).

inquiétude *f* worry.

insatisfait, -aite *adj (personne)* dissatisfied.

inscription *f* registration; *(sur écriteau etc)* inscription; **frais d'i.** *(à l'université)* tuition fees.

inscrire *vt* to write *ou* put down; **i. qn** to enroll sb.

inscrire (s') *vpr* to put one's name down; **s'i. à** *(club)* to join; *(examen)* to enroll for, to register for.

insecte *m* insect.

insecticide *m* insecticide.

insécurité *f* insecurity.

insensé, -ée *adj (projet, idée)* crazy; *(espoir)* wild.

insensible *adj* insensitive (**à** to).

inséparable *adj* inseparable (**de** from).

insigne *m* badge.

insignifiant, -ante *adj* insignificant.

insistance *f* insistence.

insister *vt* to insist (**pour faire** on doing); **i. sur** *(détail etc)* to stress.

insolation *f* sunstroke.

insolence *f* insolence.

insolent, -ente *adj* insolent.

insomnie *f* insomnia.

insonoriser *vt* to soundproof.

insouciant, -ante *adj* carefree.

inspecter *vt* to inspect.

inspecteur, -trice *mf* inspector.

inspection *f* inspection.

inspiration *f* inspiration.

inspirer *vt* to inspire (**qch à qn** sb with sth).

instable *adj (meuble)* shaky.

installation *f* putting in; *(dans une maison)* moving in.

installer *vt (appareil etc)* to install, to put in; *(étagère)* to put up.

installer (s') *vpr (s'asseoir, s'établir)* to settle (down); **s'i. dans** *(maison)* to move into.

instant *m* moment; **à l'i.** a moment ago; **pour l'i.** for the moment.

instaurer *vt* to establish.

instinct *m* instinct.

instinctif, -ive *adj* instinctive.

instituteur, -trice *mf* elementary school teacher.

institution *f (organisation, structure)* institution.

instructif, -ive *adj* instructive.

instruction *f* education; **instructions** *(ordres)* instructions.

instruire *vt* to teach, to educate.

instruire (s') *vpr* to educate oneself.

instrument *m* instrument; *(outil)* implement.

insuffisant, -ante *adj* inadequate.

insulte *f* insult (**à** to).

insulter *vt* to insult.

insupportable *adj* unbearable.

intact, -e *adj* intact.

intégral, -e, -aux *adj (paiement)* full; *(édition)* unabridged; **version intégrale** *(de film)* uncut version.

intégralement *adv* in full.

intégrer (s') *vpr* to become integrated.

intellectuel, -elle *adj & mf* intellectual.

intelligemment *adv* intelligently.

intelligence *f* intelligence.

intelligent, -ente *adj* intelligent.

intempéries *fpl* **les i.** bad weather.

intense *adj* intense; *(circulation)* heavy.

intensifier *vt*, **s'intensifier** *vpr* to intensify.

intensité *f* intensity.

intention *f* intention; **avoir l'i. de faire** to intend to do.

interchangeable *adj* interchangeable.

interdiction *f* ban (**de** on); **'i. de fumer'** 'no smoking'.

interdire* *vt* to forbid, not to allow (**qch à qn** sb sth); **i. à qn de faire** not to allow sb to do.

interdit, -ite *adj* forbidden; **'stationnement i.'** 'no parking'.

intéressant, -ante *adj* interesting; *(prix etc)* attractive.

intéresser *vt* to interest.

intéresser (s') *vpr* **s'i. à** to take an interest in.

intérêt *m* interest; **intérêts** *(argent)* interest; **tu as i. à faire** you'd do well to do.

intérieur, -e *adj* inner; *(poche)* inside; *(politique)* domestic. **2** *m* inside (**de** of); **à l'i. (de)** inside.

intérim *m* *(travail temporaire)* temporary work; **président par i.** acting president.

intérimaire 1 *adj* *(fonction, employé)* temporary. **2** *mf* *(travailleur)* temporary worker; *(secrétaire)* temp.

interlocuteur, -trice *mf* **mon i.** the person I am/was/*etc* speaking to.

intermédiaire *mf* **par l'i. de** through (the medium of).

interminable *adj* endless.

international, -e, -aux *adj* international.

internaute *mf* Internet surfer.

interne *mf* *(élève)* boarder.

Internet *m* the Internet; **sur l.** on the Internet.

interpeller *vt* *(appeler)* to shout at.

interphone *m* intercom.

interposer (s') *vpr* to intervene (**dans** in).

interprète *mf* interpreter; *(chanteur)* singer.

interpréter *vt* *(expliquer)* to interpret; *(chanter)* to sing.

interrogatif, -ive *adj & m Grammaire* interrogative.

interrogation *f* question; *(à l'école)* test.

interrogatoire *m* interrogation.

interroger *vt* to question.

interrompre* *vt* to interrupt.

interrupteur *m* *(électrique)* switch.

interruption *f* interruption.

intersection *f* intersection.

intervalle *m* *(écart)* gap; *(temps)* interval.

intervenir* *vi* to intervene; *(survenir)* to occur.

intervention *f* intervention; **i. (chirurgicale)** operation.

interview *f* interview.

interviewer *vt* to interview.

intestin *m* bowel.

intime *adj* intimate; *(journal, mariage)* private.

intimider *vt* to intimidate.

intimité *f* *(familiarité)* intimacy; *(vie privée)* privacy; **dans l'i.** in private.

intituler (s') *vpr* to be entitled.

intolérable *adj* intolerable (**que** + *subjonctif* that).

intoxication *f* *(empoisonnement)* poisoning; **i. alimentaire** food poisoning.

intraduisible *adj* impossible to translate.

intransitif, -ive *adj Grammaire* intransitive.

intrépide *adj* fearless.

intrigue *f* intrigue; *(de film, roman)* plot.

introduction *f* introduction.

introduire* *vt* *(insérer)* to put in (**dans** to); *(faire entrer)* to show in.

introduire (s') *upr* s'i. dans to get into.

introuvable *adj* nowhere to be found.

intrus, -use *mf* intruder.

inusable *adj* durable.

inutile *adj* useless.

inutilement *adv* needlessly.

inutilisable *adj* unusable.

invalide 1 *adj* disabled. **2** *mf* disabled person.

invariable *adj* invariable.

invasion *f* invasion.

inventer *vt* to invent; *(imaginer)* to make up.

inventeur, -trice *mf* inventor.

invention *f* invention.

inverse *adj (sens)* opposite; *(ordre)* reverse.

inverser *vt (ordre)* to reverse.

investir *vti* to invest (**dans** in).

investissement *m* investment.

invisible *adj* invisible.

invitation *f* invitation.

invité, -ée *mf* guest.

inviter *vt* to invite.

inviter (s') *upr* s'i. **(chez qn)** to (gate)crash (sb's house/*etc*).

involontaire *adj (geste etc)* unintentional.

invraisemblable *adj (extraordinaire)* incredible; *(alibi)* implausible.

ira, irai(t) *voir* **aller**[1].

irlandais, -aise 1 *adj* Irish. **2** *mf* **I.** Irishman, Irishwoman; **les I.** the Irish. **3** *m (langue)* Irish.

ironie *f* irony.

ironique *adj* ironic(al).

iront *voir* **aller**[1].

irréel, -elle *adj* unreal.

irrégulier, -ière *adj* irregular.

irremplaçable *adj* irreplaceable.

irréparable *adj (véhicule etc)* beyond repair.

irréprochable *adj* irreproachable.

irrésistible *adj* irresistible.

irriguer *vt* to irrigate.

irritable *adj* irritable.

irritation *f* irritation.

irriter *vt* to irritate.

irruption *f* **faire i. dans** to burst into.

islamique *adj* Islamic.

isolant *m* insulation (material).

isolé, -ée *adj* isolated (**de** from).

isolement *m (de personne)* isolation.

isoler *vt* to isolate (**de** from); *(du froid etc)* to insulate.

issu, -ue *adj* **être i. de** to come from.

issue *f* exit; **rue**/*etc* **sans i.** dead end.

italien, -ienne 1 *adj* Italian. **2** *mf* **I.** Italian. **3** *m (langue)* Italian.

italique *m* italics.

itinéraire *m* route.

IUT *m abréu (institut universitaire de technologie)* = vocational higher education college.

ivoire *m* ivory.

ivre *adj* drunk.

ivresse *f* drunkenness.

ivrogne *mf* drunk, drunkard.

J

jaillir *vi (liquide)* to spurt (out); *(lumière)* to beam out, to shine (forth).

jalousie *f* jealousy.

jaloux, -ouse *adj* jealous (**de** of).

jamais *adv* never; **elle ne sort j.** she never goes out; **j. de la vie!** (absolutely) never!; **si j.** if ever.

jambe *f* leg.

jambon *m* ham.

janvier *m* January.

japonais, -aise 1 *adj* Japanese. **2** *mf* **J.** Japanese man, Japanese woman, Japanese *inv*; **les J.** the Japanese. **3** *m (langue)* Japanese.

jardin m garden; **j. public** park.

jardinage m gardening.

jardinier m gardener.

jardinière f (caisse à fleurs) window box.

jaune 1 adj yellow. **2** m yellow; **j. d'œuf** (egg) yolk.

jaunir vti to turn yellow.

jaunisse f jaundice.

Javel (eau de) f bleach.

jazz m jazz.

je pron (**j'** before vowel or mute h) I.

jean m (pair of) jeans.

jeep® f jeep®.

jerrycan m gasoline can; (pour l'eau) water can.

jet m (de vapeur) burst; (de tuyau d'arrosage) nozzle; **j. d'eau** fountain.

jetable adj disposable.

jetée f pier.

jeter vt to throw (**à** to; **dans** into); (à la poubelle) to throw away.

jeter (se) vpr **se j. sur** to pounce on; **le fleuve se jette dans la mer** the river flows into the sea.

jeton m (pièce) token; (de jeu) chip.

jeu, -x m game; (amusement) play; (d'argent) gambling; (série complète) set; (de cartes) deck; **j. de mots** play on words; **jeux de société** parlor ou indoor games; **j. télévisé** quiz show.

jeudi m Thursday.

jeun (à) adv **être à j.** to have eaten no food.

jeune 1 adj young. **2** mf young person; **les jeunes** young people.

jeûner vi to fast.

jeunesse f youth; **la j.** (jeunes) the young.

jockey m jockey.

jogging m jogging; **faire du j.** to jog.

joie f joy.

joindre* vt to join; (envoyer avec) to enclose (**à** with); **j. qn** to get in touch with sb.

joindre (se) vpr **se j. à** (un groupe etc) to join.

joint, -ointe 1 adj **à pieds joints** with feet together; **pièces jointes** (de lettre) enclosures. **2** m joint; (d'étanchéité) seal; (de robinet) washer; **j. de culasse** gasket.

joker m Cartes joker.

joli, -ie adj nice; (femme, enfant) pretty.

jongler vi to juggle (**avec** with).

jongleur, -euse mf juggler.

jonquille f daffodil.

joue f cheek.

jouer 1 vi to play; (acteur) to act; (au tiercé etc) to gamble, to bet; **j. au tennis/aux cartes/etc** to play tennis/cards/etc; **j. du piano/etc** to play the piano/etc. **2** vt to play; (risquer) to bet (**sur** on); (pièce, film) to put on.

jouet m toy.

joueur, -euse mf player; (au tiercé etc) gambler; **bon j.** good loser.

jour m day; (lumière) (day)light; **il fait j.** it's light; **en plein j.** in broad daylight; **de nos jours** nowadays; **du j. au lendemain** overnight; **le j. de l'An** New Year's Day.

journal, -aux m (news)paper; (intime) diary; **j. (télévisé)** television news.

journaliste mf journalist.

journée f day; **toute la j.** all day (long).

joyeux, -euse adj merry, happy; **j. Noël!** merry Christmas!; **j. anniversaire!** happy birthday!

jubiler vi to be jubilant.

judo m judo.

juge m judge.

jugement m judgment; (verdict) sentence; **passer en j.** to stand trial.

juger vt to judge; (au tribunal) to try; (estimer) to consider (**que** that).

juif, juive 1 adj Jewish. **2** mf Jew.

juillet m July.

juin m June.

jumeau, -elle, pl **-eaux, -elles** mf & adj twin; **frère j.** twin brother;

sœur jumelle twin sister; **lits jumeaux** twin beds.

jumelles *fpl (pour regarder)* binoculars.

jument *f* mare.

jungle *f* jungle.

jupe *f* skirt.

jupon *m* slip, petticoat.

juré, -ée *mf* juror.

jurer 1 *vi (dire un gros mot)* to swear (**contre** at). **2** *vt (promettre)* to swear (**que** that; **de faire** to do).

juron *m* swearword.

jury *m* jury.

jus *m* juice; *(de viande)* gravy.

jusque 1 *prép* **jusqu'à** *(espace)* as far as; *(temps)* until; **jusqu'à cinquante euros** *(limite)* up to fifty euros; **jusqu'en mai** until May; **jusqu'où?** how far?; **jusqu'ici** *(temps)* up till now. **2** *conj* **jusqu'à ce qu'il vienne** until he comes.

juste 1 *adj (équitable)* fair; *(légitime)* just; *(exact)* right; *(étroit)* tight. **2** *adv (deviner etc)* right; *(chanter)* in tune; *(seulement)* just.

justement *adv* exactly.

justesse *f (exactitude)* accuracy; **de j.** *(éviter, gagner)* just.

justice *f* justice; *(autorités)* law.

justifier *vt* to justify.

juteux, -euse *adj* juicy.

K

kangourou *m* kangaroo.

karaoké *m* karaoke.

karaté *m* karate.

képi *m* cap, kepi.

kidnapper *vt* to kidnap.

kilo *m* kilo.

kilogramme *m* kilogram.

kilométrage *m* ≃ mileage.

kilomètre *m* kilometer.

kilo-octet, *pl* **kilo-octets** *m* kilobyte.

kinésithérapeute *mf* physical therapist.

kiosque *m (à journaux)* kiosk.

kit *m* **meuble en k.** (piece of) flat-pack furniture.

klaxon® *m* horn.

klaxonner *vi* to honk.

K.-O. *adj inv* **mettre K.** to knock out.

L

l', la *voir* **le.**

là 1 *adv (lieu)* there; *(chez soi)* in; *(temps)* then; **je reste là** I'll stay here; **c'est là que** that's where; **à cinq mètres de là** 16 feet away; **jusque-là** *(lieu)* as far as that; *(temps)* up till then. **2** *int* **oh là là!** oh my goodness!

là-bas *adv* over there.

laboratoire *m* laboratory.

labourer *vt* to plow.

labyrinthe *m* maze.

lac *m* lake.

lacet *m* (shoe-)lace; *(de route)* twist.

lâche 1 *adj* cowardly. **2** *mf* coward.

lâcher 1 *vt* to let go of; *(bombe)* to drop. **2** *vi (corde)* to give way.

lâcheté *f* cowardice.

là-dedans *adv* in there.

là-dessous *adv* underneath.

là-dessus *adv* on there.

là-haut *adv* up there; *(à l'étage)* upstairs.

laid, laide *adj* ugly.

laideur *f* ugliness.

lainage *m* woolen garment.

laine *f* wool; **en l.** woolen.

laisse *f* lead, leash.

laisser *vt* to leave; **l. qn partir/etc** to let sb go/etc; **l. qch à qn** to let sb have sth.

lait m milk.

laitier adj produit l. dairy product.

laitue f lettuce.

lambeau, -x m shred, bit.

lame f (de couteau etc) blade; (vague) wave.

lamentable adj (mauvais) terrible.

lamenter (se) vpr to moan.

lampadaire m floor lamp; (de rue) street lamp.

lampe f lamp; (au néon) light; l. de poche flashlight.

lance f spear; (extrémité de tuyau) nozzle; l. d'incendie fire hose.

lancement m (de fusée etc) launch(ing).

lancer vt to throw (à to); (avec force) to hurl; (fusée, produit etc) to launch; (appel etc) to issue.

lancer (se) vpr (se précipiter) to rush.

landau, pl **-aus** m baby carriage.

langage m language.

langouste f (spiny) lobster.

langue f tongue; (langage) language; l. maternelle mother tongue; langues vivantes modern languages.

lanière f strap.

lanterne f lantern; lanternes (de véhicule) parking lights.

lapin m rabbit.

laque f lacquer.

lard m (fumé) bacon; (gras) (pig's) fat.

large 1 adj wide, broad; (vêtement) loose; l. de six mètres 20 feet wide. **2** m breadth, width; avoir six mètres de l. to be 20 feet wide; le l. (mer) the open sea; au l. de Cherbourg off Cherbourg.

largement adv (ouvrir) wide; (au moins) easily; avoir l. le temps to have plenty of time.

largeur f width, breadth.

larme f tear; en larmes in tears.

laser m laser.

lasser vt, **se lasser** vpr to tire (de of).

latéral, -e, -aux adj side.

latin m (langue) Latin.

lavabo m washbasin, sink.

lave-auto, pl lave-autos m car wash.

lave-linge m inv washing machine.

laver vt to wash.

laver (se) vpr to wash up; se l. les mains to wash one's hands.

laverie f (automatique) laundromat.

lavette f dishcloth.

lave-vaisselle m inv dishwasher.

layette f baby clothes.

le, la, pl **les** (le and la become l' before a vowel or mute h) **1** art déf (à + le = au, à + les = aux; de + le = du, de + les = des) the. ■ (généralisation) la beauté beauty; la France France; les hommes men; aimer le café to like coffee. ■ (possession) il ouvrit la bouche he opened his mouth; avoir les cheveux blonds to have blond hair. ■ (mesure) dix dollars la livre ten dollars a pound. ■ (temps) ell vient le lundi she comes on Monday(s); l'an prochain next year; une fois l'an once a year. **2** pron (homme) him; (femme) her; (chose, animal) it; pl them; es-tu fatigué? – je le suis are you tired?– I am; je le crois I think so.

lécher vt to lick.

lécher (se) vpr se l. les doigts to lick one's fingers.

leçon f lesson.

lecteur, -trice mf reader; l. de cassettes/CD/DVD cassette/CD/DVD player.

lecture f reading; lectures (livres) books.

légal, -e, -aux adj legal.

légende f (histoire) legend; (de plan) key; (de photo) caption.

léger, -ère adj light; (bruit, fièvre etc) slight; (café, thé) weak; (bière, tabac) mild.

légèrement adv (un peu) slightly.

légèreté f lightness.

légitime *adj* être en état de l. défense to act in self-defense.

légume *m* vegetable.

lendemain *m* le l. the next day; le l. de the day after; le l. matin the next morning.

lent, lente *adj* slow.

lentement *adv* slowly.

lenteur *f* slowness.

lentille *f* (graine) lentil; (verre) lens.

léopard *m* leopard.

lequel, laquelle, *pl* **lesquels, lesquelles** (+ à = auquel, à laquelle, auxquel(le)s; + de = duquel, de laquelle, desquel(le)s) *pron* (chose, animal) which; (personne) who, (indirect) whom; (interrogatif) which (one); dans l. in which; parmi lesquels (choses, animaux) among which; (personnes) among whom.

les *voir* **le**.

lessive *f* (laundry) detergent; (linge) laundry; faire la l. to do the laundry.

lettre *f* letter; en toutes lettres (mot) in full.

leur 1 *adj poss* their. **2** *pron poss* le l., la l., les leurs theirs. **3** *pron inv* (indirect) (to) them; il l. est facile de it's easy for them to.

levé, -ée *adj* être l. (debout) to be up.

lever 1 *vt* to lift (up); l. les yeux to look up. **2** *m* le l. du soleil sunrise.

lever (se) *vpr* to get up; (soleil, rideau) to rise; (jour) to break.

levier *m* lever; (pour soulever) crowbar.

lèvre *f* lip.

lézard *m* lizard.

liaison *f* (routière etc) link; (entre mots) liaison.

liasse *f* bundle.

libération *f* freeing, release.

libérer *vt* to (set) free, to release (de from).

libérer (se) *vpr* to free oneself (de from).

liberté *f* freedom; en l. provisoire on bail; mettre en l. to free.

libraire *mf* bookseller.

librairie *f* bookshop.

libre *adj* free (de qch from sth; de faire to do); (voie) clear.

libre-échange *m* free trade.

librement *adv* freely.

libre-service, *pl* **libres-services** *m* self-service.

licence *f* (diplôme) (Bachelor's) degree; (sportive) license.

licencié, -ée *adj & mf* graduate; l. ès lettres/sciences Bachelor of Arts/Science.

licenciement *m* dismissal.

licencier *vt* (ouvrier) to lay off, to dismiss.

liège *m* (matériau) cork.

lien *m* (rapport) link; (ficelle) tie; l. de parenté family tie.

lier *vt* (attacher) to tie (up); (relier) to link (up).

lierre *m* ivy.

lieu, -x *m* place; (d'un accident) scene; les lieux (locaux) the premises; avoir l. to take place; au l. de instead of.

lièvre *m* hare.

ligne *f* line; (belle silhouette) figure; (se) mettre en l. to line up; en l. (au téléphone) connected; grandes lignes (de train) main line (services); à la l. new paragraph; l. d'arrivée finish line.

ligoter *vt* to tie up.

lilas *m* lilac.

limace *f* slug.

lime *f* file.

limer *vt* to file.

limitation *f* (de vitesse, poids) limit.

limite 1 *f* limit (à to); (frontière) boundary. **2** *adj* (cas) extreme; (vitesse etc) maximum; date l. latest date; date l. de vente sell-by date.

limiter *vt* to limit (à to).

limoger *vt* to dismiss.

limonade *f* lemon-lime soda.

limpide *adj* (crystal) clear.

lin *m* (tissu) linen.

linge *m* linen; (à laver) laundry.

lingerie f underwear.
lion m lion.
lionne f lioness.
liqueur f liqueur.
liquide 1 adj liquid; **argent l.** ready cash. **2** m liquid; **du l.** (argent) ready cash.
lire* vti to read.
lis m lily.
lis, lisant, lise(nt) etc voir **lire**.
lisible adj (écriture) legible.
lisse adj smooth.
lisser vt to smooth.
liste f list; **sur la l. rouge** (numéro de téléphone) unlisted.
lit¹ m bed; **l. d'enfant** crib; **lits superposés** bunk beds.
lit² voir **lire**.
literie f bedding.
litre m liter.
littéraire adj literary.
littérature f literature.
littoral m coast(line).
livraison f delivery.
livre¹ m book; **l. de poche** paperback (book).
livre² f (monnaie, poids) pound.
livrer vt to deliver (à qn); **l. qn à** (la police etc) to give sb over to.
livret m **l. scolaire** report card; **l. de caisse d'épargne** bankbook, passbook.
livreur, -euse mf delivery man, delivery woman.
local, -ale, -aux adj local.
local, -aux m room; **locaux** premises.
locataire mf tenant.
location f (de maison, voiture) rental; (par propriétaire) renting (out), letting; (loyer) rental.
locomotive f (de train) engine.
locution f phrase.
loge f (de concierge) lodge; (d'acteur) dressing room; (de spectateur) box.
logement m accommodations; (appartement) apartment; (maison) house; **le l.** housing.

loger 1 vt to accommodate; (héberger) to put up. **2** vi (à l'hôtel etc) to put up; (habiter) to live.
logiciel m software inv.
logique adj logical.
logiquement adv logically.
loi f law; (du Parlement) act; **projet de l.** bill.
loin adv far (away ou off); **Boston est l. (de Paris)** Boston is a long way away (from Paris); **plus l.** further, farther; **de l.** from a distance.
lointain, -aine adj distant.
loisirs mpl spare time, leisure (time); (distractions) leisure activities.
long, longue 1 adj long; **être l. (à faire)** to be a long time ou slow (in doing); **l. de deux mètres** seven feet long. **2** m avoir deux mètres **de l.** to be seven feet long; **(tout) le l. de** (espace) (all) along; **de l. en large** (marcher) up and down; **à la longue** in the long run.
longer vt to go along; (forêt, mer) to skirt; (mur) to hug.
longtemps adv (for) a long time; **trop l.** too long.
longuement adv (expliquer) at length; (réfléchir) for a long time.
longueur f length; **à l. de journée** all day long; **l. d'ondes** wavelength.
lors adv **l. de** at the time of.
lorsque conj when.
losange m (forme) diamond.
lot m (de loterie) prize; **gros l.** grand prize, jackpot.
loterie f lottery.
lotion f lotion.
lotissement m (habitations) housing development.
louche f ladle.
loucher vi to squint.
louer vt (prendre en location) to rent; (donner en location) to rent (out), to let; **maison à l.** house to let.
loup m wolf; **avoir une faim de l.** to be ravenous.
loupe f magnifying glass.
lourd, lourde 1 adj heavy;

(temps) close; (faute) gross. **2** adv
peser l. to be heavy.
loyal, -e, -aux adj (honnête) fair
(envers to).
loyauté f fairness.
loyer m rent.
lu, lue pp of **lire**.
lucarne f (fenêtre) skylight.
luceur f glimmer.
luge f sled, toboggan.
lui 1 pron mf (complément indirect)
(to) him; (femme) (to) her; (chose,
animal) to it; **il lui est facile de** it's
easy for him/her to. **2** pron m (complément direct) him; (chose, animal) it; (sujet emphatique) he.
lui-même pron himself; (chose,
animal) itself.
luisant, -ante adj shiny.
lumière f light.
lumineux, -euse adj (idée, ciel
etc) bright.
lundi m Monday.
lune f moon; **l. de miel** honeymoon.
lunettes fpl glasses, spectacles;
(de protection, de plongée) goggles;
l. de soleil sunglasses.
lustre m (éclairage) chandelier.
lutte f fight, struggle; (sport) wrestling.
lutter vi to fight, to struggle.
luxe m luxury; **article de l.** luxury
article.
luxueux, -euse adj luxurious.
lycée m = high school.
lycéen, -enne mf = high school
student.

M

ma voir **mon**.
macaroni(s) m(pl) macaroni.
macédoine f **m. (de légumes)**
mixed vegetables.
mâcher vt to chew.

machin m Fam (chose) whatchamacallit.
machinalement adv instinctively.
machine f machine; **m. à coudre**
sewing machine; **m. à écrire** typewriter; **m. à laver** washing machine.
mâchoire f jaw.
maçon m bricklayer.
madame, pl **mesdames** f madam;
bonjour mesdames good morning
(ladies); **Madame** ou **Mme Legras**
Mrs Legras; **Madame** (dans une lettre) Dear Madam.
madeleine f (small) sponge cake.
mademoiselle, pl **mesdemoiselles** f miss; **bonjour mesdemoiselles**
good morning (ladies); **Mademoiselle** ou **Mlle Legras** Miss Legras;
Mademoiselle (dans une lettre)
Dear Madam.
magasin m store; **grand m.** department store; **en m.** in stock.
magazine m magazine.
magicien, -ienne mf magician.
magie f magic.
magique adj (baguette etc) magic;
(mystérieux) magical.
magnétophone (Fam **magnéto**)
m tape recorder; **m. à cassettes**
cassette recorder.
magnétoscope m VCR, video (recorder).
magnifique adj magnificent.
mai m May.
maigre adj (personne) thin;
(viande) lean.
maigrir vi to get thin(ner).
maille f (de tricot) stitch; (de filet)
mesh.
maillon m (de chaîne) link.
maillot m (de sportif) jersey, shirt;
m. (de corps) undershirt; **m. (de
bain)** (de femme) bathing costume;
(d'homme) bathing trunks.
main f hand; **tenir à la m.** to hold in
one's hand; **à la m.** (faire, coudre
etc) by hand; **haut les mains!** hands
up!; **donner un coup de m. à qn** to

lend sb a (helping) hand; **sous la m.** handy.

main-d'œuvre, pl **mains-d'œuvre** f labor.

maintenant adv now; **m. que** now that.

maintenir* vt (conserver) to keep; (retenir) to hold.

maire m mayor.

mairie f city hall.

mais conj but; **m. oui, m. si** yes of course; **m. non** definitely not.

maïs m (céréale) corn.

maison f (bâtiment) house; (chezsoi) home; (entreprise) firm; **à la m.** at home; **aller à la m.** to go home; **m. de la culture** arts center; **m. des jeunes** youth center.

maître m (d'un chien etc) master; **m. d'école** teacher; **m. d'hôtel** (restaurant) head waiter; **m. nageur** swimming instructor (and lifeguard).

maîtresse f mistress; **m. d'école** teacher.

maîtrise f (diplôme) Master's degree (**de** in).

maîtriser vt (incendie) to (bring under) control; **m. qn** to overpower sb.

majesté f Votre M. (titre) Your Majesty.

majeur, -e 1 adj être m. to be of age. **2** m (doigt) middle finger.

majorette f majorette.

majoritaire adj majority; **être m.** to be in the majority.

majorité f majority (**de** of); (âge) coming of age.

majuscule f capital letter.

mal, maux 1 m (douleur) pain; **dire du m. de qn** to say bad things about sb; **m. de dents** toothache; **m. de gorge** sore throat; **m. de tête** headache; **m. de ventre** stomachache; **avoir le m. de mer** to be seasick; **avoir m. à la tête/gorge/etc** to have a headache/sore throat/etc; **ça (me) fait m., j'ai m.** it hurts (me); **faire du m. à** to hurt; **avoir du m. à**

faire to have trouble doing; **le bien et le m.** good and evil. **2** adv (travailler etc) badly; (entendre, comprendre) not too well; **pas m.!** not bad!; **c'est m. de mentir** it's wrong to lie.

malade 1 adj ill, sick; **être m. du cœur** to have a bad heart. **2** mf sick person; (d'un médecin) patient.

maladie f illness.

maladresse f clumsiness.

maladroit, -droite adj clumsy.

malaise m avoir un m. to feel dizzy.

malaria f malaria.

malbouffe f Fam junk food.

malchance f bad luck.

malchanceux, -euse adj unlucky.

mâle adj & m male.

malentendant, -ante 1 adj hearing-impaired. **2** mf person who is hard of hearing.

malentendu m misunderstanding.

malfaiteur m criminal.

malgré prép in spite of; **m. tout** after all.

malheur m (événement, malchance) misfortune.

malheureusement adv unfortunately.

malheureux, -euse 1 adj (triste) miserable. **2** mf (pauvre) poor person.

malhonnête adj dishonest.

malice f mischievousness.

malicieux, -euse adj mischievous.

malin, -igne adj (astucieux) clever.

malle f (coffre) trunk; (de véhicule) trunk.

mallette f small suitcase; (pour documents) attaché case.

malmener vt to manhandle, to treat badly.

malpoli, -ie adj rude.

malsain, -saine adj unhealthy.

maltraiter vt to ill-treat.

malveillant, -ante adj malevolent.

maman *f* mom(my).

mamie *f Fam* grandma.

mammifère *m* mammal.

manche¹ *f (de vêtement)* sleeve; *(d'un match)* round; **la M.** the English Channel.

manche² *m (d'outil)* handle; **m. à balai** broomstick; *(d'avion etc)* joystick.

manchette *f (de chemise)* cuff.

manchot *m (oiseau)* penguin.

mandarine *f* tangerine.

mandat *m (postal)* money order.

manège *m (à la foire)* merry-go-round.

manette *f* lever.

mangeable *adj (médiocre)* eatable.

mangeoire *f* (feeding) trough.

manger *vti* to eat; **donner à m. à** to feed.

maniable *adj* easy to handle.

manie *f* craze.

manier *vt* to handle.

manière *f* way; **de toute m.** anyway; **à ma m.** (in) my own way; **la m. dont elle parle** the way (in which) she talks; **faire des manières** *(chichis)* to make a fuss.

maniéré, -ée *adj* affected.

manifestant, -ante *mf* demonstrator.

manifestation *f (défilé)* demonstration.

manifester 1 *vt (sa colère etc)* to show. **2** *vi (dans la rue)* to demonstrate.

manifester (se) *vpr (maladie)* to show itself.

manipulation *f (d'appareils, de produits)* handling; **manipulations génétiques** genetic engineering.

manipuler *vt (manier)* to handle.

mannequin *m (personne)* (fashion) model; *(statue)* dummy, mannequin.

manœuvre 1 *m (ouvrier)* laborer.

2 *f (action)* maneuver.

manœuvrer *vti (véhicule)* to maneuver.

manque *m* lack *(de of)*.

manquer 1 *vt (cible, train etc)* to miss. **2** *vi (faire défaut)* to be short; *(être absent)* to be absent *(à from)*; **m. de** *(pain, argent etc)* to be short of; *(attention)* to lack; **ça manque de sel** there isn't enough salt; **elle/ cela lui manque** he misses her/ that; **elle a manqué (de) tomber** she nearly fell; **il manque/il nous manque dix tasses** there are/we are ten cups short.

mansarde *f* attic.

manteau, -x *m* coat.

manuel, -elle 1 *adj (travail)* manual. **2** *m* handbook, manual; *(scolaire)* textbook.

mappemonde *f* map of the world; *(sphère)* globe.

maquereau, -x *m (poisson)* mackerel.

maquette *f* (scale) model.

maquillage *m (fard)* make-up.

maquiller *vt (visage)* to make up.

maquiller (se) *vpr* to put one's make-up on.

marais *m* marsh.

marathon *m* marathon.

marbre *m* marble.

marchand, -ande *mf* storekeeper; *(de voitures, meubles)* dealer; **m. de journaux** *(dans un magasin)* newspaper vendor; **m. de légumes** grocer.

marchander *vi* to haggle.

marchandise(s) *f(pl)* goods.

marche *f (d'escalier)* step; *(trajet)* walk; **la m.** *(sport)* walking; **faire m. arrière** *(en voiture)* to reverse; **un train en m.** a moving train; **mettre qch en m.** to start sth (up).

marché *m (lieu)* market; **faire son ou le m.** to do one's shopping *(in the market)*; **bon m.** cheap.

marcher *vi (à pied)* to walk; *(poser le pied)* to step *(dans* in); *(fonction-*

ner) to work; **faire m.** (*machine*) to work; **ça marche?** *Fam* how's it going?

mardi *m* Tuesday; **M. gras** Shrove Tuesday, Mardi Gras.

mare *f* (*étang*) pond.

marécage *m* swamp.

marécageux, -euse *adj* swampy.

marée *f* tide; **m. noire** oil slick.

marelle *f* hopscotch.

margarine *f* margarine.

marge *f* (*de cahier etc*) margin.

marginal, -e, aux 1 *adj* (*secondaire*) marginal; (*personne*) on the fringes of society. **2** *mf* dropout.

marguerite *f* daisy.

mari *m* husband.

mariage *m* marriage; (*cérémonie*) wedding.

marié, -ée 1 *adj* married. **2** *m* (bride)groom; **les mariés** the bride and (bride)groom. **3** *f* bride.

marier *vt* **m. qn** (*prêtre etc*) to marry sb.

marier (se) *vpr* to get married (**avec qn** to sb).

marin, -ine 1 *adj* air/*etc* **m.** sea air/*etc.* **2** *m* sailor.

marine 1 *f* **m.** (**de guerre**) navy. **2** *m & adj inv* (*couleur*) (**bleu**) **m.** navy (blue).

marionnette *f* puppet.

marmelade *f* **m.** (**de fruits**) stewed fruit.

marmite *f* (cooking) pot.

marmonner *vti* to mutter.

maroquinerie *f* (*magasin*) leather goods store.

marquant, -ante *adj* (*remarquable*) outstanding; (*épisode*) significant.

marque *f* (*trace*) mark; (*de produit*) make, brand; (*points*) score; **m. de fabrique** trademark; **m. déposée** (registered) trademark.

marquer 1 *vt* (*par une marque*) to mark; (*écrire*) to note down; (*but*) to score; **m. les points** to keep (the)

score. **2** *vi* (*trace*) to leave a mark; (*joueur*) to score.

marqueur *m* (*crayon*) marker.

marraine *f* godmother.

marrant, -ante *adj Fam* funny.

marre *f* **en avoir m.** *Fam* to be fed up (**de** with).

marron 1 *m* chestnut. **2** *m & adj inv* (*couleur*) brown.

mars *m* March.

marteau, -x *m* hammer; **m. piqueur** jackhammer.

martien, -ienne *mf & adj* Martian.

martyriser *vt* (*enfant*) to batter, to abuse.

mascara *m* mascara.

mascotte *f* mascot.

masculin, -ine 1 *adj* male. **2** *adj & m Grammaire* masculine.

masque *m* mask.

massacre *m* slaughter.

massacrer *vt* to slaughter.

massage *m* massage.

masse *f* (*volume*) mass; **en m.** in large numbers.

masser *vt* (*frotter*) to massage.

masser (se) *vpr* (*gens*) to (form a) crowd.

masseur *m* masseur.

masseuse *f* masseuse.

massif, -ive 1 *adj* (*or, bois etc*) solid. **2** *m* (*de fleurs*) clump; (*de montagnes*) massif.

mastic *m* (*pour vitres*) putty.

mastiquer *vt* (*vitre*) to putty; (*mâcher*) to chew.

mat, mate *adj* (*papier, couleur*) mat(t).

mât *m* (*de navire*) mast; (*poteau*) pole.

match *m Sport* match, game.

matelas *m* mattress; **m. pneumatique** air mattress.

matelot *m* sailor.

matériaux *mpl* (building) materials.

matériel, -ielle 1 *adj* (*dégâts*) material. **2** *m* (*de camping etc*) equipment; *(d'ordinateur)* hardware *inv.*

maternel, -elle 1 *adj (amour, femme etc)* maternal. **2** *f (école)* **maternelle** kindergarten.

maternité *f (hôpital)* labor ward.

mathématiques *fpl* mathematics.

maths *fpl* math.

matière *f (à l'école)* subject; *(substance)* material; **m. première** raw material.

matin *m* morning; **le m.** *(chaque matin)* in the morning; **à sept heures du m.** at seven in the morning.

matinal, -e, -aux *adj* être m. to be an early riser.

matinée *f* morning; **faire la grasse m.** to sleep late.

matraque *f (de policier)* billy club; *(de malfaiteur)* club.

maussade *adj (personne)* bad-tempered, moody; *(temps)* gloomy.

mauvais, -aise *adj* bad; *(méchant)* wicked; *(mal choisi)* wrong; *(mer)* rough; **plus m.** worse; **le plus m.** the worst; **il fait m.** the weather's bad; **m. en** *(anglais etc)* bad at.

mauve *adj & m (couleur)* mauve.

maximal, -e *adj* maximum.

maximum *m* maximum; **le m. de** *(force etc)* the maximum (amount of); **au m.** *(tout au plus)* at most.

mayonnaise *f* mayonnaise.

mazout *m (fuel)* oil.

me (**m'** before vowel or mute *h*) *pron (complément direct)* me; *(indirect)* to me; *(réfléchi)* myself.

mécanicien *m* mechanic; *(de train)* engineer.

mécanique *adj* mechanical; **jouet m.** wind-up toy.

mécanisme *m* mechanism.

méchanceté *f* malice; **une m.** *(parole)* a malicious word.

méchant, -ante *adj (cruel)* wicked; *(enfant)* naughty.

mèche *f (de cheveux)* lock; *(de bougie)* wick; *(de pétard)* fuse.

méconnaissable *adj* unrecognizable.

mécontent, -ente *adj* dissatisfied (**de** with).

mécontentement *m* dissatisfaction.

mécontenter *vt* to displease.

médaille *f (décoration)* medal; *(bijou)* medallion; **être m. d'or** to be a gold medalist.

médecin *m* doctor.

médecine *f* medicine; **étudiant en m.** medical student.

médias *mpl* (mass) media.

médical, -e, -aux *adj* medical.

médicament *m* medicine.

médiéval, -e, -aux *adj* medieval.

médiocre *adj* second-rate.

médisance(s) *f(pl)* malicious gossip.

Méditerranée *f* **la M.** the Mediterranean.

méditerranéen, -enne *adj* Mediterranean.

méduse *f* jellyfish.

meeting *m* meeting.

méfiance *f* distrust.

méfiant, -ante *adj* suspicious.

méfier (se) *vpr* **se m. de** to distrust; *(faire attention à)* to watch out for; **méfie-toi!** watch out!; **je me méfie** I'm suspicious.

mégaoctet *m* megabyte.

mégarde (par) *adv* inadvertently.

mégot *m* cigarette butt.

meilleur, -e 1 *adj* better (**que** than); **le m. résultat/etc** the best result/etc. **2** *mf* **le m., la meilleure** the best (one).

mélange *m* mixture.

mélanger *vt*, **se mélanger** *vpr (mêler)* to mix.

mêlée *f* fight, scuffle; *Rugby* scrum.

mêler *vt* to mix (**à** with).

mêler (se) *vpr* to mix (**à** with); **se m. à** *(la foule)* to join; **mêle-toi de ce qui te regarde!** mind your own business!

mélodie f melody.

melon m (fruit) melon; (chapeau) m. derby.

membre m (bras, jambe) limb; (d'un groupe) member.

même 1 adj same; **en m. temps** at the same time (**que** as). **2** pron **le m., la m.** the same (one); **les mêmes** the same (ones). **3** adv even; **m. si** even if; **ici m.** in this very place.

mémoire f memory; **à la m. de** in memory of.

mémorable adj memorable.

menaçant, -ante adj threatening.

menace f threat.

menacer vt to threaten (**de faire** to do).

ménage m housekeeping; (couple) couple; **faire le m.** to do the housework.

ménager, -ère adj (appareil) domestic; **travaux ménagers** housework.

ménagère f housewife.

mendiant, -ante mf beggar.

mendier vti to beg (for).

mener 1 vt (personne, vie etc) to lead; (enquête etc) to carry out; **m. qn à** to take sb to. **2** vi (en sport) to lead.

menottes fpl handcuffs.

mensonge m lie.

mensuel, -elle adj monthly.

mensurations fpl measurements.

mental, -e, -aux adj mental.

menteur, -euse mf liar.

menthe f mint.

mention f (à un examen) distinction.

mentir* vi to lie (**à** to).

menton m chin.

menu m menu.

menuiserie f carpentry.

menuisier m carpenter.

mépris m contempt (**pour** for).

méprisant, -ante adj contemptuous.

méprise f mistake.

mépriser vt to despise.

mer f sea; **en m.** at sea; **aller à la m.** to go to the seaside.

mercerie f (magasin) notions store.

merci int & m thank you (**de, pour** for).

mercredi m Wednesday.

merde! int Fam shit!

mère f mother; **m. de famille** mother (of a family).

mérite m merit; (honneur) credit; **avoir du m. à faire qch** to deserve credit for doing sth.

mériter vt (être digne de) to deserve.

merle m blackbird.

merveille f wonder.

merveilleux, -euse adj wonderful.

mes voir **mon**.

mésaventure f slight mishap.

mesdames voir **madame**.

mesdemoiselles voir **mademoiselle**.

mesquin, -ine adj mean, petty.

message m message; **m. vocal** voicemail (message); **messages publicitaires** (e-mails) spam.

messager m messenger.

messagerie f courier company; **m. électronique** e-mail service; **m. instantanée** instant messaging; **m. vocale** voicemail (service).

messe f mass (church service).

messieurs voir **monsieur**.

mesure f (dimension) measurement; (action) measure; (cadence) time.

mesurer vt to measure; **m. 1 mètre 83** (personne) to be six feet tall; (objet) to measure six feet.

métal, -aux m metal.

métallique adj **échelle/etc m.** metal ladder/etc.

métallurgie f (industrie) steel industry.

météo f (bulletin) weather forecast.

météorologique adj bulletin/ etc m. weather report/etc.

méthode f (manière, soin) method.

méthodique adj methodical.

métier m (travail) job.

mètre m (mesure) meter; (règle) (meter) stick; **m. carré** square meter; **m. (à ruban)** tape measure.

métrique adj metric.

métro m subway.

metteur m **m. en scène** (de cinéma) director.

mettre* vt to put; (table) to set, to lay; (vêtement) to put on; (chauffage etc) to put on, to switch on; (réveil) to set (à for); **j'ai mis une heure** it took me an hour; **m. en colère** to make angry.

mettre (se) vpr to put oneself; (debout) to stand; (assis) to sit; (objet) to go; **se m. en short/etc** to put on one's shorts/etc; **se m. à faire** to start doing; **se m. à table** to sit (down) at the table.

meuble m piece of furniture; **meubles** furniture.

meublé m furnished apartment.

meubler vt to furnish.

meugler vi (vache) to moo.

meule f (de foin) haystack.

meurtre m murder.

meurtrier, -ière mf murderer.

mi- préfixe la **mi-mars/etc** mid-March/etc.

miauler vt to miaow.

miche f round loaf.

mi-chemin (à) adv halfway.

mi-côte (à) adv halfway up ou down (the hill).

micro m microphone.

microbe m germ.

micro-ondes m inv microwave; **four à m.** microwave (oven).

micro-ordinateur, pl **micro-ordinateurs** m microcomputer.

microscope m microscope.

midi m (heure) twelve o'clock, noon; (heure du déjeuner) lunchtime.

mie f la m. the soft part of the bread; **pain de m.** sandwich loaf.

miel m honey.

mien, mienne pron poss le m., la mienne, les miens, les miennes mine; **les deux miens** my two.

miette f (de pain) crumb.

mieux adv & adj inv better (que than); **le m., la m., les m.** the best; (de deux) the better; **tu ferais m. de partir** you had better leave.

mignon, -onne adj (joli) cute; (agréable) nice.

migraine f headache.

mijoter 1 vt (lentement) to simmer. **2** vi to simmer.

mil m inv (dans les dates) **l'an deux m.** the year two thousand.

milieu, -x m (centre) middle; **au m. de** in the middle of.

militaire 1 adj military. **2** m soldier.

mille adj & m inv thousand; **m. hommes/etc** a ou one thousand men/etc.

mille-pattes m inv centipede.

milliard m billion.

millième adj & mf thousandth.

millier m thousand; **un m. (de)** a thousand or so.

millimètre m millimeter.

million m million; **un m. d'euros/ etc** a million euros/etc; **deux millions** two million.

millionnaire mf millionaire.

mime mf (acteur) mime.

mimer vti to mime.

minable adj shabby.

mince adj thin; (élancé) slim.

mincir vi to get thin.

mine¹ f appearance; **avoir bonne m.** to look well.

mine² f (de charbon etc) mine; (de crayon) lead; (engin explosif) mine.

miner vt (terrain) to mine.

minerai m ore.

minéral, -e, -aux adj & m mineral.

mineur m (ouvrier) miner.

miniature *adj inv (train etc)* miniature.

minimal, -e *adj* minimum.

minimum *m* minimum; **le m. de** *(force etc)* the minimum (amount of); **au (grand) m.** at the very least.

ministère *m* ministry.

ministre *m* minister.

minorité *f* minority.

minou *m (chat)* kitty.

minuit *m* midnight.

minuscule *adj (petit)* tiny.

minute *f* minute.

minuterie *f* timer *(for lighting in a stairway)*.

minuteur *m* timer.

minutieux, -euse *adj* meticulous.

miracle *m* miracle; **par m.** miraculously.

miraculeux, -euse *adj* miraculous.

miroir *m* mirror.

mis, mise *pp of* **mettre**.

mise¹ *f (action)* putting; **m. en marche** starting up; **m. en scène** *(de film)* direction.

mise² *f (argent)* stake.

misérable 1 *adj (très pauvre)* destitute. **2** *mf (personne pauvre)* pauper.

misère *f* (grinding) poverty.

missile *m (fusée)* missile.

mission *f* mission.

mite *f* (clothes) moth.

mi-temps *f (pause) (en sport)* half-time; *(période) (en sport)* half; **à m.** *(travailler)* part-time.

mitigé, -ée *adj (accueil)* lukewarm; *(sentiments, impressions)* mixed.

mitraillette *f* machinegun *(portable)*.

mitrailleuse *f* machinegun.

mi-voix (à) *adv* in a low voice.

mixe(u)r *m (pour mélanger)* (food) mixer.

mixte *adj (école)* co-educational, mixed.

mobile *adj (pièce)* moving; *(personne)* mobile.

mobilier *m* furniture.

mobylette® *f* moped.

moche *adj (laid)* ugly.

mode 1 *f* fashion; **à la m.** fashionable. **2** *m Grammaire* mood; **m. d'emploi** directions (for use).

modèle *m* model; **m. (réduit)** (scale) model.

modération *f* moderation.

modéré, -ée *adj* moderate.

modérer *vt (vitesse, chaleur etc)* to reduce.

moderne *adj* modern.

moderniser *vt*, **se moderniser** *vpr* to modernize.

modeste *adj* modest.

modestie *f* modesty.

modification *f* alteration.

modifier *vt* to alter.

moelle *f (d'os)* marrow; **m. épinière** spinal cord.

moelleux, -euse *adj (lit, tissu)* soft.

mœurs *fpl (morale)* morals; *(habitudes)* customs; **entrer dans les m.** to become part of everyday life.

moi *pron (complément direct)* me; *(indirect)* (to) me; *(sujet emphatique)* I.

moi-même *pron* myself.

moindre *adj* **la m.** erreur/*etc* the slightest mistake/*etc*; **le m.** *(de mes problèmes etc)* the least (**de** of).

moine *m* monk.

moineau, -x *m* sparrow.

moins 1 *adv* less (**que** than); **m. de** *(temps, travail)* less (**que** than); *(gens, livres)* fewer (**que** than); *(cent euros)* less than; **m. grand** not as big (**que** as); **de m. en m.** less and less; **le m.** *(travailler)* the least; **le m. grand, la m. grande, les m. grand(e)s** the smallest; **au m., du m.** at least; **de m., en m.** *(qui manque)* missing; **dix ans de m.** ten years less; **en m.** *(personne, objet)* less; *(personnes, objets)* fewer; **à**

m. que *(+ subjonctif)* unless. **2** *prép (en calcul)* minus; **deux heures m. cinq** five to two; **il fait m. dix (degrés)** it's minus ten (degrees).

mois *m* month; **au m. de juin** in (the month of) June.

moisi, -ie 1 *adj* moldy. **2** *m* mold; **sentir le m.** to smell musty.

moisir *vi* to go moldy.

moisson *f* harvest.

moissonner *vt* to harvest.

moite *adj* sticky.

moitié *f* half; **la m. de la pomme** half (of) the apple; **à m. fermé** half closed; **à m. prix** (at) half-price; **de m.** by half.

mol *voir* **mou**.

molaire *f* back tooth.

molette *f* **clé à m.** adjustable wrench.

molle *voir* **mou**.

mollet *m (de jambe)* calf.

moment *m (instant)* moment; *(période)* time; **en ce m.** at the moment; **par moments** at times; **au m. de partir** when just about to leave; **au m. où** just as; **du m. que** *(puisque)* seeing that.

momentanément *adv (temporairement)* temporarily; *(brièvement)* briefly.

mon, ma, *pl* **mes** (**ma** becomes **mon** before a vowel or mute *h*) *adj poss* my; **m. père** my father; **ma mère** my mother; **m. ami(e)** my friend.

monde *m* world; **du m.** *(beaucoup de gens)* a lot of people; **le m. entier** the whole world; **tout le m.** everybody.

mondial, -e, -aux *adj (crise etc)* worldwide; **guerre mondiale** world war.

mondialisation *f* globalization.

moniteur, -trice *mf* instructor; *(de colonie de vacances)* camp counselor.

monnaie *f (devise)* currency; *(pièces)* change; **faire de la m.** to get

change; **faire de la m. à qn** to give sb change (**sur un billet** for a bill).

monopoliser *vt* to monopolize.

monotone *adj* monotonous.

monotonie *f* monotony.

monsieur, *pl* **messieurs** *m (homme)* man, gentleman; **oui m.** yes sir; **oui messieurs** yes gentlemen; **M. Legras** Mr Legras; **Monsieur** *(dans une lettre)* Dear Sir.

monstre *m* monster.

monstrueux, -euse *adj (abominable)* hideous.

mont *m (montagne)* mount.

montage *m (d'un appareil)* assembling; *(d'un film)* editing; *(image truquée)* montage.

montagnard, -arde *mf* mountain dweller.

montagne *f* mountain; **la m.** *(zone)* the mountains.

montagneux, -euse *adj* mountainous.

montant *m (somme)* amount; *(de barrière)* post.

montée *f (ascension)* climb; *(chemin)* slope.

monter 1 *vi (aux* **être**) *(personne)* to go *ou* come up; *(s'élever) (ballon, prix etc)* to go up; *(grimper)* to climb (up) (**sur** onto); *(marée)* to come in; **m. dans un véhicule** to get in(to) a vehicle; **m. dans un train** to get on(-to) a train; **m. sur** *ou* **à** *(échelle)* to climb up; **m. en courant/etc** to run/ *etc* up; **m. (à cheval)** to ride (a horse). **2** *vt (aux* **avoir**) *(côte)* to climb (up); *(objet)* to bring *ou* take up; *(cheval)* to ride; *(tente)* to set up; **m. l'escalier** to go *ou* come up the stairs.

montre *f* watch.

montrer *vt* to show (**à** to); **m. du doigt** to point to.

montrer (se) *vpr* to show oneself.

monture *f (de lunettes)* frame.

monument *m* monument; **m. aux morts** war memorial.

moquer (se) *vpr* **se m. de** to make

fun of; **je m'en moque!** I couldn't care less!

moquette f wall-to-wall carpeting.

moqueur, -euse adj mocking.

moral m spirits, morale.

morale f (d'histoire) moral.

morceau, -x m piece; (de sucre) lump.

morceler vt (terrain) to divide up.

mordiller vt to nibble.

mordre vt to bite.

morne adj (temps) dismal; (silence) gloomy; (personne) glum.

morse m (animal) walrus.

morsure f bite.

mort f death.

mort, morte (pp of mourir) **1** adj (personne, plante etc) dead. **2** mf dead man, dead woman; **les morts** the dead; **de nombreux morts** (victimes) many casualties ou dead.

mortel, -elle adj (hommes, ennemi etc) mortal; (accident) fatal.

morue f cod.

mosquée f mosque.

mot m word; **envoyer un m. à** to drop a line to; **mots croisés** crossword (puzzle); **m. de passe** password.

motard m motorcyclist.

moteur (de véhicule etc) engine, motor.

motif m (raison) reason (**de** for).

motivé, -ée adj motivated.

motiver vt (inciter, causer) to motivate; (justifier) to justify.

moto f motorcycle.

motocycliste mf motorcyclist.

motte f (de terre) lump.

mou (or **mol** before vowel or mute h), **molle** adj soft; (sans énergie) feeble.

mouche f (insecte) fly.

moucher (se) vpr to blow one's nose.

moucheron m midge.

mouchoir m handkerchief; (en papier) tissue.

moudre* vt (café) to grind.

moue f long face; **faire la m.** to pull a (long) face.

mouette f (sea)gull.

moufle f mitten.

mouillé, -ée adj wet (**de** with).

mouiller vt to (make) wet; **se faire m.** to get wet.

mouiller (se) vpr to get (oneself) wet.

moulant, -ante adj (vêtement) tight-fitting.

moule¹ m mold; **m. à gâteaux** cake pan.

moule² f (animal) mussel.

mouler vt to mold; **m. qn** (vêtement) to fit sb tightly.

moulin m mill; **m. à vent** windmill; **m. à café** coffee grinder.

moulu (pp of moudre) adj (café) ground.

mourir* vi (aux être) to die (**de** of, from); **m. de froid** to die of exposure; **je meurs de faim!** I'm starving!

mousse f (plante) moss; (écume) foam; (de bière) froth; (de savon) lather; (dessert) mousse.

mousser vi (bière) to froth; (savon) to lather; (eau) to foam.

mousseux 1 adj (vin) sparkling. **2** m sparkling wine.

moustache f mustache; **moustaches** (de chat) whiskers.

moustachu, -ue adj **être m.** to have a mustache.

moustique m mosquito.

moutarde f mustard.

mouton m sheep inv; (viande) mutton.

mouvement m (geste, groupe etc) movement; (de colère) outburst.

mouvementé, -ée adj (vie, voyage etc) eventful.

moyen, -enne 1 adj average; (format etc) medium(-sized); **classe moyenne** middle class. **2** f average; (dans un examen, un devoir) passing grade; **en moyenne** on average.

moyen *m (procédé, façon)* means, way (**de faire** of doing, to do); **il n'y a pas m. de faire** it's not possible to do; **je n'ai pas les moyens** *(argent)* I can't afford it.

MP3 *f abrév (MPEG1 Audio Layer)* **lecteur M.** MP3 player.

muer *vi (animal)* to molt; *(voix)* to break.

muet, -ette 1 *adj (infirme)* mute; *(film, voyelle)* silent. **2** *mf* mute person.

mufle *m (d'animal)* muzzle.

mugir *vi (bœuf)* to bellow.

mugissement(s) *m(pl)* bellow(-ing).

muguet *m* lily of the valley.

mule *f (pantoufle)* mule; *(animal)* (she-)mule.

multicolore *adj* multicolored.

multiculturel, -elle *adj* multicultural.

multiple *m (nombre)* multiple.

multiplexe *m* multiplex.

multiplication *f* multiplication.

multiplier *vt* to multiply.

municipal, -e, -aux *adj* municipal; **conseil m.** city council.

municipalité *f (maires et conseillers)* city council; *(commune)* municipality.

munir *vt* **m. de** to equip with.

munir (se) *vpr* **se m. de** to provide oneself with.

munitions *fpl* ammunition.

mur *m* wall; **m. du son** sound barrier.

mûr, mûre *adj (fruit)* ripe.

muraille *f (high)* wall.

mûre *f (baie)* blackberry.

mûrir *vti (fruit)* to ripen.

murmure *m* murmur.

murmurer *vti* to murmur.

muscle *m* muscle.

musclé, -ée *adj (bras)* muscular.

museau, -x *m (de chien, chat)* nose, muzzle.

musée *m* museum.

museler *vt (animal, presse)* to muzzle.

muselière *f (appareil)* muzzle.

musical, -e, -aux *adj* musical.

musicien, -ienne *mf* musician.

musique *f* music.

musulman, -ane *adj & mf* Muslim.

muter *vt* to transfer.

mutuel, -elle *adj (réciproque)* mutual.

myope *adj & mf* shortsighted (person).

myrtille *f (baie)* bilberry.

mystère *m* mystery.

mystérieux, -euse *adj* mysterious.

N

nage *f* (swimming) stroke; **traverser à la n.** to swim across; **en n.** sweating.

nageoire *f (de poisson)* fin.

nager 1 *vi* to swim. **2** *vt (crawl etc)* to swim.

nageur, -euse *mf* swimmer.

naïf, -ïve *adj* naïve.

nain, naine *mf* dwarf.

naissance *f (de personne, animal)* birth.

naître* *vi* to be born.

nappe *f (sur une table)* table cloth; **n. de pétrole** oil slick.

napperon *m (pour vase etc)* (cloth) mat, doily.

narguer *vt* to taunt.

narine *f* nostril.

naseau, -x *m (de cheval)* nostril.

natal, -e, -als *adj (pays)* native; **sa maison natale** the house where he/she was born.

natation *f* swimming.

nation *f* nation.

national, -e, -aux *adj* national; **(route) nationale** highway.

nationalité f nationality.

natte f (de cheveux) braid; (tapis) mat.

nature 1 f (monde naturel, caractère) nature. **2** adj inv (omelette, yaourt etc) plain; (café) black.

naturel, -elle adj natural.

naufrage m shipwreck; **faire n.** to be shipwrecked.

naufragé, -ée adj & mf shipwrecked (person).

nausée f nausea, sickness; **avoir la n.** to feel nauseous.

nautique adj ski/etc n. water skiing/etc.

naval, -e, -als adj naval.

navet m (plante) turnip.

navette f **faire la n.** to shuttle back and forth (**entre** between); **n. spatiale** space shuttle.

navigateur, -trice mf (marin) navigator.

navigation f (trafic de bateaux) shipping.

naviguer vi (bateau) to sail; (sur Internet) to surf.

navire m ship.

navrant, -ante adj appalling.

navré, -ée adj **je suis n.** I'm (terribly) sorry (**de faire** to do).

ne (n' before vowel or mute h; used to form negative verb with **pas, jamais, personne, rien, que** etc) adv (+ pas) not; **il ne boit pas** he doesn't drink.

né, -ée adj (pp of **naître**) born; **elle est née** she was born.

néanmoins adv nevertheless.

nécessaire 1 adj necessary. **2** m n. **de toilette** (d'homme) shaving kit; (de femme) cosmetic case; **faire le n.** to do what's necessary.

nécessité f necessity.

nécessiter vt to require.

nectarine f nectarine.

néerlandais, -aise 1 adj Dutch. **2** mf N. Dutchman, Dutchwoman; **les N.** the Dutch. **3** m (langue) Dutch.

néfaste adj harmful (**à** to).

négatif, -ive 1 adj negative. **2** m (de photo) negative.

négation f Grammaire negation; (mot) negative.

négligence f (défaut) carelessness.

négligent, -ente adj careless.

négliger vt (personne, travail etc) to neglect; **n. de faire** to neglect to do.

négociant, -ante mf merchant, dealer.

négociation f negotiation.

négocier vti to negotiate.

neige f snow; **n. fondue** sleet.

neiger vi to snow.

nénuphar m water lily.

néon m éclairage au n. neon lighting.

nerf m nerve; **du n.!** buck up!; **ça me tape sur les nerfs** it gets on my nerves.

nerveux, -euse adj (agité) nervous.

nescafé® m instant coffee.

n'est-ce pas? adv isn't he?/don't you?/etc; **tu l'as, n?** you've got it, haven't you?; **elle vient, n.?** she's coming, isn't she?

net, nette 1 adj (image, refus) clear; (coupure, linge) clean; (soigné) neat; (poids, prix) net. **2** adv (s'arrêter) dead; (casser, couper) clean.

nettement adv (bien plus) definitely.

nettoyage m cleaning; **n. à sec** dry cleaning.

nettoyer vt to clean (up).

neuf, neuve 1 adj new; **quoi de n.?** what's new? **2** m **remettre à n.** to make as good as new.

neuf adj & m nine.

neutre adj (pays) neutral.

neuvième adj & mf ninth.

neveu, -x m nephew.

nez m nose; **n. à n.** face to face (**avec** with).

ni conj ni...ni (+ ne) neither...nor; **il**

n'a ni faim ni soif he's neither hungry nor thirsty; **sans manger ni boire** without eating or drinking; **ni l'un(e) ni l'autre** neither (of them).

niche f (de chien) doghouse.

nicher vi, **se nicher** vpr (oiseau) to nest.

nid m nest.

nièce f niece.

nier vt to deny (**que** that).

niveau, -x m level; **au n. de qn** (élève etc) up to sb's standard.

noble 1 adj noble. **2** mf nobleman, noblewoman.

noce(s) f(pl) wedding.

nocif, -ive adj harmful.

Noël m Christmas; **le père N.** Santa Claus.

nœud m knot; (ruban) bow; **n. coulant** slipknot, noose; **n. papillon** bow tie.

noir, noire 1 adj black; (nuit, lunettes etc) dark; **il fait n.** it's dark. **2** m (couleur) black; (obscurité) dark; **N.** (homme) black. **3** f **Noire** (femme) black.

noircir 1 vt to make black. **2** vi, **se noircir** vpr to turn black.

noisetier m hazel (tree).

noisette f hazelnut.

noix f (du noyer) walnut; **n. de coco** coconut.

nom m name; Grammaire noun; **n. de famille** last name, surname; **n. propre** Grammaire proper noun.

nombre m number.

nombreux, -euse adj (amis, livres) numerous, many; (famille) large; **peu n.** few; **venir n.** to come in large numbers.

nombril m navel.

nommer vt (appeler) to name; **n. qn** (désigner) to appoint sb (**à un poste** to a post).

nommer (se) vpr to be called.

non adv & m inv no; **tu viens ou n.?** are you coming or not?; **n. seulement** not only; **je crois que n.** I don't

think so; **(ni) moi n. plus** neither do/am/can/etc I.

nonante adj & m (en Belgique, en Suisse) ninety.

non-fumeur, -euse mf nonsmoker.

non-voyants mpl **les n.** the unsighted.

nord m north; **au n. de** north of; **du n.** (vent) northerly; (ville) northern.

nord-africain, -aine 1 adj North African. **2** mf **N.-A.** North African.

nord-américain, -aine 1 adj North American. **2** mf **N.-A.** North American.

nord-est m & adj inv northeast.

nord-ouest m & adj inv northwest.

normal, -e, -aux adj normal.

normale f **au-dessus/au-dessous de la n.** above/below normal.

normalement adv normally.

norvégien, -ienne 1 adj Norwegian. **2** mf **N.** Norwegian. **3** m (langue) Norwegian.

nos voir **notre**.

notaire m lawyer.

notamment adv particularly.

note f (de musique, remarque) note; (à l'école) grade; (facture) bill; **prendre n. de** to make a note of.

noter vt to note; (un devoir) to grade.

notice f (mode d'emploi) instructions.

notoriété f (renom) fame; **il est de n. publique que...** it's common knowledge that...

notre, pl nos adj poss our.

nôtre pron poss **le** ou **la n., les nôtres** ours.

nouer vt (chaussure etc) to tie.

nouilles fpl noodles.

nounours m teddy bear.

nourrice f (assistante maternelle) nanny.

nourrir vt to feed.

nourrissant, -ante adj nourishing.

nourrisson *m* infant.

nourriture *f* food.

nous *pron (sujet)* we; *(complément direct)* us; *(indirect)* (to) us; *(réfléchi)* ourselves; *(réciproque)* each other.

nous-mêmes *pron* ourselves.

nouveau (or **nouvel** before vowel or mute h), **nouvelle**, *pl* **nouveaux, nouvelles 1** *adj* new. **2** *mf (dans une classe)* new boy, new girl. **3** *m* **de n., à n.** again.

nouveau-né, -née *mf* new-born baby.

nouveauté *f* novelty; **nouveautés** *(livres)* new books; *(disques)* new releases.

nouvelle *f (information)* **nouvelle(s)** news; **une n.** a piece of news.

novembre *m* November.

noyade *f* drowning.

noyau, -x *f (fruit)* pit.

noyé, -ée *mf* drowned person.

noyer[1] *vt,* **se noyer** *vpr* to drown.

noyer[2] *m (arbre)* walnut tree.

nu, nue *adj (personne)* naked; *(mains)* bare; **tout nu** (stark) naked; **tête nue, nu-tête** bareheaded.

nuage *m* cloud.

nuageux, -euse *adj* cloudy.

nuance *f (de couleurs)* shade.

nucléaire *adj* nuclear.

nuire* *vi* **n. à qn** to harm sb.

nuisible *adj* harmful.

nuit *f* night; *(obscurité)* dark(ness); **il fait n.** it's dark; **la n.** *(se promener etc)* at night; **cette n.** *(aujourd'hui)* tonight; *(hier)* last night; **bonne n.** *(au coucher)* good night.

nul, nulle *adj (médiocre)* hopeless; **faire match n.** to tie; **nulle part** nowhere.

numérique *adj* numerical; *(montre, clavier, données)* digital.

numéro *m* number; *(de journal)* issue; *(au cirque)* act; **un n. de danse** a dance number; **n. vert** *(au*

téléphone) = tollfree number.

numéroter *vt (page etc)* to number.

nuque *f* back of the neck.

nylon® *m* nylon; **chemise/etc en n.** nylon shirt/etc.

O

obéir *vi* to obey; **o. à qn** to obey sb.

obéissance *f* obedience.

obéissant, -ante *adj* obedient.

objectif *m (but)* objective; *(d'appareil photo)* lens.

objet *m (chose)* object; **objets trouvés** *(bureau)* lost and found.

obligation *f* obligation.

obligatoire *adj* compulsory.

obliger *vt* to force, to compel (**à faire** to do); **être obligé de faire** to have to do.

oblique *adj* oblique.

obscène *adj* obscene.

obscur, -e *adj (noir)* dark.

obscurcir *vt (pièce)* to make dark(er).

obscurcir (s') *vpr (ciel)* to get dark(er).

obscurité *f* dark(ness).

obséder *vt* to obsess.

obsèques *fpl* funeral.

observation *f (étude)* observation; *(reproche)* (critical) remark.

observatoire *m (endroit élevé)* lookout (post).

observer *vt (regarder)* to watch; *(remarquer, respecter)* to observe.

obstacle *m* obstacle.

obstiné, -ée *adj* stubborn, obstinate.

obstiner (s') *vpr* **s'o. à faire** to persist in doing.

obstruer *vt* to obstruct.

obtenir* *vt* to get, to obtain.

obus *m (arme)* shell.

occasion *f* chance (**de faire** to do); *(prix avantageux)* bargain; **d'o.** second-hand, used.

occasionner *vt* to cause.

Occident *m* l'O. the West.

occidental, -e, -aux *adj* western.

occupation *f (activité etc)* occupation.

occupé, -ée *adj* busy (**à faire** doing); *(place, maison etc)* occupied; *(téléphone)* busy; *(taxi)* hired.

occuper *vt (maison, pays etc)* to occupy; *(place, temps)* to take up; **o. qn** *(travail, jeu)* to keep sb busy.

occuper (s') *vpr* to keep (oneself) busy (**à faire** doing); **s'o. de** *(affaire, problème)* to deal with; **s'o. de qn** *(malade etc)* to take care of sb; **occupe-toi de tes affaires!** mind your own business!

océan *m* ocean.

octet *m* byte; **milliard d'octets** gigabyte.

octobre *m* October.

oculiste *mf* eye specialist.

odeur *f* smell.

odieux, -euse *adj* horrible.

odorat *m* sense of smell.

œil, *pl* **yeux** *m* eye; **lever/baisser les yeux** to look up/down; **coup d'o.** look, glance; **jeter un coup d'o. sur** to (have a) look at; **o. poché, o. au beurre noir** black eye.

œillet *m (fleur)* carnation.

œuf, *pl* **œufs** *m* egg; **o. sur le plat** fried egg.

œuvre *f (travail, livre etc)* work.

offenser *vt* to offend.

office *m (messe)* service.

officiel, -ielle *adj* official.

officier *m (dans l'armée etc)* officer.

offre *f* offer; **l'o. et la demande** supply and demand; **offres d'emploi** job vacancies, positions vacant.

offrir* *vt* to offer (**de faire** to do); *(cadeau)* to give;

offrir (s') *vpr* **s'o. qch** to treat oneself to sth.

oh! *int* oh!

oie *f* goose *(pl* geese).

oignon *m (légume)* onion; *(de fleur)* bulb.

oiseau, -x *m* bird.

oisif, -ive *adj (inactif)* idle.

oisiveté *f* idleness.

olive *f* olive; **huile d'o.** olive oil.

olivier *m* olive tree.

olympique *adj (jeux)* Olympic.

ombragé, -ée *adj* shady.

ombre *f (d'arbre etc)* shade; *(de personne, objet)* shadow; **à l'o.** in the shade.

omelette *f* omelet(te); **o. au fromage/etc** cheese/etc omelet(te).

omettre* *vt* to omit (**de faire** to do).

omnibus *adj & m (train)* **o.** slow *ou* local train.

omoplate *f* shoulder blade.

on *pron (les gens)* they, people; *(nous)* we; *(vous)* you; **on frappe** someone's knocking; **on m'a dit que** I was told that.

oncle *m* uncle.

onde *f (de radio)* wave; **grandes ondes** long wave; **ondes courtes** short wave.

ondulation *f (de cheveux)* wave.

onduler *vi (cheveux)* to be wavy.

ongle *m (finger)* nail.

ont *voir* **avoir.**

ONU *f abrév (Organisation des Nations Unies)* UN.

onze *adj & m* eleven.

onzième *adj & mf* eleventh.

opaque *adj* opaque.

opéra *m (musique)* opera; *(édifice)* opera house.

opération *f* operation.

opérer *vt (en chirurgie)* to operate on (**de** for); **se faire o.** to have an operation.

opinion *f* opinion (**sur** about, on).

opportun, -une *adj* opportune, timely.

EXPRIMER SON OPINION

Qu'est-ce que tu en penses/vous en pensez ?
What do you think?

Ça me plaît beaucoup/Ça m'a beaucoup plu.
I really like it/liked it.

C'était génial/beau !
It was great/beautiful!

Ce n'était pas mal.
It was OK.

La visite du château était assez intéressant.
The tour of the castle was quite interesting.

J'adore les croissants/faire de la randonné.
I love croissants/hiking.

Je déteste la neige/faire les magasins.
I hate snow/shopping.

Je préférerais du café.
I'd rather have coffee.

Tu préfères/Vous préférez lequel/laquelle ?
Which do you prefer?

Je la trouve très sympa.
I think she's very nice.

Je suis d'accord (avec toi/vous).
I agree (with you).

Absolument !
Absolutely!

Je suis sûr(e) qu'il fera beau demain.
I'm sure it'll be nice tomorrow.

C'est vrai.
That's true.

J'ai changé d'avis.
I've changed my mind.

Je ne sais pas.
I don't know.

Ah bon ?/C'est vrai ?
Really?

Quelle surprise !
What a surprise!

Le musée d'art t'a/vous a plu ?
Did you like the art gallery?

Ça ne me plaît pas/Ça ne m'a pas plu.
I don't like it/didn't like it.

C'était un peu ennuyeux/trop touristique.
It was a bit boring/too touristy.

La nourriture n'a rien d'exceptionnel.
The food's nothing special.

On s'est éclatés !
We had a great time!

Je n'aime pas le jazz/faire du vélo.
I don't like jazz/cycling.

C'est délicieux/dégoûtant !
This is delicious/disgusting!

Je préfère les petits hôtels aux grands.
I prefer small hotels to big ones.

Je préfère le (la) plus grand(e)/le (la) plus petit(e).
I prefer the bigger/smaller one.

Je crois que c'est/Je ne crois pas que ce soit possible.
I think/I don't think it's possible.

Je ne suis pas d'accord (avec toi/vous).
I disagree (with you).

Bien sur (que non) !
Of course (not)!

Tu en es sûr(e)/Vous en êtes sûr(e) ?
Are you sure?

Je ne te/vous crois pas.
I don't believe you.

Je ne suis pas sûr(e).
I'm not sure.

Ça dépend.
It depends.

C'est étrange/bizarre !
That's strange!

Quel dommage !
What a pity!

opposé, -ée 1 *adj (direction, opinion etc)* opposite; *(équipe)* opposing; **o. à** opposed to. **2** *m* **l'o.** the opposite *(de* of); **à l'o.** *(côté)* on the opposite side *(de* from, to).

opposer *vt (résistance)* to put up *(à* against); *(équipes)* to bring together; **o. qn à qn** to set sb against sb.

opposer (s') *vpr (équipes)* to play against each other; **s'o. à** *(mesure, personne)* to be opposed to, to oppose.

opposition *f* opposition *(à* to).

oppressant, -ante *adj* oppressive.

opticien, -ienne *mf* optician.

optimiste *adj* optimistic.

optique 1 *adj (nerf)* optic; *(verre, fibres)* optical. **2** *f* optics; **d'o.** *(instrument)* optical. ▪ *(point de vue)* perspective.

or 1 *m* gold; **montre/etc en or** gold watch/*etc;* **d'or** golden; **mine d'or** goldmine. **2** *conj (cependant)* now, well.

orage *m* (thunder)storm.

orageux, -euse *adj* stormy.

oral, -e, -aux 1 *adj* oral. **2** *m (examen)* oral.

orange 1 *f (fruit)* orange. **2** *adj & m inv (couleur)* orange.

orangeade *f* orangeade.

orbite *f (d'astre)* orbit; *(d'œil)* socket.

orchestre *m (classique)* orchestra; *(jazz, pop)* band; *(places)* orchestra.

ordinaire *adj (habituel, normal)* ordinary, regular; *(médiocre)* ordinary; **d'o.** usually.

ordinateur *m* computer.

ordonnance *f (de médecin)* prescription.

ordonné, -ée *adj* tidy.

ordonner *vt* to order *(que* (+ *subjonctif)* that); *(médicament etc)* to prescribe; **o. à qn de faire** to order sb to do.

ordre *m (commandement, classe-

ment)* order; *(absence de désordre)* tidiness *(of room, person etc);* **en o.** *(chambre etc)* tidy; **mettre en o., mettre de l'o. dans** to tidy (up); **jusqu'à nouvel o.** until further notice.

ordures *fpl (débris)* garbage.

oreille *f* ear; **faire la sourde o.** to take no notice, to refuse to listen.

oreiller *m* pillow.

oreillons *mpl* mumps.

organe *m (de corps)* organ.

organisateur, -trice *mf* organizer.

organisation *f* organization.

organiser *vt* to organize.

organiser (s') *vpr* to get organized.

organisme *m (corps)* body; *(bureaux etc)* organization.

orge *f* barley.

orgue 1 *m (instrument)* organ. **2** *fpl* **grandes orgues** great organ.

orgueil *m* pride.

orgueilleux, -euse *adj* proud.

oriental, -e, -aux *adj (côte, pays etc)* eastern; *(du Japon, de la Chine)* far-eastern, oriental.

orientation *f* direction; *(de maison)* orientation; **o. professionnelle** career counseling.

orienté, -ée *adj (appartement etc)* **o. à l'ouest** facing west.

orienter *vt (lampe etc)* to position; *(voyageur, élève)* to direct.

orienter (s') *vpr* to find one's bearings *ou* direction.

originaire *adj* **être o. de** *(natif)* to be a native of.

original, -e, -aux 1 *adj (idée, artiste etc)* original. **2** *m (texte)* original.

originalité *f* originality.

origine *f* origin; **à l'o.** originally; **d'o.** *(pneu etc)* original; **pays d'o.** country of origin.

ornement *m* ornament.

orner *vt* to decorate *(de* with).

orphelin, -ine *mf* orphan.

orphelinat m orphanage.

orteil m toe; **gros o.** big toe.

orthographe f spelling.

ortie f nettle.

os m bone; **trempé jusqu'aux os** soaked to the skin.

osé, -ée adj daring.

oser vti to dare; **o. faire** to dare (to) do.

osier m wicker; **panier d'o.** wicker basket.

otage m hostage; **prendre qn en o.** to take sb hostage.

OTAN f abrév (Organisation du traité de l'Atlantique Nord) NATO.

otarie f (animal) sea lion.

ôter vt to take away (**à qn** from sb); (vêtement) to take off; (déduire) to take away.

otite f ear infection.

ou conj or; **ou bien** or else; **ou elle ou moi** either her or me.

où adv & pron where; **le jour où** the day when; **la table où** the table on which; **par où?** which way?; **d'où?** where from?; **le pays d'où** the country from which.

oubli m **l'o. de qch** forgetting sth; **un o.** (dans une liste etc) an oversight.

oublier vt to forget (**de faire** to do).

ouest m & adj inv west; **d'o.** (vent) west(erly); **de l'o.** western.

ouf! int (whew,) what a relief!

oui adv & m inv yes; **tu viens, o. ou non?** are you coming or aren't you?; **je crois que o.** I think so.

ouïe f hearing.

ouïes fpl (de poisson) gills.

ouille! int ouch!

ouragan m hurricane.

ourlet m hem.

ours m bear; **o. blanc** polar bear.

outil m tool.

outillage m tools.

outre 1 prép besides. **2** adv **en o.** besides.

outre-mer adv overseas; **d'o.** (marché) overseas; **territoires d'o.** overseas territories.

outré, -ée adj (révolté) outraged.

ouvert, -erte (pp de ouvrir) adj open; (robinet, gaz) on.

ouvertement adv openly.

ouverture f opening; (trou) hole.

ouvrage m (travail, livre) work; (couture) (needle)work; **un o.** (travail) a piece of work.

ouvre-boîtes m inv can opener.

ouvre-bouteilles m inv bottle opener.

ouvreuse f usherette.

ouvrier, -ière 1 mf worker; **o. qualifié/spécialisé** skilled/unskilled worker. **2** adj (quartier) working-class; **classe ouvrière** working class.

ouvrir* 1 vt to open (up); (gaz, radio etc) to turn on, to switch on. **2** vi to open; (ouvrir la porte) to open (up).

ouvrir (s') vpr (porte, boîte etc) to open (up).

ovale adj & m oval.

OVNI m abrév (objet volant non identifié) UFO.

oxygène m oxygen.

P

pacifique 1 adj (manifestation etc) peaceful; (côte etc) Pacific. **2** m **le P.** the Pacific.

pagaie f paddle.

pagaille f (désordre) mess; **en p.** in a mess.

pagayer vi to paddle.

page f (de livre etc) page; **p. web** web page.

paie f pay, wages.

paiement m payment.

paillasson m (door)mat.

paille f straw; (pour boire) (drinking) straw; **tirer à la courte p.** to draw lots *ou* straws.

paillette *f (d'habit)* sequin; **paillettes** *(de savon)* flakes.

pain *m* bread; **un p.** a loaf (of bread); **p. grillé** toast; **p. complet** whole-wheat bread; **p. d'épice** gingerbread; **p. de seigle** rye bread; **petit p.** roll.

pair, -e *adj (numéro)* even.

paire *f* pair **(de** of).

paisible *adj (vie, endroit)* peaceful.

paître* *vi* to graze.

paix *f* peace; *(traité)* peace treaty; **en p.** in peace; **avoir la p.** to have (some) peace and quiet.

palais¹ *m (château)* palace; **P. de justice** courthouse; **p. des sports** sports stadium.

palais² *m (dans la bouche)* palate.

pâle *adj* pale.

paletot *m* (knitted) cardigan.

palette *f (de peintre)* palette.

pâleur *f* paleness.

palier *m (d'escalier)* landing; **être voisins de p.** to live on the same floor.

pâlir *vi* to turn pale **(de** with).

palissade *f* fence *(of stakes)*.

palmarès *m* prize list; *(de chansons)* charts.

palme *f* palm (leaf); *(de nageur)* flipper.

palmier *m* palm (tree).

palper *vt* to feel.

palpitant, -ante *adj* thrilling.

palpiter *vi (cœur)* to throb.

pamplemousse *m* grapefruit.

pan! *int* bang!

panaché *adj & m* **(demi) p.** shandy *(beer and lemonade)*.

pancarte *f* sign; *(de manifestant)* placard.

pané, -ée *adj* breaded.

panier *m* basket; **p. à salade** *(ustensile)* salad basket.

panique *f* panic.

paniqué, -ée *adj* panic-stricken.

paniquer *vi* to panic.

panne *f* breakdown; **tomber en p.** to break down; **être en p.** to have broken down; **p. d'électricité** blackout, power outage.

panneau, -x *m (écriteau)* sign; *(de porte etc)* panel; **p. (de signalisation)** road sign; **p. (d'affichage)** billboard.

panoplie *f (jouet)* outfit.

panorama *m* view.

pansement *m* dressing, bandage; **p. adhésif** Band-Aid®.

panser *vt (main etc)* to dress, to bandage.

pantalon *m* (pair of) pants; **en p.** in pants.

pantin *m* puppet, jumping jack.

pantoufle *f* slipper.

paon *m* peacock.

papa *m* dad(dy).

pape *m* pope.

papeterie *f (magasin)* stationery store.

papi *m* *Fam* grand(d)ad.

papier *m (matière)* paper; **un p. (feuille)** a sheet of paper; *(formulaire)* a form; **sac/etc en p.** paper bag/etc; **papiers (d'identité)** (identity) papers; **p. hygiénique** toilet paper; **p. à lettres** writing paper; **du p. journal** (some) newspaper; **p. peint** wallpaper; **p. de verre** sandpaper.

papillon *m* butterfly; **p. (de nuit)** moth.

paquebot *m* (ocean) liner.

pâquerette *f* daisy.

Pâques *m sing & fpl* Easter.

paquet *m (de bonbons etc)* packet; *(colis)* package; *(de cigarettes)* pack; *(de cartes)* pack, deck.

par *prép (agent, manière, moyen)* by; **choisi p.** chosen by; **p. le train** by train; **p. le travail** by *ou* through work; **apprendre p.** un ami to learn from *ou* through a friend; **commencer p. qch** to begin with sth. ▪ *(lieu)* through; **p. la porte** through *ou* by the door; **jeter p. la fenêtre** to throw out (of) the window; **p. ici/là** *(aller)* this/that way; *(habiter)* around here/there. ▪ *(motif)* out of, from; **p. pitié** out of *ou* from pity. ▪ *(temps)* on; **p. un jour d'hiver** on a winter day; **p. ce froid** in this cold. ▪ *(distributif)* **dix fois p. an** ten times a year; **deux p. deux** two by two.

parachute *m* parachute.

parachutisme *m* parachute jumping.

paradis *m* heaven, paradise.

paragraphe *m* paragraph.

paraître* *vi (sembler)* to seem; *(livre)* to come out; **il paraît qu'il va partir** it appears *ou* seems he's leaving.

parallèle *adj* parallel (**à** with, to).

paralyser *vt* to paralyze.

parapente *m (activité)* paragliding; **faire du p.** to go paragliding.

parapluie *m* umbrella.

parasite *m* parasite; **parasites** *(à la radio)* interference.

parasol *m* sunshade.

paravent *m* (folding) screen.

parc *m* park; *(de château)* grounds; *(de bébé)* playpen; **p. (de stationnement)** parking lot.

parce que *conj* because.

parcelle *f* fragment; *(terrain)* plot.

par-ci par-là *adv* here, there and everywhere.

parcmètre *m* parking meter.

parcourir* *vt (region)* to travel all over; *(distance)* to cover; *(texte)* to glance through.

parcours *m (itinéraire)* route; *(distance)* distance.

par-dessous *prép & adv* under(-neath).

pardessus *m* overcoat.

par-dessus *prép & adv* over (the top of); **p. tout** above all.

pardon *m* **p.!** *(excusez-moi)* sorry!; **demander p.** to apologize (**à** to).

pardonner *vt* to forgive; **p. qch à qn/à qn d'avoir fait qch** to forgive

sb for sth/for doing sth.

pare-brise *m inv* windshield.

pare-chocs *m inv* bumper.

pareil, -eille 1 *adj* similar; **p. à** the same as; **être pareils** to be the same; **un p. désordre/etc** such a mess/etc. **2** *adv Fam* the same.

parent, -ente 1 *mf* relative. **2** *mpl (père et mère)* parents. **3** *adj* related (**de** to).

parenté *f* relationship; **avoir un lien de p.** to be related.

parenthèse *f (signe)* bracket.

paresse *f* laziness.

paresseux, -euse 1 *adj* lazy. **2** *mf* lazy person.

parfait, -aite *adj* perfect; **p.!** excellent!

parfaitement *adv* perfectly; *(certainement)* certainly.

parfois *adv* sometimes.

parfum *m (odeur)* fragrance; *(goût)* flavor; *(liquide)* perfume.

parfumé, -ée *adj (savon, fleur)* scented; **p. au café/etc** coffee/etc-flavored.

parfumer *vt* to perfume; *(glace, crème)* to flavor (**à** with).

parfumer (se) *vpr* to put on perfume.

parfumerie *f* perfume shop.

pari *m* bet; **p. mutuel urbain** = parimutuel.

parier *vti* to bet (**sur** on; **que** that).

parisien, -ienne 1 *adj* Parisian; **la banlieue parisienne** the outskirts of Paris. **2** *mf* P. Parisian.

parking *m* parking lot.

parlement *m* parliament.

parlementaire *mf* member of parliament, = Congressman.

parler 1 *vi* to talk, to speak (**de** about, of; **à** to). **2** *vt (langue)* to speak.

parler (se) *vpr (langue)* to be spoken.

parmi *prép* among(st).

paroi *f* (inside) wall; *(de rocher)* (rock) face.

paroisse f parish.
paroissial, -e, -aux adj église/
etc paroissiale parish church/etc.
parole f (mot, promesse) word;
adresser la p. à to speak to; prendre la p. to speak; demander la p.
to ask to speak.
parquet m (parquet) floor.
parrain m godfather.
parrainer vt (course etc) to sponsor.
parsemé, -ée adj p. de (sol)
strewn (all over) with.
part f (portion) share; (de gâteau)
portion; (de cartes) to
take part in; (la joie etc de qn) to
share; de toutes parts from ou on
all sides; de p. et d'autre on both
sides; d'autre p. (d'ailleurs) moreover; de la p. de (provenance)
from; quelque p. somewhere; nulle
p. nowhere; autre p. somewhere
else; à p. (mettre) aside; (excepté)
apart from; (personne) different.
partage m (de gâteau, trésor etc)
sharing.
partagé, -ée adj (amour) mutual;
les avis sont partagés opinions are
divided.
partager vt (repas, joie etc) to
share (avec with).
partance (en) adj (train) about to
depart; en p. pour... for...
partenaire mf partner.
partenariat m partnership.
parterre m (de jardin) flower bed.
parti m (politique) party.
partial, -e, -aux adj biased.
participant, -ante mf participant.
participation f participation; p.
(aux frais) contribution (towards
expenses).
participe m Grammaire participle.
participer vi p. à (jeu etc) to take
part in; (frais, joie) to share (in).
particularité f peculiarity.
particulier, -ière adj (spécial)
particular; (privé) private; (bizarre)

peculiar; en p. (surtout) in particular.
particulièrement adv particularly.
partie f part; (de cartes, tennis etc)
game; en p. partly; faire p. de to be
a part of; (club etc) to belong to.
partiel, -elle adj partial.
partir* vi (aux être) (aller) to go;
(s'en aller) to go, to leave; (coup de
feu) to go off; (tache) to come out; à
p. de (date, prix) from.
partisan m supporter; être p. de
qch/de faire to be in favor of sth/of
doing.
partition f (musique) score.
partout adv everywhere; p. où tu
vas ou iras everywhere ou wher-
ever you go.
parvenir* vi (aux être) p. à (lieu)
to reach; p. à faire to manage to do.
pas¹ adv (négatif) not; (ne)...p. not;
je ne sais p. I don't know; pas de
pain/etc no bread/etc; p. encore
not yet; p. du tout not at all.
pas² m step; (allure) pace; (bruit)
footstep; (trace) footprint; rouler
au p. (véhicule) to go dead slow; au
p. (cadencé) in step; faire les cent
p. to walk up and down, to pace;
faux p. (en marchant) stumble; (erreur) blunder; le p. de la porte the
doorstep.
passable adj (travail, résultat)
(just) average.
passage m passing; (traversée en
bateau) crossing; (extrait, couloir)
passage; (droit) right of way; (chemin) path; p. clouté ou pour piétons (pedestrian) crosswalk; p.
souterrain underground passage
(for pedestrians); p. à niveau grade
crossing; 'p. interdit' 'no through
traffic'; 'cédez le p.' (au carrefour)
'yield'.
passager, -ère mf passenger.
passant, -ante mf passer-by.
passe f Sport pass.
passé, -ée 1 adj (temps) past; (cou-

leur) faded; **la semaine passée** last week; **dix heures passées** after ten (o'clock); **être passé** *(personne)* to have been here/there; *(orage)* to be over; **avoir vingt ans passés** to be over twenty. **2** *m* past; *Grammaire* past (tense).

passe-passe *m inv* **tour de p.** magic trick.

passeport *m* passport.

passer 1 *vi (aux* **être** *ou* **avoir)** to pass (**à** to; **de** from); *(traverser)* to go through *ou* over; *(facteur)* to come; *(temps)* to pass, to go by; *(film)* to be shown; *(douleur)* to pass; *(couleur)* to fade; **p. devant** *(maison etc)* to go past, to pass (by); **p. à la boulangerie** *ou* **chez le boulanger** to go to *ou* by the bakery; **laisser p.** *(personne, lumière)* to let through; **p. prendre** to pick up; **p. voir qn** to drop in on sb; **p. pour** *(riche etc)* to be taken for; **p. en** *(seconde etc)* (*à l'école)* to advance to; *(en voiture)* to shift into. **2** *vt (aux* **avoir)** *(frontière etc)* to cross; *(donner)* to pass, to hand (**à** to); *(temps)* to spend (**à faire** doing); *(CD, chemise, film)* to put on; *(examen)* to take; *(thé)* to strain; *(café)* to filter; *(limites)* to go beyond; *(visite médicale)* to have; **p. qch à qn** *(caprice etc)* to grant sb sth; **p. un coup d'éponge/etc à qch** to go over sth with a sponge/*etc.*

passer (se) *vpr* to take place, to happen; *(douleur)* to go (away); **se p. de** to do *ou* without; **ça s'est bien passé** it went off well.

passerelle *f* footbridge; *(d'avion, de bateau)* gangway.

passe-temps *m inv* pastime.

passif, -ive 1 *adj* passive. **2** *m* *Grammaire* passive.

passion *f* passion; **avoir la p. des voitures/d'écrire** to have a passion for cars/writing.

passionnant, -ante *adj* thrilling.

passionné, -ée *adj* passionate; **p.**

de qch passionately fond of sth.

passionner *vt* to thrill.

passionner (se) *vpr* **se p. pour** to have a passion for.

passoire *f (à thé)* strainer; *(à légumes)* colander.

pastèque *f* watermelon.

pasteurisé, -ée *adj* pasteurized.

pastille *f* pastille, lozenge.

patauger *vi* to wade *(in the mud etc)*; *(barboter)* to splash around.

pâte *f* paste; *(à pain)* dough; *(à tarte)* pastry; **pâtes (alimentaires)** pasta; **p. à modeler** modeling clay.

pâté *m (charcuterie)* pâté; **p. (en croûte)** meat pie; **p. (de sable)** sand castle; **p. de maisons** block of houses.

pâtée *f (pour chien, chat)* pet food.

paternel, -elle *adj* paternal.

pathétique *adj* moving.

patiemment *adv* patiently.

patience *f* patience.

patient, -ente 1 *adj* patient. **2** *mf (malade)* patient.

patienter *vi* to wait.

patin *m* **p. (à glace)** (ice) skate; **p. à roulettes** roller skate.

patinage *m* skating; **p. artistique** figure skating.

patiner *vi (en sport)* to skate; *(roue)* to spin round.

patineur, -euse *mf* skater.

patinoire *f* skating rink.

pâtisserie *f* pastry; *(magasin)* cake shop.

pâtissier, -ière *mf* pastry cook.

patrie *f (native)* country.

patrimoine *m* heritage; *(biens)* property.

patriote 1 *mf* patriot. **2** *adj* patriotic.

patriotique *adj (chant etc)* patriotic.

patron, -onne 1 *mf (chef)* boss. **2** *m (modèle de papier)* pattern.

patronat *m* employers.

patrouille *f* patrol.

patrouiller *vi* to patrol.

patte f leg; (de chat, chien) paw; **marcher à quatre pattes** to crawl.

pâturage m pasture.

paume f (de main) palm.

paupière f eyelid.

pause f (arrêt) break.

pauvre 1 adj poor. **2** mf poor person; **les pauvres** the poor.

pauvreté f (besoin) poverty.

pavé m (de rue) paving stone.

paver vt to pave.

pavillon m (maison) (detached) house; (drapeau) flag.

payant, -ante adj (hôte, spectateur) paying; (place, entrée) that one has to pay for.

paye f pay, wages.

payer 1 vt (personne, somme) to pay; (service, objet) to pay for; **p. qn pour faire** to pay sb to do ou for doing. **2** vi (personne, métier) to pay.

pays m country; **du p.** (vin, gens) local.

paysage m landscape.

paysan, -anne mf (small) farmer.

PC m abrév (personal computer) PC.

PCV abrév (paiement contre vérification) **téléphoner en P.** to call collect.

PDA m abrév (personal digital assistant) PDA.

PDG m abrév (président directeur général) CEO.

péage m (droit) toll; (lieu) tollbooth.

peau, -x f skin; (de fruit) peel, skin; (cuir) hide.

pêche[1] f fishing; (poissons) catch; **p. (à la ligne)** angling; **aller à la p.** to go fishing.

pêche[2] f (fruit) peach.

péché m sin.

pêcher[1] **1** vi to fish. **2** vt (attraper) to catch.

pêcher[2] m peach tree.

pêcheur m fisherman; (à la ligne) angler.

pédale f pedal; **p. de frein** footbrake (pedal).

pédaler vi to pedal.

pédalo m paddle boat.

pédiatre mf children's doctor.

pédicure mf chiropodist.

pédomètre m pedometer.

peigne m comb; **se donner un coup de p.** to give one's hair a comb.

peigner vt (cheveux) to comb; **p. qn** to comb sb's hair.

peigner (se) vpr to comb one's hair.

peignoir m bathrobe; **p. (de bain)** bathrobe.

peindre* vti to paint; **p. en bleu/** etc to paint blue/etc.

peine f (à) adv hardly.

peine f (châtiment) **la p. de mort** the death penalty; **p. de prison** prison sentence. ▪ (chagrin) sorrow; **avoir de la p.** to be upset; **faire de la p. à** to upset. ▪ (effort, difficulté) trouble; **se donner de la p.** to go ou to a lot of trouble (**pour faire** to do); **avec p.** with difficulty; **ça vaut la p. d'attendre/**etc it's worth(while) waiting/etc; **ce n'est pas** ou **ça ne vaut pas la p.** it's not worth it.

peintre m painter; **p. (en bâtiment)** (house) painter.

peinture f (tableau, activité) painting; (matière) paint; **'p. fraîche'** 'wet paint'.

pelage m (d'animal) coat, fur.

peler 1 vt (fruit) to peel. **2** vi (peau bronzée) to peel.

pelle f shovel; (d'enfant) spade; **p. à poussière** dustpan.

pelleteuse f steam shovel.

pellicule f (pour photos) film; (couche) layer; **pellicules** (dans les cheveux) dandruff.

pelote f (de laine) ball.

peloton m (cyclistes) pack.

pelotonner (se) vpr to curl up (into a ball).

pelouse f lawn.

peluche f **peluches** (flocons) fluff; **jouet en p.** = stuffed animal; **chien**

en p. *(jouet)* stuffed dog; **ours en p.** teddy bear.

penalty *m Football* penalty.

penchant *m (préférence)* penchant (**pour** for); *(tendance)* propensity (**pour** for).

penché, -ée *adj* leaning.

pencher 1 *vt (objet)* to tilt; *(tête)* to lean. **2** *vi (arbre etc)* to lean (over).

pencher (se) *vpr* to lean (over *ou* forward); **se p. par** *(fenêtre)* to lean out of.

pendant *prép* during; **p. la nuit** during the night; **p. deux mois** for two months; **p. que** while.

penderie *f* closet.

pendre *vti* to hang (**à** from); **p. qn** to hang sb (**pour** for).

pendre (se) *vpr* to hang (**à** from).

pendu, -ue *adj (objet)* hanging (**à** from).

pendule *f* clock.

pénétrer *vi* **p. dans** to enter; *(profondément)* to penetrate (into).

pénible *adj* difficult; *(douloureux)* painful.

péniblement *adv* with difficulty.

péniche *f* barge.

pénicilline *f* penicillin.

pensée *f (idée)* thought.

penser 1 *vi* to think (**à** of, about); **p. à qch/à faire qch** *(ne pas oublier)* to remember sth/to do sth. **2** *vt* to think (**que** that); **je pensais rester** I was thinking of staying; **je pense réussir** I hope to succeed; **que pensez-vous de?** what do you think of *ou* about?

pensif, -ive *adj* thoughtful, pensive.

pension[1] *f* boarding school; *(somme à payer)* board; **être en p.** to board (**chez** with); **p. complète** full board.

pension[2] *f (de retraite etc)* pension.

pensionnaire *mf (élève)* boarder; *(d'hôtel)* resident; *(de famille)* lodger.

pensionnat *m* boarding school.

pente *f* slope; **en p.** sloping.

Pentecôte *f* Pentecost.

pénurie *f* shortage (**de** of).

pépin *m (de fruit)* seed, pit.

perçant, -ante *adj (cri, froid)* piercing; *(yeux)* sharp.

percepteur *m* tax collector.

percer 1 *vt* to pierce; *(avec une perceuse)* to drill (a hole in); *(ouverture)* to make. **2** *vi (avec un outil)* to drill.

perceuse *f (outil)* drill.

percevoir* *vt (sensation)* to perceive; *(son)* to hear. ▪ *(impôt)* to collect.

perche *f (bâton)* pole.

percher (se) *vpr (oiseau)* to perch.

perchoir *m* perch.

percuter *vt (véhicule)* to crash into.

perdant, -ante *mf* loser.

perdre 1 *vt* to lose; *(gaspiller)* to waste; **p. de vue** to lose sight of. **2** *vi* to lose.

perdre (se) *vpr (s'égarer)* to get lost; **je m'y perds** I'm lost *ou* confused.

perdrix *f* partridge.

perdu, -ue *adj* lost; *(gaspillé)* wasted; **c'est du temps p.** it's a waste of time.

père *m* father.

perfection *f* perfection; **à la p.** perfectly.

perfectionné, -ée *adj (machine)* advanced.

perfectionnement *m* improvement (**de** in; **par rapport à** on); **cours de p.** proficiency course.

perfectionner *vt* to improve.

perfectionner (se) *vpr* **se p. en anglais/etc** to improve one's English/etc.

perforeuse *f (paper)* punch.

performance *f* performance.

performant, -ante *adj* highly efficient.

péril *m* danger, peril.

périlleux, -euse *adj* dangerous.

périmé, -ée *adj (billet)* expired.

période *f* period.

périphérique *adj & m* (**boulevard**) **p.** beltway.

perle *f(bijou)* pearl; *(de bois, verre)* bead.

permanence *f (salle d'étude)* study hall; **être de p.** to be on duty; **en p.** permanently.

permanent, -ente 1 *adj* permanent; *(spectacle)* continuous. **2** *f (coiffure)* perm.

permettre* *vt* to allow; **p. à qn de faire** to allow sb to do; **vous permettez?** may I?; **je ne peux pas me p. de l'acheter** I can't afford (to buy) it.

permis, -ise 1 *adj* allowed. **2** *m* license; **p. de conduire** driver's license; **passer son p. de conduire** to take one's driving test.

permission *f* permission; *(congé de soldat)* leave; **demander la p.** to ask permission (**de faire** to do).

perpendiculaire *adj* perpendicular (**à** to).

perpétuel, -elle *adj (incessant)* continual, non-stop.

perplexe *adj* perplexed, puzzled.

perquisitionner *vi* to make a search.

perron *m* (front) steps.

perroquet *m* parrot.

perruche *f* parakeet.

perruque *f* wig.

persécuter *vt* to persecute.

persécution *f* persecution.

persévérance *f* perseverance.

persévérer *vi* to persevere (**dans** in).

persil *m* parsley.

persister *vi* to persist (**à faire** in doing; **dans qch** in sth).

personnage *m* (important) person; *(de livre, film)* character.

personnalité *f* personality.

personne 1 *f* person; **personnes** people; **grande p.** grown-up; **en p.**

in person. **2** *pron (négatif)* nobody; **je ne vois p.** I don't see anybody; **mieux que p.** better than anybody.

personnel, -elle *adj* personal. **2** *m* staff.

personnellement *adv* personally.

perspective *f (idée, possibilité)* prospect (**de** of).

perspicace *adj* shrewd.

persuader *vt* to persuade (**qn de faire** sb to do); **être persuadé que** to be convinced that.

persuasion *f* persuasion.

perte *f* loss; *(gaspillage)* waste (**de temps/d'argent** of time/money).

pertinemment *adv* **savoir qch p.** to know sth for a fact.

perturbation *f* disruption.

perturber *vt (trafic etc)* to disrupt; *(personne)* to disturb.

pervers, -erse 1 *adj* perverse. **2** *mf* pervert.

pesant, -ante *adj* heavy.

pesanteur *f (force)* gravity.

pèse-personne, *pl* **pèse-personne(s)** *m* (bathroom) scales.

peser *vti* to weigh; **p. lourd** to be heavy.

pessimiste *adj* pessimistic.

peste *f(maladie)* plague.

pétale *m* petal.

pétanque *f* (French) bowling game.

pétard *m* firecracker.

pétillant, -ante *adj* fizzy; *(vin, yeux)* sparkling.

pétiller *vi (champagne)* to fizz; *(yeux)* to sparkle.

petit, -ite 1 *adj* small, little; *(de taille)* short; *(bruit, coup)* slight; *(jeune)* little; **tout p.** tiny; **un p. Français** a (little) French boy. **2** *mf* (little) boy/girl; *(personne)* small person; **petits** *(d'animal)* young. **3** *adv* **p. à p.** little by little.

petite-fille, *pl* **petites-filles** *f* granddaughter.

petit-fils, pl petits-fils m grandson.

petits-enfants mpl grandchildren.

petit-suisse m soft cheese (for dessert).

pétrole m oil.

pétrolier m (navire) (oil) tanker.

peu adv (manger etc) not much, little; **un p.** a little, a bit; **p. de sel/ de temps/etc** not much salt/time/ etc; **un p. de fromage/etc** a little cheese/etc; **p. de gens/etc** few people/etc; **un (tout) petit p.** a (tiny) little bit; **p. intéressant/etc** not very interesting/etc; **p. de chose** not much; **p. à p.** little by little; **à p. près** more or less; **p. après** shortly after.

peuple m people.

peuplé, -ée adj très/peu/etc **p.** highly/sparsely/etc populated; **p. de** populated by.

peur f fear; **avoir p.** to be afraid ou frightened (**de qch/qn** of sth/sb; **de faire** to do, of doing); **faire p. à** to frighten; **de p. que** (+ subjonctif) for fear that.

peureux, -euse adj easily frightened.

peut, peuvent, peux voir **pouvoir**.

peut-être adv perhaps, maybe; **p. qu'il viendra** perhaps ou maybe he'll come.

phare m (pour bateaux) lighthouse; (de véhicule) headlight; **faire un appel de phares** to flash one's lights.

pharmacie f drugstore, pharmacy; (armoire) medicine cabinet.

pharmacien, -ienne mf pharmacist.

philatélie f stamp collecting.

philatéliste mf stamp collector.

philosophe 1 mf philosopher. **2** adj (résigné) philosophical.

philosophie f philosophy.

phonétique adj phonetic.

phoque m (animal) seal.

photo f photo; (art) photography; **prendre une p. de** to take a photo of; **se faire prendre en p.** to have one's photo taken.

photocopie f photocopy.

photocopier vt to photocopy.

photocopieuse f (machine) photocopier.

photographe mf photographer.

photographier vt to photograph.

photographique adj photographic.

photomaton® m photo booth.

phrase f sentence.

physique 1 adj physical. **2** m (corps, aspect) physique; (science) physics.

physiquement adv physically.

pianiste mf pianist.

piano m piano.

pic m (cime) peak.

pic (à) adv **couler à p.** to sink to the bottom.

pichet m jug.

pickpocket m pickpocket.

picorer vti to peck.

picoter vt (yeux) to make sting; **les yeux me picotent** my eyes are stinging.

pièce f (de maison etc) room; (de pantalon) patch; **p. (de monnaie)** coin; **p. (de théâtre)** play; **p. d'identité** identity card; **pièces détachées** (de véhicule etc) spare parts; **cinq dollars p.** five dollars each.

pied m foot (pl feet); (de meuble) leg; (de verre, lampe) base; **à p.** on foot; **au p. de** at the foot of; **coup de p.** kick; **donner un coup de p.** to kick (**à qn** sb).

piège m trap.

piéger vt (animal) to trap; (voiture) to booby-trap.

piercing m (body) piercing.

pierre f stone; (précieuse) gem; **p. (à briquet)** flint.

piétiner 1 vt to trample (on). **2** vi to stamp (one's) feet.

piéton m pedestrian.

piétonne *adj* **rue p.** pedestrian street.

pieu, -x *m* post, stake.

pieuvre *f* octopus.

pigeon *m* pigeon.

pile 1 *f* (*électrique*) battery; (*tas*) pile; **radio à piles** battery radio; **en p.** in a pile; **p. (ou face)?** heads (or tails)? **2** *adv* **s'arrêter p.** to stop short; **à deux heures p.** at two o'clock sharp *ou* on the dot.

pilier *m* pillar.

pillage *m* looting.

piller *vti* to loot.

pilotage *m* **poste de p.** cockpit.

pilote *m* (*d'avion*) pilot; (*de voiture*) driver.

piloter *vt* (*avion*) to fly; (*voiture*) to drive.

pilule *f* pill; **prendre la p.** to be on the Pill.

piment *m* (chili) pepper.

pimenté, -ée *adj* spicy.

pin *m* (*arbre*) pine; **pomme de p.** pine cone.

pince *f* (*outil*) pliers; (*de cycliste*) clip; (*de crabe*) pincer; **p. (à linge)** (clothes) pin; **p. (à épiler)** tweezers; **p. (à sucre)** (sugar) tongs; **p. à cheveux** bobby pin.

pinceau, -x *m* (paint)brush.

pincée *f* (*de sel etc*) pinch (**de** of).

pincer *vt* to pinch.

pincer (se) *vpr* **se p. le doigt** to get one's finger caught (**dans** in).

pingouin *m* penguin.

ping-pong *m* table tennis.

pin's *m inv* button, lapel pin.

pintade *f* guinea fowl.

pioche *f* pick(ax).

piocher *vti* to dig (with a pick).

pion *m* (*au jeu de dames*) piece; *Échecs* pawn.

pipe *f* pipe; **fumer la p.** to smoke a pipe.

pipi *m* **faire p.** *Fam* to take a pee.

piquant, -ante *adj* (*plante, barbe*) prickly.

pique *m* (*couleur*) *Cartes* spades.

pique-nique, *pl* pique-niques *m* picnic.

pique-niquer *vi* to picnic.

piquer 1 *vt* (*percer*) to prick; (*langue, yeux*) to sting; (*coudre*) to (machine-)stitch; **p. qn** (*abeille*) to sting sb; **p. qch dans** (*enfoncer*) to stick sth into; **p. une colère** to fly into a rage. **2** *vi* (*avion*) to dive; (*moutarde etc*) to be hot.

piquet *m* (*pieu*) stake; (*de tente*) peg.

piqûre *f* (*d'abeille*) sting; (*avec un seringue*) injection, shot.

pirate *m* pirate; **p. de l'air** hijacker; **p. informatique** hacker.

pire 1 *adj* worse (**que** than); **le p. moment**/*etc* the worst moment/*etc.* **2** *mf* **le** *ou* **la p.** the worst.

piscine *f* swimming pool.

pissenlit *m* dandelion.

pistache *f* pistachio.

piste *f* (*traces*) trail; (*de course*) racetrack; (*de cirque*) ring; (*de patinage*) rink; **p. (d'envoi)** runway; **p. cyclable** bicycle path; **p. de danse** dance floor; **p. de ski** ski run *ou* slope.

pistolet *m* gun; **p. à eau** water pistol.

pitié *f* pity; **j'ai p. de lui** I feel sorry for him.

pitoyable *adj* pitiful.

pittoresque *adj* picturesque.

pivoter *vi* (*personne*) to swing round; (*fauteuil*) to swivel.

pizza *f* pizza.

pizzeria *f* pizzeria.

placard *m* (*dans la cuisine*) cupboard, cabinet; (*pour linge, vêtements etc*) closet.

place *f* (*endroit, rang*) place; (*espace*) room; (*lieu public*) square; (*siège*) seat, place; (*emploi*) job; **p. de parking** parking place *ou* space; **à la p. (de)** instead (of); **à votre p.** in your place; **sur p.** on the spot; **en p.** in place; **mettre en p.** (*installer*) to set up; **changer de p.** to change pla-

ces; **changer qch de p.** to move sth.
placement m (d'argent) investment.
placer vt to place; (invité, spectateur) to seat; (argent) to invest
(**dans** in).
placer (se) vpr (debout) to (go
and) stand; (s'asseoir) to (go and)
sit; **se p. troisième/etc (en sport)** to
come third/etc.
plafond m ceiling.
plage f beach; **p. arrière** (de voiture) (back) window shelf.
plaider vti (défendre) to plead; **p.
coupable** to plead guilty.
plaie f wound; (coupure) cut.
plaindre* vt to feel sorry for.
plaindre (se) vpr to complain (**de**
about; **que** that); **se p. de** (douleur)
to complain of.
plaine f plain.
plainte f complaint; (cri) moan.
plaire* vi **p. à qn** to please sb; **elle
lui plaît** he likes her; **ça me plaît** I
like it; **s'il vous** ou **te plaît** please.
plaire (se) vpr (dans un endroit) to
like ou enjoy it.
plaisanter vi to joke (**sur** about).
plaisanterie f joke; **par p.** as a
joke.
plaisir m pleasure; **faire p. à** to
please; **pour le p.** for fun.
plan m (projet, dessin) plan; (de
ville) map; **au premier p.** in the
foreground.
planche f board; **p. à repasser** ironing board; **p. (à roulettes)** skate-
board; **p. (à voile)** sailboard; **faire
de la p.** (à voile) to go windsurfing.
plancher m floor.
planer vi (oiseau, avion) to glide.
planète f planet.
planeur m (avion) glider.
planifier vt to plan.
plante¹ f plant; **p. verte** house
plant.
plante² f **p. du pied** sole (of the foot).
planter vt (fleur etc) to plant; (clou,
couteau) to drive in.

planter (se) vpr **se p. devant** to
come ou go and stand in front of, to
plant oneself in front of.
plaque f plate; (de verre, métal,
verglas) sheet; (de chocolat) bar; **p.
chauffante** hotplate; **p. d'immatriculation** license plate.
plaqué, -ée adj **p. or** gold-plated.
plaquer vt Sport to tackle; (aplatir)
to flatten (**contre** against).
plastique adj & m (matière) f
plastic; **en p.** (bouteille etc) plastic.
plat, plate 1 adj flat; **à p. ventre**
flat on one's face; **à p.** (pneu, batterie) flat; **poser à p.** to put down
flat; **assiette plate** dinner plate;
eau plate still water. **2** m (récipient,
nourriture) dish; (partie du repas)
course; **'p. du jour'** 'today's special'.
platane m plane tree.
plateau, -x m (pour servir) tray; **p.
à fromages** cheeseboard.
plate-forme, pl **plates-formes** f
platform; **p. pétrolière** oil rig.
plâtre m (matière) plaster; **un p.** a
(plaster) cast; **dans le p.** in plaster.
plâtrer vt (bras, jambe) to put a
cast on.
plein, pleine 1 adj full (**de** of); **en
pleine mer** out at sea; **en pleine figure** right in the face. **2** prép & adv
des bonbons p. les poches pockets
full of candy; **du chocolat p. la figure** chocolate all over one's face;
p. de lettres/d'argent/etc Fam lots
of letters/money/etc. **3** m **faire le p.
(d'essence)** to fill up (the tank).
pleurer vi to cry.
pleuvoir* vi to rain; **il pleut** it's
raining.
pli m (de papier) fold; (de jupe)
pleat; (de pantalon) crease; **(faux)
p.** crease; **mise en plis** (coiffure)
set.
pliable adj foldable.
pliant, -ante adj (chaise etc) folding.
plier 1 vt to fold; (courber) to bend.
2 vi (branche) to bend.

plier (se) *vpr (lit, chaise etc)* to fold (up).

plissé, -ée *adj (tissu, jupe)* pleated.

plisser *vt (front)* to wrinkle; to crease, to fold; **p. les yeux** to squint.

plomb *m (métal)* lead; *(fusible)* fuze; **plombs** *(de chasse)* lead shot.

plombage *m (de dent)* filling.

plomber *vt (dent)* to fill.

plomberie *f* plumbing.

plombier *m* plumber.

plongée *f (sport)* diving.

plongeoir *m* diving board.

plongeon *m* dive.

plonger 1 *vi (personne)* to dive. **2** *vt (mettre)* to plunge (**dans** into).

plongeur, -euse *mf* diver.

plu *voir* **plaire, pleuvoir**.

pluie *f* rain; **sous la p.** in the rain.

plume *f (d'oiseau)* feather; *(de stylo)* (pen) nib; **stylo à p.** (fountain) pen.

plumer *vt (volaille)* to pluck.

plupart (la) *f* most; **la p. des cas** most cases; **la p. du temps** most of the time; **la p. d'entre eux** most of them; **pour la p.** mostly.

pluriel, -ielle *adj & m* plural; **au p.** in the plural.

plus¹ *adv comparatif (travailler etc)* more (**que** than); **p. d'une livre/de dix** more than a pound/ten; **p. de thé** more tea; **p. beau** more beautiful (**que** than); **p. tard** later; **p. petit** smaller; **de p. en p.** more and more; **p. ou moins** more or less; **en p.** in addition (**de** to); **de p.** more (**que** than); *(en outre)* moreover; *(âgé)* **de p. de dix ans** over ten; **j'ai dix ans de p. qu'elle** I'm ten years older than she is; **il est p. de cinq heures** it's after five. **2** *adv superlatif* **le p.** *(travailler etc)* (the) most; **le p. beau** the most beautiful (**de** in); **le p. grand** the biggest (**de** in); **j'ai le p. de livres** I have (the) most books.

plus² *adv de négation* **p. de** *(pain, argent)* no more; **il n'a p. de pain**

he has no more bread, he doesn't have any more bread; **tu n'es p. jeune** you're not young any more; **je ne la reverrai p.** I won't see her again.

plus³ *prép* plus; **deux p. deux** two plus two; **il fait p. deux (degrés)** it's two degrees above freezing.

plusieurs *adj & pron* several.

plutôt *adv* rather (**que** than).

pluvieux, -euse *adj* rainy.

pneu *m (pl -s)* tire.

pneumatique *adj* **matelas p.** air mattress; **canot p.** rubber dinghy.

poche *f* pocket; *(de kangourou)* pouch.

pocher *vt (œufs)* to poach; **p. l'œil à qn** to give sb a black eye.

pochette *f (sac)* bag; *(d'allumettes)* book; *(de disque)* sleeve; *(sac à main)* (clutch) bag.

podcast *m* podcast.

poêle 1 *m* stove. **2** *f* **p. (à frire)** frying pan.

poème *m* poem.

poésie *f (art)* poetry; *(poème)* poem.

poète *m* poet.

poétique *adj* poetic.

poids *m* weight; **au p.** by weight.

poids lourd *m* (heavy) truck.

poignard *m* dagger.

poignarder *vt* to stab.

poignée *f (quantité)* handful (**de** of); *(de porte etc)* handle; **p. de main** handshake; **donner une p. de main à** to shake hands with.

poignet *m* wrist; *(de chemise)* cuff.

poil *m* hair; *(pelage)* fur.

poilu, -ue *adj* hairy.

poinçonner *vt (billet)* to punch.

poing *m* fist; **coup de p.** punch.

point *m (lieu, score etc)* point; *(sur i, à l'horizon)* dot; *(tache)* spot; *(de couture)* stitch; **sur le p. de faire** about to do; **p. (final)** period; **p. d'exclamation** exclamation point; **p. d'interrogation** question mark; **points de suspension** ellipsis; **p.**

de vue (*opinion*) point of view; **à p.** (*steak*) medium rare; **au p. mort** (*véhicule*) in neutral; **p. de côté** (*douleur*) stitch (in one's side).

pointe *f* (*extrémité*) tip; (*clou*) nail; **sur la p. des pieds** on tiptoe; **en p.** pointed.

pointer 1 *vt* (*cocher*) to check (off); (*braquer*) to point (**sur** at). **2** *vi* **p. vers** to point (upwards) towards.

pointillé *m* dotted line.

pointu, -ue *adj* (*en pointe*) pointed.

pointure *f* (*de chaussure, gant*) size.

point-virgule, *pl* **points-virgules** *m* semicolon.

poire *f* pear.

poireau, -x *m* leek.

poirier *m* pear tree.

pois *m* pea; **petits p.** peas; **p. chiche** garbanzo, chickpea.

poison *m* poison.

poisseux, -euse *adj* sticky.

poisson *m* fish; **p. rouge** goldfish.

poissonnerie *f* fish market.

poissonnier, -ière *mf* fish merchant.

poitrine *f* chest; (*de femme*) bust.

poivre *m* pepper.

poivré, -ée *adj* (*piquant*) peppery.

poivrer *vt* to pepper.

poivrière *f* peppershaker.

poivron *m* (*légume*) pepper.

pôle *m* **p. Nord/Sud** North/South Pole.

polémique 1 *adj* polemical. **2** *f* heated debate.

poli, -ie *adj* (*courtois*) polite (**avec** to, with); (*lisse*) polished.

police[1] *f* police; **p. secours** police emergency services.

police[2] *f* **p.** (d'assurance) (insurance) policy.

policier, -ière 1 *adj* **enquête/etc policière** police investigation/*etc*, **roman p.** mystery novel. **2** *m* policeman, detective.

poliment *adv* politely.

polio 1 *f* (*maladie*) polio. **2** *mf* (*personne*) polio victim.

polir *vt* to polish.

politesse *f* politeness.

politique 1 *adj* political; **homme p.** politician. **2** *f* (*activité*) politics; **une p.** a policy.

pollen *m* pollen.

polluer *vt* to pollute.

pollution *f* pollution.

polo *m* (*chemise*) polo shirt.

polochon *m* bolster.

polonais, -aise 1 *adj* Polish. **2** *mf* **P.** Pole. **3** *m* (*langue*) Polish.

polycopié *m* duplicated course notes.

polyester *m* polyester; **chemise/ etc en p.** polyester shirt/*etc*.

polyvalent, -ente *adj* (*salle*) multi-purpose; (*personne*) versatile.

pommade *f* ointment.

pomme *f* apple; **p. de terre** potato; **pommes frites** French fries; **pommes chips** potato chips.

pommier *m* apple tree.

pompe *f* pump; **p. à essence** gas station; **pompes funèbres** undertaker's; **entrepreneur de pompes funèbres** undertaker.

pomper *vt* (*eau*) to pump out (**de** of).

pompier *m* fireman; **voiture des pompiers** fire engine.

pompiste *mf* gas station attendant.

pompon *m* pompon.

poncer *vt* to rub down, to sand.

ponctuation *f* punctuation.

ponctuel, -elle *adj* (*à l'heure*) punctual.

pondre 1 *vt* (*œuf*) to lay. **2** *vi* (*poule*) to lay (eggs *ou* an egg).

poney *m* pony.

pont *m* bridge; (*de bateau*) deck.

pop *m & adj inv* (*musique*) pop.

populaire *adj* (*qui plaît*) popular; (*quartier*) working-class; (*expression*) colloquial.

population *f* population.

porc *m* pig; *(viande)* pork.
porcelaine *f* china.
porche *m* porch.
porcherie *f* (pig)sty.
port *m* port, harbor.
portable 1 *adj (portatif)* portable.
2 *m (ordinateur)* laptop; *(téléphone)*
cellphone.
portail *m (de jardin)* gate(way).
portant, -ante *adj* **bien p.** in
good health.
portatif, -ive *adj* portable.
porte *f* door; *(de jardin)* gate; *(de
ville)* entrance; **p. (d'embarquement)** *(d'aéroport)* (departure)
gate; **p. d'entrée** front door; **p. coulissante** sliding door; **mettre à la p.**
to throw out.
porte-avions *m inv* aircraft carrier.
porte-bagages *m inv* luggage
rack.
porte-bonheur *m inv* (lucky)
charm.
porte-clefs *m inv* key ring.
porte-documents *m inv* briefcase.
portée *f (de fusil etc)* range; *(animaux)* litter; **à p. de la main** within
(easy) reach; **à p. de voix** within
earshot; **hors de p.** out of reach.
porte-fenêtre, *pl* **portes-fenê-
tres** *f* French door *ou* window.
portefeuille *m* wallet.
portemanteau, -x *m* coatrack;
(crochet) coat hook.
porte-monnaie *m inv* purse.
porte-parole *m inv* spokesman;
(femme) spokeswoman.
porter 1 *vt* to carry; *(vêtement, lunettes, barbe etc)* to wear; **p. qch à**
(apporter) to take sth to; **p. bon-
heur/malheur** to bring good/bad
luck. **2** *vi (voix)* to carry.
porter (se) *vpr (vêtement)* to be
worn; **se p. bien/mal** to be well/ill;
comment te portes-tu? how are
you?
porte-revues *m inv* newspaper
rack.

porte-savon *m inv* soapdish.
porte-serviettes *m inv* towel
rack.
porteur *m (à la gare)* porter.
porte-voix *m inv* loudspeaker,
megaphone.
portier *m* doorman.
portière *f (de véhicule, train)* door.
portion *f (partie)* portion; *(de
nourriture)* helping.
portique *m (de balançoire etc)*
crossbar.
portrait *m* portrait.
portrait-robot, *pl* **portraits-
robots** *m* composite picture.
portugais, -aise 1 *adj* Portuguese. **2** *mf* **P.** Portuguese man, Portuguese woman, Portuguese *inv*;
les P. the Portuguese. **3** *m (langue)*
Portuguese.
pose *f (installation)* putting up;
putting in; laying; *(attitude de modèle)* pose.
posé, -ée *adj (calme)* composed.
poser 1 *vt* to put (down); *(papier
peint, rideaux)* to put up; *(sonnette,
chauffage)* to put in; *(moquette)* to
lay; *(question)* to ask (**à qn** sb). **2** *vi
(modèle)* to pose (**pour** for).
poser (se) *vpr (oiseau, avion)* to
land.
positif, -ive *adj* positive.
position *f* position.
posséder *vt* to possess; *(maison
etc)* to own.
possessif, -ive *adj & m* Gram-
maire possessive.
possibilité *f* possibility.
possible 1 *adj* possible (**à faire** to
do); **il (nous) est p. de le faire** it is
possible (for us) to do it; **il est p.
que** (+ *subjonctif*) it is possible
that; **si p.** if possible; **le plus tôt p.**
as soon as possible; **autant que p.**
as far as possible; **le plus p.** as much
ou as many as possible. **2** *m* **faire
son p.** to do one's best (**pour faire**
to do).
postal, -e, -aux *adj* postal; **boîte**

postale PO Box; **code p.** zip code.

poste 1 f *(service)* post; *(bureau de)* **p.** post office; **la P.** the Post Office; **par la p.** by post; **p. aérienne** airmail. **2** m *(lieu, emploi)* post; *(radio, télévision)* set; **p. de secours** first aid station; **p. de police** police station.

poster vt *(lettre)* to mail.

postier, -ière mf postal worker.

postuler vi **p. à un emploi** to apply for a job.

pot m pot; *(à confiture)* jar; *(à lait)* jug; *(à bière)* mug; *(de crème, yaourt)* carton; *(de bébé)* potty; **p. de fleurs** flower pot.

potable adj drinkable; **'eau p.'** 'drinking water'.

potage m soup.

potager adj & m **(jardin) p.** vegetable garden.

pot-au-feu m inv beef stew.

pot-de-vin, pl **pots-de-vin** m bribe.

poteau, -x m post; **p. indicateur** signpost; **p. d'arrivée** winning post; **p. télégraphique** telegraph pole.

poterie f *(art)* pottery; **une p.** a piece of pottery; **des poteries** *(objets)* pottery.

potier m potter.

potiron m pumpkin.

pou, -x m louse; **poux** lice.

poubelle f garbage can.

pouce m thumb; *(mesure)* inch.

poudre f powder; *(explosif)* gunpowder; **en p.** *(lait)* powdered; **chocolat en p.** cocoa powder.

poudrer (se) vpr *(femme)* to powder one's face.

poudrier m *(powder)* compact.

pouf m *(siège)* (cushioned) ottoman ou footstool.

poulailler m henhouse.

poulain m *(cheval)* foal.

poule f hen.

poulet m chicken.

poulie f pulley.

pouls m pulse.

poumon m lung; **à pleins poumons** *(respirer)* deeply; *(crier)* loudly.

poupée f doll.

pour 1 prép for; **p. toi/***etc* for you/*etc*; **partir p.** *(Paris, cinq ans)* to leave for; **elle est p.** she's in favor; **p. faire** (in order) to do; **p. que tu saches** so (that) you know; **p. quoi faire?** what for?; **trop petit/***etc* **p. faire** too small/*etc* to do; **assez grand/***etc* **p. faire** big/*etc* enough to do. **2** m **le p. et le contre** the pros and cons.

pourboire m *(argent)* tip.

pourcentage m percentage.

pourchasser vt to pursue.

pourparlers mpl negotiations, talks.

pourquoi adv & conj why; **p. pas?** why not?

pourra, pourrai(t) etc voir **pouvoir.**

pourri, -ie adj *(fruit, temps etc)* rotten.

pourriel m spam e-mail; **des pourriels** spam.

pourrir vi to rot.

poursuite f chase; **se mettre à la p. de** to go after, to chase (after).

poursuivant, -ante mf pursuer.

poursuivre* vt to chase, to go after; *(lecture, voyage etc)* to continue (with).

poursuivre (se) vpr to continue, to go on.

pourtant adv yet.

pourvu que conj *(condition)* provided ou providing (that); *(souhait)* **p. qu'elle soit là!** I only hope (that) she's there!

pousser 1 vt to push; *(cri)* to utter; *(soupir)* to heave; **p. qn à faire** to urge sb to do. **2** vi *(croître)* to grow; **faire p.** *(plante etc)* to grow.

poussette f stroller.

poussière f dust.

poussiéreux, -euse adj dusty.

poussin m *(poulet)* chick.

poutre f *(en bois)* beam; *(en acier)* girder.

pouvoir* 1 v aux *(capacité)* can, be able to; *(permission, éventualité)* may, can; **je peux deviner** I can guess; **tu peux entrer** you may ou can come in; **il peut être sorti** he may ou might be out; **elle pourrait/pouvait venir** she might/could come; **j'ai pu l'obtenir** I managed to get it; **j'aurais pu l'obtenir** I could have gotten it; **je n'en peux plus** I'm utterly exhausted. 2 m *(capacité, autorité)* power; **les pouvoirs publics** the authorities; **au p.** in power.

pouvoir (se) vpr **il se peut qu'elle parte** (it's possible that) she might leave.

prairie f meadow.

pratique 1 adj practical. 2 f *(exercice, procédé)* practice; **la p. de la natation/du golf** swimming/golfing.

pratiquement adv *(presque)* practically.

pratiquer vt *(sport, art etc)* to practice.

pré m meadow.

préalable 1 adj prior, previous; **p. à** prior to. 2 m precondition, prerequisite; **au p.** beforehand.

préau, -x m *(d'école)* covered playground.

préavis m (advance) notice (**de** of); **p. de grève** strike notice; **p. de licenciement** notice of dismissal.

précarité f precariousness; **p. de l'emploi** lack of job security.

précaution f precaution (**de faire** of doing); *(prudence)* caution.

précédent, -ente 1 adj previous. 2 m f previous one.

précéder vti to precede.

précieux, -euse adj precious.

précipice m chasm, precipice.

précipitamment adv hastily.

précipitation f haste.

précipiter vt *(hâter)* to rush.

précipiter (se) vpr to throw oneself; *(foncer)* to rush (**à, sur** on to); *(s'accélérer)* to speed up.

précis, -ise adj precise; **à deux heures précises** at two o'clock sharp.

préciser vt to specify (**que** that).

préciser (se) vpr to become clear(er).

précision f precision; *(explication)* explanation.

précoce adj *(fruit etc)* early; *(enfant)* precocious.

prédécesseur m predecessor.

prédiction f prediction.

prédire* vt to predict (**que** that).

préfabriqué, -ée adj prefabricated.

préface f preface.

préfecture f prefecture; **la P. de police** police headquarters.

préféré, -ée adj & m f favorite.

préférence f preference (**pour** for); **de p.** preferably.

préférer vt to prefer (**à** to); **p. faire** to prefer to do.

préfet m prefect *(chief administrator in a department)*.

préfixe m prefix.

préhistorique adj prehistoric.

préjudice m *(à une cause)* prejudice; *(à une personne)* harm; **porter p. à qn** to do sb harm.

préjugé m prejudice; **être plein de préjugés** to be full of prejudice.

prélèvement m *(d'échantillon)* taking; *(de somme)* deduction; **p. automatique** automatic deduction.

premier, -ière 1 adj first; *(étage)* second; **nombre p.** prime number; **le p. rang** the front row; **P. ministre** Prime Minister. 2 m f first (one); **arriver le p.** to arrive first; **être le p. de la classe** to be (at the) head of the class. 3 m *(date)* first; *(étage)* second floor; **le p. de l'an** New Year's Day. 4 f *(wagon, billet)* first class; *(au lycée)* = junior year; *(de véhicule)* first (gear).

premièrement adv firstly.

prendre* 1 vt to take (**à qn** from

sb); *(attraper)* to catch; *(voyager par)* to take *(train etc)*; *(douche, bain)* to take, to have; *(repas)* to have; *(photo)* to take; *(temps)* to take (up); **p. qn pour** *(un autre)* to mistake sb for; *(considérer)* to take sb for; **p. feu** to catch fire; **p. de la place** to take up room; **p. du poids** to put on weight. **2** *vi (feu)* to catch; *(ciment)* to set; *(vaccin)* to take.

prendre (se) *vpr (objet)* to be taken; *(s'accrocher)* to get caught; **se p. pour un génie** to think one is a genius; **s'y p.** to go about it; **s'en p. à** to attack; *(accuser)* to blame.

prénom *m* first name.

prénommer *vt* to name.

prénommer (se) *vpr* to be called; **il se prénomme Daniel** his first name is Daniel.

préoccupation *f* worry.

préoccupé, -ée *adj* worried.

préoccuper *vt (inquiéter)* to worry.

préoccuper (se) *vpr* **se p. de** to be worried about.

préparatifs preparations (**de** for).

préparation *f* preparation.

préparer *vt* to prepare (**qch pour** sth for; **qn à** sb for); *(examen)* to prepare for.

préparer (se) *vpr* to get (oneself) ready (**à, pour qch** for sth); **se p. à faire** to prepare to do.

préposition *f* Grammaire preposition.

préretraite *f* early retirement.

près *adv* **p. de** *(qn, qch)* near (to); **p. de deux ans/etc** nearly two years/ *etc*; **tout p.** nearby (**de qn/qch** sb/ sth); **de p.** *(lire, suivre)* closely.

presbyte *adj* long-sighted.

prescrire* *vt (médicament)* to prescribe.

présence *f* presence; *(à l'école etc)* attendance (**à** at); **feuille de p.** attendance sheet; **en p. de** in the presence of.

présent, -ente 1 *adj (non absent)*

present (**à** at; **dans** in); *(actuel)* present. **2** *m* Grammaire present (tense); **à p.** at present.

présentateur, -trice *mf* announcer.

présentation *f* presentation; *(d'une personne à une autre)* introduction.

présenter *vt* to present; **p. qn à qn** to introduce sb to sb.

présenter (se) *vpr* to introduce oneself (**à** to); **se p. à** *(examen)* to take; *(élections)* to run in.

préservatif *m* condom.

préserver *vt* to protect (**de, contre** from).

présidence *f (de nation)* presidency; *(de firme)* chairmanship.

président, -ente *mf (de nation)* president; *(de réunion, firme)* chairman, chairwoman; **p. directeur général** chief executive officer.

présidentiel, -ielle *adj* presidential.

presque *adv* almost.

presqu'île *f* peninsula.

presse *f (journaux, appareil)* press; **conférence/etc de p.** press conference/*etc*.

presse-citron *m inv* lemon juicer.

pressé, -ée *adj (personne)* in a hurry; *(travail)* urgent.

pressentir* *vt* to sense (**que** that).

presser 1 *vt (serrer)* to squeeze; *(bouton)* to press; *(fruit)* to squeeze, to juice. **2** *vi (temps)* to press; **rien ne presse** there's no hurry.

presser (se) *vpr (se serrer)* to squeeze (together); *(se hâter)* to hurry (**de faire** to do).

pressing *m (magasin)* dry cleaner's.

pression *f* pressure.

prestation *f (allocation)* benefit; **prestations** *(services)* services; **prestations sociales** welfare payments. ▪ *(de comédien)* performance.

prestidigitateur, -trice *mf* magician.

prestidigitation *f* tour de p. magic trick.

prêt *m (emprunt)* loan.

prêt, prête *adj (préparé)* ready (**à faire** to do; **à qch** for sth).

prêt-à-porter *m inv* ready-to-wear clothes.

prétendre *vt* to claim (**que** that; **être** to be).

prétendre (se) *vpr* elle se prétend riche she claims to be rich.

prétendu, -ue *adj* so-called.

prétentieux, -euse *adj & mf* conceited (person).

prêter *vt (argent, objet)* to lend (**à** to); **p. attention** to pay attention (**à** to).

prétexte *m* excuse; **sous p. de/que** on the pretext of/that.

prêtre *m* priest.

preuve *f* **preuve(s)** proof, evidence; **faire p. de** to show.

prévenir *vt (avertir)* to warn (**que** that); *(aviser)* to inform (**que** that).

prévention *f* prevention; **p. routière** road safety.

prévisible *adj* foreseeable.

prévision *f* forecast.

prévoir* *vt (anticiper)* to foresee (**que** that); *(prédire)* to forecast (**que** that); *(temps)* to forecast; *(organiser)* to plan; *(préparer)* to provide, to make provision for.

prévoyant, -ante *adj* farsighted.

prévu, -ue *adj* un repas est p. a meal is provided; **au moment p.** at the appointed time; **comme p.** as expected; **p. pour** *(véhicule, appareil)* designed for.

prier 1 *vti* to pray (**pour** for). **2** *vt* **p. qn de faire** to ask sb to do; **je vous en prie** *(faites donc)* please; *(en réponse à 'merci')* you're welcome.

prière *f* prayer; **p. de répondre/etc** please reply/etc.

primaire *adj* primary.

prime *f (d'employé)* bonus; **en p.** *(cadeau)* as a free gift; **p. (d'assurance)** (insurance) premium.

primevère *f* primrose.

primitif, -ive *adj (société etc)* primitive.

primordial, -e, -aux *adj* vital (**de faire** to do).

prince *m* prince.

princesse *f* princess.

principal, -e, -aux 1 *adj* main. **2** *m (de collège)* principal; **le p.** *(essentiel)* the main thing.

principe *m* principle; **en p.** theoretically; *(normalement)* as a rule.

printemps *m (saison)* spring.

prioritaire *adj* **être p.** to have priority; *(en voiture)* to have the right of way.

priorité *f* priority (**sur** over); **la p.** *(sur la route)* the right of way; **la p. à droite** right of way to traffic coming from the right; **'cédez la p.'** 'yield'.

pris, prise *(pp of* **prendre***) adj (place)* taken; *(crème, ciment)* set; *(nez)* congested; **être (très) p.** to be (very) busy; **p. de** *(peur, panique)* stricken with.

prise *f (de judo etc)* hold; *(objet saisi)* catch; **p. (de courant)** *(mâle)* plug; *(femelle)* outlet, socket; **p. multiple** *(électrique)* adaptor; **p. de sang** blood test.

prison *f* prison, jail; **en p.** in prison ou jail.

prisonnier, -ière *mf* prisoner; **faire qn p.** to take sb prisoner.

privé, -ée *adj* private.

priver *vt* to deprive (**de** of).

priver (se) *vpr* se p. de to do without.

prix¹ *m (d'un objet etc)* price; **à tout p.** at all costs; **à aucun p.** on no account.

prix² *m (récompense)* prize.

probable *adj* likely, probable (**que** that); **peu p.** unlikely.

probablement *adv* probably.

problème *m* problem.

procédé *m* process.

procéder *vi (agir)* to proceed; **p. à** *(enquête, arrestation)* to carry out; **p. par élimination** to follow a process of elimination.

procès *m (criminel)* trial; *(civil)* lawsuit; **faire un p.** à to take to court.

procès-verbal, -aux *m (contravention)* (traffic) ticket.

prochain, -aine *adj* next.

prochainement *adv* shortly.

proche *adj (espace)* near, close; *(temps)* close (at hand); *(parent, ami)* close; **p. de** near (to), close to.

procuration *f* power of attorney; **par p.** by proxy.

procurer *vt* **p. qch à qn** *(personne)* to obtain sth for sb.

procurer (se) *vpr* **se p. qch** to obtain sth.

prodigieux, -euse *adj* extraordinary.

producteur, -trice 1 *mf* producer. **2** *adj* **pays p. de pétrole** oil-producing country.

production *f* production.

produire* *vt (fabriquer, causer etc)* to produce.

produire (se) *vpr (événement etc)* to happen.

produit *m (article etc)* product; *(pour la vaisselle)* liquid; **produits** *(de la terre)* produce; **p. (chimique)** chemical; **p. de beauté** cosmetic.

prof *mf* Fam teacher; *(à l'université)* professor.

proférer *vt* to utter.

professeur *m* teacher; *(à l'université)* professor.

profession *f* occupation; *(de médecin etc)* profession; *(manuelle)* trade.

professionnel, -elle 1 *adj* professional; *(école)* vocational. **2** *mf* professional.

profil *m* **de p.** (viewed) from the side, in profile.

profit *m* profit; **tirer p. de** to benefit from *ou* by.

profitable *adj (utile)* beneficial (**à** to).

profiter *vi* **p. de** to take advantage of; **p. à qn** to profit sb.

profond, -onde 1 *adj* deep; **p. de deux mètres** seven feet deep. **2** *adv (pénétrer etc)* deep.

profondément *adv* deeply; *(dormir)* soundly.

profondeur *f* depth; **à six mètres de p.** at a depth of 20 feet.

progiciel *m* (software) package.

programmateur *m (de four etc)* timer.

programme *m* program; *(scolaire)* syllabus; *(d'ordinateur)* program.

programmer *vt (ordinateur)* to program.

progrès *m & mpl* progress; **faire des p.** to make progress.

progresser *vi* to progress.

progressif, -ive *adj* gradual.

progressivement *adv* gradually.

proie *f* prey.

projecteur *m (de monument)* floodlight; *(de film etc)* projector.

projectile *m* missile.

projection *f (de film)* projection; *(séance)* showing.

projet *m* plan.

projeter *vt (lancer)* to hurl; *(film)* to project; *(voyage, fête etc)* to plan; **p. de faire** to plan to do.

prolonger *vt* to extend.

prolonger (se) *vpr (séance, rue)* to continue.

promenade *f (à pied)* walk; *(en voiture)* drive; *(en vélo, à cheval)* ride; **faire une p.** to (go for a) walk; *(en voiture)* to (go for a) drive.

promener *vt* to take for a walk *ou* drive.

promener (se) *vpr* to (go for a) walk; *(en voiture)* to (go for a) drive.

promeneur, -euse *mf* stroller.

promesse *f* promise.

promettre* *vt* to promise (**qch à qn** sb sth; **que** that); **p. de faire** to promise to do; **c'est promis** it's a promise.

promotion *f* **en p.** *(produit)* on (special) offer.

pronom *m* pronoun.

prononcer *vt (articuler)* to pronounce; *(dire)* to utter; *(discours)* to deliver.

prononcer (se) *vpr (mot)* to be pronounced.

prononciation *f* pronunciation.

pronostic *m* forecast; *(d'un médecin)* prognosis.

propager *vt*, **se propager** *vpr* to spread.

propice *adj* favorable (**à** to); **le moment p.** the right moment.

proportion *f* proportion; *(rapport)* ratio.

propos **1** *mpl (paroles)* remarks. **2** *prép* **à p. de** about. **3** *adv* **à p.!** by the way!

proposer *vt* to suggest, to propose (**qch à qn** sth to sb; **que** (+ *subjonctif)* that); *(offrir)* to offer (**qch à qn** sb sth; **de faire** to do); **je te propose de rester** I suggest you stay.

proposer (se) *vpr* **se p. pour faire** to offer to do.

proposition *f* *Grammaire* clause.

propre¹ **1** *adj* clean; *(soigné)* neat. **2** *m* **mettre qch au p.** to make a clean copy of sth.

propre² *adj* own; **mon p. argent** my own money.

proprement *adv* cleanly; *(avec netteté)* neatly.

propreté *f* cleanliness; *(netteté)* neatness.

propriétaire *mf* owner; *(qui loue)* landlord, landlady.

propriété *f* *(bien, maison)* property.

prose *f* prose.

prospectus *m* leaflet.

prospère *adj* thriving.

protecteur, -trice **1** *mf* protector.

2 *adj (geste etc)* protective.

protection *f* protection; **de p.** *(écran etc)* protective.

protège-cahier, *pl* **protège-cahiers** *m* note book cover.

protéger *vt* to protect (**de** from; **contre** against).

protestant, -ante *adj & mf* Protestant.

protestataire *mf* protester.

protestation *f* protest (**contre** against).

protester *vi* to protest (**contre** against).

prothèse *f* prosthesis; **p. auditive** hearing aid; **p. dentaire** false teeth.

prouver *vt* to prove (**que** that).

provenance *f* origin; **en p. de** from.

provenir* *vi* **p. de** to come from.

proverbe *m* proverb.

province *f* province; **la p.** the provinces; **en p.** in the provinces; **de p.** *(ville etc)* provincial.

provincial, -e, -aux *adj & mf* provincial.

proviseur *m (de lycée)* principal.

provision *f* supply; **provisions** *(achats)* shopping; *(nourriture)* food; **sac à provisions** shopping bag; **chèque sans p.** bad check.

provisoire *adj* temporary.

provisoirement *adv* temporarily.

provoquer *vt (causer)* to bring *(sth)* about; *(défier)* to provoke *(sb)*.

proximité *f* closeness; **à p.** close by; **à p. de** close to.

prudemment *adv* cautiously, carefully.

prudence *f* caution, care.

prudent, -ente *adj* cautious, careful.

prune *f (fruit)* plum.

pruneau, -x *m* prune.

prunier *m* plum tree.

psychiatre *mf* psychiatrist.

psychologique *adj* psychological.

psychologue *mf* psychologist.

PTT *fpl abrév (Postes, Télégraphes, Téléphones)* Post Office.

pu *voir* **pouvoir**.

puanteur *f* stink.

public, -ique 1 *adj* public. **2** *m* public; (*de spectacle*) audience; **en p.** in public.

publication *f* publication.

publicité *f* advertising, publicity; (*annonce*) advertisement; (*filmée*) commercial.

publier *vt* to publish.

puce *f* flea; (*d'ordinateur*) chip; **marché aux puces** flea market.

pudeur *f* modesty; **par p.** out of a sense of decency.

pudique *adj* modest.

puer 1 *vi* to stink. **2** *vt* to stink of.

puéricultrice *f* pediatric nurse.

puis *adv* then.

puiser *vt* to draw (**dans** from).

puisque *conj* since, as.

puissance *f* (*force, nation*) power.

puissant, -ante *adj* powerful.

puisse(s), puissent *etc voir* **pouvoir**.

puits *m* well; (*de mine*) shaft.

pull(-over) *m* sweater.

pulluler *vi* (*abonder*) to swarm.

pulvérisateur *m* spray.

pulvériser *vt* (*liquide*) to spray.

punaise *f* (*insecte*) bug; (*clou*) thumbtack.

punir *vt* to punish (**de qch** for sth; **pour avoir fait** for doing).

punition *f* punishment.

pupille *f* (*d'œil*) pupil.

pupitre *m* (*d'écolier*) desk; (*d'orateur*) lectern.

pur, -e *adj* pure.

purée *f* purée; **p. (de pommes de terre)** mashed potatoes.

pureté *f* purity.

pus *m* (*liquide*) pus.

puzzle *m* (*jigsaw*) puzzle.

p.-v. *m inv abrév* (*procès-verbal*) (traffic) ticket.

pyjama *m* pajamas; **un p.** a pair of pajamas.

pylône *m* pylon.

pyramide *f* pyramid.

Q

QI *m inv abrév* (*quotient intellectuel*) IQ.

quadrillé, -ée *adj* (*papier*) squared.

quai *m* (*de port*) (*pour passagers*) quay; (*pour marchandises*) wharf; (*de fleuve*) embankment; (*de gare*) platform.

qualifié, -ée *adj* (*équipe etc*) that has qualified; (*ouvrier*) skilled.

qualifier *vt* (*équipe*) to qualify (**pour qch** for sth; **pour faire** to do); (*décrire*) to describe (**de** as).

qualifier (se) *vpr* (*en sport*) to qualify (**pour** for).

qualité *f* quality.

quand *conj & adv* when; **q. je viendrai** when I come; **q. même** all the same.

quant à *prép* as for.

quantité *f* quantity; **une q.** (*beaucoup*) a lot (**de** of).

quarantaine *f* **une q. (de)** about forty.

quarante *adj & m* forty.

quarantième *adj & m/f* fortieth.

quart *m* quarter; **q. (de litre)** quarter liter (*= one cup*); **q. d'heure** quarter of an hour; **une heure et q.** an hour and a quarter; **il est une heure et q.** it's a quarter after one; **une heure moins le q.** quarter to one.

quartier¹ *m* (*de ville*) neighborhood, district; (*chinois etc*) quarter; **de q.** (*cinéma etc*) local.

quartier² *m* (*de pomme*) quarter; (*d'orange*) segment.

quartz *m* montre/*etc* à q. quartz watch/*etc*.

quasiment *adv* almost.

quasoze *adj & m* fourteen.

quatorze *adj & m* fourteen.

quatre *adj & m* four; **q. heures**

(goûter) afternoon snack.

quatre-quatre *m* SUV.

quatre-vingt(s) *adj & m* eighty; **q.-vingts** an eighty years; **q.-vingt-un** eighty-one; **page quatre-vingt** page eighty.

quatre-vingt-dix *adj & m* ninety.

quatrième *adj & mf* fourth.

que (**qu'** *before a vowel or mute h*) **1** *conj* that; **je pense qu'elle restera** I think (that) she'll stay; **qu'elle vienne ou non** whether she comes or not; **qu'il s'en aille!** let him leave! ■ **(ne)...q.** only; **tu n'as qu'un euro** you only have one euro. ■ *(comparaison)* than; *(avec aussi, même, tel, autant)* as; **plus âgé q.** older than; **aussi sage q.** as wise as; **le même q.** the same as. **2** *adv* **(ce) qu'il est bête!** how silly he is! **3** *pron rel (chose)* that, which; *(personne)* that; *(temps)* when; **le livre q. j'ai** the book (that *ou* which) I have; **l'ami q. j'ai** the friend (that) I have; **un jour q.** one day when. **4** *pron interrogatif* what; **q. fait-il?**, **qu'est-ce qu'il fait?** what is he doing?; **qu'est-ce qui est dans ta poche?** what's in your pocket?

quel, quelle 1 *adj interrogatif* what, which; *(qui)* who; **q. livre/acteur?** what *ou* which book/actor?; **je sais q. est ton but** I know what your aim is. **2** *pron interrogatif* which (one); **q. est le meilleur?** which (one) is the best? **3** *adj exclamatif* **q. idiot!** what a fool!

quelconque *adj* any (whatever); **une raison q.** any reason (whatever).

quelque 1 *adj* **quelques femmes/ livres/**etc some *ou* a few women/ books/*etc*; **les quelques amies qu'elle a** the few friends she has. **2** *pron* **q. chose** something; *(interrogation)* anything, something; **il a q. chose** *(un problème)* there's something the matter with him; **q. chose d'autre/de grand/**etc

something else/big/*etc*. **3** *adv* **q. part** somewhere; *(interrogation)* anywhere, somewhere.

quelquefois *adv* sometimes.

quelques-uns, -unes *pron pl* some.

quelqu'un *pron* someone; *(interrogation)* anyone, someone; **q. d'intelligent/**etc someone smart/ *etc*.

question *f* question; *(problème)* matter; **il est q. de** there's some talk about (**faire** doing); **il a été q. de vous** we/they/*etc* talked about you; **il n'en est pas q.** it's out of the question.

questionner *vt* to question (**sur** about).

quête *f (collecte)* collection; **faire la q.** to collect money.

quêter *vi* to collect money.

queue¹ *f (d'animal etc)* tail; *(de fleur)* stem; *(de fruit)* stalk; *(de poêle)* handle; *(de train)* rear; **q. de cheval** *(coiffure)* ponytail; **à la q. leu leu** in single file.

queue² *f (file)* line; **faire la q.** to line up.

qui *pron (personne)* who, that; *(interrogatif)* who; *(chose)* which, that; **l'homme q.** the man who *ou* that; **la maison q.** the house which *ou* that; **q. est là?** who's there?; **q. désirez-vous voir?**, **q. est-ce que vous désirez voir?** who do you want to see?; **la femme de q. je parle** the woman I'm talking about; **l'ami sur l'aide de q. je compte** the friend on whose help I rely; **à q. est ce livre?** whose book is this?

quiche *f* quiche.

quiconque *pron (sujet)* whoever; *(complément)* anyone.

quille *f (de jeu)* (bowling) pin; **jouer aux quilles** to bowl.

quincaillerie hardware store.

quincaillier, -ière *mf* hardware store owner.

quinzaine f une q. (de) about fifteen; q. (de jours) two weeks.

quinze adj & m fifteen; q. jours two weeks.

quinzième adj & mf fifteenth.

quittance f (reçu) receipt.

quitte adj even (envers with).

quitter 1 vt to leave; q. qn des yeux to take one's eyes off sb. 2 vi ne quittez pas! (au téléphone) hold on!

quitter (se) vpr (se séparer) to part, to say goodbye.

quoi pron what; (après prép) which; à q. penses-tu? what are you thinking about?; de q. manger something to eat; de q. couper/écrire something to cut/write with; il n'y a pas de q.! (en réponse à 'merci') don't mention it!

quoique conj (al)though; q. je le sache déjà (al)though I already know.

quotidien, -ienne 1 adj daily. 2 m daily (paper).

R

rabâcher 1 vt to repeat endlessly. 2 vi to say the same thing over and over again.

rabais m reduction, discount.

rabattre* vt to pull down; (refermer) to close (down).

rabattre (se) vpr (barrière) to come down; (après avoir doublé un véhicule) to cut in.

rabbin m rabbi.

rabot m (outil) plane.

raboter vt to plane.

raccommodage m mending; (de chaussette) darning.

raccommoder vt to mend; (chaussette) to darn.

raccompagner vt to see ou accompany back (home); r. à la porte to see to the door.

raccord m (dispositif) connection, connector; (de papier peint) seam.

raccourci m (chemin) short cut.

raccourcir 1 vt to shorten. 2 vi to get shorter.

raccrocher 1 vt (objet tombé) to hang back up; (téléphone) to put down. 2 vi (au téléphone) to hang up.

race f (groupe ethnique) race; (d'animal) breed.

rachat m (de voiture, d'appartement) repurchase; (de firme) buy-out.

racheter vt r. un manteau/une voiture/etc to buy another coat/car/etc; r. des chaussettes/du pain/etc to buy some more socks/bread/etc.

racial, -e, -aux adj racial.

racine f root; prendre r. (plante) to take root.

racisme m racism.

raciste adj & mf racist.

racler vt to scrape; (enlever) to scrape off.

racler (se) vpr se r. la gorge to clear one's throat.

racontars mpl gossip.

raconter vt (histoire) to tell; r. qch à qn (vacances etc) to tell sb about sth; r. à qn que to tell sb that.

radar m radar.

radeau, -x m raft.

radiateur m heater; (de chauffage central, voiture) radiator.

radieux, -euse adj (personne, visage) beaming; (soleil) brilliant; (temps) glorious.

radio[1] f radio; (poste) radio (set); à la r. on the radio.

radio[2] f (examen, photo) X-ray; passer une r. to have an X-ray.

radioactif, -ive adj radioactive.

radiodiffuser vt to broadcast (on the radio).

radiographier vt to X-ray.
radis m radish.
radoucir (se) vpr (temps) to become milder.
radoucissement m r. (du temps) milder weather.
rafale f (vent) gust.
raffiné, -ée adj refined.
raffoler vi r. de (aimer) to be crazy about.
rafistoler vt Fam to patch up.
rafraîchir vt to cool (down).
rafraîchir (se) vpr (boire) to refresh oneself; (temps) to get cooler.
rafraîchissant, -ante adj refreshing.
rafraîchissement m (de température) cooling; (boisson) cold drink; **rafraîchissements** (glaces etc) refreshments.
rage f (colère) rage; (maladie) rabies; **r. de dents** violent toothache.
ragoût m stew.
raid m raid.
raide adj (rigide) stiff; (côte) steep; (cheveux) straight; (corde) tight.
raidir vt, **se raidir** vpr to stiffen; (corde) to tighten.
raie f (trait) line; (de tissu, zèbre) stripe; (de cheveux) part.
rail m (barre) rail (for train).
rainure f groove.
raisin m (grain de) r. grape; **du r., des raisins** grapes; **r. sec** raisin.
raison f reason; **la r. de/pour laquelle...** the reason for/why...; **en r. de** on account of; **avoir r.** to be right (**de faire** to do).
raisonnable adj reasonable.
raisonnement m reasoning.
raisonner 1 vi (penser) to reason. **2** vt **r. qn** to reason with.
rajeunir vt to make (feel ou look) younger.
rajouter vt to add (**à** to).
ralenti m au r. (filmer) in slow motion; **tourner au r.** (moteur) to turn over.
ralentir vti to slow down.

ralentissement m slowing down; (embouteillage) hold-up.
rallonge f (de table) extension; (électrique) extension cord.
rallonger vti to lengthen.
rallumer vt (feu, pipe) to light again; (lampe) to switch on again.
rallye m (automobile) rally.
ramassage m (de par terre) picking up; (d'ordures, de copies) collection; (de fruits, de coquillages) gathering; **r. scolaire** school bus service.
ramasser vt (prendre par terre, réunir) to pick up; (ordures, copies) to collect; (fruits, coquillages) to gather.
rame f (aviron) oar; (de métro) train.
ramener vt to bring ou take (sb) back.
ramer vi to row.
ramollir vt, **se ramollir** vpr to soften.
ramoner vt (cheminée) to sweep.
rampe f (d'escalier) banister(s); **r. (d'accès)** ramp; **r. de lancement** (de fusées) launching pad.
ramper vi to crawl.
ranch m ranch.
rançon f (argent) ransom.
rancune f grudge; **garder r. à qn** to bear sb a grudge.
rancunier, -ière adj spiteful.
randonnée f (à pied) hike; (en voiture) drive; (en vélo) ride.
rang m (rangée) row, line; (classement) rank; **se mettre en rang(s)** to line up (**par trois/etc** in threes/etc).
rangé, -ée adj (chambre etc) tidy.
rangée f row, line.
rangements mpl (placards) storage space.
ranger vt (papiers etc) to put away; (chambre etc) to tidy (up); (chiffres, mots) to arrange; (voiture) to park.
ranger (se) vpr (élèves etc) to line

up; *(s'écarter)* to stand aside; *(voiture)* to pull over.

ranimer *vt (réanimer)* to revive *(sb), (feu)* to poke, to stir.

rapace *m* bird of prey.

râpe *f (à fromage etc)* grater.

râper *vt (fromage, carottes)* to grate.

rapetisser *vi* to get smaller.

rapide 1 *adj* fast, quick. **2** *m (train)* express (train).

rapidement *adv* fast, quickly.

rapidité *f* speed.

rapiécer *vt* to patch (up).

rappeler *vt* to call back; *(souvenir)* to recall; **r. qch à qn** to remind sb of sth.

rappeler (se) *vpr* to remember (**que** that).

rapport *m (lien)* connection; *(récit)* report; **rapports** *(entre personnes)* relations; **par r. à** compared to; **ça n'a aucun r.!** it has nothing to do with it!

rapporter 1 *vt* to bring *ou* take back; *(profit)* to bring in. **2** *vi (dénoncer) Fam* to tell tales; *(investissement)* to bring in a good return.

rapporter (se) *vpr* **se r. à** to relate to.

rapporteur, -euse 1 *mf* telltale. **2** *m (en géométrie)* protractor.

rapprocher *vt* to bring closer (**de** to); *(chaise)* to pull up (**de** to).

rapprocher (se) *vpr* to come *ou* get closer (**de** to).

raquette *f (de tennis)* racket; *(de ping-pong)* paddle.

rare *adj* rare; **il est r. que** (+ *subjonctif*) it's rare that.

rarement *adv* rarely, seldom.

ras, rase *adj (cheveux)* close-cropped; *(herbe, poil)* short; **en rase campagne** in the open country; **à r. bord** *(remplir)* to the brim.

rasé, -ée *adj* **être bien r.** to have shaved; **mal r.** unshaven.

raser *vt (menton, personne)* to shave; *(barbe, moustache)* to shave off; *(démolir)* to knock down; *(frôler)* to skim.

raser (se) *vpr* to (have a) shave.

rasoir *m* razor; *(électrique)* shaver.

rassemblement *m* gathering.

rassembler *vt (gens, objets)* to gather (together).

rassembler (se) *vpr* to gather.

rassis, f rassie *adj (pain etc)* stale.

rassurant, -ante *adj* reassuring.

rassurer *vt* to reassure; **rassure-toi** don't worry.

rat *m* rat.

ratatiner (se) *vpr* to shrivel up.

râteau, -x *m (outil)* rake.

rater *vt (bus, cible etc)* to miss; *(travail, gâteau etc)* to ruin; *(examen)* to fail.

ration *f* ration.

rationnement *m* rationing.

rationner *vt* to ration.

ratisser *vt (allée etc)* to rake; *(feuilles etc)* to rake up.

rattacher *vt (lacets etc)* to tie up again.

rattrapage *m* **cours de r.** remedial class.

rattraper *vt* to catch; *(prisonnier)* to recapture; *(temps perdu)* to make up for; **r. qn** *(rejoindre)* to catch up with sb.

rature *f* crossing out.

raturer *vt* to cross out.

rauque *adj (voix)* hoarse.

ravager *vt* to devastate.

ravages *mpl* havoc; **faire des r.** to cause havoc *ou* widespread damage.

ravaler *vt (façade etc)* to clean (and restore).

ravi, -ie *adj* delighted (**de** with; **de faire** to do).

ravin *m* ravine.

ravioli(s) *mpl* ravioli.

ravir *vt (plaire)* to delight.

raviser (se) *vpr* to change one's mind.

ravissant, -ante *adj* beautiful.

ravisseur, -euse *mf* kidnapper.
ravitaillement *m* supplying; *(denrées)* supplies.
ravitailler *vt* to supply (**en** with).
ravitailler (se) *vpr* to stock up (with supplies).
rayé, -ée *adj* scratched; *(tissu)* striped.
rayer *vt (érafler)* to scratch; *(mot etc)* to cross out.
rayon *m (de lumière, soleil)* ray; *(de cercle)* radius; *(de roue)* spoke; *(planche)* shelf; *(de magasin)* department.
rayonnant, -ante *adj (visage etc)* beaming (**de** with).
rayure *f* scratch; *(bande)* stripe; **à rayures** striped.
raz-de-marée *m inv* tidal wave.
re-, ré- *préfixe* re-.
réacteur *m (d'avion)* jet engine; *(nucléaire)* reactor.
réaction *f* reaction; **avion à r.** jet (aircraft).
réagir *vi* to react (**contre** against; **à** to).
réalisateur, -trice *mf (de film)* director.
réaliser *vt (projet etc)* to carry out; *(rêve)* to fulfill; *(fabriquer)* to make; *(film)* to direct.
réaliser (se) *vpr (vœu)* to come true; *(projet)* to materialize.
réaliste *adj* realistic.
réalité *f* reality; **en r.** in fact.
réanimation *f* **en r.** in intensive care.
réanimer *vt* to revive, to resuscitate.
rebond *m* bounce.
rebondir *vi* to bounce.
rebord *m* **r. de (la) fenêtre** windowsill.
reboucher *vt (flacon)* to put the top back on; *(trou)* to fill in again.
rébus *m inv* rebus *(word guessing game)*.
récemment *adv* recently.
récent, -ente *adj* recent.

réception *f (réunion, de radio etc)* reception; *(d'hôtel)* reception (desk); **dès r. de** on receipt of.
recette *f (de cuisine)* recipe (**de** for); *(argent, bénéfice)* takings.
recevoir* 1 *vt* to receive; *(accueillir)* to welcome; **être reçu (à) (examen)** to pass. **2** *vi* to have guests.
rechange (de) *adj (outil etc)* spare; **vêtements de r.** a change of clothes.
recharge *f (de stylo)* refill.
recharger *vt (fusil, appareil photo)* to reload; *(briquet, stylo)* to refill; *(batterie)* to recharge.
réchaud *m (portable)* stove.
réchauffement *m (de température)* rise (**de** in).
réchauffer *vt* to warm up.
réchauffer (se) *vpr* **se r.** to warm oneself up; *(temps)* to get warmer.
recherche *f* **la r., des recherches** *(scientifique etc)* research (**sur** on, into); **faire des recherches** to (do) research; *(enquêter)* to investigate.
recherché, -ée *adj* **r. pour meurtre** wanted for murder.
rechercher *vt (personne, objet)* to search for.
rechute *f* relapse.
récif *m* reef.
récipient *m* container.
réciproque *adj* mutual.
récit *m (histoire)* story.
récitation *f (poème)* poem *(learned by heart and recited aloud)*.
réciter *vt* to recite.
réclamation *f* complaint.
réclame *f* advertising; *(annonce)* advertisement; **en r.** on (special) offer.
réclamer 1 *vt (demander)* to ask for *(sth)* back. **2** *vi* to complain.
recoin *m* nook.
recoller *vt (objet cassé)* to stick back together; *(enveloppe)* to reseal.

récolte f (action) harvest; (produits) crop.

récolter vt to harvest.

recommandation f recommendation.

recommander vt to recommend (à to; pour for); **r. à qn de faire** to recommend to sb to do; **lettre recommandée** certified letter; **en recommandé** (envoyer) by certified mail.

recommencer vti to start again.

récompense f reward (pour for).

récompenser vt to reward (de, pour for).

réconciliation f reconciliation.

réconcilier (se) vpr to settle one's differences, to make it up (avec that).

reconduire* vt **r. qn** to see sb back.

réconfort m comfort.

réconfortant, -ante adj comforting.

réconforter vt to comfort.

reconnaissance f (gratitude) gratitude.

reconnaissant, -ante adj grateful (à qn de qch to sb for sth).

reconnaître vt to recognize (à qch by sth); (admettre) to admit (que that); **reconnu coupable** found guilty.

reconstruire* vt (ville) to rebuild.

reconvertir (se) vpr (personne) to retrain.

recopier vt to copy out.

record m & adj inv (en sport etc) record.

recoudre* vt (bouton) to sew (back) on; (vêtement) to stitch (up).

recourbé, -ée adj (clou etc) bent; (nez) hooked.

recourir* vi **r. à** (moyen, violence) to resort to; (personne) to turn to.

recours m recourse; **avoir r. à** (chose) to resort to; (personne) to turn to; **en dernier r.** as a last resort.

recouvrir* vt (livre, meuble etc) to cover.

récréation f (à l'école) recess.

recroquevillé, -ée adj (personne, papier etc) curled up.

recrue f recruit.

rectangle m rectangle.

rectangulaire adj rectangular.

rectification f correction.

rectifier vt to correct.

recto m front (of the page).

reçu, reçue 1 pp of **recevoir**. **2** m (écrit) receipt.

recueil m anthology, collection (de of).

recueillir* vt to collect; (prendre chez soi) to take (sb) in.

recul m (d'armée, de négociateur, de maladie) retreat; (de canon) recoil; (déclin) decline; **avoir un mouvement de r.** to recoil; **manquer de r.** to be too closely involved; **prendre du r.** to stand back from things.

reculer 1 vi to move back; (véhicule) to reverse. **2** vt to push back.

reculons (à) adv backwards.

récupérer 1 vt (objet prêté) to get back. **2** vi to get one's strength back.

récurer vt (casserole etc) to scrub.

recyclage m (de matériaux) recycling; (de personne) retraining.

recycler vt (matériaux) to recycle.

rédacteur, -trice mf (de journal) editor; **r. en chef** editor(-in-chief).

rédaction f (devoir de français) essay, composition.

redescendre 1 vi (aux être) to come ou go back down. **2** vt (aux avoir) to bring ou take back down.

rediffusion f (de film etc) repeat, rerun.

rédiger vt to write.

redire* vt to repeat.

redonner vt (donner plus) to give more; **r. un euro/etc** to give another euro/etc.

redoublant, -ante mf student repeating a grade.

redoublement *m* repeating a grade.

redoubler *vti* r. (une classe) to repeat a grade.

redoutable *adj* formidable.

redouter *vt* to dread (de faire doing).

redresser *vt (objet tordu etc)* to straighten (out).

redresser (se) *upr* to sit up; *(debout)* to stand up.

réduction *f* reduction (de in); *(prix réduit)* discount; **en r.** *(copie, modèle)* small-scale.

réduire* *vt* to reduce (à to; de by); **r. en cendres** to reduce to ashes.

réduit, -uite *adj (prix, vitesse)* reduced; *(modèle)* small-scale.

rééducation *f (de personne)* rehabilitation; **faire de la r.** to have physical therapy.

réel, -elle *adj* real.

réellement *adv* really.

réexpédier *vt (faire suivre)* to forward *(letter)*.

refaire* *vt (exercice, travail)* to do again, to redo; *(chambre etc)* to redecorate.

réfectoire *m* refectory.

référence *f* reference.

refermer *vt*, **se refermer** *upr* to close (again).

réfléchir 1 *vt (image)* to reflect; **verbe réfléchi** reflexive verb. **2** *vi (penser)* to think (à about).

réfléchir (se) *upr* to be reflected.

reflet *m (image)* reflection; **reflets** *(couleurs)* highlights.

refléter *vt (image etc)* to reflect.

refléter (se) *upr* to be reflected.

réflexe *m* reflex.

réflexion *f (méditation)* thought; *(remarque)* remark.

réforme *f (changement)* reform.

refrain *m (de chanson)* chorus.

réfrigérateur *m* refrigerator.

refroidir *vti* to cool (down).

refroidir (se) *upr (prendre froid)* to catch cold; *(temps)* to get cold.

refroidissement *m (rhume)* chill; **r. de la température** fall in the temperature.

refuge *m* refuge; *(pour piétons)* median; *(de montagne)* (mountain) hut.

réfugié, -ée *mf* refugee.

réfugier (se) *upr* to take refuge.

refus *m* refusal.

refuser 1 *vt* to refuse (qch à qn sth; **de faire** to do); *(candidat)* to fail. **2** *vi* to refuse.

regagner *vt* to regain, to get back; *(revenir à)* to get back to.

régaler (se) *upr* to have a feast.

regard *m* look; *(fixe)* stare; **jeter un r. sur** to glance at.

regarder¹ 1 *vt* to look at; *(fixement)* to stare at; *(observer)* to watch; **r. qn faire** to watch sb do. **2** *vi* to look; to stare; to watch.

regarder² *vt (concerner)* to concern; **ça ne te regarde pas!** it's none of your business!

régime¹ *m (politique)* (form of) government; *(alimentaire)* diet; **se mettre au r.** to go on a diet; **suivre un r.** to be on a diet.

régime² *m (de bananes, dattes)* bunch.

régiment *m (soldats)* regiment.

région *f* region, area.

régional, -e, -aux *adj* regional.

registre *m* register.

réglable *adj (siège)* adjustable.

réglage *m* adjustment; *(de moteur)* tuning.

règle *f* rule; *(instrument)* ruler; **en r. générale** as a rule; **règles** *(de femme)* (monthly) period.

règlement *m (règles)* regulations; *(paiement)* payment; **contraire au r.** against the rules.

réglementation *f (règles)* regulations.

régler 1 *vt (problème etc)* to settle; *(mécanisme)* to adjust; *(moteur)* to tune. **2** *vti (payer)* to pay; **r. qn** to settle up with sb.

réglisse f licorice.

règne m (de roi) reign.

régner vi (roi, silence) to reign (**sur** over).

regret m regret; **à r.** with regret.

regrettable adj unfortunate, regrettable.

regretter vt to regret; **r. qn** to miss sb; **r. que** (+ subjonctif) to be sorry that; **je (le) regrette** I'm sorry.

regrouper vt, **se regrouper** vpr to gather together.

régularité f regularity; (de progrès, vitesse) steadiness.

régulier, -ière adj regular; (progrès, vitesse) steady.

regulièrement adv regularly.

réhabituer (se) vpr se **r. à qch/à faire qch** to get used to sth/to doing sth again.

rein m kidney; **les reins** (dos) the (small of the) back.

reine f queen.

réinsertion f reintegration; **r. sociale** rehabilitation.

rejeter vt to throw back; (refuser) to reject.

rejoindre* vt (famille, lieu etc) to get back to; **r. qn** (se joindre à) to join sb; (rattraper) to catch up with sb.

rejoindre (se) vpr (personnes, routes) to meet.

réjouir (se) vpr to be delighted (**de** at, about; **de faire** to do).

réjouissances fpl festivities.

relâcher vt (corde etc) to slacken; **r. qn** to release sb.

relais m **prendre le r.** to take over (**de** from).

relancer vt (lancer à nouveau) to throw again; (rendre) to throw back; (production) to boost; (moteur) to restart.

relatif, -ive adj relative.

relation f relation(ship); (ami) acquaintance; **entrer en relations avec** to come into contact with.

relativement adv (assez) relatively.

relayer vt to take over from (sb).

relayer (se) vpr to take (it in) turns (**pour faire** to do).

relevé m (de compteur) reading; **r. de compte** (bank) statement.

relever vt to raise; (personne tombée) to help up; (col) to turn up; (manches) to roll up; (compteur) to read.

relever (se) vpr (personne tombée) to get up.

relief m (forme) relief; **en r.** (cinéma) 3-D.

relier vt to connect (**à** to); (livre) to bind.

religieux, -euse 1 adj religious. **2** f nun.

religion f religion.

relire* vt to read again, to reread.

reliure f (de livre) binding.

reluire vi to shine.

remarquable adj remarkable (**par** for).

remarquablement adv remarkably.

remarque f remark; (écrite) note.

remarquer vt to notice (**que** that); **faire r.** to point out (**à** to; **que** that); **se faire r.** to attract attention; **remarque!** mind you!, you know!

rembobiner vt, **se rembobiner** vpr to rewind.

rembourré, -ée adj (fauteuil etc) padded.

remboursement m repayment; (dans un magasin etc) refund.

rembourser vt to pay back, to repay; (billet) to refund.

remède m cure; (médicament) medicine.

remédier vi **r. à qch** to remedy sth.

remémorer (se) vpr to remember.

remerciements mpl thanks.

remercier vt to thank (**de qch, pour qch** for sth); **je vous remercie d'être venu** thank you for coming.

remettre* vt to put back; (vêtement) to put back on; (donner) to hand over (**à** to); (*démission, devoir*) to hand in; (*différer*) to postpone (**à** until); **r. en question** to call into question; **r. en état** to repair.

remettre (se) *vpr* **se r. à** (*activité*) to go back to; **se r. à** faire to start to do again; **se r. de** (*chagrin, maladie*) to get over.

remise *f* (*rabais*) discount.

remonte-pente, *pl* **remonte-pentes** *m* ski lift.

remonter 1 *vi* (*aux être*) to come *ou* go back up; **r. dans** (*voiture*) to get back in(to); (*bus, train*) to get back on(to); **r. sur** (*cheval, vélo*) to get back on(to). **2** *vt* (*aux avoir*) (*escalier, pente*) to come *ou* go back up; (*porter*) to bring *ou* take back up; (*montre*) to wind; (*relever*) to raise; (*col*) to turn up; (*objet démonté*) to put back together.

remords *m & mpl* remorse; **avoir des r.** to feel remorse.

remorque *f* (*de voiture etc*) trailer; **prendre en r.** to tow; **en r.** in tow.

remorquer *vt* to tow.

remorqueur *m* tug(boat).

remplaçant, -ante *mf* (*personne*) replacement; (*enseignant*) substitute teacher; (*en sport*) reserve.

remplacement *m* replacement; **assurer le r. de qn** to stand in for sb.

remplacer *vt* to replace (**par** with, by); (*succéder*) to take over from.

rempli, -ie *adj* full (**de** of).

remplir *vt* to fill (up) (**de** with); (*fiche etc*) to fill in *ou* out.

remplir (se) *vpr* to fill (up).

remporter *vi* (*objet*) to take back; (*prix, victoire*) to win.

remuant, -ante *adj* (*enfant*) restless.

remuer 1 *vt* to move; (*café etc*) to stir; (*salade*) to toss. **2** *vi* to move; (*gigoter*) to fidget.

renard *m* fox.

rencontre *f* meeting; (*en sport*) game; **aller à la r. de qn** to go to meet sb.

rencontrer *vt* to meet; (*équipe*) to play.

rencontrer (se) *vpr* to meet.

rendez-vous *m inv* appointment; (*d'amoureux*) date; (*lieu*) meeting place; **donner r. à qn** to make an appointment with sb.

rendormir* (se) *vpr* to go back to sleep.

rendre 1 *vt* to give back; (*monnaie*) to give; (*vomir*) to bring up; **r. célèbre/plus grand/**etc to make famous/bigger/etc. **2** *vti* (*vomir*) to throw up.

rendre (se) *vpr* to surrender (**à qn** to sb); (*aller*) to go (**à** to); **se r. utile/**etc to make oneself useful/etc.

rênes *fpl* reins.

renfermé *m* **sentir le r.** (*chambre etc*) to smell stuffy.

renfermer *vt* to contain.

renflement *m* bulge.

renforcer *vt* to strengthen.

renforts *mpl* (*troupes*) reinforcements.

renier *vt* (*ami, pays*) to disown; (*foi*) to deny.

renifler *vti* to sniff.

renne *m* reindeer.

renommé, -ée *adj* famous (**pour** for).

renommée *f* fame.

renoncer *vi* **r. à qch/à faire** to give up sth/doing.

renouvelable *adj* renewable.

renouveler *vt* to renew; (*erreur, question*) to repeat.

renouveler (se) *vpr* (*incident*) to happen again.

renseignement *m* (piece of) information; **des renseignements** information; **les renseignements** (*au téléphone*) directory assistance, information.

renseigner *vt* to inform, to give some information to (**sur** about).

renseigner (se) *vpr* to find out, to inquire (**sur** about).

rentable *adj* profitable.

rentrée *f* return; **r. (des classes)** beginning of the school year.

rentrer 1 *vi* (*aux* **être**) to go *ou* come back; (*chez soi*) to go *ou* come (back) home; (*entrer de nouveau*) to go *ou* come back in; (*élèves*) to go back to school; **r. dans** to go *ou* come back into; (*pays*) to return to; (*heurter*) to crash into; (*s'emboîter dans*) to fit into. **2** *vt* (*aux* **avoir**) to bring *ou* take in; (*voiture*) to put away; (*chemise*) to tuck in; (*griffes*) to draw in.

renverse (à la) *adv* (*tomber*) backwards.

renverser *vt* (*mettre à l'envers*) to turn upside down; (*faire tomber*) to knock over; (*piéton*) to knock down; (*liquide*) to spill.

renverser (se) *vpr* (*vase etc*) to fall over; (*liquide*) to spill.

renvoi *m* (*d'un employé*) dismissal; (*rot*) burp.

renvoyer* *vt* to send back; (*employé*) to dismiss; (*élève*) to expel; (*balle etc*) to throw back.

réorganiser *vt* to reorganize.

repaire *m* den.

répandre *vt* (*liquide*) to spill; (*nouvelle*) to spread.

répandre (se) *vpr* se r. dans (*fumée, odeur*) to spread through.

répandu, -ue *adj* (*opinion etc*) widespread.

reparaître *vi* to reappear.

réparateur, -trice *mf* repairer.

réparation *f* repair; **en r.** under repair.

réparer *vt* to repair, to mend; (*erreur*) to correct.

repartir* *vi* (*aux* **être**) to set off again; (*s'en retourner*) to go back.

répartir *vt* (*partager*) to share (out).

repas *m* meal; **prendre un r.** to have a meal.

repassage *m* ironing.

repasser 1 *vi* to come *ou* go back. **2** *vt* (*traverser*) to go back over; (*leçon*) to go over; (*film*) to show again; (*linge*) to iron.

repêcher *vt* (*objet*) to fish out.

repentir* (se) *vpr* to be sorry (**de** for).

repère *m* (*guide*) mark; **point de r.** (*espace, temps*) landmark.

repérer *vt* to locate.

repérer (se) *vpr* to get one's bearings.

répertoire *m* r. d'adresses address book.

répéter *vti* to repeat; (*pièce de théâtre*) to rehearse.

répéter (se) *vpr* (*événement*) to happen again.

répétitif, -ive *adj* repetitive.

répétition *f* repetition; (*au théâtre*) rehearsal.

répit *m* rest, respite; **sans r.** ceaselessly.

replacer *vt* to put back.

repli *m* fold.

replier *vt* to fold (up); (*couverture*) to fold back; (*ailes, jambes*) to tuck in.

replier (se) *vpr* (*siège*) to fold up; (*couverture*) to fold back.

réplique *f* (sharp) reply; (*au théâtre*) lines.

répliquer 1 *vt* to reply (sharply) (**que** that). **2** *vi* to answer back.

répondeur *m* (*téléphonique*) answering machine.

répondre 1 *vi* to answer; (*être impertinent*) to answer back; (*réagir*) to respond (**à** to); **r. à qn** to answer sb; (*avec impertinence*) to answer sb back; **r. à** (*lettre, question*) to answer. **2** *vt* **r. que** to answer that.

réponse *f* answer.

reportage *m* (news) report; (*en direct*) (live) commentary.

reporter[1] *vt* to take back; (*différer*) to put off (**à** until).

reporter[2] *m* reporter.

repos *m* rest; (*tranquillité*) peace

(and quiet); **jour de r.** day off.
reposant, -ante *adj* restful.
reposer *vt* (*objet*) to put back
down; (*délasser*) to relax.
reposer (se) *vpr* to rest.
repousser 1 *vt* to push back; (*écarter*) to push away; (*différer*) to put
off. **2** *vi* (*cheveux, feuilles*) to grow
again.
reprendre* 1 *vt* (*objet*) to take
back; (*évadé*) to recapture; (*souffle,
forces*) to get back; (*activité*) to take
up again; (*refrain*) to take up; **r.
de la viande/un œuf**/*etc* to take
(some) more meat/another egg/
etc. **2** *vi* (*recommencer*) to start (up)
(again); (*affaires*) to pick up; (*dire*)
to go on.
reprendre (se) *vpr* to correct
oneself; **s'y r. à deux fois** to give it
another try.
représentant, -ante *mf* represe-
ntative; **r. de commerce** (traveling) salesman, saleswoman.
représentation *f* (*au théâtre*)
performance.
représenter *vt* to represent;
(*pièce de théâtre*) to peform.
réprimander *vt* to reprimand.
reprise *f* (*d'émission de télévision*)
rerun, repeat; (*de tissu*) mend; *Boxe*
round; (*économique*) recovery;
(*pour nouvel achat*) trade-in; **à plusieurs reprises** on several occa-
sions.
repriser *vt* (*chaussette etc*) to
mend.
reproche *m* criticism; **faire des re-
proches à qn** to criticize sb.
reprocher *vt* **r. qch à qn** to criticize sb for sth.
reproduction *f* breeding; (*copie*)
copy.
reproduire* *vt* (*modèle etc*) to
copy.
reproduire (se) *vpr* (*animaux*) to
breed; (*incident etc*) to happen
again.
reptile *m* reptile.

républicain, -aine *adj & mf* republican.
république *f* republic.
réputation *f* reputation; **avoir la r.
d'être** to have a reputation for being.
requin *m* (*poisson*) shark.
rescapé, -ée *mf* survivor.
réseau, -x *m* network.
réservation *f* reservation, booking.
réserve *f* (*provision*) stock, reserve; (*entrepôt*) storeroom; **en r.**
in reserve; **r. naturelle** nature reserve.
réservé, -ée *adj* (*personne, place*)
reserved.
réserver *vt* (*garder*) to save, to reserve (**à** for); (*place, table*) to book,
to reserve.
réserver (se) *vpr* **se r. pour** to
save oneself for.
réservoir *m* (*citerne*) tank; **r. d'essence** gas tank.
résidence *f* residence; **r. secondaire** second home.
résidentiel, -ielle *adj* (*quartier*)
residential.
résider *vi* to be resident (**à, en,
dans** in).
résigner (se) *vpr* to resign oneself (**à qch** to sth; **à faire** to doing).
résistance *f* resistance (**à** to);
(*électrique*) (heating) element; **plat
de r.** main dish.
résistant, -ante *adj* tough; **r. à la
chaleur** heat-resistant; **r. au choc**
shockproof.
résister *vi* **r. à** to resist; (*chaleur, fatigue*) to withstand.
résolu, -ue *adj* determined (**à
faire** to do).
résolution *f* (*décision*) decision.
résonner *vi* (*cris etc*) to ring out;
(*salle*) to echo (**de** with).
résoudre* *vt* (*problème*) to solve;
(*difficulté*) to clear up.
respect *m* respect (**pour, de** for).
respecter *vt* to respect.
respectueux, -euse *adj* res-
pectful (**envers** to).

respiration f breathing; *(haleine)* breath.

respirer 1 vi to breathe; *(reprendre haleine)* to get one's breath back. **2** vt to breathe (in).

resplendissant, -ante adj *(visage)* glowing (**de** with).

responsabilité f responsibility.

responsable 1 adj responsible (**de qch** for sth; **devant qn** to sb). **2** mf *(chef)* person in charge; *(coupable)* person responsible (**de** for).

ressaisir (se) vpr to pull oneself together.

ressemblance f likeness (**avec** to).

ressembler vi **r. à** to look ou be like.

ressembler (se) vpr to look ou be alike.

ressentir* vt to feel.

resserrer vt, **se resserrer** vpr *(nœud etc)* to tighten.

resservir* vi *(outil etc)* to come in useful (again).

resservir (se) vpr **se r. de** *(plat)* to have another helping of.

ressort m *(objet)* spring.

ressortir* vi *(aux être)* to go ou come back out; *(se voir)* to stand out.

ressources fpl *(moyens, argent)* resources.

restaurant m restaurant.

restauration f *(hôtellerie)* catering; *(de tableau)* restoration.

restaurer vt *(réparer)* to restore.

reste m rest (**de** of); **restes** *(de repas)* leftovers; **un r. de fromage/** etc some leftover cheese/etc.

rester vi *(aux être)* to stay; *(calme etc)* to keep, to stay; *(subsister)* to be left; **il reste du pain/**etc there's some bread/etc left (over); **il me reste une minute** I have one minute left; **l'argent qui lui reste** the money he ou she has left.

restreindre* vt to limit (**à** to).

résultat m *(score, d'examen etc)* results; *(conséquence)* outcome, result.

résumé m summary.

résumer vt to summarize; *(situation)* to sum up.

rétablir vt to restore.

rétablir (se) vpr *(malade)* to recover.

rétablissement m *(de malade)* recovery.

retard m *(sur un programme etc)* delay; **en r.** late; **en r. dans qch** behind in sth; **en r. sur qn/qch** behind sb/sth; **rattraper son r.** to catch up; **avoir du r.** to be late; *(sur un programme)* to be behind; *(montre)* to be slow; **avoir une heure de r.** to be an hour late.

retardataire mf latecomer.

retarder 1 vt to delay; *(date, montre)* to put back; **r. qn** *(dans une activité)* to put sb behind. **2** vi *(montre)* to be slow; **r. de cinq minutes** to be five minutes slow.

retenir* vt *(empêcher d'agir)* to hold back; *(souffle)* to hold; *(réserver)* to book; *(se souvenir de)* to remember; *(fixer)* to hold (in place); *(chiffre)* to carry; *(chaleur, odeur)* to retain; **r. qn prisonnier** to keep sb prisoner.

retenir (se) vpr *(se contenir)* to restrain oneself; **se r. de faire** to stop oneself (from) doing; **se r. à** to cling to.

retentir vi to ring (out) (**de** with).

retenue f *(punition)* detention.

retirer vt *(sortir)* to take out; *(ôter)* to take off; *(éloigner)* to take away; **r. qch à qn** *(permis etc)* to take sth away from sb.

retomber vi to fall (again); *(pendre)* to hang (down); *(après un saut etc)* to land.

retouche f *(de vêtement)* alteration.

retoucher vt *(vêtement)* to alter.

retour m return; **être de r.** to be back (**de** from); **à mon r.** when I get ou got back.

retourner 1 vt (aux **avoir**) (mate-las, steak etc) to turn over; (terre etc) to turn; (vêtement, sac etc) to turn inside out. **2** vi (aux **être**) to go back, to return.

retourner (se) vpr to turn around, to look around; (sur le dos) to turn over; (voiture) to overturn.

retrait m withdrawal; (de bagages, de billets) collection; (des eaux) receding; **en r.** (maison) set back; **rester en r.** to stay in the background.

retraite f (d'employé) retirement; (pension) (retirement) pension; **prendre sa r.** to retire; **à la r.** retired.

retraité, -ée 1 adj retired. **2** mf senior citizen, pensioner.

retransmettre vt to broadcast.

retransmission f broadcast.

rétrécir vi (au lavage) to shrink.

rétrécir (se) vpr (rue etc) to narrow.

rétro adj inv (personne, idée etc) old-fashioned.

rétrograder vi (automobiliste) to change down.

retrousser vt (manches) to roll up.

retrouver vt to find (again); (rejoindre) to meet (again); (forces, santé) to get back; (se rappeler) to recall.

retrouver (se) vpr to find oneself (back); (se rencontrer) to meet (again); **s'y r.** to find one's way.

rétroviseur m (de véhicule) rearview mirror.

réunion f (séance) meeting.

réunir vt (objets) to gather; (convoquer) to call together.

réunir (se) vpr to meet, to get together.

réussi, -ie adj successful.

réussir 1 vi to succeed (**à faire** in doing); **r. à** (examen) to pass; **r. à qn** (aliment, climat) to agree with sb. **2** vt to make a success of.

réussite f success.

revanche f (en sport) rematch; **en r.** on the other hand.

rêve m dream; **faire un r.** to have a dream (**de** about); **maison**/etc **de r.** dream house/etc.

réveil m (pendule) alarm (clock); **à son r.** when he wakes (up)/woke (up).

réveillé, -ée adj awake.

réveiller vt, **se réveiller** vpr to wake (up).

réveillon m midnight supper (on Christmas Eve or New Year's Eve).

réveillonner vi to see in Christmas/the New Year (with a midnight supper and party).

révéler vt to reveal (**que** that).

revenant m ghost.

revendication f claim; (exigence) demand.

revendiquer vt to claim; (exiger) to demand.

revenir* vi (aux **être**) to come back; (coûter) to cost (**à qn** sb); **r. à** (activité, sujet) to go back to; **r. à qn** (forces, mémoire) to come back to sb; **r. à soi** to come to; **r. de** (surprise) to get over; **r. sur** (décision, promesse) to go back on.

revenu m income (**de** from).

rêver 1 vi to dream (**de** of; **de faire** of doing). **2** vt to dream (**que** that).

rêverie f daydream.

revers m (de veste) lapel; (de pantalon) cuff.

revêtement m (de route etc) surface.

rêveur, -euse mf dreamer.

revient m prix de r. (production) cost.

réviser vt (leçon) to revise; (machine, voiture) to service.

révision f (de leçon) revision; (de machine, voiture) service.

revoir* vt to see (again); (texte, leçon) to revise; **au r.** goodbye.

révoltant, -ante adj revolting.

révolte f rebellion, revolt.

révolté, -ée mf rebel.

révolter vt to sicken.

révolter (se) *vpr* to rebel (**contre** against).

révolution *f* revolution.

révolutionnaire *adj & mf* revolutionary.

revolver *m* gun.

revue *f (magazine)* magazine.

rez-de-chaussée *m inv* first floor.

rhabiller (se) *vpr* to get dressed again.

rhinocéros *m* rhinoceros.

rhubarbe *f* rhubarb.

rhum *m* rum.

rhumatisme *m* rheumatism; **avoir des rhumatismes** to have rheumatism.

rhume *m* cold; **r. des foins** hay fever.

ri, riant *pp & pres p of* **rire**.

ricaner *vi* to snicker.

riche 1 *adj* rich. **2** *mf* rich person; **les riches** the rich.

richesse *f* wealth; **richesses** *(trésor)* riches.

ricocher *vi* to ricochet.

ricochet *m (de pierre)* ricochet.

ride *f* wrinkle.

ridé, -ée *adj* wrinkled.

rideau, -x *m* curtain; *(de magasin)* shutter.

ridicule *adj* ridiculous.

ridiculiser (se) *vpr* to make a fool of oneself.

rien 1 *pron* nothing; **il ne sait r.** he knows nothing, he doesn't know anything; **r. du tout** nothing at all; **r. d'autre/de bon**/*etc* nothing else/ good/*etc*; **de r.!** *(je vous en prie)* don't mention it!; **ça ne fait r.** it doesn't matter; **r. que** just. **2** *m* (mere) nothing.

rigide *adj* rigid; *(carton, muscle)* stiff.

rigoler *vi Fam* to laugh; *(s'amuser)* to have fun.

rigolo, -ote *adj Fam* funny.

rigoureux, -euse *adj (analyse)* rigorous; *(climat, punition)* harsh;

(personne, morale, neutralité) strict.

rigueur *f (d'analyse)* rigor; *(de climat)* harshness; *(de personne)* strictness; **être de r.** to be the rule; **à la r.** if need be.

rillettes *fpl* potted ground pork.

rime *f* rhyme.

rimer *vi* to rhyme (**avec** with).

rinçage *m* rinsing.

rincer *vt* to rinse; *(verre)* to rinse (out).

ring *m* (boxing) ring.

ringard, -e *Fam* **1** *adj* uncool, geeky. **2** *mf* geek.

riposter **1** *vt* **r. que...** to retort that... **2** *vi* to counterattack; **r. à** *(attaque)* to counter; *(insulte)* to reply to.

rire* 1 *vi* to laugh (**de** at); *(s'amuser)* to have a good time; *(plaisanter)* to joke; **pour r.** as a joke. **2** *m* laugh; **rires** laughter; **le fou r.** the giggles.

risque *m* risk (**de faire** of doing; **à faire** in doing); **assurance tous risques** comprehensive insurance.

risqué, -ée *adj* risky.

risquer *vt* to risk; **r. de faire** to stand a good chance of doing.

rivage *m* shore.

rival, -e, -aux *adj & mf* rival.

rivaliser *vi* to compete (**avec** with; **de** in).

rive *f (de fleuve)* bank; *(de lac)* shore.

riverain, -aine *mf (près d'une rivière)* riverside resident; *(près d'un lac)* lakeside resident; *(de rue)* resident.

rivière *f* river.

riz *m* rice; **r. au lait** rice pudding.

RN *abrév = route nationale.

robe *f (de femme)* dress; **r. du soir**/ **de mariée** evening/wedding dress; **r. de chambre** bathrobe.

robinet *m* tap, faucet; **eau du r.** tap water.

robot *m* robot.

robuste *adj* sturdy.

roche *f*, **rocher** *m* rock.

rocheux, -euse *adj* rocky.

rock *m (musique)* rock.

roder *vt (moteur, voiture)* to break in.

rôder *vi* to prowl (about).

rôdeur, -euse *mf* prowler.

rognon *m (d'animal)* kidney.

roi *m* king.

rôle *m (au théâtre)* role, part; *(d'un père etc)* job; **à tour de r.** in turn.

romain, -aine *adj & mf* Roman.

roman *m* novel; **r. d'aventures** adventure story.

romancier, -ière *mf* novelist.

romantique *adj* romantic.

romarin *m* rosemary.

rompre* (se) *vpr (corde etc)* to break; *(digue)* to burst.

ronces *fpl* brambles.

ronchonner *vi Fam* to grumble.

rond, ronde 1 *adj* round; **dix euros tout r.** ten euros exactly. **2** *m (cercle)* circle, ring; **en r.** *(s'asseoir etc)* in a ring *ou* circle; **tourner en r.** to go round and round.

ronde *f (de soldat)* round; *(de policier)* beat, round.

rondelle *f (tranche)* slice.

rondin *m* log.

rond-point, *pl* **ronds-points** *m* traffic circle.

ronflement *m* snore; **ronflements** snoring.

ronfler *vi* to snore.

ronger *vt* to gnaw (at); *(ver, mer, rouille)* to eat into.

ronger (se) *vpr* **se r. les ongles** to bite one's nails.

ronronnement *m* purr(ing).

ronronner *vi* to purr.

rosbif *m* **du r.** roast beef; *(à rôtir)* (beef) roast; **un r.** (beef) roast.

rose 1 *f (fleur)* rose. **2** *adj & m (couleur)* pink.

rosé *adj & m (vin)* rosé.

roseau, -x *m (plante)* reed.

rosée *f* dew.

rosier *m* rose bush.

rossignol *m* nightingale.

rot *m Fam* burp.

roter *vi Fam* to burp.

rôti *m* **du r.** roast; *(cuit)* meat roast; **un r.** a roast; **r. de porc** pork roast.

rotin *m* cane.

rôtir *vti*, **se rôtir** *vpr* to roast; **faire r.** to roast.

roue *f* wheel.

rouge 1 *adj* red; *(fer)* red-hot. **2** *m (couleur)* red; **r. (à lèvres)** lipstick; **le feu est au r.** the (traffic) light is red.

rouge-gorge, *pl* **rouges-gorges** *m* robin.

rougeole *f* measles.

rougir *vi (de honte)* to blush; *(de colère)* to flush (**de** with).

rouille *f* rust.

rouillé, -ée *adj* rusty.

rouiller *vi*, **se rouiller** *vpr* to rust.

roulant, -ante *adj (escalier)* moving; *(meuble)* on wheels.

rouleau, -x *m (outil)* roller; *(de papier etc)* roll; **r. à pâtisserie** rolling pin; **r. compresseur** steamroller.

rouler 1 *vt* to roll; *(brouette)* to push; *(crêpe, ficelle etc)* to roll up. **2** *vi* to roll; *(train, voiture)* to go; *(conducteur)* to drive.

rouler (se) *vpr* to roll; **se r. dans** *(couverture etc)* to roll oneself (up) in.

roulette *f (de meuble)* castor; *(de dentiste)* drill.

roulotte *f (de gitan)* caravan.

round *m Boxe* round.

rouspéter *vi Fam* to complain.

rousse *voir* **roux**.

rousseur *f* **tache de r.** freckle.

roussir *vt (brûler)* to scorch.

route *f* road (**de** to); *(itinéraire)* way; **r. nationale/départementale** main/secondary road; **en r.!** let's go!; **par la r.** by road; **mettre en r.** *(voiture etc)* to start (up); **se mettre en r.** to set out (**pour** for); **une heure de r.** an hour's drive; **bonne r.!** have a good trip!

routier, -ière 1 *adj* carte/sécurité **routière** road map/safety. **2** *mf* (long-distance) truck driver.

roux, rousse 1 *adj (cheveux)* red; *(personne)* red-haired. **2** *mf* red-head.

royal, -e, -aux *adj (famille, palais)* royal.

royaume *m* kingdom.

ruban *m* ribbon; **r. adhésif** (adhesive) tape.

rubéole *f* German measles.

rubis *m* ruby; *(montre)* jewel.

rubrique *f (article de journal)* column; *(catégorie, titre)* heading.

ruche *f* (bee)hive.

rude *adj (pénible)* tough; *(hiver, voix)* harsh; *(grossier)* crude; *(rêche)* rough.

rudement *adv (parler, traiter)* harshly; *(très) Fam* awfully.

rue *f* street; **à la r.** *(sans domicile)* on the streets.

ruelle *f* alley(way).

ruer *vi (cheval)* to kick (out).

ruer (se) *vpr* to rush (**sur** at).

rugby *m* rugby.

rugbyman, *pl* **-men** *m* rugby player.

rugir *vi* to roar.

rugissement *m* roar.

rugueux, -euse *adj* rough.

ruine *f* ruin; **en r.** in ruins; **tomber en r.** *(bâtiment)* to become a ruin, to crumble; *(mur)* to crumble.

ruiner *vt (personne, santé etc)* to ruin.

ruiner (se) *vpr* se **r.** to be(come) ruined.

ruisseau, -x *m* stream.

ruisseler *vi* to stream (**de** with).

rumeur *f (murmure)* murmur; *(nouvelle)* rumor.

rupture *f* breaking; *(de fiançailles, de relations)* breaking off; *(de pourparlers)* breakdown (**de** in); *(dispute)* break-up; **être en r. de stock** to be out of stock.

rural, -e, -aux *adj* vie/école/*etc*

rurale country life/school/*etc*.

ruse *f (subterfuge)* trick; **la r.** *(habileté)* cunning.

rusé, -ée *adj & mf* cunning (person).

russe 1 *adj* Russian. **2** *mf* R. Russian. **3** *m (langue)* Russian.

rythme *m* rhythm; *(de travail)* rate; **au r. de trois par jour** at a rate of three a day.

rythmé, -ée *adj* rhythmical.

S

sa *voir* **son**.

sable *m* sand.

sabler *vt (rue)* to sand.

sablier *m (de cuisine)* egg timer.

sablonneux, -euse *adj* sandy.

sabot *m (de cheval etc)* hoof; *(chaussure)* clog; **s. (de Denver)** (Denver) boot.

sac *m* bag; *(grand et en toile)* sack, tote; **s. (à main)** purse; **s. à dos** backpack.

saccadé, -ée *adj* jerky.

saccager *vt (détruire)* to wreck.

sachant, sache(s), sachent *etc voir* **savoir**.

sachet *m* (small) bag; **s. de thé** teabag.

sacoche *f* bag; *(de vélo)* saddlebag.

sacré, -ée *adj (saint)* sacred; **un s. menteur**/*etc Fam* a damned liar/*etc*.

sacrifice *m* sacrifice.

sacrifier *vt* to sacrifice (**à** to; **pour** for).

sacrifier (se) *vpr* to sacrifice oneself.

sage *adj* wise; *(enfant)* good.

sage-femme, *pl* **sages-femmes** *f* midwife.

sagement *adv* wisely; *(avec calme)* quietly.

sagesse f (philosophie) wisdom; (calme) good behavior.

saignant, -ante adj (viande) rare.

saignement m bleeding; **s. de nez** nosebleed.

saigner vti to bleed.

sain, saine adj healthy; **s. et sauf** safe and sound.

saint, sainte 1 adj holy; **s. Jean** Saint John; **la Sainte Vierge** the Blessed Virgin. **2** mf saint.

Saint-Sylvestre f New Year's Eve.

sais, sait voir **savoir**.

saisir vt to grab (hold of); (occasion) to jump at; (comprendre) to understand.

saisir (se) vpr se **s. de** to grab (hold of).

saison f season.

salade f (laitue) lettuce; **s. (verte)** (green) salad; **s. de fruits/etc** fruit/ etc salad.

saladier m salad bowl.

salaire m wage(s).

salarié, -ée mf wage earner.

sale adj dirty; (dégoûtant) filthy.

salé, -ée adj (goût, plat) salty; (aliment) salted.

saler vt to salt.

saleté f dirtiness; filthiness; (crasse) dirt, filth; **saletés** (détritus) garbage.

salière f saltshaker.

salir vt to (make) dirty.

salir (se) vpr to get dirty.

salissant, -ante adj dirty; (étoffe) that shows the dirt.

salive f saliva.

salle f room; (très grande) hall; (de théâtre) theater, auditorium; (de cinéma) cinema; (d'hôpital) ward; **s. à manger** dining room; **s. de bain(s)** bathroom; **s. d'opération** operating room.

salon m sitting room, lounge; (exposition) show.

salopette f (d'enfant, d'ouvrier) overalls.

saluer vt to greet; (de la main) to

wave to; (de la tête) to nod to.

salut 1 m greeting; (de la main) wave; (de la tête) nod. **2** int hi!; (au revoir) bye!

samedi m Saturday.

SAMU m abrév (service d'aide médicale d'urgence) emergency medical service.

sanctionner vt (approuver) to sanction; (punir) to punish.

sandale f sandal.

sandwich m sandwich; **s. au fromage/etc** cheese/etc sandwich.

sandwicherie f sandwich shop.

sang m blood.

sang-froid m self-control; **garder son s.** to keep calm; **avec s.** calmly.

sanglant, -ante adj bloody.

sangle f strap.

sanglier m wild boar.

sanglot m sob.

sangloter vi to sob.

sanguin adj **groupe s.** blood group.

sans prép without; **s. faire** without doing; **s. qu'il le sache** without him ou his knowing; **s. cela** otherwise; **s. importance** unimportant.

sans-abri mf inv homeless person.

sans-gêne 1 adj inv ill-mannered. **2** m inv ill manners.

sans-papiers mf inv illegal immigrant.

santé f health; (à votre) **s.!** cheers!

sapeur-pompier, pl **sapeurs-pompiers** m fireman, firefighter.

sapin m (arbre, bois) fir; **s. de Noël** Christmas tree.

sardine f sardine.

satellite m satellite.

satin m satin.

satisfaction f satisfaction.

satisfaire* vt to satisfy (sb); **satisfait (de)** satisfied (with).

satisfaisant, -ante adj satisfactory.

sauce f sauce; (jus de viande) gravy; **s. tomate** tomato sauce.

saucisse f sausage.

saucisson m (cold) sausage.

sauf prép except (**que** that).

saule m willow.

saumon m salmon.

sauna m sauna.

saupoudrer vt to sprinkle (**de** with).

saura, saurai(t) etc voir **savoir**.

saut m jump, leap; **faire un s.** to jump, to leap; **faire un s. chez qn** to drop in on sb, to pop over to see sb.

sauter 1 vi to jump, to leap; (détruire) to blow up; **s. à la corde** to jump rope; **ça saute aux yeux** it's obvious. **2** vt to jump (over); (mot, repas) to skip.

sauterelle f grasshopper.

sauvage adj (animal, plante) wild; (tribu, homme) primitive.

sauvegarder vt to safeguard; (fichier) to save.

sauver vt to save; (d'un danger) to rescue (**de** from); **s. la vie à qn** to save sb's life.

sauver (se) vpr to run away ou off.

sauvetage m rescue.

sauveteur m rescuer.

sauveur m savior.

savant m scientist.

savate f old slipper.

saveur f flavor.

savoir* vt to know; **s. lire/nager/** etc to be able to read/swim/etc; **faire s. à qn que** to inform sb that; **je n'en sais rien** I have no idea.

savon m soap; (morceau) (bar of) soap.

savonner vt to wash with soap.

savonnette f bar of soap.

savonneux, -euse adj soapy.

savourer vt to enjoy.

savoureux, -euse adj tasty.

saxophone m saxophone.

scandale m scandal; **faire un s.** to make a scene.

scandaleux, -euse adj shocking.

scandaliser vt to shock.

scandinave 1 adj Scandinavian. **2** mf S. Scandinavian.

scanner m (appareil) scanner.

scarlatine f scarlet fever.

scénario m (dialogues etc) movie script.

scénariste mf scriptwriter.

scène f (plateau) stage; (décors, partie de pièce, dispute) scene; **mettre en s.** to direct.

sceptique 1 adj skeptical. **2** mf skeptic.

schéma m diagram.

scie f saw.

science f science; **étudier les sciences** to study science.

science-fiction f science fiction.

scientifique 1 adj scientific. **2** mf scientist.

scier vt to saw.

scintiller vi to sparkle; (étoiles) to twinkle.

scission f (de parti) split (**de** in).

scolaire adj année/etc s. school year/etc.

scolarité f schooling; **pendant ma s.** during my school years.

score m (de match) score.

scotch® m (ruban) scotch tape®.

scrutin m voting, ballot.

sculpter vt to carve, to sculpt.

sculpteur m sculptor.

sculpture f (art, œuvre) sculpture.

SDF mf abrév (sans domicile fixe) homeless person.

se (**s'** before vowel or mute h) pron (complément direct) himself; (féminin) herself; (non humain) itself; (indéfini) oneself, pl themselves. ■ (indirect) to himself; (féminin) to herself; (non humain) to itself; (indéfini) to oneself. ■ (réciproque) each other, one another; (indirect) to each other, to one another. ■ (possessif) **il se lave les mains** he washes his hands.

séance f (au cinéma) screening.

seau, -x m bucket.

sec, sèche 1 adj dry; (légumes)

dried; *(ton)* harsh; **coup s.** (sharp) knock, bang; **frapper un coup s.** to knock (sharply), to bang; **bruit s.** *(rupture)* snap. **2** *m* **à s.** *(rivière)* dried up; **au s.** in a dry place.

sécateur *m* pruning shears.

sèche-cheveux *m inv* hair dryer.

sèche-linge *m inv* tumble dryer.

sécher 1 *vti* to dry. **2** *vt (cours)* to skip.

sécheresse *f (période)* drought.

séchoir *m* **s. à linge** drying rack.

second, -onde 1 *adj* second; *(étage)* third. **2** *mf* second (one) **3** *m (étage)* third floor. **4** *f (de lycée)* = sophomore year; *(vitesse)* second (gear).

secondaire *adj* secondary.

seconde *f (instant)* second.

secouer *vt* to shake.

secourir *vt* to assist.

secouriste *mf* first-aid worker.

secours *m* assistance, help; **(premiers) s.** first aid; **au s.!** help!; **sortie de s.** emergency exit; **roue de s.** spare tire.

secousse *f* jolt.

secret, -ète 1 *adj* secret. **2** *m* secret; **en s.** in secret.

secrétaire 1 *mf* secretary; *(de médecin etc)* receptionist. **2** *m (meuble)* writing desk.

secrétariat *m (bureau)* secretary's office.

secteur *m (électricité)* mains.

sectionner *vt (couper)* to sever.

sécurité *f* safety; **en s.** safe; **S. sociale** = Social security.

séduire* *vt* to charm; *(plaire à)* to appeal to; *(abuser de)* to seduce.

séduisant, -ante *adj* attractive.

segment *m* segment.

seigneur *m* lord.

sein *m* breast.

séisme *m* earthquake.

seize *adj & m* sixteen.

seizième *adj & mf* sixteenth.

séjour *m* stay; **(salle de) s.** living room.

séjourner *vi* to stay.

sel *m* salt; **sels de bain** bath salts.

sélection *f* selection.

sélectionner *vt* to select.

self(-service) *m* self-service restaurant *ou* store.

selle *f* saddle.

selon *prép* according to (**que** whether).

semaine *f* week; **en s.** during the week.

semblable *adj* similar (**à** to).

semblant *m* **faire s.** to pretend (**de faire** to do).

sembler *vi* to seem (**à** to); **il (me) semble vieux** he seems *ou* looks old (to me); **il me semble que** *(+ indicatif)* I think that, it seems to me that.

semelle *f (de chaussure)* sole.

semer *vt (graines)* to sow.

semestre *m* half(year); *(scolaire)* semester.

semi-remorque *m* semi(trailer).

semoule *f* semolina.

sénat *m* senate.

sens¹ *m (signification)* meaning, sense; **avoir du bon s.** to have sense, to be sensible; **avoir un s.** to make sense; **ça n'a pas de s.** that doesn't make sense.

sens² *m (direction)* direction; **s. giratoire** traffic circle; **s. unique** *(rue)* one-way street; **'s. interdit'** 'no entry'; **s. dessus dessous** upside down; **dans le s./le s. inverse des aiguilles d'une montre** clockwise/counterclockwise.

sensation *f* feeling.

sensationnel, -elle *adj* sensational.

sensé, -ée *adj* sensible.

sensibilité *f* sensitivity.

sensible *adj* sensitive (**à** to); *(douloureux)* tender; *(progrès etc)* noticeable.

sentier *m* path.

sentiment *m* feeling.

sentimental, -e, -aux *adj* senti-

mental; **vie sentimentale** love life.
sentir* vt to feel; (odeur) to smell;
(goût) to taste; **s. le parfum**/etc to
smell of perfume/etc; **s. le poisson**/
etc (avoir le goût de) to taste of fish/
etc; Fam **je ne peux pas le s.** (supporter) I can't stand him.
sentir (se) vpr **se s. fatigué**/etc to
feel tired/etc.
séparément adv separately.
séparer vt to separate (**de** from).
séparer (se) vpr (se quitter) to
part; (couple) to separate; **se s. de**
(chien etc) to part with.
sept adj & m seven.
septante adj & m (en Belgique, en
Suisse) seventy.
septembre m September.
septième adj & mf seventh.
sera, serai(t) etc voir **être**.
serein, -eine adj serene.
série f series; (ensemble) set.
sérieusement adv seriously;
(travailler) conscientiously.
sérieux, -euse 1 adj serious. 2 m
prendre au s. to take seriously; **garder son s.** to keep a straight face.
seringue f syringe.
serment m oath; **faire le s. de
faire** to promise to do.
sermonner vt (faire la morale à)
to lecture.
séropositif, -ive adj HIV positive.
serpent m snake.
serpillière f floor cloth.
serre f greenhouse; **effet de s.**
greenhouse effect.
serré, -ée adj (nœud etc) tight;
(gens) packed (together).
serrer 1 vt (tenir) to grip; (presser)
to squeeze; (nœud, vis) to tighten;
(poing) to clench; (frein) to apply;
s. la main à qn to shake hands with
sb; **s. qn** (embrasser) to hug sb. 2 vi
s. à droite to keep (to the) right.
serrer (se) vpr to squeeze up ou
together; **se s. contre** to squeeze
up against.

serrure f lock.
serveur, -euse mf waiter, wait-
ress; (au bar) bartender, barmaid.
serviable adj helpful.
service m service; (pourboire) service (charge); (dans une entreprise)
department; **un s.** (aide) a favor;
rendre s. to be of service (**à qn** to
sb); **s. (non) compris** service (not)
included; **s. après-vente** aftersales
service; **être de s.** to be on duty.
serviette f towel; (sac) briefcase;
s. hygiénique sanitary napkin; **s.
(de table)** napkin, serviette.
servir* 1 vt to serve (**qch à qn** sb
with sth, sth to sb). 2 vi (être utile)
to be useful; **s. à qch/à faire** (objet)
to be used for sth/to do; **ça ne sert à
rien** it's useless (**de faire** doing); **ça
me sert à faire/de qch** I use it to do/
as sth.
servir (se) vpr (à table) to help oneself (**de** to); **se s. de** (utiliser) to use.
ses voir **son**.
set m Tennis set; **s. (de table)** place
mat.
seuil m doorstep.
seul¹, -e 1 adj alone; **tout s.** by oneself, on one's own; **se sentir s.** to feel
lonely. 2 adv (tout) **s.** (rentrer, vivre
etc) by oneself, on one's own, alone;
(parler) to oneself.
seul², -e adj (unique) only; **la seule
femme**/etc the only woman/etc; **un
s. chat**/etc only one cat/etc; **pas un
s. livre**/etc not a single book/etc. 2
mf **le s., la seule** the only one; **un
s., une seule** only one; **pas un s.**
not (a single) one.
seulement adv only.
sévère adj severe; (parents etc) strict.
sévérité f severeness, severity; (de
parents etc) strictness.
sévices mpl ill-treatment; **s. à enfant** child abuse.
sexe m sex.
sexuel, -elle adj sexual; **éduca-
tion/vie sexuelle** sex education/
life.

shampooing m shampoo; **faire un s. à qn** to shampoo sb's hair.

short m (pair of) shorts.

si¹ 1 (s' *before* **il, ils**) *conj* if; **je me demande si** I wonder whether *ou* if; **si on restait?** what if we stayed? **2** *adv* (*tellement*) so; **pas si riche que toi** not as rich as you; **un si bon dîner** such a good dinner; **si bien que** (+ *indicatif*) with the result that.

si² *adv* (*après négative*) yes; **tu ne viens pas? – si!** you're not coming? – yes (I am)!

SIDA m *abrév* (*syndrome immuno-déficitaire acquis*) AIDS.

sidérurgie f iron and steel industry.

siècle m century; (*époque*) age.

siège m seat; (*de parti etc*) headquarters; **s. (social)** head office.

sien, sienne *pron poss* **le s., la sienne,** **les sien(ne)s** his; (*de femme*) hers; (*de chose*) its; **les deux siens** his *ou* her two.

sieste f **faire la s.** to take a nap.

sifflement m whistling; (*de gaz, serpent*) hiss(ing).

siffler 1 *vi* to whistle; (*avec un sifflet*) to blow one's whistle; (*gaz, serpent*) to hiss. **2** *vt* (*chanson*) to whistle; (*chien*) to whistle to; (*acteur*) to boo.

sifflet m whistle; **(coup de) s.** (*son*) whistle; **sifflets** (*des spectateurs*) boos.

sigle m acronym.

signal, -aux m signal; **s. d'alarme** (*de train*) alarm.

signaler *vt* to point out (**à qn** to sb; **que** that); (*à la police etc*) to report (**à** to).

signature f signature.

signe m sign; **faire s. à qn** (*geste*) to motion (to) sb (**de faire** to do).

signer *vt* to sign.

signification f meaning.

signifier *vt* to mean (**que** that).

silence m silence; **en s.** in silence;

garder le s. to keep silent (**sur** about).

silencieusement *adv* silently.

silencieux, -euse *adj* silent.

silhouette f outline; (*ligne du corps*) figure.

sillonner *vt* (*parcourir*) to criss-cross.

similitude f similarity.

simple *adj* simple.

simplement *adv* simply.

simplifier *vt* to simplify.

simultané, -ée *adj* simultaneous.

simultanément *adv* simultaneously.

sincère *adj* sincere.

sincèrement *adv* sincerely.

sincérité f sincerity.

singe m monkey, ape.

singeries fpl antics.

singulier, -ière *adj & m* (*non pluriel*) singular; **au s.** in the singular.

sinistre 1 *adj* sinister. **2** m disaster.

sinon *conj* (*autrement*) otherwise, or else.

sirène f (*d'usine etc*) siren.

sirop m syrup; **s. contre la toux** cough medicine *ou* syrup.

site m (*endroit*) site; (*pittoresque*) beauty spot; **s. touristique** place of interest; **s. classé** conservation area; **s. Web** website.

situation f situation.

situé, -ée *adj* situated, located.

situer (se) *vpr* to be situated, to be located.

six *adj & m* six.

sixième *adj & mf* sixth.

sketch, pl sketches m (*de théâtre*) sketch.

ski m ski; (*sport*) skiing; **faire du s.** to ski; **s. nautique** water skiing.

skier *vi* to ski.

skieur, -euse *mf* skier.

slip m (*d'homme*) briefs, underwear; (*de femme*) panties, underwear; **s. de bain** (bathing) trunks.

slogan *m* slogan.

SMIC *m abrév (salaire minimum interprofessionnel de croissance)* guaranteed minimum wage.

smoking *m (veston, costume)* tuxedo.

SMS *m abrév (short message service)* text (message); **envoyer un s. à qn** to text sb, to send sb a text.

SNCF *f abrév (Société nationale des chemins de fer français)* = French railroad system.

social, -e, -aux *adj* social.

socialiste *adj & mf* socialist.

société *f* society; *(compagnie)* company.

socquette *f* anklet.

sœur *f* sister.

soi *pron* oneself; **cela va de soi** it's evident (**que** that).

soi-disant 1 *adj inv* so-called. **2** *adv* supposedly.

soie *f* silk.

soient *voir* **être**.

soif *f* thirst; **avoir s.** to be thirsty; **donner s. à qn** to make sb thirsty.

soigné, -ée *adj (vêtement)* neat; *(travail)* careful.

soigner *vt* to look after, to take care of; *(maladie)* to treat; **se faire s.** to get (medical) treatment, to be treated.

soigneusement *adv* carefully.

soigneux, -euse *adj* careful (**de** with); *(propre)* neat.

soi-même *pron* oneself.

soin *m* care; *(à un malade)* treatment, care; **avec s.** carefully; **prendre s. de qch** to take care of sth; **les premiers soins** first aid.

soir *m* evening; **le s.** *(chaque soir)* in the evening; **à neuf heures du s.** at nine in the evening.

soirée *f* evening; *(réunion)* party.

sois, soit *voir* **être**.

soit *conj* **s.... s....** either... or...

soixantaine *f* **une s. (de)** about sixty.

soixante *adj & m* sixty.

soixante-dix *adj & m* seventy.

soixante-dixième *adj & mf* seventieth.

soixantième *adj & mf* sixtieth.

soja *m (plante)* soya; **germes** *ou* **pousses de s.** beanshoots.

sol *m* ground; *(plancher)* floor.

solaire *adj* solar; **crème/huile s.** sun(tan) lotion/oil.

soldat *m* soldier.

solde *m (de compte)* balance; **en s.** *(acheter)* on sale; **soldes** *(marchandises)* sale goods; *(vente)* (clearance) sale(s).

soldé, -ée *adj (article etc)* reduced.

solder *vt (articles)* to put on sale.

sole *f (poisson)* sole.

soleil *m* sun; *(chaleur, lumière)* sunshine; **au s.** in the sun; **il fait (du) s.** it's sunny; **coup de s.** sunburn.

solennel, -elle *adj* solemn.

solidarité *f (de personnes)* solidarity.

solide *adj & m* solid.

solidement *adv* solidly.

solitaire *adj (tout seul)* all alone.

solitude *f* **aimer la s.** to like being alone.

solliciter *vt (audience)* to request; *(emploi)* to apply for; **s. qn** *(faire appel à)* to appeal to sb (**de faire** to do).

sombre *adj* dark; **il fait s.** it's dark.

sombrer *vi (bateau)* to sink; **s. dans** *(folie, sommeil)* to sink into.

sommaire 1 *adj* summary; *(repas)* basic. **2** *m (table des matières)* contents.

somme 1 *f* sum; **faire la s. de** to add up. **2** *m (sommeil)* nap; **faire un s.** to take a nap.

sommeil *m* sleep; **avoir s.** to be *ou* feel sleepy.

sommes *voir* **être**.

sommet *m* top.

sommier *m (de lit)* base.

somnifère *m* sleeping pill.

somnoler *vi* to doze.

son *m (bruit)* sound.

son, sa, *pl* **ses** (**sa** *becomes* **son** before a vowel or mute *h*) *adj poss* his; *(de femme)* her; *(de chose)* its; *(indéfini)* one's; **s. père** his/her/ one's father; **sa mère** his/her/one's mother; **son ami(e)** his/her/one's friend; **sa durée** its duration.

sondage *m* **s. (d'opinion)** opinion poll.

songer *vi* **s. à qch/à faire** to think of sth/of doing.

songeur, -euse *adj* thoughtful, pensive.

sonner *vi* to ring; **on a sonné** *(à la porte)* someone's at the door.

sonnerie *f (son)* ring(ing); *(appareil)* bell; *(au téléphone)* ring; **s. 'occupé'** busy signal.

sonnette *f* bell; **coup de s.** ring.

sonore *adj (rire)* loud; *(salle)* resonant.

sont *voir* **être**.

sorcière *f* witch.

sort *m (destin, hasard)* fate; *(condition)* lot.

sorte *f* sort, kind (**de** of); **toutes sortes de** all sorts ou kinds of; **de (telle) s. que** (+ *subjonctif*) so that; **faire en s. que** (+ *subjonctif*) to see to it that.

sortie *f (promenade à pied)* walk; *(en voiture)* drive; *(excursion)* outing; *(porte)* exit, way out; *(de disque, film)* release; **à la s. de l'école** when the children get out of school.

sortir* **1** *vi (aux* **être**) to go out, to leave; *(venir)* to come out; *(pour s'amuser, danser etc)* to go out; *(film etc)* to come out; **s. de table** to leave the table; **s'en s.** to pull ou come through. **2** *vt (aux* **avoir**) to take out (**de** of).

sottise *f (action, parole)* foolish thing; **faire des sottises** *(enfant)* to misbehave.

sou *m* **sous** *(argent)* money; **elle n'a pas un s.** she doesn't have a bean;

appareil *ou* **machine à sous** slot machine.

souche *f (d'arbre)* stump.

souci *m* worry; *(préoccupation)* concern (**de** for); **se faire du s.** to worry; **ça lui donne du s.** it worries him/her.

soucier (se) *vpr* **se s. de** to be worried about. .

soucieux, -euse *adj* worried (**de qch** about sth).

soucoupe *f* saucer; **s. volante** flying saucer.

soudain *adv* suddenly.

souder *vt* to weld.

souffle *m* puff; *(haleine)* breath; *(respiration)* breathing; *(de bombe etc)* blast.

souffler **1** *vi* to blow. **2** *vt (bougie)* to blow out; *(chuchoter)* to whisper.

souffrance(s) *f(pl)* suffering.

souffrant, -ante *adj* unwell.

souffrir* *vi* to suffer (**de** from); **faire s. qn** to hurt sb.

souhait *m* wish; **à vos souhaits!** *(après un éternuement)* bless you!, gesundheit!

souhaitable *adj* desirable.

souhaiter *vt* to wish for; **s. qch à qn** to wish sb sth; **s. faire** to hope to do; **s. que** (+ *subjonctif*) to hope that.

soûl, soûle *adj* drunk.

soulagement *m* relief.

soulager *vt* to relieve (**de** of).

soulever *vt* to lift (up); *(poussière, question)* to raise.

soulier *m* shoe.

souligner *vt* to underline; *(faire remarquer)* to emphasize.

soumettre *vt (pays, rebelles)* to subdue; *(rapport, demande)* to submit (**à** to); **s. qn à** *(assujettir)* to subject sb to.

soumis, -ise *adj (docile)* submissive; **s. à** subject to.

soupçon *m* suspicion.

soupçonner *vt* to suspect (**de** of; **d'avoir fait** of doing; **que** that).

soupe f soup.

souper 1 m supper. **2** vi to have supper.

soupir m sigh.

soupirer vi to sigh.

souple adj supple; (tolérant) flexible.

souplesse f suppleness; (tolérance) flexibility.

source f (point d'eau) spring; (origine) source; **eau de s.** spring water.

sourcil m eyebrow.

sourd, sourde 1 adj deaf; (douleur) dull; **bruit s.** thump. **2** mf deaf person.

sourd-muet, sourde-muette, pl sourds-muets, sourdes-muettes adj & mf deaf-mute.

sourire* 1 vi to smile (**à qn** at sb). **2** m smile; **faire un s. à qn** to give sb a smile.

souris f mouse (pl mice).

sournois, -oise adj sly, underhand.

sous prép (position) under(neath), beneath; **s. la pluie** in the rain; **s. Charles X** under Charles X; **s. peu** (bientôt) shortly.

sous-développé, -ée adj (pays) underdeveloped.

sous-entendre vt to imply.

sous-entendu, pl sous-entendus m insinuation.

sous-estimer vt to underestimate.

sous-marin, pl sous-marins m submarine.

sous-sol, pl sous-sols m (d'immeuble) basement.

sous-titre, pl sous-titres m subtitle.

soustraction f subtraction.

soustraire* vt (nombre) to take away, to subtract (**de** from).

sous-traitant, pl sous-traitants m subcontractor.

sous-vêtements mpl underwear.

soutenir* vt to support; **s. que** to maintain that.

soutenir (se) vpr (blessé etc) to hold oneself up.

souterrain, -aine 1 adj underground. **2** m underground passage.

soutien m support; (personne) supporter.

soutien-gorge, pl soutiens-gorge m bra.

souvenir m memory; (objet) memento; (cadeau) keepsake; (pour touristes) souvenir.

souvenir* (se) vpr se s. de to remember; **se s. que** to remember that.

souvent adv often; **peu s.** seldom; **le plus s.** usually.

soyeux, -euse adj silky.

soyez, soyons voir être.

spacieux, -euse adj spacious.

spaghetti(s) mpl spaghetti.

sparadrap m Band-Aid®.

speaker, speakerine mf (à la radio etc) announcer.

spécial, -e, -aux adj special.

spécialement adv specially.

spécialiste mf specialist.

spécialité f specialty.

spécimen m specimen.

spectacle m (vue) sight; (représentation) show.

spectaculaire adj spectacular.

spectateur, -trice mf spectator; (témoin) onlooker; **les spectateurs** (le public) the audience.

sphère f sphere.

spirale f spiral.

spirituel, -elle adj (amusant) witty.

splendide adj splendid.

spontané, -ée adj spontaneous.

sport m sport; **faire du s.** to play sports; **voiture/veste/terrain de s.** sports car/jacket/ground.

sportif, -ive 1 adj (personne) fond of sports. **2** mf sportsman, sportswoman, athlete.

spot m (lampe) spotlight; **s. (publicitaire)** commercial.

squash m (jeu) squash.

squelette m skeleton.

stable *adj* stable.

stade *m* stadium.

stage *m (cours)* (training) course; *(en entreprise)* internship.

stagiaire *mf* intern.

stand *m (d'exposition etc)* stand.

standard 1 *m (téléphonique)* switchboard. **2** *adj inv (modèle etc)* standard.

station *f* station; *(de ski etc)* resort; *(d'autobus)* stop; **s. de taxis** taxi stand.

stationnement *m* parking.

stationner *vi (se garer)* to park; *(être garé)* to be parked.

station-service, *pl* **stations-service** *f* service station, gas station.

statistique *f (donnée)* statistic.

statue *f* statue.

steak *m* steak.

stéréo *adj inv* stereo.

stériliser *vt* to sterilize.

stock *m* stock, supply (**de** of); **en s.** in stock.

stocker *vt (provisions etc)* to store.

stop 1 *int* stop. **2** *m (panneau)* stop sign; *(feu arrière)* brake light; **faire du s.** to hitchhike.

stopper *vti* to stop.

store *m* (window) shade.

stress *m inv* stress.

stressant, -ante *adj* stressful.

stressé, -ée *adj* stressed.

strict, -e *adj* strict.

strictement *adv* strictly.

string *m* thong.

structure *f* structure.

studieux, -euse *adj* studious; *(vacances)* devoted to study.

studio *m* studio; *(logement)* studio apartment.

stupéfaction *f* amazement.

stupéfait, -faite *adj* amazed (**de** at, by).

stupéfiant, -ante 1 *adj* amazing. **2** *m* drug, narcotic.

stupide *adj* stupid.

stupidité *f* stupidity; *(action, parole)* stupid thing.

style *m* style.

stylo *m* pen; **s. à bille** ballpoint (pen); **s.-plume** fountain pen.

su, sue *pp* of **savoir**.

subir *vt* to undergo; *(conséquences, défaite)* to suffer; *(influence)* to be under.

subit, -ite *adj* sudden.

subitement *adv* suddenly.

subjonctif *m Grammaire* subjunctive.

submergé, -ée *adj* flooded (**de** with); **s. de travail** overwhelmed with work.

substance *f* substance.

subtil, -e *adj* subtle.

subvention *f* subsidy.

succéder *vi* **s. à qch** to follow sth.

succéder (se) *vpr* to follow one another.

succès *m* success; **avoir du s.** to be successful.

successif, -ive *adj* successive.

succession *f (série)* sequence (**de** of).

succursale *f (de magasin)* branch; **magasin à succursales multiples** chain store.

sucer *vt* to suck.

sucette *f* lollipop; *(tétine)* pacifier.

sucre *m* sugar; *(morceau)* sugar lump; **s. cristallisé** granulated sugar; **s. en morceaux** lump sugar; **s. en poudre, s. semoule** fine sugar.

sucré, -ée *adj* sweet.

sucrer *vt* to sugar.

sucreries *fpl* candy.

sucrier *m* sugar bowl.

sud *m* south; **au s. de** south of; **du s.** *(vent)* southerly; *(ville)* southern.

sud-est *m & adj inv* southeast.

sud-ouest *m & adj inv* southwest.

suédois, -oise 1 *adj* Swedish. **2** *mf* **S.** Swede. **3** *m (langue)* Swedish.

suer *vi* to sweat; **faire s. qn** *Fam* to get on sb's nerves.

sueur *f* sweat; **en s.** sweating.

suffire* *vi* to be enough (**à** for); **ça suffit!** that's enough!; **il suffit**

d'une goutte/*etc* **pour faire** a drop/*etc* is enough to do.

suffisamment *adv* sufficiently; **s. de** enough.

suffisant, -ante *adj* sufficient.

suffocant, -ante *adj* stifling.

suggérer *vt* to suggest (**à** to; **de faire** doing; **que** (+ *subjonctif*) that).

suggestion *f* suggestion.

suicide *m* suicide.

suicider (se) *vpr* to commit suicide.

suis *voir* **être, suivre**.

suisse 1 *adj* Swiss. **2** *mf* **S.** Swiss *inv*; **les Suisses** the Swiss.

Suissesse *f* Swiss woman/girl, Swiss *inv*.

suite *f* (*reste*) rest; (*de film, roman*) sequel; (*série*) series; **faire s.** (**à**) to follow; **par la s.** afterwards; **à la s.** one after another; **à la s. de** (*événement etc*) as a result of; **de s.** (*deux jours etc*) in a row.

suivant, -ante 1 *adj* next, following. **2** *mf* next (one); **au s.!** next!

suivre* **1** *vt* to follow; (*accompagner*) to go with; (*classe*) to attend, to go to; **s. des yeux** *ou* **du regard**) to watch. **2** *vi* to follow; **faire s.** (*courrier*) to forward; **'à s.'** 'to be continued'.

suivre (se) *vpr* to follow each other.

sujet *m* (*question*), Grammaire subject; (*d'examen*) question; **au s. de** about; **à quel s.?** about what?

super 1 *adj inv* (*bon*) great. **2** *m* (*essence*) premium gas.

superbe *adj* superb.

supercherie *f* deception.

supérette *f* convenience store.

superficie *f* surface.

superficiel, -ielle *adj* superficial.

supérieur, -e *adj* upper; (*qualité etc*) superior (**à** to); (*études*) higher; **l'étage s.** the floor above.

supériorité *f* superiority.

supermarché *m* supermarket.

superposer *vt* (*objets*) to put on top of each other.

superstitieux, -euse *adj* superstitious.

superstition *f* superstition.

supplément *m* (*argent*) extra charge; **en s.** extra.

supplémentaire *adj* extra.

supplier *vt* **s. qn de faire** to beg sb to do.

support *m* support; (*d'instrument etc*) stand.

supporter¹ *vt* to bear; (*résister à*) to withstand; (*soutenir*) to support.

supporter² *m* supporter.

supposer *vti* to suppose (**que** that).

supposition *f* assumption.

suppositoire *m* suppository.

suppression *f* removal; (*de train*) cancellation.

supprimer *vt* to get rid of; (*mot*) to cut out; (*train*) to cancel.

sur *prép* on, upon; (*par-dessus*) over; (*au sujet de*) on, about; **six s. dix** six out of ten; **un jour s. deux** every other day; **six mètres s. dix** 20 by 33 feet.

sûr, sûre *adj* sure, certain (**de** of; **que** that); (*digne de confiance*) reliable; (*lieu*) safe; **c'est s. que** (+ *indicatif*) it's certain that; **s. de soi** self-assured; **bien s.!** of course!

sûrement *adv* certainly.

sûreté *f* safety; **être en s.** to be safe; **mettre en s.** to put in a safe place.

surexcité, -ée *adj* overexcited.

surf *m* surfing; **faire du s.** to go surfing.

surface *f* surface; (*dimensions*) (surface) area; (**magasin à**) **grande s.** hypermarket.

surgelé, -ée *adj* (*viande etc*) frozen.

surgelés *mpl* frozen foods.

surgir *vi* to appear suddenly (**de** from); (*problème*) to arise.

sur-le-champ *adv* immediately.

surlendemain *m* **le s.** two days

LES SUGGESTIONS, LES INVITATIONS ET LES DÉSIRS

Qu'est-ce que tu veux/vous voulez faire ?
What do you want to do?

On va prendre un café ?
Shall we go for a coffee?

Tu veux/Vous voulez allez au restaurant ?
Do you want to go to a restaurant?

Ça te/vous dit d'aller boire un verre ?
Would you like to go for a drink?

Et si on allait faire une promenade ?
How about going for a walk?

Allons nous baigner !
Let's go for a swim!

On se retrouve à midi/devant le cinéma ?
Let's meet at noon/outside the movie theater.

J'aimerais aller à la plage.
I'd like to go to the beach.

Je ne veux pas aller au musée d'art.
I don't want to go to the art gallery.

Je préférerais faire les magasins.
I'd rather go shopping.

J'ai envie d'une glace.
I feel like an ice-cream.

Je n'ai pas envie d'aller au marché.
I don't feel like going to the market.

Qu'est-ce que tu préfères/vous préférez faire ?
What would you rather do?

Je propose qu'on parte vers six heures et demie.
I think we should leave around 6.30.

J'aimerais apprendre le français.
I'd like to learn French.

J'aimerais bien habiter ici.
I wouldn't mind living here.

Ça m'est égal.
I don't mind.

C'est comme tu veux/vous voulez.
It's up to you.

Avec plaisir !
I'd love to!

C'est une bonne idée.
That's a good idea.

Je n'en ai pas envie.
I don't feel like it.

Je suis désolé(e), je ne peux pas.
I'm sorry, I can't.

Est-ce que tu es/vous êtes libre demain soir ?
Are you free tomorrow night?

Je regrette, j'ai déjà quelque chose de prévu.
I'm afraid I already have plans.

C'est très gentil.
That's very kind of you.

Merci de m'avoir invité.
Thank you for inviting me.

later; **le s. de** two days after.

surligneur *m* highlighter (pen).

surmener (se) *vpr* to overwork.

surmonter *vt (obstacle etc)* to get over.

surnom *m* nickname.

surnommer *vt* to nickname.

surpasser (se) *vpr* to surpass oneself.

surprenant, -ante *adj* surprising.

surprendre* *vt (étonner)* to surprise; *(prendre sur le fait)* to catch; *(conversation)* to overhear.

surpris, -ise *adj* surprised *(de* at; *que* (+ *subjonctif*) that); **je suis surpris de te voir** I'm surprised to see you.

surprise *f* surprise.

sursauter *vi* to jump, to start.

surtout *adv* especially; *(avant tout)* above all; **s. pas** certainly not; **s. que** especially since.

surveillant, -ante *mf (au lycée)* monitor; *(au prison)* (prison) guard.

surveiller *vt* to watch; *(contrôler)* to supervise.

survêtement *m* tracksuit.

survivant, -ante *mf* survivor.

survivre* *vi* to survive *(à qch* sth).

survoler *vt* to fly over.

susceptibilité *f* touchiness, sensitivity.

susceptible *adj* touchy, sensitive.

susciter *vt (sentiment)* to arouse; *(ennuis, obstacles)* to create.

suspect, -ecte 1 *adj* suspicious. **2** *mf* suspect.

suspendre *vt (accrocher)* to hang (up) *(à* on).

suspendre (se) *vpr* **se s. à** to hang from.

suspendu, -ue *adj* **s. à** hanging from.

suspense *m* suspense.

suspension *f (de véhicule)* suspension.

suture *f* **point de s.** stitch *(in wound)*.

SVP *abrév (s'il vous plaît)* please.

syllabe *f* syllable.

symbole *m* symbol.

symbolique *adj* symbolic.

sympa *adj inv Fam* = **sympathique**.

sympathie *f* liking; **avoir de la s. pour qn** to be fond of sb.

sympathique *adj* nice, pleasant.

sympathiser *vi* to get along well *(avec* with).

symphonie *f* symphony.

symptôme *m* symptom.

synagogue *f* synagogue.

syndicat *m (d'ouvriers)* (labor) union; **s. d'initiative** tourist (information) office.

syndiqué, -ée *mf* union member.

synonyme 1 *adj* synonymous *(de* with). **2** *m* synonym.

système *m* system.

T

ta *voir* **ton**.

tabac *m* tobacco; *(magasin)* tobacco store.

table *f* table; *(d'école)* desk; **t. de nuit** bedside table; **t. basse** coffee table; **t. à repasser** ironing board; **t. roulante** (serving) cart; **t. des matières** table (of contents); **à t.** sitting at the table; **à t.!** (food's) ready!

tableau, -x *m (image)* picture; *(panneau)* board; *(liste)* list; *(graphique)* chart; **t. (noir)** (black) board; **t. d'affichage** bulletin board; **t. de bord** dashboard.

tablette *f (de chocolat)* bar; *(petite planche)* shelf.

tablier *m* apron; *(d'écolier)* smock.

tabouret *m* stool.

tache *f* spot; *(salissure)* stain.

tâche f task, job; **tâches ménagères** housework.

tacher vti, **se tacher** vpr to stain.

tâcher vi t. **de faire** to try to do.

tact m tact; **avoir du t.** to be tactful.

tactique f **la t.** tactics; **une t.** a tactic.

tag m graffiti tag.

taie d'oreiller f pillowcase.

taille f (hauteur) height; (dimension, mesure) size; (ceinture) waist; **tour de t.** waist measurement.

taille-crayon, pl **taille-crayons** m pencil sharpener.

tailler vt to cut; (haie, barbe) to trim; (arbre) to prune; (crayon) to sharpen.

tailleur m (personne) tailor; (vêtement) suit.

taire* (se) vpr (ne rien dire) to keep quiet (**sur qch** about sth); (cesser de parler) to stop talking; **tais-toi!** be quiet!

talent m talent; **avoir du t. pour** to have a talent for.

talentueux, -euse adj talented.

talon m heel; (de chèque, carnet) stub.

talus m slope, embankment.

tambour m drum; (personne) drummer.

tambourin m tambourine.

tamis m sieve.

tamiser vt (farine) to sift.

tampon m (marque, instrument) stamp; (de coton) wad; **t. hygiénique** tampon; **t. à récurer** scrubbing pad.

tamponner vt (lettre, document) to stamp; (visage) to dab; (plaie) to swab; (train, voiture) to crash into.

tandis que conj while.

tant adv (travailler etc) so much (**que** that); **t. de** (temps etc) so much (**que** that); (gens etc) so many (**que** that); **t. que** (aussi longtemps que) as long as; **t. mieux!** good!; **t. pis!** too bad!

tante f aunt.

tantôt adv **t.... t....** sometimes... sometimes...

tapage m din, uproar.

tape f slap.

taper[1] **1** vt (enfant, cuisse) to slap; (table) to bang. **2** vi t. **sur qch** to bang on sth; **t. du pied** to stamp one's foot.

taper[2] vti **t.** (à la machine) to type.

tapis m carpet; **t. roulant** (pour marchandises) conveyor belt.

tapisser vt (mur) to (wall)paper.

tapisserie f (papier peint) wallpaper; (broderie) tapestry.

tapoter vt to tap; (joue) to pat.

taquiner vt to tease.

tard adv late; **plus t.** later (on); **au plus t.** at the latest.

tarder vi **t. à faire** to take one's time doing; **elle ne va pas t.** she won't be long; **sans t.** without delay.

tardif, -ive adj late; (regrets) belated.

tarif m (prix) rate; (de train) fare; (tableau) price list.

tarte f (open) pie, tart.

tartine f slice of bread; **t. (de beurre/de confiture)** slice of bread and butter/jam.

tartiner vt (beurre etc) to spread.

tas m pile, heap; **un** ou **des t. de** (beaucoup) Fam lots of; **mettre en t.** to pile ou heap up.

tasse f cup; **t. à café** coffee cup; **t. à thé** teacup.

tasser vt to pack, to squeeze (**dans** into).

tasser (se) vpr (se serrer) to squeeze together.

tâter vt to feel.

tâtonner vi to grope around.

tâtons (à) adv **avancer à t.** to feel one's way (along); **chercher à t.** to grope for.

tatouage m (dessin) tattoo.

tatouer vt to tattoo.

taudis m slum.

taupe f mole.

taureau, -x m bull.

taux *m* rate; **t. d'alcool** alcohol level.

taxe *f (impôt)* tax; *(de douane)* duty; **t. à la valeur ajoutée** sales tax.

taxé, -ée *adj* taxed.

taxi *m* taxi.

te (**t'** before vowel or mute *h*) *pron (complément direct)* you; *(indirect)* (to) you; *(réfléchi)* yourself.

technicien, -ienne *mf* technicien.

technique 1 *adj* technical. **2** *f* technique.

technologie *f* technology.

tee-shirt *m* tee-shirt.

teindre* *vt* to dye; **t. en rouge** to dye red.

teindre (se) *vpr* to dye one's hair.

teint *m* complexion.

teinte *f* shade.

teinture *f (produit)* dye.

teinturerie *f (boutique)* (dry) cleaner's.

teinturier, -ière *mf* (dry) cleaner.

tel, telle *adj* such; **un t. livre/etc** such a book/etc; **un t. intérêt/etc** such interest/etc; **de tels mots/ etc**, such words/etc; **rien de t. que** (there's) nothing like.

télé *f* TV; **à la t.** on TV.

téléchargement *m* download.

télécharger *vt* to download.

télécommande *f* remote control.

télécopie *f* fax.

télécopieur *m* fax (machine).

téléfilm *m* TV movie.

télégramme *m* telegram.

téléphérique *m* cable car.

téléphone *m* (tele)phone; **coup de t.** (phone) call; **passer un coup de t. à qn** to give sb a call; **au t.** on the (tele)phone.

téléphoner *vi* to (tele)phone; **t. à qn** to (tele)phone sb.

téléphonique *adj* **appel/etc t.** (tele)phone call/etc.

télescope *m* telescope.

télésiège *m* chair lift.

téléspectateur, -trice *mf* (television) viewer.

télévisé *adj* **journal t.** television news.

téléviseur *m* television (set).

télévision *f* television; **à la t.** on (the) television; **t. en circuit fermé** CCTV.

telle *voir* **tel**.

tellement *adv (si)* so; *(tant)* so much; **t. de** *(travail etc)* so much; *(soucis etc)* so many; **pas t.!** not much!

téméraire *adj* reckless.

témoignage *m* evidence; *(récit)* account.

témoigner *vi* to give evidence (**contre** against).

témoin *m* witness; **être t. de** to witness.

température *f* temperature; **avoir de la t.** to have a fever.

tempête *f* storm; **t. de neige** snowstorm.

temple *m (romain, grec)* temple.

temporaire *adj* temporary.

temps¹ *m* time; *(de verbe)* tense; **il est t. (de faire)** it's time (to do); **ces derniers t.** lately; **de t. en t.** from time to time; **à t.** *(arriver)* in time; **à plein t.** *(travailler)* full-time; **à t. partiel** *(travailler)* part-time; **dans le t.** *(autrefois)* once.

temps² *m (climat)* weather; **quel t. fait-il?** what's the weather like?

tenailles *fpl (outil)* pincers.

tendance *f* tendency; **avoir t. à faire** to tend to do.

tendeur *m (à bagages)* bungee (cord).

tendre¹ *vt* to stretch; *(main)* to hold out (**à qn** to sb); *(bras, jambe)* to stretch out; *(piège)* to set, to lay; **t. qch à qn** to hold out sth to sb; **t. l'oreille** to prick up one's ears.

tendre² *adj (viande etc)* tender; *(personne)* affectionate (**avec** to).

tendrement *adv* tenderly.

tendresse *f* affection.

TÉLÉPHONER

Allô ?
Hello?

Allô, Alain Petit à l'appareil ?
Hello, Alain Petit speaking?

Salut Claire, c'est Alex.
Hi Claire, it's Alex.

Éditions Libro, bonjour !
Good morning/afternoon, Éditions Libro!

Bonjour, pouvez-vous me passer le service clientèle, s'il vous plaît ?
Hello, could you put me through to Customer Services, please?

Est-ce que je peux parler à Steve Brown, s'il vous plaît ? C'est Julie Rey de la part de CPS.
Can I speak to Steve Brown, please? This is Julie Rey from CPS.

C'est moi !
Speaking!

C'est de la part de qui ?
Who's calling, please?

Vous pouvez répéter/l'épeler ?
Could you repeat that/spell it?

Un instant, je vais le/la chercher.
Just a moment, I'll get him/her.

Ne quittez pas, je vous le/la passe.
Hold the line please, I'll put you through.

Je regrette, elle est en réunion/elle n'est pas là.
I'm afraid she's in a meeting/she's not here.

Ça sonne occupé, voulez-vous patienter ?
The line's busy, would you like to hold?

Ça ne répond pas.
There's no reply.

Voulez-vous laisser un message ?
Would you like to leave a message?

Veuillez laisser un message après le bip.
Please leave a message after the tone.

Non merci, je rappellerai plus tard.
No thanks, I'll call back later.

Vous pouvez lui dire que j'ai appelé ?
Could you tell him/her I called?

Pouvez-vous lui demander de me rappeler dès que possible ?
Can you ask him/her to call me back as soon as possible?

Mon numéro est le quarante-deux, trente-cinq, cinquante-neuf, zéro-un.
My number is 42-35-59-01.

Merci d'avoir appelé.
Thank you for calling.

On s'appelle !
Talk to you later!

Je peux avoir votre/ton numéro?
Can I take your number?

Vous pouvez/Tu peux me joindre sur mon portable.
You can reach me on my cell.

Je vous/t'envoie un SMS plus tard.
I'll text you later.

Je ne capte pas ici.
I can't get a signal in here.

Il ne me reste plus beaucoup de crédit.
I don't have many minutes left.

J'ai besoin de recharger mon portable.
I need to charge my cellphone.

Vous vous êtes trompé(e) de numéro.
You've got the wrong number.

Désolé(e), j'ai dû me tromper de numéro.
Sorry, I must have the wrong number.

Je vous/t'entends très mal.
I can barely hear you.

On a été coupés.
We got cut off.

Est-ce qu'il y a une cabine téléphonique par ici ?
Is there a payphone around here?

Je voudrais appeler en PCV.
I'd like to call collect.

tendu, -ue *adj* (corde) tight; (personne, situation, muscle) tense; (main) held out.

tenir* **1** *vt* to hold; (promesse, comptes, hôtel) to keep; (rôle) to play; **t. sa droite** (conducteur) to keep to the right. **2** *vi* to hold; (résister) to hold out; **t. à** (personne, jouet etc) to be attached to; **t. à faire** to be anxious to do; **t. dans qch** (être contenu) to fit into sth; **tenez!** (prenez) here (you are)!; **tiens!** (surprise) well!

tenir (se) *upr* (avoir lieu) to be held; **se t. (debout)** to stand (up); **se t. droit** to stand up *ou* sit up straight; **se t. par la main** to hold hands; **se t. bien** to behave oneself.

tennis *m* tennis; (terrain) (tennis) court; (chaussure) sneaker; **t. de table** table tennis.

tension *f* tension; **t. (artérielle)** blood pressure; **avoir de la t.** to have high blood pressure.

tentant, -ante *adj* tempting.

tentation *f* temptation.

tentative *f* attempt.

tente *f* tent.

tenter[1] *vt* to try (**de faire** to do).

tenter[2] *vt* (faire envie à) to tempt.

tenue *f* (vêtements) clothes; (conduite) (good) behavior; **t. de soirée** evening dress.

tergal® *m* Dacron®.

terme *m* (mot) term; (fin) end; **mettre un t. à** to put an end to; **à court/long t.** (conséquences) short-/long-term; **en bons/mauvais termes** on good/bad terms (avec with).

terminaison *f* (de mot) ending.

terminal, -e, -aux **1** *adj & f* (classe) **terminale** = senior year. **2** *m* **t.** (d'ordinateur) (computer) terminal.

terminer *vt* to end.

terminer (se) *vpr* to end (par with; en in).

terne *adj* dull.

terrain *m* ground; (étendue) land; (à bâtir) plot; Football etc field; **t. de camping** campsite; **t. de jeux** (pour enfants) playground; (stade) playing field; **t. vague** vacant lot.

terrasse *f* terrace; (de café) sidewalk area.

terre *f* (matière, monde) earth; (sol) ground; (opposé à mer) land; **par t.** (poser, tomber) to the ground; (assis, couché) on the ground; **sous t.** underground.

terre-à-terre *adj inv* down-to-earth.

terrestre *adj* **la surface t.** the earth's surface; **globe t.** globe (model).

terreur *f* terror.

terrible *adj* awful, terrible; (formidable) Fam terrific.

terrifiant, -ante *adj* terrifying.

terrifier *vt* to terrify.

territoire *m* territory.

terroir *m* (sol) soil; (région) region.

terroriser *vt* to terrorize.

terroriste *adj & mf* terrorist.

tes *voir* **ton**.

test *m* test.

testament *m* (en droit) will.

tester *vt* to test.

tête *f* head; (visage) face; (d'arbre) top; **tenir t. à** to stand up to; **faire la t.** to sulk; **à la t. de** (entreprise) at the head of; (classe) at the top *ou* head of; **en t.** (sportif) in the lead.

tête-à-tête *adv* (**en**) **t.** alone together.

téter **1** *vt* to suck. **2** *vi* **le bébé tète** the baby is feeding; **donner à t. à** to feed.

tétine *f* (de biberon) nipple; (sucette) pacifier.

têtu, -ue *adj* stubborn.

texte *m* text.

textile *adj & m* textile.

texto *m* text (message); **envoyer un t. à qn** to text sb, to send sb a text.

TGV *m abrév* = **train à grande vitesse**.

thé *m* tea.

théâtre *m* theater; *(œuvres)* drama; **faire du t.** to act.

théière *f* teapot.

théorie *f* theory; **en t.** in theory.

thérapie *f* therapy.

thermomètre *m* thermometer.

thermos® *m ou f* Thermos®.

thermostat *m* thermostat.

thèse *f (proposition, ouvrage)* thesis.

thon *m* tuna (fish).

tibia *m* shin (bone).

ticket *m* ticket.

tiède *adj* (luke)warm.

tien, tienne *pron poss* **le t., la tienne, les tien(ne)s** yours; **les deux tiens** your two.

tiens, tient *voir* tenir.

tiercé *m* **jouer/gagner au t.** = to bet/win on the horses.

tiers *m (fraction)* third.

tiers-monde *m* **le t.** the Third World.

tige *f (de plante)* stem; *(barre)* rod.

tigre *m* tiger.

tilleul *m (arbre)* lime tree; *(infusion)* lime blossom tea.

timbre *m* stamp.

timbre-poste, *pl* **timbres-poste** *m* (postage) stamp.

timbrer *vt (lettre)* to stamp.

timide *adj* shy.

timidement *adv* shyly.

timidité *f* shyness.

tinter *vi (cloche)* to ring; *(clefs)* to jingle.

tir *m* shooting; *Sport* shot; **t. à arc** archery.

tirage *m (de journal)* circulation; *(de loterie)* draw; **t. au sort** drawing of lots.

tire-bouchon, *pl* **tire-bouchons** *m* corkscrew.

tirelire *f* coin bank.

tirer 1 *vt* to pull; *(langue)* to stick out; *(trait, rideaux)* to draw; *(balle,*

canon) to shoot; **t. de** *(sortir)* to pull *ou* draw out of; *(obtenir)* to get from; **t. qn de** *(danger, lit)* to get sb out of. **2** *vi* to pull *(sur* on, at*)*; *(faire feu)* to shoot *(sur* at*)*; *Sport* to shoot; **t. au sort** to draw lots; **t. à sa fin** to draw to a close.

tirer (se) *vpr* **se t. de** *(travail)* to cope with; *(situation)* to get out of; **se t. d'affaire** to get out of trouble.

tiret *m (trait)* dash.

tireur *m (au fusil)* gunman.

tiroir *m* drawer.

tisane *f* herbal tea.

tisonnier *m* poker.

tisser *vt* to weave.

tissu *m* material, cloth; **du t.-éponge** toweling.

titre *m* title; *(gros) t. (de journal)* headline; **à t. d'exemple** as an example; **à juste t.** rightly.

tituber *vi* to stagger.

titulaire 1 *adj (enseignant)* tenured; **être t. de** *(permis)* to be the holder of; *(poste)* to hold. **2** *mf (de permis, de poste)* holder (**de** of).

toast *m (pain grillé)* piece *ou* slice of toast.

toboggan *m* slide; *(pour voitures)* overpass.

toc *int* **t. t.!** knock knock!

toi *pron (complément, sujet)* you; *(réfléchi)* **assieds-t.** sit (yourself) down; **dépêche-t.** hurry up.

toile *f* cloth; *(à voile, sac etc)* canvas; *(tableau)* painting; **t. d'araignée** spider's web.

toilette *f (action)* wash(ing); *(vêtements)* clothes; **eau de t.** eau de toilette; **faire sa t.** to wash (and dress); **les toilettes** the bathroom, the men's/ladies' room; **aller aux toilettes** to go to the bathroom *ou* to the men's/ladies' room.

toi-même *pron* yourself.

toit *m* roof; **t. ouvrant** *(de voiture)* sunroof.

tôle *f* **une t.** a piece of sheet metal; **t. ondulée** corrugated iron.

tolérant, -ante adj tolerant (**à l'égard de** of).

tolérer vt to tolerate.

tomate f tomato.

tombe f grave.

tombeau, -x m tomb.

tombée f **t. de la nuit** nightfall.

tomber vi (aux **être**) to fall; **t. malade** to fall ill; **t. (par terre)** to fall (down); **faire t. (personne)** to knock over; **laisser t.** to drop; **tu tombes bien/mal** you've come at the right/wrong time; **t. sur (trouver)** to come across.

tombola f raffle.

ton, ta, pl **tes** (**ta** becomes **ton** before a vowel or mute h) adj poss your; **t. père** your father; **ta mère** your mother; **t. ami(e)** your friend.

ton m (de voix etc) tone.

tonalité f (téléphonique) dial tone.

tondeuse f **t. (à gazon)** (lawn)-mower.

tondre vt (gazon) to mow.

tongs fpl thongs, flip-flops.

tonne f metric ton; **des tonnes de (beaucoup)** Fam tons of.

tonneau, -x m barrel.

tonner vi **il tonne** it's thundering.

tonnerre m thunder; **coup de t.** clap of thunder.

tonton m Fam uncle.

top model m supermodel.

torche f (flamme) torch; **t. électrique** flashlight.

torchon m (à vaisselle) dish towel; (de ménage) dust cloth.

tordre vt to twist; (linge) to wring (out); (barre) to bend.

tordre (se) vpr to twist; (barre) to bend; **se t. la cheville** to twist ou sprain one's ankle, **se t. de douleur** to be doubled up with pain; **se t. (de rire)** to split one's sides (laughing).

tordu, -ue adj twisted; (esprit) warped.

torrent m (mountain) stream; **il pleut à torrents** it's pouring (down).

torse m chest; **t. nu** stripped to the waist.

tort m **avoir t.** to be wrong (**de faire** to do, in doing); **être dans son t.** to be in the wrong; **donner t. à qn (accuser)** to blame sb; **à t.** wrongly; **parler à t. et à travers** to talk nonsense.

torticolis m **avoir le t.** to have a stiff neck.

tortiller vt to twist, to twirl.

tortue f turtle.

torture f torture.

torturer vt to torture.

tôt adv early; **le plus t. possible** as soon as possible; **t. ou tard** sooner or later; **je n'étais pas plus t. sorti que** no sooner had I gone out than.

total, -e, -aux adj & m total.

totalement adv totally.

totaliser vt to total.

totalité f **en t. (détruit etc)** entirely; (payé) fully.

touchant, -ante adj moving; touching.

touche f (de clavier) key; (de téléphone) (push-)button; **téléphone à touches** touch-tone phone.

toucher 1 vt to touch; (paie) to draw; (chèque) to cash; (cible) to hit; (émouvoir) to touch, to move. **2** vi **t. à** to touch. **3** m (sens) touch.

toucher (se) vpr (lignes, mains etc) to touch.

touffe f (de cheveux, d'herbe) tuft.

toujours adv always; (encore) still; **pour t.** for ever.

tour¹ f tower; (immeuble) high-rise; Echecs castle, rook.

tour² m turn; (de magie etc) trick; **t. de poitrine/etc** chest/etc measurement; **faire le t. de** to go around; **faire un t.** to go for a walk; (en voiture) to go for a drive; (voyage) to go on a trip; **jouer un t. à qn** to play a trick on sb; **c'est mon t.** it's my turn; **à t. de rôle** in turn.

tourbillon m (de vent) whirlwind; (d'eau) whirlpool; (de sable) swirl.

tourisme *m* tourism; **faire du t.** to go sightseeing.

touriste *mf* tourist.

touristique *adj* **guide/etc t.** tourist guide/*etc.*

tourmenter (se) *vpr* to worry.

tournage *m (de film)* shooting.

tournant *m (de route)* bend.

tourne-disque *m* record player.

tournée *f (de livreur, boissons)* round; *(de spectacle)* tour.

tourner 1 *vt* to turn; *(film)* to shoot. **2** *vi* to turn; *(tête)* to spin; *(moteur)* to run; *(lait)* to go off; **t. autour de** *(objet)* to go around.

tourner (se) *vpr* to turn (**vers** to).

tournesol *m* sunflower.

tournevis *m* screwdriver.

tournoi *m* tournament.

Toussaint *f* All Saints' Day.

tousser *vi* to cough.

tout, toute, *pl* **tous, toutes 1** *adj* all; **tous les livres** all the books; **l'argent/le temps** all the money/time; **t. le village** the whole village; **toute la nuit** all night; **tous (les) deux** both; **tous les trois** all three. ■ *(chaque)* every; **tous les ans** every *ou* each year; **tous les cinq mois/mètres** every five months/16 feet. **2** *pron pl* all; **ils sont tous là** they're all there. **3** *pron m sing* everything; **t. ce que** everything that, all that; **en t.** *(au total)* in all. **4** *adv (tout à fait)* quite, very; **t. simplement** quite simply; **t. petit** very small; **t. neuf** brand new; **t. seul** all alone; **t. autour** all around; **t. en chantant/etc** while singing/etc; **t. à coup** suddenly; **t. à fait** completely; **t. de même** all the same; **t. de suite** at once. **5** *m* **le t.** everything; **pas du t.** not at all; **rien du t.** nothing at all.

toutefois *adv* nevertheless, however.

toux *f* cough.

toxique *adj* poisonous.

trac *m* **avoir le t.** to be *ou* become nervous.

tracasser *vt*, **se tracasser** *vpr* to worry.

trace *f* trace (**de** of); *(marque)* mark; **traces** *(de bête, pneus)* tracks; **traces de pas** footprints.

tracer *vt (dessiner)* to draw.

tracteur *m* tractor.

tradition *f* tradition.

traditionnel, -elle *adj* traditional.

traducteur, -trice *mf* translator.

traduction *f* translation.

traduire* *vt* to translate (**de** from; **en** into).

trafic *m* traffic.

trafiquant, -ante *mf* trafficker, dealer.

tragédie *f* tragedy.

tragique *adj* tragic.

trahir *vt* to betray.

trahir (se) *vpr* to give oneself away.

trahison *f* betrayal.

train¹ *m* train; **t. à grande vitesse** high-speed train; **t. couchettes** sleeper.

train² *m* **être en t. de faire** to be (busy) doing.

traîneau, -x *m* sled.

traînée *f (de peinture etc)* streak.

traîner 1 *vt* to drag. **2** *vi (jouets etc)* to lie around; *(s'attarder)* to lag behind; **t. (par terre)** *(robe etc)* to trail (on the ground).

traîner (se) *vpr (par terre)* to crawl.

train-train *m* routine.

traire* *vt* to milk.

trait *m* line; *(en dessinant)* stroke; *(caractéristique)* feature; **t. d'union** hyphen.

traité *m (accord)* treaty; *(ouvrage)* treatise (**sur** on); **t. de paix** peace treaty.

traitement *m* treatment; *(salaire)* salary; **t. de texte** word processing; **machine de t. de texte** word processor.

traiter 1 *vt* to treat; *(problème)* to deal with; **t. qn de lâche/etc** to call sb a coward/*etc.* **2** *vi* **t. de** (*sujet*) to deal with.

traiteur *m* **chez le t.** at the delicatessen.

traître *m* traitor.

trajectoire *f* path.

trajet *m* trip; (*distance*) distance; (*itinéraire*) route.

tramway *m* streetcar, trolley.

tranchant, -ante *adj* (*couteau, voix*) sharp.

tranche *f* (*morceau*) slice.

tranchée *f* trench.

trancher *vt* to cut.

tranquille *adj* quiet; (*mer*) calm; (*conscience*) clear; **laisser t.** to leave alone.

tranquillement *adv* calmly.

tranquillisant *m* tranquilizer.

tranquilliser *vt* to reassure.

tranquillité *f* (peace and) quiet.

transat *m* (*chaise*) deckchair.

transférer *vt* to transfer (**à** to).

transfert *m* transfer.

transformation *f* change.

transformer *vt* to change; (*maison*) to remodel; **t. en** to turn into.

transfusion *f* **t. (sanguine)** (blood) transfusion.

transgresser *vt* (*ordres*) to disobey; (*loi*) to infringe.

transistor *m* transistor (radio).

transitif, -ive *adj* Grammaire transitive.

transmettre* *vt* (*message etc*) to pass on (**à** to).

transparent, -ente *adj* clear, transparent.

transpercer *vt* to pierce.

transpiration *f* sweat.

transpirer *vi* to sweat.

transport *m* transportation (**de** of); **moyen de t.** means of transportation; **les transports en commun** public transportation.

transporter *vt* to transport; (*à la main*) to carry; **t. d'urgence à l'hôpital** to rush to the hospital.

trappe *f* trap door.

trapu, -ue *adj* (*personne*) stocky, thickset.

traquer *vt* to hunt (down).

traumatisant, -ante *adj* traumatic.

traumatisme *m* (*choc*) trauma.

travail, -aux *m* (*activité, lieu*) work; (*à effectuer*) job, task; (*emploi*) job; **travaux** (*dans la rue*) roadwork, construction; (*aménagement*) alterations; **travaux pratiques** (*à l'école etc*) practical work.

travailler *vi* to work (**à qch** at ou on sth).

travailleur, -euse 1 *adj* hardworking. **2** *mf* worker.

travers 1 *prép & adv* **à t.** through; **en t.** (**de**) across. **2** *adv* **de t.** (*chapeau etc*) crooked; (*comprendre*) badly; **j'ai avalé de t.** it went down the wrong way.

traversée *f* crossing.

traverser *vt* to cross, to go across; (*foule, période*) to go through.

traversin *m* bolster.

trébucher *vi* to stumble (**sur** over); **faire t. qn** to trip sb (up).

trèfle *m* Cartes clubs.

treize *adj & m inv* thirteen.

treizième *adj & mf* thirteenth.

tréma *m* dieresis.

tremblement *m* shaking, trembling; **t. de terre** earthquake.

trembler *vi* to shake, to tremble (**de** with).

tremper 1 *vt* to soak; (*plonger*) to dip (**dans** in). **2** *vi* to soak; **faire t. qch** to soak sth.

tremplin *m* springboard.

trentaine *f* **une t. (de)** about thirty.

trente *adj & m* thirty; **un t.-trois tours** an album.

trentième *adj & mf* thirtieth.

très *adv* very; **t. aimé**/*etc* (*with past participle*) much ou greatly liked/*etc.*

trésor *m* treasure.

tresse *f* (*cheveux*) braid.

tresser *vt* to braid.

tri *m* sorting (out); **faire le t. de** to

sort (out); **centre de t.** *(des postes)* sorting office.

triangle *m* triangle.

triangulaire *adj* triangular.

tribu *f* tribe.

tribunal, -aux *m* court.

tribune *f (de stade)* (grand)stand.

tricher *vi* to cheat.

tricheur, -euse *mf* cheater.

tricolore *adj* red, white and blue; **feu t.** traffic light.

tricot *m (activité)* knitting; *(chandail)* sweater.

tricoter *vti* to knit.

tricycle *m* tricycle.

trier *vt* to sort (out).

trimestre *m (période)* quarter; *(scolaire)* term.

trimestriel, -ielle *adj (revue)* quarterly; **bulletin t.** (quarter) report card.

tringle *f* rail, rod.

trinquer *vi* to clink glasses; **t. à la santé de qn** to drink to sb's health.

triomphe *m* triumph (**sur** over).

triompher *vi* to triumph (**de** over).

triple *m* **le t.** three times as much (**de** as).

tripler *vti* to treble, to triple.

tripoter *vt* to fiddle around with.

triste *adj* sad; *(couleur, temps)* gloomy.

tristement *adv* sadly.

tristesse *f* sadness; *(du temps)* gloom(iness).

trivial, -e, -aux *adj* coarse, vulgar.

trognon *m (de fruit)* core.

trois *adj & m* three.

troisième *adj & mf* third.

troisièmement *adv* thirdly.

trombone *m* trombone; *(agrafe)* paper clip.

trompe *f (d'éléphant)* trunk.

tromper *vt* to deceive; *(être infidèle à)* to be unfaithful to.

tromper (se) *vpr* to be mistaken; **se t. de route/etc** to take the wrong road/etc, **se t. de date/etc** to get the date/etc wrong.

trompette *f* trumpet.

trompeur, -euse *adj (apparences)* deceptive, misleading; *(personne)* deceitful.

tronc *m* trunk.

tronçonneuse *f* chain saw.

trône *m* throne.

trop *adv* too; too much; **t. dur/etc** too hard/etc; **t. fatigué pour jouer** too tired to play; **boire/etc t.** to drink/etc too much; **t. de sel/etc** *(quantité)* too much salt/etc; **t. de gens/etc** *(nombre)* too many people/etc; **un euro/etc de t.** *ou* **en t.** one euro/etc too many.

tropical, -e, -aux *adj* tropical.

trot *m* trot; **aller au t.** to trot.

trotter *vi (cheval)* to trot.

trottinette *f (jouet)* scooter.

trottoir *m* sidewalk.

trou *m* hole; **t. de (la) serrure** keyhole; **t. (de mémoire)** lapse (of memory).

troublant, -ante *adj (détail)* disturbing, disquieting.

trouble *adj (liquide)* cloudy; *(image)* blurred; **voir t.** to see things blurred.

troubler *vt* to disturb; *(vue)* to blur.

troubles *mpl (de santé)* trouble; *(désordres)* disturbances.

trouer *vt* to make a hole *ou* holes in.

troupe *f (groupe)* group; *(de théâtre)* company; **troupes** *(armée)* troops.

troupeau, -x *m (vaches)* herd; *(moutons, oies)* flock.

trousse *f (étui)* case, kit; *(d'écolier)* pencil case; **t. à outils** toolkit; **t. à pharmacie** first-aid kit; **t. de toilette** *(de femme)* cosmetic case; *(d'homme)* shaving kit.

trousseau, -x *m (de clefs)* bunch.

trouver *vt* to find; **aller/venir t. qn** to go/come and see sb; **je trouve que** I think that.

trouver (se) *vpr* to be; *(être situé)* to be located; *(se sentir)* to feel; *(dans une situation)* to find oneself.

truc *m (astuce)* trick; *(moyen)* way; *(chose) Fam* thing.

truite f trout.

truquer vt (photo) to fake; (élections, match) to rig.

TTC abrév (toutes taxes comprises) inclusive of tax.

tu pron you (familiar form of address).

tu, tue voir **taire**.

tuba m (instrument de musique) tuba; (de plongée) snorkel.

tube m tube; (chanson) Fam hit.

tuberculose f TB.

tue-tête (à) adv at the top of one's voice.

tuer vti to kill.

tuer (se) vpr to kill oneself; (dans un accident) to be killed.

tuile f tile.

tulipe f tulip.

tunisien, -ienne 1 adj Tunisian. **2** mf T. Tunisian.

tunnel m tunnel.

turbulent, -ente adj (enfant) disruptive.

tutoyer vt t. qn to use the familiar tu form with sb.

tutu m tutu, ballet skirt.

tuyau, -x m pipe; **t. d'arrosage** hose(pipe); **t. d'échappement** tailpipe.

TVA f abrév (taxe à la valeur ajoutée) sales tax.

type m type; (individu) fellow, guy.

typique adj typical (**de** of).

tzigane 1 adj gipsy. **2** mf T. gipsy.

U

UE f abrév (Union Européenne) EU.

ulcère m ulcer.

ULM m inv abrév (ultraléger motorisé) microlight.

ultérieurement adv later (on), subsequently.

ultime adj last; (préparatifs) final.

ultramoderne adj ultramodern.

ultra-secret, -ète adj top-secret.

un, une 1 art indéf a; (devant voyelle) an; **une page** a page; **un ange** an angel. **2** adj one; **la page un** page one; **un mètre** one metre. **3** pron & mf one; **l'un** one; **les uns** some; **j'en ai un** I have one; **l'un d'eux, l'une d'elles** one of them; **la une** (de journal) the front page.

unanime adj unanimous.

unanimité f à l'u. unanimously.

uni, -ie adj united; (famille) close; (surface) smooth; (couleur) plain.

unième adj (after a number) (-)first; **trente et u.** thirty-first; **cent u.** hundred and first.

uniforme m uniform.

union f union.

Union Européenne f European Union.

unique adj (fille, espoir etc) only; (prix, marché) single; (exceptionnel) unique.

uniquement adv only.

unir vt (efforts, forces) to combine; (deux pays etc) to unite, to join together; **u. deux personnes** (amitié) to unite two people.

unir (s') vpr (étudiants etc) to unite.

unité f (mesure, élément) unit.

univers m universe.

universel, -elle adj universal.

universitaire adj ville/etc u. university town/etc.

université f university; **à l'u.** at college, at school.

urgence f (cas) emergency; (de décision etc) urgency; **faire qch d'u.** to do sth urgently; **(service des) urgences** (d'hôpital) emergency room.

urgent, -ente adj urgent.

urne f ballot box; **aller aux urnes** to go to the polls, to vote.

usage m use; (habitude) custom;

faire u. de to make use of; **hors d'u.** not in service.

usagé, -ée adj worn.

usager m user.

usé, -ée adj (tissu etc) worn (out).

user vt, **s'user** vpr (vêtement) to wear out.

usine f factory.

ustensile m utensil.

usuel, -elle adj everyday.

usure f wear (and tear).

utile adj useful (à to).

utilisateur, -trice mf user.

utilisation f use.

utiliser vt to use.

utilité f use(fulness); **d'une grande u.** very useful.

V

va voir **aller¹**.

vacances fpl vacation; **en v.** on vacation; **les grandes v.** the summer vacation.

vacancier, -ière mf vacationer.

vacarme m din, uproar.

vaccin m vaccine; **faire un v. à** to vaccinate.

vaccination f vaccination.

vacciner vt to vaccinate.

vache 1 f cow. **2** adj (méchant) Fam mean.

vachement adv Fam (très) damned; (beaucoup) a hell of a lot.

vaciller vi to sway; (flamme, lumière) to flicker.

vagabond, -onde mf tramp, hobo.

vague 1 adj vague; (regard) vacant. **2** f wave; **v. de chaleur** heat wave; **v. de froid** cold spell.

vaguement adv vaguely.

vain (en) adv in vain.

vaincre* vt to beat.

vaincu, -ue mf (sportif) loser.

vainqueur m (sportif) winner.

vais voir **aller¹**.

vaisselle f dishes; (à laver) dirty dishes; **faire la v.** to wash the dishes.

valable adj (billet etc) valid.

valet m Cartes jack.

valeur f value; **avoir de la v.** to be valuable; **objets de v.** valuables.

valide adj (personne) fit, ablebodied; (billet) valid.

valise f (suit)case; **faire ses valises** to pack (one's bags).

vallée f valley.

valoir* vi to be worth; **v. cher** to be worth a lot; **un vélo vaut bien une auto** a bicycle is just as good as a car; **il vaut mieux rester** it's better to stay; **il vaut mieux que j'attende** I'd better wait; **ça ne vaut rien** it's no good; **ça vaut le coup** it's worth it (**de faire** to do).

valoir (se) vpr to be as good as each other; **ça se vaut** it's all the same.

valse f waltz.

vandale mf vandal.

vanille f vanilla; **glace à la v.** vanilla ice cream.

vaniteux, -euse adj conceited.

vantard, -arde mf braggart.

vanter (se) vpr to boast (**de** about, of).

vapeur f v. (d'eau) steam.

vaporisateur m (appareil) spray.

variable adj (humeur, temps) changeable.

varicelle f chicken pox.

varié, -ée adj varied; (divers) various.

varier vti to vary.

variété f variety; **spectacle de variétés** variety show.

vas voir **aller¹**.

vase m vase.

vaste adj vast, huge.

vaut voir **valoir**.

veau, -x m calf; (viande) veal;

(cuir) calfskin, (calf) leather.

vécu, -ue *(pp of* **vivre***) adj (histoire etc)* true.

vedette *f (de cinéma etc)* star.

végétarien, -ienne *adj & mf* vegetarian.

végétation *f* vegetation.

véhicule *m* vehicle; **v. tout terrain** all-terrain *ou* four-wheel drive vehicle.

veille *f* **la v. (de)** the day before; **la v. de Noël** Christmas Eve.

veiller *vi* to stay up; *(sentinelle)* to keep watch; **v. à qch** to see to sth; **v. sur qn** to watch over sb.

veilleur *m* **v. de nuit** night watchman.

veilleuse *f (de voiture)* parking light; *(de cuisinière)* pilot light; *(lampe allumée la nuit)* nightlight.

veine *f* vein; *(chance) Fam* luck.

vélo *m* bike, bicycle; *(activité)* cycling; **faire du v.** to cycle; **v. tout terrain** mountain bike.

vélomoteur *m* motorcycle.

velours *m* velvet; **v. côtelé** corduroy.

velu, -ue *adj* hairy.

vendange *f (récolte)* grape harvest; *(raisin récolté)* grapes (harvested); **vendanges** *(période)* grape-harvesting time; **faire les vendanges** to pick the grapes.

vendeur, -euse *mf* sales clerk; *(de voitures etc)* salesman, saleswoman.

vendre *vt* to sell (**qch à qn** sb sth, sth to sb); **à v.** for sale.

vendre (se) *vpr* to sell; **ça se vend bien** it sells well.

vendredi *m* Friday; **V. saint** Good Friday.

vénéneux, -euse *adj* poisonous.

vengeance *f* revenge.

venger (se) *vpr* to get one's revenge, to get one's own back (**de qn** on sb; **de qch** for sth).

venimeux, -euse *adj* poisonous.

venin *m* poison.

venir* *vi (aux* **être***)* to come (**de** from); **v. faire** to come to do; **viens me voir** come and see me; **je viens/venais d'arriver** I've/I'd just arrived; **où veux-tu en v.?** what are you getting at?; **faire v.** to send for, to get.

vent *m* wind; **il y a du v.** it's windy; **coup de v.** gust of wind.

vente *f* sale; **v. (aux enchères)** auction; **en v.** on sale; **prix de v.** selling price.

ventilateur *m* fan.

ventre *m* stomach; **avoir mal au v.** to have a stomach ache.

venu, -ue *mf* **nouveau v., nouvelle venue** newcomer; **le premier v.** anyone.

ver *m* worm; *(de fruits etc)* maggot; **v. de terre** (earth)worm.

véranda *f (en verre)* sunroom *(attached to house).*

verbe *m* verb.

verdict *m* verdict.

verdure *f (végétation)* greenery.

verger *m* orchard.

verglas *m* (black) ice.

véridique *adj* truthful.

vérification *f* check(ing).

vérifier *vt* to check.

véritable *adj* true, real; *(non imité)* real.

véritablement *adv* really.

vérité *f* truth.

vernir *vt* to varnish.

vernis *m* varnish; **v. à ongles** nail polish.

verra, verrai(t) *etc voir* **voir**.

verre *m* glass; **boire** *ou* **prendre un v.** to have a drink; **v. de bière** glass of beer; **v. à bière** beer glass.

verrou *m* bolt; **fermer au v.** to bolt.

verrouiller *vt (porte)* to bolt; *(quartier)* to seal off.

verrue *f* wart.

vers¹ *prép (direction)* toward(s).

vers² *m (de poème)* line.

verse (à) *adv* pleuvoir à v. to pour (down).

versement *m* payment.

verser *vt* to pour; *(larmes)* to shed; *(argent)* to pay.

version *f (de film, d'incident etc)* version.

verso *m* 'voir au v.' 'see over'.

vert, verte 1 *adj* green; *(pas mûr)* unripe. **2** *m* green.

vertical, -e, -aux *adj* vertical.

vertige *m* avoir le v. to be *ou* feel dizzy; **donner le v. à qn** to make sb (feel) dizzy.

vessie *f* bladder.

veste *f* jacket.

vestiaire *m* locker room.

veston *m* (suit) jacket.

vêtement *m* garment; **vêtements** clothes; **vêtements de sport** sportswear.

vétérinaire *f* vet.

vêtu, -ue *adj* dressed (**de** in).

vétuste *adj* dilapidated.

veuf, veuve 1 *adj* widowed. **2** *mf* widower, widow.

veuille(s), veuillent etc voir **vouloir.**

veulent, veut, veux voir **vouloir.**

vexant, -ante *adj* upsetting.

vexer *vt* to upset.

VF *f abrév (version française)* film en VF film dubbed into French.

viande *f* meat.

vibration *f* vibration.

vibrer *vi* to vibrate.

vice *m* vice.

vicieux, -euse *adj (pervers)* depraved; *(perfide)* underhand.

victime *f* victim; *(d'un accident)* casualty; **être v. de** to be the victim of.

victoire *f* victory; *(en sports)* win.

victorieux, -euse *adj* victorious; *(équipe)* winning.

vidange *f (de véhicule)* oil change.

vide 1 *adj* empty. **2** *m* emptiness; *(trou)* gap.

vidéo *adj inv* video.

vidéocassette *f* video cassette.

vide-ordures *m inv* garbage chute.

vide-poches *m inv* glove compartment.

vider *vt,* **se vider** *vpr* to empty.

vie *f* life; *(durée)* lifetime; **le coût de la v.** the cost of living; **gagner sa v.** to earn one's living; **en v.** living.

vieil voir **vieux.**

vieillard *m* old man.

vieille voir **vieux.**

vieillesse *f* old age.

vieillir 1 *vi* to get old; *(changer)* to age. **2** *vt* v. qn *(vêtement etc)* to make sb look old(er).

vierge 1 *adj (femme, neige)* virgin; *(feuille de papier, film)* blank; **être v.** *(femme, homme)* to be a virgin. **2** *f* virgin.

vieux (*or* **vieil** before vowel or mute h), **vieille,** *pl* **vieux, vieilles 1** *adj* old. **2** *m* old man; **les vieux** old people; **mon v.!** *(mon ami)* buddy!, pal! **3** *f* old woman; **ma vieille!** *(ma chère)* dear!

vif, vive *adj (enfant)* lively; *(couleur, lumière)* bright; *(froid)* biting; **brûlé v.** burned alive.

vignette *f (de véhicule)* road tax sticker.

vignoble *m* vineyard.

vilain, -aine *adj (laid)* ugly; *(enfant)* bad; *(impoli)* rude.

villa *f* (detached) house.

village *m* village.

villageois, -oise *mf* villager.

ville *f* town; *(grande)* city; **aller/ être en v.** to go (in)to/be in town.

vin *m* wine.

vinaigre *m* vinegar.

vinaigrette *f* oil-and-vinegar dressing, vinaigrette.

vingt *adj & m* twenty; **v. et un** twenty-one.

vingtaine *f* **une v. (de)** about twenty.

vingtième *adj & mf* twentieth.

viol *m* rape.

violemment *adv* violently.

violence f violence.

violent, -ente adj violent.

violer vt to rape.

violet, -ette adj & m purple.

violeur m rapist.

violon m violin.

violoncelle m cello.

vipère f adder.

virage m (de route) bend; (de véhicule) turn.

virement m transfer.

virgule f comma; (de nombre) (decimal) point; **2 v. 5** 2 point 5.

virus m virus.

vis¹ voir **vivre, voir**.

vis² f screw.

visa m (de passeport) visa.

visage m face.

viser 1 vi to aim (à to). **2** vt (cible) to aim at.

visible adj visible.

visite f visit; **rendre v. à** to visit; **v. (médicale)** medical examination; **v. guidée** guided tour.

visiter vt to visit.

visiteur, -euse mf visitor.

visser vt to screw on.

vit voir **vivre, voir**.

vitamine f vitamin.

vite adv quickly.

vitesse f speed; (sur un véhicule) gear; **boîte de vitesses** transmission; **à toute v.** at full speed.

viticulteur, -trice mf wine grower.

vitrail, -aux m stained-glass window.

vitre f (window)pane; (de véhicule, train) window.

vitrine f (shop) window; (meuble) display cabinet.

vivace adj (plante) perennial; (tradition, sentiment) deep-rooted; (souvenir) vivid.

vivant, -ante adj living; (récit, rue) lively.

vive int **v. le roi/etc!** long live the king/etc!; **v. les vacances!** bring on the vacation!

vivement adv quickly; (répliquer) sharply; (regretter) deeply.

vivre*¹ 1 vi to live; **v. vieux** to live to be old; **v. de** (fruits etc) to live on; (travail etc) to live by. **2** vt (vie) to live; (aventure) to live through.

VO f abrév (version originale) **film en VO** film in the original language.

vocabulaire m vocabulary.

vodka f vodka.

vœu, -x m wish.

voici prép here is, this is, pl here are, these are; **me v.** here I am; **v. dix ans que** it's ten years since.

voie f road; (rails) track; (partie de route) lane; (chemin) way; (de gare) platform; **v. sans issue** dead end; **sur la bonne v.** on the right track.

voilà prép there is, that is, pl there are, those are; **les v.** there they are; **v., j'arrive!** all right, I'm coming!; **v. dix ans que** it's ten years since.

voile¹ m (tissu) veil.

voile² f (de bateau) sail; (sport) sailing; **faire de la v.** to sail.

voilier m (de plaisance) sailboat.

voir* vti to see; **faire v. qch** to show sth; **fais v.** let me see; **v. qn faire** to see sb do ou doing; **je ne peux pas la v.** Fam I can't stand (the sight of) her; **ça n'a rien à v. avec** that's got nothing to do with.

voir (se) vpr (se fréquenter) to see each other; **ça se voit** that's obvious.

voisin, -ine 1 adj neighboring; (maison, pièce) next (**de** to). **2** mf neighbor.

voisinage m neighborhood.

voiture f car.

voix f voice; (d'électeur) vote; **à v. basse** in a whisper.

vol¹ m (d'avion, d'oiseau) flight.

vol² m (délit) theft; (hold-up) robbery; **v. d'identité** identity theft.

volaille f **une v.** a fowl.

volant m (steering) wheel.

volcan m volcano.

voler[1] vi (oiseau, avion etc) to fly.

voler[2] vti (prendre) to steal (**à** from).

volet m (de fenêtre) shutter.

voleur, -euse mf thief; **au v.!** stop thief!

volontaire 1 adj (voulu) (geste etc) deliberate. **2** mf volunteer.

volontairement adv (exprès) deliberately.

volontariat m voluntary work.

volonté f will; **bonne v.** goodwill; **mauvaise v.** ill will.

volontiers adv gladly.

volume m (de boîte, de son, livre) volume.

volumineux, -euse adj bulky.

vomir 1 vt to bring up. **2** vi to be sick, to vomit.

vomissements mpl **avoir des v.** to vomit.

vont voir **aller**[1].

vos voir **votre**.

vote m vote; (de loi) passing; **bureau de v.** polling place.

voter 1 vi to vote. **2** vt (loi) to pass.

votre, pl **vos** adj poss your.

vôtre pron poss **le** ou **la v., les vôtres** yours; **à la v.!** cheers!

voudra, voudrai(t) etc voir **vouloir**.

vouloir* vt to want (**faire** to do); **je veux qu'il parte** I want him to go; **v. dire** to mean (**que** that); **je voudrais rester** I'd like to stay; **je voudrais un pain** I'd like a loaf of bread; **voulez-vous me suivre** will you follow me; **si tu veux** if you like ou wish; **en v. à qn d'avoir fait qch** to be angry with sb for doing sth; **je veux bien (attendre)** I don't mind (waiting); **sans le v.** unintentionally.

vous pron (sujet, complément direct) you; (complément indirect) (to) you; (réfléchi) yourself, pl yourselves; (réciproque) each other.

vous-même pron yourself.

vous-mêmes pron pl yourselves.

vouvoyer vt **v. qn** to use the formal vous form with sb.

voyage m trip, journey; **aimer les voyages** to like traveling; **faire un v., partir en v.** to go on a trip; **bon v.!** have a good trip!; **v. organisé** (package) tour; **agent/agence de voyages** travel agent/agency.

voyager vi to travel.

voyageur, -euse mf traveler; (passager) passenger.

voyant, -ante 1 adj (couleur) gaudy, loud. **2** m (signal) (warning) light; (d'appareil électrique) pilot light.

voyelle f vowel.

voyou m hooligan.

vrac (en) adv (en désordre) in a muddle, haphazardly; (non emballé) loose.

vrai, -e adj true; (réel) real; (authentique) genuine.

vraiment adv really.

vraisemblable adj (probable) likely.

VTT m inv abrév (vélo tout terrain) mountain bike.

vu, vue pp of **voir**.

vue f (spectacle) sight; (sens) (eye)sight; (panorama, photo) view; **en v.** (proche) in sight; **de v.** (connaître) by sight.

vulgaire adj vulgar.

W

wagon m (de voyageurs) car; (de marchandises) freight car.

wagon-lit, pl **wagons-lits** m sleeping car.

wagon-restaurant, pl **wagons-restaurants** m dining car.

WAP m abbr (Wireless Application Protocol) WAP.

waters *mpl* bathroom, men's/ladies' room.

w-c *mpl* bathroom, men's/ladies' room.

Web *m* le W. the Web.

webcam *m* webcam.

week-end *m* weekend.

western *m* (*film*) western.

whisky, *pl* **-ies** *m* whiskey.

pron (= *à cela*) **je m'y attendais** I was expecting it; **ça y est!** that's it!

yacht *m* yacht.

yaourt *m* yogurt.

yeux *voir* **œil**.

Z

zèbre *m* zebra.

zéro *m* zero; **deux buts à z.** two zero.

zeste *m* **un z. de citron** a piece of lemon peel.

zigzag *m* zigzag; **en z.** (*route etc*) zigzag(ging).

zigzaguer *vi* to zigzag.

zone *f* zone, area; **z. bleue** restricted parking area; **z. industrielle** industrial park.

zoo *m* zoo.

zut! *int* oh dear!

Y

y 1 *adv* there; **allons-y** let's go; **j'y suis!** now I get it!; **je n'y suis pour rien** I have nothing to do with it. **2**